# Giovanni Bellini

# Giovanni Bellini

RONA GOFFEN

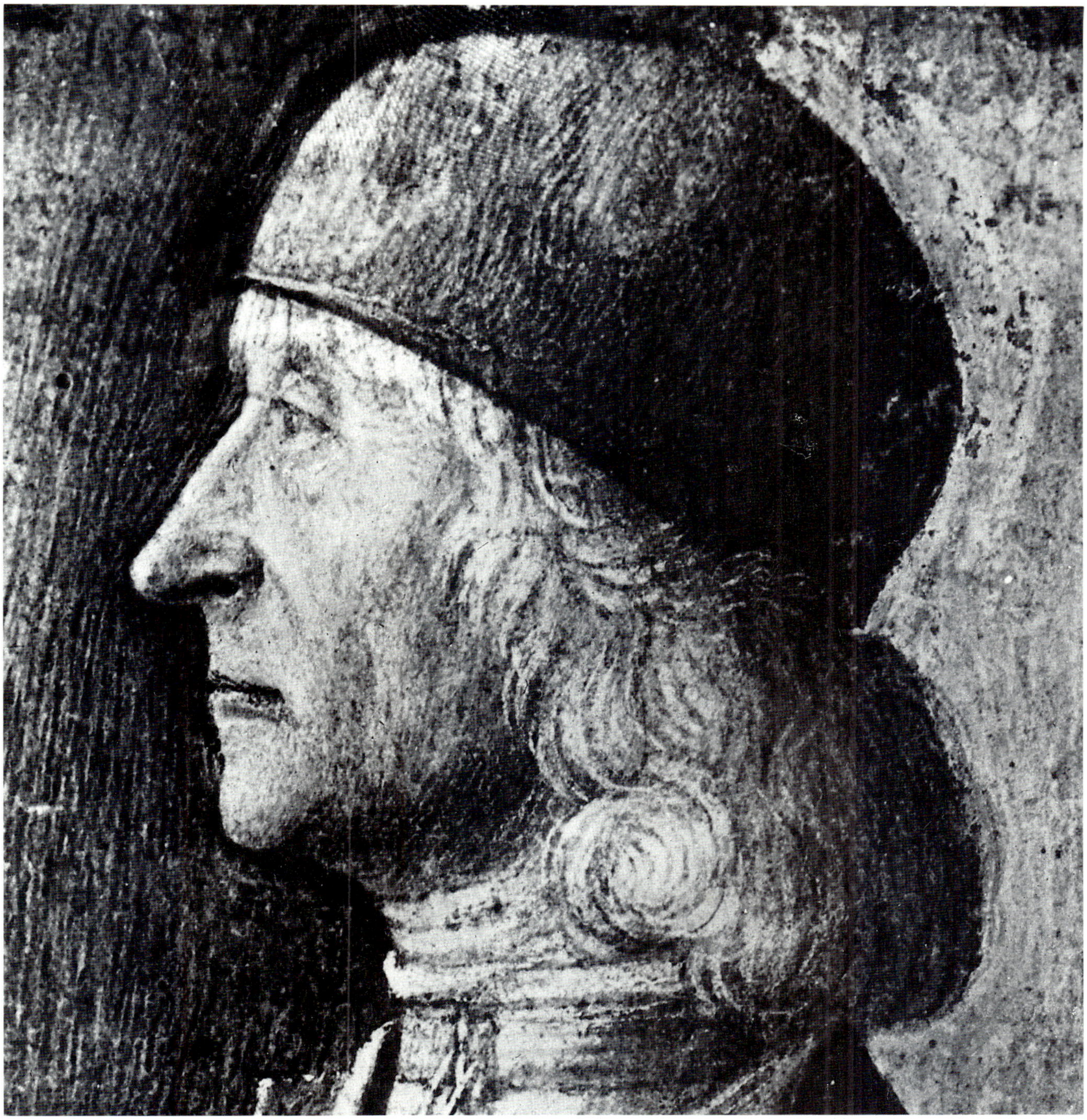

*Yale University Press New Haven & London*

Designed by Richard Hendel
and set in Galliard type
by Tseng Information Systems, Inc.
Printed in Japan by Dai Nippon
Printing Company.

FRONTISPIECE:
*Vittore Belliniano,*
Giovanni Bellini, *Musée Condé, Chantilly. Photo: Archivio Fotografico del Museo Correr, Venice.*

Library of Congress
Cataloging-in-Publication Data
Goffen, Rona, 1944–
Giovanni Bellini / Rona Goffen.
p. cm.
Bibliography: p.
Includes index.
ISBN 0–300–04334–1
(alk. paper)
1. Bellini, Giovanni, d. 1516—
Criticism and interpretation.
I. Title.
ND623.B39G64 1989
759.5—dc 20 89-33263
CIP

# Contents

# Preface and Acknowledgments

Born in the early 1430s, Bellini was active for close to seven decades—from about 1450, the approximate date of his earliest known works, until 1516, the year of his death. The history of Bellini's career is tantamount to a history of the greatest Venetian art in those years, involving a development from the traditional International Style and the art of Bellini's father, Jacopo, to the revolutionary works of Giorgione and Titian in the early sixteenth century.

The organizational difficulties inherent in any monographic treatment of an artist are particularly problematic in Bellini's case, largely because of his extraordinary productivity and the success of his shop: well over 220 surviving paintings have been attributed to him with greater or lesser degrees of certainty. Yet serious controversies surround key works by him. For example, are the Pesaro *Coronation of the Virgin* and the Vatican *Pietà* parts of the same altarpiece or two separate commissions? Some of his most important works, such as the SS. Giovanni e Paolo altarpiece and the Ducal Palace murals, have been destroyed. Furthermore, though many pictures bear his signature, no one with eyes has ever believed that all of the signed paintings were actually by Bellini. And in spite of all those signatures, Bellini did not usually date his compositions: the first surviving painting to be both signed and dated by him alone appears in 1487, when he was over fifty years old. One is forced to conclude that Giovanni Bellini was unconcerned about the eventual needs of art historians.

My solution to the familiar problem of chronological versus thematic organization has been to combine both schemes in the following way: The book's two parts deal with the sacred works and with secular works. The Introduction and chapter 1 set the scene and provide a chronological frame of reference for the chapters that follow, which are organized thematically. The Introduction contains an abbreviated biography, historiography, and survey of Bellini's early stylistic development. Chapter 1 begins with a discussion of Bellini's paintings of the Madonna and Child, which he produced throughout his long career with comparatively little change in iconography—but with remarkable diversity of style and technique. In effect, these images of the Virgin Mother chart Bellini's stylistic development from his earliest years until almost the end of his life. In the succeeding chapters, the approach is thematic and contextual—which is not to say that matters of stylistic interest are ignored. Documentation and various special problems are considered in the appendixes. Finally, there are checklists of autograph works, works by Bellini with assistance, and lost works.

The first—and almost certainly the last—great exhibition of Giovanni Bellini was held in Venice in 1949: such a retrospective will probably not be repeated, given the dangers of transporting panel paintings. But knowledge about Bellini and his milieu has been greatly enriched in recent years. While I was writing this book, Meyer zur Capellen published his monograph on Gentile Bellini, Colin Eisler was preparing his volume on Jacopo, and numerous paintings by Giovanni were in restoration, including such works as the early Ducal Palace *Pietà* and the late *Feast of the Gods*.

This book is not meant to be an inclusive catalogue raisonné of Bellini's art but rather is concerned with his undisputed masterpieces, surviving works, and inventions of particular distinction and importance. I realize that few if any readers will agree with all of my decisions in these particulars but hope nonetheless that they will find that I have done justice to a great master.

Writing this book would have been far more difficult if not impossible were it not for the help I received from various institutions and individuals. My research was assisted by grants from the National Endowment for the Humanities in 1986 and from the Duke University Research Council. Fellowships from the John Simon Guggenheim Memorial Foundation and the National Humanities Center during the academic year 1986–87 enabled me to complete the book.

Doing research in Venice is a great pleasure, thanks to the excellent staffs of the Archivio di Stato, Biblioteca Correr, and Biblioteca Nazionale Marciana. In particular, I wish to thank Dr. Giustiniana Colasanti Migliardi O'Riordan, Dr. Francesca Romanelli, and Dr. Alessandra Schiavon of the Archivio; Dr. Giandomenico Romanelli, Director of the Correr Library, where Sr. Urbano Pasquon was especially helpful; and Dr. Francomario Colasanti, Director of the Marciana. With the generosity and skill typical of him, Gianfranco Spinazzi produced some beautiful new photographs for this book. Francesco Valcanover, former Ministro Generale di Cultura, has facilitated my research on many occasions. I am deeply grateful to Dr. Giovanna Nepi Scirè, Soprintendente ai Beni Culturali and Director of the Gallerie dell'Accademia in Venice, for her great professional and personal generosity during my visits to Venice. To her, *Grazie veramente infinite*.

Particular thanks are due the curators and conservators of several museums who shared their files and expertise with me: David Alan Brown, Curator of Early Italian Painting, and David Bull, Conservator, National Gallery of Art, Washington; Francis W. Greenacre, Curator of the Bristol Museum and Art Gallery; Rollin van N. Hadley, Director, and Kristin Mortimer, Curator, Isabella Stewart Gardner Museum, Boston; Professor Hamish Miles, Director of the Barber Institute of Fine Arts at Birmingham University; Charlotte Nichols, Assistant Curator, the Frick Art Collection; Wolfgang Prohaska, Curator of the Gemäldegalerie, Kunsthistorisches Museum, Vienna; Sante Luigi Savio, Conservator, Gallerie dell'Accademia, Venice; Alistair J. W. Smith, Deputy Keeper of the National Gallery, London; and Gloria C. Williams, Assistant Curator, the Norton Simon Museum, Pasadena.

For their helpfulness in obtaining photographs, I thank Mary L. Myers, Associate Curator of Prints and Drawings, Metropolitan Museum of Art, New York; Görel Cavalli-Björkman, Curator, Nationalmuseum, Stockholm; Erich Schleier, Curator, Gemäldegalerie, Berlin; Dott.ssa Fiorella Superbi, Fototeca Berenson, Villa I Tatti; Dott.ssa Rosalba Tardito, Soprintendente, and her colleague at the Pinacoteca di Brera, Milan, Dante Pini; and Professor Fulvio Zuliani of the University of Udine.

I have also profited from conversations and correspondence with friends and colleagues, among them Stanley Chojnacki, Keith Christiansen, Everett Fahy, Michael Hirst, David Rosand, Craig Hugh Smyth, and especially Sarah Blake McHam. My cousin Diane Goffen Bylciw taught me indirect but powerful lessons about the meaning of Bellini's imagery.

Professor Fred Licht read an earlier version of this book and offered many valuable suggestions that I have incorporated as though they were my own: to have acknowledged his help in each instance would have meant a notable inflation of the endnotes. Patricia Fortini Brown's perceptive criticisms have also been of great benefit. Finally, I thank Judy Metro and Laura Jones Dooley at Yale University Press, who did much to improve this book.

# Introduction: Young Bellini

*Giovanni Bellini may be called the springtime of all the world in the art of painting, for all freshness is derived from him, and without him art would be winter.*
—Marco Boschini

Giovanni Bellini—Giambellino—is an anomaly in the history of art. The traditional view presents Bellini as a contradictory figure: undeniably one of the greatest masters of painting, yet dependent on others for direction; innovative, yet slow to develop at the beginning of his career, and at the end somewhat reluctant or unable to accept challenge and change. It is assumed that Bellini at first depended on his brother-in-law Andrea Mantegna. Then the direction of Bellini's art is supposed to have changed by his contact with the art of Piero della Francesca and Antonello da Messina in the 1470s; changed again in the later years of the century when Leonardo da Vinci introduced the principles of High Renaissance art to Venice; and changed a final time by the impact of Bellini's younger Venetian compatriots, Giorgione and Titian, in the first years of the sixteenth century. Just as Mantegna left Bellini behind at the start of his career, we are told, so Giorgione and Titian surpassed him at the end of his life: although Bellini continued to paint until his death in 1516, he remained mired in the quattrocento, responsive to the new art of these young masters but unable or unwilling to assimilate their innovations. So we are told, and so we read in authors from Dolce and Vasari in the sixteenth century to Longhi, Freedberg, Boskovits, and others in the twentieth.[1] But the facts present a different picture of Giovanni Bellini and his art. Cultural campanilismo, partisanship, and tenacious bad habit explain the negative views of Bellini put forward by the Tuscan Vasari, by Dolce, the great admirer and publicist of Titian, and by many modern art historians. When we consider Bellini in his historical and cultural context, we find a different reality.

By the time Bellini was about forty years old, at least one contemporary considered him a great master who would always "be dignified by celestial honors,"[2] while others called him "the most noble painter" and "the most famous painter in the world."[3] In a sonnet in praise of Bellini, Nicolò Liburnio declaimed that Alexander the Great would have chosen Bellini over Apelles as his artist had they been contemporaries: an elegant emendation of the traditional humanist compliment to painters praised as a "second Apelles."[4] Bellini was "still the best in painting" in his extreme old age, according to no less a judge of artistic merit than Albrecht Dürer, who knew Bellini and his work in Venice in 1506 and praised him in a letter to Willibald Pirckheimer.[5] And Joachim Camerarius (1500–1574), Dürer's friend and a pupil of Philipp Melancthon, considered the Venetian the measure against which he might demonstrate the superior genius of the German artist. Camerarius was writing in 1532, sixteen years after Bellini's death, and yet—for all that the purpose of the anecdote was clearly to assert Dürer's greatness—Bellini remained the "man to beat."[6] Nonetheless, within fewer than twenty years, when Vasari published the first edition of his Lives (1550), Bellini had been eclipsed by Giorgione and Titian, at least according to that author, who criticized the "dryness" of Bellini's art. This negative view of Bellini is due in part to Vasari's national prejudice, his Tuscan pride in the achievements of his compatriots Leonardo and especially Michelangelo—a prejudice compounded by his comparative ignorance of Venetian art and his dependence on Titian (who was anything but disinterested) for information about it. Although the "critical misfortune" of Giovanni Bellini is important for the history of taste and of ideas, his real achievement must be recognized by those who wish to understand the Renaissance in Italy.

This is easier said than done. And it is Bellini's great success during his lifetime that has made him difficult to know.[7] Several knotty problems confront us: Bellini's shop may be reckoned one of the largest and most prolific in the history of art, full of assistants—not a few of them mediocre—whose contributions must be separated from the master's; he was productive for an extraordinary sixty-five years or more and capable throughout those many decades of remarkable, frequently contemporaneous, variations in style and technique; he was "economical," sometimes recycling motifs, poses, and gestures; and his work, like that of other great masters, has suffered terrible distortion at the hands of well-intentioned restorers, to say nothing of destruction through natural and man-made disasters. Two of his first major altarpieces and all of his narrative paintings for the Palazzo Ducale di San Marco have been destroyed—these are the greatest, but by no means the only, losses—and other critical works have been scraped, abraded, bleached, overpainted, and torn apart, all in the name of restoration.

Sometimes it seems as though Bellini has told us too much: the multivalence of his artistic personality throughout his career is undeniable. But in another sense Bellini has told us almost nothing of himself: he is among the least documented of the great masters. Far less is known about Bellini than about his brother Gentile, or indeed about any other important painter of the Renaissance in Venice.[8] The written record is meager: no will, few documents alluding to commissions, and only two letters—formal communications to Francesco Gonzaga and to Isabella d'Este that conceal the author in polite tropes. But however significant the history of criticism, the conservation and restoration of works of art, and the connoisseurship of the belliniani, they are nonetheless coincidental to the central issue, which is to understand Bellini's creative processes and appreciate his art in its cultural and historical context. This context is Venetian humanism and spirituality, with its particular references to the social and political interests of the Serene Republic and its long-standing ties with Byzantium. The styles and iconography of Bellini's oeuvre, the achievements of his career, can best be understood in connection with Venetian Renaissance civilization.

The Golden Age of Venetian painting began with Giovanni Bellini. Ironically, however, the period of Venice's greatest cultural achievement coincided with its loss of hegemony, signaled by the fall of Constantinople to the Ottoman Turks in 1453. This loss was of incalculable psychological and symbolic significance to the Christian West, above all to the Venetian Republic, and other humiliating and strategic defeats, including the Turkish capture of Negroponte in 1470, soon followed. By the end of hostilities in 1479, Venice had lost almost all its holdings on the Greek mainland. In the following year, Venice lost the Ionian Islands—briefly recaptured some twenty years later by Bellini's patron Benedetto Pesaro before they were ceded forever. Venetians responded to these military losses with a renewed Byzantinism in arts and letters, in the publications of Aldus Manutius, in the architecture of Mauro Codussi, and in the painting of Giovanni Bellini. Art thus regained what had been lost in reality.

During those frightening decades of the later fifteenth century, the Venetians were also expanding on the Italian mainland. The republic was thus constantly at odds with other Italian states, engaged sometimes in overt hostilities, sometimes in battles of words. The culmination came at the turn of the new century with the formation of the League of Cambrai (1504–17), a European alliance against Venice. The republic survived, but Venetian self-confidence and esteem were casualties.[9] These terrible events formed and colored Giovanni Bellini's age and shaped his art in ways that are often ineffable but present nonetheless in his awareness of the fragility of human existence.

The son of a painter, destined from childhood for a painter's career, Giovanni Bellini must have been working in his father's shop from the time he was old enough to hold a brush. But when was that? Although Bellini's death on 29 November 1516 was noted by contemporaries, there is no record of his birth.[10] It seems, however, that he was born after 1433, perhaps two or three years later, the fourth and youngest child of Jacopo Bellini and Anna Rinversi (see the Family Tree in app. 1).[11] And this chronological sequence is probably correct whether or not Giovanni Bellini was illegitimate, as has frequently been argued, primarily because Anna omitted him from her second known will, dated 1471.[12] Unless Anna's "sin of omission" is interpreted as sinister, there is nothing to indicate that Giovanni was treated or regarded as illegitimate.[13] On the contrary, he seems to have enjoyed all the benefits of the Bellini family's status as members of the *cittadinanza originaria,* the class second only to the patriciate in dignity and privileges. Like his brother Gentile, Giovanni Bellini was always identified as "our faithful citizen" in state documents, and his son, Alvise, served in the chancellery, where employment was restricted to the citizen class.[14]

Giovanni Bellini was painting independently (that is, completing works of his own) by 1450 and possibly even as early as the later 1440s: he was as precocious as Andrea Mantegna, albeit in a different genre of art, working on small-scale panel paintings and probably miniatures while the Paduan was executing large-scale commissions. The Barber Institute's *Saint Jerome in the Wilderness*, Bellini's earliest surviving independent work, is universally dated circa 1450—that is, when the artist was between fifteen and seventeen (fig. 1). The awkwardness of the signature is explained by this early dating: a still uncertain command of calligraphy combined with an idiosyncratic spelling of the name, IHOVANES BELINVS, inscribed on a white panel in the foreground.[15]

Bellini's precocity and independence are proved by this small panel, which is almost a miniature. Jerome is living as a hermit in the desert, with only his wounded lion as audience for his theological discourse. The saint sits at the left of the picture space, his figure buttressed by rocks that rise to the top of the panel. The varied contour of these coral pink rocks divides the picture diagonally, almost but not quite into two steep triangular sections. Bellini combined asymmetry with a juxtaposition of open and closed spaces, setting Jerome and his lion in the closed space of the foreground while leaving empty the open areas of midground and sky. The composition is not balanced by the traditional—and contemporary, mid-quattrocento—symmetrical distribution of forms. A more subtle and varied arrangement here counterbalances solid with void and combines irregular shapes in an abstract design. Color and light unify the composition, the warm blond palette and brown resin glazes creating the sunlit atmosphere that permeates the scene, so that we must temper our understanding of the void in Bellini's world, where emptiness is suffused with atmospheric light.

Bellini generally represented atmosphere by naturalistic means and by applying color and glazes in thin, translucent layers. But in the rock at the left of the *Saint Jerome* he also used touches of silver and gold paint to suggest sunlight glistening on stone and gold to highlight the bare trees and the grazing donkey. He applied metallic paint in a naturalistic way, giving the primary impression of light, not artificial embellishment. Concomitant with this interest in pictorial light, including effects of atmospheric perspective in the distant right landscape, is concern for illusionistic space. The receding plane and far mountains show Bellini's early mastery of landscape, whereas the foreshortening of Jerome's halo and book are spatial incidents that betoken the artist's interest in—if not yet his command of—mathematical perspective.

The *Saint Jerome* is a small picture, measuring only 48 by 35.8 centimeters, but its originality is remarkable. Already Bellini had endowed his landscape with the prominence and poetic force of a protagonist in the composition. To be sure,

Jerome in the wilderness, a theme popular throughout the fifteenth century, requires a landscape setting. But just as that setting can be depicted in many ways, so can other, related choices be made to illustrate Jerome's life of solitary penitence. Jerome himself had provided the text for these images, the letter written to his disciple Eustochium:

> How often, when I was living in the desert, in the vast solitude which gives to hermits a savage dwelling-place, parched by a burning sun, how often did I fancy myself among the pleasures of Rome! . . . I had no companions but scorpions and wild beasts. . . . Helpless, I cast myself at the feet of Jesus . . . and ceased not from beating my breast till tranquility returned at the chiding of the Lord. . . . I still could not bring myself to forego the library which I had formed for myself at Rome. . . . I would fast only that I might afterwards read Cicero. . . . And when at times I returned to my right mind, and began to read the prophets, their style seemed rude and repellent. I failed to see the light with my blinded eyes; but I attributed the fault not to them, but to the sun. . . . about the middle of Lent a deep-seated fever fell upon my weakened body. . . . Suddenly I was caught up in the spirit and dragged before the judgement seat of the Judge; and here the light was so bright, and those who stood around were so radiant, that I cast myself upon the ground. . . . Asked who and what I was I replied, "I am a Christian." But He who presided said: "Thou liest, thou art a follower of Cicero and not of Christ."[16]

Most masters, including Jacopo Bellini, visualized the penitential saint beating his breast, "scorpions and wild beasts" his only companions.[17] The architectural, botanical, and zoological adornments of Jacopo Bellini's compositions are all but eliminated from Giovanni Bellini's *Saint Jerome*. Giovanni Bellini saw only the saint's "savage dwelling-place, parched by a burning sun," yet also illuminated by the light that Jerome had first "failed to see with my blinded eyes," for this scene clearly represents the aftermath of his visionary trial. Now the saint reads the Bible, not Cicero: his conversion is complete. Bellini represented Jerome this way in compositions produced throughout his career, with varying degrees of studio assistance (fig. 2); only once, in a predella panel, did he depict Jerome beating his breast "at the feet of Jesus" (fig. 98). Bellini's choices, both stylistic and iconographic, are revealingly characteristic and not to be taken for granted.

Bellini treats the viewer-worshiper as the unseen witness of Jerome's saintly isolation; no glance or gesture acknowledges our presence, no anecdotal detail attracts (or distracts) our imagination, but the artist engages our spiritual involvement by conveying the mood of the scene, which we are invited to share and emulate. This quality is also typical of Bellini's mature works—and the contemplative tenor of the composition is determined as much or more by the landscape as by the action of the two animate protagonists. We sense both the weight of

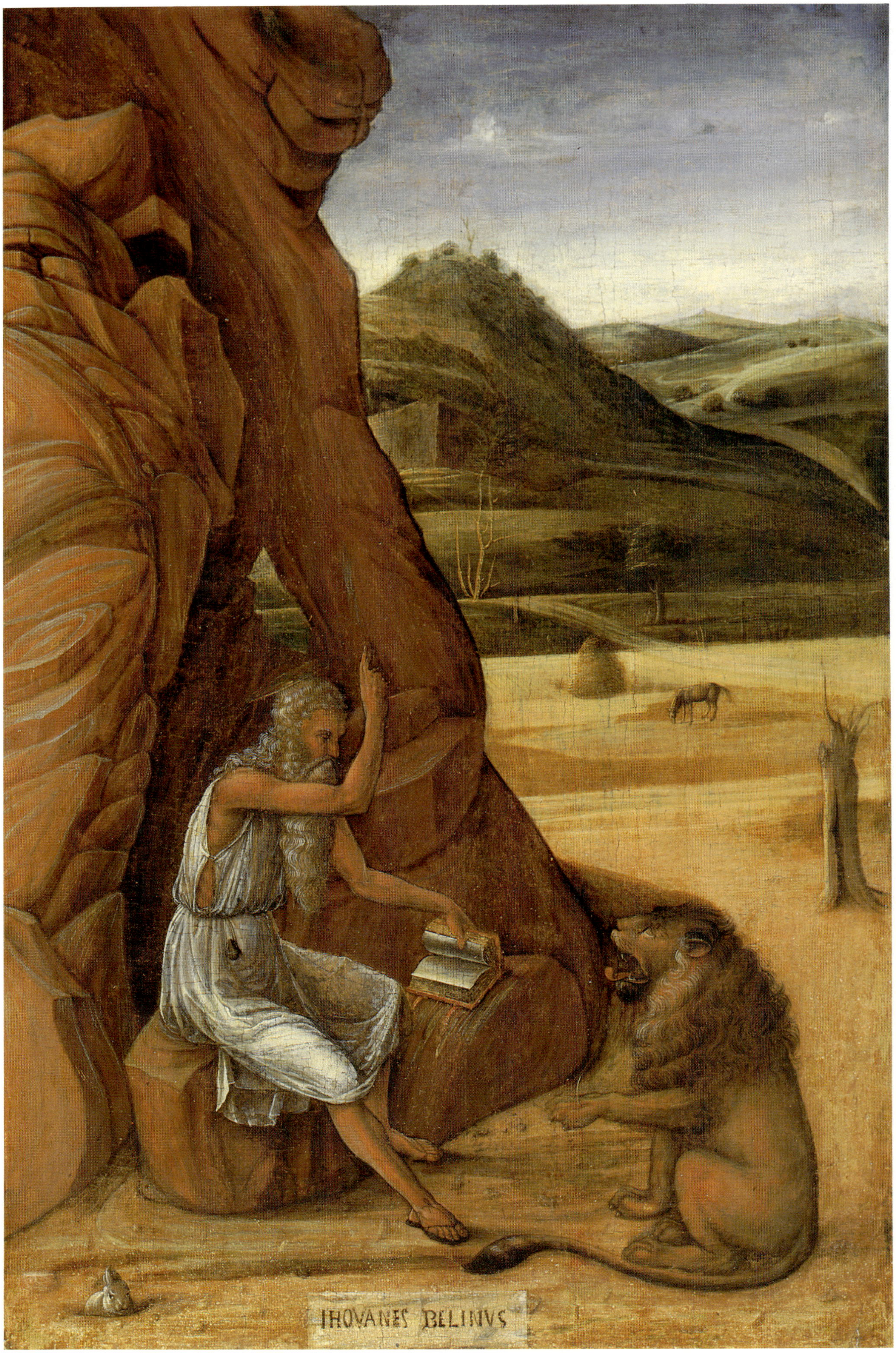
IHOVANES BELINVS

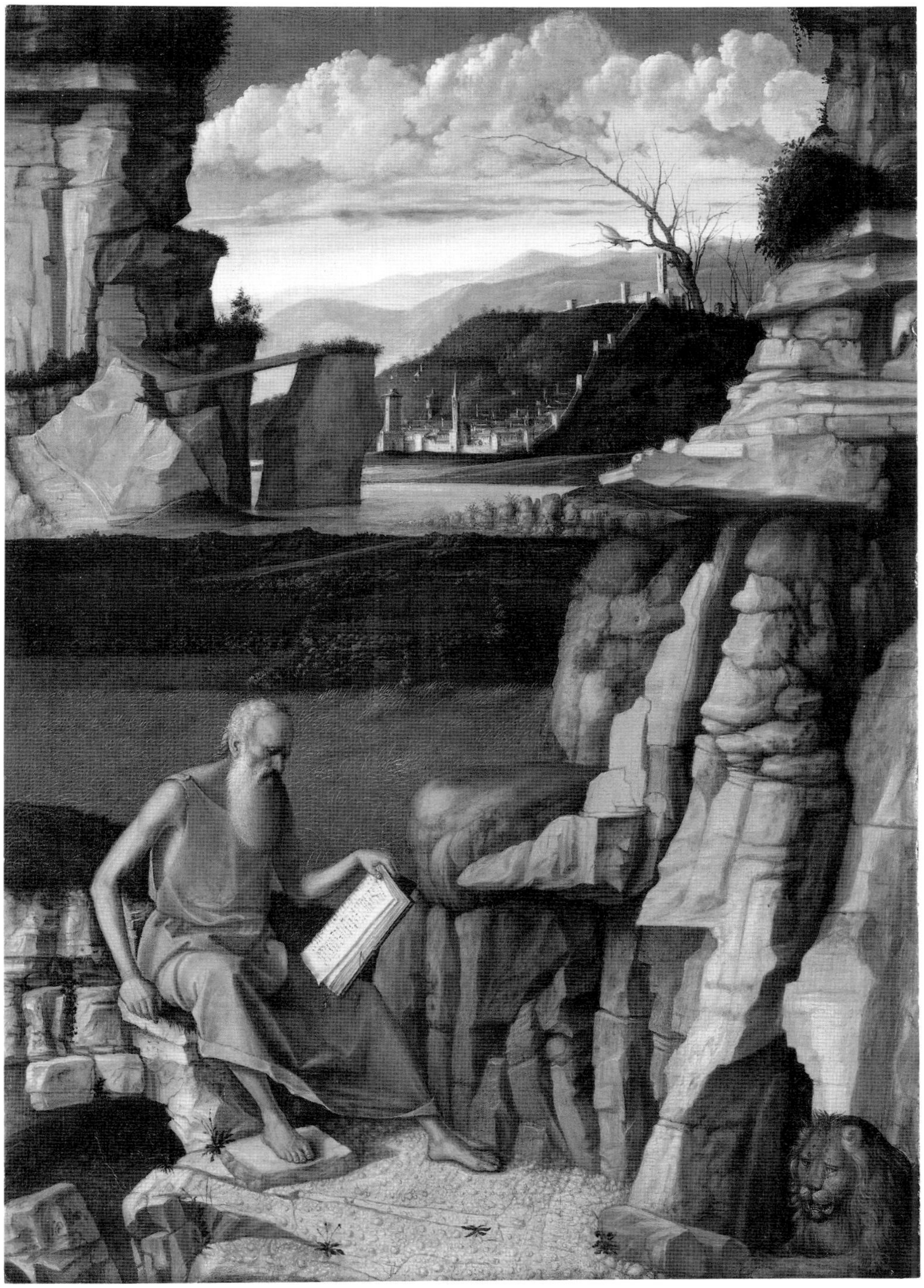

2. *Giovanni Bellini and assistants,* Saint Jerome, *National Gallery, London.*

Jerome's isolation and the spiritual tranquility he achieved in the wilderness. The landscape seems the inevitable environment for the saint, and neither setting nor figure seems fully defined without the other.

One could argue that some or all of these qualities in Bellini's panel were determined by, or related to, its miniature scale, and to an extent this is so, although Bellini's later development proves that scale was not the whole of the matter.[18] But it is important to recognize that the work's size, together with its delicacy and the small scale of many forms within it, such as the curls of Jerome's hair and

*1.* Saint Jerome in the Wilderness, *Barber Institute of Fine Arts, Birmingham. Courtesy The Barber Institute of Fine Arts, The University of Birmingham.*

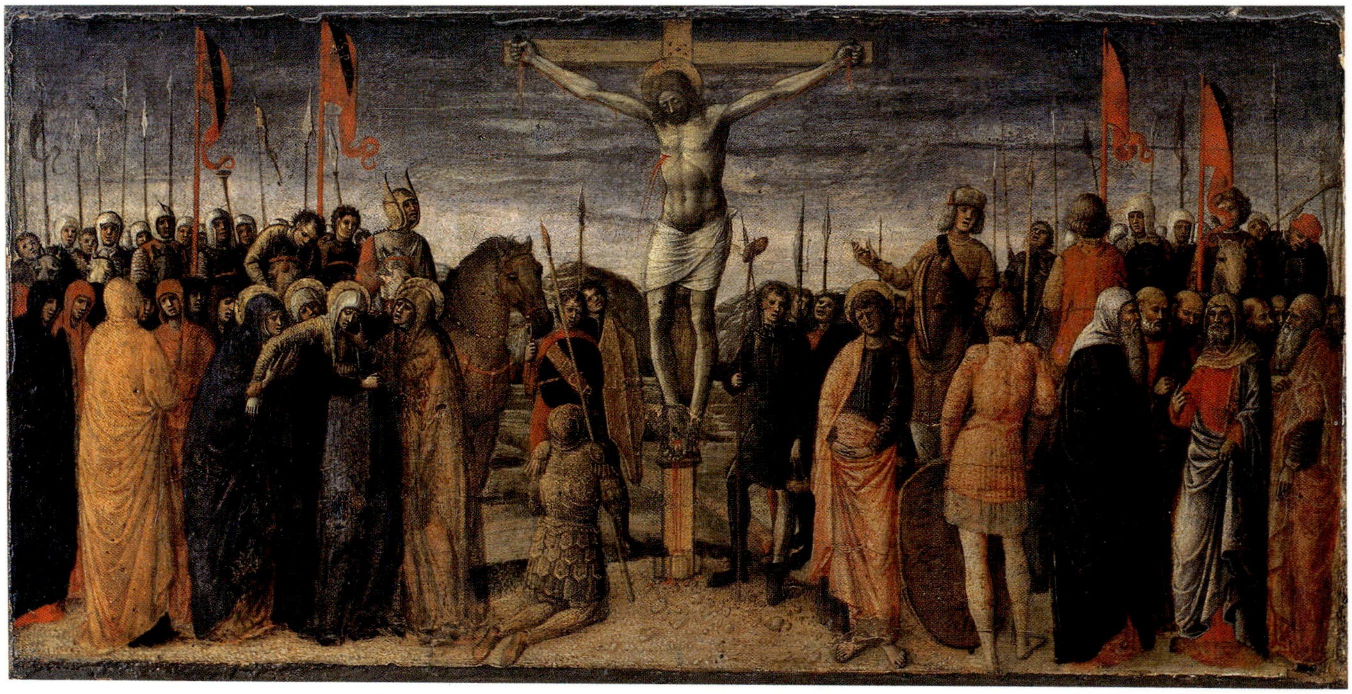

3. *Jacopo Bellini with probable assistance of Giovanni Bellini,* Crucifixion, *predella, Civico Museo Correr, Venice. Photo: Gianfranco Spinazzi, Venice.*

beard or the lion's mane, and even the use of silver and gold all endow the panel with a miniaturistic quality. It seems likely that Bellini's career started this way—that this is no mere accident of survival—and that his first works were manuscript illuminations, perhaps guided by his older cousin Leonardo, a miniaturist who is documented as working in Jacopo's shop in 1443 (Family Tree).[19] As one might expect, the young Giovanni also collaborated with his father: the three related predella panels representing the *Adoration of the Magi*, the *Crucifixion*, and the *Descent of Christ into Limbo* were designed by Jacopo but executed largely by Giovanni himself (figs. 3, 4).[20]

Colin Eisler and Miklós Boskovits have recently shown that these three predella panels are associated with the left wing of a dismembered altarpiece depicting Saints Anthony Abbot and Bernardino of Siena, convincingly attributed by Eisler to Jacopo and Gentile Bellini.[21] But are these fragments all that remain of the work signed and dated by the three Bellini in 1459 or 1460 for the Gattamelata Chapel of Saints Francis and Bernardino in Sant'Antonio, as has been argued?[22] Bernardino's cult was celebrated in non-Franciscan churches in Venice and the Veneto, including San Marco, where the saint stands next to Anthony Abbot—his companion in Jacopo Bellini's panel—in a mid-fifteenth-century mosaic adorning the arch of the south transept of San Marco.[23] And by 1459 Giovanni Bellini was in his twenties and living on his own in the parish of San Lio in Venice.[24] Artists, like musical prodigies, develop early, not late, a proclivity encouraged in the Middle Ages and Renaissance by childhood apprenticeship and workshop practice. How, then, can these Jacopo Bellinesque predella panels represent Giovanni Bellini's work at such a late date? This anomaly can be explained in two ways.

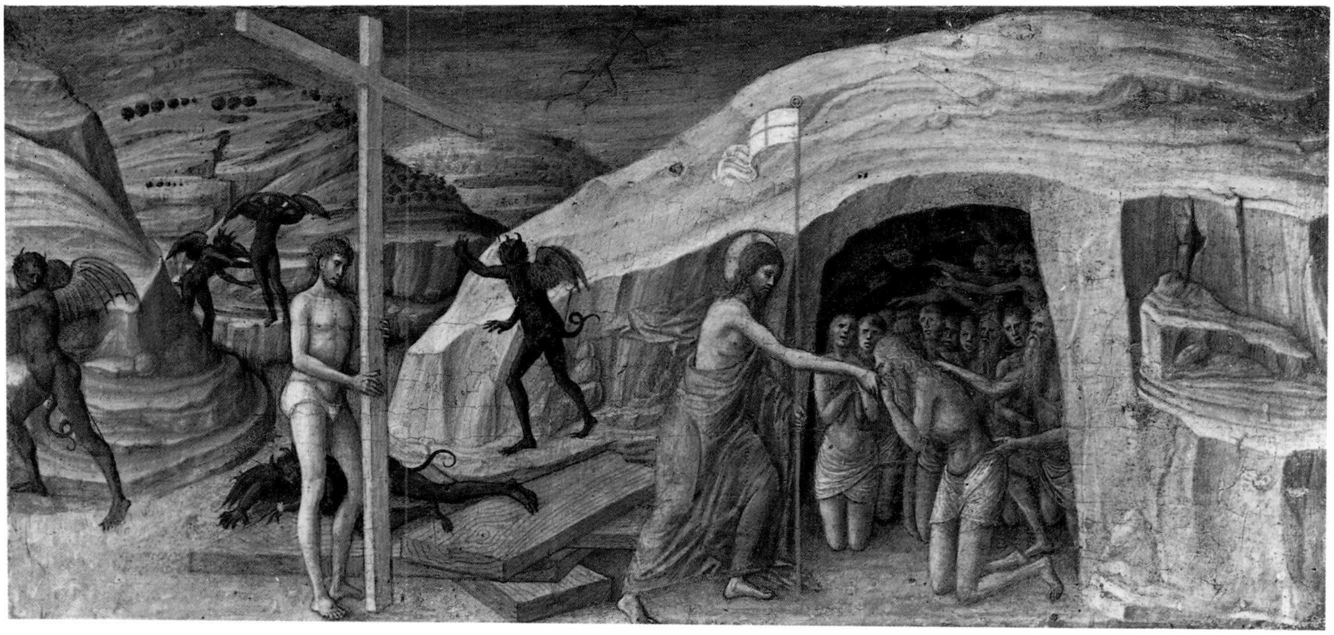

4. *Jacopo Bellini, with probable assistance of Giovanni Bellini,* Descent of Christ into Limbo, *Museo Civico, Padua. Photo: Archivio Fotografico del Museo Correr, Venice.*

If these panels are fragments of the Gattamelata altarpiece, then Giovanni Bellini subsumed his artistic personality to accommodate his father's style. For precisely this reason the predella panels are considered Jacopo Bellini's designs with the collaboration of his son in the execution. If this is the predella of the altarpiece that Giovanni, his father, and his brother signed in 1459 or 1460, then it is an early instance of Bellini's remarkable and characteristic stylistic flexibility, his ability to paint in more than one manner or to adapt himself to the stylistic exigencies of a commission. Moreover, the predella may have been completed several years earlier than the main panels of the altarpiece.[25] But another explanation may be that the altarpiece fragments are not associated with the Gattamelata commission but are the predella and left wing of a different, undocumented work, most likely dated earlier in the 1450s.[26]

The difference between Giovanni Bellini's artistic collaborations with his father and his independent work is illustrated by a small devotional image, the *Crucifixion* in the Museo Correr (fig. 5). The *Crucifixion* may be dated circa 1453–55, slightly later than the *Saint Jerome* (fig. 1), and close in both composition and date to one of Jacopo Bellini's drawings (fig. 6)—minus the landscape, probably the younger Bellini's most significant achievement in this panel.[27] Trees, a bridge, and other forms cast shimmering reflections in the distant river, which is possibly the wettest water painted in Italian art up to its time; atmosphere envelops and softens contours and colors in the midground and distance, effects Bellini evidently achieved here with oil. Mourning putti hover above Christ not as corporeal bodies but as embodiments of light. Bellini had used silver and gold in the *Saint Jerome* and gold in the *Crucifixion* predella for naturalistic highlights; here metallic

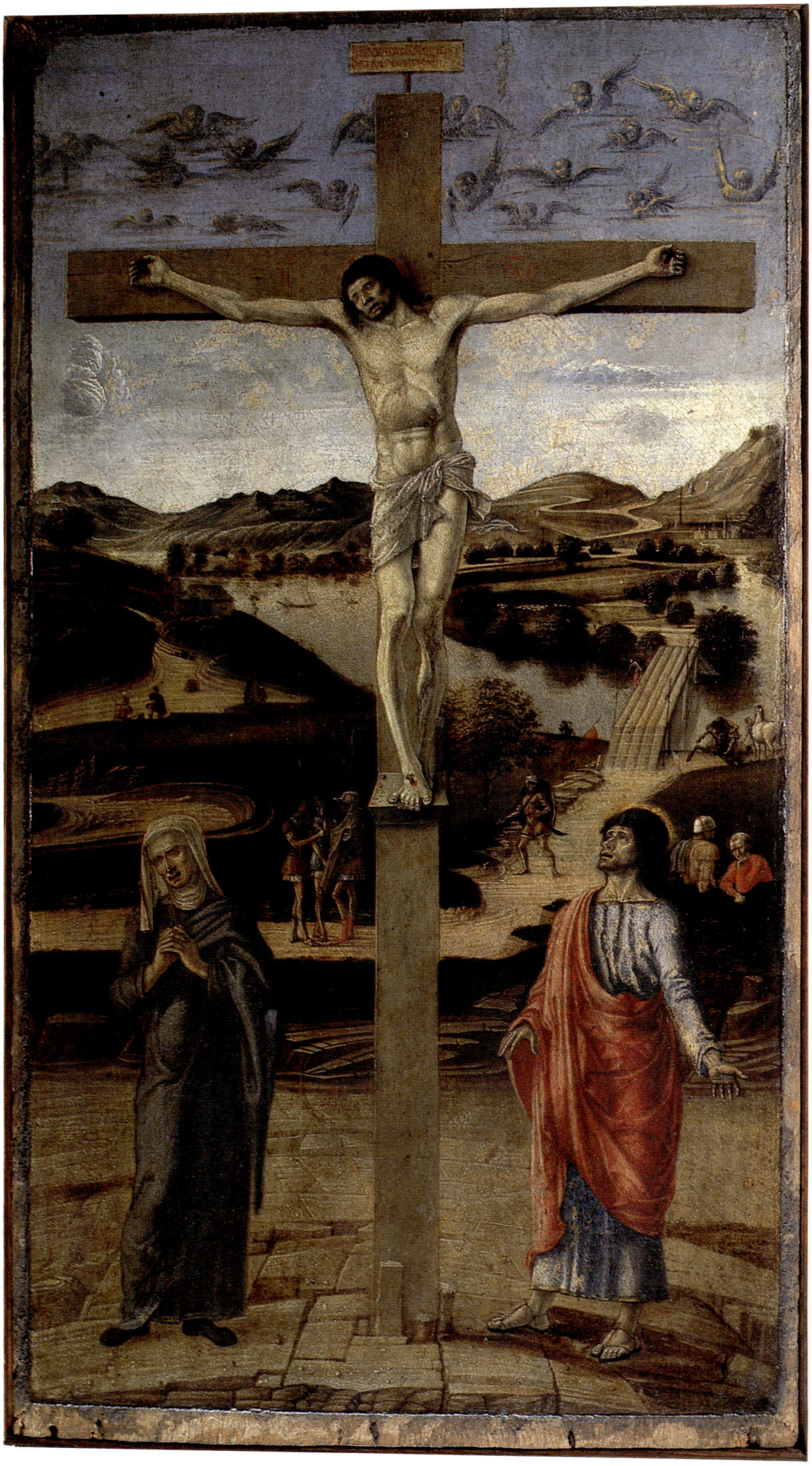

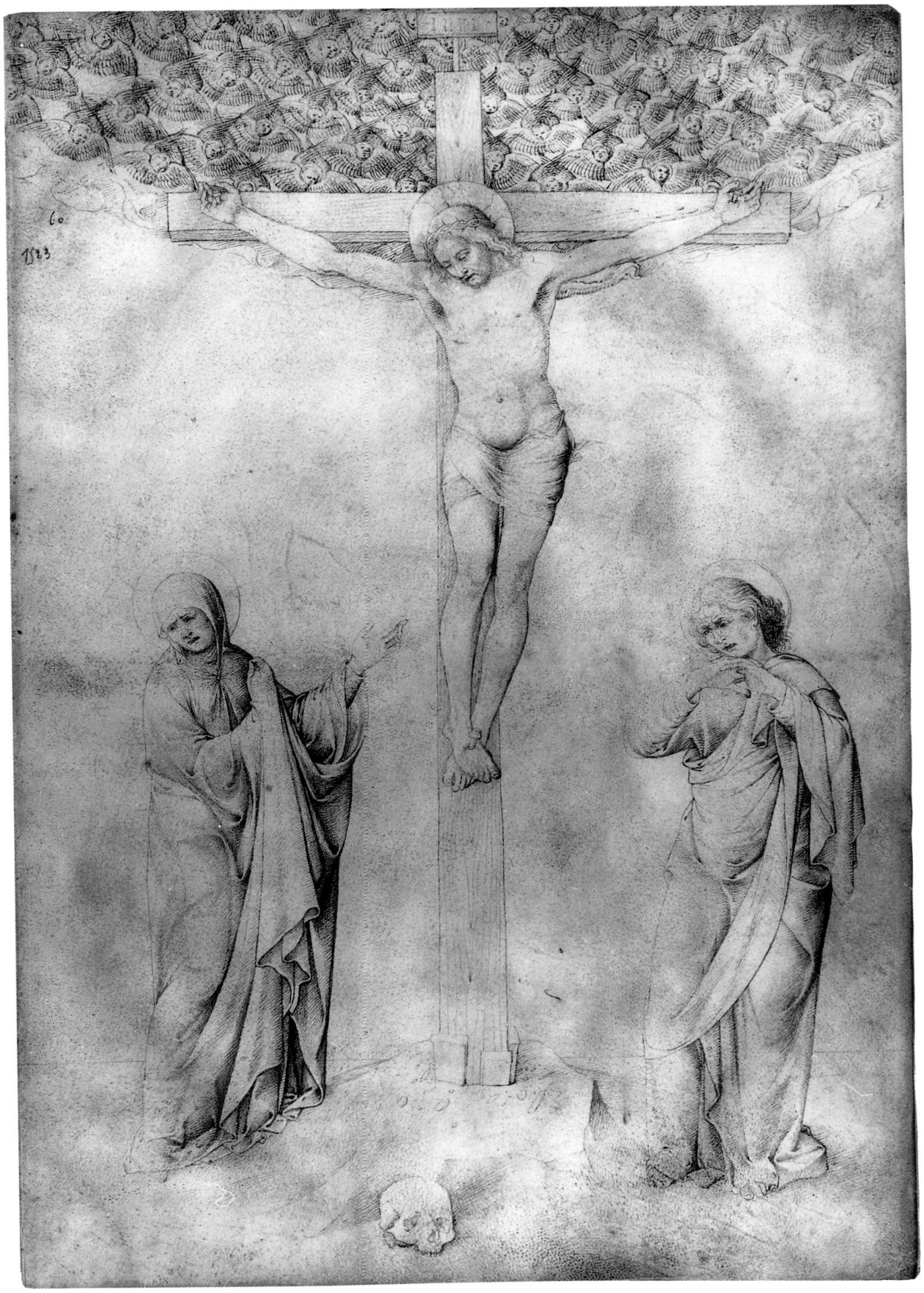

6. *Jacopo Bellini,* Crucifixion, *drawing book, folio 55, Musée du Louvre, Paris. Photo: Musées Nationaux, Paris.*

gold has a purely supernatural association, in accordance with Byzantine tradition. Golden striations painted over shades of blue slightly darker than the sky define the shapes and the otherworldly essence of these putti, evanescent flickers of light in the heavens. Birdlike, they bend and twist in the air, some in complicated foreshortened positions, and no two alike, affirming both their own presence and the reality of the sky through which they flutter.

The landscape, unlike that behind Jerome, is populated: soldiers seated, standing, walking, or riding, solitary or in groups, inhabit this world. (Some background figures are so thinly painted that they have become transparent.) The three

5. Crucifixion, *Civico Museo Correr, Venice.*

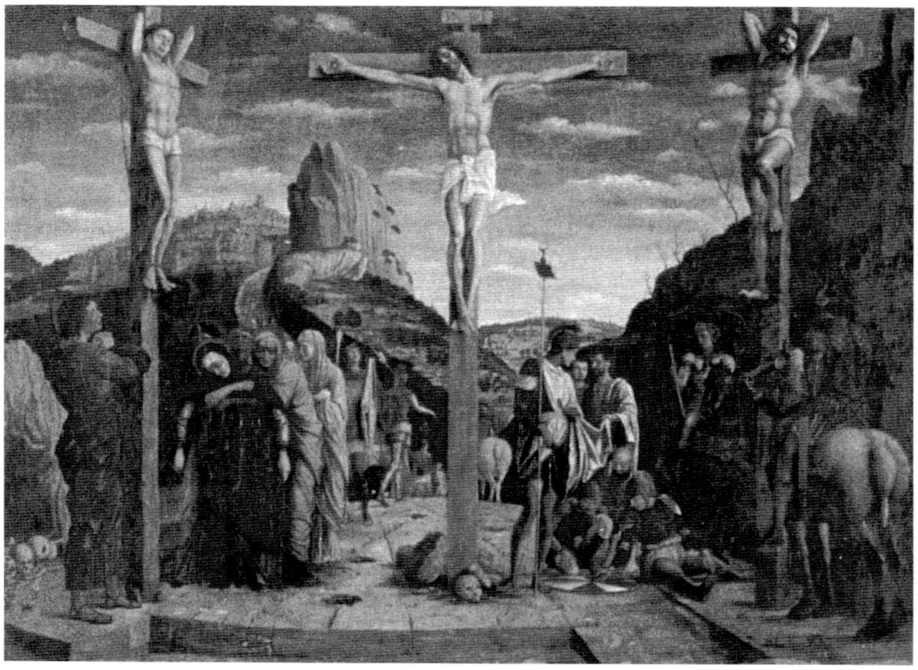

*7. Andrea Mantegna,* Crucifixion, *predella, San Zeno altarpiece, San Zeno, Verona. Photo: Scala/Art Resource, New York.*

men next to the cross seem more closely associated with the Crucifixion than the rest, and we are probably meant to imagine that the subject of their conversation is indeed Christ's death. But others go about their business with no awareness of this momentous event: they are as detached from the Crucifixion spiritually and psychologically as they are spatially by the great contrast in scale between them and the large figures of Mary, John, and Christ. This suggestion of historicity, the location of the death of Christ in a continuum of time, space, and human affairs, is subjugated to the ahistorical, iconic depiction of the three protagonists whose tragedy is set against—not within—intimations of time and limitations of space. Although light and atmosphere envelop every form and figure, the disjunction of scale separates them, a pictorial device that Bellini developed and exploited in later devotional images of the Madonna and of the dead Christ.

Giovanni Bellini's conception of the composition and its drama contrast with his father's in Jacopo's drawing or in the *Crucifixion* predella panel, and these differences are not entirely explained by the different formats and functions of the two works (figs. 3, 5, 6). What was hinted in the treatment of landscape in the predella had become a primary expressive feature of Giovanni Bellini's painting. At the same time, the narrative approach of his father's work—its straightforward, traditional storytelling—has been redefined. Mantegna explored similar effects in his contemporary or slightly later work, notably in the *Crucifixion* predella of his San Zeno altarpiece, painted between 1457 and 1459 (fig. 7). Soldiers leave the scene on foot and on horseback, literally turning their backs on the Crucifixion, and their procession into the distance begins just behind the cross of Christ himself. Both Mantegna and Bellini could find the inspiration for this

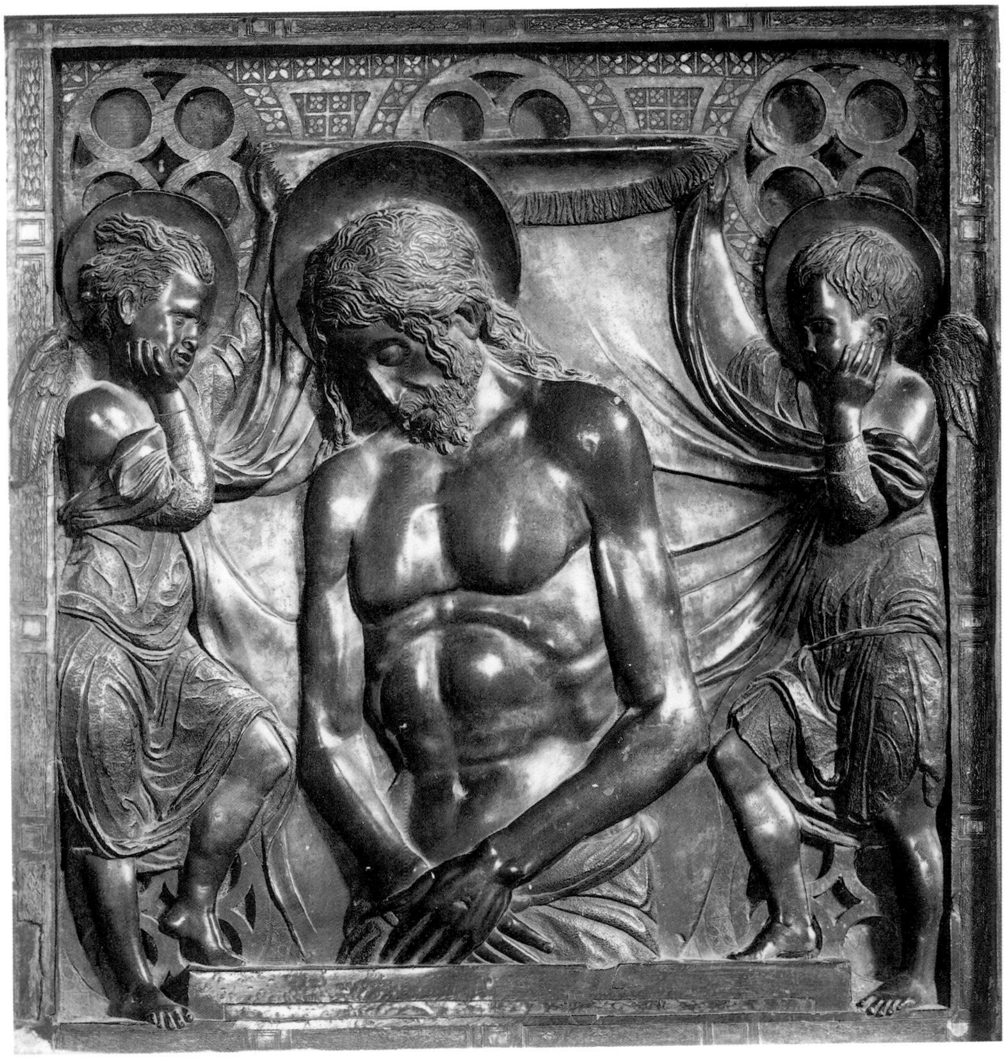

8. *Donatello,* Dead Christ Supported by Putti, *bronze relief, high altar, Sant'Antonio, Padua. Courtesy Museo Civico, Padua. Photo: Alinari/Art Resource, New York.*

powerful conception in a common source: the works of Jan van Eyck.[28] But what is important here is not so much the historical tracing of an artistic conception as the recognition that the younger generation learned from older artists (as always) and that Andrea Mantegna and Giovanni Bellini were turning to the same sources at about the same time. In addition to Jan van Eyck, they also studied Jacopo Bellini and Donatello, whose high altar for the Santo in Padua provided models of figure types, patterns of drapery, and in some cases composition (fig. 8).

By the time Bellini was perhaps twenty, he was executing commissions not only for small, private devotional images but for major altarpieces, which represented a greater financial commitment by the donor and reflected the painter's fast-growing reputation. Of course, the donation of an altarpiece to a church signifies much more than a gift of monetary value: as donors repeatedly remind us in their testaments and in the inscriptions of their altars, which are almost always the altars of funerary chapels, these images were intended as the focal point of prayers to be offered in perpetuity for the immortal souls of the patron and his family. In spite of such exhortations and various practical measures—the provision of funds, contractual obligations notarized and filed with the authorities—it often happened that funerary chapels changed hands and that new owners wished to honor different saints or to patronize other artists. The original altarpiece, now liturgically superfluous, could be preserved elsewhere, but removed from its original context, it may lose comprehensibility. Bellini's first known altarpiece is one of these fragmentary survivals, the Museo Correr's *Transfiguration of Christ*, which would have been the central panel of a triptych or polyptych (fig. 9).[29]

The feast of the Transfiguration had been celebrated in the West since at least the eighth century. It was extended to the universal church only in 1457, by Callistus III Borgia, to commemorate the Christian victory over the Turks at Belgrade.[30] It is tempting to associate Giovanni Bellini's painting of the Transfiguration with this momentous event, though the style may justify an earlier date. Whether the panel was painted in the mid- or late 1450s, it is Bellini's earliest surviving altarpiece, presumably intended for an altar or chapel of the Transfiguration.

During his earthly existence, Christ appeared in glory, or transfigured, and accompanied by Moses and Elijah in a vision witnessed by the Apostles Peter, James, and John (Matt. 17:1–13, Mark 9:2–13, Luke 9:28–36). Here is how the miracle is described in the Gospel of Matthew, chapter 17, verses 1–13:

> Jesus took with him Peter and James and John his brother, and led them up a high mountain apart. And he was transfigured before them, and his face shone like the sun, and his garments became white as light. And behold, there appeared to them Moses and Elijah, talking with him. And Peter said to Jesus, "Lord, it is well that we are here; if you wish, I will make three booths here, one for you and one for Moses and one for Elijah." He was still speaking, when lo, a bright cloud overshadowed them, and a voice from the cloud said, "This is my beloved Son, with whom I am well pleased; listen to him." When the disciples heard this, they fell on their faces, and were filled with awe. But Jesus came and touched them, saying, "Rise, and have no fear." And when they lifted up their eyes, they saw no one but Jesus only.

Then the apostles heard the voice of God the Father, repeating the words first spoken of Christ at the Baptism: "This is my beloved Son, with whom I am well pleased."

As in the *Saint Jerome*, a white plaque in the immediate foreground carries an inscription—not, as one might expect here, in reference to the Transfiguration, but rather the plaintive words of Job (19:21): "Miseremini Mei Saltem Vos Amici Mei," "Have pity on me, O you my friends (for the hand of God has touched me)." The quotation suggests that the Old Testament figure, venerated as a saint in Venice, would have been represented in one of the flanking panels that originally accompanied the *Transfiguration*.[31]

A sudden rise in the land, a kind of outcropping, provides a raised platform for the three apostles who witness the miracle. Their poses, no less than their location,

9. Transfiguration of Christ, *Civico Museo Correr, Venice. Photo: Gianfranco Spinazzi, Venice.*

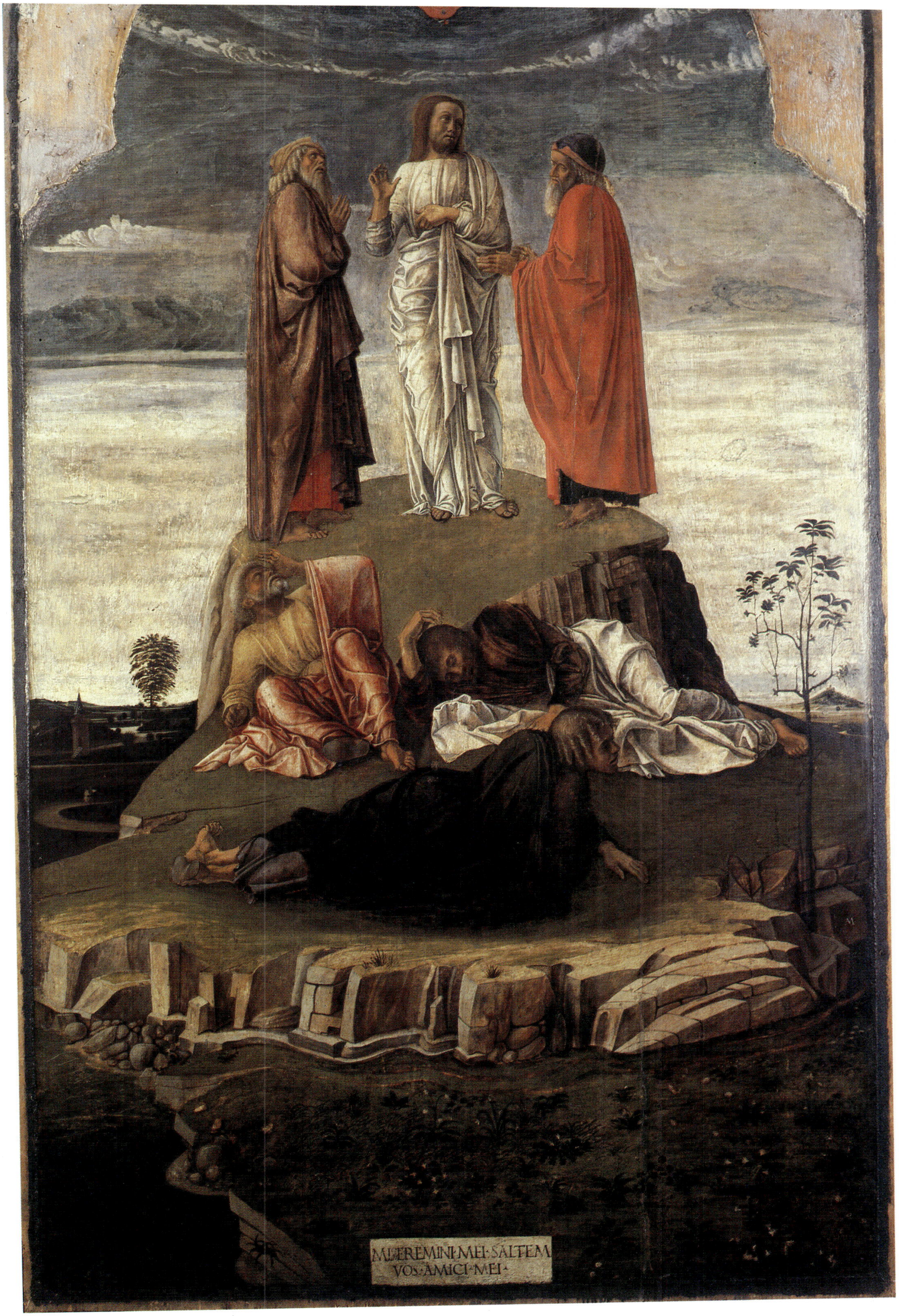
M EREMINI·MEI·SALTEM
VOS·AMICI·MEI·

clearly distinguish between their human nature and the celestial character of the Transfigured Christ and his prophets. The apostles cling to the ground, seeming literally to sink into the earth, whereas the sacred figures stand upright above them, aware only of one another and of God. John, for example, turns away from the apparition toward a leafy sapling that flourishes next to the cut stump of a large tree; his face and posture express his yearning for this new plant, by which Bellini meant to remind us that the Transfiguration prefigured the Resurrection. Christ himself suggested this in words ascribed to him by Matthew immediately after the Transfiguration is described: "And as they were coming down the mountain, Jesus commanded them, 'Tell no one the vision, until the Son of man is raised from the dead'" (Matt. 17:9).[32]

Whereas the Resurrection betokened Christ's eternal glory, which became possible only after his suffering and death on the cross, the Transfiguration was momentary and revealed only to three witnesses—the three who later accompanied Christ on the Mount of Olives. James, his reclining position the counterpoint of John's, appears to sleep (though his eyes are slightly open), anticipating his oblivion during Christ's Agony in the Garden (fig. 73).[33] Peter, meanwhile, the only one of the three apostles to whom the Gospels assign an active role, shields his eyes to look up at Christ and the prophets, and awestruck, falls back from the sight. In spite of his fear, as the Gospels explain, Peter is about to offer to construct "booths" (tents or tabernacles) to honor them.

Christ, Elijah, and Moses stand, or hover, above another platform of rocks created by Bellini to represent Mount Tabor (the traditional site of the Transfiguration) and to raise their figures above the others. Above Christ's head, the clouds form a slender arc that echoes the circular shapes of the rocks below, an arc that was originally completed above by the arched lobe of the panel itself, which has been cut. Within this elliptic space defined by clouds, Bellini had painted God the Father (or perhaps the Dove) surrounded by a glory of red cherubim: natural forms accompany the manifestation of the supernatural in the sky.[34] To be sure, a heavenly background is appropriate for the figures of the vision, but Bellini used this fact to give over half of the setting to sky, that is, not solid form but atmosphere.

Even before he painted this altarpiece, Bellini had used outdoor settings in his early images for private devotion in which landscape and sky provide the naturalistic raison d'être for his explorations of the palpable and coloristic essence of atmosphere. The large scale of the *Transfiguration* enhances these atmospheric effects, and the use of oil probably made them possible. Bellini's emphasis on colored light and air allows him to exploit their influence on form, most notably in the distant horizon to the right, where the mountains are so shrouded in mist that they have all but dissolved into air. This effect is both intentional—the surface is in good condition—and critical in setting Bellini's work apart from Mantegna's (fig. 7).

10. *Grand Canal, Venice.*

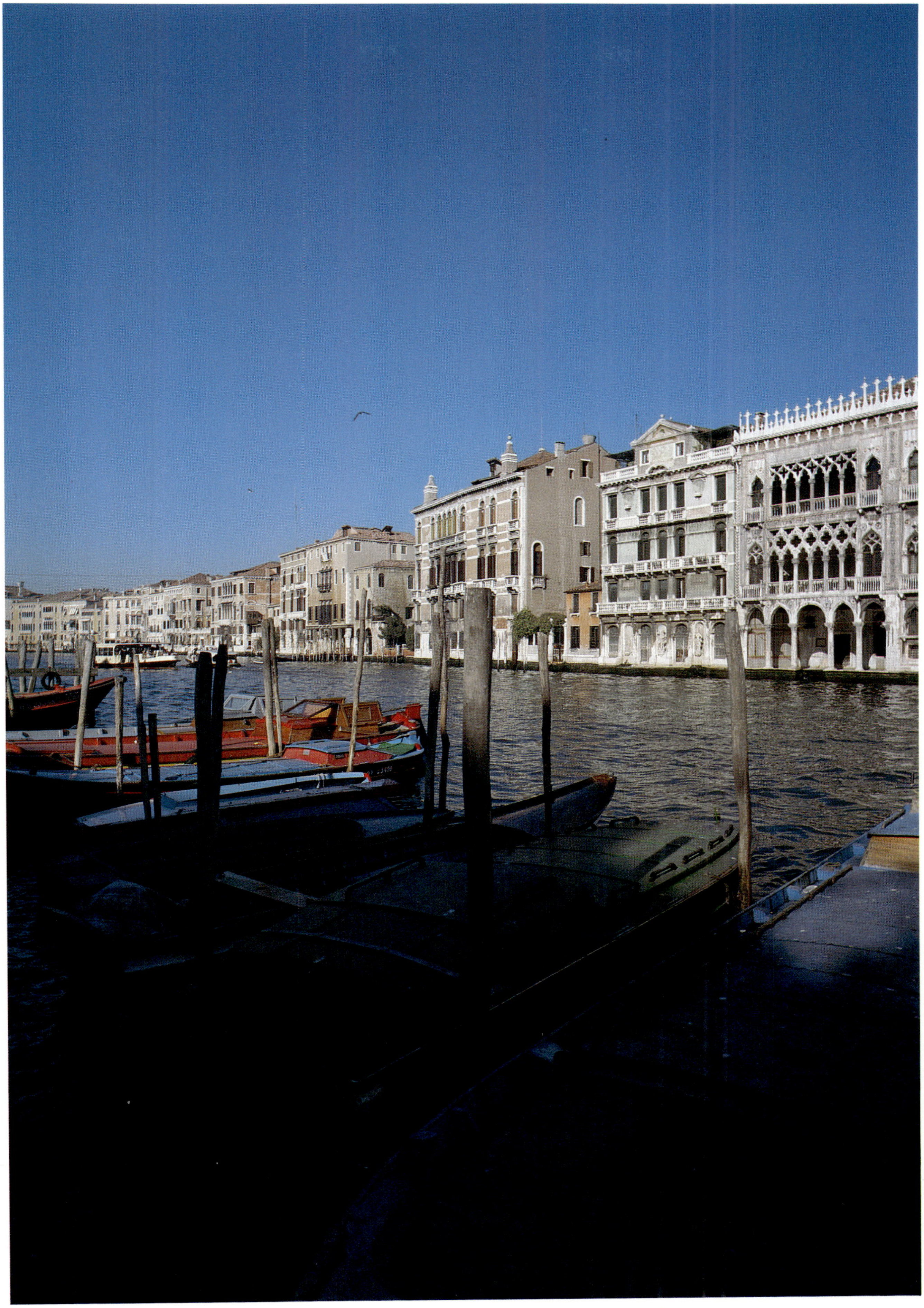

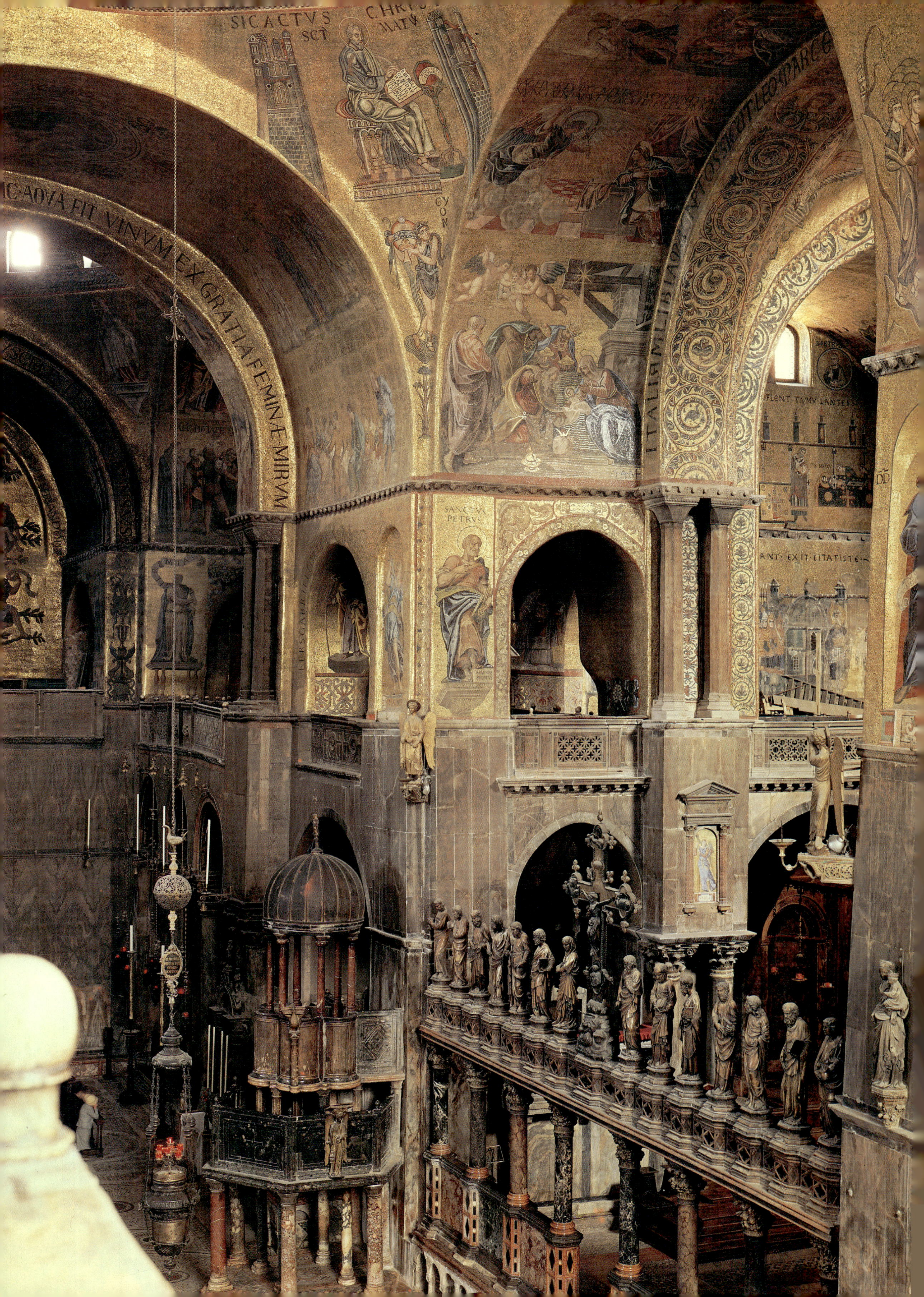
SIC ACTVS
IC AQVA FIT VINVM EX GRATIA FEMINE MIRVM
SANCTVS PETRVS

Mantegna's style of this time is represented by the *Agony in the Garden* (fig. 75).[35] The formal similarities between the two young artists so impressed some past observer that he carved the false monogram of Mantegna "AM" in the face of the rock at the right edge of Bellini's *Transfiguration* panel. But the differences are striking as well, and most important is the disparate conception of light, or rather its effect. In the Mantegna, everything is solid and precise, the sky no less than the rocks, the distance no less than the foreground. In the Bellini, atmosphere all but absorbs forms and colors on the horizon, and the clouds are amorphous manifestations of light and air.

Bellini's luminous vision was determined by the extraordinary experience of his native city, for in Venice solid forms are almost subsumed in the miasma of sky and water: light reaches the eye both from above and from below. Buildings, low on the horizon, shimmer against the ambient light that seems to erode the very contours of the stone, and in their watery reflections, these solid structures cease to exist as masonry and survive only as broken patches of color (fig. 10). Comparable to this natural phenomenon is the man-made miracle of San Marco, the most sacred monument of Venice. In its golden mosaics, as in the reflections of the canals, forms are defined not by contours but by irregular patches of golden light and color, and ambient light both penetrates the translucent surfaces of these tesserae and is refracted by them to the dazzled eye of the beholder (fig. 11).[36] Bellini saw these effects in his mind's eye as he painted.

*11. Interior, Basilica di San Marco, Venice. Photo: Scala/Art Resource, New York.*

# Part One: Sacred Painting

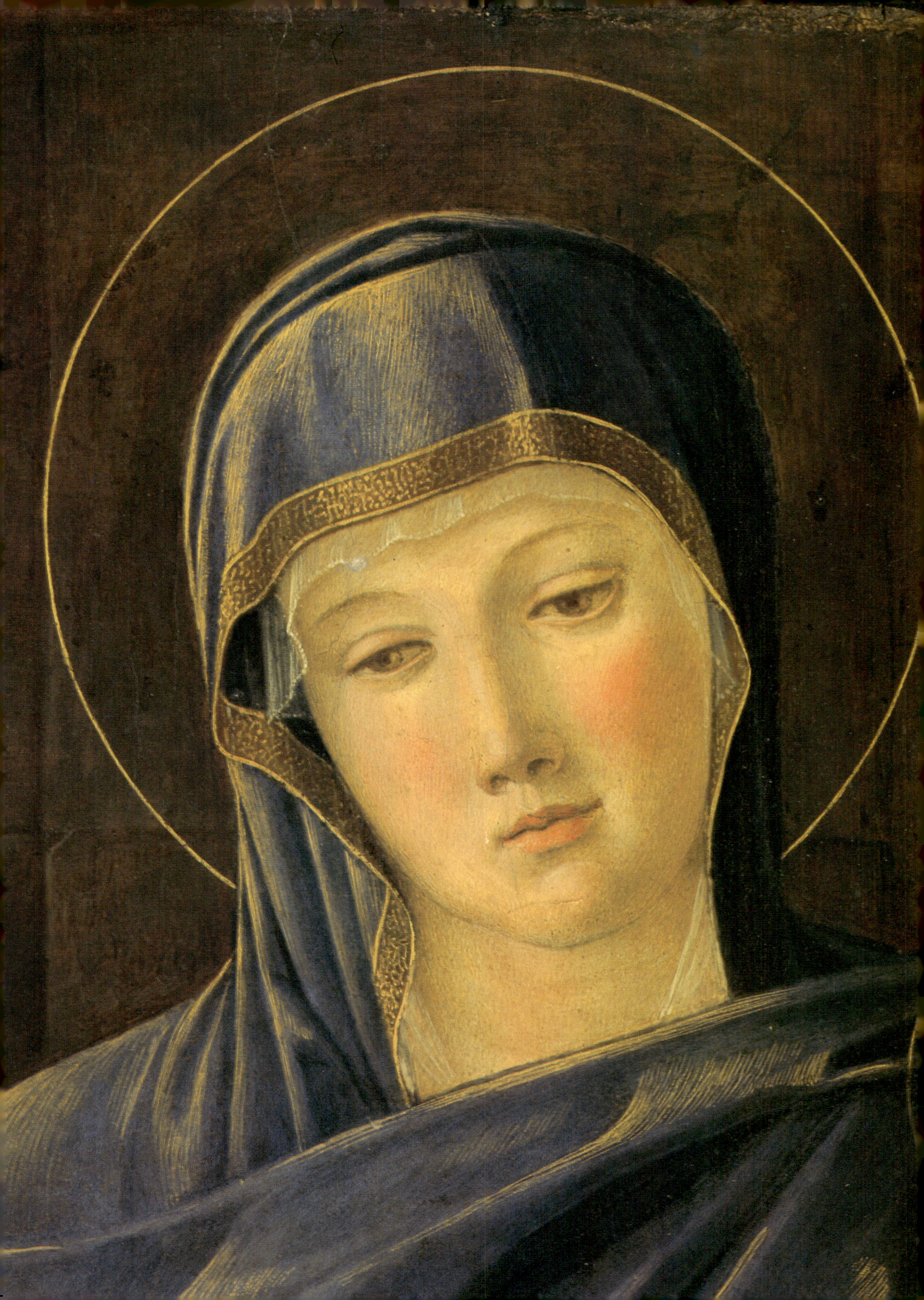

# 1 Images for Private Devotion

*Very beautiful and very devout*
—Francesco Sansovino

## Alpha: The Madonna and Child

Giovanni Bellini painted every kind of picture, sacred and secular, known to the Venetian Renaissance: histories and saints' lives, Madonnas and nudes, altarpieces, portraits, and murals. Above all else, however, he was a painter of private devotional images, especially the Virgin and Child. Thus Francesco Sansovino, in his *Dialogue on All the Notable Things in Venice*, particularly mentioned among Bellini's works his paintings for the republic, his altarpieces in San Giobbe (figs. 108–10) and in San Zaccaria (figs. 126, 127)—and his Madonnas, "very beautiful and very devout."[1]

Perhaps no artist is more intimately associated with the Madonna and Child theme than Bellini, and this is not merely a matter of sheer numbers, of the great success with his patrons that these numbers reflect, or of his extraordinary inventiveness in treating the subject. Even more than these facts—which are of obvious significance—the close association of artist and subject is founded on Bellini's ability to imbue his sacred images with conviction, which is perhaps the primary reason the Madonna paintings stir our imaginations and spiritual longings today, even when they rarely serve their original purpose. Few artists have equaled and none has surpassed Bellini's ability to engender a profoundly religious response in the viewer. His contemporaries conspicuously acknowledged his accomplishment: the great number of Madonna paintings produced by Bellini and his shop—more than eighty compositions are known—must closely parallel the number of patrons who commissioned or purchased them—a remarkable commercial success indeed.

Yet the explanation of the Madonna paintings does not lie solely in the demands of the Venetian marketplace, which reflected but did not motivate the production of these images. Innovative in style, yet traditional in imagery and meaning, the Madonna paintings reflect Bellini's proclivities and professional self-awareness. For this reason, some scholars have sought to understand Bellini's Madonnas by hypothesizing the artist's illegitimacy. This putative explanation implicitly acknowledges the force of his imagery, but the suggestion, however tempting in its touching and romantic picture of the unloved artist-bastard, remains unproven and improbable.[2] Almost nothing can be known or intuited about Bellini's rapport with Jacopo's wife, Anna Rinversi—whether or not she was Giovanni's mother—and it is far too speculative to base analysis of his Madonna paintings or his interpretation of the Virgin mourning her dead Son on the artist's supposed illegitimacy or even on the possibility that Anna did not love Giovanni very much.

Bellini's conception of sacred or earthly motherhood is not the only issue, however; it is bound with the foreseen death of the Son. Premonition of this fate determines the actions and demeanor of Mother and Child. Mary and Christ often seem remote from each other in spite of physical proximity. Their comportment is more hierarchic than maternal or childlike, their relationship seemingly more theological than human: in presenting her Child for our veneration, the Virgin offers the eucharistic sacrifice for our redemption. Bellini visualized this fundamental belief not with symbols or inscriptions but with the form and psychology of his images. In an age of devastating infant mortality rates, the Virgin Mother's certainty that her Child will predecease her would have been understood also in human terms. Any mother may dread the possibility of such tragic loss—but the Mother of Christ knows that in giving him life she has also assured his death: he is mortal because of her. Perhaps the maternal embrace remains psychologically uncertain because of Mary's realization that her possession of her Child endures only in death.[3]

The first thing one notices about Bellini's Madonna paintings may be their self-imposed formulaic quality within or against which Bellini set forth different interpretations of his favored theme. His followers' replicas and variants obscure this fact, like an accretion of barnacles concealing a treasure. Bellini is at once present and hidden in his images, self-aware in asserting his professional and spiritual role yet self-abnegating, masking himself and his guidance of our emotions from us. Like the most subtle of spiritual advisers, Bellini leads us to understanding while reiterating the phrases of the sacred text that he himself had written. Bellini never forgot that these are devotional images intended to inspire a contemplative mood of reverence. This spirituality verifies the authenticity of his Madonnas as much as (if not more than) their stylistic or technical features or the typical compositional limitations that Bellini imposed.

The primary restriction, both in composition and in meaning, was to depict the Madonna as a partial figure, almost always half-length and frontal and seen behind a ledge or parapet that supports her Child. Although the half-length was being used less and less for sacred images in Italian art, it remained the traditional format of portraiture until the end of the fifteenth century, and therein lies the key to Bellini's imagery.

The art history of Madonna painting begins with a legend. The first artist to have portrayed Mary, according to tradition, was the Apostle and Evangelist Luke, the patron saint of painters. Mary signaled her approbation of his efforts in a practical way: she appeared before Luke, so that his picture of her was in fact a portrait, painted in the presence of the model (fig. 12).[4] This conception of a

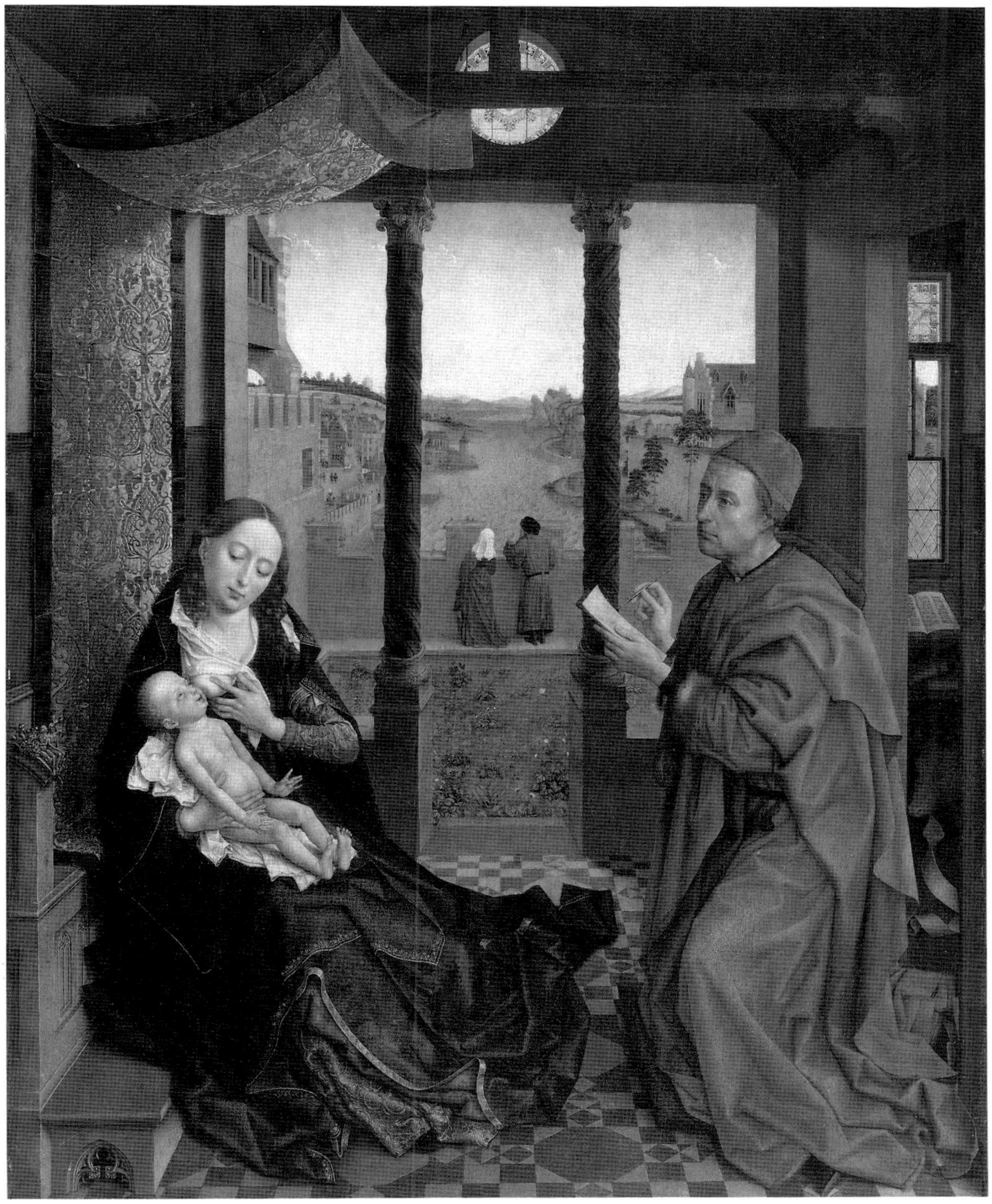

12. *Attributed to Rogier van der Weyden,* Saint Luke Portraying the Virgin Mary, *Museum of Fine Arts, Boston. Courtesy Museum of Fine Arts, Boston, Gift of Mr. and Mrs. Henry Lee Higginson.*

sacred image as a likeness was fundamental to Byzantine understanding of the icon (image), which can assist in the transmission of prayer because it resembles the holy being it represents. The repetition of facial features, of specific colors and details of appearance in Byzantine icon painting is explained by the pious necessity to adhere to the appearance of the sacred figure recorded in images that supposedly originated as portrait likenesses. The half- or bust-length format was appropriate for these holy images because it was also the format of ancient secular portraiture: icons are portraits, portraits are bust-length, therefore icons are also bust-length, with the further advantage of focusing attention on that part of the body—the upper part—considered the more spiritual.

Bishop Durandus explained this apt symbolism in his *Rationale Divinorum Officiorum*, an authoritative compendium of liturgy and imagery. "The Greeks," Durandus informed his readers, "employ painted representations, painting . . .

only from the navel upwards, that all occasion of vain thoughts may be removed."[5] Thus, when the legend of Luke's painting the Virgin Mary was associated with particular icons, those icons were and are appropriately bust portraits—including the *Nikopeia*, the miraculous palladium brought from Constantinople to Venice after the Fourth Crusade and still venerated in San Marco.[6] When Luke's icon of the Madonna was represented as his saintly attribute, it was represented as a half- or bust-length picture (fig. 13). And when Luke's act of portraying the Virgin itself became a subject of paintings, the image that he creates is a partial figure, even though the Madonna frequently appears standing full-length before him.

Luke's purported images of the Virgin Mary commemorate her appearance. We understand, as ancient and Renaissance people did when they made or viewed portraits, that a likeness signifies actual presence. Thus, if the emperor himself could not be present to pass judgment, as required by Roman law, then his portrait bust became his proxy. With this ancient precedent in mind, when the humanist Raffaele Zovenzoni would not go to the bishop of Trent, he sent instead his portrait by Bellini.[7] And with similar reasoning, albeit with a less literal insistence on its meaning, portraits of contemporary rulers are displayed today; whether elected, hereditary, or tyrannically imposed, heads of state are present in their government offices by virtue of their portraits, which are typically half- or bust-length. The medium may have changed from sculpture or painting to photography, but the format and intent remain the same.

The half-length, which is literally a partial disembodiment, may also connote a vision or, in the case of Saint Luke's Madonnas, the record of a vision. This visionary aspect of the half-length is inherently related to its portrait function: the absent may be present (like the emperor of Rome), the dead may live, through their likenesses. In ancient Rome, the portrait of one's ancestor—sometimes a death mask or an image based on such a mask—was preserved in order that both the individual and his *gens* might continue to live. These wonderful possibilities were appreciated by Leon Battista Alberti in the fifteenth century. "Through painting," he declared, "the faces of the dead go on living for a very long time."[8] For related reasons, in Christian art, when a saint or God himself appears in a vision, the apparition is characteristically a half-length. Thus God the Father appears in the skies to welcome the Virgin Mary in Titian's *Assunta*; thus the Madonna appears to honor the saints in Carpaccio's San Vitale altarpiece; thus an angel appears from heaven to unite Joachim and Anna in the *Meeting at the Golden Gate* by Bartolomeo Vivarini.

To be sure, all of these related themes may be associated with any half-length image of the Virgin: portraiture, presence, vision, and the legend of Saint Luke are all evoked. When Bellini started to produce his half-length Madonna paintings in the mid-fifteenth century, the format soon became a distinguishing feature of his works and those produced by artists associated with him. Yet throughout most of that century, the half-length figure continued in use for portraiture in the usual

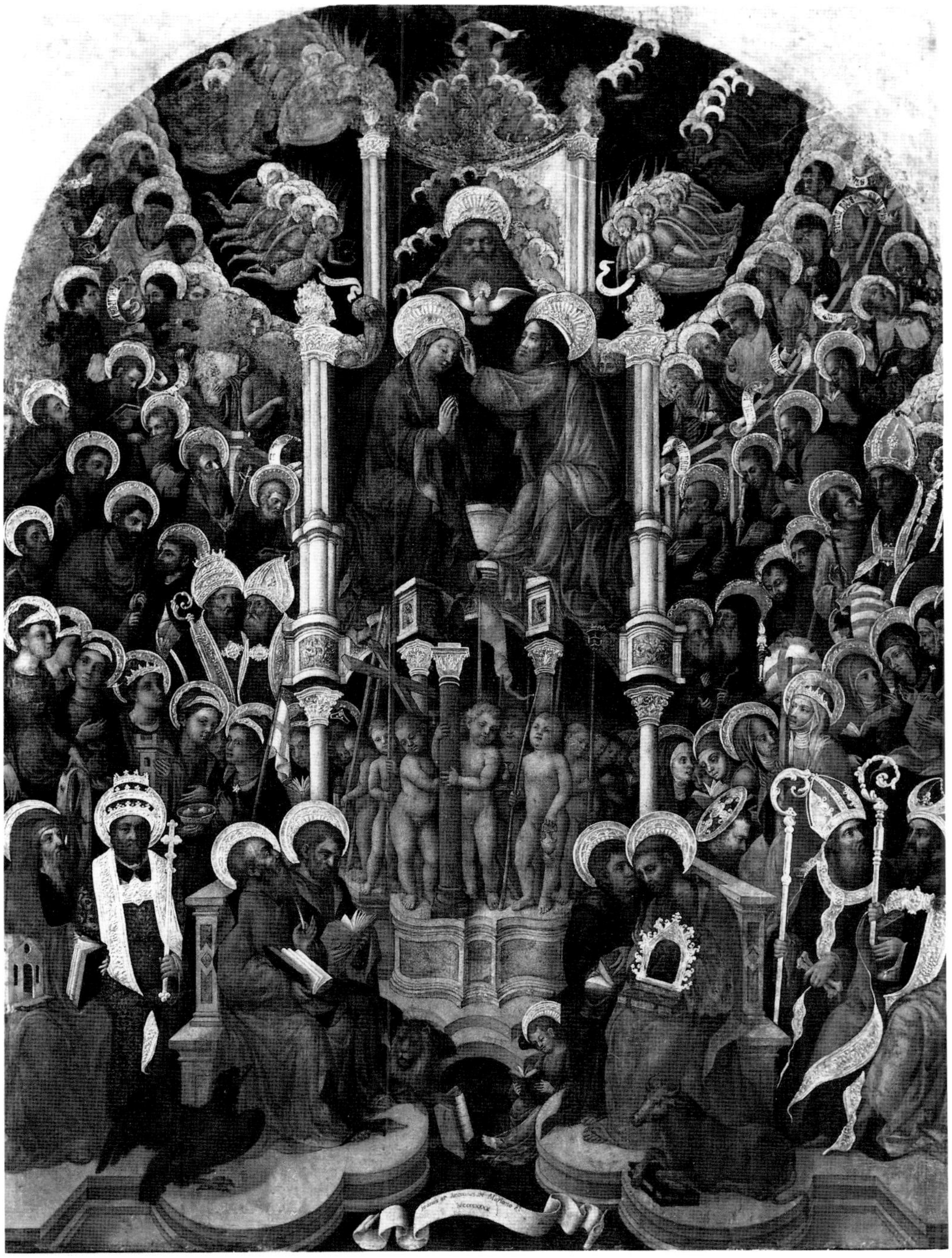

13. *Michele Giambono,* Coronation of the Virgin, *Gallerie dell'Accademia, Venice. Photo: Soprintendenza ai Beni Artistici e Storici, Venice.*

sense, for likenesses of contemporaries and of secular historical figures of the recent past, for actual men and women, rulers and poets, condottieri and courtesans.[9] This almost exclusive association of the half-length figure with portraiture confirms Bellini's intentions: the half-length implies portraiture, in particular Luke's first portrait(s) of the Virgin Mary. Nor is this allusion to the legend and form of icon painting surprising, for it was in Venice that the models of the Byzantine East were considered more sacrosanct than elsewhere in the West, in Venice that the Greek Christians settled when they were expelled from Constantinople in 1453, in Venice that they found, in Cardinal Bessarion's words, "quasi alterum Byzantium," almost another Byzantium.[10]

First coming to prominence as a colony of the Byzantine Empire, Venice was infused with the spirit and culture of the East, and these psychological and intellectual ties were reinforced by continuing financial and military concerns from the time of the Fourth Crusade, when the Venetians reversed their ancient client-patron relationship with Byzantium, until 1570–71, when they lost Cyprus, their last colonial stronghold there, to the Turks.[11] But even then Venetian reverence for Byzantium never ceased. Bellini's patrons did not need to be reminded of the icon tradition, or of the sanctity of their mythologized Byzantine past. To any Venetian, the Byzantine allusions of a sacred image were appropriate and rich with significance: this was a heritage to be cherished, not discarded; and no Venetian would have written of the sterility of the Greek modes, as the Tuscans Ghiberti and Vasari did in their summaries of Italian art history.

Bellini's use of the half-length format for the Virgin, then, is a purposeful reference to the legend of Luke's image of the Madonna, the first ever painted, and to the icon tradition that embodied this legendary history of art. Details of Mary's costume in Bellini's paintings, such as the wimple that covers her brow or the fold of her mantle over her shoulder, also evoke the Byzantine images associated with Luke and with icons in general. Unlike his saintly predecessor, however, Bellini provided a logical explanation for the half-length figure by including a parapet or ledge in the foreground. This admixture of supernatural and natural or illusionistic elements is typical of the Renaissance mentality.

The parapet, the only significant perspectival form in Bellini's Madonna paintings, asserts the immediacy of Mary and Christ in the foreground while separating their sacred realm from our world. The Christ Child who appears on this ledge is thrust toward us, almost out of the picture space, an effect heightened by the relation of image to frame. The Madonna is immediately behind the parapet and her proximity to us emphasized by her size. Moreover, the parapet resembles the form that it symbolizes in Bellini's art, namely the altar, where the sacred and earthly spheres meet, where one is accessible to the other, when Christ's sacrifice is reenacted in the celebration of the Mass. The altar-parapet is also the metaphoric equivalent of the tomb and of the Virgin Mother herself, because in each of these Christ was enshrined and from each he was born, as the newborn in the Nativity, as the reborn Savior of the Resurrection, and as the eucharistic sacrifice of the Mass.

Bellini introduced his compositional formula with his first essay on this theme, the Davis *Madonna* (circa 1455), which is also his first surviving monumental figure—monumental in conception, not in size (fig. 14).[12] The *Madonna* presents us at once with the typical problems of studying Bellini: in its present condition, the painting is the poorly preserved relic of a once-powerful work, and we must attempt to restore its visual appearance in the mind's eye just as we attempt to restore its historical context in the informed imagination. The handling of the figures represents the most notable development over Bellini's slightly earlier works,

*14.* Madonna and Sleeping Child *(Davis* Madonna*), Metropolitan Museum of Art, New York, Bequest of Theodore M. Davis, 1915. Theodore M. Davis Collection.*

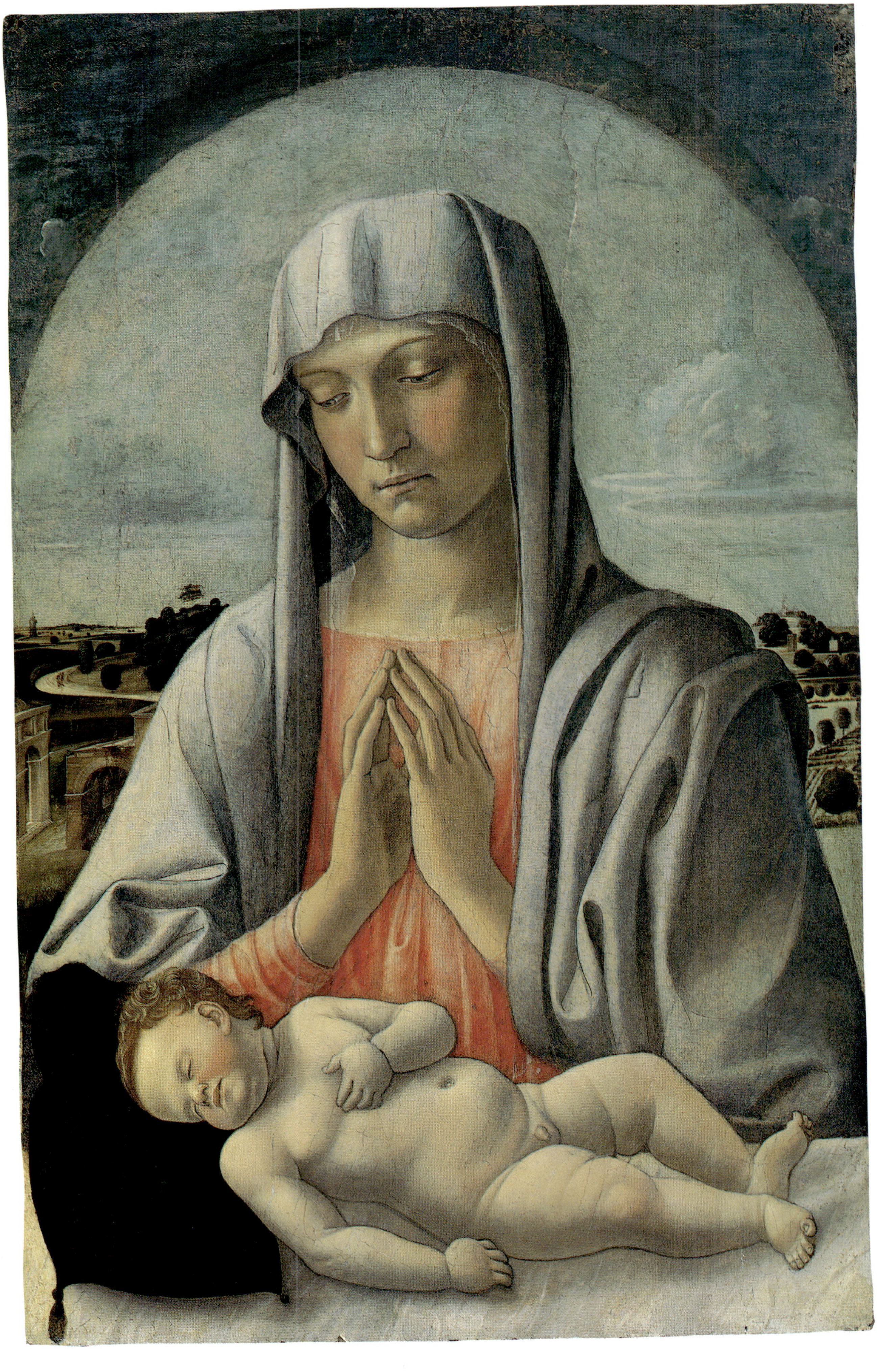

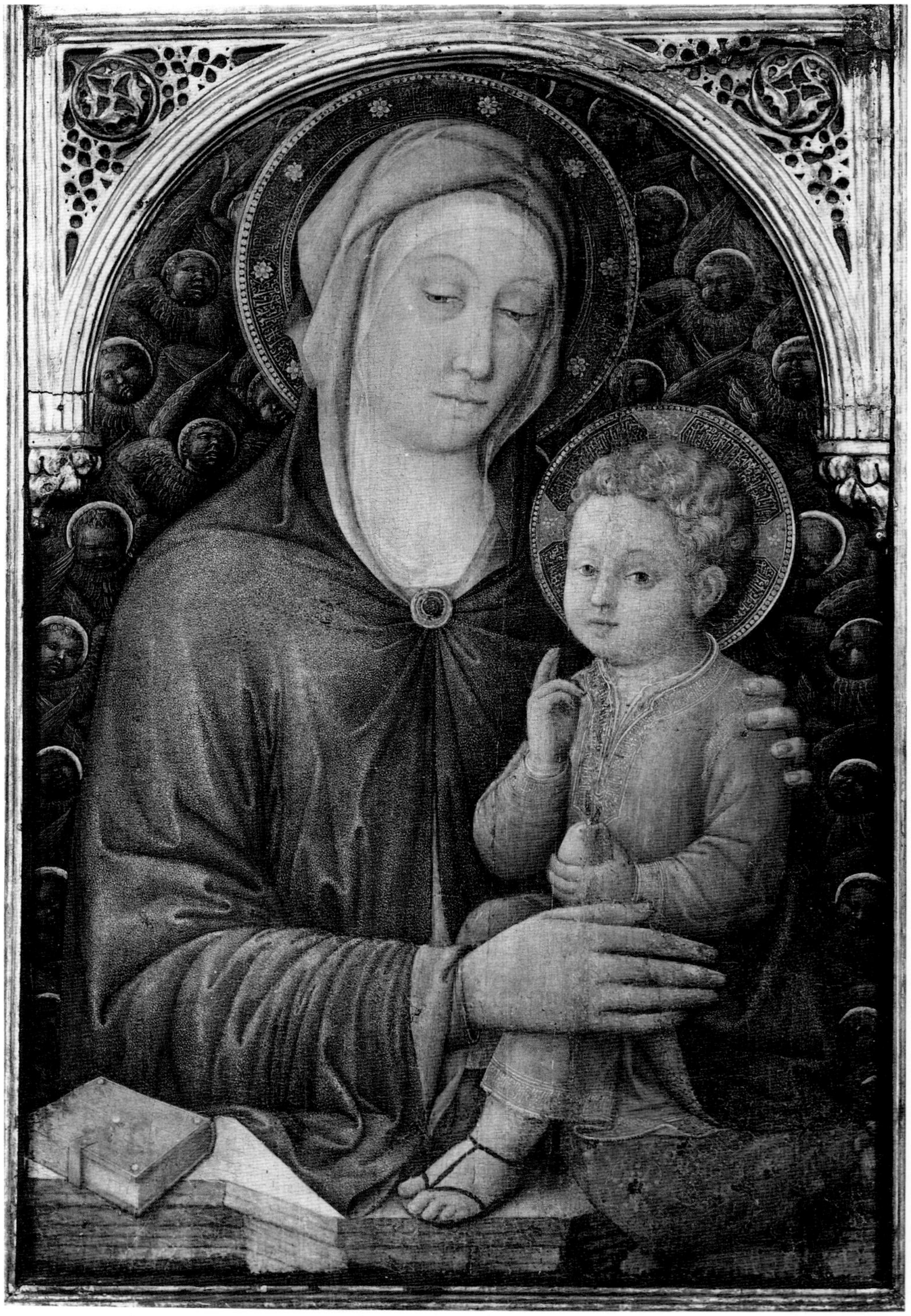

15. *Jacopo Bellini,* Madonna dei cherubini, *Gallerie dell'Accademia, Venice. Photo: Soprintendenza ai Beni Artistici e Storici, Venice.*

in the spatial construction of Mary's praying hands, for example, or in the movement of her mantle, now more naturalistically varied than in the *Crucifixion* (fig. 5) and corresponding to the bend of her head as she looks down at her Son.

The Virgin prays over the sleeping figure of the Child, whose sleep prefigures his sacrifice and death. This subject was not new: the Vivarini, among others, also represented such images. In spite of this iconographical kinship, Bellini broke with the Venetian heritage. His strong, severe personification of the Virgin and his stylistic austerity signify a rejection of the Venetian International Style of Jacopo

Bellini, Antonio Vivarini, Michele Giambono, and their contemporaries (fig. 13). These qualities distinguish Giovanni Bellini's painting from the contemporary *Madonna dei cherubini* by his father, for example, in spite of compositional similarities between the two, notably the use of the half-length figure and the parapet (fig. 15). Jacopo's image is luxurious, with gold stippling to highlight the Virgin's mantle, punched patterns in her halo, gold striations for the cherubim that fill the background; every detail, including the parapet, is elaborated. Not so in Giovanni's painting. Here instead is a bold image stripped of all adornment: a restricted palette, powerful forms, nothing courtly, elegant, or purely decorative. In spite of these restrictions, the painting was costly, because Bellini used ultramarine blue, now almost lost, for the Virgin's mantle. But the only ornamental forms are, de facto, the halos, defined by concentric gold striations, recalling Bellini's similar use of gold in his other early works. Here visual simplicity is inextricably bound with psychological force.

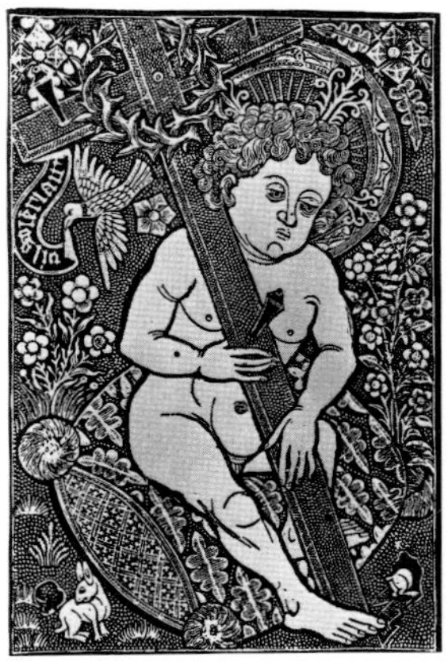

*16. Anonymous Fifteenth-Century German,* Infant Christ with Instruments of the Passion, *woodcut. Reprinted from Henrik Cornell,* The Iconography of the Nativity of Christ *(Uppsala, 1924).*

The horizon coincides with Mary's shoulders, so that her head is set against the cloudy sky, providing her with a luminous aura of sanctity. However, the landscape itself, minute in scale, cannot be understood as a natural environment for the Virgin and Child: they are outside its spatial restrictions, as they are also removed from any historical or temporal limitations. In spite of the great contrast in scale, the background is unified with the foreground—not by perspective, but by light and air. The low horizon permits a background largely given over to sky, an insubstantial substance of color, light, and air—an ephemeral compound. The atmosphere makes its force felt on the softened forms and contours of the distant landscape. As in the *Transfiguration*, this effect is intentional: the landscape is the best preserved part of the composition.

The Child is nude—a youthful, heroic nude, a Christian infant Hercules, his heroism made vulnerable, however, by his sleep and by the revelation of his humanity. By depicting the Infant nude, thereby demonstrating his likeness to all male infants, Bellini reminded the viewer-worshiper of Christ's mortality, the means of our salvation. Christ's death, prefigured by his sleep, was possible only because he had taken human form. Thus when Bellini represented the symbolic sleep of the Infant, he represented him naked: the Child's sex, the primary attribute of his humanity, signifies the possibility of his eventual suffering and death on the cross.[13] Whatever else may be involved in depictions of Christ's nudity—intimations of mortality may be combined with recollections of antiquity, for example—surely Leo Steinberg is correct about this theological and devotional significance of the Lord's nakedness.[14] Christ's nudity and his sacrifice are conflated in this imagery, as, for example, when Francis and his friars spoke of their nakedness to follow the naked Lord, referring specifically to Jesus naked on the cross.[15] In this way are combined the themes of Christ's Incarnation and his sacrificial death, commemorated in the eucharistic offering of the Mass.

Bellini reiterated his eucharistic theme by other means as well. In the Davis

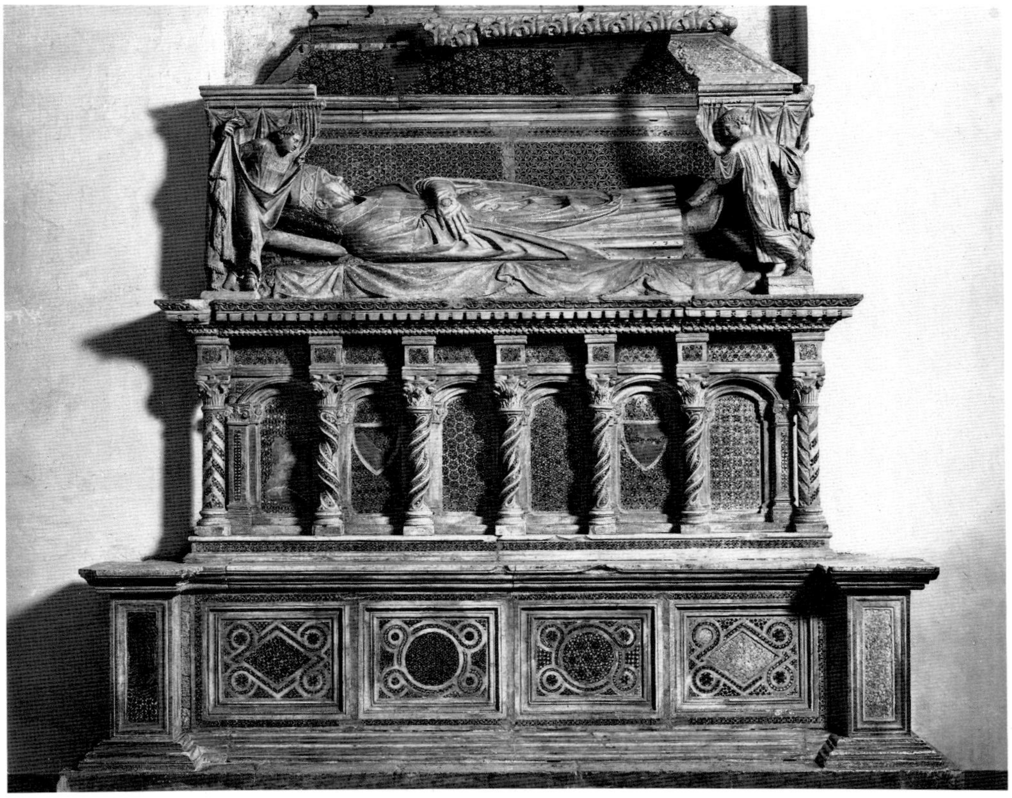

*17. Arnolfo di Cambio, detail, tomb of Guillaume, cardinal de Braye, San Domenico, Orvieto. Photo: Anderson/Art Resource, New York.*

*Madonna*, for example, the Child's head rests on a tasseled pillow, recalling contemporary images of the Child seated on a cushion with instruments of the Passion (fig. 16). This is also reminiscent of the imagery of funerary monuments in which the deceased reclines on a bier, the head resting on a pillow (fig. 17). Sculptors were recording reality: tomb effigies generally depict precisely how the deceased was interred.[16] Bellini alluded to death even more explicitly in the pose of the Christ Child. With one arm at his side and the other bent across his chest, the Infant resembles effigies of the deceased and even more resembles images of himself in countless Lamentations, Entombments, and Pietàs.

The Child casts shadows on the parapet, and the light that causes them must come from outside the picture, from the viewer's world, as distinguished from the illumination of the landscape setting. Light, spatial illusion, and the relation of picture to frame thus combine to create two disparate realms while establishing an intimate bond between them, hence between viewer and image. The two spheres join at the parapet, where the eucharistic Christ is presented for our veneration, exemplified by the Madonna. And here, on the parapet, Bellini conspicuously placed his signature in many paintings, either inscribed directly into the fictive stone surface of the ledge or written on a *cartellino* (an illusionistic paper label) seemingly affixed to its surface.

*18.* Madonna and Child, *Pinacoteca Malaspina, Civici Musei, Castello Visconteo, Pavia. Photo: Chiolini & Pozzi di Pozzi Dario, Pavia.*

Bellini evidently used the cartellino for the first time in the Pavia *Madonna and Child* (fig. 18), painted shortly after the Davis picture: the cartellino is inscribed with his signature, IOANNES. BELLINVS. P., written with a surer classicizing

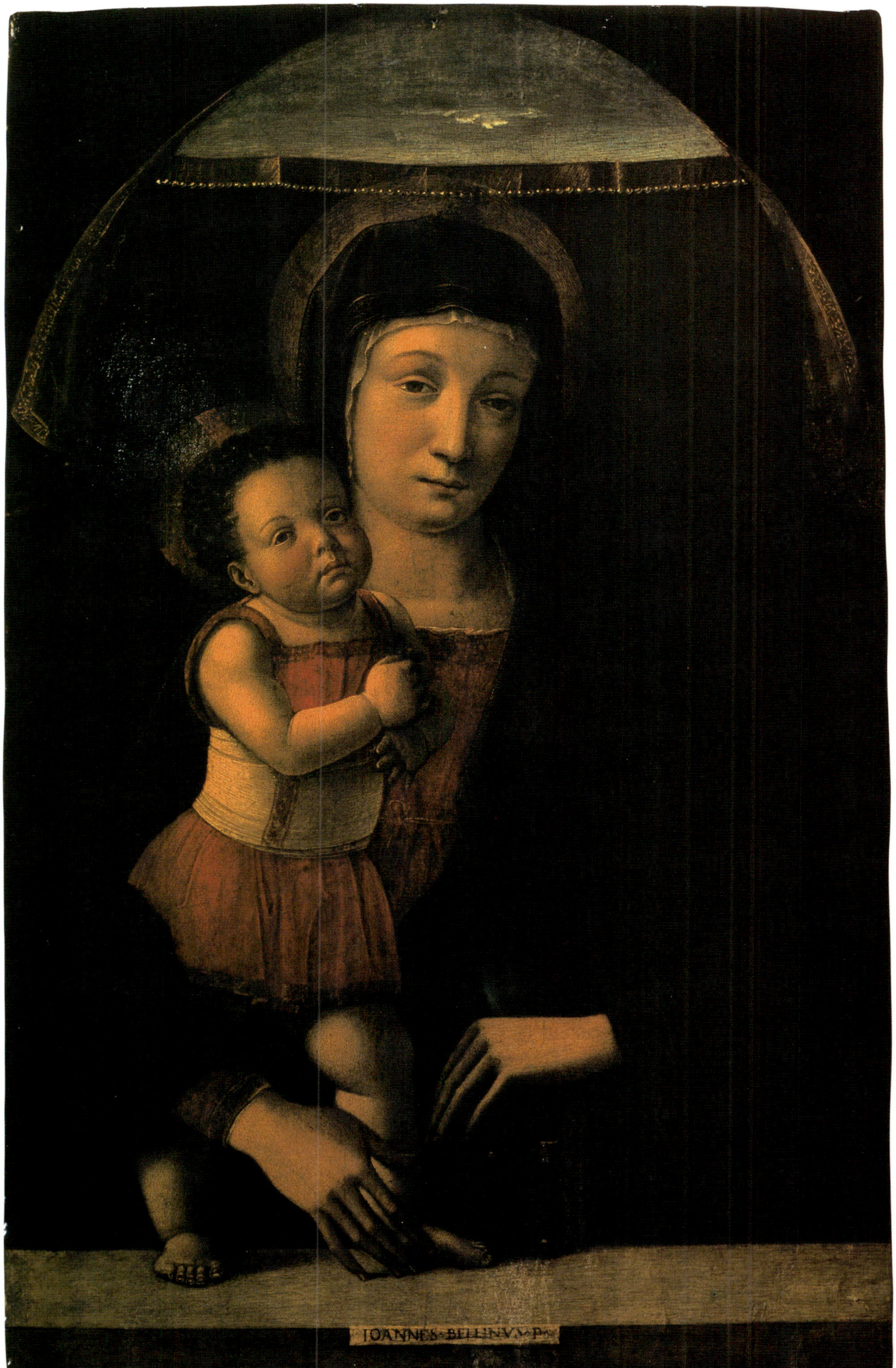
IOANNES·BELLINVS·P·

hand than in the *Saint Jerome* (fig. 1) and in the form and spelling that became customary in his work.[17] In the *Saint Jerome*, as in the *Transfiguration* altarpiece (fig. 9), Bellini had signed his name on a white panel or plaque, superimposed on the painting, as it were, and not integral to the composition. But now, and from now on, by associating his signature with the parapet, pretending that his name is inscribed on a piece of paper attached to, and sometimes casting shadows on, the stone ledge, Bellini exploited illusionism to make his presence felt. And the signature becomes even more than a testimony of his professional identity and an avowal of his faith: by writing his name, he bears witness to the reality of the Virgin and Child whose appearance before us is made possible by his skill.[18]

Certain technical details relate the Pavia *Madonna* to the Davis panel and to the other earliest works: the halos are defined by concentric dashes of gold, Mary's white veil is translucent, painted with short, vertical strokes, and the highlights of her dark mantle are suggested by gold stippling, recalling the use of gilding in the Barber *Saint Jerome* and the Correr *Crucifixion*. As in the Davis *Madonna* and many others, in the Pavia composition the Infant's presence is confirmed by the shadows he casts on the parapet, shadows that pretend to be caused by light from outside the picture. The Infant is no longer nude, however, but clothed as a princeling. Mary, too, is more elegant and courtly: Bellini has abandoned the broad, almost square face and strong features of the earlier image for smaller, more delicate features in a tapered, oval face. Whether because Bellini's Venetian clients preferred loveliness to strength in their images of the Virgin Mary or because the young master had redefined his conception of the holy Mother—or, as seems likely, for both reasons—his characterization of the Madonna had already changed even though the compositional formula remained the same.

In Bellini's images, Mary's loveliness is poignant, tinged with tragic understanding but never distorted by it. Resembling Byzantine icons (fig. 19), both physically and psychologically, her oval face is dominated by large, usually dark eyes that look inward, rarely at the Child and almost never at the viewer. This detachment is not indifference; it is prescience, commingled with sadness and seriousness of purpose, for the Virgin not only anticipates and accepts Christ's sacrifice, she shares his Passion as our co-redeemer. At the same time, her restraint expresses the stated Venetian ideal of decorous comportment, a patrician desideratum of behavior extolled by Francesco Barbaro and Pietro Bembo, among others.[19]

These early Madonnas introduce Bellini's two major categories of Marian imagery, the Mother who presents her Child for our worship, and the Virgin who herself worships her sleeping Son. The import is the same in each: the Passion is prefigured in the Child. This meaning is encapsulated in the symbolic form of the parapet/altar-tomb and inherent in the Christ's eucharistic identity, although the sacrificial role is more explicitly visualized in images of the nude, sleeping Infant.

In the 1460s and early 1470s, Bellini seems to have preferred the more conservative imagery of the clothed Child held in his Mother's arms. None of the

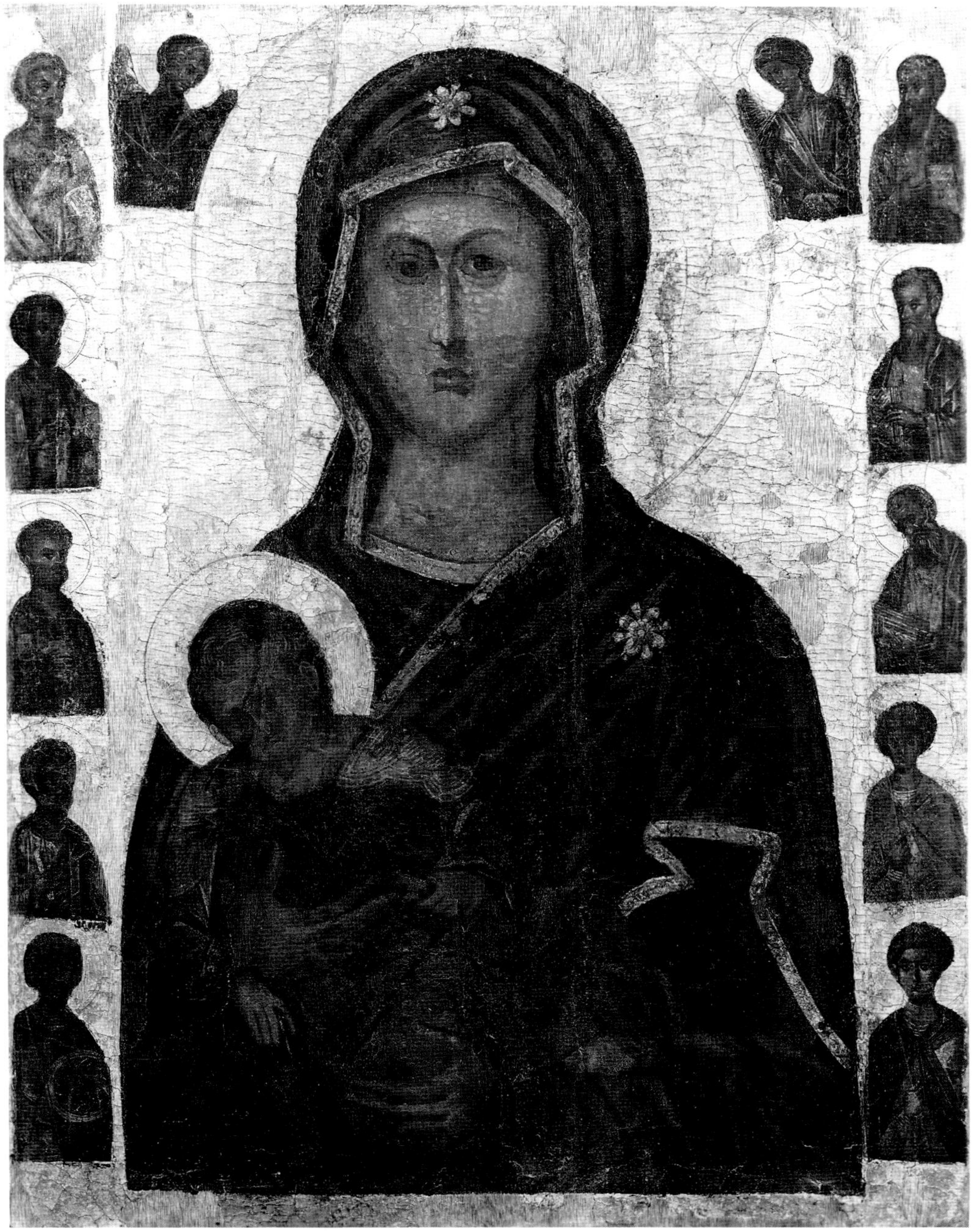

19. *Byzantine,* Madonna, *Istituto Ellenico, Venice. Photo: Istituto Ellenico, Venice.*

Madonnas associated with his style in the 1460s seems worthy of him, however, not even the three most commonly accepted as autograph: the paintings in the Johnson Collection, in the Lehman Collection, and in the Castello Sforzesco (figs. 20–22). They recall the Davis and Pavia Madonnas but are markedly inferior to these works and to other paintings of the 1450s and 1460s. These three Madonna paintings are either copies or variants of his compositions by other masters or by Bellini himself but with considerable assistance—possibly supplied by restorers. This would explain the early distortions of the heads in the Lehman painting; the uncertainty of Christ's pose and the inept drawing of Mary's hands in the Johnson *Madonna*; and the misshapen neck and hand of the Virgin in the Sforzesco panel.[20] The presence of Giovanni Bellini's name does not guarantee authorship,

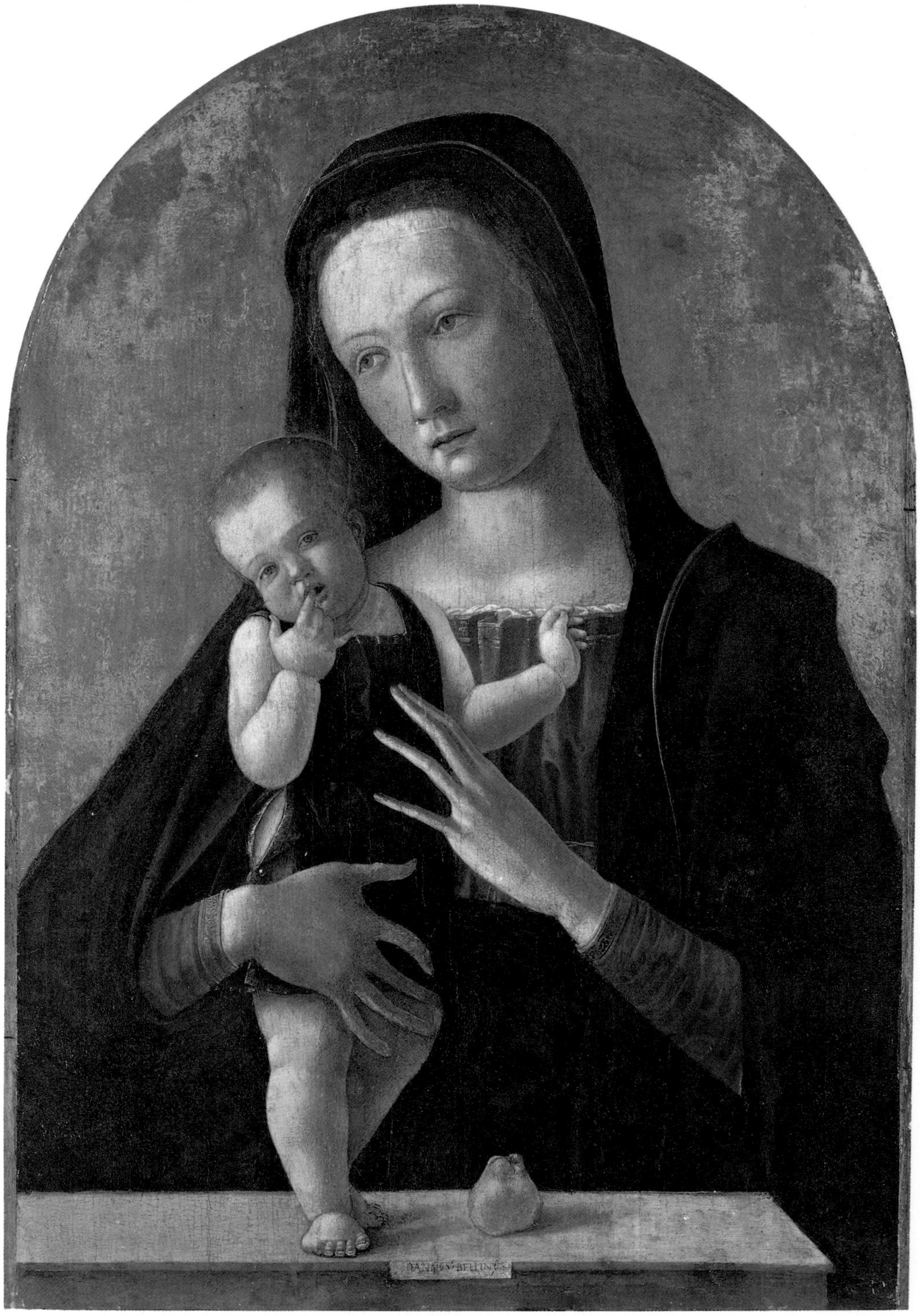

20. *Giovanni Bellini with assistance,* Madonna and Child, *Philadelphia Museum of Art, The John G. Johnson Collection of Philadelphia.*

in the Johnson panel or in numerous other "signed" works.[21] Nonetheless, the Bellinesque origin of these pictures is indisputable. They reveal Bellini's response to other artists, notably Donatello and Mantegna, absorbing some ideas—such as the type used for the Christ Child—while merely experimenting with others, such as the vivid colors and decorative garland of the Lehman *Madonna*. The luxurious elaboration of the Sforzesco picture is related to Jacopo Bellini's art (fig. 15). Perhaps this flurry of derivative activity owed something to the demands of Bellini's patrons, and surely it reflects his self-aware concern with style and his flexibility of

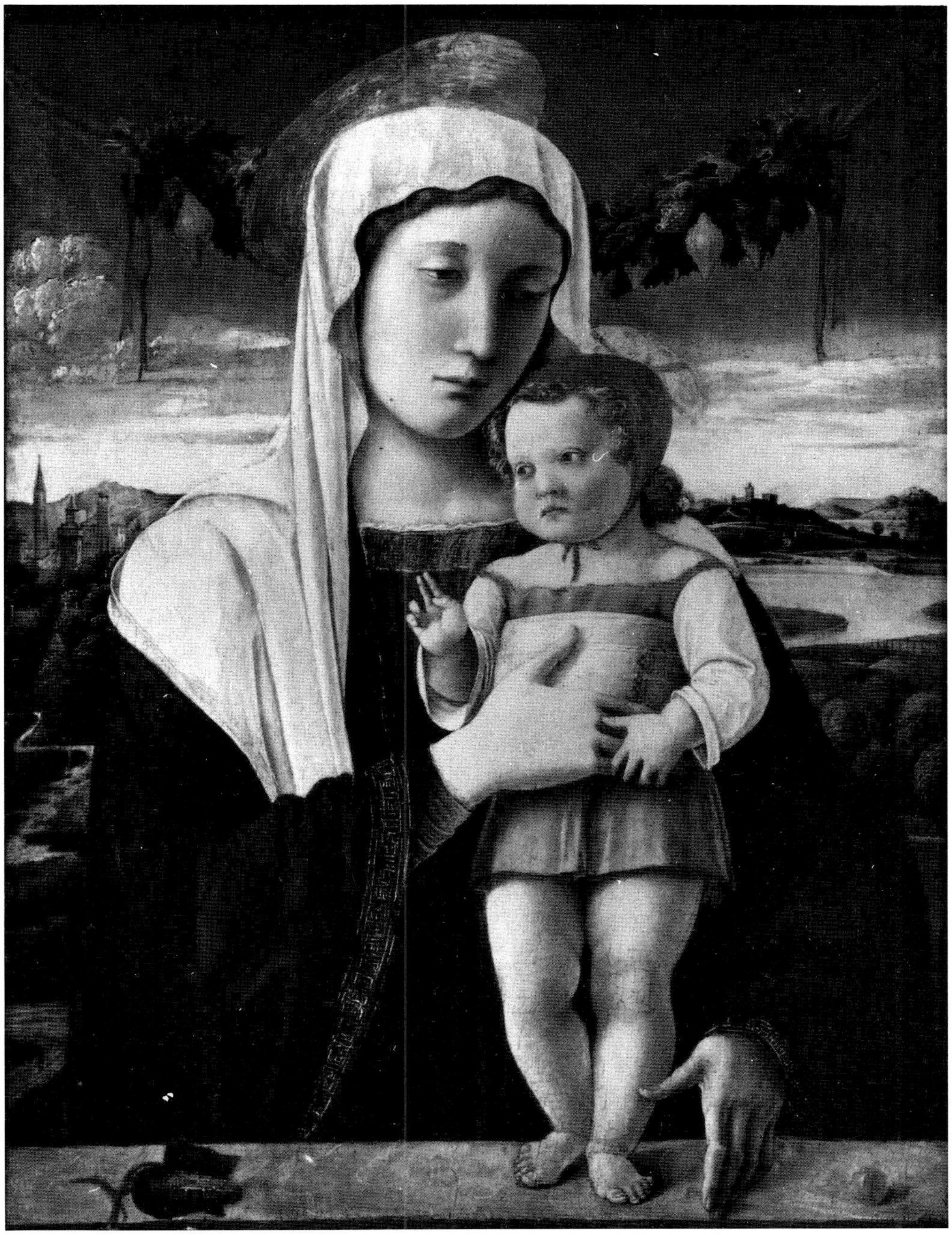

21. *Giovanni Bellini (repainted),* Madonna and Blessing Child, *Metropolitan Museum of Art, New York, Robert Lehman Collection, 1975.*

mind. But these ideas offered only temporary or partial solutions to the problems of style and iconography that concerned him.

As we have seen, in addition to the traditional image of the Child fully clothed and alert, Bellini depicted the Infant naked and asleep. The elegant *Madonna and Child* in the Gardner Museum, which is the poorly preserved and heavily restored remnant of a composition of the early 1470s, is a case in point (fig. 23).[22] Here the Passion is evoked with even greater intimacy and emotion than in the Davis *Madonna*: Mary supports her Son's head and takes his limp hand in hers; his other arm falls over the pillows on which he rests as he will rest on his mother's lap in the Pietà; he sinks back on the cushion as though lifeless. Mary looks into his face, but he cannot return her glance. When she lifts the Child's hand in her own,

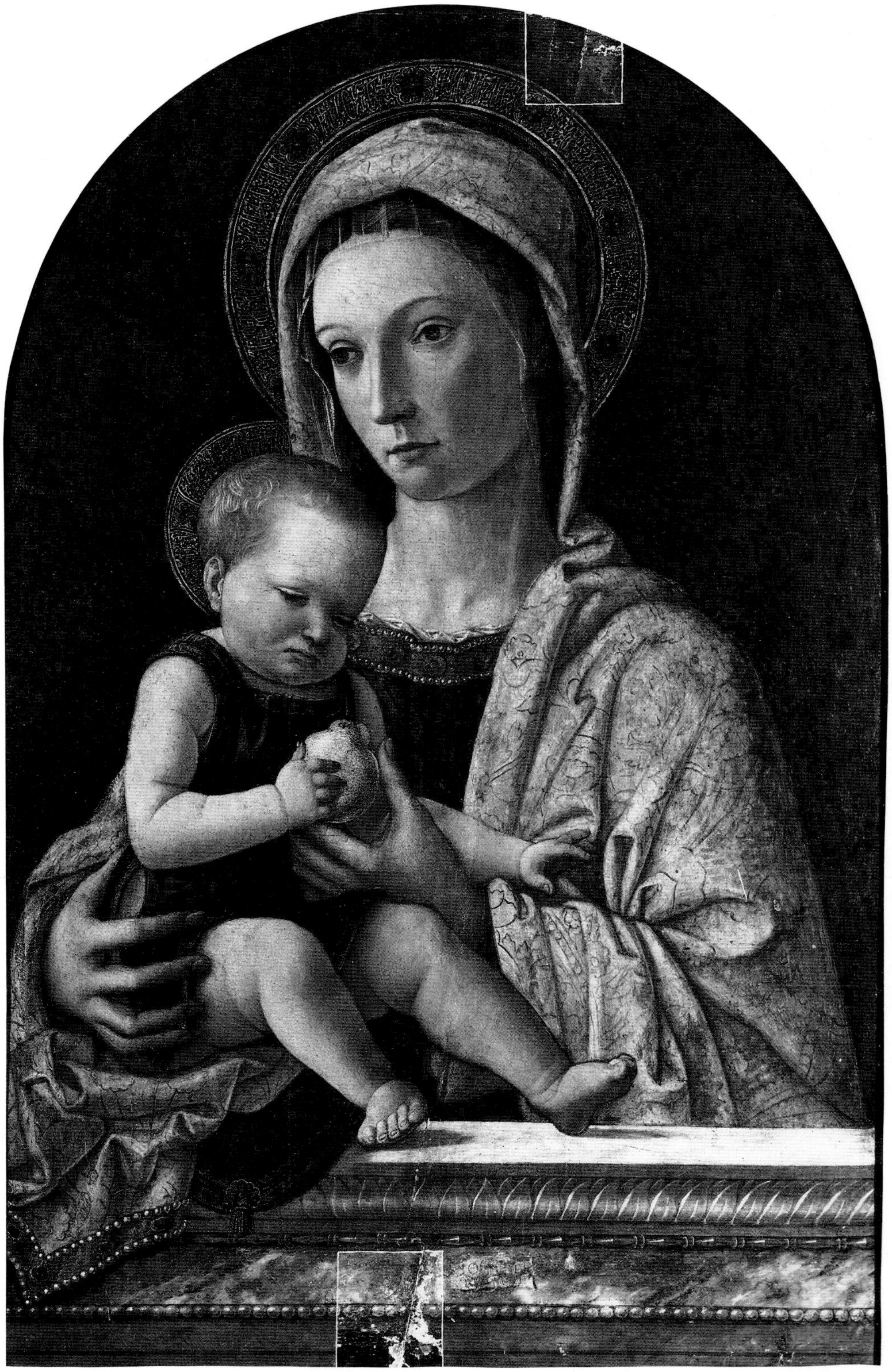

22. *Giovanni Bellini with assistance,* Madonna and Child *(Trivulzio* Madonna*), Civiche Raccolte d'Arte, Castello Sforzesco, Milan. Courtesy Pinacoteca, Civico Museo d'Arte Antica, Castello Sforzesco, Milan. Photo: Foto Saporetti, Milan.*

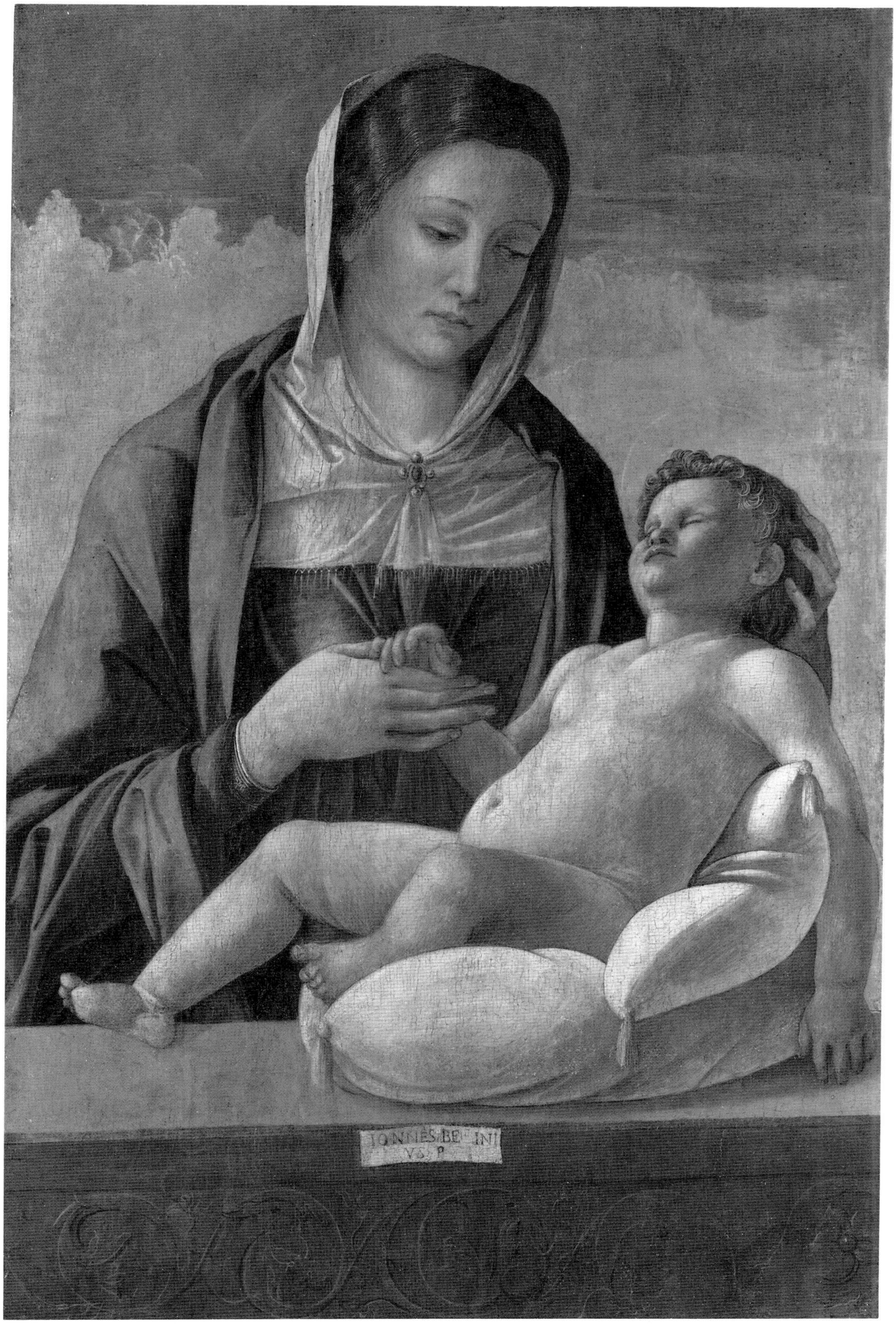


23. *Giovanni Bellini (repainted)*, Madonna and Sleeping Child, *Isabella Stewart Gardner Museum, Boston. Photo: Isabella Stewart Gardner Museum, Boston.*

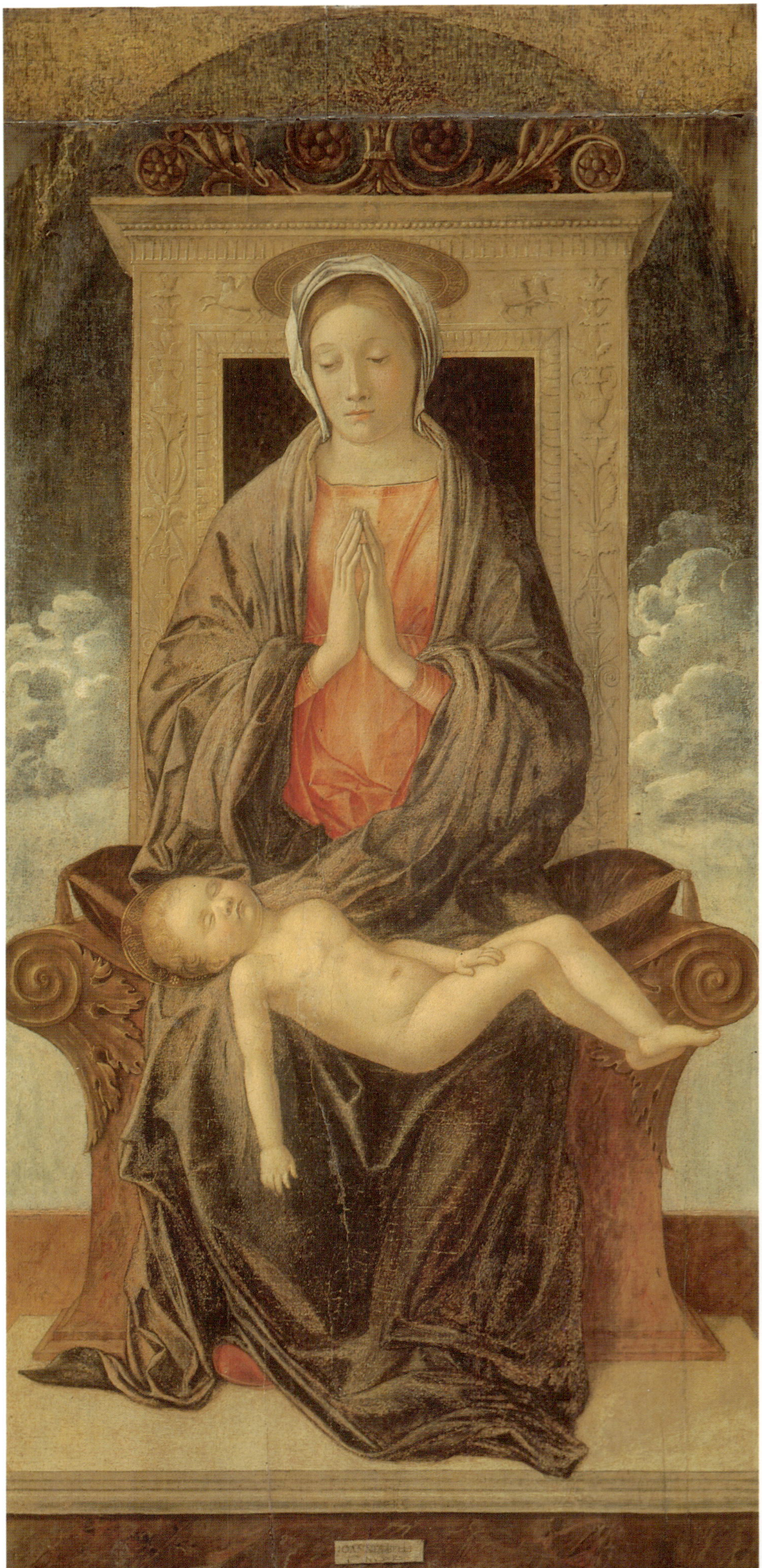

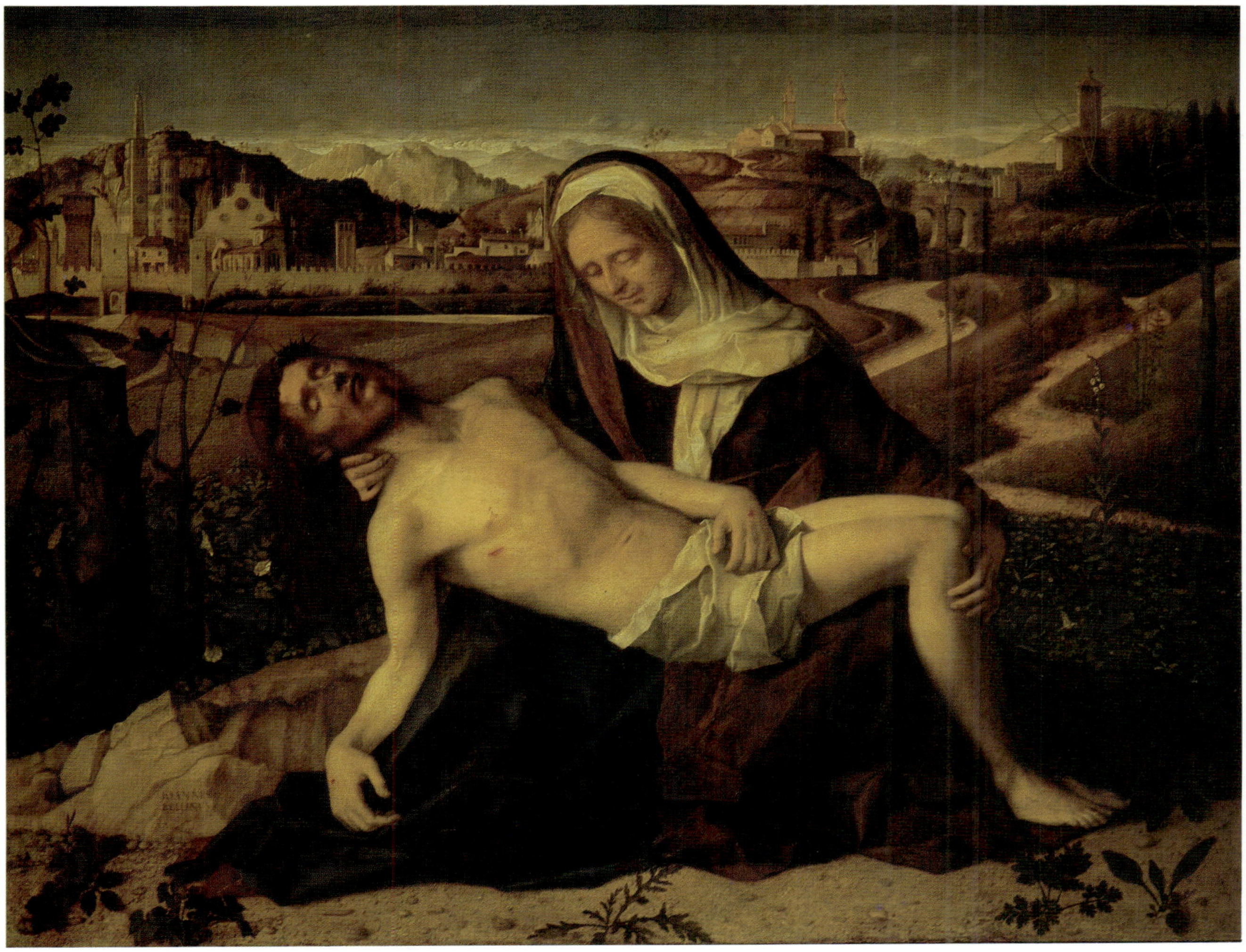

25. Pietà, *Gallerie dell'Accademia, Venice. Photo: Giacomelli Fotografia, Venice.*

as in the Gardner *Madonna*, or touches his feet, she may be indicating the future sites of the wounds of crucifixion. Christ's mourners take his hands and caress his feet in this way in numerous Lamentations, Entombments, and Pietàs, including a work by Bellini himself (fig. 88).

Bellini repeated the theme of symbolic sleep in a painting of the *Madonna and Sleeping Child Enthroned*, which appears to have been the central panel of a triptych or polyptych painted early in the 1470s (fig. 24).[23] Gold striations were used to highlight the throne (see figs. 1, 5, 9), and the Virgin's refined face resembles the Gardner *Madonna*, whereas the "sketchier" handling is probably explained by the larger scale of this work—and by its abraded condition. This damage reveals how Bellini constructed his image, modeling from dark to light and manipulating the brushstroke to follow (or create) form. Again the Virgin prays and looks down at the Infant sleeping in her lap; but now the pose of the Child and even his large size are further, unmistakable references to the Pietà. Indeed, much later Bellini depicted the dead Christ in essentially the same position used for this Child (fig. 25).

24. Madonna and Sleeping Child Enthroned, *Gallerie dell'Accademia, Venice. Photo: Giacomelli Fotografia, Venice.*

The *Madonna Enthroned* marks Bellini's farewell to the imagery of Christ's sleep, with one late exception (fig. 43). The overt symbolism of the Infant's sleep as

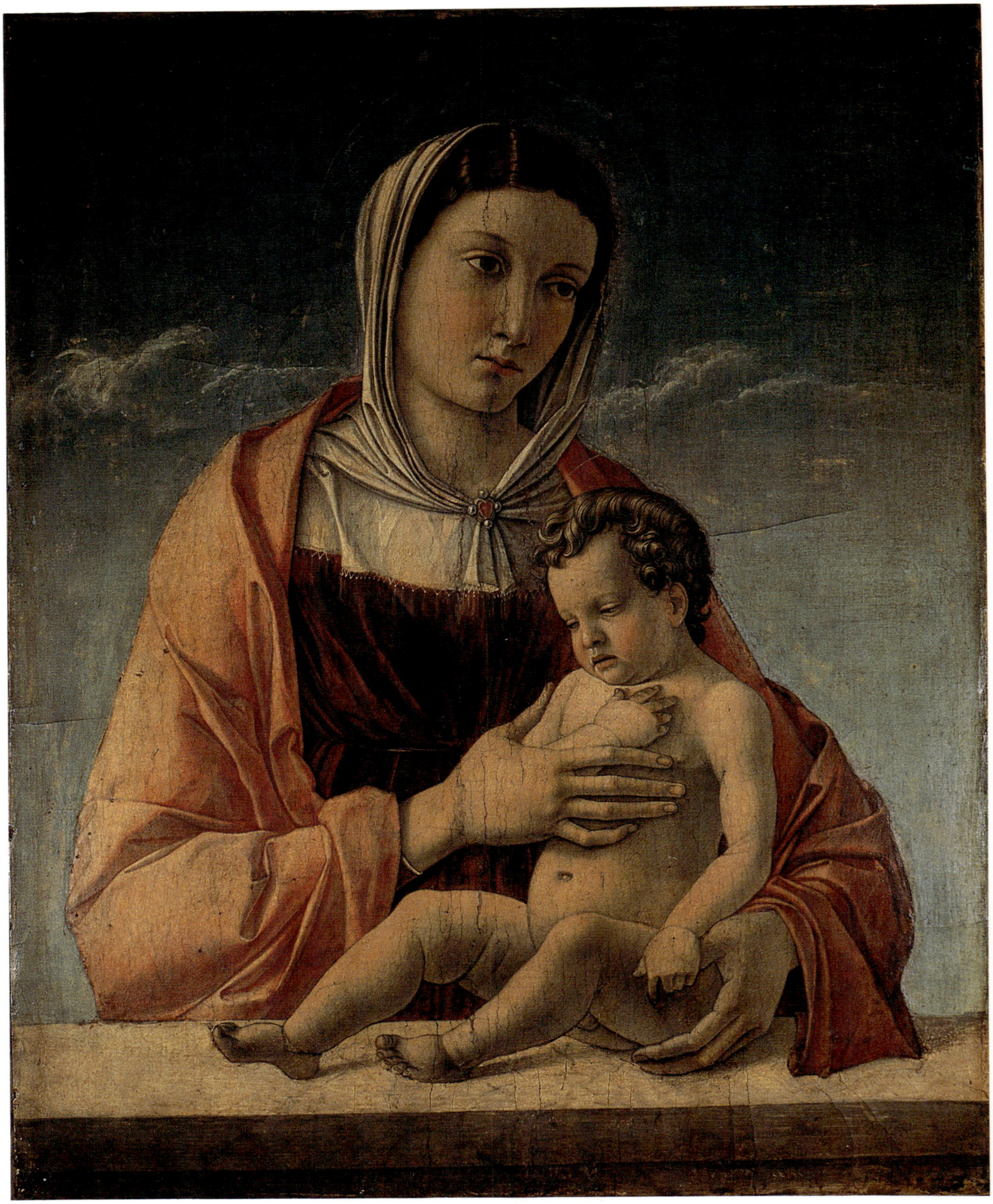

an adumbration of his Passion was replaced by its concomitant in Bellini's art, the nakedness of Christ. In effect, Bellini's two early types of imagery merged: the Child clothed and awake is stripped of his garments, and his nudity, at first associated exclusively with his sleep, is now displayed in depictions in which he is alert.

Bellini's Frizzoni *Madonna*, painted at about the same time as the Gardner painting, illustrates the point (fig. 26).[24] Mary stares sadly into the distance while her Child looks down and inward with an expression of ineffable tragedy; the expression seems precocious on his baby features. The Infant sits upright and naked on the parapet, one arm at his side, the hand grasping his mother's thumb in a childlike way as she supports him. His other hand is on his chest, in a gesture of self-indication and self-recognition, locked into place by Mary's large hand, evocative of the traditional gesture of the Byzantine *Hodegetria*, the Indicator of the Way. Christ seems to accept his adult responsibility with his remarkable action, suggestive of the penitential gesture of mea culpa, and the Virgin enforces his decision. Their demeanor expresses their acknowledgment and acceptance of the sacrifice, but each is alone in this; they move in opposite directions and are oblivious to each other, in spite of their proximity.

By the mid-1470s, the Christ Child's nudity had become as much a feature of Bellini's Madonna paintings as his use of the half-length figure or the parapet. Thereafter, his occasional insistence on clothing the Child may be understood in part as another intentional archaism, like his adherence to the Byzantinizing half-length format itself. Bellini sometimes referred to Byzantine prototypes even more directly, with such motifs as the pull of Mary's mantle across her breast, the fall of the fabric over her shoulder, and the placement of her veil and mantle low on the brow to conceal her hair.

The greatest of these Byzantinizing images and one of Bellini's most moving characterizations of the Virgin and Child is the Brera *Madonna greca* (fig. 27). Even were it not for the Greek monograms of Mary and Christ, the arrangement of her mantle and the patterns of light and shade on her face would justify the picture's popular name (fig. 19).[25] Yet the composition departs from tradition in other ways. More of the Madonna's figure is shown—she is seated—and the parapet is only suggested by the way in which the Child's feet seem to be supported on the panel's edge. The space behind them is closed by a brown cloth hanging, which reveals strips of sky to either side and at the top and resembles the cloths used to honor earthly monarchs (fig. 28). The cloth of honor pushes the sacred figures forward, toward the picture plane. When the painting was complete in its frame, the effect must have been extraordinary: the Infant almost falls out of the picture into the viewer's space and is pulled back only by the embrace of his mother's large hands.

Christ's right arm hangs helplessly over Mary's (another Byzantine motif), shadowing her wrist. In his left hand he holds a fruit, possibly an apple, resting

26. Madonna and Child (*Frizzoni* Madonna), *Civico Museo Correr, Venice. Photo: Gianfranco Spinazzi, Venice.*

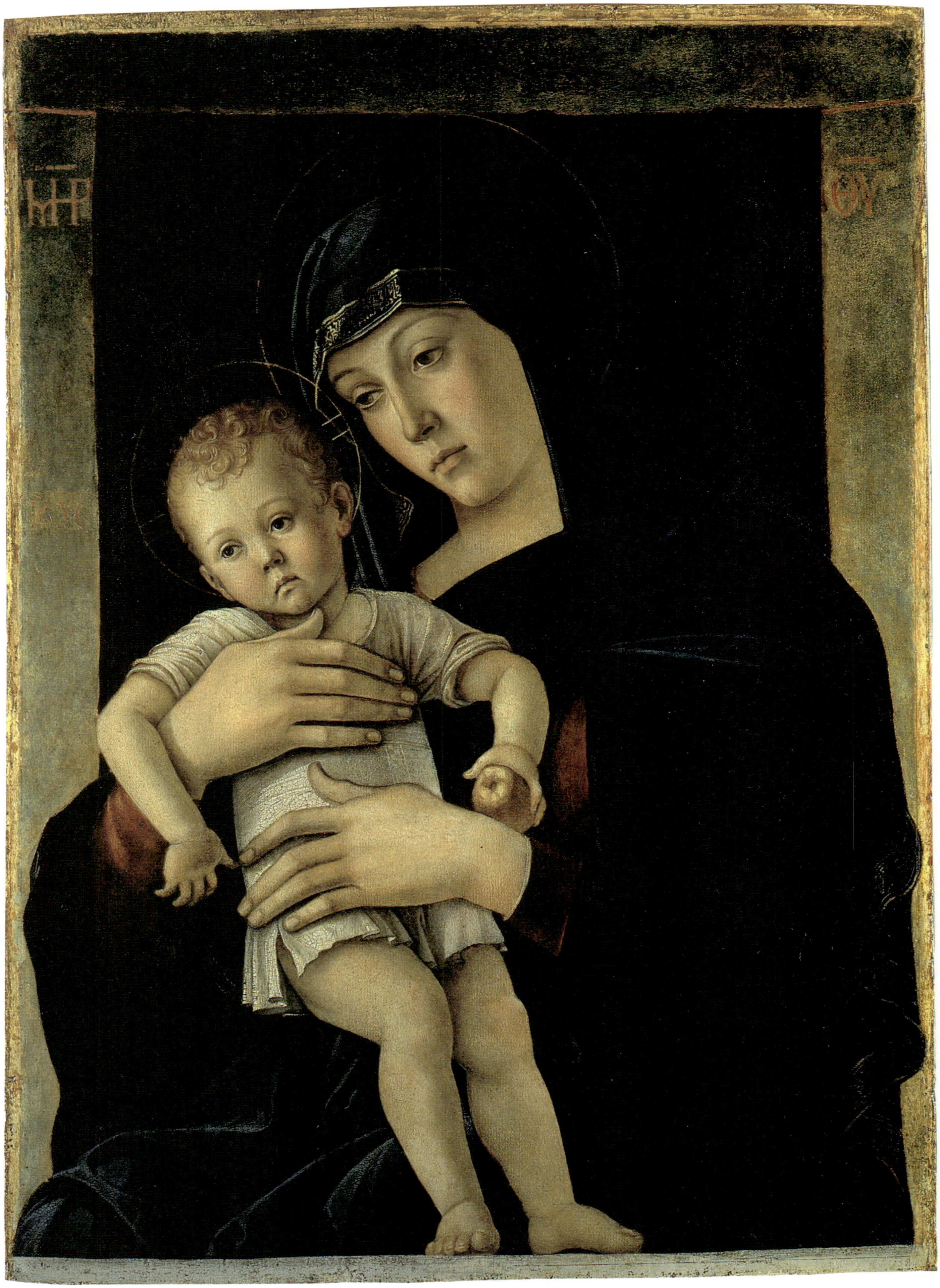

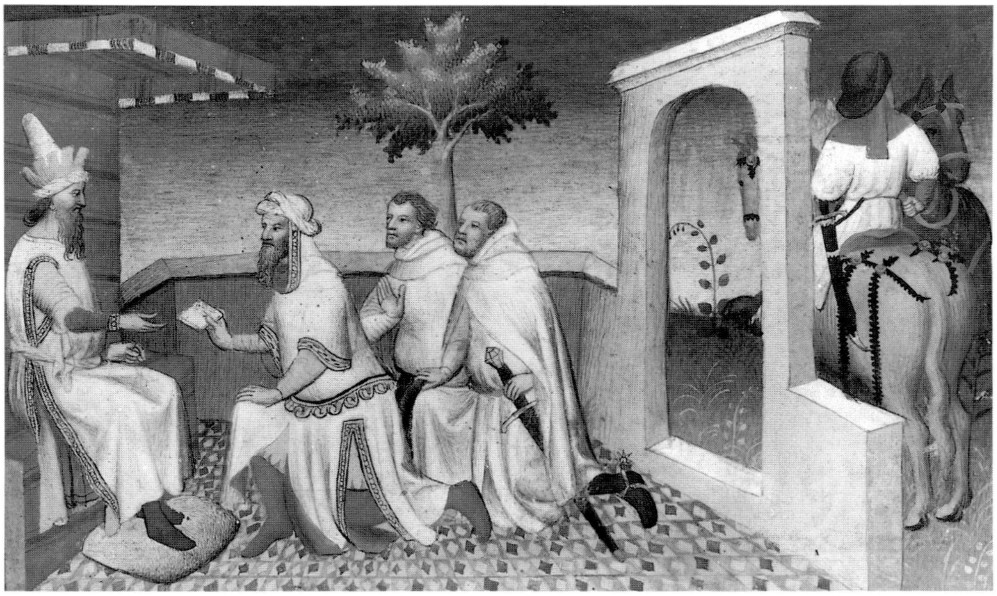

28. *Anonymous French, c. 1413,* The Polo Brothers before the Khan, *from* Livre des Merveilles, *folio 3v, MS Fr. 2810, Bibliothèque Nationale, Paris. Photo: Bibl. Nat. Paris.*

on her other wrist. The image is tragic: the tilt of Christ's head, his expression, his helpless posture, as though he were a marionette—all is calculated to arouse compassion. Mary, too, is an affective and introspective figure, bending toward her Son but looking beyond him, holding him in her great hands with tenderness yet distractedly, preoccupied by thoughts of their fate, symbolized in the fruit at the center of the composition.

Bellini adapted elements of this group in the much-repainted Accademia *Madonna and Blessing Child* (fig. 29).[26] But now the posture and characterization of Mother and Son are more assertive. No longer unsteady and helpless, the Child moves of his own volition, blessing the worshiper and grasping Mary's thumb with his left hand (cf. fig. 26). The Virgin looks at us with unsentimental forthrightness, her glance crossing the boundary of the parapet. Christ's feet actually overlap this division between the two realms. With this detail, which asserts the Child's physical immediacy, Bellini reiterates the spiritual nearness signified by the Lord's blessing.

The illusionistic tension between the worlds of the beholder and of the sacred beings becomes the dramatic focus of the Lochis *Madonna*, which dates circa 1475 (fig. 30). The panel is smaller than most of its predecessors discussed here, yet it is more monumental in conception than any of them. Mary's mantle is painted with deep tubular folds and wells of shadow, contrasted with highlights painted in apparent obedience to the laws of nature but achieved with the archaizing, abstract means of gold striations. This metallic gold is applied in thin parallel strokes of varied lengths to represent patterns of light, similar in effect and technique to the putti in Bellini's earlier *Crucifixion* (fig. 5), while the fold of drapery at Mary's neck recalls the motif in the *Madonna greca* and the *Madonna and Blessing Child* (figs. 27, 29). The background cloth, with its strict geometry of rectangular folds, encloses the scene, heightening tension by restricting the space allocated to the

27. Madonna greca, *Pinacoteca di Brera, Milan. Photo: Sovrintendenza per i Beni Artistici e Storici, Milan, and Color Dielle, Milan.*

*Overleaf:*
29. Madonna and Blessing Child, *Gallerie dell'Accademia, Venice. Photo: Giacomelli Fotografia, Venice.*

30. Madonna and Child *(Lochis* Madonna*), Galleria dell'Accademia Carrara, Bergamo. Photo: Stefano Paolillo, Venice and New York.*

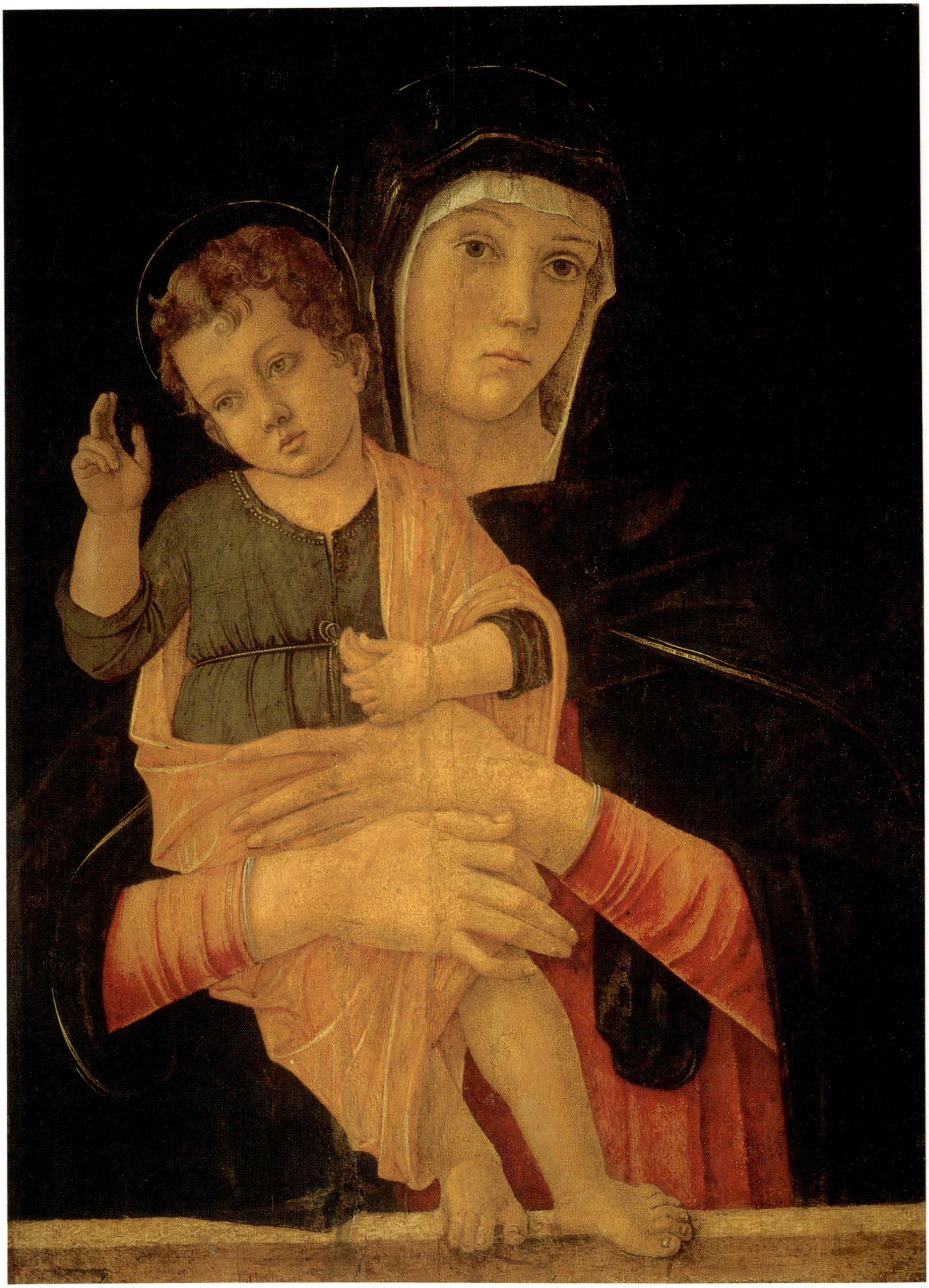

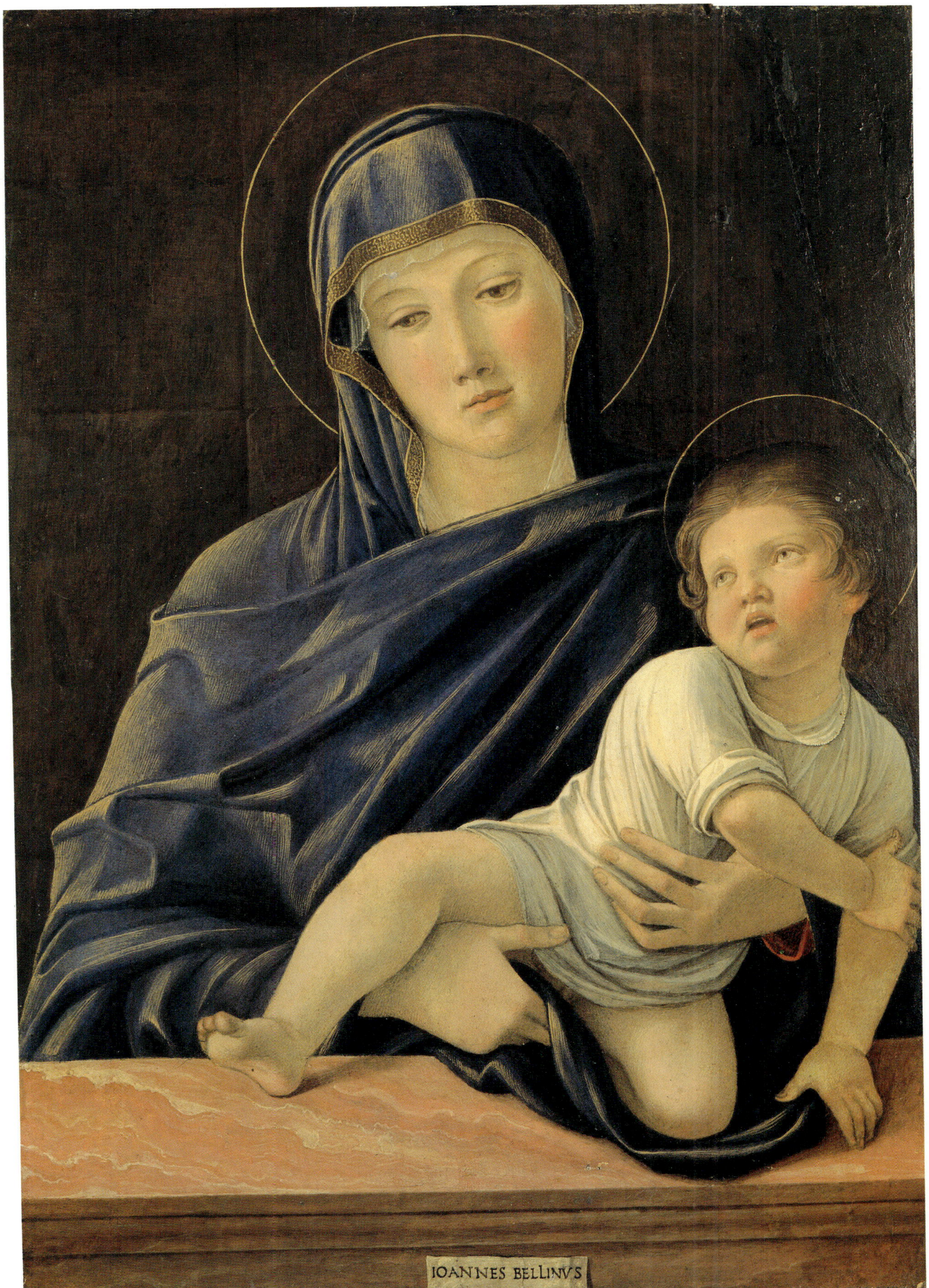
IOANNES BELLINVS

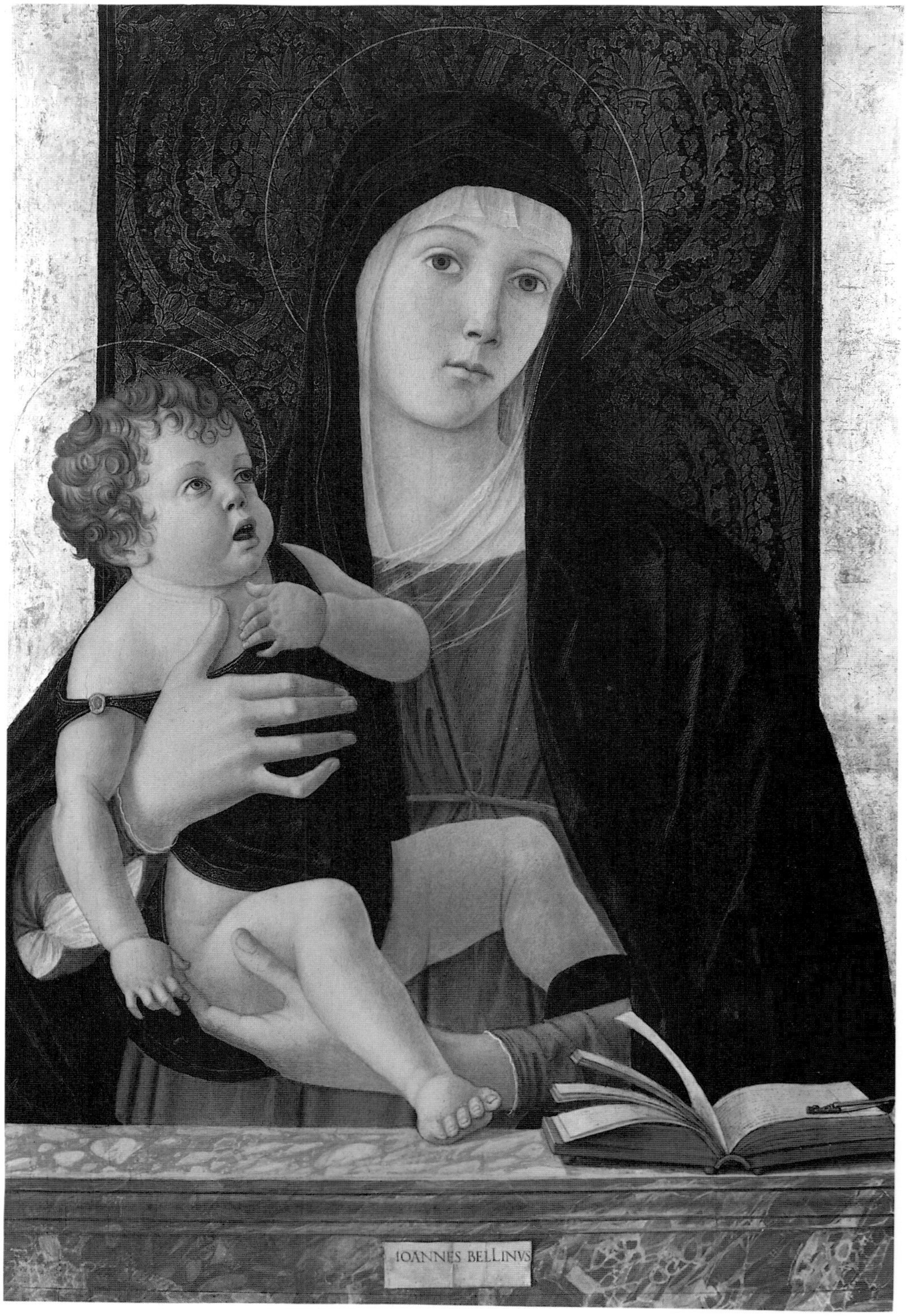


31. *Giovanni Bellini with assistance,* Madonna and Child, *Kimbell Art Museum, Fort Worth. Photo: Michael Bodycomb.*

Madonna and Child, who are pushed forward, almost but not quite out of the picture space: Mary's mantle brushes the edge of the parapet, and the Child's action suggests that he would move forward if his mother did not restrain him.

What are we to make of Christ's strange posture and of the interaction of Madonna and Child? Although she restrains her Son, Mary seems to ignore him: her gaze is turned elsewhere, withdrawn and unfocused or focused inwardly. The Infant, meanwhile, seems to struggle on the parapet, but whether he is attempting to rise or has fallen to one knee is uncertain. Perhaps his ambivalent posture is meant to evoke an image of the adult Christ, who falls beneath the weight of the cross on the way to Calvary. The Child's loose white shift may allude to this motif of defeat: the adult Christ in scenes of the Via Crucis is similarly dressed (fig. 62).[27] The torsion of the Child's posture and the way in which he turns to look back over his shoulder, eyes upward and lips parted, suggest the profound difficulty of his situation and perhaps a plea for release. We do not know whether Christ is attempting to escape his fate or to embrace it, whether his mother restrains him on his sacrificial altar or tries to keep him from striving toward his martyrdom. The red of Mary's sleeve, seen in the shadows against the deep fold of her mantle as she pulls it around her Son, is a note of alarm: the sudden appearance of color is startling, almost like a stain of blood. The reddish tone of the marble parapet seems to take its hue from this color, and the white veins of the stone provide a diagonal counterpoint to the folds of Mary's mantle. Christ's movement, or attempted movement, is arrested here, captured by the web of these diagonals no less than by the Madonna's restraining hands.

The action of Mary's hands calls attention to the Child's partially exposed genitals. Here, as in the Davis *Madonna* and others, Christ's nudity—the revelation of his sex—seems calculated to remind the viewer-worshiper of the Lord's humanity and his foreordained sacrifice, which was possible only because he took on human flesh. Christ first shed blood for the redemption of humankind at the circumcision (fig. 135). Bellini reminds us of this sacrifice by revealing Christ's nudity and Mary's red sleeve.

Bellini modified this pattern in the Contarini *Madonna and Blessing Child*, one of his best-preserved works (fig. 32).[28] Bending her head to touch Christ's, Mary turns her eyes toward the beholder, exhorting our attention. Her large hands encase the Child, shielding his humanity. Once again the Infant is nude, but now, standing upright and frontal on the parapet, he blesses the beholder: his nudity and the slight contrapposto of his stance—even his close-cropped, curly hair—suggest a classical hero, not a helpless baby, while his serious expression invests him with morality and self-awareness. This Child anticipates in miniature Michelangelo's combination of heroic classical nudity and triumphant Christian spirit in the colossal *David*. The Florentine sculptor surely knew such works by Bellini and learned much from them.[29]

In the Contarini *Madonna*, Bellini reintroduced a landscape background, which he had used earlier in the Davis *Madonna* (fig. 14). From this point on, almost without exception, he employed landscape settings in his devotional images, and always with a low horizon, so that the background is predominantly sky.[30] In the distance, the mountain range recalls the prealpine landscape of the Veneto, essentially wild and uninhabited on the figures' left, whereas on their right, above Christ's blessing hand, Bellini painted a miniature cityscape. The suggestion is that the Lord blesses the society and endeavors of humankind. Indeed, Bellini's

*Overleaf:*
32. Madonna and Blessing Child *(Contarini* Madonna*), Gallerie dell'Accademia, Venice. Photo: Giacomelli Fotografia, Venice.*

33. Madonna dei cherubini rossi, *Gallerie dell'Accademia, Venice. Photo: Giacomelli Fotografia, Venice.*

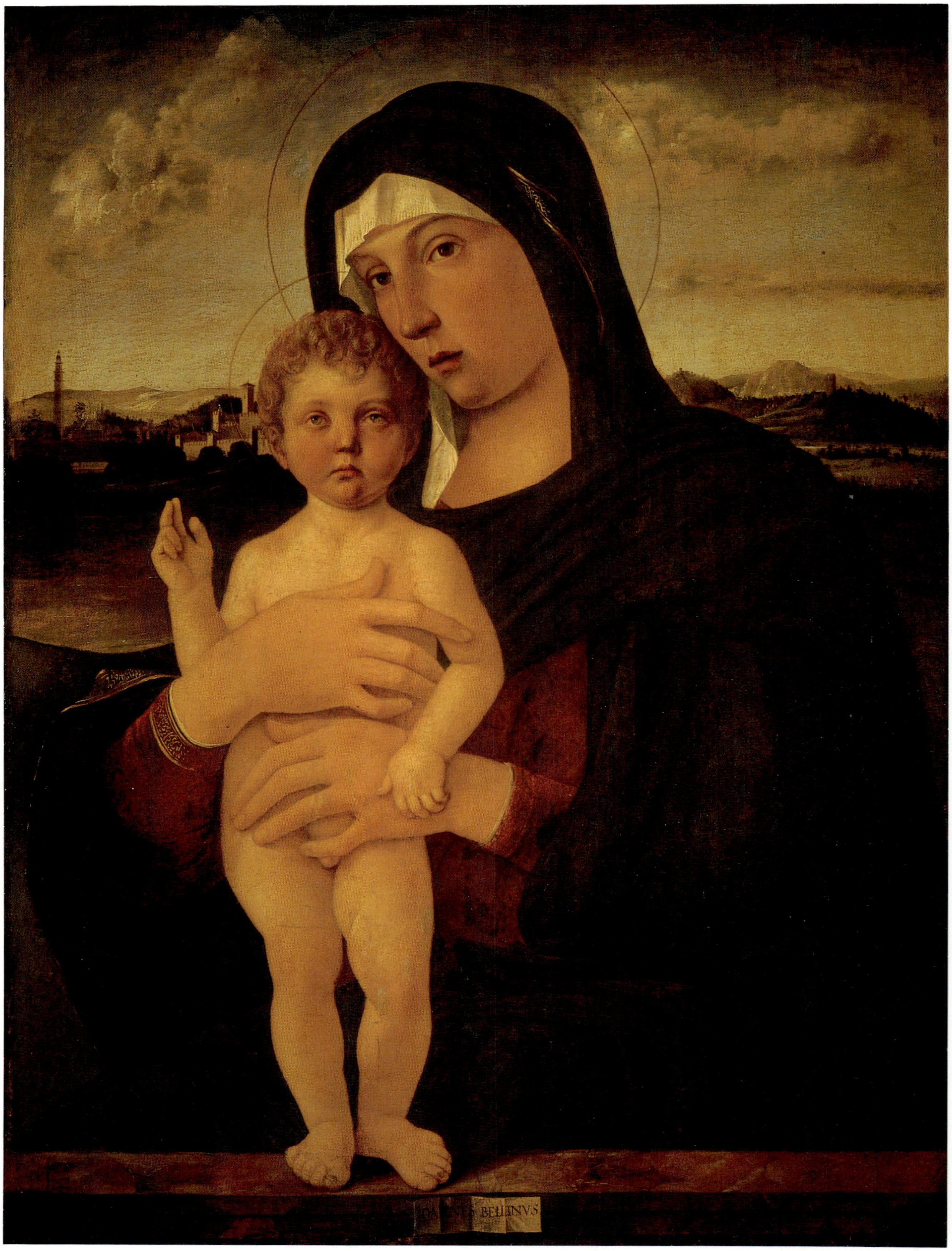
BELLINVS

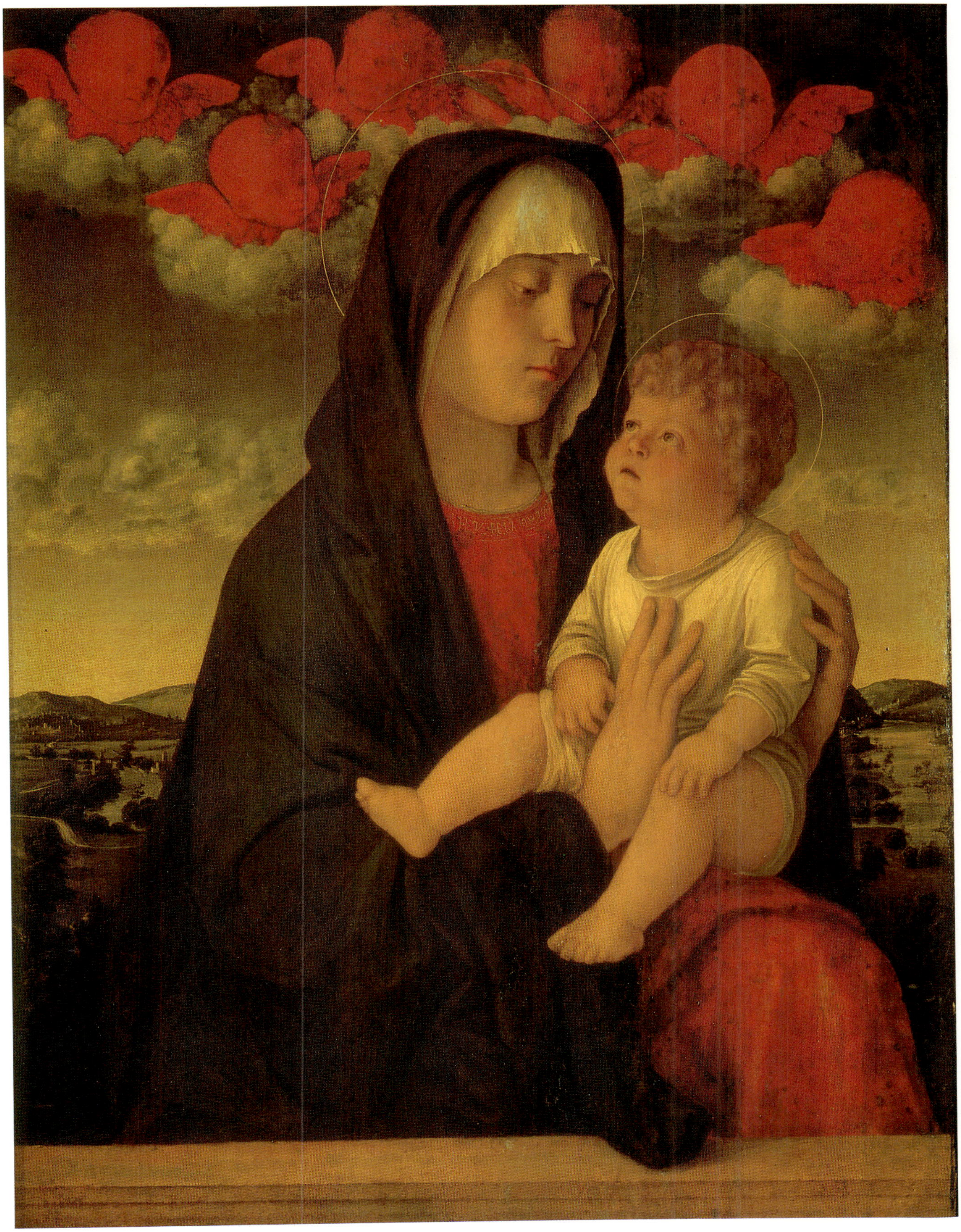

landscapes, dominated by Mary and her Son, may allude to the domination of the Venetian mainland by the republic, characterized and personified both as the Virgin and as Christ. At the same time, Bellini's conception of landscape is to be understood as the visual counterpart of ancient and contemporary bucolic literature, from Virgil's eclogues to Jacopo Sannazaro's *Arcadia*, written in the 1490s, or *Gli Asolani*, by Bellini's good friend and patron Pietro Bembo.

The middle ground of Bellini's landscape is empty, and the mountains and city on the horizon are a great but indeterminate distance from the Virgin and Child. This is no more their spatial environment than in the Davis *Madonna*; it does not contain their figures the way the landscape surrounds Saint Francis, for example (fig. 77). Yet the landscape in this and other Madonna paintings is not a spaceless backdrop. The same light and air that suffuse the landscape also surround Mary and Christ. Figures and setting are bound by this enveloping atmosphere, despite the disjunctions of scale, the emptiness of the intermediate space, and the absence of perspectival links between foreground and background. None of these is needed to unite the composition, which is fused, atom by atom, in Bellini's luminous vision.

Two compositions are related to this one, the *Madonna degli alberetti*, which is in effect a revival of the Contarini panel, and the *Madonna dei cherubini rossi*, which represents the midpoint between them. In the *Madonna dei cherubini rossi* (fig. 33), Bellini recalled a motif that his father had used in a painting of the 1450s (fig. 15).[31] But Jacopo's cherubim of gold striations, which formed an immobile backdrop for the Virgin and Child, have been transformed by Giovanni into energetic three-dimensional beings that fly above Mary's head, each with its penetrable bank of clouds, forming an animated, spatial glory. Their intense red tints the whitened sky at the horizon, warming the composition.

Bellini represented the distant landscape of mountains, trees, and winding paths with an even lower horizon than he had used previously: the background is more than half sky, and this aerial setting becomes the naturalistic warrant for his increasingly atmospheric definition of form. The relationship between the sacred beings has also changed: they turn toward each other to exchange a glance. With parted lips and head tilted upward to look into his mother's eyes, the Infant seems to question her.[32] She looks at him calmly, almost smiling, as though, more prescient than he, she seeks to infuse in her Child understanding and acceptance of his role.

The *Madonna degli alberetti* is signed and dated by an inscription on the parapet IOANNES.BELLINVS.P. / 1487—a precious point of reference, because this is the first of the artist's undisputed surviving works to be signed and dated (fig. 34).[33] The Infant seems to point with his feet at Bellini's signature, one foot above the other, as though nailed on the cross: a variation on the relationship between artist and image, servant and Lord, sinner and Redeemer, which the master repeated elsewhere (figs. 18, 84). Because the Child is intended to remind us of

Christ Crucified, his nudity is exposed. In the similar Contarini *Madonna*, by contrast, Mary all but conceals Christ's genitals, protecting his humanity: the blessing Infant is thus less vulnerable than his counterpart.

Behind the Virgin in the *Madonna degli alberetti* are the two trees that give the painting its name. Placed almost like sentinels, these alberetti may perhaps symbolize the Old and New Testaments. The large folds of Mary's mantle interrupt the trees, and at the right her silhouette all but coincides with the line of one of them: these visual games reinforce the spatial separation of the figures from their setting. Atmosphere envelops the Madonna and Child, has become palpable, softening the modeling of their flesh and the draperies, blurring them in sympathy with the hazy mist on the horizon. Even the closest forms are defined not by line but by color and ambient light. This is most readily apparent in the treatment of Mary's veil, no longer an opaque white cloth as in earlier works but now painted with varied brushstrokes, the density of pigment adjusted as though in response to light. But Bellini's luminosity is not merely illusionism; he exploits light and space to establish the meaning of his sacred image.

Cast shadows assert the reality of the Madonna and Child's presence, his shadows on the parapet and on her neck, hers conspicuous on the cloth of honor. The light that causes these shadows comes from in front of them, from outside the painting, perforce from our world: the light that shines on Mary and her Child also shines on us. Bellini anticipated this effect in earlier works, but his treatment here is more insistent. This light binds the realms of sacred beings and worshiper. And because they are large by contrast with the small forms of the background, the Virgin and Christ seem almost to leave the pictorial realm to enter our world. As always, the parapet confirms their immediacy. The Child who stands on this ledge, physically so near to us, is psychologically immediate as well, turning toward us, lips parted as though to address us, while his mother looks down at him.

Mary presents us with Christ Incarnate, the Spirit made flesh, like all humans capable of suffering and death. For this reason, she regards her Child with an expression of extraordinary ambivalence: at once tender and wary, she perhaps does not entirely accept the role that he, by taking cognizance of the beholder, is prepared to acknowledge. Are we to see in the way her large hands enfold the Child an embrace or a restraint? Does he touch her hand with his fingertips to caress his mother or to protest her grasp? Does his right arm, which falls over her hand, imply his passivity in her arms or his active refusal to raise that arm to bless us? Seemingly simple and straightforward, the painting is profound and complex, both visually and psychologically. Mary and Christ have come before us not for casual attention but to compel contemplation and involvement. They seem still, but their postures suggest action, motion both completed and imminent: the light that illuminates them will change, the shadows will shift, they will not remain as they are. But in this instant, captured by Bellini, the Child pauses to acknowledge our presence.

*Overleaf:*
34. Madonna degli alberetti, *Gallerie dell'Accademia, Venice. Photo: Giacomelli Fotografia, Venice.*

35. Madonna of the Pear *(Morelli* Madonna*), Gallerie dell'Accademia Carrara, Bergamo. Photo: Stefano Paolillo, Venice and New York.*

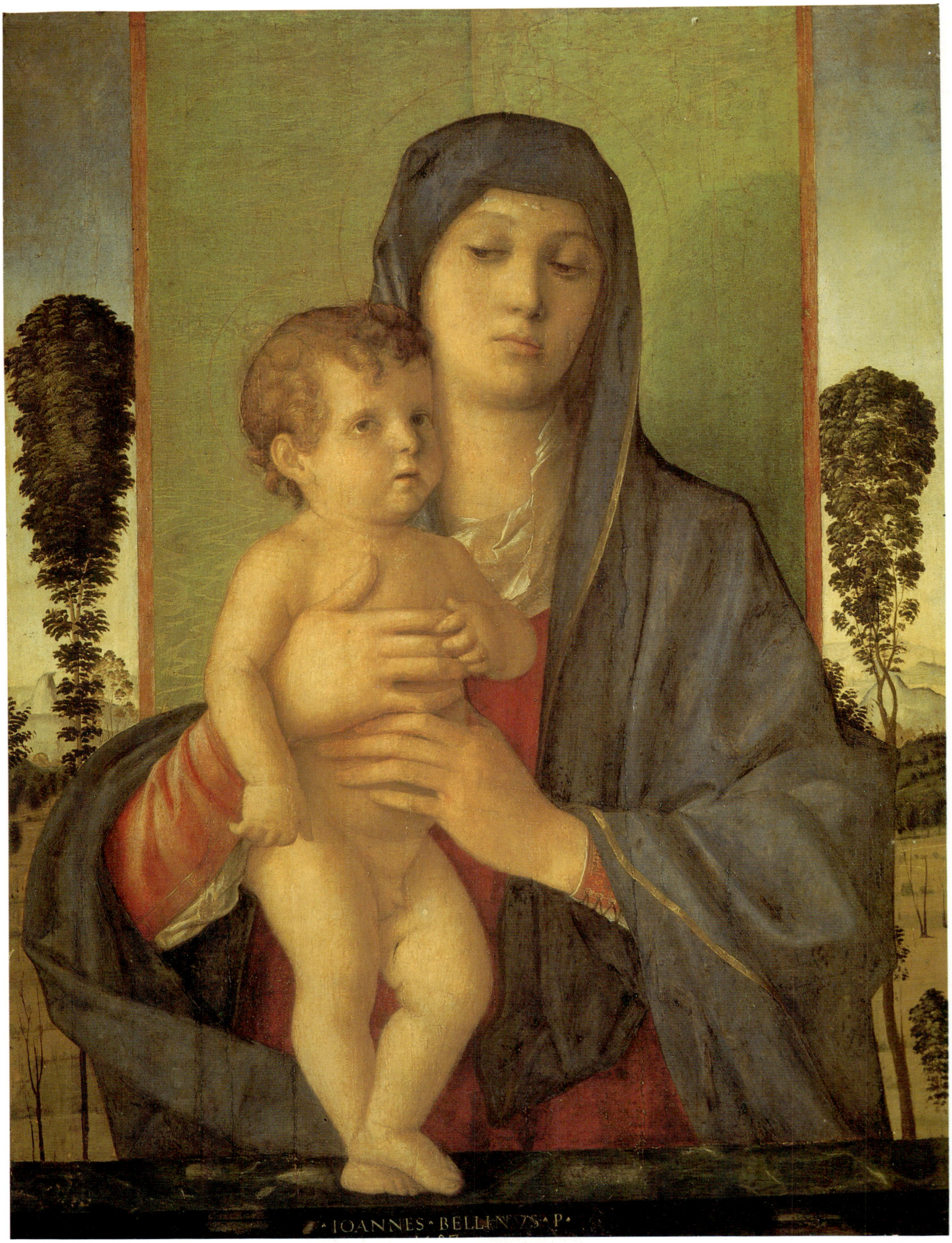
IOANNES BELLINVS P

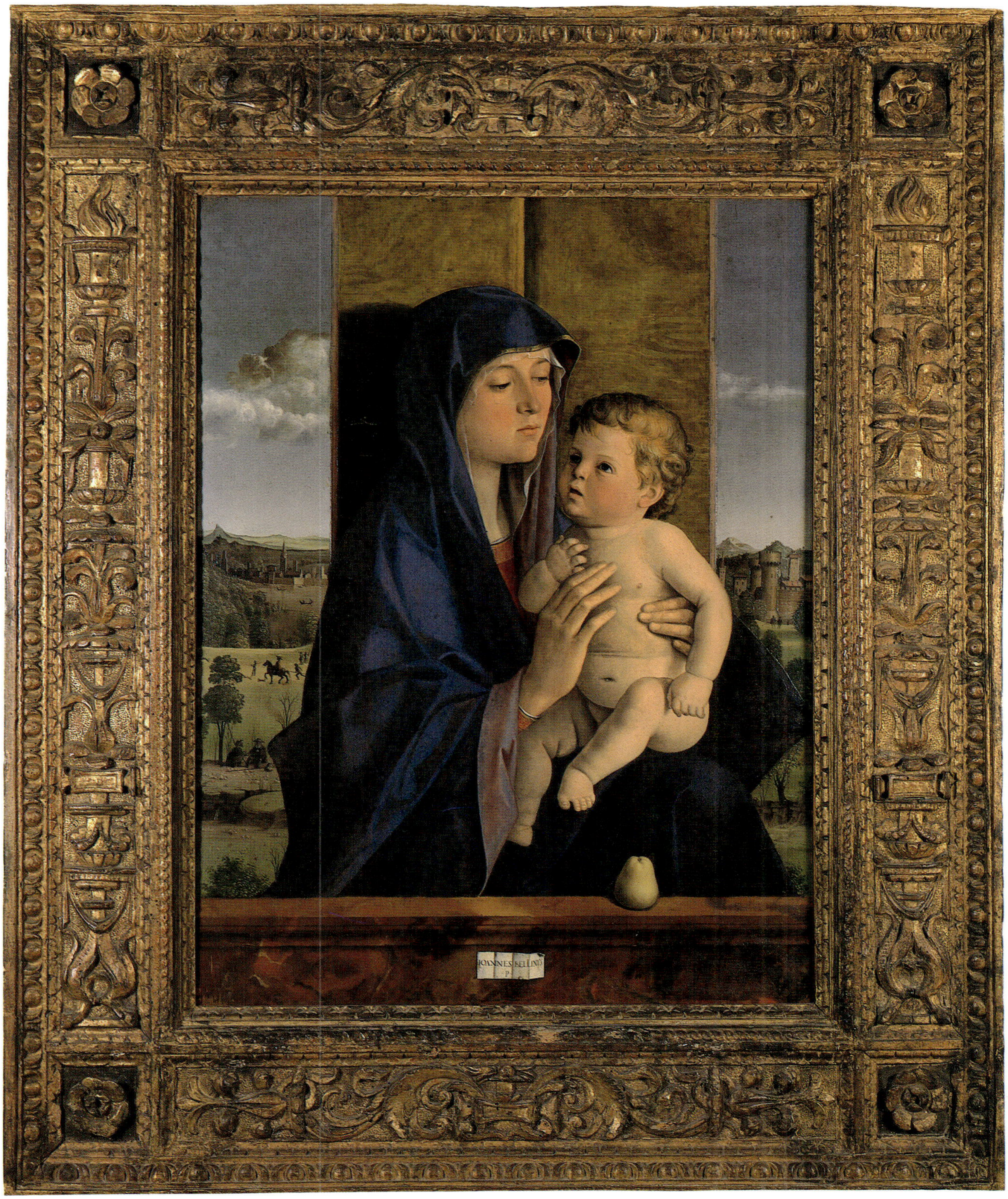
IOANNES BELLINVS
P.

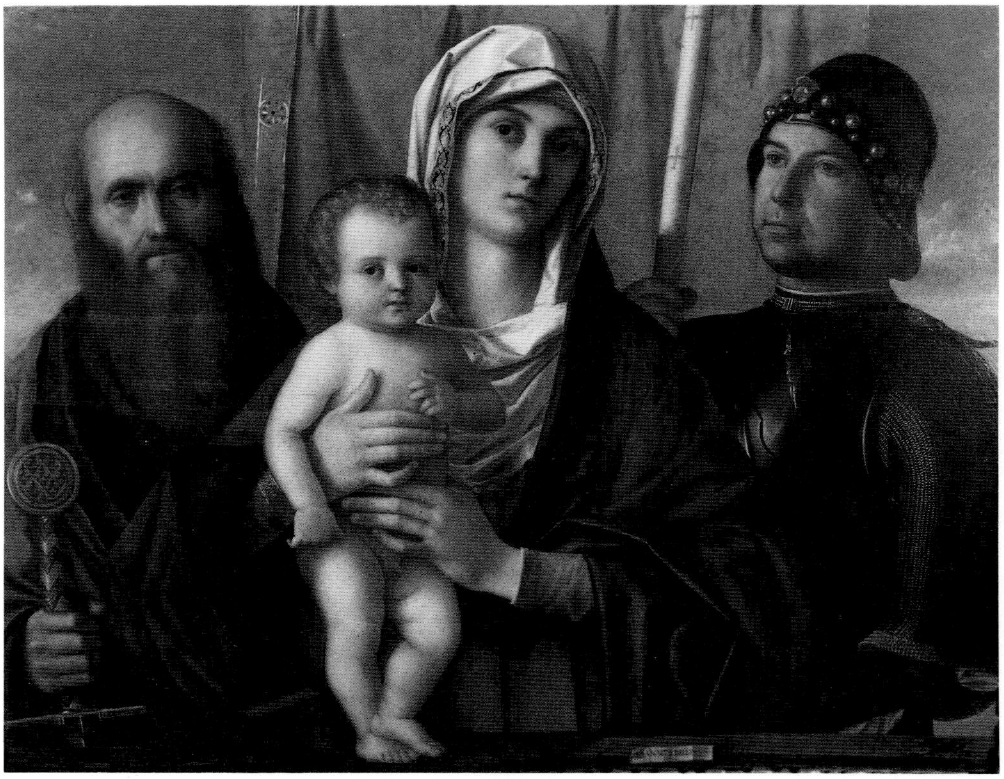

36. *Giovanni Bellini(?) with assistance,* Madonna and Child with Saints Paul and George, *Gallerie dell'Accademia, Venice. Photo: Soprintendenza ai Beni Artistici e Storici, Venice.*

In the so-called *Madonna of the Pear* (circa 1488), Christ's acknowledgment of us is combined with a gesture of self-recognition (fig. 35). Bellini revised his composition of the *Madonna dei cherubini rossi* for this work, but the landscape is now populated by small anecdotal figures, unrelated in any specific way to the Madonna and Child in the foreground.[34] These minute figures invest the landscape with hopefulness and a sense of harmonious well-being. They are the painter's visual equivalent of the bucolic characters who populate contemporary pastoral literature—Sannazaro's *Arcadia* is a notable case in point—and the predecessors of the protagonists of such later compositions by Bellini as the *Feast of the Gods* and of works by such younger masters as Giorgione and Titian.

At about the same date as the *Madonna of the Pear*, Bellini varied the theme of Virgin and Child by adding one or two saints. This probably resulted from his clients' desire to see their patron saints represented in devotional images. In at least one case, a donor is depicted in the guise of his patron (fig. 36), but more often donors are incorporated without sacred disguise, kneeling or standing next to the Virgin and Christ, sometimes receiving their blessing, sometimes ignored by them (figs. 38, 39, 68, 69).

In the *Madonna and Child with Saints Paul and George*, the idiosyncratic features of the soldier saint leave little doubt that this figure is a portrait likeness that seems almost to have been superimposed on an existing composition (fig. 36). The Virgin and Child are adapted from the *Madonna degli alberetti*, but Bellini (or a follower) has broadened the format to accommodate the two saints to either side.[35] Although a horizontal format is logical for such extended compositions, it

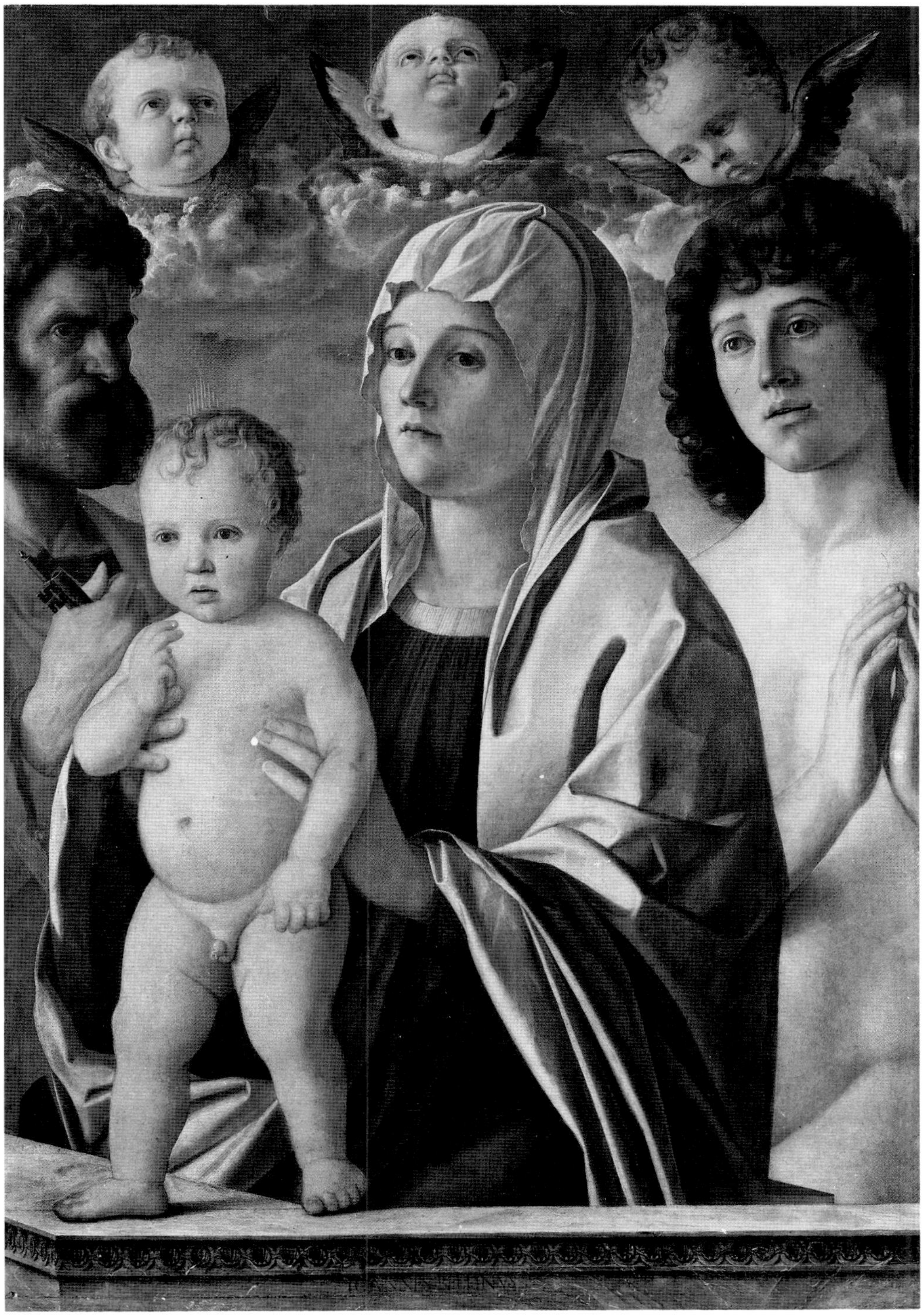

37. *Giovanni Bellini with assistance,* Madonna and Child with Saints Peter and Sebastian, *Musée du Louvre, Paris. Photo: Archivio Fotografico del Museo Correr, Venice.*

should not be taken for granted. Bellini's contemporary or slightly earlier panel in the Louvre, also painted with assistance, depicts Saints Peter and Sebastian with the Virgin in a vertical format, like the images of Mary and Christ alone (fig. 37). Similarly, Bellini used the vertical scheme in compositions with only one accompanying saint and in others with a donor figure taking the place of the saint (figs: 38, 39).[36] But in other Madonna paintings that include two flanking saints, Bellini chose the horizontal field, which makes the compositions more spatious and somehow more modern, cinquecentesque.

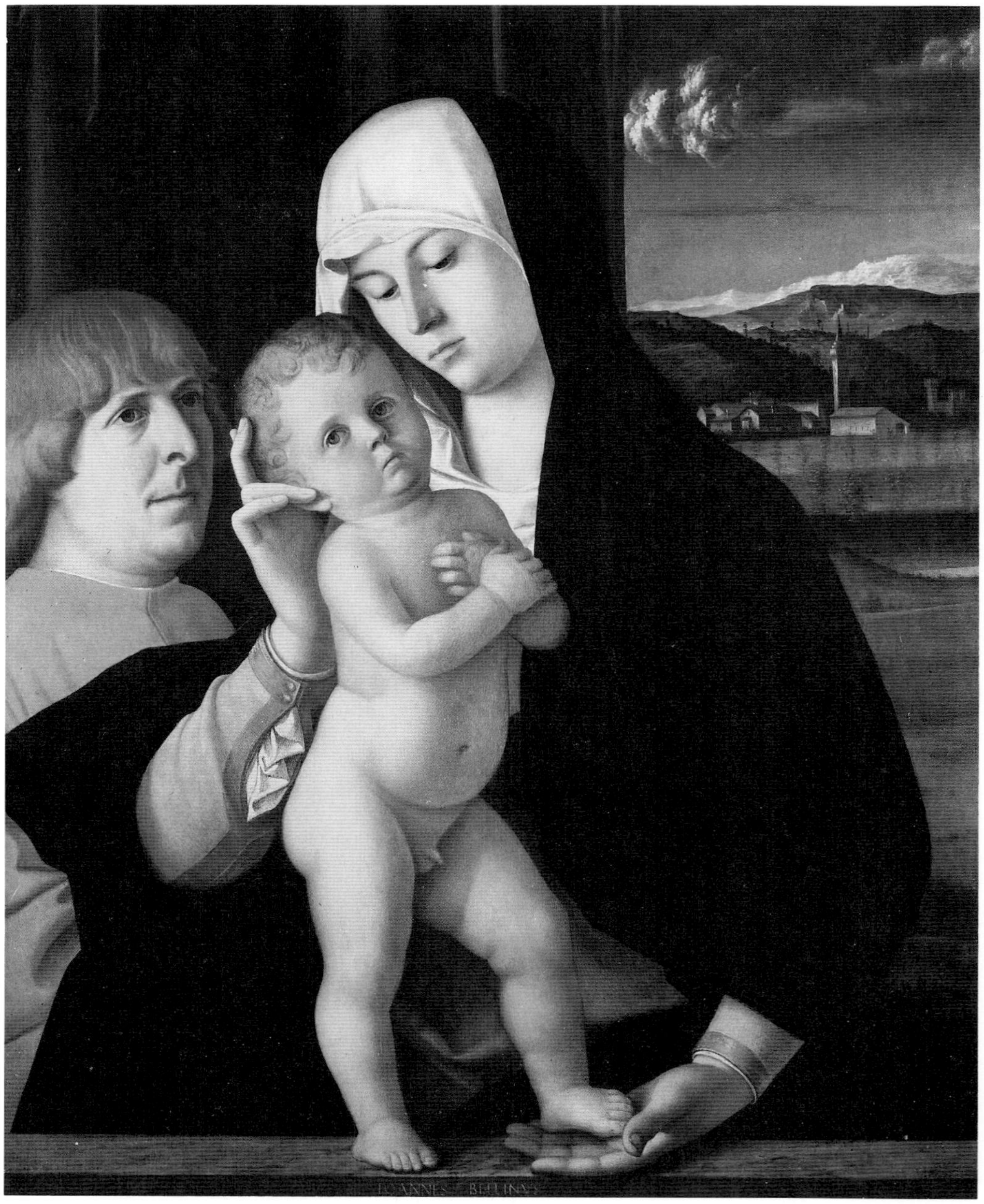

38. *Giovanni Bellini with assistance,* Madonna and Child with Donor, *Earl of Harewood, Harewood Castle, Yorkshire. Photo: Archivio Fotografico del Museo Correr, Venice.*

The *Madonna and Child with Two Female Saints* and the slightly later *Madonna and Child with Saint John the Baptist and a Female Saint* (the Giovanelli *Sacra Conversazione*) are other noteworthy examples of this type (figs. 40–42). In the *Madonna with Two Female Saints*, who are rather uncertainly identified as Catherine and Mary Magdalen, Bellini used a dark ground, but the flesh of the figures is so luminous, the pearls and gems of the saints so glowing, that the painting seems illuminated from within, as though by lamplight, as Roger Fry described it.[37] The painting is a tour de force of lighting effects, seeming both to contain and be penetrated by light.

Shades of red dominate the palette, and this harmony of reds tints the surrounding colors, warming even the indeterminate dark of the ground. Bellini had rehearsed this combination of reds in his Frizzoni *Madonna*, but here his palette

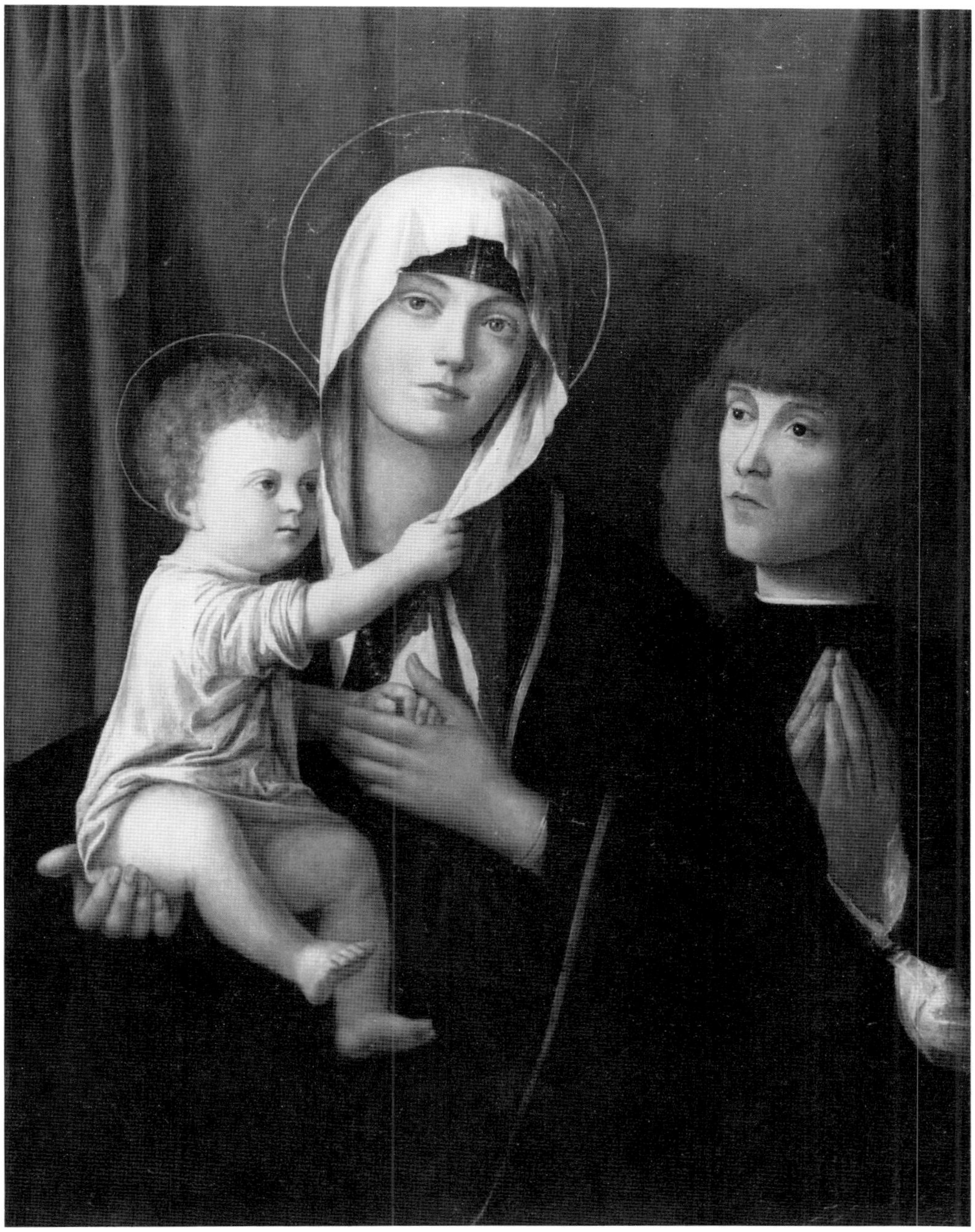

39. *Shop of Giovanni Bellini,* Madonna and Child with Donor, *Friedsam Library, Saint Bonaventure University. Courtesy Saint Bonaventure Art Collection, Saint Bonaventure, New York.*

is deeper and richer, and color has taken on a more compelling, expressive role.

The so-called Giovanelli *Sacra Conversazione* is slightly later than this *Madonna and Saints*, dating from the beginning of the sixteenth century and possibly painted with assistance (fig. 42). The palette exploits strong contrasts of bright, sharp colors, such as the Baptist's green cape or the violet,[38] red, and ochre worn by the female saint, all obscured by discolored varnish. The background, a complicated cityscape, seems to be unique in Bellini's oeuvre and may reflect the patron's wishes. Now the figures are nearly full-length: Bellini (and/or his patrons) evidently became increasingly reluctant to adhere to the half- or three-quarter-length figure, and in the first decade of the sixteenth century he all but abandoned the older format. Whereas Bellini's earlier use of the partial figure is explained in reference to Byzantine art and the story of Saint Luke, his late preference for the

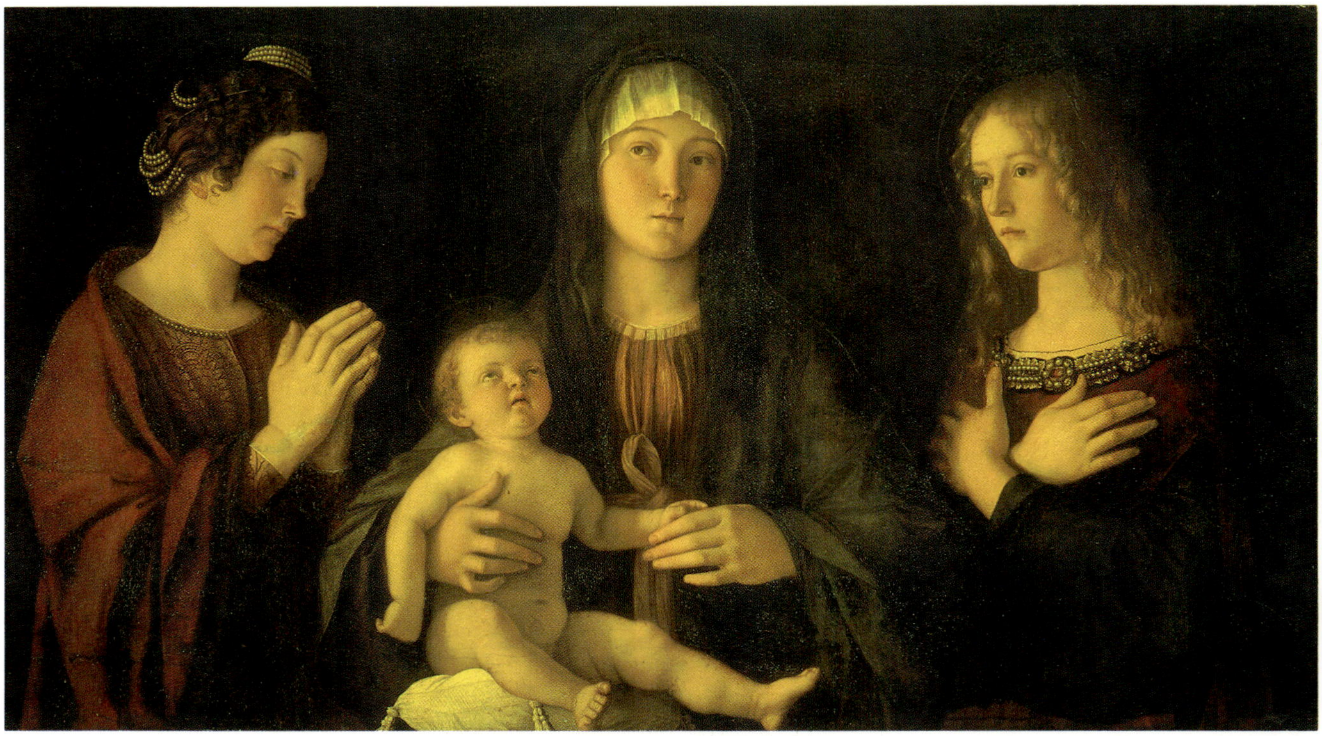

40. Madonna and Child with Two Female Saints, *Gallerie dell'Accademia, Venice. Photo: Giacomelli Fotografia, Venice.*

full-length may be understood as an attempt to westernize and modernize his imagery. Concomitant with this development is his use of the horizontal format, even for depictions of the Madonna and Child alone. These compositional changes preclude evocation of the icon tradition. Departing from this venerable formula, Bellini endowed his images with a new verisimilitude, visual and psychological.

The *Madonna of the Meadow* (circa 1500–1505) illustrates these developments (fig. 43). It represents a Madonna of Humility—Bellini's only depiction of the type—with Mary seated directly on the ground, figure and environment unified by ambient light. Her humility seems natural, not a symbol, as she sits in a space that might actually contain her.[39] That it does not results primarily from the geometric treatment of Mary's form, which, like the composition itself, appears natural but is achieved by artistic manipulation. The Virgin's garments are arranged to provide her with a physical largeness that exceeds her natural stature, endowing Mary with grandeur and providing a monumental pyramidal support for the Infant who sleeps on her lap. As in Bellini's earlier depictions of the sleeping Child, Christ's sleep prefigures his death, tragically explicit in his posture and shadowed, sunken eyes. The Virgin turns to look down at Christ, and she prays over him as in the Davis *Madonna*, Bellini's first depiction of this subject (fig. 14). Bellini's different renditions of this gesture of prayer might almost represent the remarkable course of his career *in nuce*: the closed, precise, vertical formation of the hands in the first work has become open, easy, and more horizontal in the sixteenth-century composition; the clear, almost sculptural modeling of the mid-quattrocento has become the *colorito* of the late work, in which forms are defined by modulations of color and light.

41. Madonna and Child with Two Female Saints, *detail, saint with jeweled gown. Photo: Giacomelli Fotografia, Venice.*

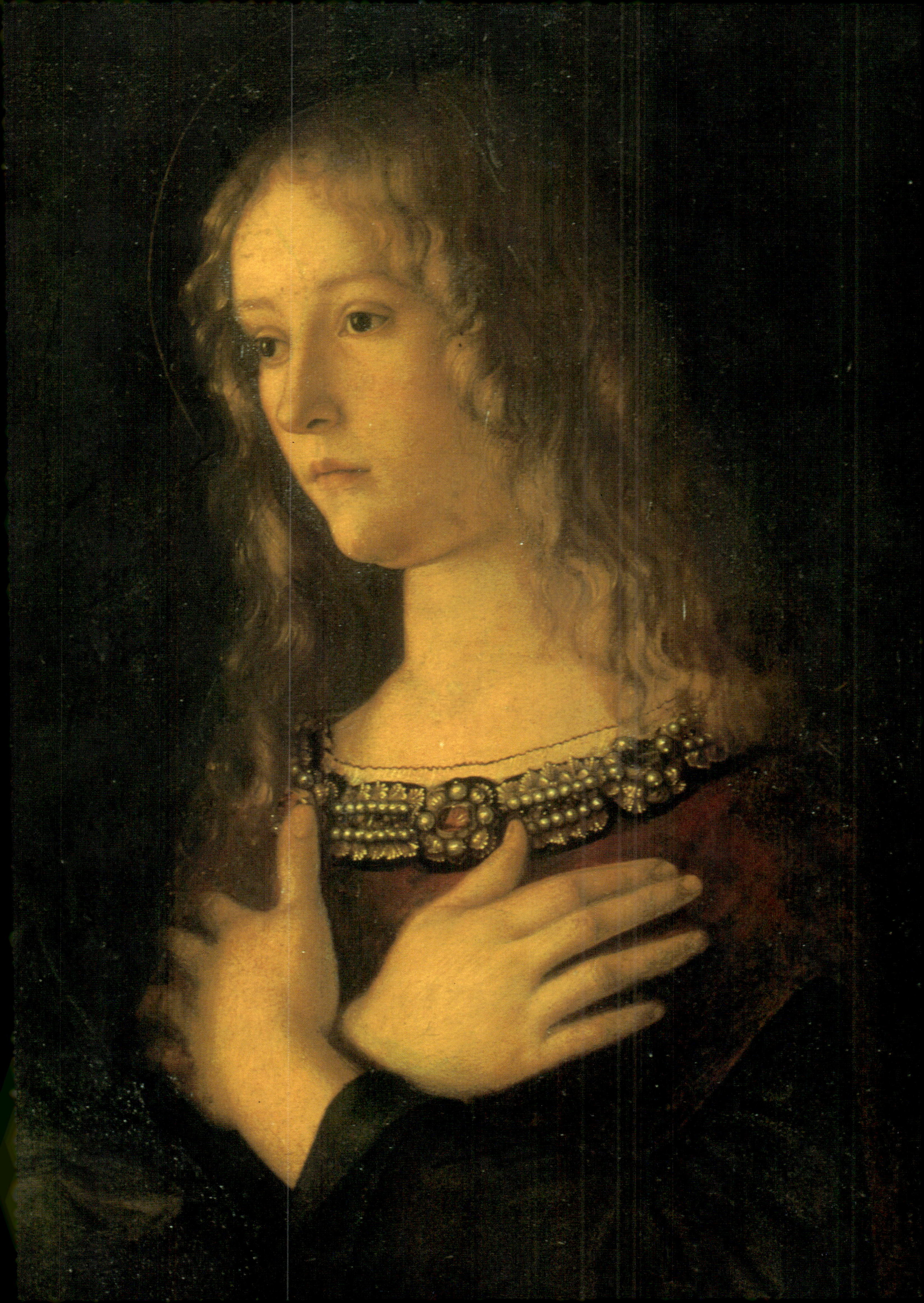

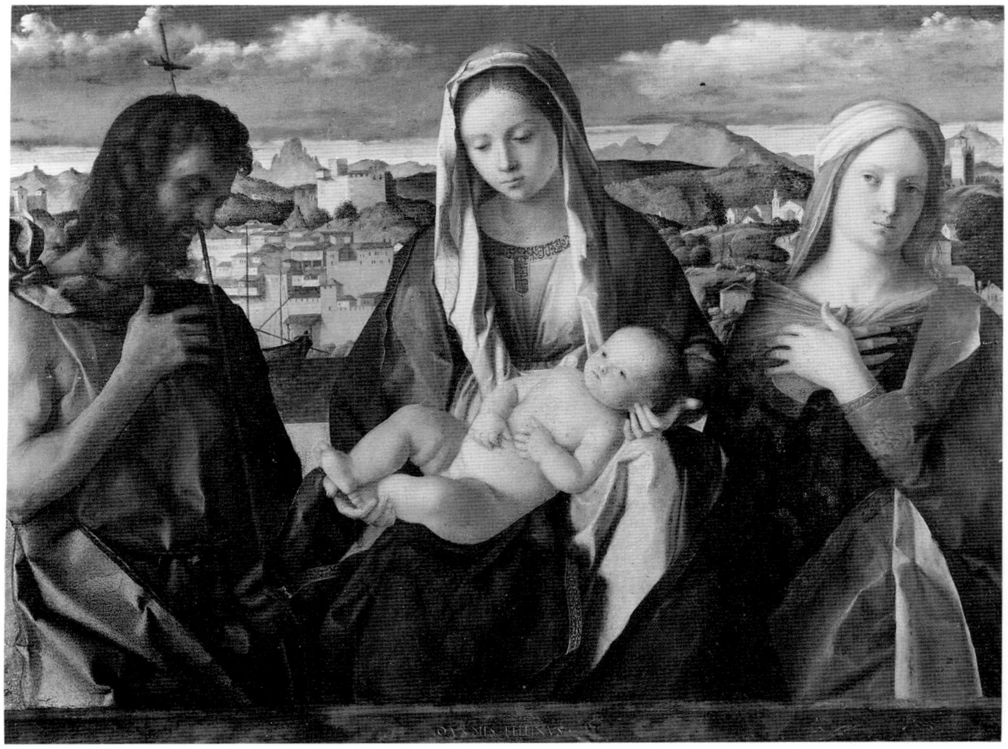

42. *Giovanni Bellini with probable assistance,* Madonna and Child with Saint John the Baptist and a Female Saint *(Giovanelli* Sacra Conversazione*), Gallerie dell'Accademia, Venice. Photo: Giacomelli Fotografia, Venice.*

In the *Madonna of the Meadow*, as in Bellini's earliest works, the landscape provides the naturalistic raison d'être for the atmosphere that surrounds the Virgin and Child, even though they are detached from this environment by their grand scale and by the visual games that Bellini played with certain details.[40] To either side of the Madonna, for example, Bellini included the head of a brown cow and the rump of a white one—implying the beginning and end of the same piebald creature, impossibly long and with its midsection concealed by Mary. The first impression of the composition is verisimilar: the Mother and Child seem to be in a meadow. What these details achieve, however, is an irrefutable insistence on the disassociation of the Virgin from the naturalistic setting, a spatial disjunction that may also imply a spiritual separation. What was hinted in the hierarchic distinctions of earlier compositions now seems explicit: Mary may sit on the ground, like a traditional Madonna of Humility, but she so dominates her setting and is so separate from it that her humility is denied by the very means that assert her lowliness. Bellini does not elevate the Holy Mother with fictive jewels and gilding but more subtly establishes her independence from this world and her exaltation above it.

One detail of Bellini's composition suggests an almost emblematic symbolism, and that is the stork attacking a snake, seen in the distance to Mary's right. This unnatural combat—for all that it is naturally represented, with the snake springing and the bird spreading its wings and arching its back—is neither anecdotal nor bucolic. Perhaps the battle represents a combat of good and evil, or perhaps it is a visualization of Religion.[41] Whatever the significance of such details may be, the import of the painting is clear: Christ's redemption of mankind requires his death on the cross, and this is adumbrated by his sleep, made poignant by his vulnerable nudity. Mary prays over her sleeping Infant because he is the eucharistic Christ, and her posture, no less than his, recalls images of the Pietà—including one (fig. 25) Bellini himself painted at about the same time as the London *Madonna*.

The mournfulness and inwardness of the Virgin Mary in this painting, and in most Bellini Madonnas, ultimately gave way to more hopeful imagery in which the Mother and Child behold the viewer-worshiper directly, acknowledging and welcoming this presence (figs. 44, 45). No longer does the Madonna compel contemplation of her Son's sacrifice by her demeanor, nor does Christ evoke his future suffering in any obvious way; rather, their beneficence promises or at least implies our salvation.

One might expect a devotional image to present Christ blessing the viewer-worshiper, but in Bellini's earlier works this is almost never the case. The Infant and his mother rarely behold the viewer directly—no recognition, to say nothing of benediction, is expected or given. Christ's blessing should not be taken for granted, Bellini seems to remind us. Even in images that include donors, even in altarpieces, the Child may deny his blessing. Bellini's two related compositions of 1509 and 1510 are thus a welcome surprise: now Christ blesses us, he and the Virgin behold us even more directly, with greater sweetness than in the earlier Contarini *Madonna and Blessing Child*, and with none of Mary's sadness. Diffidence, even disinterest, is replaced by an assured directness of attention that invites the confidence of the viewer, who is rewarded by Christ's blessing.

As in the Contarini *Madonna*, the Infant stands on his mother's knee like a small hero, nude and in classical contrapposto; his act of blessing is heroic, validated by his eventual immolation, his ultimate heroism. The import of these later images is beneficent and hopeful: and this at a time when the Venetians were facing one of the greatest threats ever mounted against them. The sixteenth-century *Madonnas*, both dated after the War of the League of Cambrai, are contemporary with that assertive and optimistic rewriting of history with which the Venetians sought to restore prestige and self-confidence. This patriotic assertion of grandeur and success, as even an ardent citizen must have recognized, was *campanilismo* and braggadocio.[42] In this troubled context, Bellini's images represent both a prayer for salvation and its fulfillment in the generosity of Virgin and Child.

The earlier of the two sixteenth-century works, now in Detroit, was painted with assistance, which is evident especially in the hands, head, and neck of the Madonna, in the proportions of the Infant, and perhaps even in the slightly irregular lettering of the inscription (fig. 45). But when Bellini decided to vary the composition one year later, it seems that he worked alone (figs. 44, 46). In each composition, Mary and Christ are frontal and look directly at the beholder.

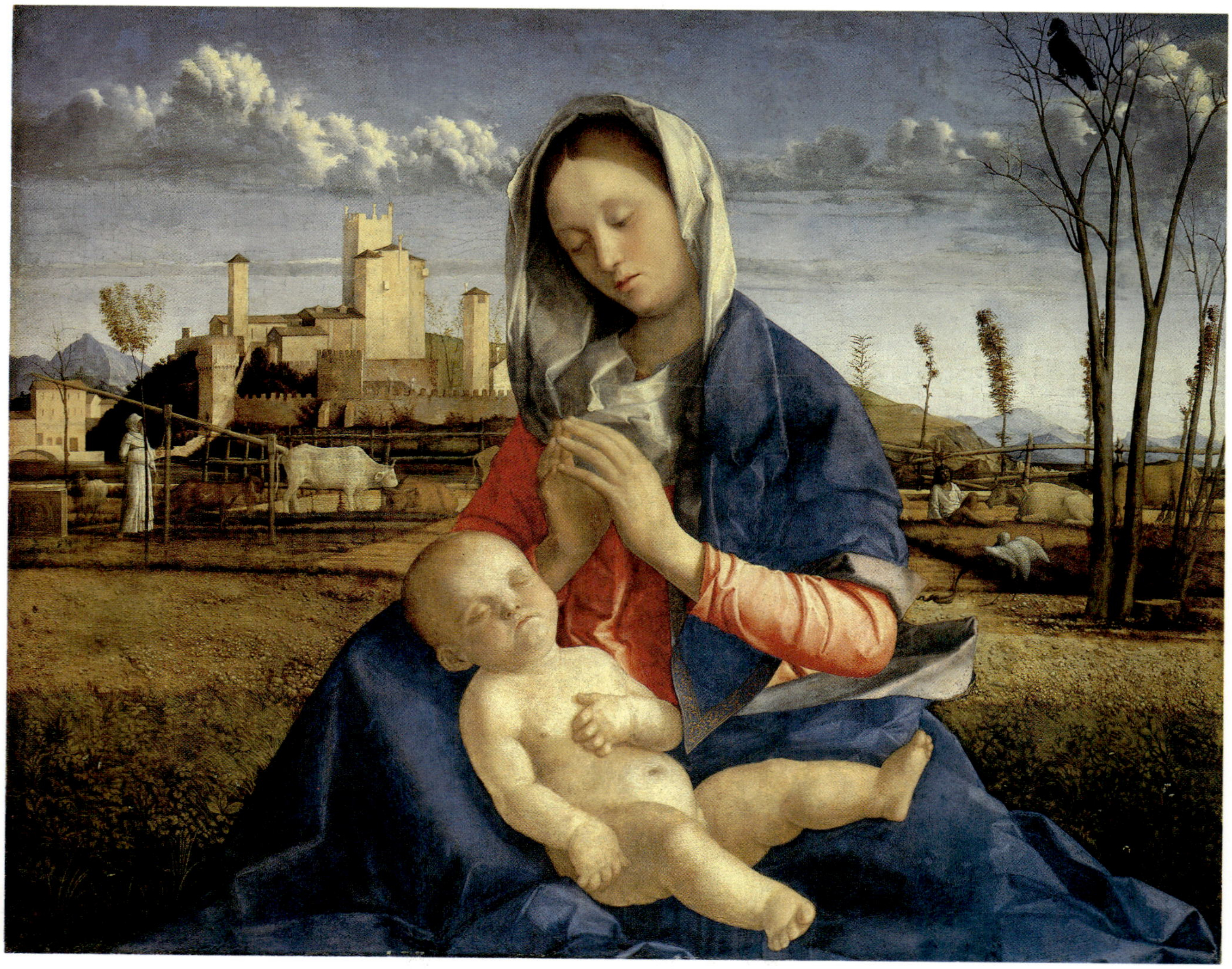

43. Madonna of the Meadow, *National Gallery, London.*

The Virgin is a partial figure, standing in the foreground with one knee raised to support the Child, an "extension" of the posture Bellini had already used in such earlier works as the *Madonna greca* and the *Madonna dei cherubini rossi*.

The two sixteenth-century compositions differ in several details, however. The first is an asymmetrical scene with a cloth of honor—or perhaps now merely a drapery—pulled to one side to reveal a landscape vista, as in the Metropolitan Museum *Madonna* or the Harewood *Madonna and Child with Donor* (fig. 38), both dating some twenty years earlier, or in the contemporary panel in Atlanta. The Madonna holds a book, and on it is the artist's signature and date, IOANNES BELLINVS/MDVIIII, their placement implying the Virgin's approbation and equating Bellini's image with the written word of the sacred text.

In the Brera *Madonna*, Bellini used the traditional cloth of honor, watered green silk with a red border, as in the *Madonna degli alberetti*, revealing landscape views to either side. Bellini's name and the date 1510 are inscribed on a stone block that resembles an ancient altar, on which sits a spotted cat.[43] Because the painting surface was badly abraded in an early attempt at restoration, Bellini's sketchy underdrawing is visible in parts: seemingly random lines, for example, indicate the

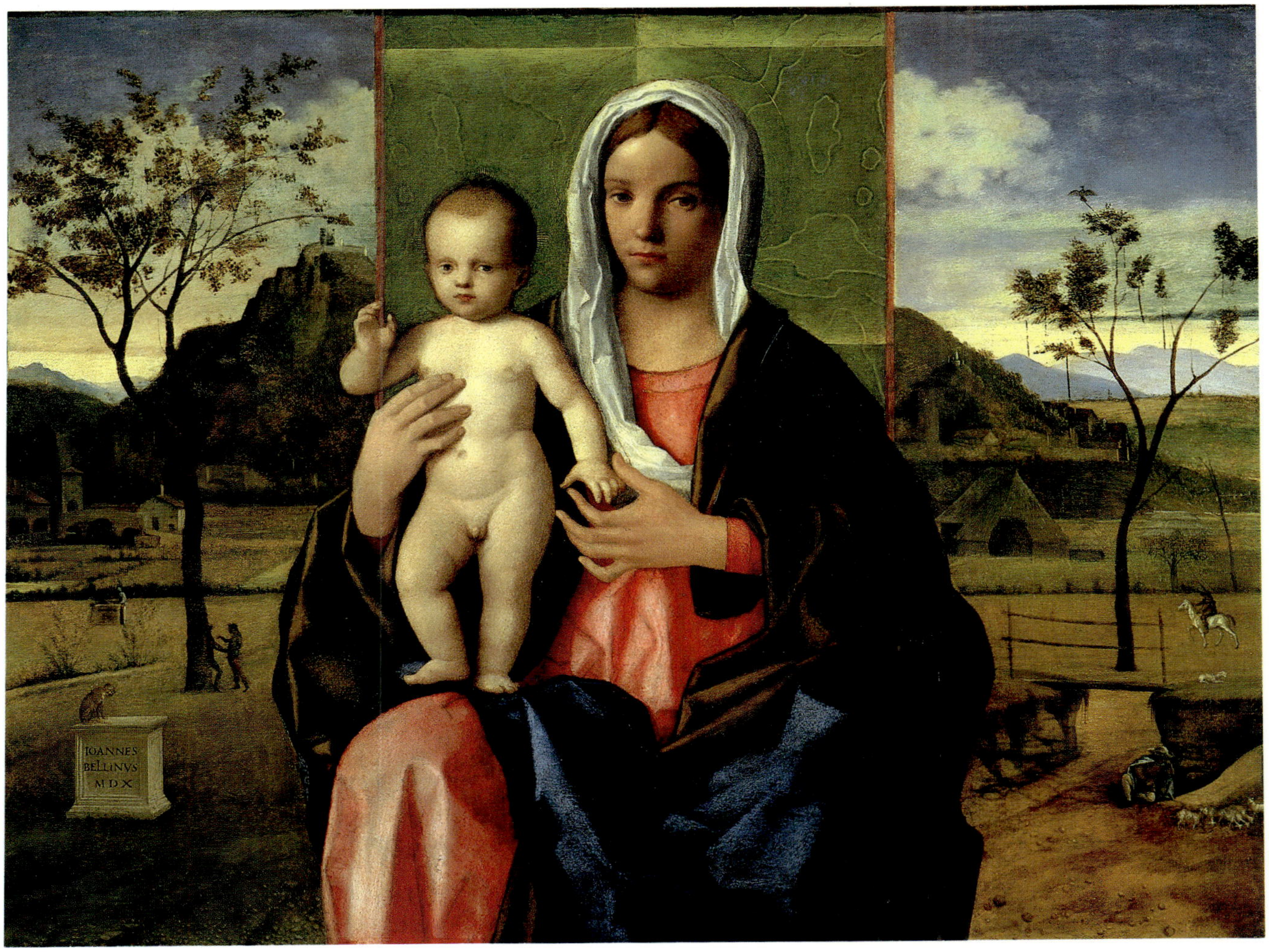


44. Madonna and Child *(Brera* Madonna*)*, *Pinacoteca di Brera, Milan. Photo: Sovrintendenza per i Beni Artistici e Storici, Milan, and Color Dielle, Milan.*

placement of shadowed folds in Mary's mantle.[44] Other parts of the composition were evidently not drawn at all but defined in paint on the prepared surface of the panel. Moreover, only traces of Bellini's rose and yellow glazes survive; the surface was originally much richer than it appears today. What is now visible of Mary's red gown, for instance, is merely Bellini's undermodeling, which was almost certainly completed by an additional stratum of lake glaze.[45]

The landscapes of both pictures are filled with activity: figures ride, stand and talk, or doze in the shade while their sheep graze. This tranquility echoes the calm of the sacred beings. Quiet self-assurance pervades these scenes; Mother and Child are no longer haunted by their future suffering but confident and attentive to the viewer-worshiper: now we are assured of their benevolence. This may explain why Bellini eliminated the parapet from these compositions and avoided all memory of it in the relationship of figures to the edge of the picture field (cf. figs. 27, 40). The symbolic form of the parapet had provided a point of access for the worshiper but also barred him or her from the sacred realm. Combined with the half-length figure, the parapet was a means of asserting the visionary presence of the sacred beings before us. These implications of presence are here replaced by a Western

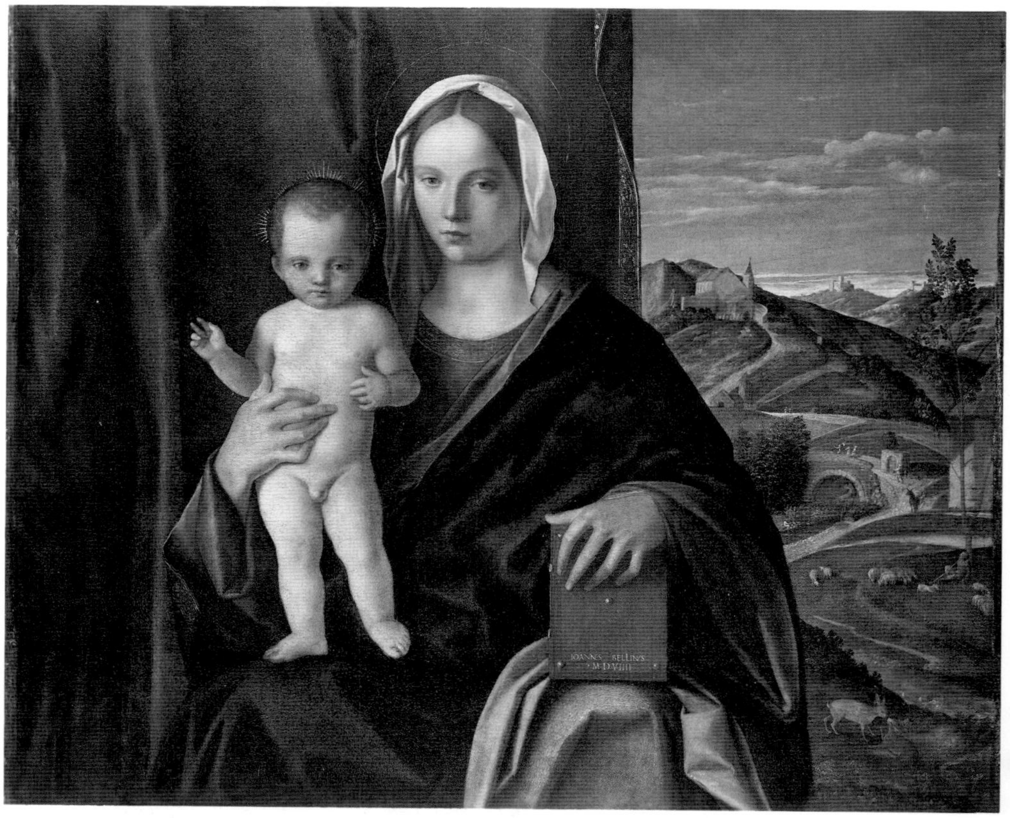

45. *Giovanni Bellini with assistance,* Madonna and Blessing Child, *Institute of Arts, Detroit. Courtesy of the Detroit Institute of Arts.*

conception of the sacred image as a representation—a painting, not an apparition, with the signature incorporated within the image, not applied illusionistically to the surface. Here nothing recalls so explicitly as the parapet Christ's identity as eucharistic offering and Mary's as the shrine that contained him. Their redemptive sacrifice is conveyed more gently by the figures themselves, by their gestures, their steady gazes, and the nakedness of the Word made flesh. The salvation they have obtained by this sacrifice is freely offered to the worshiper whom Christ blesses.

## Omega: The Dead Christ

Bellini's vision of motherhood differs in paintings of the Virgin and Child from that in his images of the dead Christ, the other most-repeated sacred theme in his oeuvre. When Mary embraces her dead Son, she expresses the unbearable grief of one bereft of both her Lord and her beloved Child. The bond between Mary and Christ in these paintings is always more intimate than that between Christ and John the Evangelist, a frequent companion, and it is always represented as a paroxysm of pathos and intimacy disrupted by death. Yet the memory of that intimacy survives death, whereas the young Mother who embraces her Child seems comparatively distant and aloof. They rarely exchange a glance; their intimacy is primarily physical, a matter of practicality. Mary's embrace sometimes seems a restraint, and her expression is almost always abstract regardless of Christ's action:

whether he seems to sing, attempts to escape her arms, or lifts his hand in blessing —nothing elicits a response. Only when he sleeps does she respond with prayer. And in each case, she contemplates what her Child will achieve on the cross. Bellini's imagery does not offer easy solace but sorrowful compassion for the suffering of Mary and Christ. The fulfillment of Christ's fate, the tragic omega of his earthly existence, is the subject of Bellini's images of the dead Savior.

Sometimes alone, sometimes supported by weeping putti or angels, sometimes mourned by his mother and John the Evangelist, the half-length crucified Christ is the central figure in all of these compositions, and in all but one he is seen within a sarcophagus or behind a parapet.[46] This imagery, combined with the use of the partial figure, is the same as in the fifteenth-century Madonna paintings: the half-length suggests a vision, and the parapet is the symbolic equivalent of the altar, the tomb, and the Virgin Mary, because Christ is contained in and emerges from each. Indeed, a Christian altar is a tomb, the burial place of a sacred relic. The symbolism is clear: the dead Christ is the Eucharist, and his flesh-and-blood sacrifice has made unnecessary the blood sacrifice of the Old Testament. The author of the Letter to Hebrews explains that "such a high priest [as Christ] . . . has no need to offer sacrifices daily . . . ; for this he did once and for all when he offered up himself. . . . the blood of his sacrifice is his own blood . . . ; and thus he has entered the sanctuary once and for all and secured an eternal deliverance" (Heb. 7:26–28, 8:5).[47]

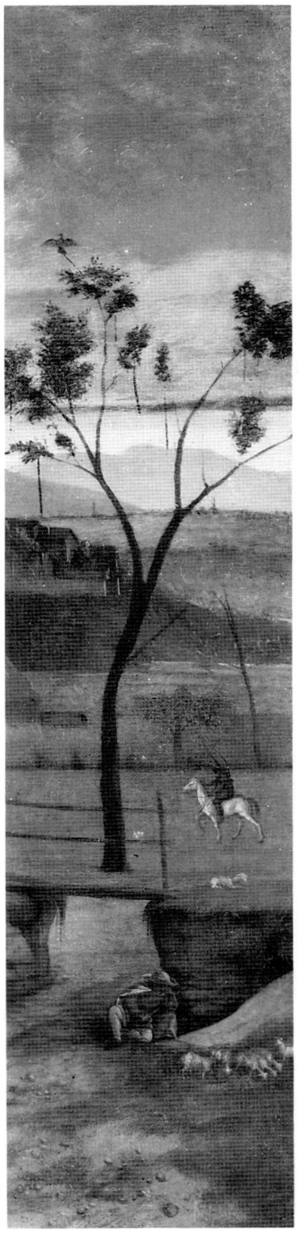

46. *Brera* Madonna, *detail, landscape. Photo: Sovrintendenza per i Beni Artistici e Storici, Milan.*

This and similar passages in the Bible provide the ultimate source for such images of the sacrificial Christ as Bellini's. In fact, the very word *pietà*, which describes such images in Medieval and Renaissance writings, also finds precedent in scripture.[48] According to modern art historical habit, however, *pietà* is used specifically to describe Mary holding the crucified Christ in her lap. Such compositions may be visually and emotionally quite different from half-length images of the dead Christ, but the underlying spiritual and theological significance is the same, as fifteenth-century people understood when they used the same word to characterize both scenes. The choice of word, the pious emotion that it signified —both piety and pity—is directly related to the meaning of these images and to their original function as perceived by their first viewers.

In these images of the Crucified Christ with Mary, as in the Madonna paintings, the Virgin is seen as participating in the Lord's work of redemption by offering her own sacrifice: her Son.[49] But whereas the Madonna paintings cannot be associated with any particular narrative moment, and are indeed sometimes anachronistic,[50] some images of the dead Christ have specific historical resonance and narrative implications. Depictions of the Pietà in which Mary holds her dead Son on her lap are perforce associated with the Lamentation or Deposition: the two central figures have been removed from larger narrative groupings, but the sequence of events is remembered.

Bellini's half-length compositions of the dead Christ with the Madonna and

Saint John, however, are related to the preceding and successive historical moments in narrations of the Passion, namely, the Crucifixion and the Entombment. The Madonna and John the Evangelist were the chief mourners at the Crucifixion, and with his dying words, Christ entrusted his Mother to John. Thus Mary and John are represented in countless scenes of the Crucifixion, whether alone with Christ or in a crowd of mourners and bystanders. Medieval crosses encapsulate this drama with half-length figures of the Virgin and John in the arms of the rood, their weeping faces juxtaposed with the visage of the Crucified Christ. Such paintings as Bellini's Pietàs in Bergamo or in the Brera, therefore, have a historical resonance, while isolating the characters to emphasize their theological and spiritual significance. Narrative is abbreviated, the cast limited to half-length figures seen behind a parapet; space is restricted; and time is suspended. Mourners support Christ in his sepulcher, evoking yet not enacting the Entombment. All that is extraneous has been removed from the drama, and historical recollection is subsumed in our empathetic contemplation of the eucharistic Christ, out of time and out of space. Bellini's interpretation is thus both narrative and non-narrative, history painting and ahistorical *Andachtsbild* (devotional picture). His theme derives from the historical Passion—Crucifixion, Deposition, Lamentation, and Entombment conflated in the pathetic image of Christ and his mourners—but it is also the perpetual reenactment of this sacrifice in the celebration of the Mass.[51]

The earliest of Bellini's *imagines pietatis,* the panel in Bergamo (fig. 47), is also one of his earliest surviving works, and it is closely related in date and conception to one of his father's drawings in the Louvre (fig. 48). Giovanni's painting isolates the central group from Jacopo's drawing, focusing attention on the three protagonists. Signed on the parapet with the abbreviated signature IOHANNES. B., the picture is also inscribed at the top with Greek characters identifying the three figures, the Mother of God (*Mater Theoi*), Jesus Christ, and Saint John. Each figure is half-length and in the immediate foreground, defined and delimited by a parapet. Mary and John, moreover, are cropped by the sides of the panel, which emphasizes their proximity to the picture plane and hence to the beholder.[52] They stand slightly behind Christ; he is the most complete figure in this powerful, intimate composition. His head falls of its own weight, pressing against his mother's, while she inclines her head and her eyes toward him: seldom beholding him in life, as the Infant in her arms, now she contemplates him in death, when he cannot return her gaze.

47. Dead Christ with the Virgin Mary and Saint John the Evangelist *(Bergamo* Pietà*), Gallerie dell'Accademia Carrara, Bergamo. Photo: Stefano Paolillo, Venice and New York.*

Mary's face is youthful but aged by extreme grief, her eyes moist with tears and red from crying. With her right hand she supports Christ's right arm, grasping his wounded hand. John the Evangelist holds Christ's left arm at the elbow, so that the Savior's arms assume the traditional pose of the deceased in countless funerary monuments: Christ is in effect entombed here, behind the parapet. John supports his head in his right hand, evoking his comportment in Crucifixion scenes; thus

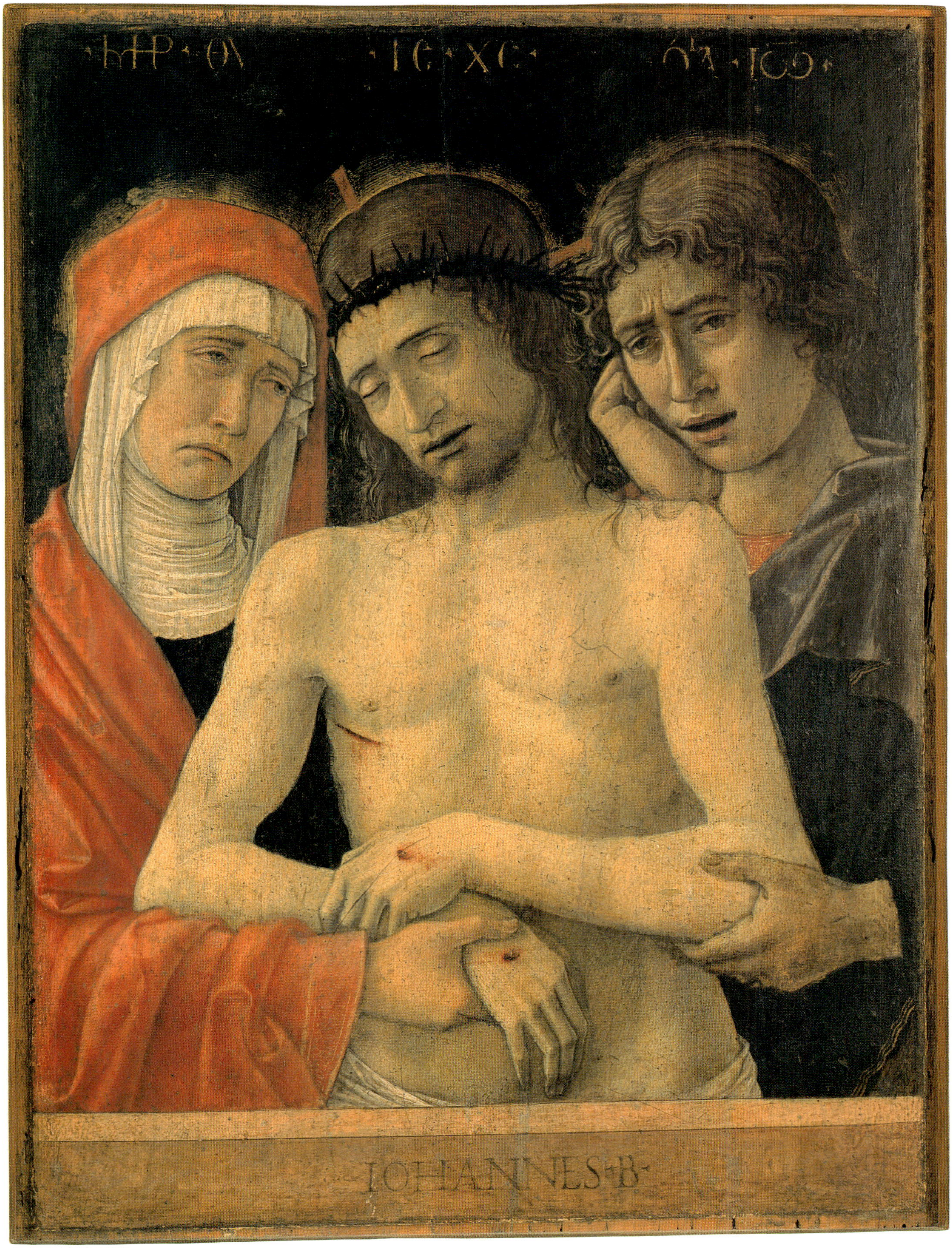
IC XC
IOHANNES·B·

the preceding, causative event is remembered in this moment of Lamentation and Entombment (cf. figs. 3, 5).

The color, now obscured by dirt and discolored varnish, is extraordinary. Bellini used dark green for the background, and combined with its complement, red, for Mary's mantle.[53] This red becomes brighter by contrast with the white veil and wimple, painted with heavy impasto that remains apparent in Mary's veil and in Christ's loincloth, and with the dark gown, too discolored to name, but presumably a shade of blue or purple, for mourning, as in the *Madonna Enthroned* or the late *Pietà*. The Evangelist's mantle is also obscured by discolored varnish, but the color of the lining is blue with lavender highlights, and his gown, visible at the neck, is red with a gold border. Three lines of gold at the edge of his mantle below John's left hand ripple in response to his movement and seem the abstract equivalent of weeping.

John's eyes, like Mary's, are reddened and moist. He looks toward us and his lips are parted, sobbing or perhaps to address us. Expressive faces are matched by expressive hands, contrasted in color—the pallor of death against the warmth of life—and distinguished in energy. The hands of Mary and John are active, while those of Christ fall or preserve the spasm of crucifixion in their rigor. A pentimento for Christ's right index finger reveals the attention Bellini gave to the arrangement of these hands and shows something of his working method, rethinking even on the panel surface.

In many ways, this composition anticipates the Brera *Dead Christ with the Virgin Mary and Saint John the Evangelist* (fig. 49).[54] In the Brera painting, the background opens to landscape and sky, the panel is a horizontal rectangle—apparently Bellini's first use of this format and perhaps a narrative echo—and the intimacy between Mary and Christ is even more intense, heightened by separation from the Evangelist. Christ's body, with broad shoulders and articulated torso, athletic and well muscled, is more classicizing in its beauty compared to earlier works (cf. figs. 5, 47).[55]

The top of the parapet is exploited as the support for Christ's left hand. His fingers are still clenched as if on the cross—in effect, this is the back of one of Christ's hands in the Correr *Crucifixion* (fig. 5). Blood from the stigma has bled down the arm and dried there, and this wounded hand becomes the viewer-worshiper's access into the composition. Resting at the edge of the parapet, Christ's hand almost touches the line that demarcates the structure's highlighted top and shadowed face, which is also the border between the pictorial realm and the world of the beholder. But a light source that can come only from our world causes the shadow of Christ's hand on the symbolic parapet, where the two spheres, sacred and mundane, meet. Christ's hand, dead but not relaxed, rests directly above the inscription that includes the artist's signature. Perhaps this is a purposeful juxtaposition between the visible, wounded hand of the Redeemer, whose power resides

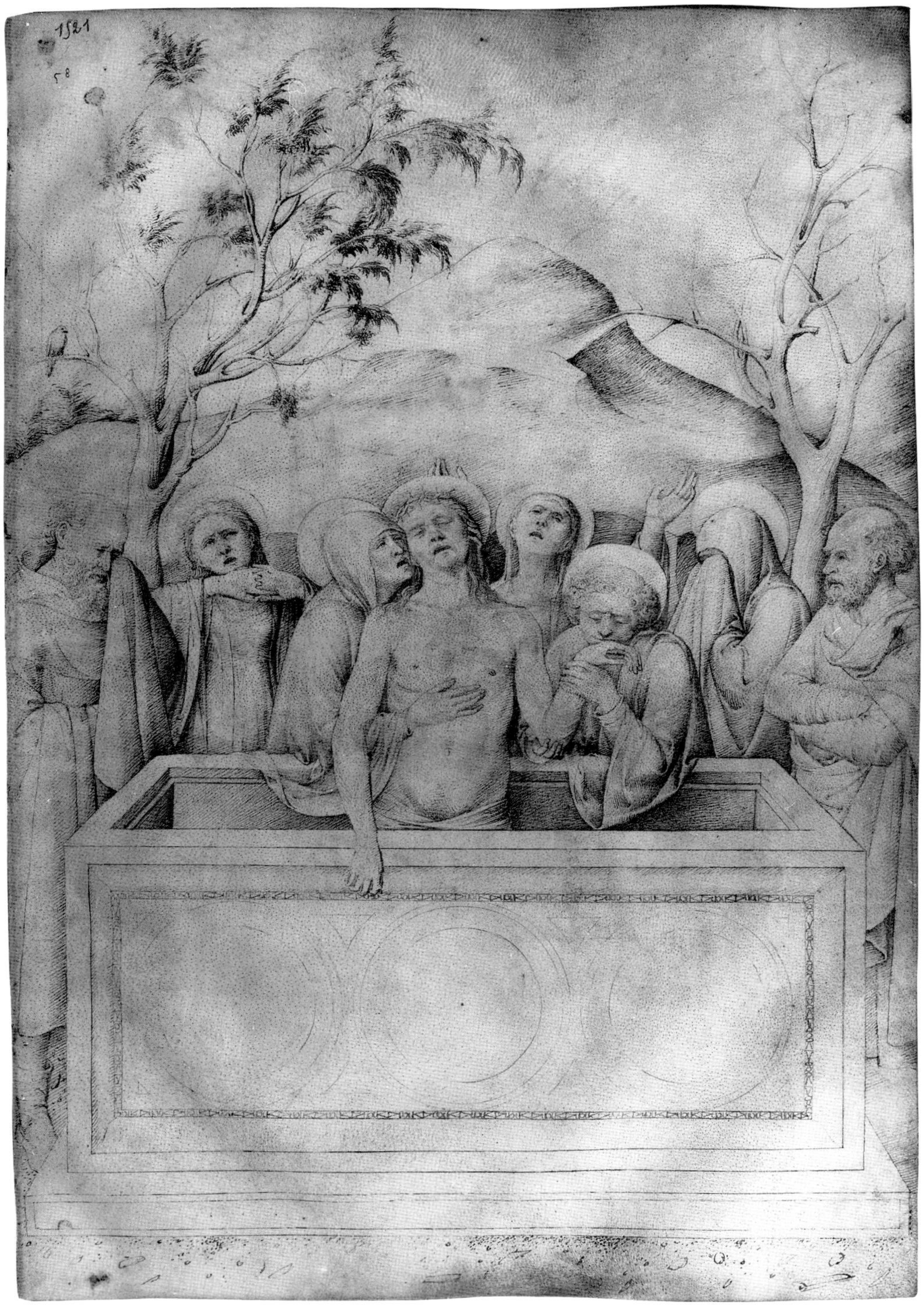

48. *Jacopo Bellini,* Dead Christ, *drawing book, folio 53r, Musée du Louvre, Paris. Photo: Musées Nationaux, Paris.*

in his sacrifice, and the invisible hand of the artist, the hand that expresses his skill and devotion.

The professional and spiritual self-awareness of this situation is confirmed by the discursive context of the signature, unique in Bellini's work. He incorporated his name in a Latin couplet adapted from an elegy by Propertius: HAEC FERE QUUM GEMITUS TURGENTIA LUMINA PROMANT/BELLINI POTERAT FLERE IOANNIS OPUS ("When these swelling eyes evoke groans this

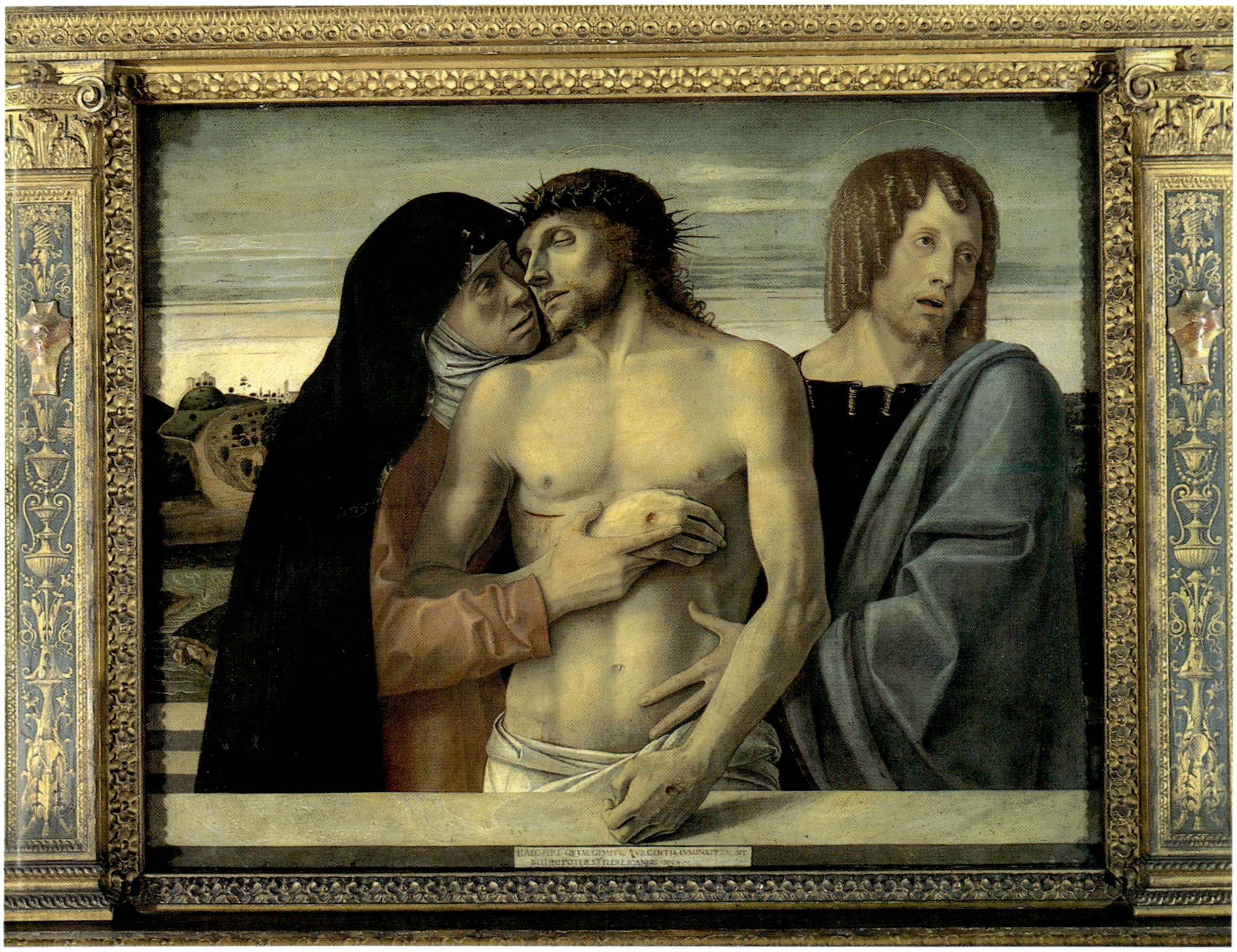

49. Dead Christ with the Virgin Mary and Saint John the Evangelist *(Brera* Pietà*), Pinacoteca di Brera, Milan. Photo: Sovrintendenza per i Beni Artistici e Storici, Milan, and Color Dielle, Milan.*

work of Giovanni Bellini could shed tears").[56] The idea of images that are endowed with human powers—like the ancient topos of the image that lacks only a voice to be alive—is by implication related to those miraculous images of the Virgin that weep. Bellini's image, too, may shed tears, moved by the agonizing grief of Christ's mourners. All the lips are parted here, in the silence of death, in the gasps of weeping, or in the groans of sorrow.

Christ's closed, almost clenched, left hand is juxtaposed with the splayed fingers of John's hand, which supports the Lord's torso, while Mary holds Christ's right hand in hers and presses her face to his, their intimacy frustrated by death. Two calligraphic swirls of drapery at Mary's brow transform an International Style motif into the visualization of her crying, recalling John in the Bergamo *Pietà*. Meanwhile, John turns away and groans, as the inscription suggests, as though contemplation of the Crucified is too painful. The distant landscape rises to their shoulders, and then the background is given over to sky. The variegated atmosphere reflects Bellini's observation of nature and his concern with color and light, but the landscape itself is comparatively primitive (cf. figs. 5, 9, 14). This suggests an early date, circa 1460, an impression confirmed by the forms of the drapery,

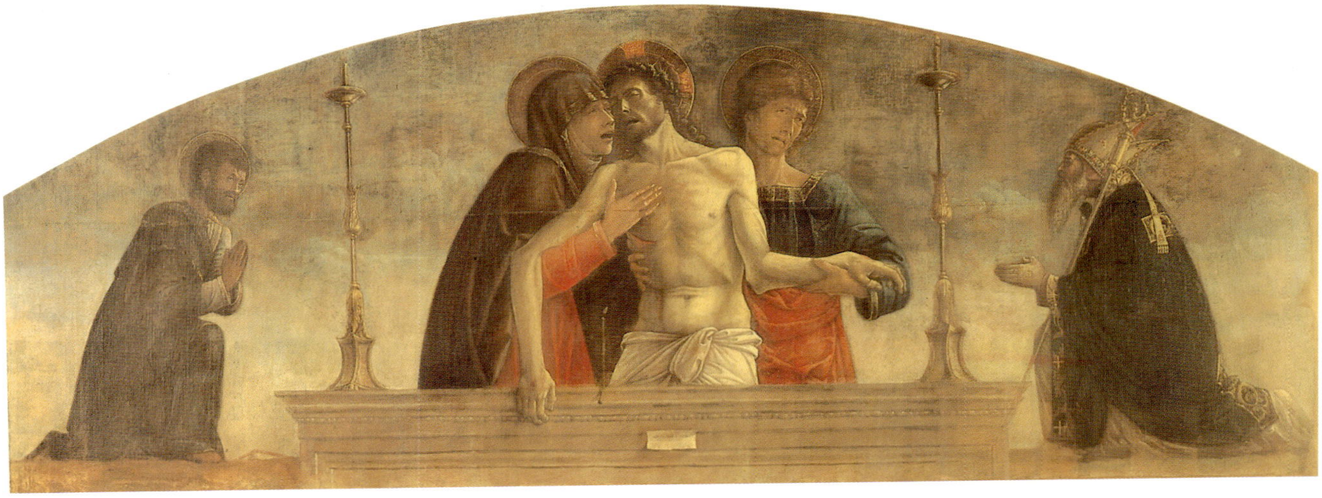

50. Dead Christ with the Virgin Mary and Saint John the Evangelist and Saints Mark and Nicholas, *Palazzo Ducale, Venice. Photo: Scala/Art Resource, New York.*

especially the Evangelist's, which resemble the Davis *Madonna* and other early works (figs. 5, 9, 14, 18).

The canvas in the Ducal Palace is in some ways a variant of the Brera *Dead Christ* composition, but with figure types that recall a still earlier period of Bellini's career (fig. 50). Both Christ and John the Evangelist, for example, resemble themselves in the Correr *Crucifixion*. One might even see the Ducal Palace picture as a predecessor of the Brera pānel, except for a reference by A. M. Zanetti, writing in the late eighteenth century. According to Zanetti, the painting carried the date 1472, now lost but formerly inscribed with the signature.[57] But both the form of the name, IOHANES.BELLINVS, and the style of the painting tempt one to suspect that Zanetti may have mistaken the year. The painting is poorly preserved, especially the flanking figures of Saints Mark and Nicholas, included in deference to the site for which the picture was probably made, the Church or Chapel of Saint Nicholas in the Ducal Palace of Saint Mark.[58] In spite of these problems, however, the picture warrants consideration for both its distinguished provenance and its imagery, which is more explicit than that of the related compositions and hence clarifies their meaning.

In 1571, nearly a hundred years after it was painted, the picture was "modernized" by the addition of an extensive landscape background by Paolo Farinati (fig. 51).[59] The noblemen responsible for this "updating" had Farinati include their coats of arms on shields in the foreground. This artist's other additions clarify the sixteenth-century understanding of Bellini's work, for the parapet was enlarged to become a sarcophagus, and three crosses were painted on a hill in the landscape, thereby expanding its narrative context and recalling compositions by Jacopo Bellini (fig. 48). Although these ideas were inherent in Bellini's conception, narrative evocations of the Crucifixion and Entombment were subsidiary to the imagery of the crucified Christ as eucharistic offering. Including only the molded cornice of the "parapet," Bellini made ambivalent its identity as altar or tomb: it is both,

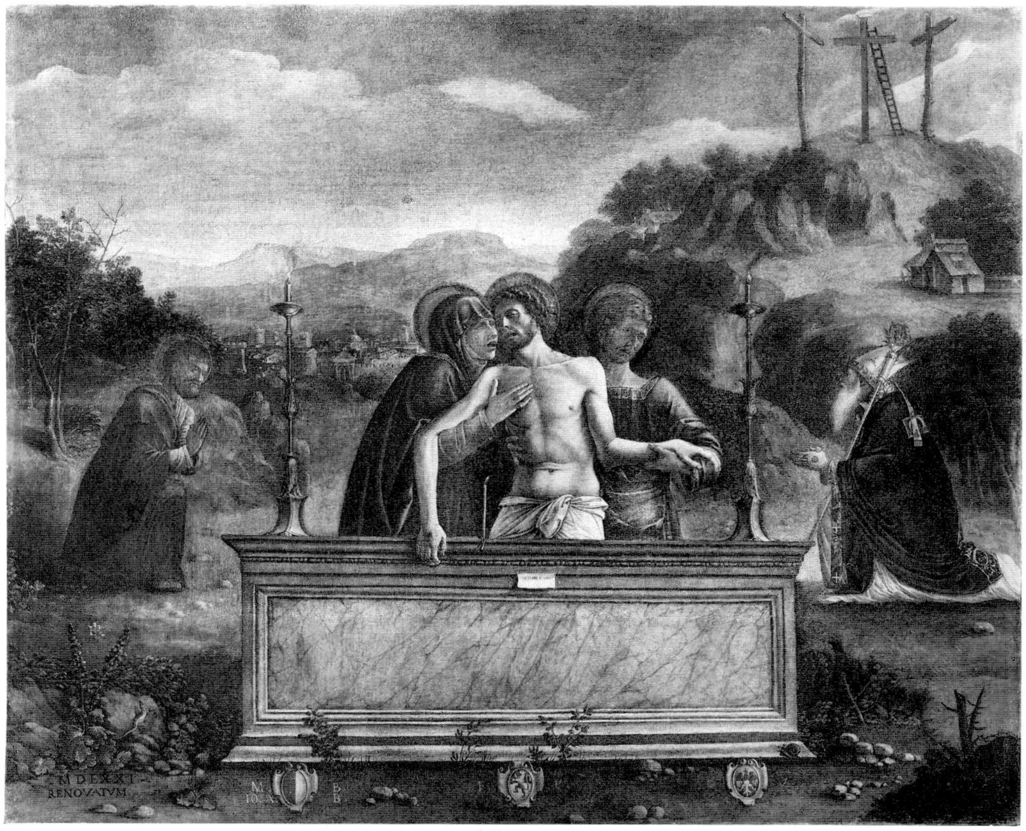


*51. Giovanni Bellini and Paolo Farinati,* Dead Christ with the Virgin Mary and Saint John the Evangelist and Saints Mark and Nicholas, *before restoration, Palazzo Ducale, Venice. Photo: Alinari/Art Resource, New York.*

and if Farinati saw primarily a sarcophagus, at least he did not obliterate Bellini's elegant allusions to the altar, the two candelabra with lighted candles.

In addition to these characteristic and obligatory altar furnishings at either end of the altar-tomb, Bellini affixed a burning taper to its surface, between the figures of Christ and Mary. This taper suggests a votive candle, perhaps offered by Bellini himself, given its proximity to his signature. Certainly this is one of his most intense, deeply felt images of the dead Christ. And so it may be somewhat disappointing to notice the flanking figures of Saints Mark and Nicholas: they disconcert, they distract from the tragic drama of the central group, and they disappoint stylistically, seeming inferior to Bellini's work of the early 1470s.

Much of this apparent inferiority, however, is surely due to the ruinous condition of these two figures, in particular the Evangelist. We must restore the canvas in the mind's eye, imagining the former brilliance of the pearls and gems that embellish Nicholas's glove and mitre, which we can picture by reference to the contemporary *Saint Giustina* (fig. 84), and the luminous atmosphere that would unify the figures while also expressing their emotion, as in Bellini's earlier *Agony in the Garden* (fig. 73).

Although it is possible that Bellini may have been assisted in the execution,[60] one thing is certain: he never hesitated to reuse figure types and compositions, and whether this work was painted in 1472, as Zanetti wrote, or before the Brera *Pietà*, the two paintings are closely related. Another conclusion is justified, however problematic the evidence: Giovanni Bellini was employed in the Ducal Palace

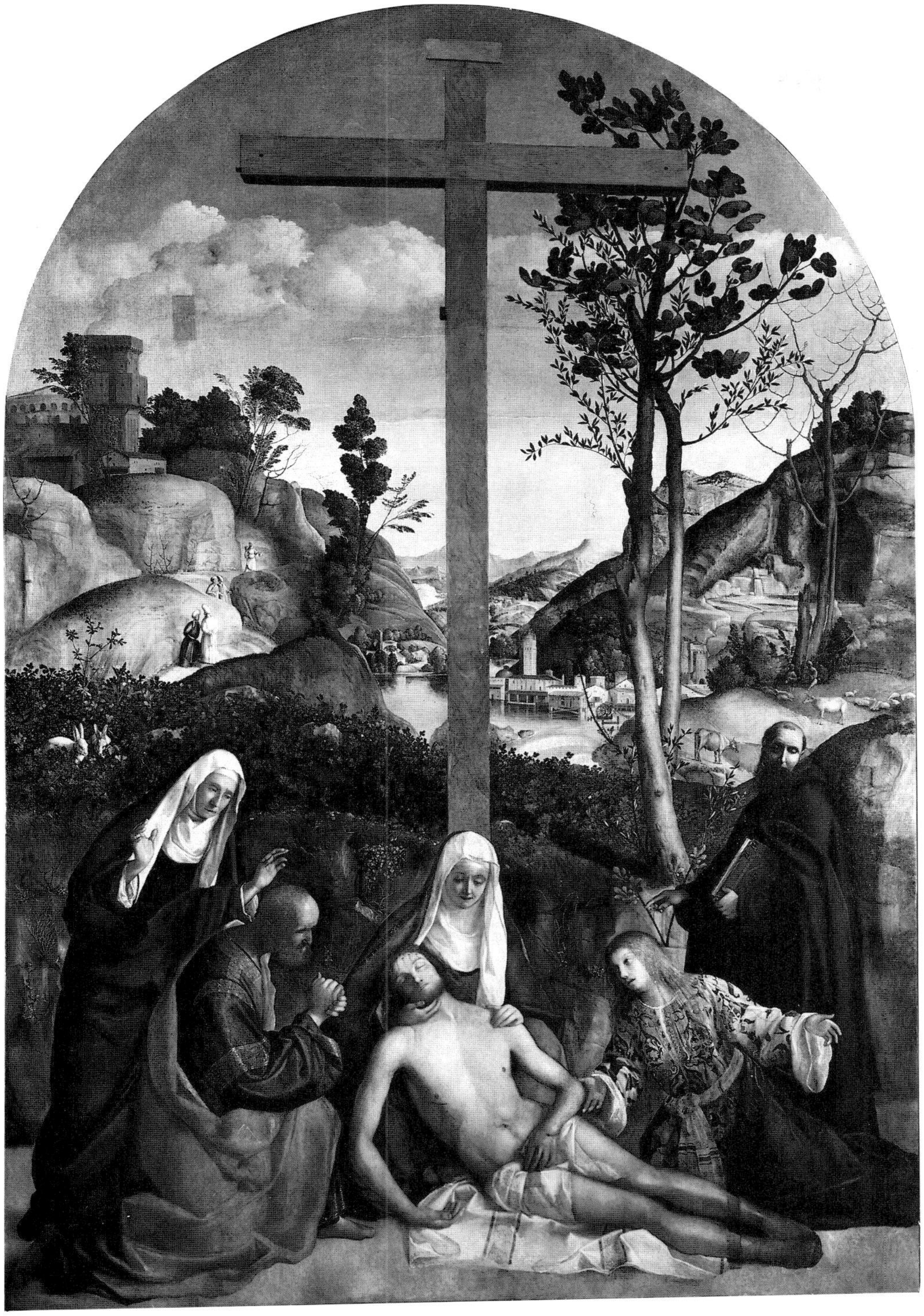

52. *Rocco Marconi with possible participation of Giovanni Bellini,* Lamentation, *Gallerie dell'Accademia, Venice. Photo: Soprintendenza ai Beni Artistici e Storici, Venice.*

even before he substituted for his brother in the Maggior Consiglio decorative campaign when Gentile went to Constantinople in 1479. In short, the *Dead Christ* was Giovanni's first Ducal Palace commission, and it certainly predated Gentile's departure for the Sultan's court. Without placing too great a historical burden on this noble ruin of a painting, perhaps we may also deduce that Giovanni's reputation was foremost as an artist of sacred images: thus his earliest palace commission was a painting of the dead Christ. Only later did Bellini begin to paint secular historical narratives for the Maggior Consiglio, scenes of the kind for which his brother was already justly famous.[61]

*Overleaf:*
53. Dead Christ Supported by Two Putti, *Civico Museo Correr, Venice. Photo: Gianfranco Spinazzi, Venice.*

54. Dead Christ, *Museo Poldi-Pezzoli, Milan. Photo: Museo Poldi-Pezzoli, Milan.*

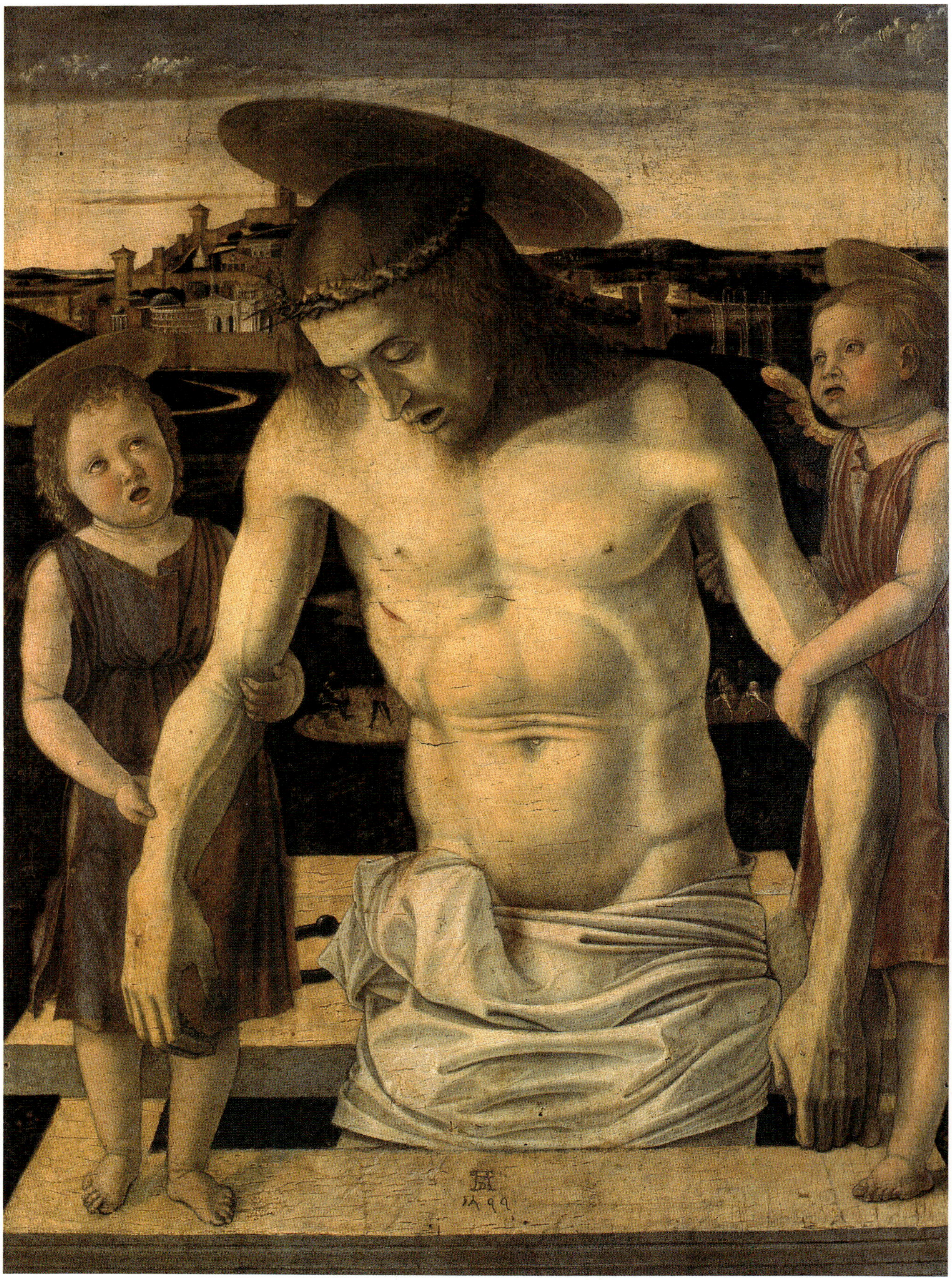

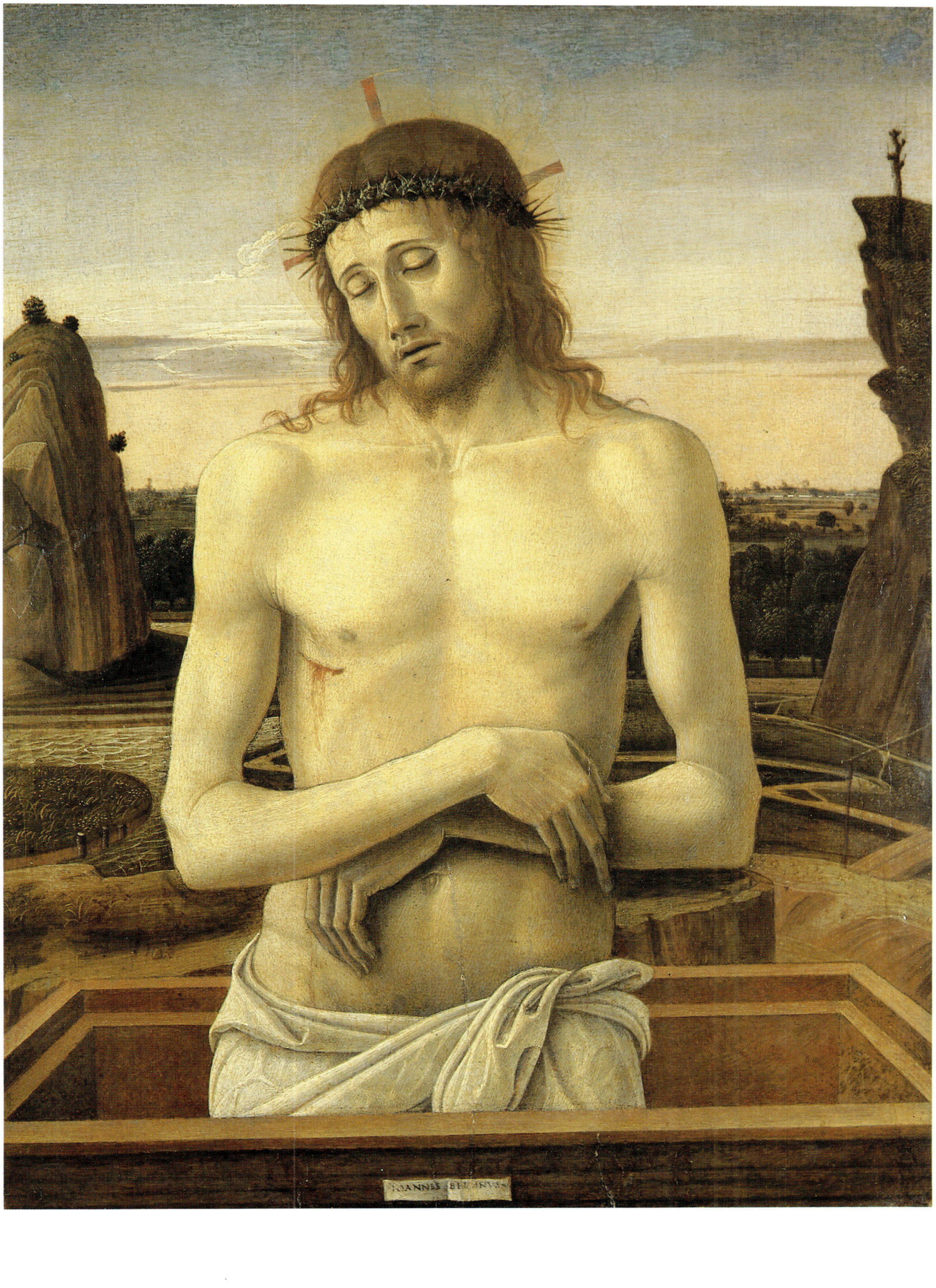

Although Farinati's additions and alterations to Bellini's *Dead Christ* were lamentable and have been removed, they nonetheless underscored an important aspect of the work: when mourning figures of Mary and John the Evangelist flank the figure of the Crucified Christ, certain sequential narrative moments from the Passion are evoked, from the Crucifixion itself, to the Deposition, the Lamentation (fig. 52), and the Entombment, or indeed a seamless interweaving of these events, but emphasizing the Entombment by means of the suggestive form of the parapet.

The theological significance of Bellini's compositions of Christ with Mary and John is the same as in those of Christ alone or with angels: all are eucharistic images. But unlike the former, the images of Christ alone or those of Christ and angels cannot be associated with any biblical episode; they are more insistently ahistorical and are understood essentially as *Andachtsbilder*, non-narrative devotional images.

Bellini's compositions of the dead Christ, alone or with angels, may allude to the legend of the Mass of Saint Gregory, when Gregory became God's agent in a miraculous demonstration of the reality of transubstantiation. Celebrating the Mass, the saint elevated the Eucharist, whereupon a figure of the Crucified Christ appeared, literally and visibly replacing the Host: one substance had become another—the miracle of transubstantiation. In depictions of the Mass of Saint Gregory, the eucharistic Christ, who is the transubstantiated Host, is shown as a half-length figure on the altar.[62] Bellini collated this literary and pictorial tradition with that of the Passion narratives, but only the eucharistic Christ remains to represent his Passion and its repetition in the Mass; mourning angels remind us of the anguish of his death and burial; and the parapet binds the two themes, the devotion celebrated at the altar and the tragic event at the tomb. Allusions to space and time are more completely suppressed than in compositions with Mary and John to compel the viewer-worshiper's contemplation of the eucharistic Christ.

This conception evolved, however; it was not inherent in Bellini's first treatment of the theme. The *Dead Christ Supported by Two Putti*, a work of the early 1450s, shows the Crucified in the foreground, held upright in his tomb by little angels that stand on its edge (fig. 53). The haloes are foreshortened gold disks, perhaps recalling Andrea del Castagno's frescoes for the San Tarasio Chapel, signed in 1442. The angels' classicizing tunics and even their facial types reflect the influence of Donatello, whose bronze relief for the high altar of the Santo in Padua provided a primary source for Bellini's composition and his treatment of the male torso (fig. 8). But whereas Donatello represented his figures against a patterned background of interlocking circles, Bellini provided a whole world, a landscape populated by soldiers who may remind us of the Crucifixion and a distant city containing classical monuments within its medieval walls, and the ruins of a triumphal arch in the countryside (cf. fig. 14). In spite of these narrative and architectural suggestions of place and time, the spatial remoteness of the setting effectively removes the figures from history. What is shown here cannot be associated with any

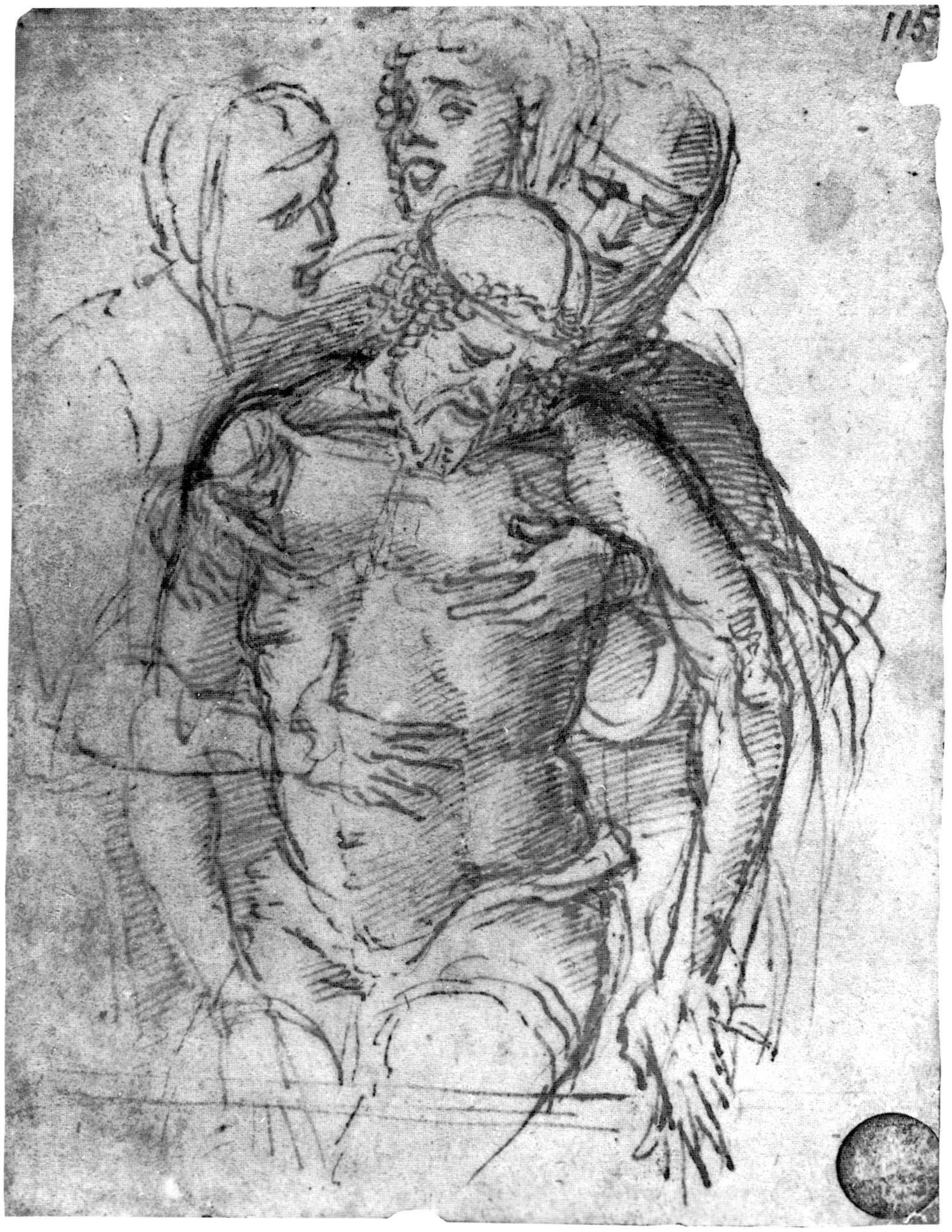

55. Dead Christ, *pen drawing, Gallerie dell'Accademia, Venice. Photo: Soprintendenza ai Beni Artistici e Storici, Venice.*

historical event, unless, in a most tenuous way, it be the Resurrection, anticipated by the opening of the tomb even as the angels weep. Bellini has represented not triumph over death but death's conquest of Jesus the Man, mourned by angels whose grief is too complete to encourage our own hopeful interpretation of the scene. To be sure, hope is implicit in any image of the Christ, but its realization is not imminent here. This explains why Bellini used a landscape setting and not the cloth of honor for his images of the Man of Sorrows: we see the dead man, not the triumphant King of Heaven, and the locus of his sacrificial death is this world.

In his next depiction of the dead Savior, the panel in the Museo Poldi Pezzoli, Bellini eschewed figural echoes of history altogether, representing the eucharistic Christ alone in his tomb, clearly crucified and dead, yet standing upright without support (fig. 54).[63] His figure is based on that in the early Bergamo *Pietà* (fig. 47), and the theme is the contemplation of Christ's redemptive sacrifice.

*Overleaf:*
56. Blessing Redeemer, *Musée du Louvre, Paris. Photo: Musées Nationaux, Paris.*

57. Blood of the Redeemer, *National Gallery, London.*

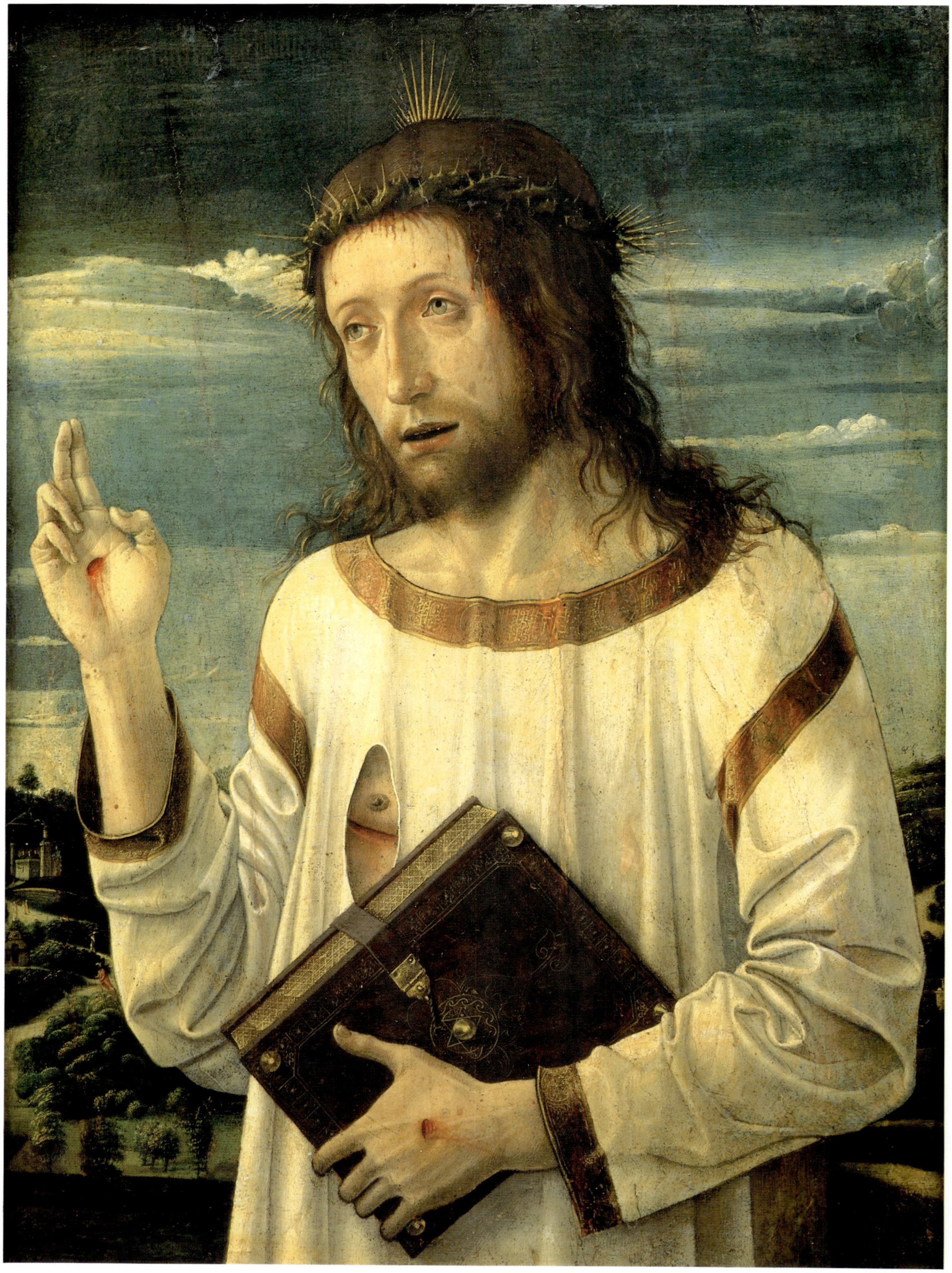

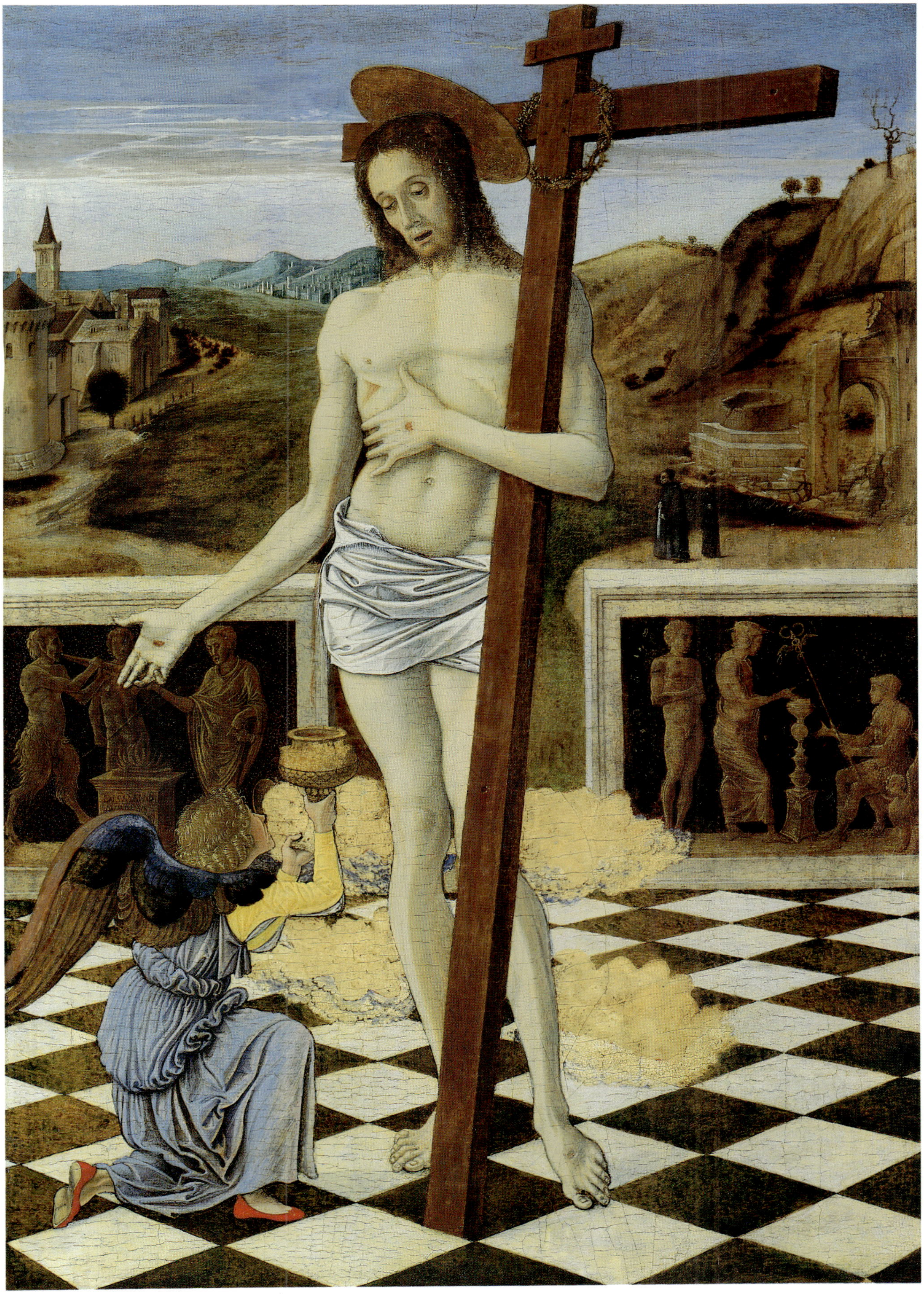

Christ's wounds are to be venerated not only in compassion for his Passion but because they bring salvation. This is the subject of two nearly contemporary works by Bellini in which Christ is crucified and yet alive, the *Blessing Redeemer* and the *Blood of the Redeemer* (figs. 56, 57). The scarred hands of the *Blessing Redeemer*, his crown of thorns, and his garment torn to reveal the wound in the side remind us that his self-sacrifice validates his benediction. In this work Bellini seems to have experimented in an almost self-conscious way with the expressive possibilities of Netherlandish art. Both the style and the psychologically explicit, "bittersweet" characterization of Christ are particularly close to Rogier van der Weyden (cf. fig. 12), though there was also an Italian precedent for Bellini's combination of apparently contradictory emotions.[64]

Like Bellini's other images of the Crucified Christ, this panel was intended for private devotion (fig. 56). The *Blood of the Redeemer*, however, seems to have had a utilitarian function and probably served as the door of a tabernacle (fig. 57).[65] The eucharistic Christ of the door would thus provide access to the sanctified Host within the shrine. Holding his cross in the bend of his left arm, as the Resurrected holds his banner (fig. 105), Christ uses his hand to press blood from the wound in his side. His right arm is extended to encourage the flow and to reveal the wound in the hand. Thus Christ offers himself again; he actively participates in renewing his sacrificial offering for our salvation, filling the chalice of the Mass with his blood.[66]

Kneeling at Christ's right is an angel who catches the blood in a chalice, recalling the text of the ordinary of the Mass: *Pecamor, ut hanc oblationem suscipias in sublimi altari tuo pro manus angelorum tuorum.*[67] God's angel will take the oblation—Christ's offering of himself—to the celestial altar. (Perhaps the angels in Bellini's Pietàs serve the same function; they would appear to do so if the paintings were set on portable altars.) Christ looks down at the angel with an expression of loving mercy, gesturing with his right hand to indicate his approbation and cooperation with the angel's act. At the same time, Christ's hand obliterates a fictive relief on a parapet behind him; another such scene adorns the parapet to his left. Apparently representing episodes of pagan sacrifice, these reliefs depict the antecedents of Christ's immolation, which has rendered them obsolete.[68]

Christ's slender body, associated by its proportions with his cross, his facial type, and his foreshortened, disklike halo may be compared with other comparatively early works by Bellini (figs. 1, 5, 53). Similarities of color appear as well, combinations of closely related pale hues, such as the whites of Christ's loincloth, his pale flesh, and the beiges of rocks or stone. These stylistic elements suggest a slightly earlier date for the London panel than is generally given, perhaps as early as 1460–62.

When Bellini returned to the theme of the dead Christ, he developed a powerful idea that he may have depicted first in drawings in Paris and Venice (figs. 55, 58).[69] In the Pietàs in Berlin and in Rimini, all barriers between viewer and image

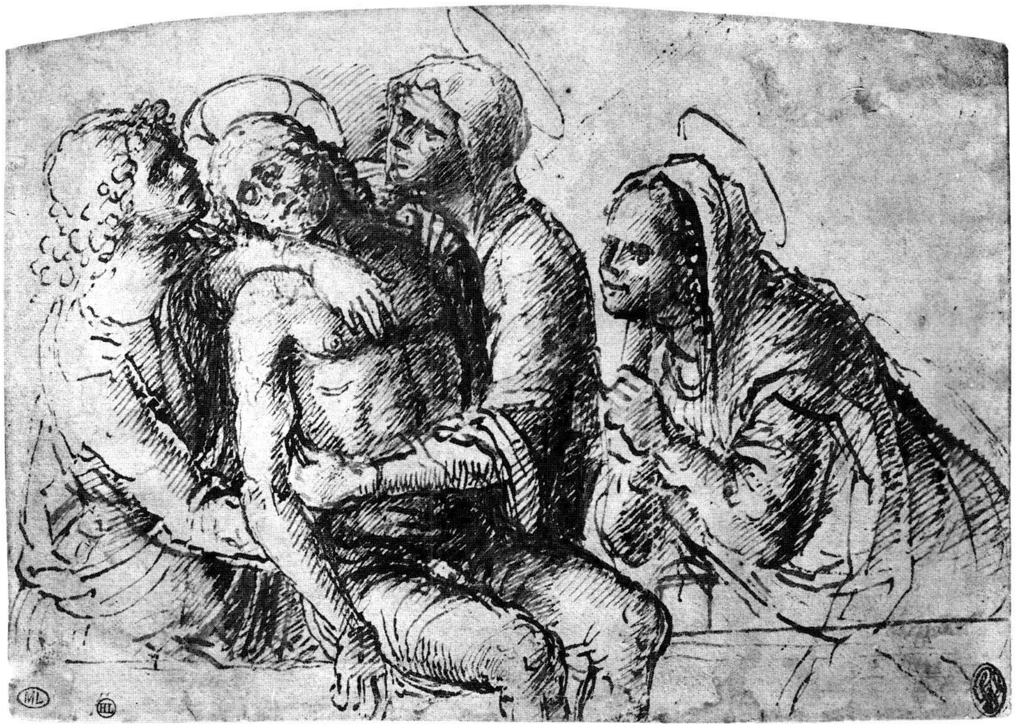

58. Lamentation, *pen drawing, Musée du Louvre, Paris. Photo: Archivio Fotografico del Museo Correr, Venice.*

have been removed (figs. 59, 60). The scene has been broadened to a horizontal rectangle in the Rimini *Pietà*, recalling the Brera *Dead Christ*, and four putti have replaced the customary two flanking figures. Three of the four putti ponder the mystery of Christ's sacrificial act of redemption while their companion struggles to support Christ's limp body. Were this putto to succeed in lifting Christ, it seems that he would fall forward, out of the picture and toward the beholder. In this composition the parapet ledge places Christ, or at least his legs, in our space; the tomb into which he is being placed becomes associated illusionistically with that space: Christ's grave is in this world. Similarly, in the Berlin *Dead Christ with Two Angels* and in the related composition in London, Christ is placed so far forward in the picture space that he seems to push through the plane, which is not defined by a parapet here but only implied by the arrangement of the figures.

In these compositions the wounded hands of Christ are also placed close to the picture plane, compelling contemplation of the stigmata and recalling the Crucifixion in the spasm of the fingers of one hand contrasted with the limp helplessness of the other. Blood from the wound in Christ's side stains the white loincloth, perhaps to remind us that Jesus first shed blood for our salvation in the circumcision. The bloodstain is unexpectedly beautiful: the delicacy of color, the subtlety of pattern are not gruesome but exquisite, and that Bellini could see loveliness in those wounds is characteristic of his spirituality.[70]

After the Ducal Palace canvas and the Rimini *Pietà*, devotional images of the Crucified Christ seem to have vanished from Bellini's oeuvre, with one notable exception. The *Christ Crowned with Thorns* in Stockholm, painted early in the sixteenth century, may be understood as the master's revival and revision of an

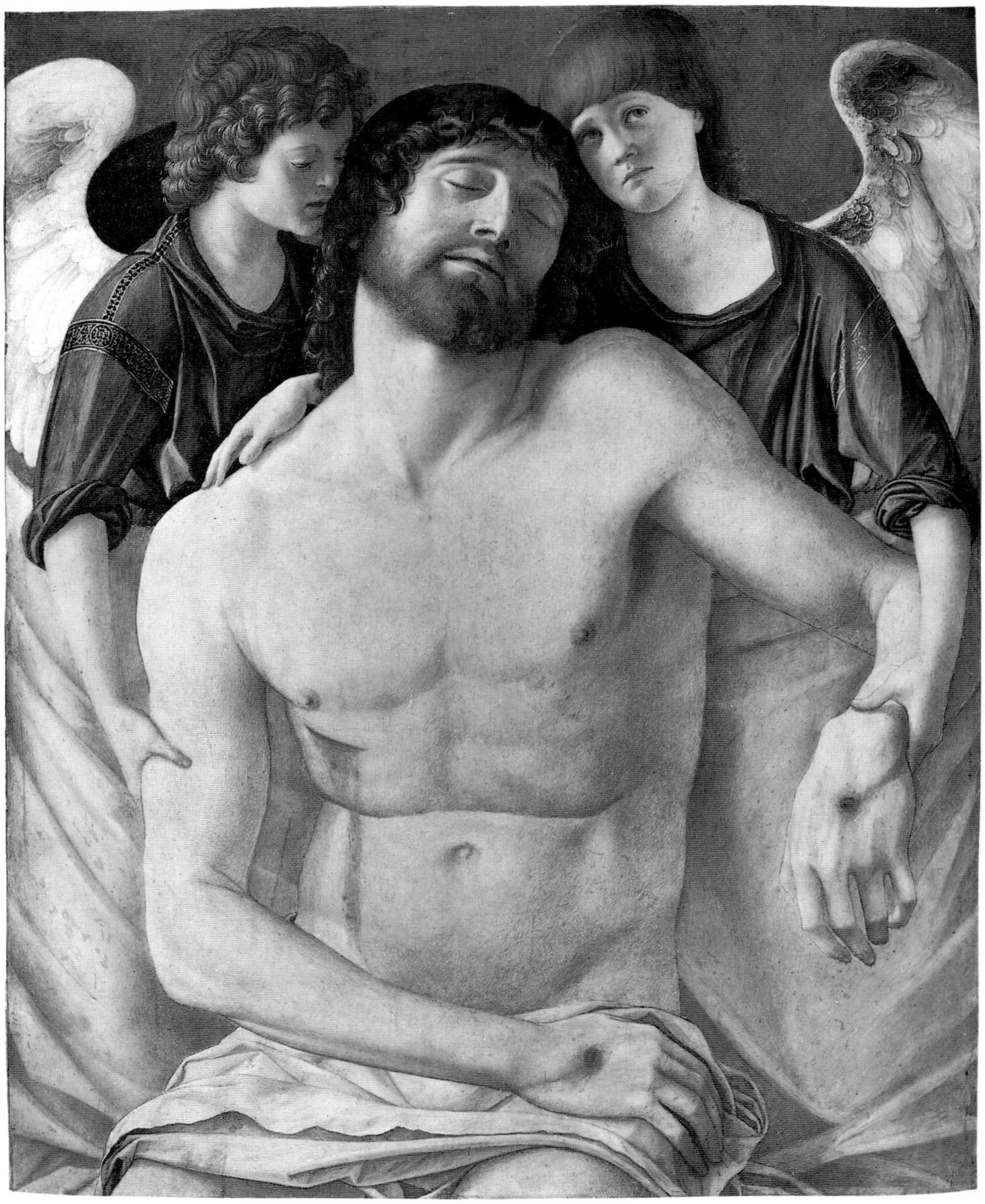

59. Dead Christ with Two Angels, *Gemäldegalerie, Staatliche Museen Preussischer Kulturbesitz, Berlin (West). Photo: Jörg P. Anders.*

old theme and his farewell to it (fig. 61).[71] Christ is seen against a background of rocks and sky, the best preserved parts of this ruined work. The luminous, almost photographic reality of the glowing figure, landscape, and intense blue sky may be appreciated by reference to Bellini's contemporary portrait of Doge Loredan, which is in excellent condition (fig. 149). With the *Loredan* as our warrant, we may restore the *Christ Crowned with Thorns* in the mind's eye, imagining Bellini's purposeful variation in the handling of paint, applied more freely in the flesh than in the setting. The comparatively imprecise definition of the figure—an effect exaggerated by damage—requires that the viewer complete the image, so to speak, and this physical involvement in the act of seeing and defining becomes a spiritual involvement as well.[72]

Christ's zigzag posture poignantly suggests the breaking of his body on the cross. Plants grow in the rocks behind him, possibly in allusion to the Resurrec-

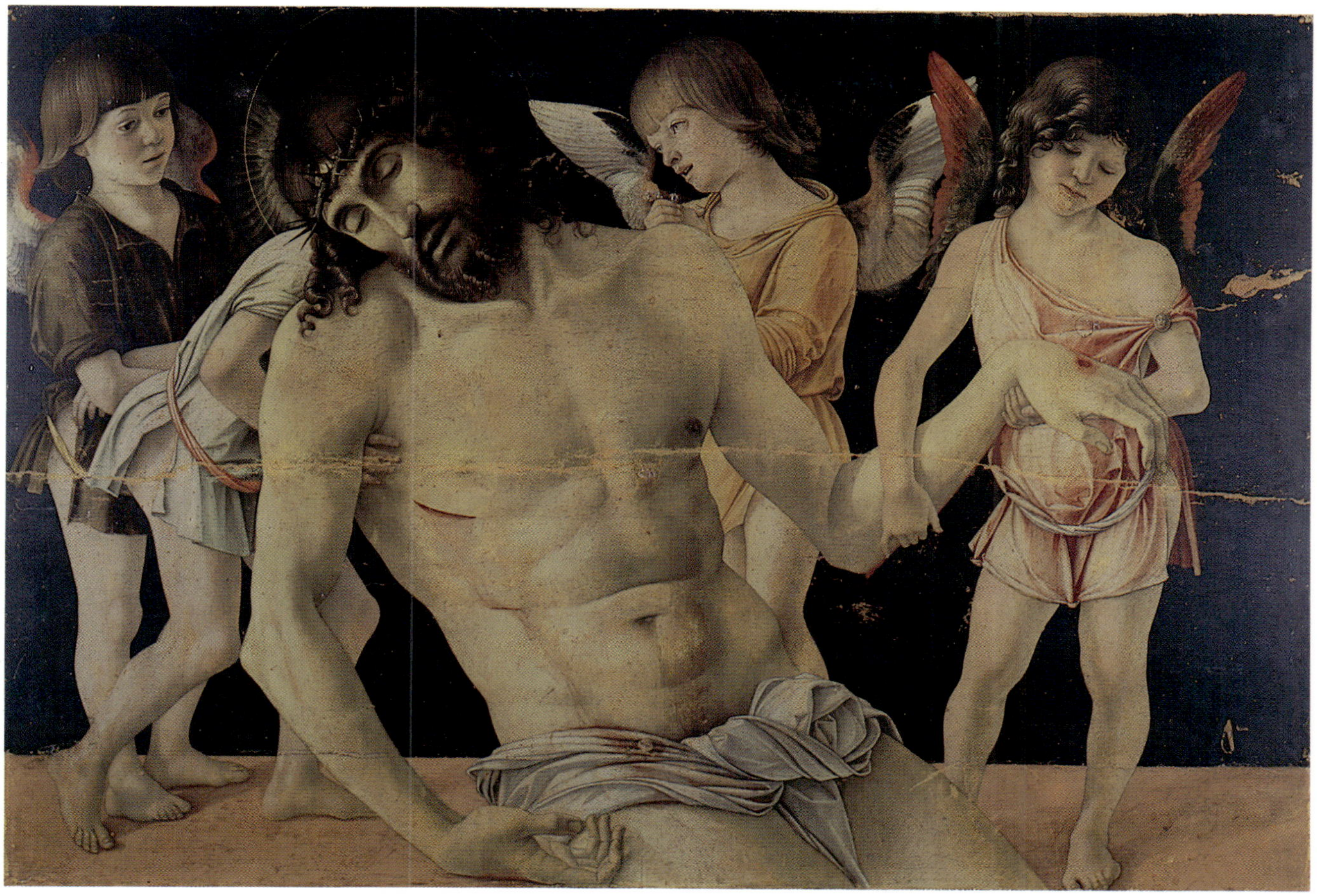

60. Dead Christ with Four Angels *(Rimini* Pietà), *Musei Communali, Rimini. Photo: Museo di Rimini.*

tion. But this veiled symbolic reference to the Lord's ultimate victory and our salvation is the only sign of hope that Bellini presents here. Christ's isolation is complete, his only mourner the beholder: no angels, no Virgin, no beloved apostle shows the way. The spiritual and emotional burden of response to the terrible sacrifice now falls solely on the worshiper.[73] There is no physical action, not even weeping, and yet this stillness heightens the emotion. Each of us alone must confront and mourn the Lord, even as Christ himself is alone in his pain and sacrifice. And because Christ's entire figure is presented, references to the Eucharist and to salvation are not implied, as in the earlier compositions of Christ seen half-length behind the parapet. We understand this late image not in terms of symbolism or even theology but only in human terms.

In contrast to the visual and psychological treatment of this panel, in which we are shocked by the sight of the entire figure of the Man of Sorrows, another of Bellini's late christological compositions, the *Portacroce*, startles us by the intimacy of "dramatic close-up," in Ringbom's words.[74] Several versions of this composition are associated with Bellini, but none is entirely autograph, even though such motifs as the folds of Christ's drapery are very close to the master's handling (fig. 62).[75] But the design and conception are Bellini's.

Christ's head casts a shadow on his cross, and both figure and cross are cut dramatically by the edges of the picture, enhancing the powerful impression of the Lord's proximity, an effect Christ himself confirms by turning his tearful gaze toward us. In the variants, this appeal to the beholder may seem overt and even manipulative. But we may imagine the power of the lost original by reference to other works by Bellini in which we are confronted by the suffering of the Lord and his mourners. Here, however, as in the *Christ Crowned with Thorns*, we are confronted by Jesus alone, and it is the Lord himself who compels us to share his pain and sorrow.

This dramatic close-up is abstracted from the narration of the *Via Crucis*, the Way to Calvary, and Bellini's separation of the protagonist from his narrative circumstances is complete. The composition is given over entirely to the figure: no setting, no subsidiary characters are included. The artistic precedent for such exclusivity is found in images of the Holy Face, alluding to the *Sudarium*, or the Veronica—that is, the True Icon, the "vera icon," the likeness of Christ's visage miraculously impressed on the cloth with which his follower wiped his face as Jesus was led to crucifixion. Here, the beholder is brought as close to the Savior as "Veronica," made a witness to his suffering, invited to share that suffering, and, if possible, to offer solace.

The turn of Christ's head in the Bellinesque compositions, the direction of his glance, and the way in which his figure is placed in the picture field all resemble another early sixteenth-century Venetian painting of *Christ Carrying the Cross*, the miraculous image admired by Vasari in the Scuola Grande di San Rocco and still venerated there today (fig. 63).[76] This scene, however, has been expanded to include two other men, one of whom holds a rope around Christ's neck, making recollection of the Via Crucis more narrative and dramatic. Thus we are forcibly reminded of the Lord's enemies, not his compassionate follower, and of the physical aspects of his suffering as much as the psychological, given primacy in Bellini's conception.

Although the connection between the San Rocco painting and Bellini's composition is undeniable, it remains problematic for two reasons: the attribution of the picture in San Rocco is debated, Vasari himself being uncertain whether to ascribe it to Giorgione or to Titian,[77] and the dates of this work and of Bellini's *Portacroce* are also uncertain, making the direction of indebtedness unclear. In my view, however, the invention was typical of Bellini, and was first put forward in a lost or unknown prototype for the panels in Boston, Rovigo, and elsewhere, was replicated in his studio and outside it, and was finally adapted by Titian (or Giorgione?), who enlarged the original composition, altered its psychological import, and translated it into the more painterly language of the sixteenth century. And if this variation enjoyed more success than its prototype—for none of the Bellinesque paintings has yet been credited with miracles—it should also be acknowledged that Bellini most likely originated the idea.

Bellini's private devotional images of the Madonna and Child and the Man

*61*. Dead Christ (Christ Crowned with Thorns), *Statens Konstmuseer, Stockholm. Photo: Philip A. Charles, Washington.*

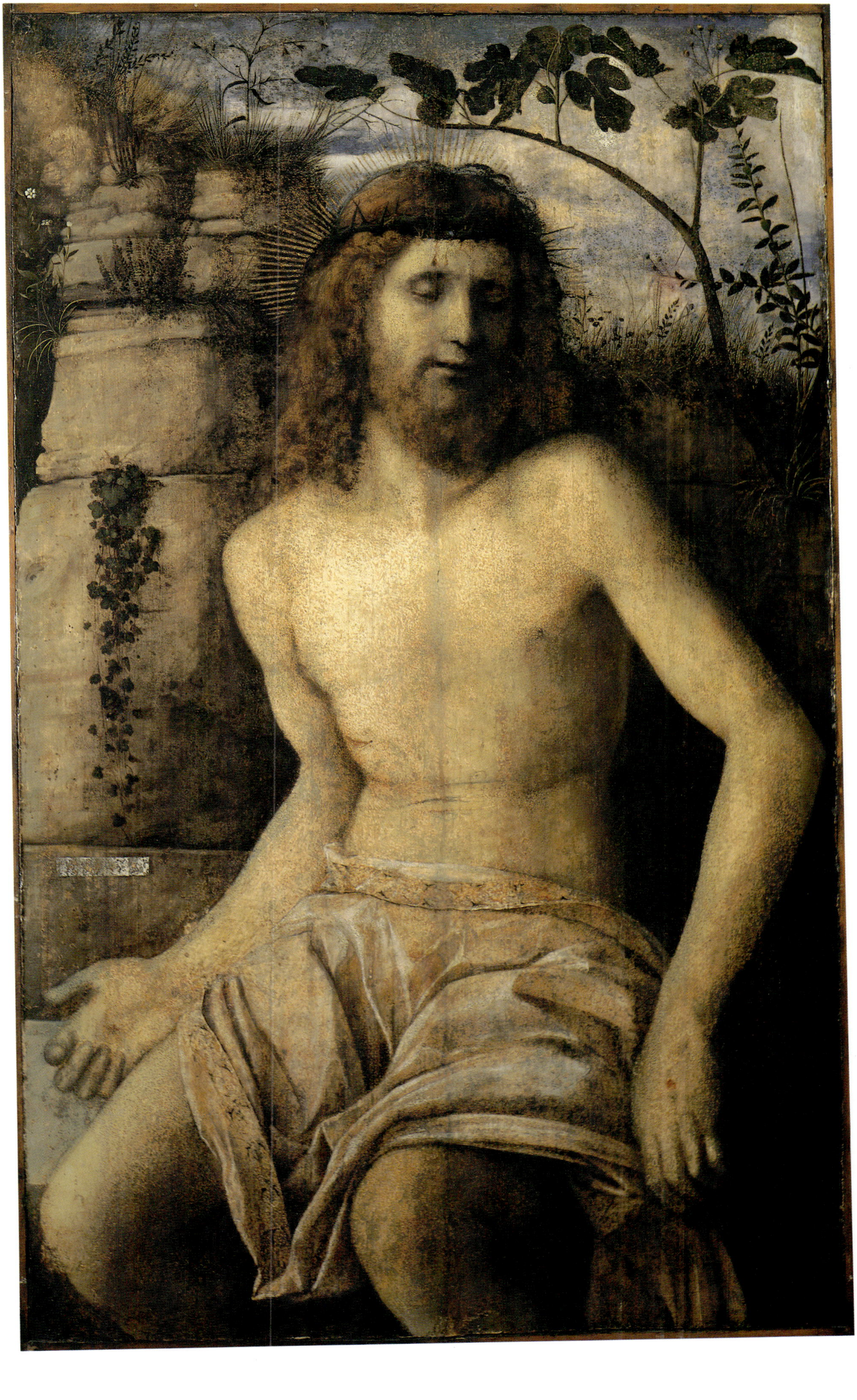

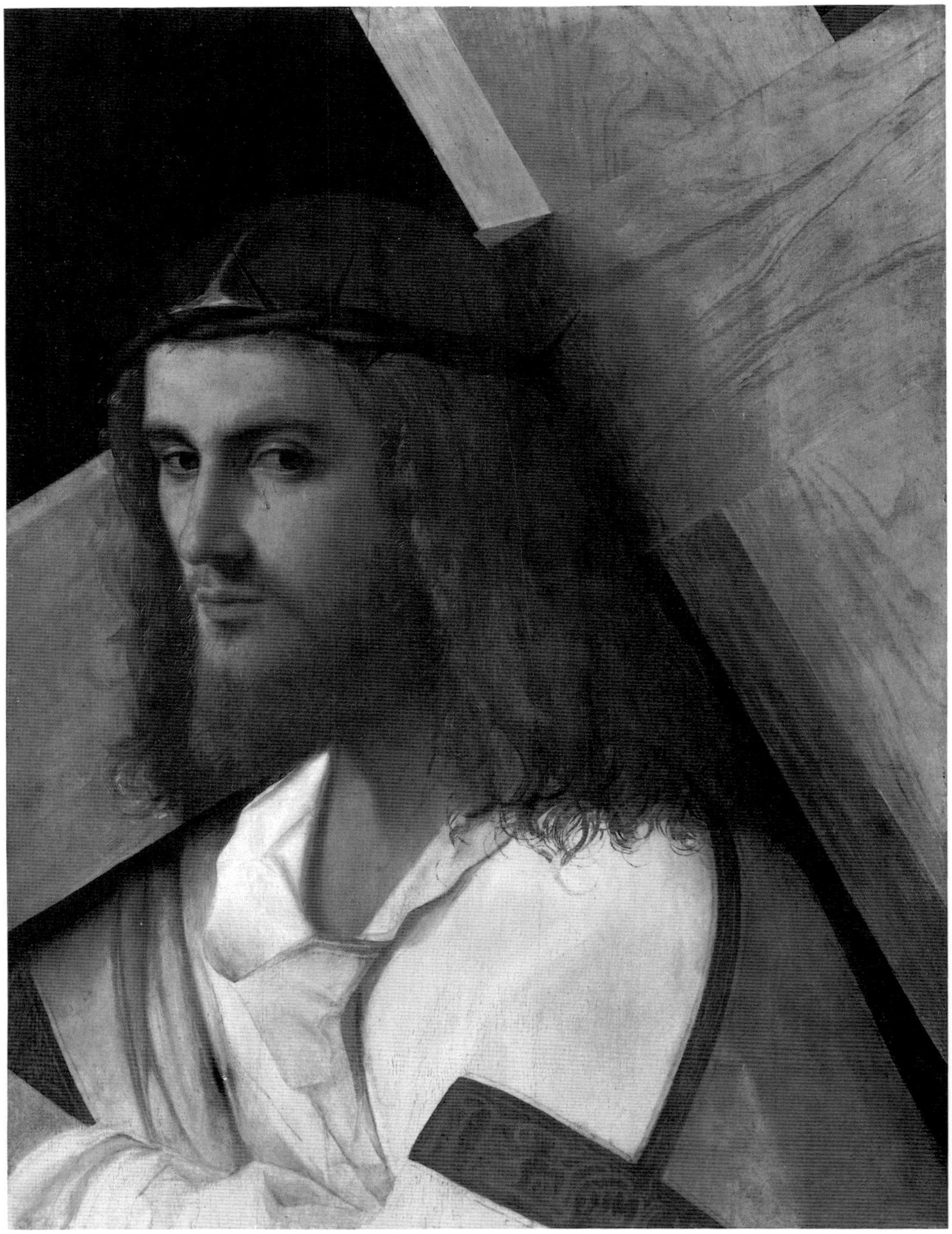

62. *Giovanni Bellini with assistance,* Portacroce, *Isabella Stewart Gardner Museum, Boston.*

of Sorrows represent two related aspects of Venetian spirituality: the affective alpha and omega of the Lord's earthly existence interpreted in essentially non-narrative form, in each case illustrating Jesus at his most vulnerable, and in each case depicting him as the embodiment of the eucharistic sacrifice offered for the salvation of humankind. In part, these interwoven emphases reflect the widespread influence of Franciscan spirituality in Venice, as indeed throughout Italy, and an emphasis on the Incarnation, the humanity of Christ.[78] But there is also a distinctive Venetian component, combining religiosity with political and social interests in a characteristic Venetian amalgamation.

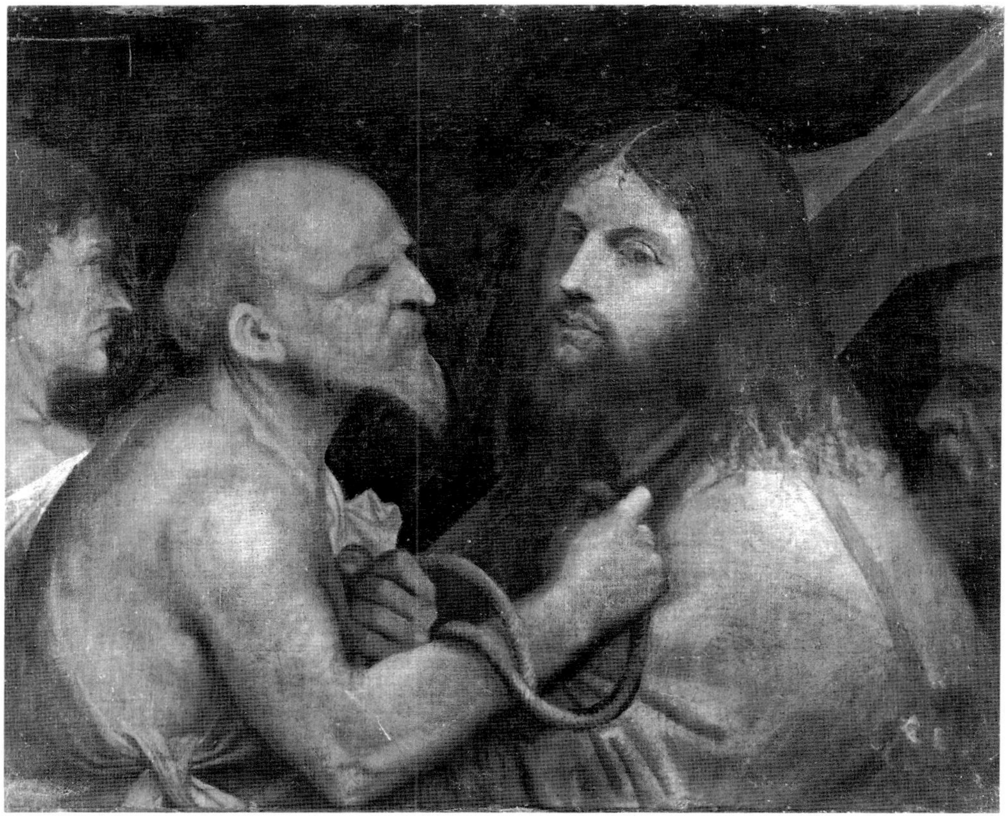

63. *Titian or Giorgione,* Portacroce, *Scuola Grande di San Rocco, Venice. Photo: Osvaldo Böhm, Venice.*

## Piety, Politics, and Patronage

How were Bellini's images for private devotion perceived by their first viewers? No contracts or sales agreements which might have provided some answer, have been found, and nothing like Lorenzo Lotto's *Libro di spese* documents Bellini's activity. Knowledge of the patronage and purpose of his devotional images must be gleaned from circumstantial evidence, primarily testaments.

Another problem hinders attempts to reconstruct the historical setting of Bellini's devotional images. None of his Madonnas remains where it was originally displayed—assuming that any of them was painted for a specific location—and almost none has a complete record of provenance that may reveal something of their purpose and the way in which they were understood. One partial exception to this discouraging list of historical exclusions is the *Virgin and Child* in the church of the Madonna dell'Orto in Venice (fig. 64).

Nothing is casual in this composition; rather, the actions of Mother and Child seem momentous. When the Child places one hand on his breast (recalling the Frizzoni *Madonna*), opens his mouth, and tilts his head back as though to sing, we imagine no childish song but an orison issuing from his lips.[79] The way Mary's mantle conceals his left foot is ominous, suggesting enclosure and enshroudment.

The painting was evidently bequeathed to the Madonna dell'Orto in the 1480s and has been there ever since, though not, unfortunately, preserved in its original Renaissance setting. This was the altar endowed by Luca Navagero at the site of his tomb, located in the pavement of the right aisle before the organ of the church. Both altar and tomb were destroyed when the church was restored in the mid-nineteenth century.[80] The dedicatory inscription, however, was recorded; it commemorated Navagero's endowment of the monument in 1485, three years before his death, for himself and for "sweetest posterity": D.M. / LUCAS NAVAIERIUS PATRICIUS / VENETUS / SIBI MONUMENTU[M] / ISTUO POSTERISQ[UE] DULCIS/SIMIS HABENDUM DICAVIT / .V[IVENS].P[OSUIT]. / MCCCCLXXXV.[81]

Navagero died in Udine in 1488, but his body was returned to Venice for burial in the tomb that he had already had constructed in the Madonna dell'Orto.[82] He must also have made provision in his testament to endow the altar itself, granting funds for its maintenance, for incense and candles, and, most important, for the performance of Mass on the anniversary of his death and possibly on certain feast days: these were standard testamentary provisions for the establishment of a funerary chapel in Renaissance Venice, as elsewhere in Italy.[83] To put the matter another way: a Renaissance church did not accept the gift—or responsibility—of an altar and tomb without appropriate financing; the arrangement was quid pro quo.

The Madonna painting that became the altarpiece of Navagero's funerary chapel was presumably one that he himself had commissioned (or perhaps merely purchased) as an image of private devotion, painted, judging stylistically, in the 1470s —and perhaps with no thought, at that early date, of using it to adorn a gravesite. A near replica of this composition, the *Madonna and Child* in the Kimbell Museum (fig. 31), and a closely related panel in Berlin may mean either that Navagero did not necessarily commission the painting but purchased it from Bellini's "studio stock" or that admiration for the composition led to its repetition for another patron—or both.[84] At any rate, like other owners of Bellini's sacred images, Navagero wished to perpetuate his private devotions before the Virgin, here by the permanent endowment of prayers and Masses to be offered in the church of the Madonna dell'Orto for the well-being of his immortal soul.

At least one other owner, Jeronimo Hollivier, made similar arrangements for his *Madonna and Child*, inherited from his brother Marin, whose portrait was included in the composition. As it happens, like Navagero, Hollivier gave his picture to the church of the Madonna dell'Orto. The Hollivier painting probably resembled the panel in the Harewood Collection, with which it is often, but inconclusively, identified (fig. 38).[85] Hollivier may have been referring to the panel now in the Friedsam Library of Saint Bonaventure University, New York (fig. 39), or to another work now lost.[86] But more important than the identification of Hollivier's panel is his own explanation of its significance.

64. Madonna and Child, *Madonna dell'Orto, Venice. Photo: Giacomelli Fotografia, Venice.*

In his holograph will of 1524, with a codicil dated four years later, 16 May 1528, Jeronimo Hollivier requested that the painting be framed for an altar in the

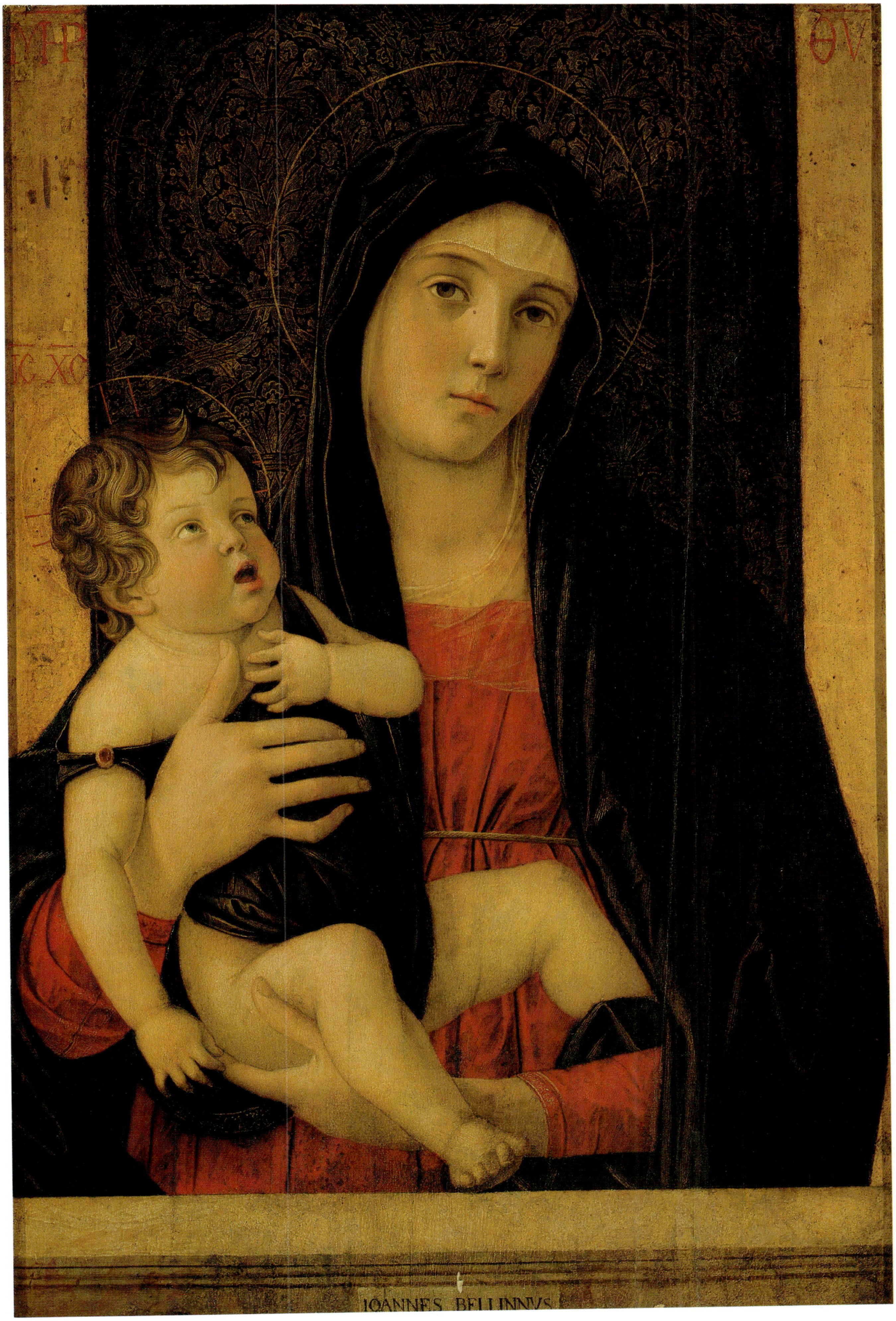
MP
ΘV
IC XC
IOANNES BELLINNVS

church or sacristy. But Jeronimo either did not wish or could not afford to endow the altar itself as his tombsite, and he merely asked to be buried in one of the sepulchers of the church, with typical deference to the wishes of the clergy:

> Item. I want and order burial in one of the tombs [*arche*] of the fathers of the Madonna dell'Orto. . . . I want and order that the painting of Our Lady made by the hand of Giovanni Bellini, which has the portrait of the blessed memory of the deceased Marin who was my brother, . . . be framed in a carved and gilded frame and made as beautiful and sumptuous as possible, and that it be placed in the church of the Madonna dell'Orto in place of an altarpiece at some one of the altars of the said church . . . or alternately [an altar] of the sacristy, according to the judgment of the fathers.[87]

For Hollivier, Bellini's *Madonna* was both sacred and precious, to be displayed on an altar in its richly carved and gilded frame. In his testament, Hollivier took care of his body by providing for his burial in a tomb of the Madonna dell'Orto, a practicality that is unavoidably a concern in almost any testament, even those made today.

Unlike many modern testators, however, Hollivier was also concerned for his soul and for the soul of his brother, who had predeceased him. Although the bequest of their *Madonna* to the church does not state this concern explicitly, it is inherent in the testamentary provisions, and Renaissance people would have understood this. Installed "in place of an altarpiece at some one of the altars" of the Madonna dell'Orto, the Hollivier painting—which included Marin's portrait—perforce became the focus of prayers and holy offices performed at the altar. For Hollivier, as for Navagero, a private devotional image could become an altarpiece in a church merely by a change of setting.[88] But how were such devotional pictures displayed before they were transformed into church altarpieces at their owners' behest? And what—aside from setting—distinguished a private devotional image in a home from an altarpiece in a church?

The answer to the second question is essentially a matter of size, but the answer to the first may seem surprising. Some of Bellini's paintings were doubtless displayed in studies: Saint Jerome had a *Madonna and Child* in his studio, as recreated by Lucas Cranach, and Carpaccio's *Saint Augustine* has a statue of Christ, showing that Italian studies were also decorated with sacred images.[89] But many more of Bellini's small Madonna paintings were probably hung over their owners' beds, part of the bedroom furnishing, as it were. Saint Ursula had such a half-length image of the Virgin on the wall near her bed, as did her father, King Maurus, at least according to Carpaccio's vision of their quarters, which clearly report the fashion of fifteenth-century Venice and not that of the saint's fourth-century Brittany (fig. 65).[90] In other fifteenth-century households, a painting of the Madonna might be attached to the head of the bed itself.[91] (Even today, sacred images are displayed near or above beds in Catholic homes and hospitals.) Perhaps we are

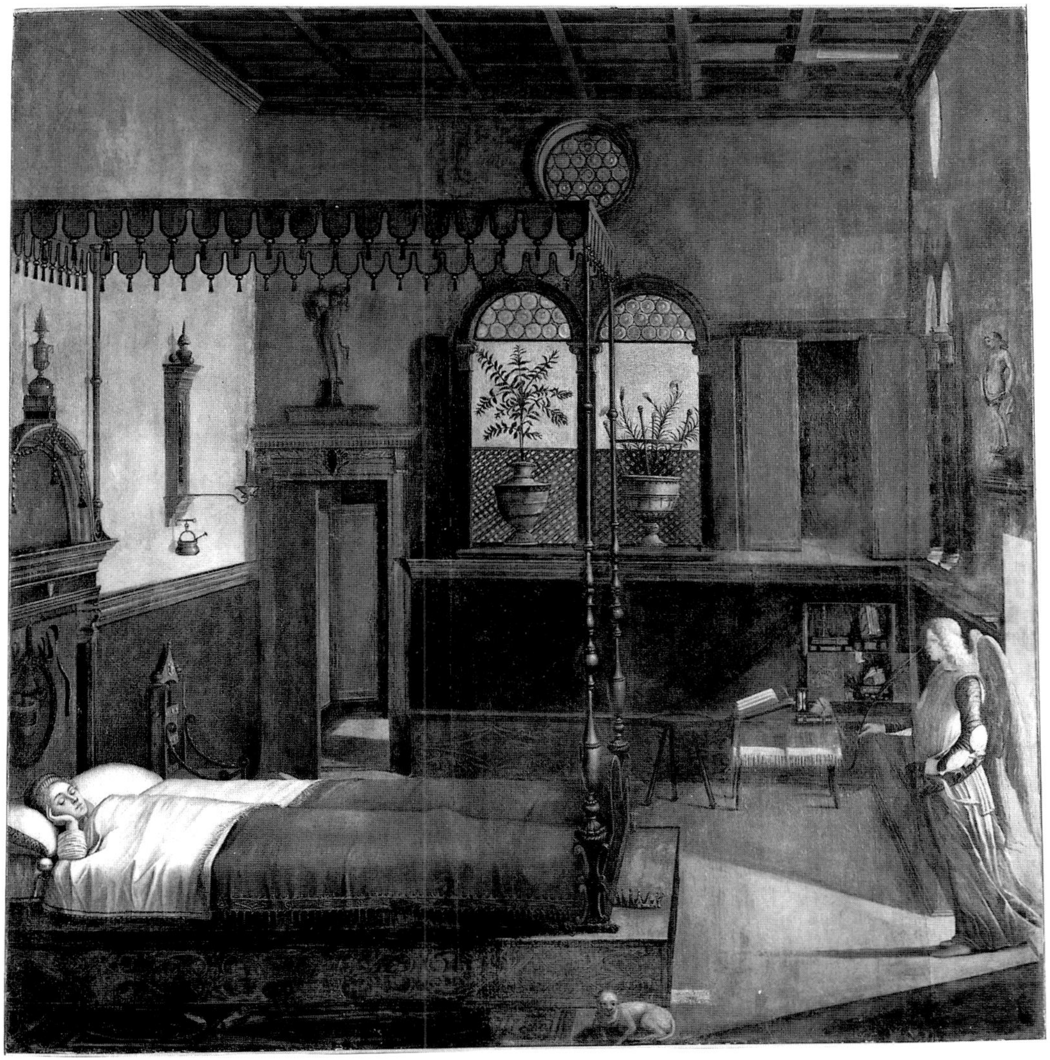

*65. Vittore Carpaccio,* Dream of Saint Ursula *(before restoration), Gallerie dell'Accademia, Venice. Photo: Soprintendenza ai Beni Artistici e Storici, Venice.*

to understand that the king's *Madonna* assists him to understand his daughter's mission—the conversion of her fiancé to Christianity and their papal pilgrimage, accompanied by eleven thousand virgins—and that Ursula's sacred image helps to call forth the holy vision that comes to her in her sleep. Perhaps those who slept beneath similar images by Bellini might also have hoped for God-sent illumination and for Mary's protection and guidance. One may recall the Humanist idea of *vacatio,* freeing the mind and spirit during sleep to facilitate inspiration. But although Bellini's patrons may have emulated (or inspired) Ursula's decorative scheme, unlike that virgin martyr, who slept alone, they were usually married and hopeful of issue.

Children, especially male children, were the sole purpose and justification of sexual intercourse, as theologians and medical doctors explained, and according to popular belief, the biological process of procreation could be assisted by images. In the fifteenth century, *cassoni,* pairs of chests commissioned for married couples and displayed in their bechambers, or *deschi da parto,* trays presented to new mothers, might be decorated discreetly, under the lid or on the bottom, with images of nude male children, meant, as inscriptions explain, to abet husbands and wives in their efforts to become fathers and mothers.[92] Similarly, the Christ Child, the prototypical male infant, whether nude or clothed, but perhaps especially when nude, might inspire the couples who slept beneath his image. The sight of the Holy Infant in images was to provide an example for human children in much the same way, as the Dominican Bl. Giovanni Dominici had explained in his *Regola del governo di cura familiare* (*Rule of government of family care*).[93] Their mothers, meanwhile, might have been given dolls of the Christ Child to cherish: role-playing with these dolls, they could emulate the Madonna's motherhood and her perfect love for Jesus. Nuns, vowed to chastity, were given the same kinds of dolls. Brides and daughters of Christ, they might also be his mothers, much as the Virgin was his mother, daughter, and consort: all female roles were defined in relation to him. And this same threefold identity was ascribed to the Madonna in the inscription below the celestial throne in Guariento's *Coronation of the Virgin* (fig. 66), formerly in the Great Council Hall of the Ducal Palace: "She who was then mother of her son / Here he makes queen of the universe" ("L'amor che mosse già l'eterno padre / Per figlia haver de sua deità trina / Chostei che fu del suo figliuol poi madre / Del'universo qui la fa Regina").[94] If such owners of Bellini's Madonna paintings as Navagero and Hollivier considered the end of life and the life hereafter, others surely contemplated the beginning of life and its guidance here on earth.

Like the Madonna paintings, Bellini's images of the adult Christ might be transformed into altarpieces of funerary chapels. Unfortunately, only one such painting, the Rimini *Pietà*, is endowed with a documented (albeit incomplete) provenance, and even here the patronage if not the use of the image is uncertain: the man who gave it to the church of San Francesco may not have been its first owner (fig. 59). At any rate, the donor was Rainerio di Lodovico Migliorati, a doctor of law and adviser to Pandolfo IV di Roberto, the last Malatesta ruler of Rimini.[95] In his will of 1499, Migliorati requested burial in the church of Sant'Antonio, near San Francesco, and provided funds to construct a funerary chapel. Migliorati wished one of his paintings to be displayed there, "a panel painted by the hand of Giovanni Bellini, in which is depicted the image of Our Lord Jesus Christ the Savior dead and taken from the Cross, in the form of a Pietà."[96]

This transformation of private devotional image to altarpiece seems to have been the exception rather than the rule, especially regarding an image of Christ. Perhaps it is significant, therefore, that it was a *Pietà* owned by a Riminese, not a Venetian, that became the altarpiece of a funerary chapel. Like the overwhelming majority of Bellini's Madonna paintings, his images of Christ remained in private possession until they were acquired by public collections; comparatively few of these pictures were bequeathed to churches, judging from sixteenth-century Venetian guidebooks.[97] Made for the private devotions of individual worshipers, they continued to serve their original function for the heirs of the first owners.

In 1521, for example, Elena Trevisan, daughter of the Venetian grand chancel-

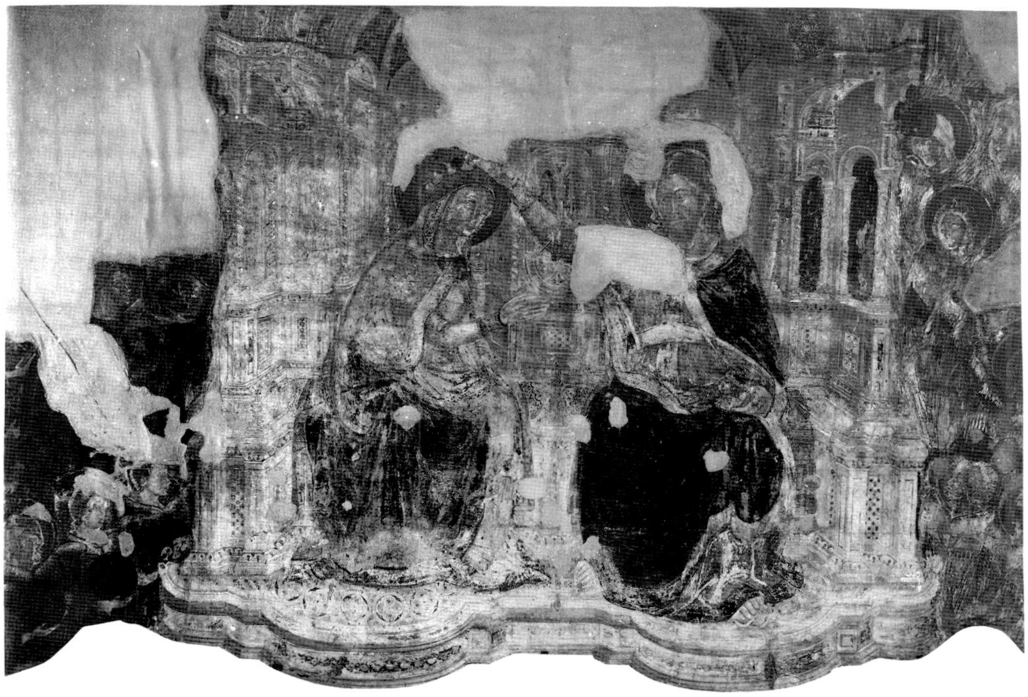

66. *Guariento,* Paradiso (Coronation of the Virgin), *Palazzo Ducale, Venice. Photo: Fototeca Berenson, Villa i Tatti, Florence.*

lor, bequeathed her painting of "Christ made by the hand of Giovanni Bellini," together with a gilded and silver crucifix and a tabernacle, to her son Domenico, "as a sign of love." In exchange, Domenico, a Camaldolese monk, was requested to pray for his mother's soul.[98] Both the request and its context make clear that Elena Trevisan considered her painting by Bellini to be a devotional image, comparable to her crucifix. Thus the *Christ* remained a private image: it did not become an altarpiece or part of a chapel decoration. So powerful is an image, however, that even without an altar it may benefit the donor's soul, as Elena Trevisan understood. At the same time, Elena appreciated the importance of her picture's authorship, which she carefully specified. Her words were used also by Jeronimo Hollivier, Rainerio Migliorati, and others: "by the hand of Giovanni Bellini"; these devotional images were also valued as works of art by an esteemed master. Which, if any, of Bellini's surviving images of Christ may have belonged to the Trevisan cannot be known: like Hollivier's *Madonna*, the *Christ* remains a provenance without a painting.

The increasing passion for collecting eventually transformed Bellini's sacred images, for some owners at least, into examples of the master's hand, perhaps cherished more for artistic value than for religiosity. Isabella d'Este, marchesa of Mantua, ordered a *Nativity* from Bellini for this reason alone—and displayed it in a bedroom.[99] Similarly, the Venetian nobleman Taddeo di Gentile Contarini, in his will of February 1578, bequeathed to his kinsman Gerolamo "a beautiful *Our Lady* by the hand of Giovanni Bellini, and another painting of *Holofernes* . . . , to be enjoyed by their brothers": Bellini's *Madonna*, perhaps a panel now in the

Accademia (fig. 32), had evidently become an object more of delight than of prayer.[100] Likewise, the Venetian Republic itself was surely concerned less with piety than with the prestige and beauty of Bellini's "Dead Christ with figures," which was purchased from Cipriano Malipiero in 1510 to be presented to Louis XII of France.[101] Five years later, the republic turned to Bellini again for such a gift, this time a *Madonna* intended for the sister of King Louis's successor, François I (1515–47).

The *Madonna*, which has been lost, was commissioned by the Heads of the Council of Ten on 31 October 1515: "We have decided . . . to give to the most illustrious Lady of Alençon a picture in painting of the image of the Glorious Virgin, this to be the most excellent and perfect as possible." To be sure, there were already "some beautiful but old" Madonna paintings in the city, but desirous of satisfying the king's sister, the Ten decided "to have a new one made, in all beauty and perfection," after learning the royal recipient's "wish and pleasure regarding the size and quality of the said painting, to be of the Glorious Virgin with her Son, which figures she [the Lady of Alençon] would like to be on either side, and of what size, and in sum, every other necessary particular."[102]

The *Madonna* must have been a splendid work, but nothing is known of it except that it was near completion when Giovanni Badoer, the Venetian orator in France, received a reassuring letter from a compatriot dated 15 January 1516. "It will be a beautiful thing," Badoer was to inform the king, "the master is Giovanni Bellini, and very little is lacking to complete it perfectly."[103] Bellini was dead within the year; thus his career ended as it had begun, with an image for private devotion.

Whatever opinion the royal recipient of this last, lost Madonna painting may have had of Bellini's work—whether it was regarded as a "collector's item" or devotional image—the intimacy of his images suits them for private devotions. Generally smaller than life-size, with the sacred beings in the immediate foreground, the compositions require scrutiny and invite solitary contemplation; they are addressed not to an audience in a public, secular setting but to worshipers in the quietude of prayer.

Two exceptions may prove the rule, the *Madonna Enthroned* and the *Pietà with Saints Mark and Nicholas*. The *Pietà* was made for a civic setting in the Palazzo Ducale, the chapel of Saint Nicholas, and this explains both Bellini's treatment of his theme and his use of canvas, the typical support for mural painting in Venice (fig. 50).[104] The low vantage point indicates that the picture was placed high on the wall. The intensity of the imagery is mitigated by official sensibilities when the faithful pay public homage to Mary and Christ in a governmental context. By extending the composition and its cast of characters, Bellini invites us to approach this scene not only directly but through the intermediating presence of Mark and Nicholas. Controlled, formalized veneration is exemplified, not the "groans" and weeping visualized and indeed described in the Brera *Pietà* (fig. 49) and similar compositions.[105] Saints Mark and Nicholas embody the official nature of the Ducal Palace canvas: the patron of the Serenissima and the patron of the chapel where the painting was displayed are understood as official representatives of the state, and not merely anachronistic worshipers of the Crucified. The redemptive sacrifice of Christ, Bellini implies, is offered to the Venetian Republic, and the republic, represented by two of its most venerated patrons, prayerfully acknowledges the sacrifice.

The mural decoration of the chapel of Saint Nicholas with the "Peace of Venice" made this more explicit.[106] The saga recounts how the Venetians restored peace between Emperor Frederick Barbarossa and Pope Alexander III and how the grateful pontiff assured the Serenissima's dominion over the seas. Every year on the feast of the Ascension, the *Sensa* in dialect, the Venetians recalled the pope's symbolic gift of a ring with which the doge "married the sea." And every year on 6 December, the feast of Saint Nicholas, the doge and Signoria attended Mass in the Cappella di San Nicolò. While they worshiped, their eyes beheld this cycle of Venetian glory—and Bellini's tragic painting of Christ's suffering.[107] The Lord's ultimate triumph over death is the more magnificent because of the reality of that death, and the continuous triumph of the republic, conflated in the Venetian mind with Christ's Resurrection, is likewise guaranteed by his conquest of mortality. In Bellini's painting, Venetian hegemony is implicit in the presence of Saints Mark and Nicholas, the apostolic protector of the regime and the great patron of those who depend on the sea, both protagonists of the celebration of the Sensa—that is, the Resurrection of Christ and the ritual confirmation of Venetian rule.

If, as Zanetti indicated, the painting was dated 1472, Bellini's patron may have been the reigning doge, Nicolò Tron, who had assumed office the previous year. The presence of his onomastic saint and the placement of the picture in the chapel of Saint Nicholas would confirm this hypothesis. Indeed, one of the responsibilities of the doge and other elected officials was to provide images for the Palazzo Ducale; and the sixteenth-century adaptation of this work, which included the addition of three patrician donors and their arms, indicates that they understood the composition in this way (fig. 51).[108] This is very different from the intensely personal situations described by Elena Trevisan and Rainerio Migliorati when they made provisions for their paintings of Christ by Bellini. The apparent discrepancy between the style of the Ducal Palace *Pietà* and the date evidently once inscribed on it, 1472, may thus be explained by the civic setting of the picture.

Gentile Bellini was undeniably more attractive to the regime than Giovanni, judging from the fact that Gentile enjoyed a near monopoly on Ducal Palace commissions, at least until the end of the 1470s, when he was sent to Constantinople and his brother was hired to replace him in decorating the Great Council Hall.[109] Of course, there was no practical reason why Giovanni could not have been assigned earlier to the ongoing work there, which continued to engage numerous artists. Moreover, although the brothers largely worked independently, they had collaborated when they were younger and planned to work together for the Scuola Grande di San Marco in their middle age. Indeed, at the end of his life, Gentile entrusted Giovanni with completing the San Marco cycle, and Giovanni's first surviving scuola paintings are those undertaken at his brother's request, the *Saint Mark Preaching in Alexandria*, which Gentile had begun, and the *Martyrdom of the Saint*, which Giovanni did not live to complete.[110] Giovanni's lack of regular employment in the Ducal Palace until after Gentile's departure implies that the regime employed him *faut de mieux*, as it were. His multivalent artistic personality has been noted: that he should have emulated the official style of his brother in his first official painting seems logical. Perhaps his patrons requested this, though it is equally plausible that Bellini chose to modify his style to suit the commission. Even Bellini's adaptation here of an earlier work, the Brera *Pietà*, may be understood in part as his intentionally conservative approach.

What then of the *Madonna Enthroned* (fig. 24), a work stylistically dated circa 1470—that is, contemporary with the Ducal Palace *Pietà*? It seems incongruous that these works should be contemporaneous, but that apparent inconsistency is typical of Bellini. If the *Madonna* were originally intended for the Ducal Palace, where it was displayed before being removed to the Accademia, perhaps elements in this painting show Bellini's adaptation of his art to the circumstances of the commission.[111]

By enthroning the Virgin, pushing her white veil back from her brow, and painting her symbolic smile, Bellini endowed her person with more worldliness than was customary in his quattrocento works, and with more hopefulness as well. The Virgin smiles as she prays over her sleeping Son, and it first appears that her prayer is inconsistent with her expression. Moreover, this smiling Virgin wears purple, for mourning, another apparent contradiction—not the traditional blue but the color of vestments worn before Easter.[112] Bellini used purple for the Madonna in only one other painting, his late *Pietà* in the Accademia (fig. 25). There Mary's sorrow is unrelieved, but in the *Madonna Enthroned*, she smiles in anticipation of the wakening of the Child and the Resurrection of the Adult. The suffering of Jesus is anticipated not as his Mother's great sorrow but as the prelude to his glorious Resurrection and the means of human redemption.[113] Perhaps the mood of this painting is related to its presumed function as a public reminder of salvation and to the political connotations of the Sensa, in which the triumph of Christ signifies Venetian dominion.

In addition to the *Dead Christ* and the *Madonna Enthroned*, at least one other devotional painting by Bellini was displayed in the Palazzo Ducale, the *Madonna greca*, formerly in the office of the Regolatori alla Scrittura (fig. 27).[114] The painting's Byzantinizing qualities may have made it seem particularly appropriate for such a purpose in a state where the Byzantine East was esteemed as nowhere else in the West and where pictorial imagery might belie political reality: a Byzantine Madonna and Child endorse the regime in spite of Venetian losses in the East. It is not known whether the *Madonna* was originally purchased or commissioned for this quasi-official purpose or as a private devotional image, only later converted to public use, as other images were transformed into altarpieces. Long after it was painted, for example, the contemporary *Madonna and Blessing Child* (fig. 29) was given to the Magistrato del Monte Novissimo in the Palazzo dei Camerlenghi, the office of the state treasurers at Rialto, established in the early sixteenth century.[115] The Child's benediction may have made the painting particularly apt for the Monte: the Lord appears to bless the financial dealings of the republic. The beneficiary is the regime, or its representatives.

Although this expression of divine sanction was evidently not Bellini's intent in the *Madonna and Blessing Child*, neither is it inconsistent with his sacred imagery or with Venetian thinking. Indeed, the implication of sacred presence in state affairs is the subject of another kind of Venetian devotional image, in which the noble servants of the regime receive divine approbation not only as individuals but ex officio, and distinctions between the state and its officials are purposefully blurred. This is the import of a painting admired by Ridolfi in the Procuratia di Ultra, the *Madonna and Child with Saints Peter and Mark Presenting Procuratori Tommaso Mocenigo, Luca Zen, and Domenico Trevisan* (fig. 67). Signed and dated by Bellini in 1510, the work was painted with studio assistance in spite of the patrons' eminence.[116] Bellini adjusted the composition to accommodate the three donors—it is horizontal, like his private devotional images that include saints and/or donors—and he used canvas, because this was a mural painting, displayed above the innermost door of the Procuratia, at least in 1646, when Ridolfi described it. These factors clearly distinguish the votive picture from the altarpieces it resembles; no Venetian would have misunderstood its purpose or intended destination.

No such distinction was made for Doge Agostino Barbarigo's votive picture, however (figs. 68, 69).[117] Essentially identical compositions were commissioned by the doge's predecessors and followers as obligatory gifts to the palace—but not the picture by Giovanni Bellini, which Barbarigo commissioned for himself.[118] Admittedly, this painting, made for the Barbarigo family palace, may have been a replica or variant of a picture that the doge would have given to the Ducal Palace, where he was required to live during his tenure; and like other votive pictures that it resembles, this may be understood in part as a monumentalization of the illuminations illustrating the manuscript *Promissione ducale*, the doge's written oath of office. In other words, Barbarigo's votive picture is both an official, political image and an image of private devotion, a peculiar yet characteristic Venetian hybrid of piety and politics.

Sunlight and atmosphere fill the composition, softening forms, glistening on

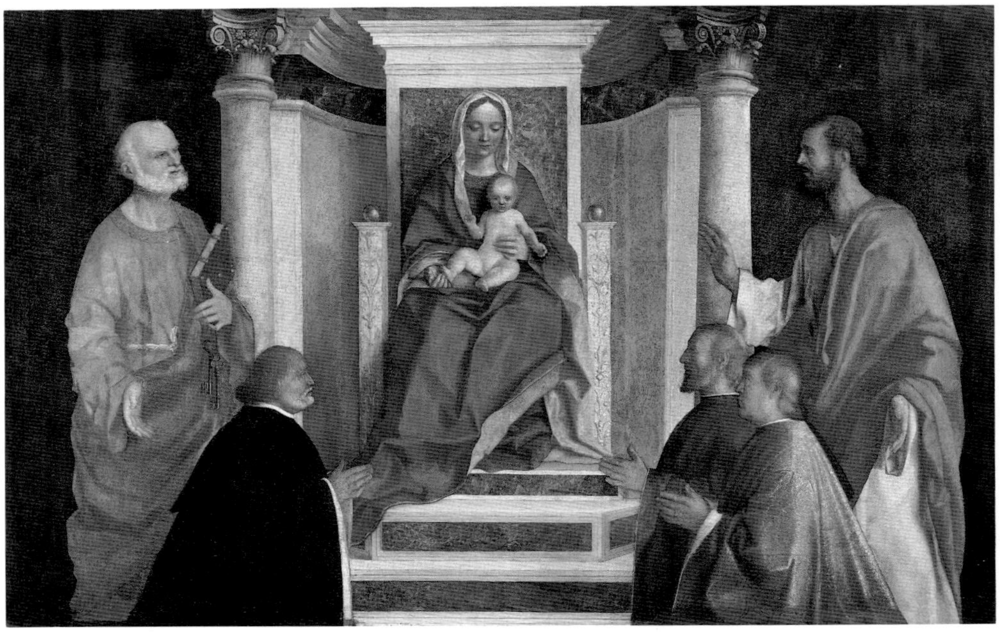

67. *Giovanni Bellini with assistance.* Madonna and Child with Saints Peter and Mark Presenting Procurators Tommaso Mocenigo, Luca Zen, and Domenico Trevisan, *Walters Art Gallery, Baltimore. Photo: Walters Art Gallery, Baltimore.*

surfaces, everywhere confirming the out-of-doors setting. Christ, standing on his mother's knee, turns to his right, toward the direction of light. The symbolic conflation of pictorial illumination and Christ's action is for the benefit of Doge Agostino Barbarigo, who kneels in prayer at the base of the throne to receive the Child's blessing. This is no formulaic gesture but a benediction given personal and gracious import by the inclination of Christ's head toward the doge. Barbarigo is also the beneficiary of Saint Mark's solicitude: the patron saint of Venice acts as Barbarigo's patron, presenting him to the Virgin and Child, while the doge's onomastic saint, Augustine, stands to the other side of the throne.

Barbarigo's votive picture glories in his rank: his ducal arms are displayed, Saint Mark concerns himself with the doge's spiritual well-being, and his official garments are emphatically resplendent. The doge even wears a luxuriant ermine cape, the *bavero,* a ducal garment worn only on solemn occasions when he "went in triumph."[119] The aggrandizing prominence with which Bellini endowed Barbarigo derives from these ducal robes—that is, from the official status in which the individual wraps himself, all but obliterating himself in the process of assuming his onerous, and splendid, responsibilities of office. Barbarigo, the only secular figure in the scene, is closest to the viewer's space, yet his mantle overlaps the celestial throne, and Christ and Mark exchange a glance as the saint bends over the doge: such details associate Barbarigo with the sacred beings, placing him in their illusionistic and psychological sphere. Spiritual hierarchy is implied in Bellini's luministic division of the scene, summarized in the pattern of light and shade on the throne canopy. Barbarigo's dogeship warrants his blessing and Mark's solicitude; his individual identity, represented by Augustine, is secondary and literally overshadowed.

Thus Bellini expressed the stated ideal of the Venetian patriciate: the nobleman serves the regime, and his individuality is subsumed in his service. Barbarigo's expression suggests neither awareness nor expectation of divine favor, but only the unassuming prayer for such acknowledgment on behalf of his state—one reason why Mark is the doge's sponsor. The other reason is, or was, more personal, an allusion to Marco Barbarigo, Agostino's brother and immediate predecessor in the dogate. On his deathbed, Marco is said to have disparaged his brother's character. Whether or not this was so, Agostino Barbarigo was disliked and mistrusted by his compatriots as ambitious and corrupt. They were not without reason. Contrary to Venetian custom, Agostino insisted on the conspicuous obeisance of his people: they were required to kneel before him and kiss his hand.[120] But here, in Bellini's painting, Barbarigo kneels before the Virgin and Child, receiving both the posthumous forgiveness and the approbation of his deceased brother and predecessor Doge Marco through Saint Mark. Self-aggrandizement and the glory of the family are transformed into Venetian piety and politics.

The significance of this choice of saintly protector and the way in which the relationship between saint and doge is realized in Bellini's image is further clarified by reference to an almost contemporary picture of the same genre, often attributed to Gentile Bellini (fig. 70).[121] Giovanni Mocenigo, doge from 1478 to 1485, kneels in prayer to the left of the Virgin and Child, both of whom turn toward him. Accompanying them are Saint Christopher, who carries a second Christ Child on his shoulder, and the doge's onomastic saint, John the Baptist.[122] Unlike Bellini's Barbarigo, whose hands are in prayer, Mocenigo firmly grasps the banner of Saint Mark, which he holds before him. Mocenigo's official identity, explicit in his garments, is thus invoked by his attribute but not exalted above his personal identity, which is embodied in the figure of Saint John.

Such compositions addressed their self-serving and perhaps self-deceiving propagandistic messages to the doge's personal circle of relatives, friends, and associates—that is, to a receptive audience. Neither an altarpiece nor a public commission, Giovanni Bellini's painting was made for Barbarigo's family palace, and the doge mentioned the painting in his will, specifying its location in the crossing (*crozola*), or intersection of the hallway on the piano nobile.[123] Bellini's picture was a mural, its function decorative and votive, not liturgical.

Barbarigo's bequest of the painting to two of his daughters, nuns at the church of Santa Maria degli Angeli in Murano, assured that these original functions of Bellini's creation would change. The doge requested that his daughters and the other nuns pray before it for his soul:

> Item. We order that our great *pala* that is in the crossing of our palace be sent to the aforesaid monastery of nuns of Santa Maria degli Angeli, this image of Our Lady with angels being well suited to be placed above the high altar of their church, but [with the provision] that our commissaries must have the painting adorned below, at the sides and above in such way as would be

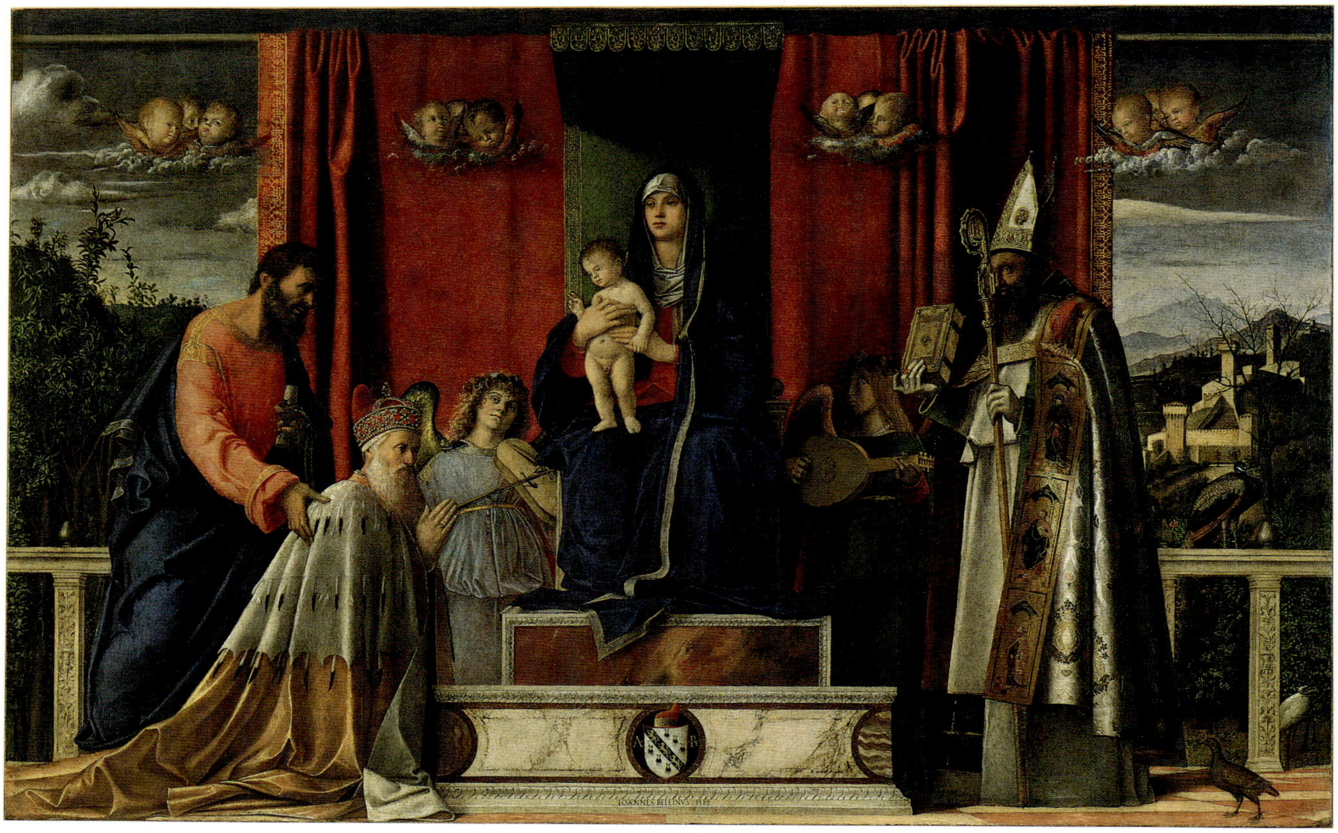

68. *Votive picture of Doge Agostino Barbarigo, San Pietro Martire, Murano. Photo: Soprintendenza ai Beni Artistici e Storici, Venice.*

69. *Votive picture of Doge Agostino Barbarigo, detail, Doge Agostino Barbarigo. Photo: Soprintendenza ai Beni Artistici e Storici, Venice.*

to our satisfaction and to that of these venerable women. And the sooner the said altarpiece is put into use [*in opera*], the sooner we shall hope in the Blessed Virgin Mary as being our advocate before God, our Creator most high. And [we order] that neither our sons-in-law nor our daughters nor our nephews be permitted to place the picture either in our palace or in any other place except above the high altar of this most devout and religious monastery, which, we are certain, will always pray to God for our soul and for the souls of all our [kinsmen] who have passed from this life.[124]

This commemorative and devotional transformation of a work conceived during the doge's lifetime and for a secular situation was entirely appropriate, given the genesis of these kinds of compositions. The tomb of Giovanni degli Angeli (d. 1481) was adorned with such an image by Lazzaro Bastiani (fig. 71). Likewise, Paolo da Venezia painted a similar lunette for the funerary monument of one of Barbarigo's predecessors, Francesco Dandolo (d. 1339) (fig. 72).[125] The deceased doge and his consort are presented to the court of heaven by their onomastic saints, Francis and Elizabeth of Hungary, a traditional and suitable motif in this funerary context. Departures from this kind of personal imagery are rare in funerary art, and the exceptions are significant. In Arnolfo di Cambio's monument of Cardinal Guillaume de Braye (d. 1282), for example, the prelate is presented by Mark, not his onomastic saint but the titular saint of his church (fig. 17). To the other side of Mary's throne is Saint Dominic, in honor of the tomb's location

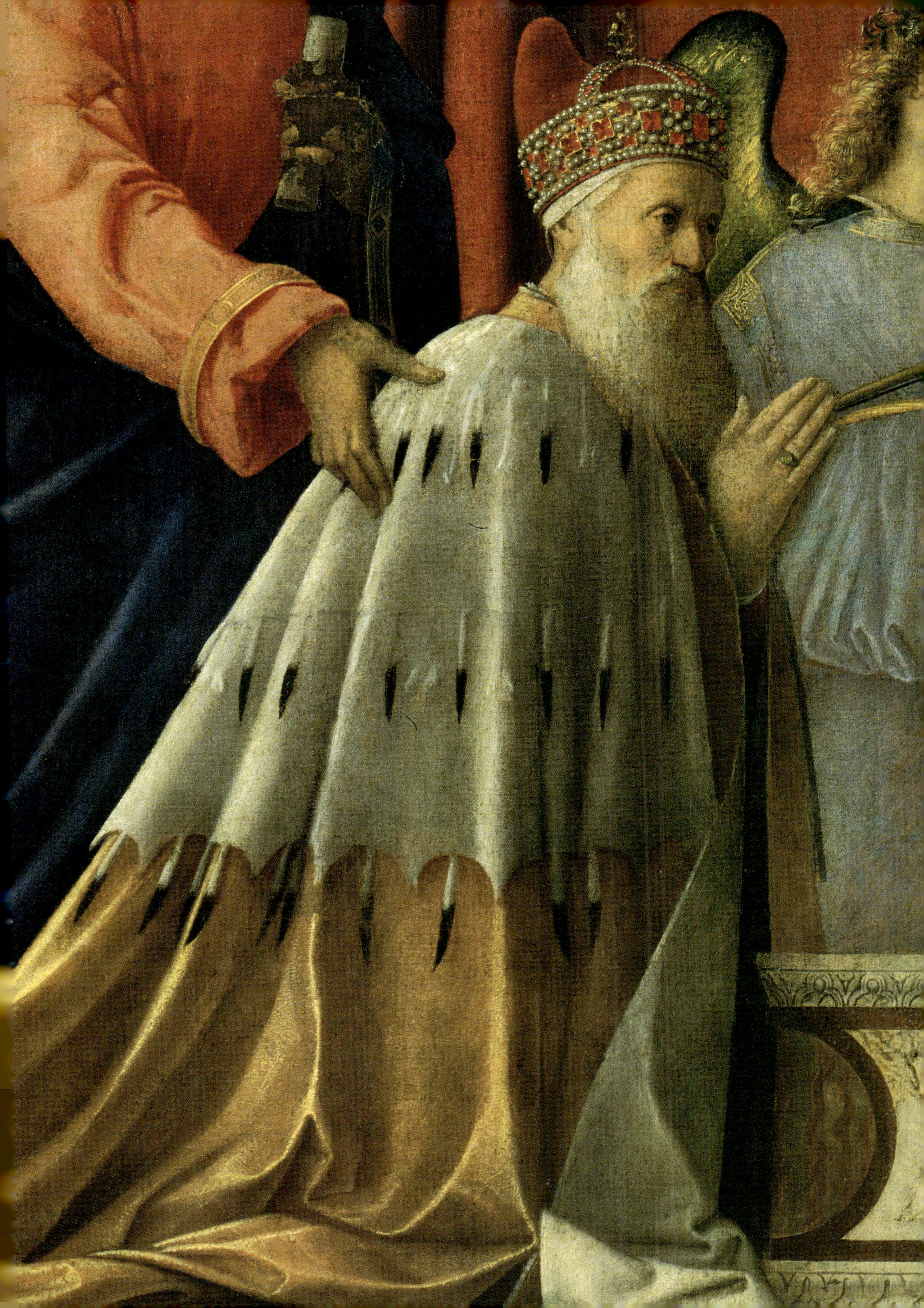

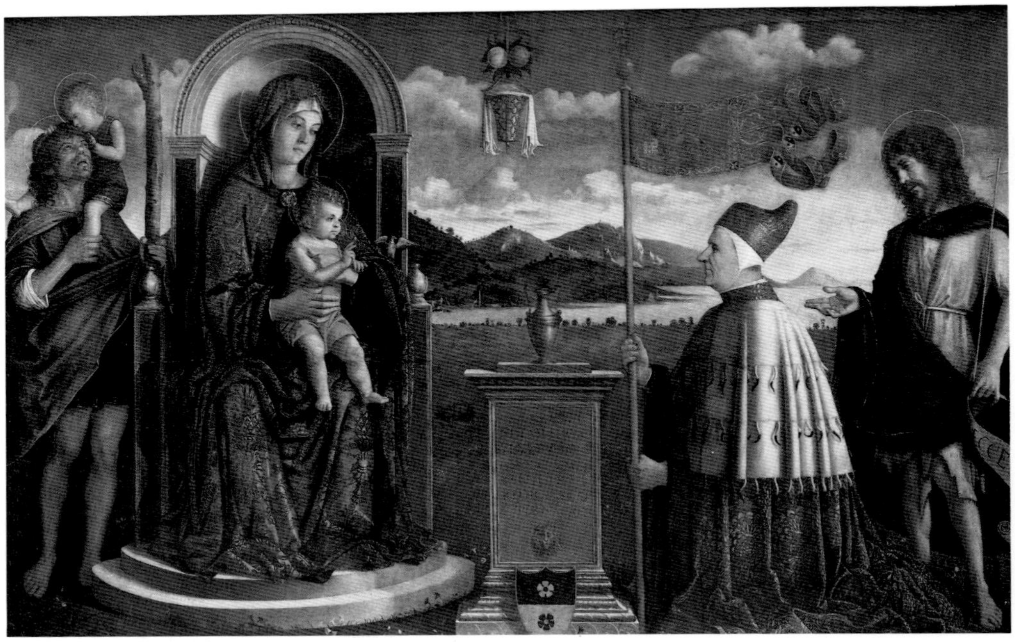

*70. Anonymous Fifteenth-Century Venetian (Gentile Bellini?), votive picture of Doge Giovanni Mocenigo, National Gallery, London.*

in the church of San Domenico in Orvieto. The tomb is self-referential, but in a more official, less personal way than the Dandolo monument. Subjugation of individual identity in official identity may have been considered particularly appropriate for the sepulchers of clerics. This would correspond to the treatment of Doge Barbarigo in Bellini's votive picture, which thus recalls the sacral character of the dogate.[126]

The setting of this picture, as in many of Bellini's small devotional paintings, is a landscape, not a cityscape or view of Venice, which might have seemed appropriate in this context. For Bellini, and perhaps for his patrons, landscape was indispensable to sacred imagery, his naturalistic visualization of God's beneficent presence. Perhaps he (and they) recalled the advice of the Venetian humanist Giovanni Caldiera that a home—modeled on the ideal state—should be open to sun and air.[127] Bellini may also have been alluding to the tradition of Horace and Virgil, revived in late quattrocento Venice by Sannazaro, which extolled country life over life in the city. But for Bellini, sky and landscape were more than compositional devices and metaphors: he made them the causation of his style, the logical explanation of his colorism, and, more than this, the affective determinant of the psychology of his images—hence the emotions of the beholder.

Bellini's atmospheric light derives its visual and emotional power from his exacting observation of light in nature—though this was less scientific than poetic in intent and mood. An insight into his creative process is provided by an unsuspected source, the conventual deliberations of the Dominican brothers of SS. Giovanni e Paolo. On 30 January 1516—ten months almost to the day before Bellini died—the Dominicans voted unanimously to grant Bellini's request to bor-

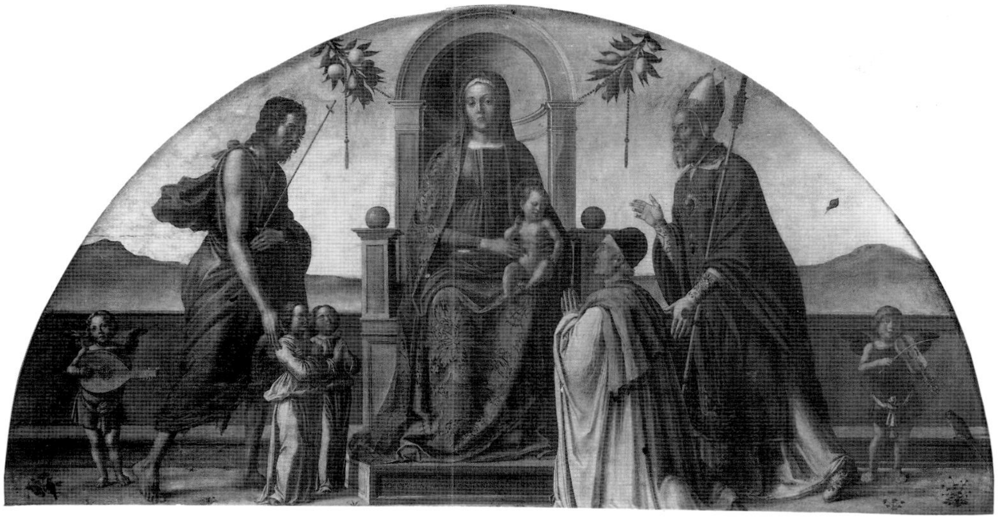

71. *Lazzaro Bastiani,* Madonna and Child with Donor Giovanni degli Angeli, *San Pietro Martire, Murano. Photo: Soprintendenza ai Beni Artistici e Storici, Venice.*

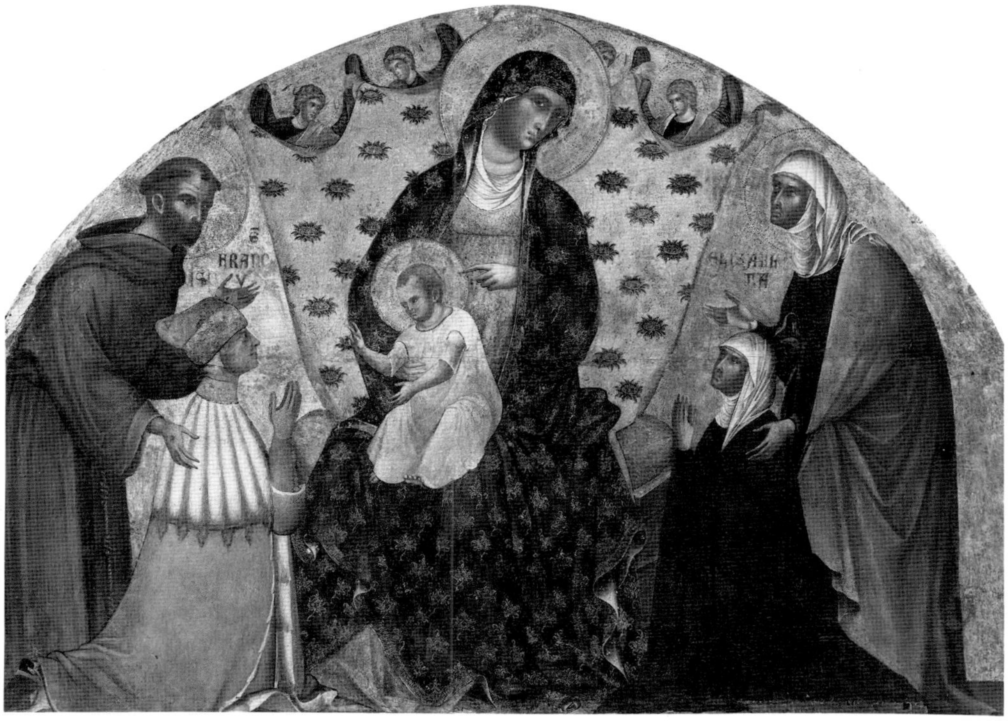

72. *Paolo da Venezia, tomb of Francesco Dandolo (*Madonna and Child with Saints Francis and Elizabeth of Hungary Presenting Doge Francesco Dandolo and Dogaressa Elisabetta*), Santa Maria Gloriosa dei Frari, Venice. Photo: Soprintendenza ai Beni Artistici e Storici, Venice.*

row a "beautiful silver crown": "A chapter was held to take counsel regarding another [*ex novo*] loan of a beautiful silver crown by Domine Giovanni Bellini, most excellent painter, and this for two days or so."[128] Bellini evidently wanted to use (or reuse) the crown as a model. As we have seen, shortly before he died in 1516, Bellini was working on a painting of the Virgin Mary, commissioned by the republic for the sister of the king of France.[129] Perhaps Bellini used the crown to make this royal commission a regal image. But whether he requested the crown for this painting is less significant than his having borrowed it.

This implies that jewels and other objects in Bellini's paintings, such as mirrors and armor, may have been based on real things.[130] Moreover, it is likely that Bellini was borrowing the silver crown not only to copy its design but to examine the effect of light on its glittering surfaces. The man who looked at shining metal indoors also observed the mutable effects of light and shade out-of-doors: his paintings themselves demonstrate this. Bellini transformed light, air, and the landscape itself into primary constituents of his art.

## God in His World: Sacred Subjects in Landscape Settings

Bellini painted a new kind of devotional picture in which the landscape setting is of the utmost importance: visually, in the composition; emotionally, in establishing the mood of the scene—and of the beholder; and symbolically, as a metaphor for God's presence. Bellini's early *Saint Jerome* and the *Crucifixion* are such images. Given their small dimensions, they seem, like the Madonnas and Pietàs, to have been made for private devotion. None of these paintings was commissioned as an altarpiece, although such distinctions were flexible in Renaissance Venice. In any case, more significant than their categorization is Bellini's affective treatment of landscape, light, and atmosphere.

Taking a drawing by Jacopo Bellini as their model, both his son Giovanni and his son-in-law Andrea Mantegna painted nearly identical panels of the *Agony in the Garden* in the later 1450s—but although the compositions are similar and contemporary they are light-years apart in style and mood (figs. 73–76).[131] Whether one or both of the young masters intended this artistic confrontation cannot be proved, but nonetheless in these two works Bellini and Mantegna have epitomized their similarities and differences. And if Mantegna's painting was done for the Venetian Jacopo Antonio Marcello, then the comparison seems inevitable, almost a gauntlet thrown, though it is uncertain who was challenging whom: neither picture is dated.[132]

From Jacopo Bellini the young artists derived the asymmetry of their compositions, high rocks rising to one side where Christ kneels, while the apostles sleep in the foreground. This grouping is counterbalanced by a tree in the midground on the other side of the composition, and a road that winds into the distance where Judas leads the Roman soldiers toward their victim. There the similarities end. For Mantegna, everything is carved of stone, the clouds no less solid than the rocks on which Christ kneels, the distant view on the horizon as sharp as the apostles sleeping by the river in the foreground. The bluish color of the mountains may suggest their distance, but their contours are precise, quite unlike Bellini's forms.

In his *Agony in the Garden* (circa 1459), Bellini represented Christ's celestial vision as a putto of disembodied white light shimmering in the sky.[133] Mante-

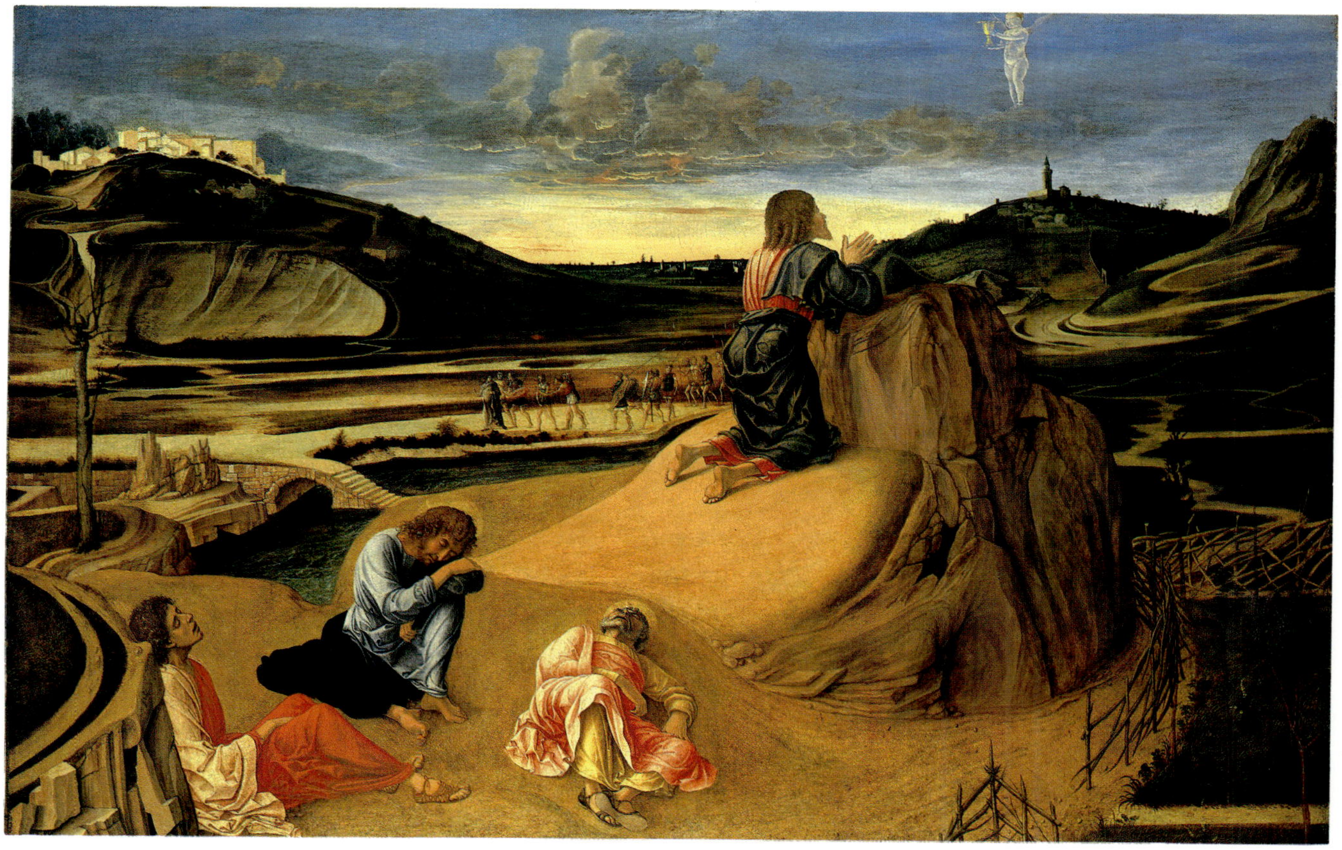

73. Agony in the Garden, *National Gallery, London.*

gna's phalanx of athletic putti, by contrast, present the Instruments of the Passion from a stony bank of clouds that easily bears their weight. Iconographically more orthodox than Mantegna, whose row of putti departs from tradition, Bellini was stylistically more adventurous. Bellini's clouds and sky exist only as immaterial color and light, so that Christ no longer needs the gold disk halo that Mantegna provided; in Bellini's version, the heavens themselves are Christ's glory. The carefully observed clouds and sky, remarkably varied in shape and color, imply the passage of time: these ephemeral phenomena represent the warmly colored sky at dawn, moments ago dark with night and soon to become bright with day. Bellini's *Agony in the Garden* is poignant—we respond emotionally to this coloristic, luminous abstraction that reminds us how the Son of Man subjected himself to history and to natural law. More than any of his Italian contemporaries, Bellini strove to recreate our visual experience of this world—the physical act of seeing—as a metaphor for our experience of the sacred. Thus, he reminds us of our fragile existence: we too are ephemera, like the changing color and light of the insubstantial sky that occupies so much of his compositions.

The conception of nature as an expression of spiritual meaning illuminates one of Bellini's most familiar works, the *Saint Francis in Ecstasy*, painted in the mid-1470s (figs. 77, 78).[134] It is also one of his most mysterious, because he seems to represent a state of mind or spirit as much as a narrative event. The problem of interpretation is compounded because the panel has been cut at the top, destroying

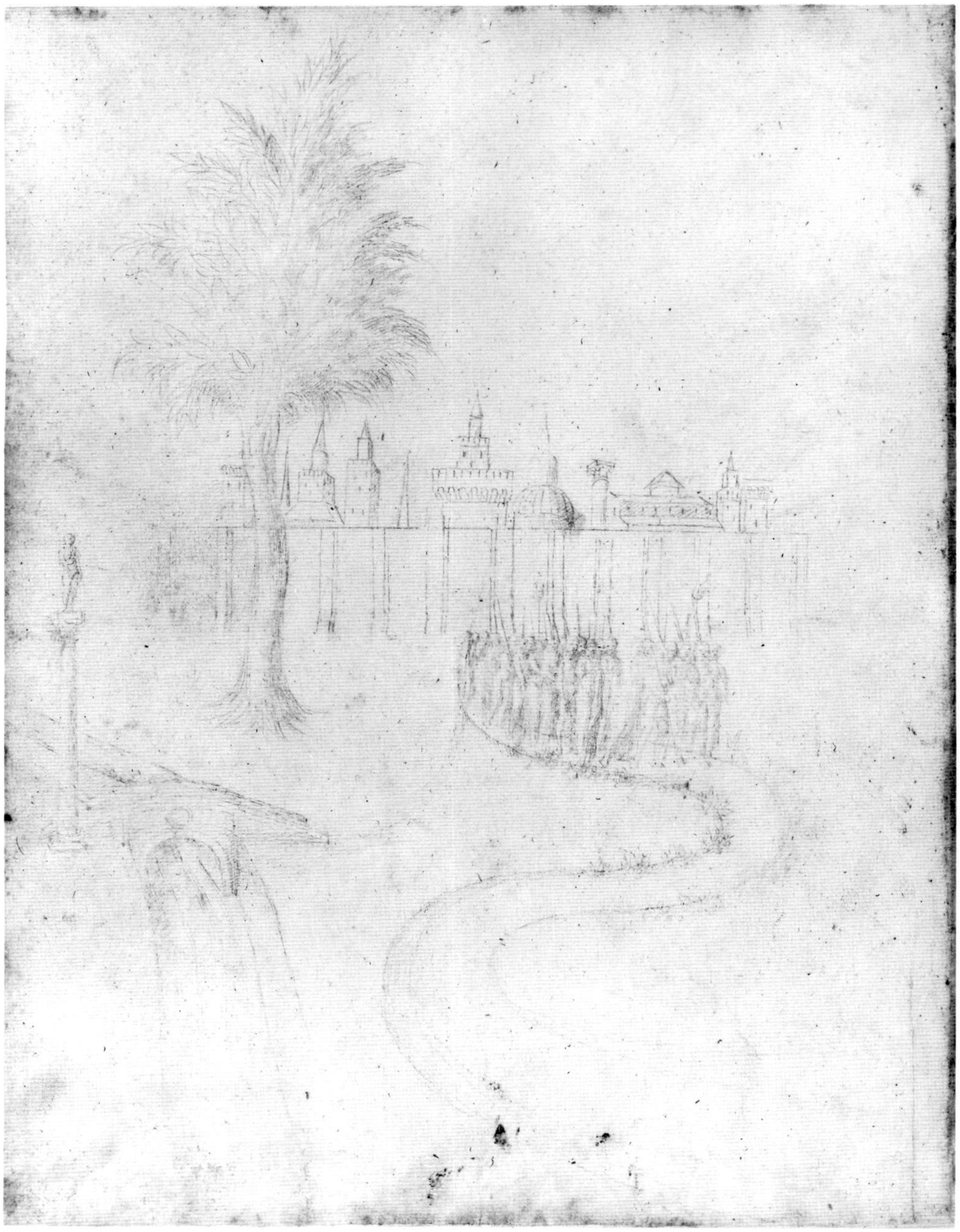

74. *Jacopo Bellini,* Agony in the Garden, *drawing book, folios 43v-44r, British Museum, London. Courtesy Trustees of the British Museum.*

whatever narrative explanation Bellini may have included there.[135] Whether the composition represents the Stigmatization, Francis singing his hymn of the sun, or his blessing Brother Leo seems peripheral to the forceful characterization of the saint himself.[136] This in itself was a typically Franciscan choice, for no other saint or religious order had ever focused so profoundly on an individual's personality.[137]

Francis himself had expounded on his spiritual experience to instill pity for Christ's suffering; gratitude for God's loving sacrifice of his Son for humanity's sake; and penance, exemplified by Francis's own repentance, as he attempted to imitate the Lord in order to share the Passion. The founder of the Friars Minor became, seemingly of his own volition, the model for his order, and his followers took Francis's experience as their spiritual prototype. According to Franciscan

belief, the validity of his example and of the rule that he wrote for his friars was proved when Francis received the wounds of crucifixion, inflicted by Christ himself in the miracle of the stigmatization (fig. 89). Just as Christ may intercede for humanity by displaying his scars to God the Father, so may Francis pray for mercy on our behalf by displaying his stigmata. Francis's prayer will be granted because of those scars, the wounds of Christ Crucified. This is the subject of Bellini's painting, which might almost be considered an illustration of the famous Franciscan prayer by Thomas of Celano, Francis's first biographer: "Remember . . . your sons crying thus sadly to you: 'Present, Father Francis, to Jesus Christ his sacred stigmata, and let him see the marks of the cross, that he may mercifully deign to show his own wounds to the Father, who because of them will indeed

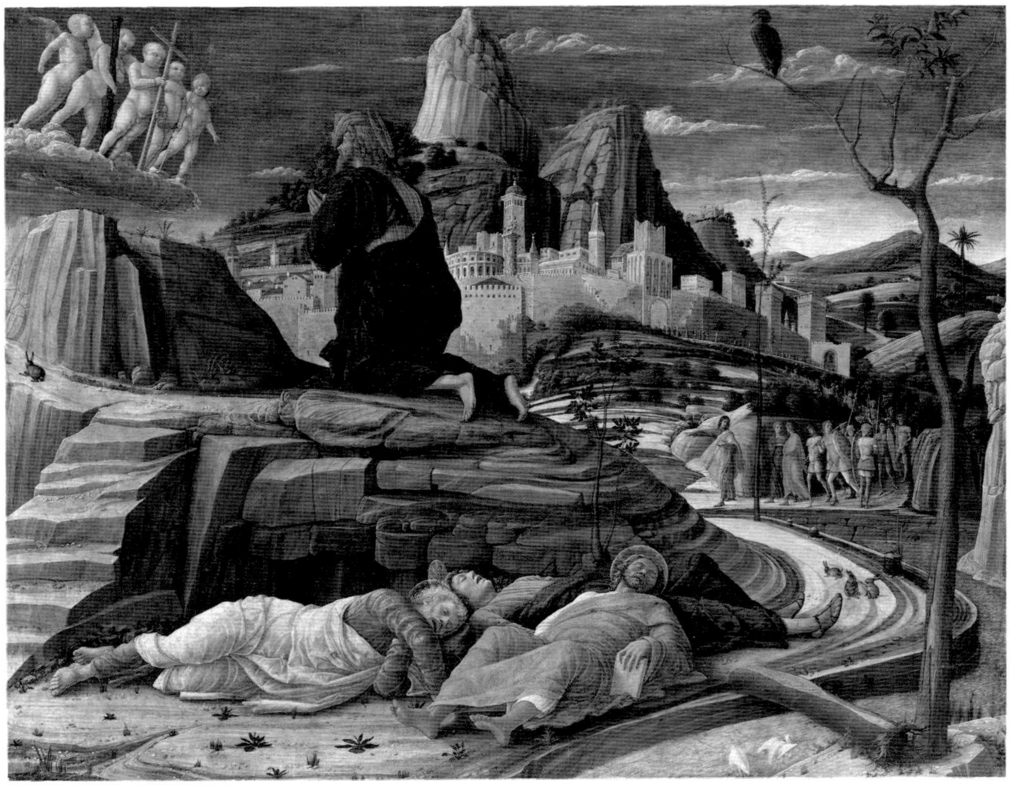

75. *Andrea Mantegna,* Agony in the Garden, *National Gallery, London.*

be ever gracious to us miserable ones.'"[138] Bellini's painting, like Celano's prayer, represents Francis's compassionate and irresistible intermediation for the faithful. Francis stands to the right of this asymmetrical composition, looking upward and spreading his arms to reveal the stigmata. His lips are parted, and his upward glance makes explicit the listener. That God responds to Francis is confirmed by a miraculous manifestation in the sky, rays of light distinct from the other, naturalistic source of illumination in the picture (fig. 78).

The saint's wounds are mere touches of pigment, and the scars in his feet and side are either concealed or omitted: perhaps Bellini's diffident painting of the stigmata reflects the controversy about them, that was still a matter of concern in the 1470s and indeed long thereafter.[139] Yet it is difficult to imagine that Bellini would have represented the act of stigmatization, were that his subject, with such reticence or that a patron requesting a depiction of the miracle would be content with such narrative ambiguity. Moreover, though the panel has been trimmed at the top, the source of the supernatural light was probably not specified, given the angle of the rays, and it seems impossible that five rays emanating from Christ's wounds inflicted identical wounds in the hands, feet, and side of the saint, as in traditional depictions of the miracle (pl. 89).[140]

In the Frick *Saint Francis*, the rays of light are not Christ's means of transmitting his wounds to his follower. The supernatural light illuminates Francis in a metaphoric and perhaps non-narrative sense. Yet these rays enter the scene with such force that the laurel tree through which they shine feels their power: the tree bends toward Francis. Laurel may signify many things, but here the tree is a symbol of Christ's cross. This was the constant theme of Francis's prayers, the leitmotif of his compassion for the Passion.[141]

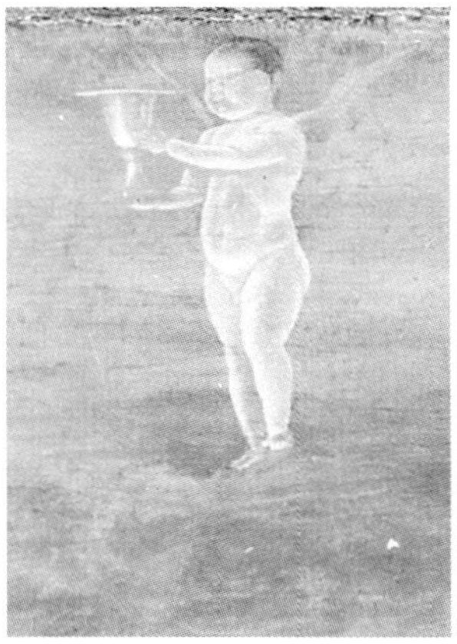

76. Agony in the Garden, *detail, putto.*

Bellini reminds us of the Passion with various symbolic objects associated with the lectern behind Francis. A death's head is displayed there, and a tall wooden cross, encircled by a crown of thorns, is set in the ground immediately behind the skull: we recall Golgotha, where Christ's cross was raised above the skull of Adam. Here, with this constant reminder of Christ's death and the fragility of earthly life, Francis reads his Bible, which also rests on the lectern. Above this, grapevines, another reference to the Passion, grow on a rough-hewn arbor of bare, pointed branches, suggesting the cross and the crown of thorns. Even the flowers that grow near Francis evoke the Passion.[142] Francis has left his Bible and the contemplative study of Christ's suffering to commune with God himself, who responds to him—it was by his empathetic meditation on the sacred text that Francis merited this privilege. He has removed his sandals, which lie near the lectern, because he stands on sacred ground. Bellini specified this place as La Verna, the mountainous retreat where Francis lived a contemplative life of penance and prayer, in contrast to his active life of preaching to the faithful in towns and cities.[143] Francis received the stigmata during one of his retreats at La Verna, and by evoking that site Bellini reiterated the theme of Christ's Passion, without representing the stigmatization itself. The saint personifies religious rapture, and his exemplary devotion is presented as a model for the beholder, who is encouraged to enter the stillness of Francis's world.

Landscape does more than provide the saintly protagonist with an appropriate setting, however: landscape is a second protagonist of Bellini's composition, as expressive of God's presence as the explicitly supernatural rays of light. Not only those golden shafts but the diffuse naturalistic light that illuminates the scene confirms God's presence in every particle of his creation. Bellini's mastery of light and atmosphere conveys this faith with ardor and conviction, and landscape is immeasurably more important in this regard than the specific symbolism of individual objects, although these too play their part.

Bellini had been rehearsing for this drama of luminosity since the beginning of his career in such works as the *Saint Jerome* and the *Agony in the Garden* (figs. 1, 73). The mountain air of the *Francis* is crystalline, and light penetrates the translucent paint surfaces so that they glow from within. This light binds the multiple forms of the landscape without sacrificing their individual formal identities. The closest parallels to Bellini's style and handling here are generally found not in Italian art but in the painting of Jan van Eyck and of Rogier van der Weyden, with which the Venetian was clearly familiar (cf. figs. 12, 56).[144] Bellini emulated Netherlandish techniques of painting with oil, which he combined with tempera, applying glazes to endow his colors with translucence and depth.

Bellini's style of landscape painting changed in the *Sacred Allegory* (circa 1488;

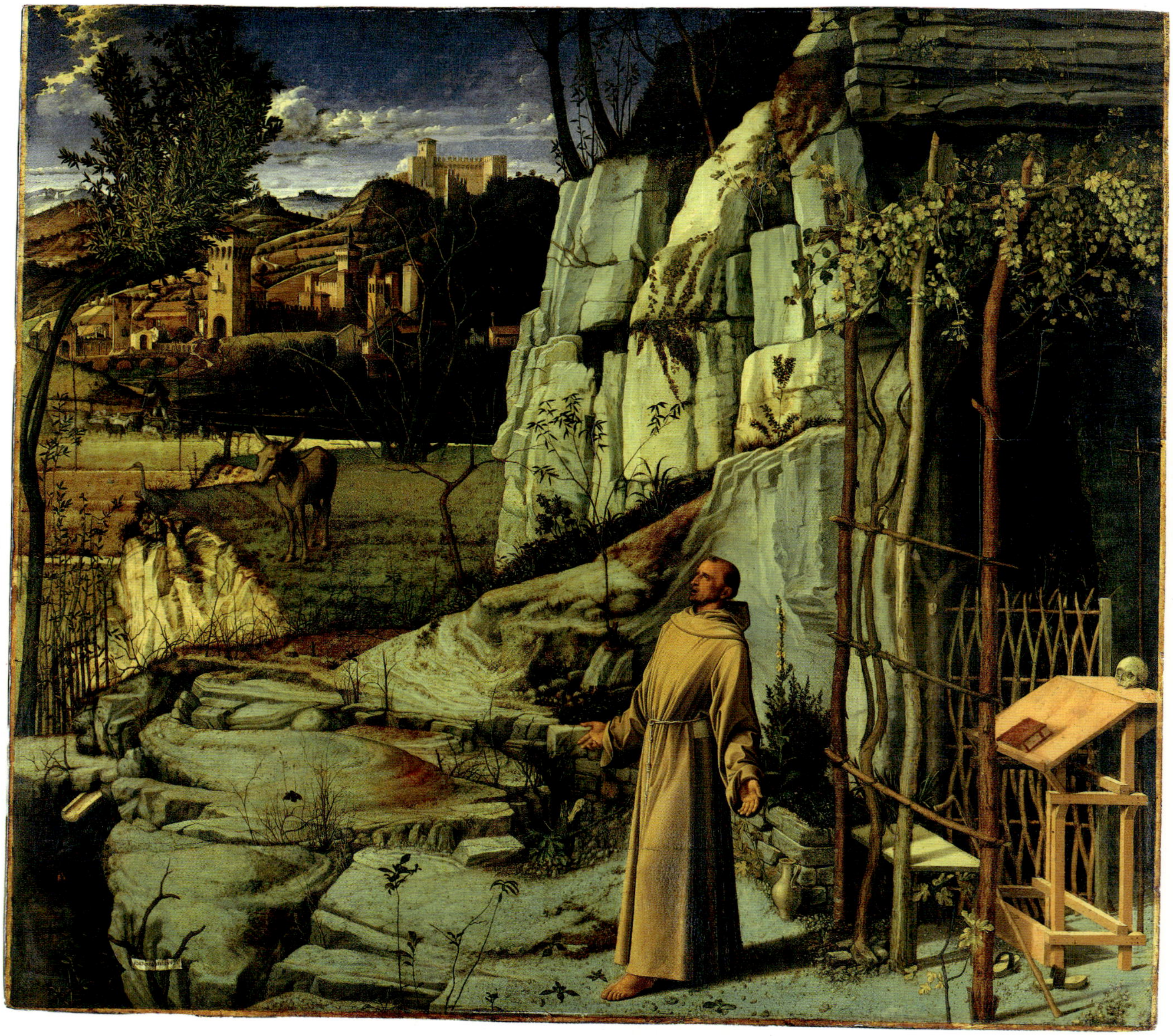

77. Saint Francis in Ecstasy, *Frick Collection, New York. Copyright © The Frick Collection, New York.*

78. Saint Francis in Ecstasy, *detail, laurel tree. Copyright © The Frick Collection, New York.*

figs. 79, 80). The scene is set on the banks of a lake, and forms are softened by mist or dissolve in the water, where reflections preserve the color of their source but almost nothing of the shape. The rocks and mountains on the far shore may recall Francis's La Verna, but the edges are rounded; the stone seems to have become pliable in the strong sunlight and air, and along the bank it is almost impossible to distinguish between solid reality and its watery reflection: one melts into the other, and they nearly become the same substance.

A sacred precinct in the foreground, with a patterned pavement and waist-high balustrade, provides the stagelike setting of the *Sacred Allegory* (cf. figs. 56, 68).[145] The figures are small in this context and set back from the picture plane so that they are contained completely by the pictorial realm. Several are readily identifiable. The Virgin Mary is enthroned at the left; in profile, she bends forward and extends her hands in prayer, as do her two female companions.[146]

The subject of their devotion is the Christ Child, the only seated figure other

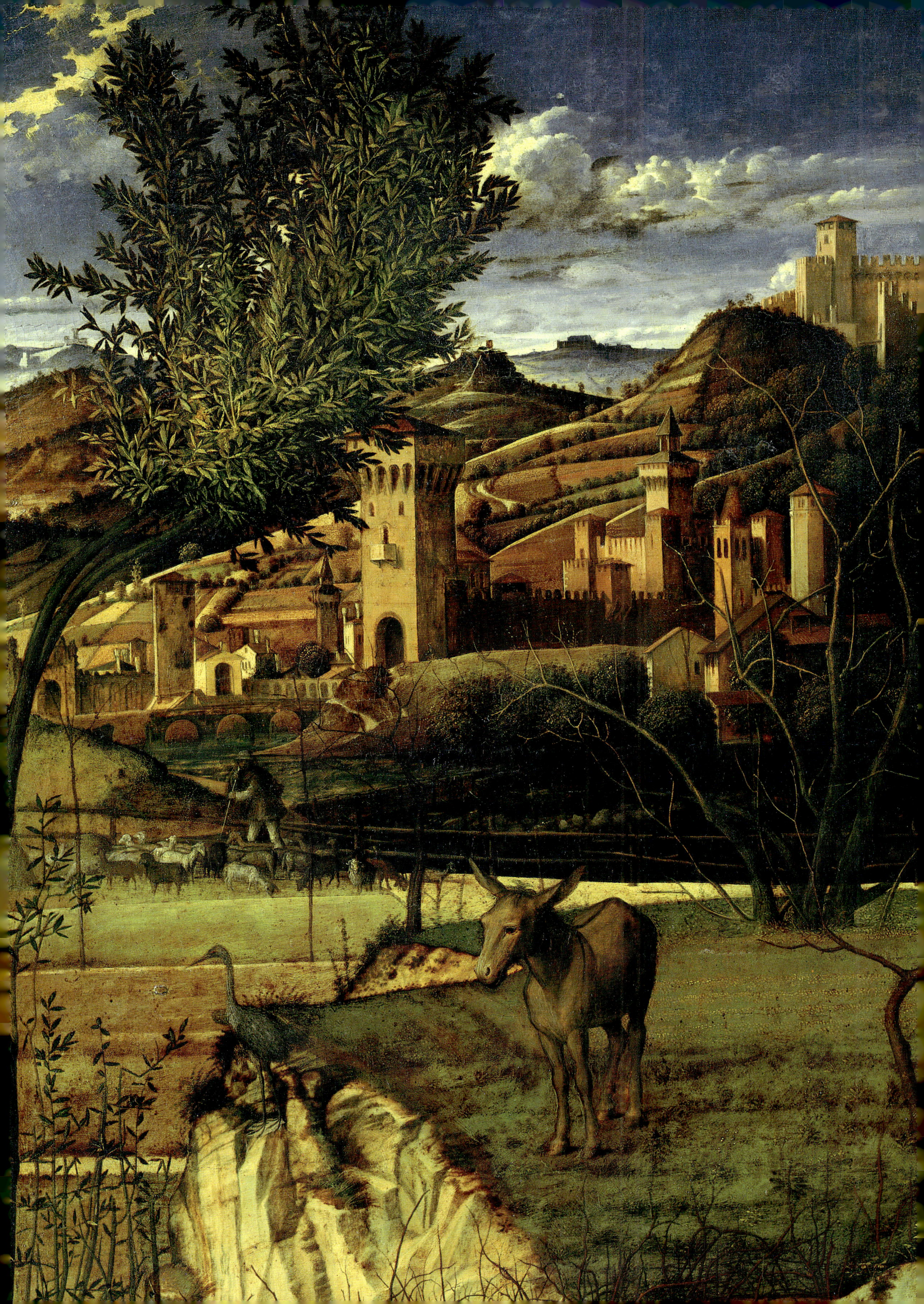

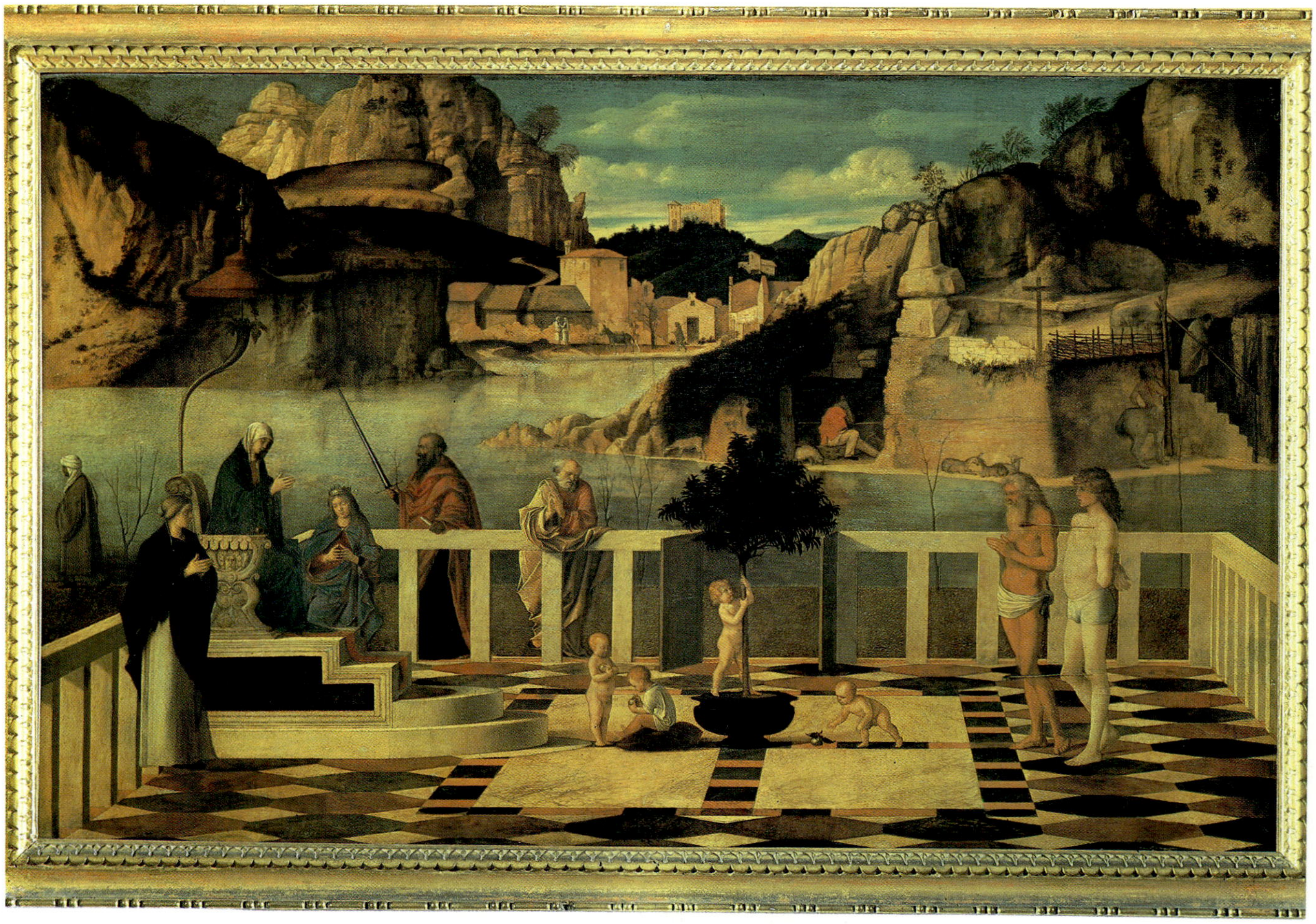

79. Sacred Allegory (Meditation on the Passion), *Galleria degli Uffizi, Florence. Photo: Scala/Art Resource, New York.*

80. Sacred Allegory (Meditation on the Passion), *detail, landscape. Photo: Scala/Art Resource, New York.*

than Mary. He contemplates a golden apple, unaware that he is the focus of attention and unaware also of the child who stands before him, holding another golden apple to his breast. This wingless boy and the two other children with Christ are the Innocents, his first martyrs, murdered by order of King Herod, who hoped to slay the Holy Infant among them (Matt. 2:16). Behind Christ, and in the center of the pavement, another Innocent shakes an apple tree planted in a vase: the child has caused an apple to fall, and one of his companions picks it up. Only the apple tree bears fruit in Bellini's pictorial world, and he emphasized its exceptional condition by placing dead trees just outside the balustrade.

Further to the right, Sebastian and Job look on. These two saints were often invoked against the plague, and their presence suggests that the painting may have been commissioned as a prayer for protection from the plague's ravages or in gratitude for survival. Outside this paved area, but related to it through the force of their actions and attention, are Peter and Paul. But who are the women who accompany the Madonna? All of the other figures in the foreground are saints, and the women also are martyrs or confessors of Christ, and not allegories or personifications of virtues, as has been suggested.[147] In a general way, and especially in their unspecificity, they resemble the two women saints who flank Mary and Christ in the Accademia *Madonna* (circa 1490), traditionally identified as Catherine and

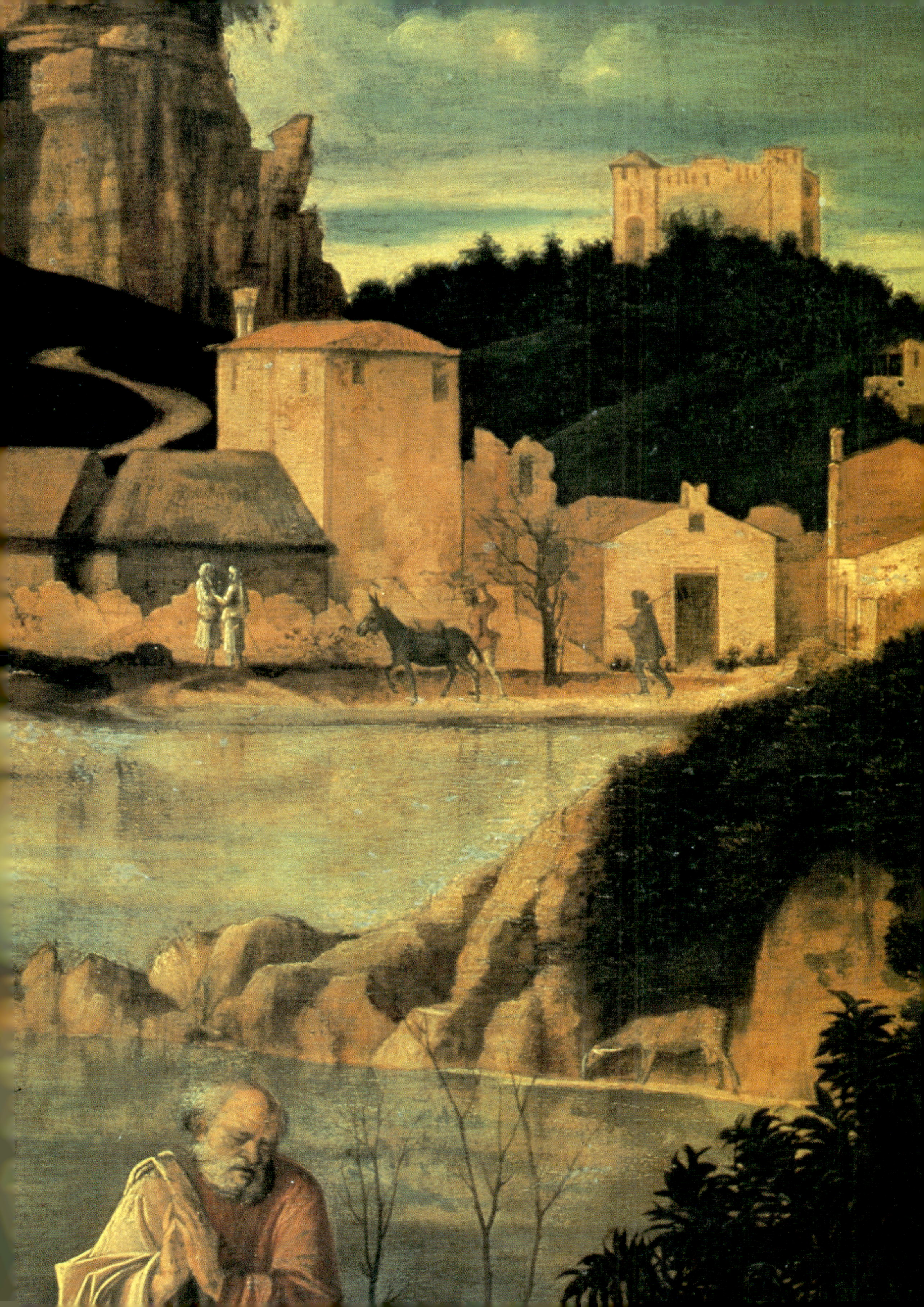

Mary Magdalen (figs. 40, 41). The royal saint of the *Sacred Allegory* might be Catherine of Alexandria or Lucy; both are often shown with diadems like the one she wears. The other woman's pearls are not a specific attribute but are included for their luminosity.

Having insisted on the human, historical identity of the figures, what can one conclude about the meaning of the *Sacred Allegory*? For it remains unique and puzzling: nothing else in Bellini's oeuvre or in the work of his contemporaries looks quite like this mysterious scene. The composition is dramatically asymmetrical; though the center of the patterned pavement is clearly marked the center of the painting is not here but to the left. Christ himself occupies this "axial" center. Thus the composition has two focal points, one where the symbolic tree stands, and the other coincident with the axis of the panel, where the Child contemplates the fruit of that tree.[148] Apples are a familiar symbol of original sin and redemption, and this explains the subject of the Infant's reverie, which is Adam's fall and his redemption by the New Adam, Christ himself. Apples and their tree also signify love, that is, Charity—the Christian emendation of a pagan association of apples and carnal love. The two symbolic meanings are inextricable in Christian thinking. Redemption is achieved by Christ's ultimate gift of love, his self-sacrifice on the cross. The cushion on which he sits underscores this meaning. A familiar accoutrement of death and burial in the Middle Ages and Renaissance, the cushion was used as such in Bellini's *Madonna* paintings as well.

Jesus embraced this self-sacrifice, as he explained to his disciples, as a twofold demonstration of God the Father's love and of his own love for humankind: "For God so loved the world, that he gave his only begotten Son, that whosoever believeth in him should not perish, but have everlasting life" (John 3:16); and again, speaking of himself at the Last Supper, "Greater love hath no man than this, that a man lay down his life for his friends" (John 15:13). If Bellini's painting has a text, perhaps it is found here, in the words of Christ himself.

Bellini manipulates light to underscore this meaning. Light in the *Sacred Allegory* comes from the left, somewhere behind Mary. Her throne, decorated with eucharistic grapes, casts shadows on Christ and the Innocent standing before him. Christ himself shadows the base of the tree's vase and the apple that an Innocent bends to gather. These cast shadows are naturalistically observed and consistent, but they are also conspicuous in a way that indicates an inherent symbolism, a suggestion of the metaphoric shadow that Christ's sacrificial role casts on him as he ponders his destiny.

Behind the apple tree the sacred precinct opens to the world that Christ's self-sacrifice will redeem. Saints Peter and Paul, the instruments of the Lord's earthly mission, stand in this world, but on the dividing edge that demarcates the holy realm. On the far shore of the lake that fills the midground, the landscape is inhabited by the sorts of bucolic figures seen in the backgrounds of other works by Bellini, including the *Saint Francis*, and they convey the same sense of well-being and harmonious existence in the natural world. But the figures in the midground of the *Sacred Allegory* are rather different.

One man departs the scene at the left. His garments lend him a foreign air, and he walks away from the sacred figures—in particular, away from Paul, who lifts his sword—suggesting that he is the pagan who turns his back on the true faith. Seeing themselves as the great defenders of the Church Militant, a Venetian audience would have recognized Bellini's reference to the continuing struggle of the faith, threatened in the East by the Moslem Turks.

The individual who has rejected Christ's gift is set against those who embrace it on the right. Here a large wooden cross makes explicit the Christian morality of the scene while reminding us of the sacrificial imagery of the central group. The rocks on the shore open to a cave or shelter which houses a shepherd and his flock. Perhaps he represents the Christian who heeds Christ's message and accepts his redeeming sacrifice.

Another man walks toward the water down a flight of stairs from the area defined by the cross and his ramshackle hermitage. That this is the hermit saint Anthony Abbot is confirmed by the centaur awaiting him on the shore. Anthony encountered this creature as he traveled to visit the first hermit, Paul, and unlike the abbot's other encounters with beasts, this meeting was amicable: the centaur gave Anthony directions to Paul's hermitage.[149] The thoughtful shepherd, however, is too young to be Paul and remains nameless. But it is worth remembering that the hermit saints Paul and Anthony were especially venerated in Venice and that Anthony—like Job and Sebastian in the foreground—was invoked against the plague. Represented in a lunette painting above the door to the right of the tribune in the Great Council Hall of the Ducal Palace, Paul and Anthony were associated, albeit at a slight distance, with the celestial court that witnessed the *Coronation of the Virgin* in Guariento's fresco above the doge's throne (fig. 66).[150] According to Sansovino, writing in 1581 but presumably recording older traditions, Anthony and Paul were represented sharing the bread brought to them by an angel, and this signified Charity, the virtue that should inspire the rulers of Venice as they meet in the Council Hall.[151] Anthony's association with Charity, the virtue of Christian love, is consonant with the meaning of the central group in Bellini's composition —the Infant Christ, the symbolic apple tree, and the Innocents.

Perhaps "allegory" is an inappropriate characterization of this scene, which might better be described as a "meditation on the Passion." To be sure, this is the title customarily associated with a painting by Carpaccio in which Saints Jerome and Job behold the Crucified Christ (fig. 81). Carpaccio's meaning is immediately recognizable because the central figure is the dead Adult, and not the Infant, as in Bellini's composition. Nonetheless, the two contemporaries were concerned with much the same subject interpreted in much the same way. Their compositions dramatize Christian spirituality in visualizations of devotion rather than traditional narratives. Like Bellini, Carpaccio exploited the expressive power

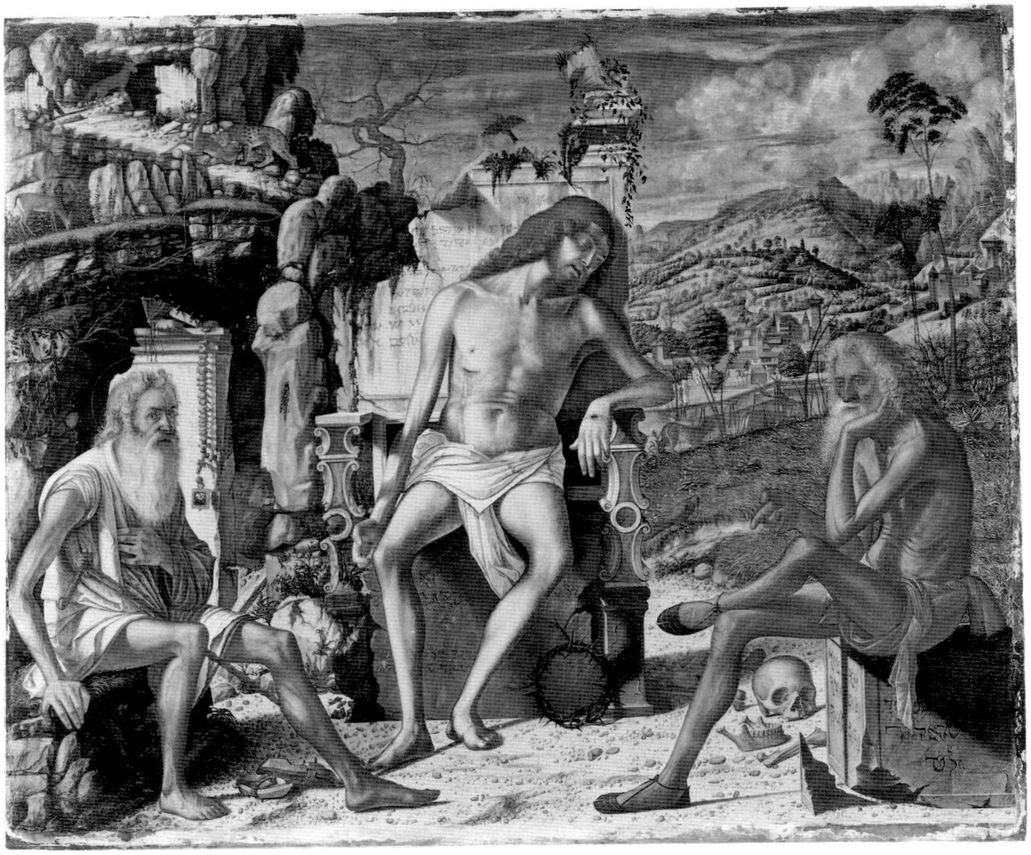

*81. Vittore Carpaccio,* Meditation on the Passion, *Metropolitan Museum of Art, New York, John Stewart Kennedy Fund, 1911.*

of his landscape setting. Like Carpaccio, Bellini interpreted Christ Incarnate as the eucharistic Christ, and whatever other themes he may have woven into his tapestry, the essential meaning is this: Christ took on human flesh to accomplish our redemption by his own death, and he did so for love of humankind. This is the mystery that Christ, Mary, and the saints contemplate and that Bellini invites us to consider and to accept in his "meditation on the Passion."

# 2 "Ravished Souls"

## Images for Public Devotion

*Their comportment is so gentle and their movements so graceful that they ravish souls.*
—Carlo Ridolfi

### The Quattrocento Altarpieces

The first quarter-century of Bellini's achievement as a painter of major altarpieces is obscured by the loss of documented works and by controversy regarding the attribution of those that survive.[1] His first undisputed altarpiece, the Correr *Transfiguration* (fig. 9), is the poorly preserved fragment of a larger work. And the master's first altarpiece of the Madonna, Child, and saints, a work of the mid-1470s, is known only from copies—it was lost in the same fire that destroyed Titian's *Saint Peter Martyr* in 1867 (figs. 82, 83).[2] But even these poor copies make clear that Bellini's picture was one of his most original and influential inventions.

In style and handling, the lost SS. Giovanni e Paolo altarpiece of Saint Catherine must have resembled the *Madonna and Sleeping Child Enthroned* and the *Saint Giustina* (figs. 24, 84).[3] Bellini exploited the image's relation to its stone enframement, which is visually, if not structurally, part of the fabric of the church itself, and in scale and effect, part of the viewer's environment. Bellini dissolved the barriers between the image and the viewer, who stands or kneels before the altarpiece in the nave: the two worlds are contiguous, one illusionistically accessible from the other. Though the pictorial world clearly does not represent an ecclesiastical setting, the sacred lamp suspended from the vault above the Virgin's throne suggests the sanctity of this locus. The fictive architecture meets the viewer's space at the altar, the only place where the faithful may see God, in the transubstantiated Eucharist of the Mass. The words of Saint Francis—relevant even in this Dominican church—explain how this can be: "In this world I cannot see the most high Son of God with my own eyes, except for his most holy Body and Blood."[4]

The Madonna and Child are raised on a high throne, surrounded to the right by male saints, led by Thomas Aquinas, and to the left by female saints, including Ursula and Catherine, titular saint of the altar. Three children standing at the base of the Madonna's throne serenade the holy congregation. In addition to the black and white of the Dominican saints' habits and the traditional blue and red worn by the Madonna, Bellini enriched his palette with the colors used for Ursula's

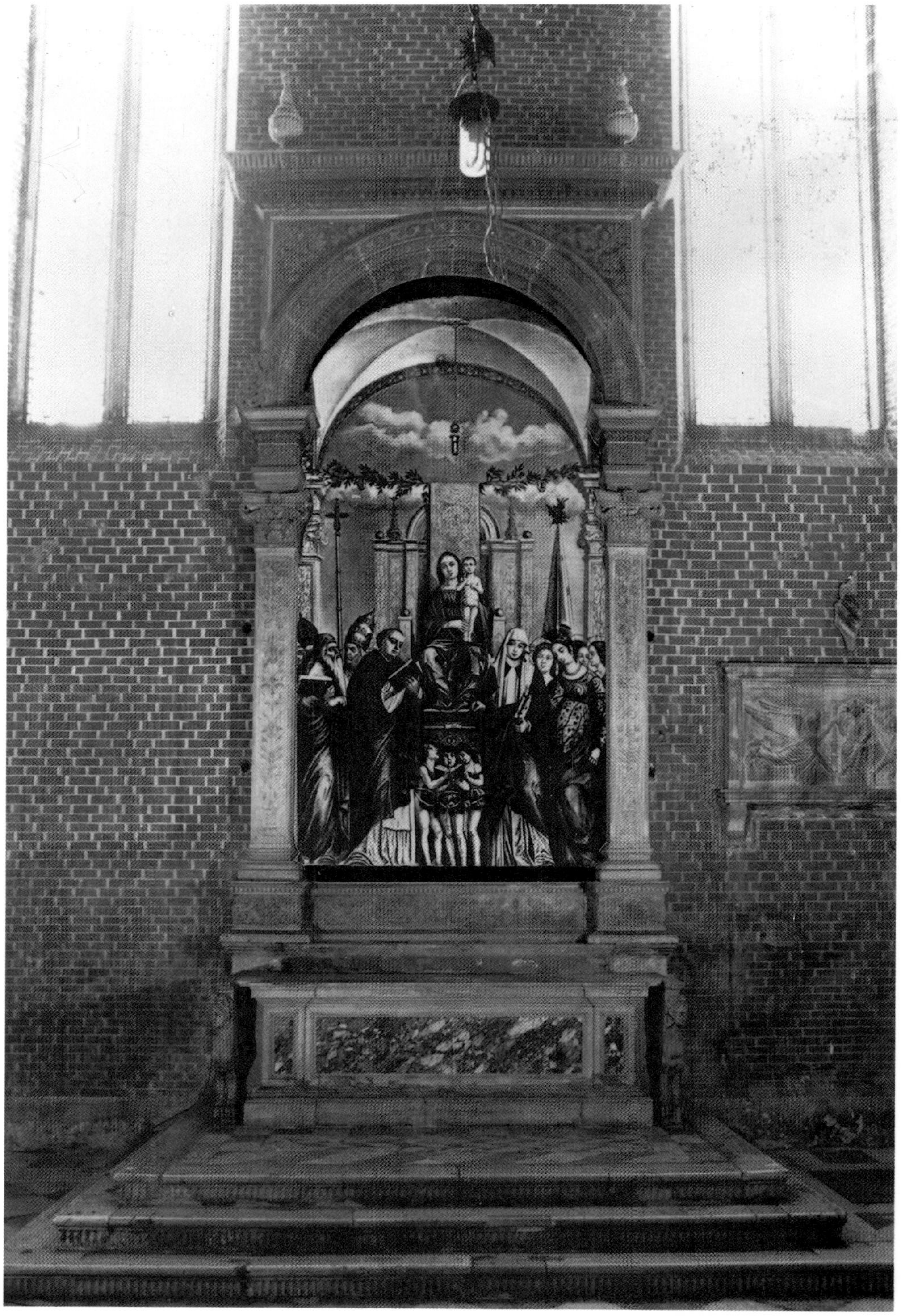

82. *After Giovanni Bellini, Saint Catherine altarpiece,* Sacra Conversazione (Madonna and Child with Saints Catherine of Siena, Ursula, Thomas Aquinas, and Other Saints), *copy of destroyed work formerly in SS. Giovanni e Paolo, Venice, reconstructed with its frame. Photo: Gianfranco Spinazzi, Venice, and Archivio Fotografico del Museo Correr, Venice. Montage: Author.*

garments—cloth of gold (*drappo d'oro*) embroidered with red, and a dark green mantle.[5] The figures are united within one bay of a loggia with round arches and a cross vault. Bellini's architecture opens in back to the sky, and surviving paintings dating from the early 1470s and even earlier reveal his richly colored and luminous handling of the heavens. Such a sky would have charged the lost pala with emotion while unifying the composition, effects that must be recreated in the mind's eye.

An art-historical red herring has traditionally confused understanding of this lost work, and in particular its relation to Antonello da Messina's contemporary San Cassiano altarpiece, dated 1475–76 (fig. 85). Carlo Ridolfi, writing in 1646, fabricated a story of Bellini's disguising himself as a gentleman to gain access to the visitor's studio—and to Antonello's technical secret, the Netherlandish use of oil.[6] This posthumous libel was regarded as *ben trovato,* "well-found," if not exactly true, to paraphrase the old Italian saying, because, though Giovanni Bellini had used oil before Antonello came to Venice in 1475—the *Jörg Fugger* of 1474 (fig. 150) is a case in point—his style clearly changed in the mid-1470s, purportedly in response to Antonello's art. And it is in the lost altarpiece for SS. Giovanni e Paolo that this influence was supposedly most obvious.

Chemical analyses of fifteenth-century and early sixteenth-century works by Bellini and his contemporaries indicate that they frequently used oil in varying combinations with tempera. However, it is not the medium that determines style but the way in which it is handled. Bellini may indeed have been inspired by the practical example of Antonello, whose familiarity with Netherlandish art encompassed technical knowledge—not just using oil to bind pigment but exploiting the medium to achieve a coloristic modeling of form. Bellini and his compatriots could view works by Rogier van der Weyden and Jan van Eyck, and certain elements in Bellini's art, as in Antonello's, derive from this common source. Parapets and inscribed cartellini, landscape settings with low horizon lines, sensitivity to the atmospheric effects of light and shade, interest in such light-reflecting surfaces as water, metal, and gems—to say nothing of the use of glazes and the oil medium —all reflect Netherlandish influence. When Antonello came to Venice he demonstrated Northern technique "in the making," and therein lies his contribution to Bellini's art. But must Bellini's lost altarpiece be dated after Antonello's Venetian commission, a documented work of 1475–76?

Only chemical analysis can reveal the artist's materials, and obviously there can be no such evidence for Bellini's lost painting. But Crowe and Cavalcaselle considered the medium to have been tempera; which means that it looked like tempera, not oil, though it now seems likely that some oil would have been mixed in the medium.[7] Sansovino did not mention Bellini's technique but in discussing slightly later works, notably the *Resurrection* and the San Giobbe altarpiece, Sansovino noted the use of oil, adding that the San Giobbe was Bellini's first oil painting.[8] Bellini did employ oil in these paintings—although it bears repeating that he may have done so in the lost altarpiece as well: the point is not that his medium contains oil but rather that the later works *appear* to have been painted in oil, even though oil was combined with tempera. Evidently the lost altarpiece did not exhibit this stylistic quality and for this reason, rather than revealing the influence of Antonello's Venetian work of 1475–76, it seems to have been completed before then.

Whatever Antonello da Messina's San Cassiano altarpiece may have looked like, it did not look quite like Bellini's pala, as surviving fragments prove. Where the

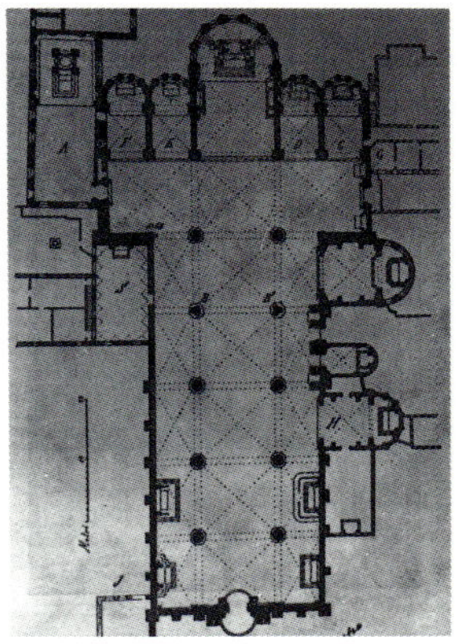

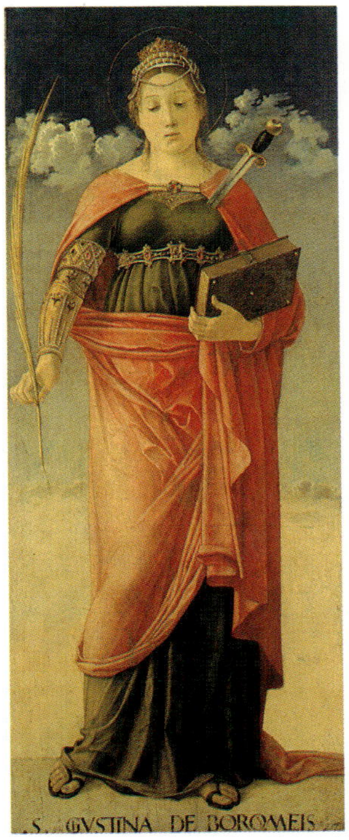

*83. SS. Giovanni e Paolo, Venice, plan, Chapels of Saint Catherine and Saint Vincent Ferrer in right aisle. Photo: Osvaldo Böhm, Venice.*

84. Saint Giustina, *Fondazione Bagatti Valsecchi, Milan. Photo: Fondazione Bagatti Valsecchi, Milan.*

Venetian painted an open sky, Antonello effectively closed his background with cloths of honor suspended behind Mary's throne. No one knows what Antonello's architecture was, and reconstructions by Mather and Wilde are based on Bellini's lost and undated work.[9] Who was copying whom?

The compositional ideas are surely Bellini's; his command of and interest in architectural settings are self-evident. The Antonello that most recalls Bellini is the San Cassiano altarpiece: nothing he had painted before that commission brings the two artists so close together. The altarpiece may fairly be called Bellinesque, an effect the foreigner probably intended to please his Venetian patrons. Antonello's composition and figure types in particular reveal his debt to Bellini's art and provide a terminus ante quem for the lost work, begun before 1475.[10] But equally clear is a change in Bellini's style in the mid-1470s: forms are more richly modeled, more volumetric than in earlier works, and yet more softly defined, with modulations of color, light, and shade replacing the clearer contours and sharper modeling of such paintings as the Brera *Pietà* or the *Saint Giustina*. Comparison of the Frizzoni *Madonna* of the early 1470s with the Lochis *Madonna*, painted in the second half of the decade, illustrates this development (figs. 26, 30). The culmination of Bellini's fascination with Netherlandish art is the *Saint Francis in Ecstasy*, painted immediately after the lost altarpiece (fig. 77). Related to this change is a shift in color, favoring warmer, richer hues, and greater variety in the palette.[11]

The direction of Bellini's development had been self-determined before Antonello's arrival in such works as the *Agony in the Garden* (fig. 73). Bellini continued to pursue this direction, toward an art of increasing grandeur and of chromatic and atmospheric subtlety, in his next great altarpiece commission, the *Coronation of the Virgin*, painted circa 1471–74 for the high altar of San Francesco in Pesaro (figs. 86–90).[12] Including the predella and elements of the frame, this altarpiece survives more nearly intact than any of Bellini's other early works.[13] Although the subject is familiar—it was much favored by the Franciscans—Bellini's interpretation is unlike any other Coronation of the Virgin in Italian art.

Mary's Coronation was considered a happy occasion, her culminating "seventh joy" as she is reunited with Christ in glory and crowned Queen of Heaven. This is how Mary's triumph was described by Jacopo da Voragine, the thirteenth-century Dominican priest whose compilation of saints' lives, the *Golden Legend*, was popular throughout the Middle Ages and Renaissance: "The assemblage of those who had stayed behind in Heaven, in admiration at the choiring of those who had ascended, went swiftly forth to meet them," Voragine explained, "and seeing their King bearing in His own arms the soul of a woman, and her leaning upon Him, they began to exclaim, saying: 'Who is this that cometh up from the desert, flowing with delights, leaning upon her beloved?' And those who accompanied her answered: 'Fair is she among the daughters of Jerusalem, as ye have seen her filled with charity and love.' And in this wise she was taken up into

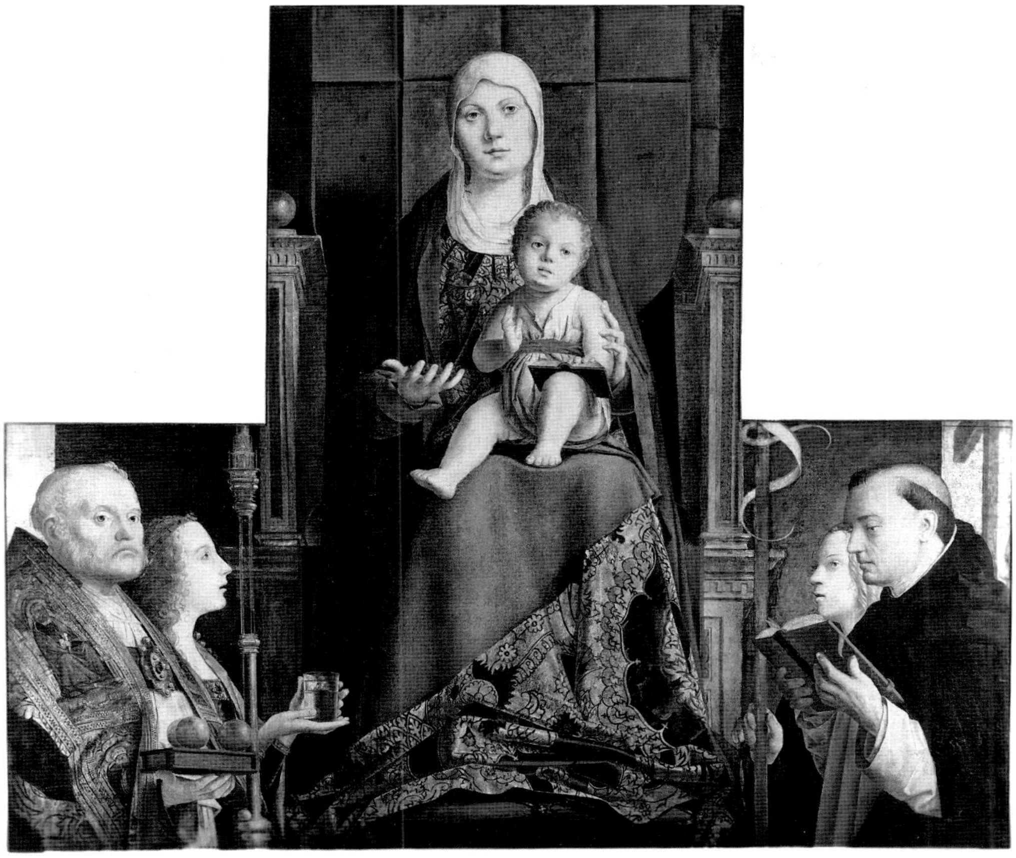

*85. Antonello da Messina, San Cassiano altarpiece (fragment), Kunsthistorisches Museum, Vienna. Photo: Kunsthistorisches Museum, Vienna.*

Heaven rejoicing, and placed upon a throne of glory at the right hand of her Son."[14]

In keeping with this traditional account, the Coronation was customarily represented in Italian art as a scene of rejoicing and wonderment in the heavens: angels greet Mary with music, the entire court of heaven comes forward to welcome her, and, she, forgetting her suffering and the sacrifice of her Son, recalls her happiness at the beginning of his life now that they are reunited in glory (figs. 13, 66). Thus Carlo Crivelli, in his *Coronation* painted for the church of San Francesco in Fabriano in 1493, included the traditional musical angels and depicted gentle smiles on the faces of some of the saints in attendance (figs. 91, 92).[15] In other respects, Crivelli's altarpiece recalls Bellini's work, which seems to have been its inspiration. But Giovanni Bellini's Coronation altarpiece has no rejoicing; no angel offers celestial music—although Bellini was evidently a knowledgeable musician.[16] None of the witnesses expresses wonder and joy at the reception of the Madonna in heaven; there is no pleasure here, but rather solemnity and sorrow in the recollection of Christ's Passion. And whereas most Coronations include a multitude of celebrating saints and angels, here there are only four, Peter and Paul, Jerome and Francis.

Bellini's reinterpretation of the Coronation theme is determined, or overshadowed, by the *Pietà* that originally crowned the composition. Placing an image of the dead Christ at the top of the altarpiece is not in itself noteworthy; this was traditional in Venetian art and in Franciscan art, including Crivelli's version of the

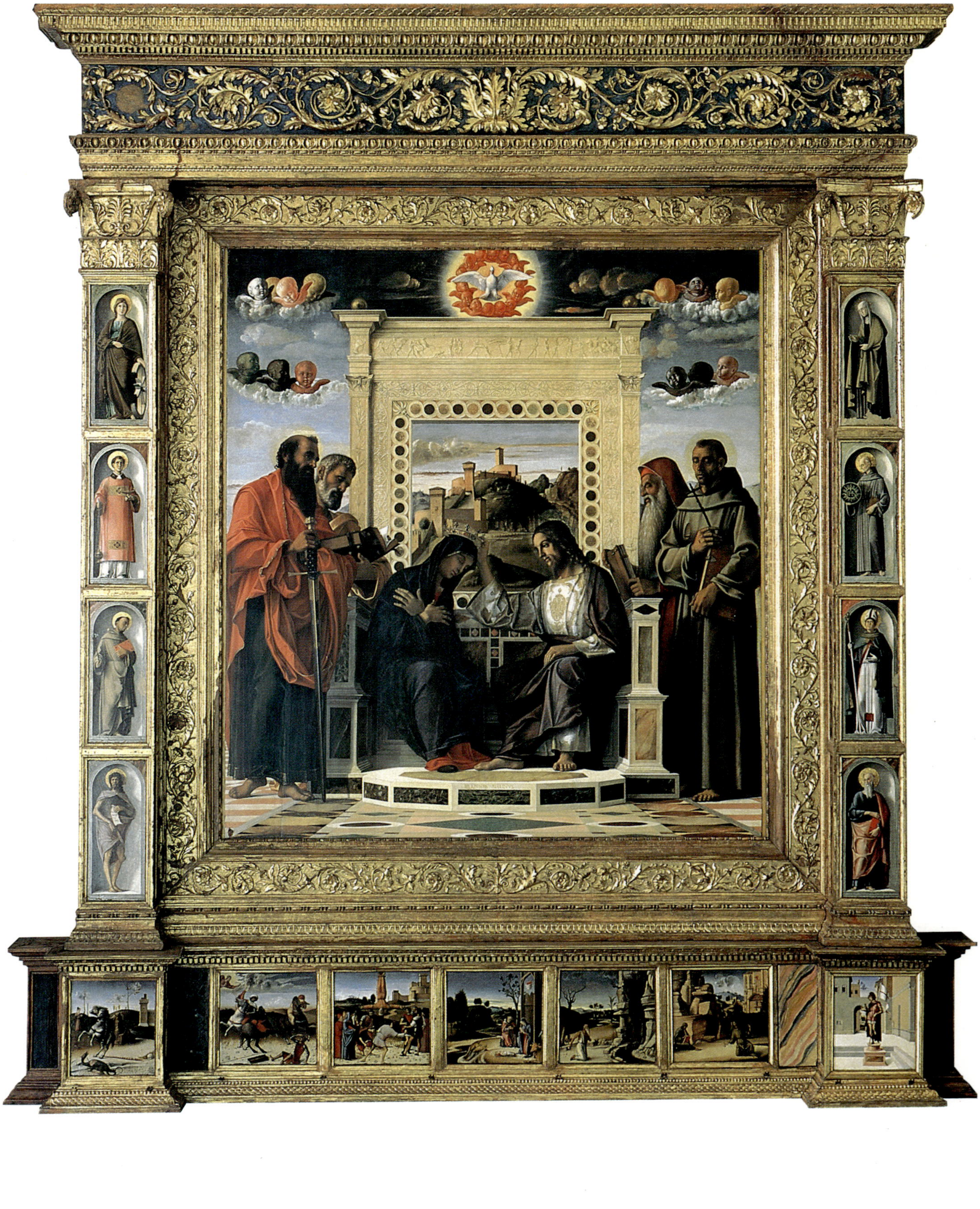

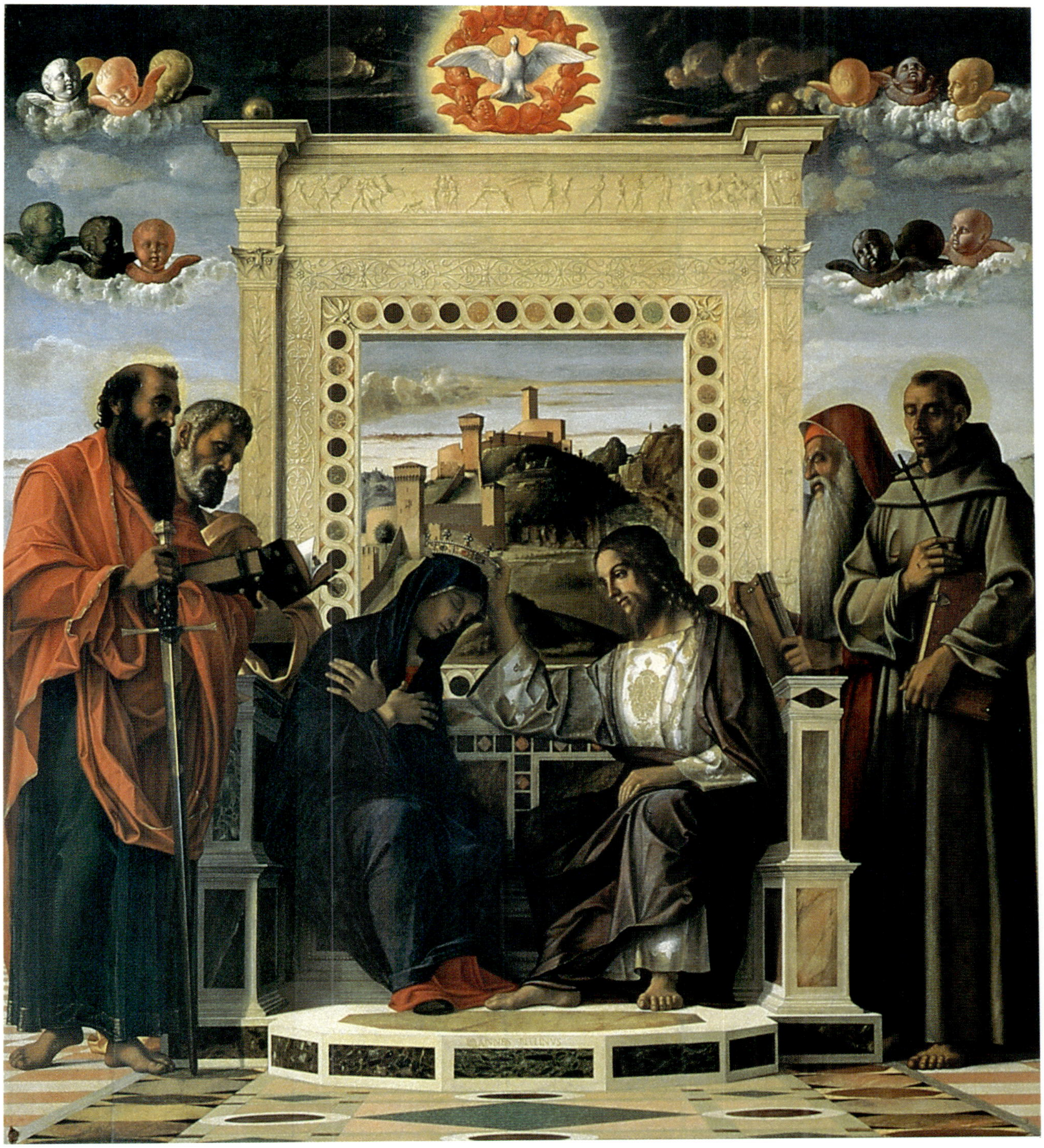

Coronation. Bellini's *Pietà*, approximately one-third the width of the *Coronation*, rested above the Virgin and Christ in the main panel and is related to the panel both psychologically and visually, through color, the low viewpoint, and lighting (fig. 93). Given the dimensions and descriptions of the altarpiece before the parts were separated, it seems that other panels, either with saints or with Gabriel and the Annunciate Virgin, may have flanked the *Pietà*, as in the polyptych of Saint Vincent Ferrer (fig. 186).[17]

Christ's body rests on the sarcophagus edge—the only spatial reference in the composition—and his legs overlap it, pushed illusionistically into the viewer's

87. *Pesaro altarpiece, detail, Christ and the Virgin Mary. Photo: Pesaro, Museo Civico.*

86. *Pesaro altarpice* (Coronation of the Virgin), *after restoration, Museo Civico, Pesaro. Photo: Pesaro, Museo Civico.*

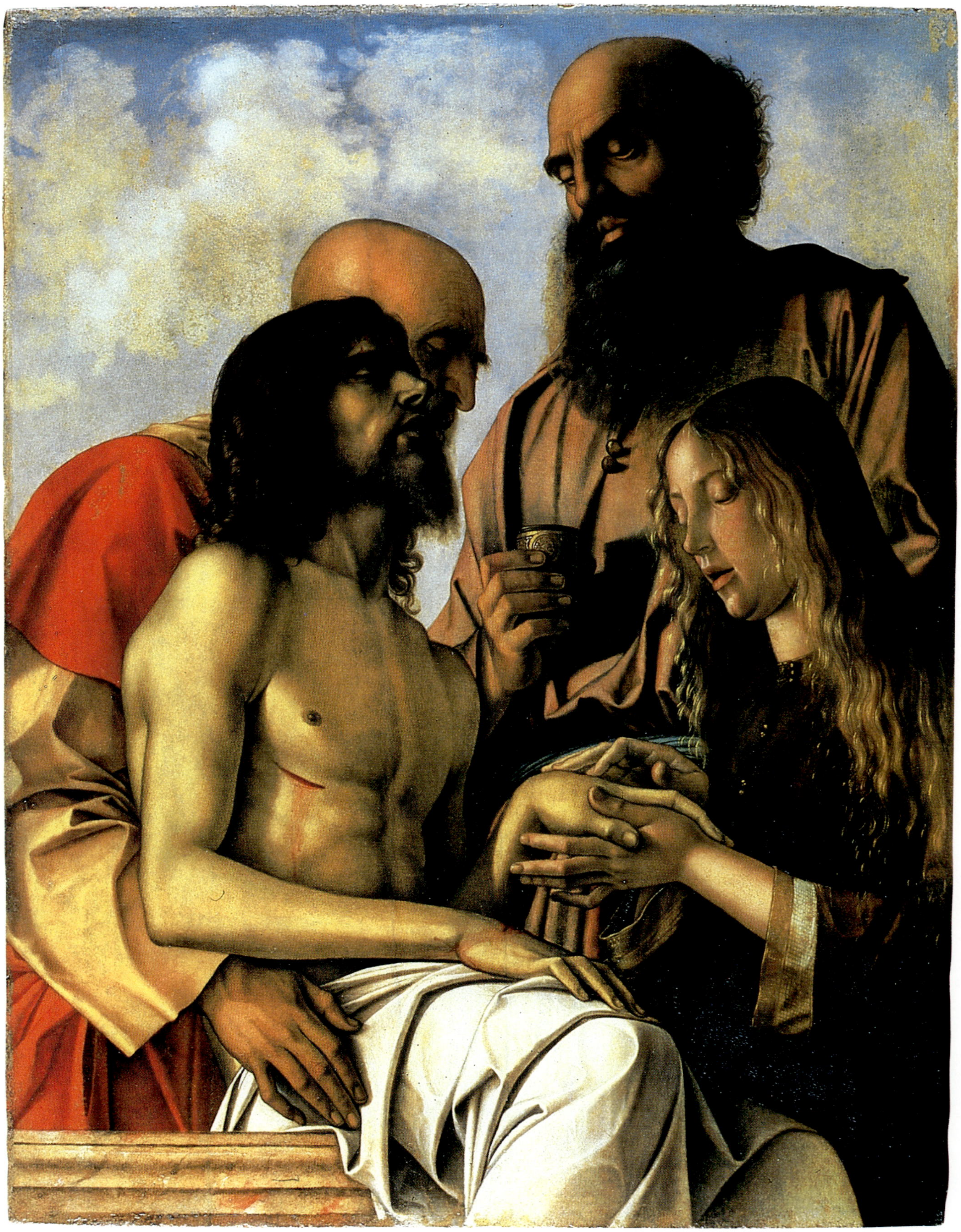

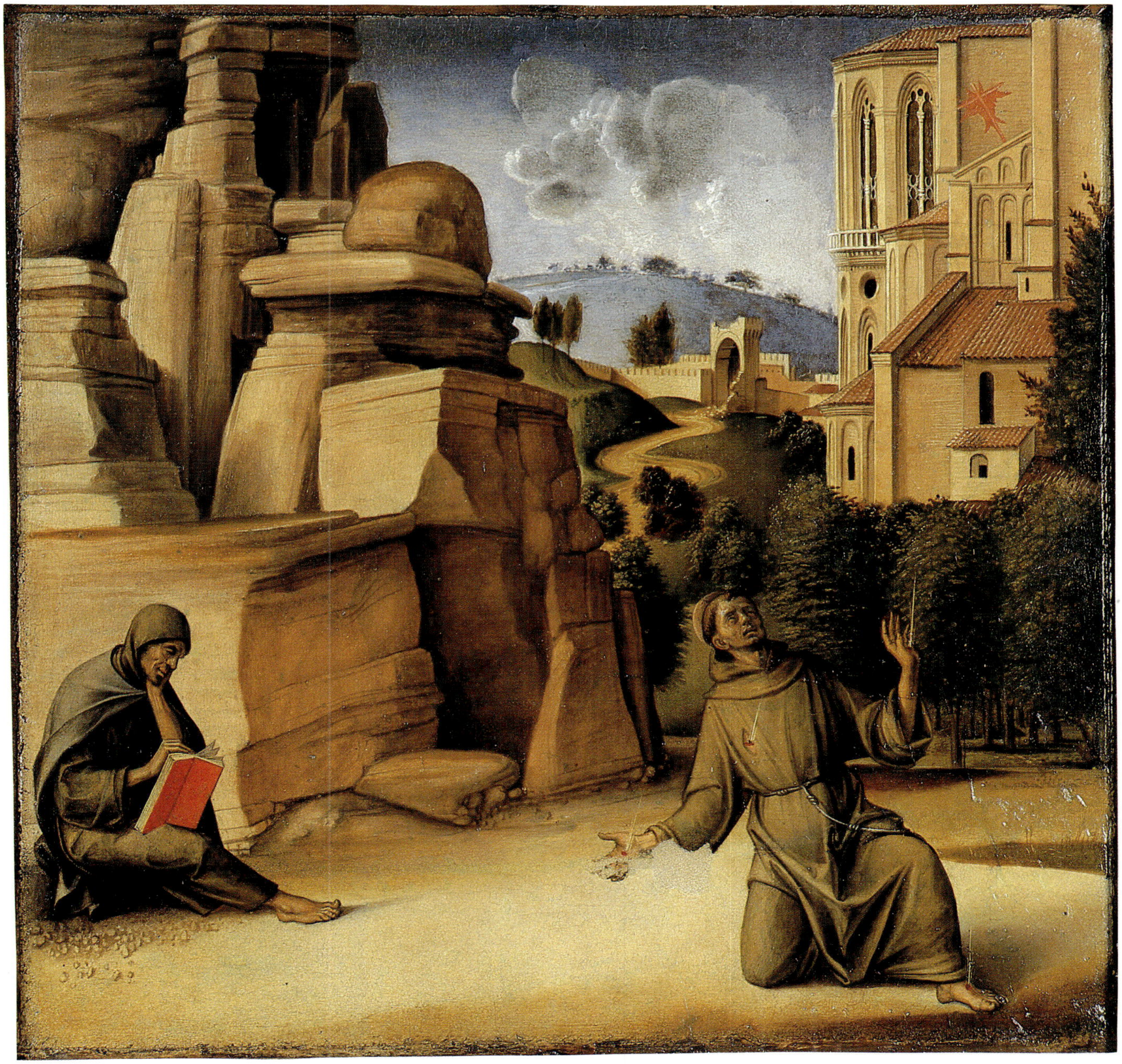

*89. Pesaro altarpiece, detail, predella,* Stigmatization of Saint Francis. *Photo: Pesaro, Museo Civico.*

space. Perhaps Bellini's drawings in Paris and Venice (figs. 55, 58) were studies for this conception, but now three figures surround Christ and prepare his body for entombment. They crowd around him near the picture plane; the composition is compressed to intensify the concentration of the mourners. An old man, Joseph of Arimathea, gently supports Christ's body from behind and has wrapped his body in a white cloth in preparation for burial, as described in the Gospels: "And Joseph took the body, and wrapped it in a clean linen shroud, and laid it in his own new tomb" (Matt. 27:59–61, also Mark 15:46–47 and Luke 23:53–56). In Bellini's interpretation, Joseph seems literally to share his tomb with Christ.

Joseph's unseeing gaze falls on the metal ointment vessel held by his companion, Nicodemus: "Nicodemus also . . . came bringing a mixture of myrrh and aloes. . . . They took the body of Jesus, and bound it in linen cloths with the spices, as is the

*88.* Pietà (Dead Christ with Joseph of Arimathea, Nicodemus, and Saint Mary Magdalen), *Pinacoteca Vaticana, Vatican City. Photo: Archivio Fotografico Coll. Mus. Vaticani.*

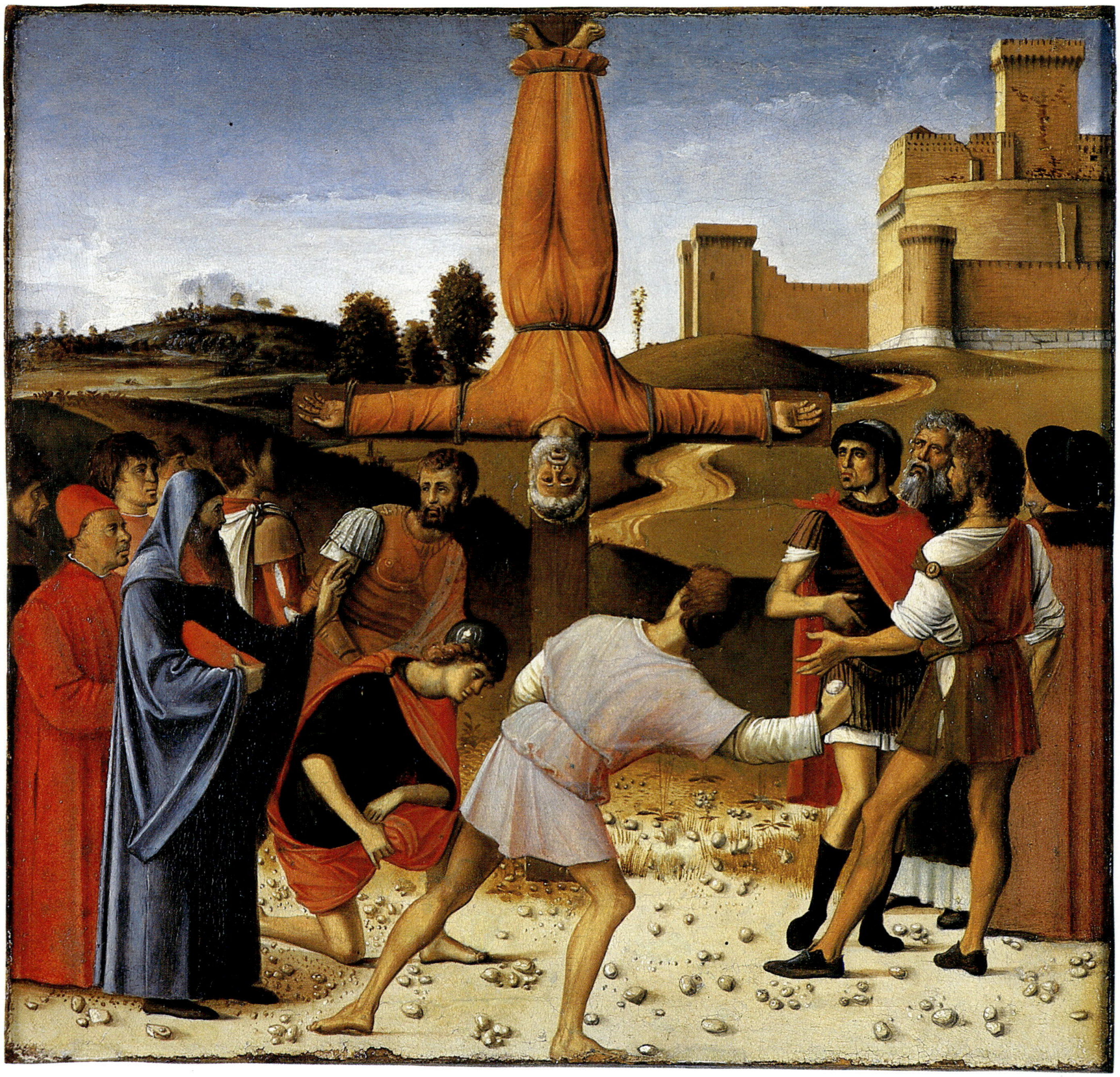

90. *Pesaro altarpiece, detail, predella,* Crucifixion of Saint Peter. *Photo: Pesaro, Museo Civico.*

burial custom of the Jews" (John 19:39–40). The Magdalen holds Christ's hand in hers, gently anointing or caressing the wound (fig. 94). Her parted lips and the movement of her long hair suggest her weeping as she performs her last service, and the slow, deliberate action of her hands expresses her grief as a controlled act of veneration. Bellini manipulated light and shade to make the anointing of the wound the focal point of the asymmetrical composition.

This emphasis on the wounded hand of the Crucified is related to the Franciscan cult of the wounds and to the belief that Christ inflicted these wounds on Francis in the miracle of the stigmatization, which is depicted in the predella (fig. 90).[18] When the *Pietà* was set above the *Coronation* (a Franciscan altarpiece), the Crucified Christ would have been turned toward Francis, who displays the identical

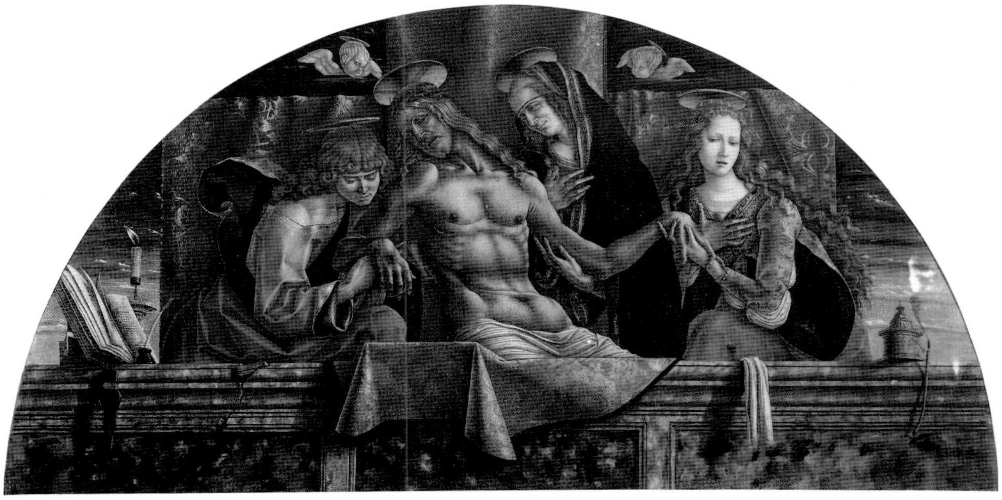

92. *Carlo Crivelli,* Pietà, *Pinacoteca di Brera, Milan. Photo: Sovrintendenza per i Beni Artistici e Storici, Milan.*

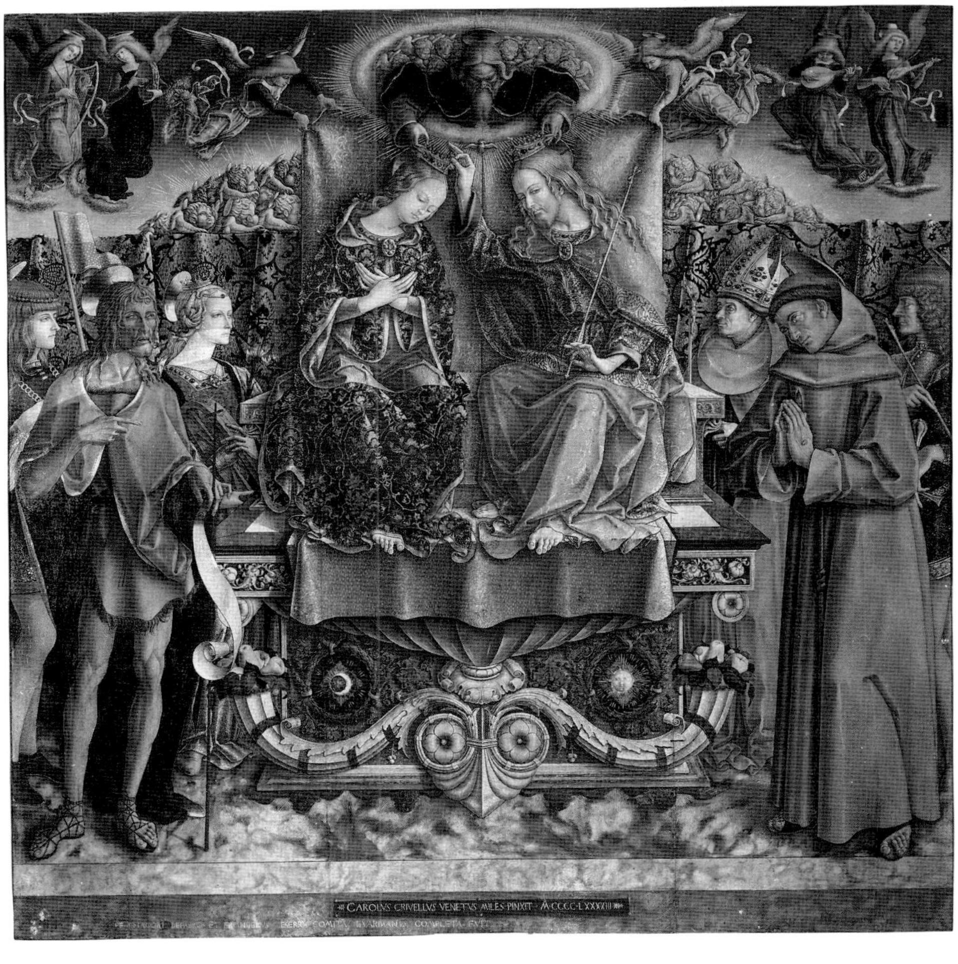

91. *Carlo Crivelli,* Coronation of the Virgin, *Pinacoteca di Brera, Milan. Photo: Sovrintendenza per i Beni Artistici e Storici, Milan.*

wounds of crucifixion. The Crucified himself effectively duplicates the posture of the Lord enthroned in heaven, though facing in the opposite direction.[19]

Christ's mourners seem to have transmitted not only their colors—warm brown tones, whites, and reds—but also their mood to those who witness the Virgin's Coronation. The inference is clear: this is a coronation of a queen by a king who achieved glory only after both had suffered. Christ's redemptive sacrifice, in which the Virgin shared as coredeemer, has made possible their reunion and triumph. Even the cherubim who hover in the sky express not joy but rather, by the directions of their glances, the poignant juxtaposition of the dead Christ with the King of Heaven. Only one putto turns toward the viewer, the cherub above the only saint who addresses us directly, Paul, Apostle to the Gentiles. His red mantle, the brightest color in the composition, reiterates the command of his gaze. Paul exhorts the Christian congregation of San Francesco as though they require conversion or the renewal of faith, and his own paroxysmatic conversion is represented beneath him in the predella (fig. 96). Paul's aggressive attribute, the sword, casts a shadow on the throne, and unlike any of the other saints, Paul steps forward, the staunch defender of the church. With Paul is Peter, the foundation stone of the church, who gazes lovingly at his Bible. His martyrdom for Christ is the subject of his predella (fig. 90).

Peter and Paul, martyrs of the church, stand to Mary's right, that is, next to the personification of the church. Next to Christ are the confessor saints Jerome and Francis, who serve the church by their exemplary penance and compassionate contemplation of Christ's suffering and by spreading Christ's word, Jerome as the translator of the Vulgate, Francis as the preacher who addressed the faithful in their own language.[20] Francis, the *Alter Christus* (Imitator of Christ), holds a crucifix, one of his traditional attributes, recalling the Passion. Of the four saints, only he completely displays his hands—marked with the wounds of Christ. Jerome reads his Bible, resting it on the arm of Christ's throne so that the book and Jerome's hand are visually locked with the silhouette of Christ himself: the Word, and the Word made flesh.[21] Jerome's predella panel illustrates his repentant contemplation of Christ's cross (fig. 98). Christ is somber as he crowns his mother, and she acquiesces with characteristic humility, bending before him with her hands crossed on her breast. This posture recalls her demeanor at the Annunciation (fig. 190), and indeed it was Mary's role in the Incarnation that merited her exemption from the corruption of death and the assumption of her body and soul into heaven as the Lord's consort. As the Venetian patriarch Lorenzo Giustinian recounted in his sermon for the feast of the Assumption, when Christ welcomed his mother as Queen of Heaven, she acceded to her honor with the words she had spoken when he became incarnate. "'Ascend to the throne that I have prepared for you,' Christ urged her, 'take the crown set with gems' [Ps. 20:4]. And the Virgin accepted, despite her sense of unworthiness: 'I shall not draw back, nor shall I contradict, but consent to your will, with a reverent acquiescence of mind, and with those same words that I spoke when I conceived you . . . "Behold the handmaid of the Lord; be it unto me according to thy word."'"[22]

Mary's humility is evident not only in her comportment but in her modest garments, their simplicity contrasted with the brocade worn by Christ and the rich colors that adorn the saints. This humble conception of the Virgin is repeated in the predella panel of the *Nativity*, in which the mother kneels before her Son, anticipating her veneration of him in heaven (fig. 97).

*93. Reconstruction of Pesaro altarpiece. Photo: Pesaro, Museo Civico.*

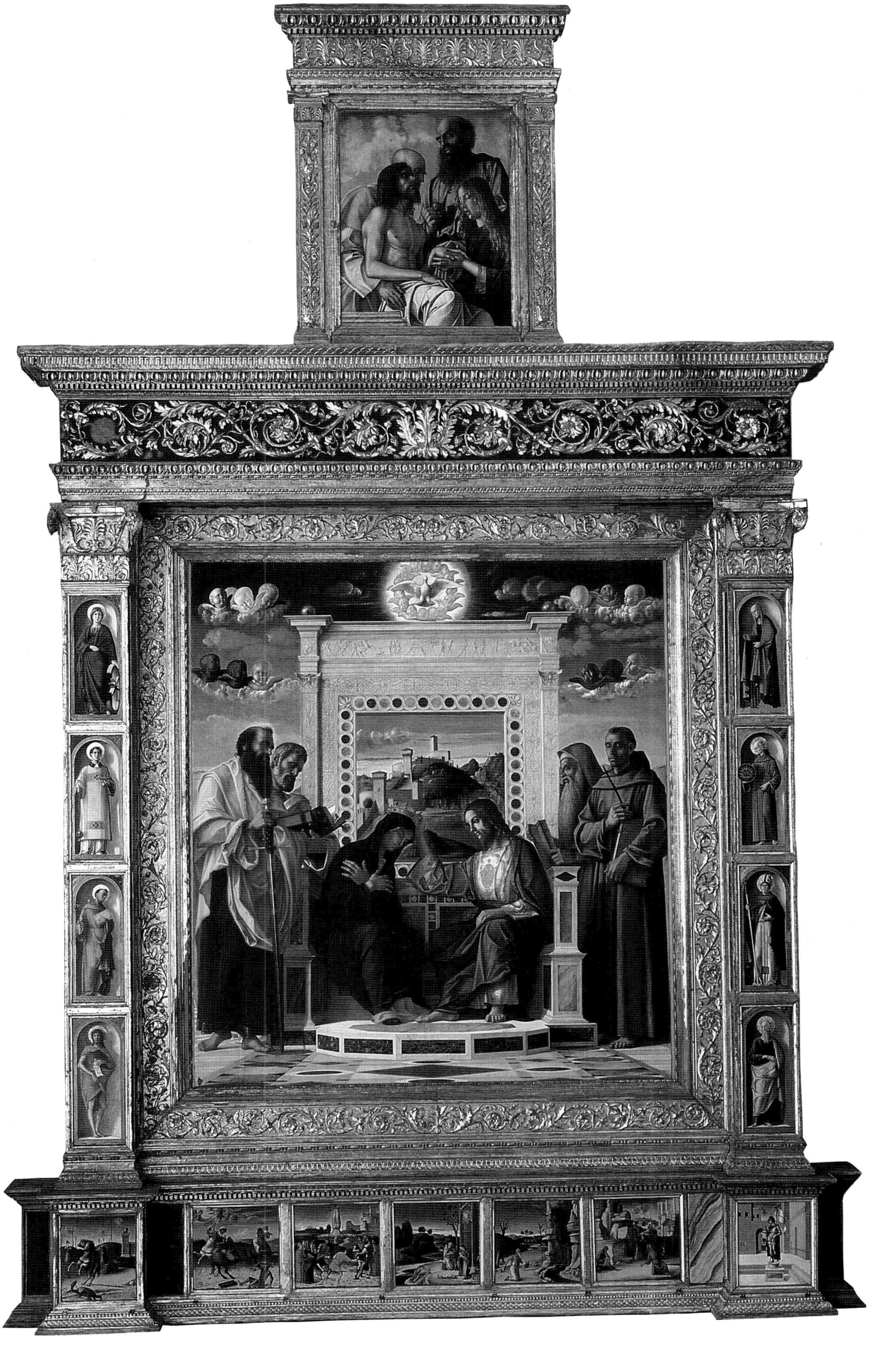

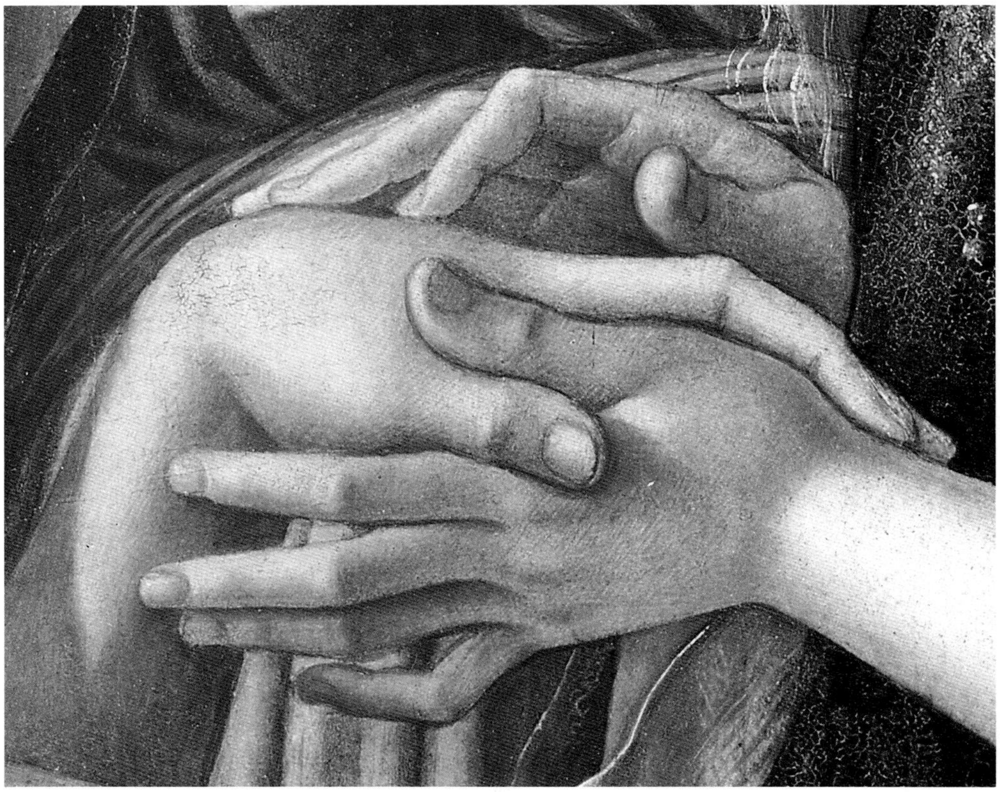

*94.* Pietà (Dead Christ with Joseph of Arimathea, Nicodemus, and Saint Mary Magdalen), *detail. Photo: Archivio Fotografico Coll. Mus. Vaticani.*

In Giustinian's sermon, as in other texts and in other Venetian depictions of the Coronation of the Virgin, God the Father is present to honor and to welcome his daughter.[23] In Crivelli's *Coronation*, which is otherwise similar in its arrangement of parts and composition to Bellini's Pesaro altarpiece, he appears as a half-length figure in a glory of cherubim above Mary and Christ, placing crowns on both their heads (figs. 91, 92). In the *Coronation of the Virgin* by Guariento, whose example was followed by Giambono, Jacobello del Fiore, and the Vivarini, the Father is enthroned with Mary and Christ, appropriately raised higher than they, and placing his hands on their shoulders to embrace them (figs. 13, 66). These compositions, like Crivelli's, all include the Dove as well, completing the Holy Trinity—but Bellini depicted only the Son and the Holy Spirit; the Father has apparently been omitted. Why is this so?

The answer may lie in the setting of Bellini's *Coronation*, for in this too the artist departed from tradition. The Virgin and Christ are enthroned together in an architectonic throne with ornamental reliefs that repeat the foliate motifs of the inner frame. The general arrangement—an inner square area surrounded by a rectangular frame with pilasters supporting a cornice or entablature—is echoed in the actual enframement.[24] The back of the throne opens to a landscape that clearly does not continue the vistas behind the saints to the left and right. The realm seen behind Mary and Christ, with its crenellated walls and fortress towers, evoking the castle of Gradara near Pesaro, represents the heavenly citadel, the celestial Jerusalem.[25] God the Father is there, and indeed the landscape seems to enclose Mary and Christ no less than the embracing arms of the Father in Coronations

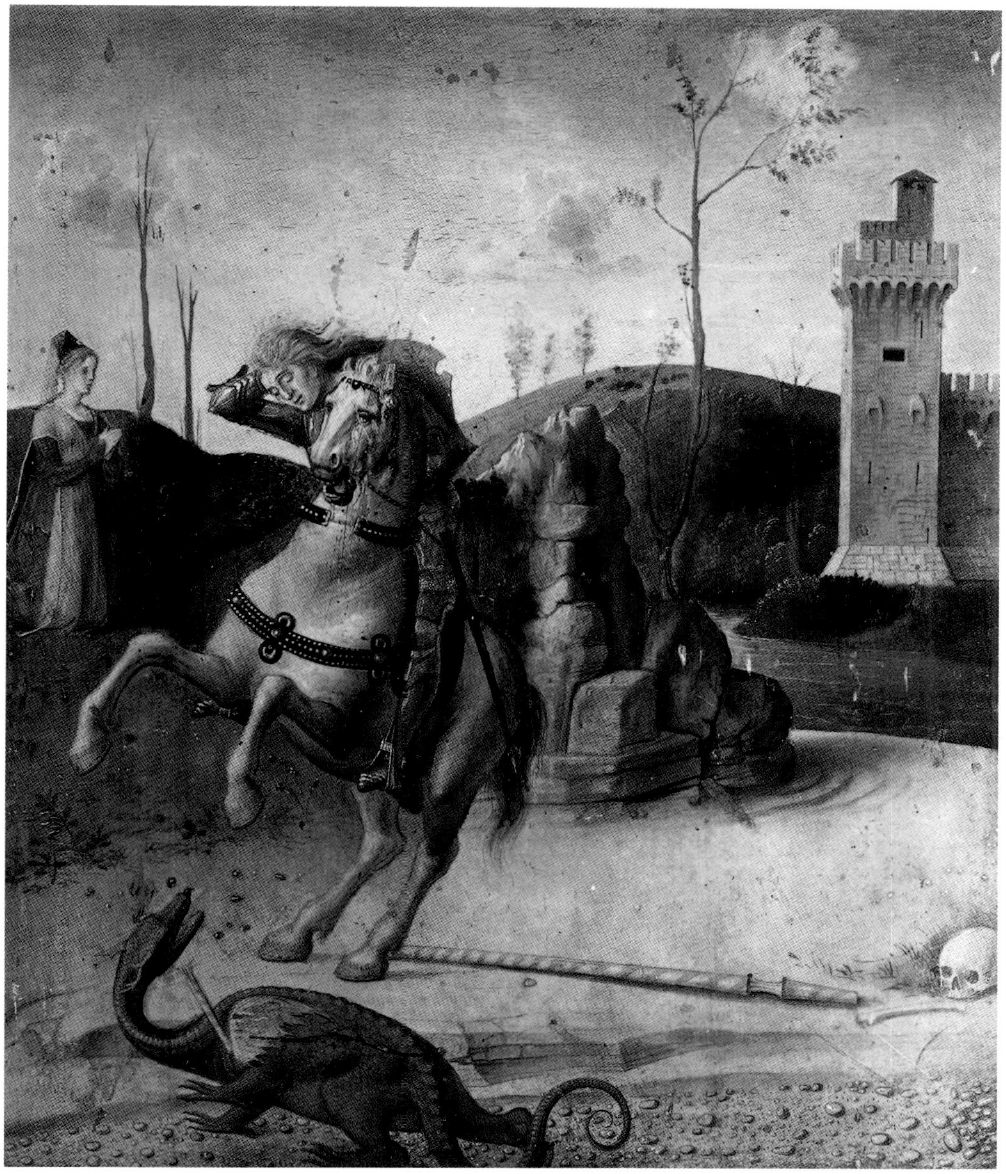

95. *Pesaro altarpiece, detail, predella,* Saint George Slaying the Dragon. *Photo: Archivio Fotografico del Museo Correr, Venice.*

by other masters. The opening in the throne alludes to the Madonna as the Gate, Portal, or Window of Heaven, the *Porta* or *Fenestra Coeli*; and the place to which she gives access, the Heavenly Jerusalem, is the Kingdom of God the Father.[26]

The format of the altarpiece is elaborate and rich, and though ornamentation and sumptuousness were not new to Venetian art, Bellini's means of achieving them here are different. In the Pesaro altarpiece, the decorative roles usually assigned to sculpture have been assumed by painting: instead of carved figures or motifs, such as those adorning altarpieces by the Vivarini or Jacobello del Fiore, Bellini embellished his frame with painted images, not only in the predella, as was customary, but in the pilasters. The altarpiece thus resembles Byzantine icons in its use of smaller figures to surround the central image and an additional frame within the pilasters. The saints who usually constitute the court of heaven have been banished to the periphery. The eight saints of the pilasters—Catherine, Lawrence, Anthony of Padua, and John the Baptist, on the left, and on the right, the

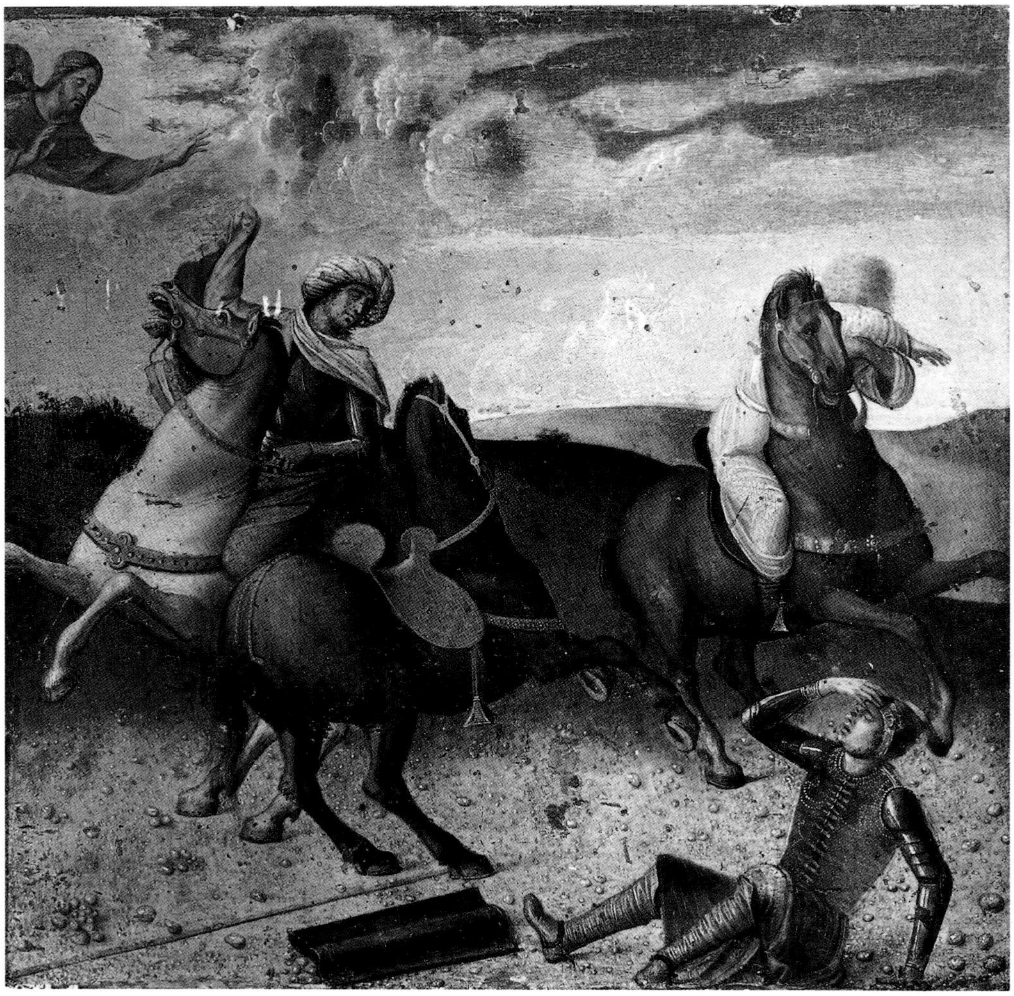

96. *Pesaro altarpiece, detail, predella,* Conversion of Saint Paul. *Photo: Archivio Fotografico del Museo Correr, Venice.*

Franciscans Bl. Michelina, Bernardino of Siena, Louis of Toulouse, with Andrew —witness the Coronation (fig. 100). Standing in illusionistic niches, the figures move and gaze in different directions, animated and independent within their limited spaces. Light comes from the left, casting shadows to the right, as in the *Coronation* and *Pietà*. The effect is remarkably spacious and luminous.

The predella narratives are likewise unified with the main panel, among themselves, and with the bases of the frame pilasters by various visual and contextual means (figs. 89, 90, 95–99). The horizon lines are essentially continuous throughout the seven scenes (five in the predella proper and two on the bases of the pilasters), lighting is consistent, and the compositions are arranged so that the one leads into the next as though they were sequential episodes. Of course, they are not: the narratives represent unrelated events from the lives of Mary and Christ (the *Nativity*), of the saints represented in the main panel above, and, in the pilaster bases, scenes of Saints George and Terentius, who otherwise do not appear in the altarpiece. Although the first three depict scenes of violence—George slaying the dragon, Paul's conversion, Peter's death—the fourth and central panel, the poetic *Nativity*, signifies a change in mood. The scenes to the right, *Saint Jerome in the Desert*, the *Stigmatization of Saint Francis*, and *Saint Terentius*, patron of Pesaro,

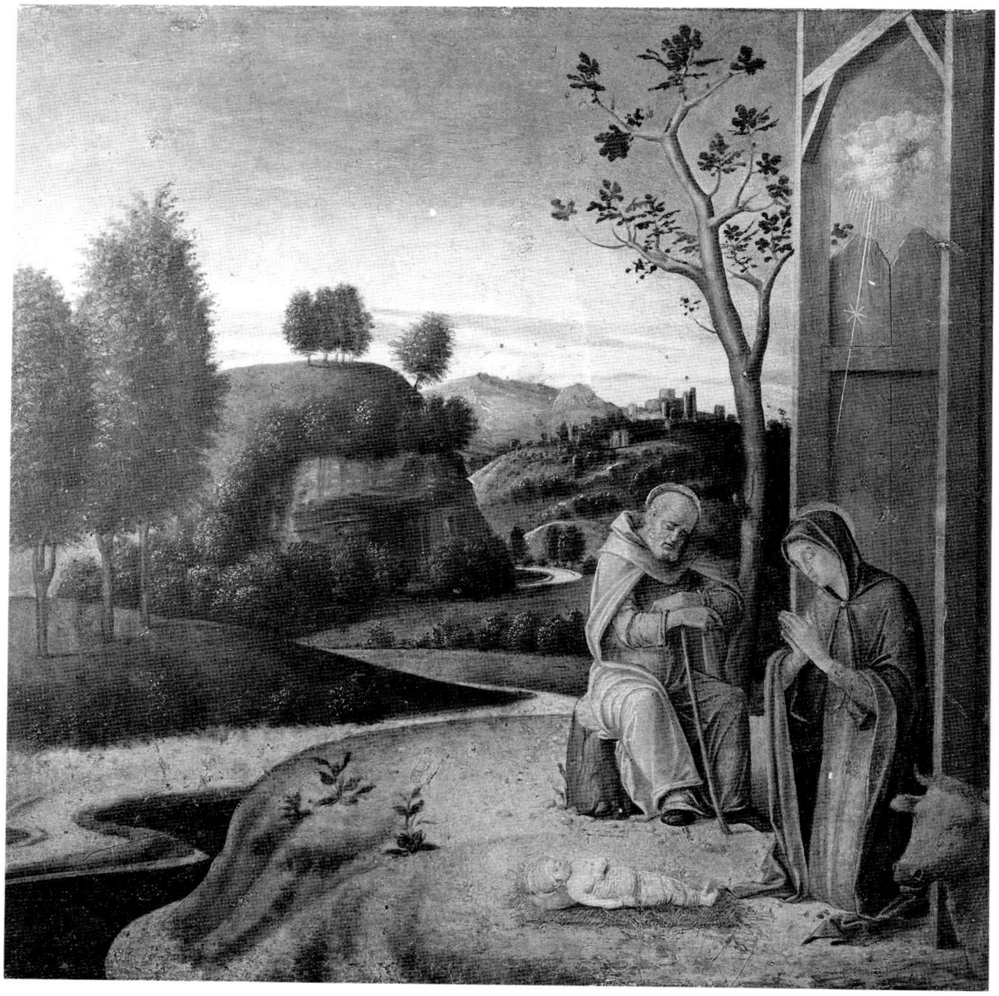

97. *Pesaro altarpiece, detail, predella,* Nativity. *Photo: Archivio Fotografico del Museo Correr, Venice.*

represent the introspection of prayer, the penitent contemplation of Christ's sacrifice, and the beneficence it brings. These compositions are remarkable for their dramatic power, the luminosity of the settings, and the variety of pose and action. In spite of their small scale, the predella panels preserve something of the quality and narrative force of Bellini's lost mural paintings for the Great Council Hall.[27]

One of the panels, the *Crucifixion of Saint Peter*, may contain a clue to the painting's commission (fig. 90). Upside-down on his cross, in cruel deference to the saint's expression of unworthiness to imitate Christ's martyrdom, Peter is being stoned by one of his executioners, a man in the central foreground, shown about to let fly one of his missiles. This is an unusual gloss on the legend of Peter's death, one not included in Voragine's description of the martyrdom.[28] Nor was it characteristic of Bellini to elaborate a scene of suffering with such a sadistic detail. It may be that the episode had historical significance. The man who was sitting on the throne of Saint Peter when Bellini painted his altarpiece was Sixtus IV della Rovere (pope, 1471–84), a patron of the Sforza of Pesaro, who had himself been stoned in Rome on his coronation day in 1471, a shocking event that must have distressed the pope's supporters.[29] Perhaps Bellini was requested to represent Peter being stoned in allusion to the appalling mistreatment suffered by Sixtus IV

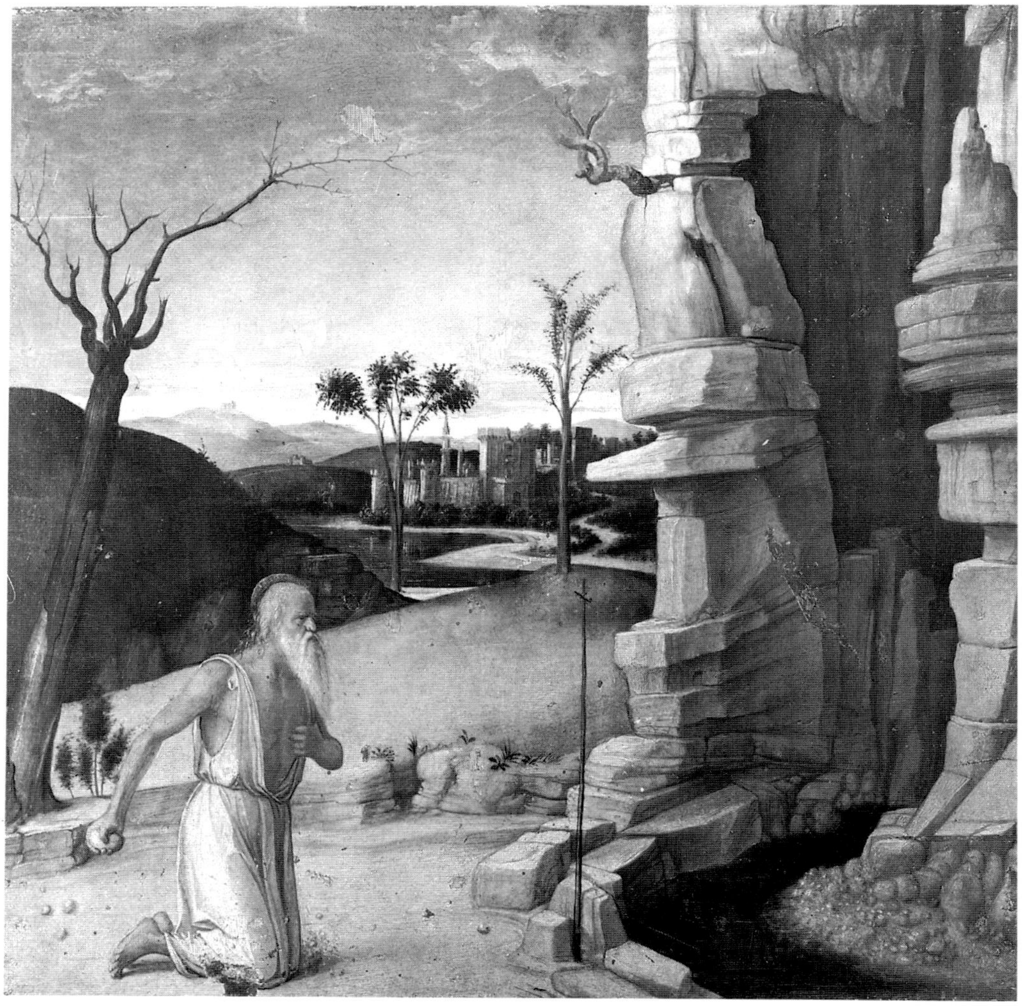

*98. Pesaro altarpiece, detail, predella,* Saint Jerome in the Desert. *Photo: Archivio Fotografico del Museo Correr, Venice.*

—in which case the altarpiece, or at least this part of it, would postdate the pope's coronation.

Another feature of Bellini's composition suggests its relevance to contemporary people and events: one witness of Peter's martyrdom, the man standing at the edge of the crowd to the left, wearing ruby red with a bright red cap, is almost certainly a portrait (fig. 101). His full lips, bulbous chin, thick, round nose, and bags under his eyes distinguish him as an individual, and his red cap resembles hats worn by men in contemporary portraits, such as the so-called self-portrait by Antonello da Messina in London, dated circa 1470–75. Perhaps the man with short dark hair behind Bellini's figure is a portrait as well. Nor should this surprise us: Masaccio had similarly included portraits, presumably of his patrons, in the *Adoration of the Magi* predella panel for the Pisa *Madonna*; Domenico Veneziano added portrait likenesses to the train of the Magi in his *Adoration* tondo; and other masters of the first half of the century, and occasionally even artists of the fourteenth century, incorporated the visages of actual men and women into their compositions. In short, by the time Bellini painted the Pesaro altarpiece, there was already a tradition of inserting portraits into sacred narratives, disguising them, so to speak, as onlookers. The donor or donors of Bellini's altarpiece might well

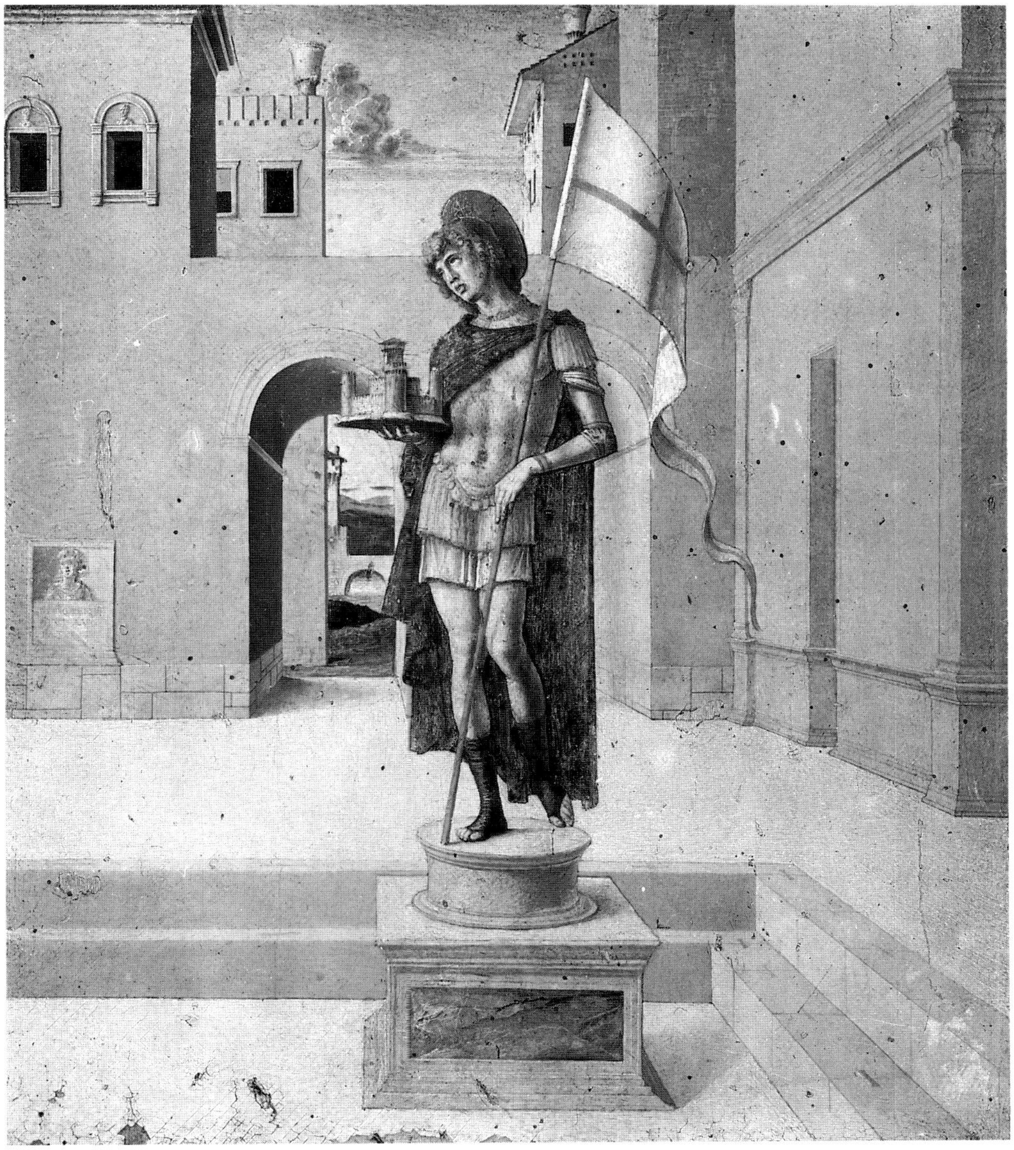

99. *Pesaro altarpiece, detail, predella,* Saint Terentius, Patron Saint of Pesaro. *Photo: Archivio Fotografico del Museo Correr, Venice.*

have considered the inclusion of their portraits in the scene of Peter's martyrdom particularly appropriate, not only because of the papal associations of the theme but because, according to legend, the crowd that witnessed the apostle's death was friendly to him and wished to save him. Perhaps Peter was the onomastic saint of Bellini's patron, but nothing is known of the commission except the original site of the painting on the high altar of the church of San Francesco, which suggests that the friars themselves were in part responsible for the work.[30]

Bellini's first altarpiece had depicted the Transfiguration of Christ, and he returned to that theme almost twenty years later. The juxtaposition of the two works is startling; the first only hints at the majesty of the second (figs. 9, 102, 103).[31] The experience of earlier commissions—notably the *Agony in the Garden*, the *Saint Francis*, and the Pesaro altarpiece—had made this possible, and Bellini's understanding of the biblical text of the Transfiguration made it inevitable, seemingly predetermined and yet innovative.

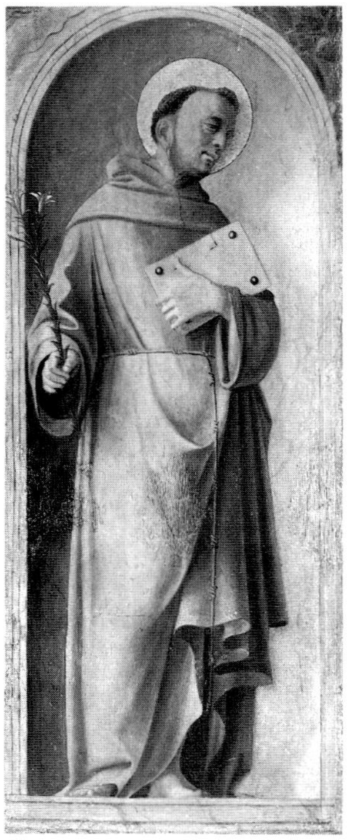

*100. Pesaro altarpiece, detail, frame pilaster,* Saint Anthony of Padua. *Photo: Archivio Fotografico del Museo Correr, Venice.*

Sky and landscape had become central to Bellini's art by the mid-1470s, no longer subsidiary but equal to figures in the communication of mood and meaning. Bellini achieved this expressive use of landscape not through symbolism but by visualizing the words of the Gospels. "A bright cloud overshadowed them," we are told, "and a voice from the cloud said, 'This is my beloved Son . . . ; listen to him'" (Matt. 17:5). Bellini abandoned the traditional, figural formula of depicting God in a supernatural glory of cherubim and instead represented the Creator in the substance of his creation, in light and color. By rendering biblical text in this naturalistic way, Bellini was revolutionizing art.

God appears in the "bright cloud," illuminating the sky, indeed the world. In Bellini's original conception, the splendor of the divine presence was still more dazzling, uninterrupted by the dense foliage of the tree to the right, added by an unknowing hand sometime in the sixteenth century. And the "bright cloud" of the divinity takes corporeal form—becomes incarnate—in the glowing figure of Christ, which is the theological point of the Transfiguration. Christ is the luminous, coloristic, and figural equivalent of the heavens, the embodiment of this light and air, and this reveals his identity: "His face shone like the sun, and his garments became white as light." Only Christ wears white here, in contrast to Bellini's earlier *Transfiguration*, where James's white mantle detracts from Christ's uniqueness. Bellini has illustrated Christ's words, "Ego sum lux mundi" ("I am the light of the world"). But Christ's white is not mere white, undiluted from the painter's pigments: the white seems to contain and reflect all the surrounding colors, as does the sky itself. Similarly, Christ's translucent gold halo forms the geometrical counterpart of the sun's golden glow in the clouds; Bellini painted this halo in part for this luminous and coloristic effect.

In Bellini's world God is manifest, his presence felt and his acknowledgment of his Son heard, not because a glory of cherubim appears but because the Holy Spirit infuses both heavens and earth. Every detail of the landscape suggests God's presence, and Bellini translates the mundane into the sacred through atmospheric light. The profound association of setting and figures—their harmonious equivalence—is new in Bellini's art, as is their relation by scale and by form and rhythm. Tree branches repeat Moses' contours, for example, and the distant mountains echo Elijah's. Above all, the surrounding atmosphere unites the composition: sunlight falls on the blond stone buildings in the background, making their illuminated geometric faces and shadowed recesses the architectural equivalent of the rocks in the foreground, and shades of the same or closely related hues are repeated—the blues worn by James are echoed in the sky, and the earth tones of John's mantle and the colors worn by Peter make them the figural equivalent of the hills.

Setting and figures have taken on a new dignity that is at once physical and spiritual. Shapes are larger and bulkier: the swelling contours of the landscape are broad and smooth; the garments that the figures wear fall in complicated but

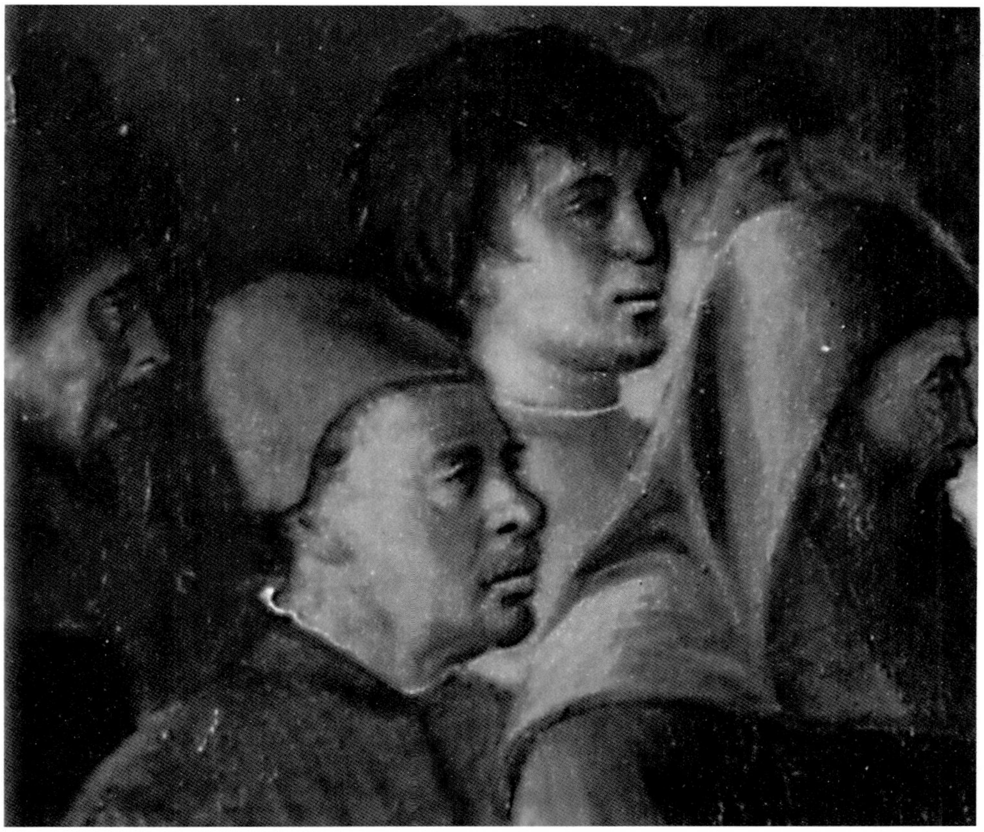

*101. Pesaro altarpiece, predella,* Crucifixion of Saint Peter, *detail, witnesses of Saint Peter's martyrdom. Photo: Pesaro, Museo Civico.*

naturalistic folds that always suggest volume and movement. Yet, remarkably, the panel is shorter than the early *Transfiguration* in the Correr Museum, although considerably wider, 115 × 150 centimeters: its monumentality is inherent and is unrelated to its measurements.

Light unifies the composition, which is centered in arrangement and spirit around the figure of Christ. Only he is seen complete: frontal and symmetrical in an otherwise asymmetrical composition. Even Bellini's abbreviated signature IOANNES BELLI. is off-center, and the diagonals of the fence play against the curving forms of the landscape and the postures of the figures while echoing their symmetry.

Bellini's conception of drama has also grown. Anecdotal and narrative behavior in the earlier *Transfiguration*, such as the suggestion that Peter is about to speak, has been restricted to the distant bucolic figures in favor of a less specific drama and more fully conceived psychology. As Christ converses with his prophets in the earlier painting, he raises his right hand in a gesture of salutation and blessing. In the later *Transfiguration*, Christ raises his hands in the ancient gesture of the orant, or praying figure. Christ's hierarchic posture and expression of calm assertiveness represent him as the Pantocrator who addresses us with formality and benevolence, and the demeanor of his Old Testament companions is determined by this. In the first *Transfiguration*, the three figures talk, as the Gospels describe, and in an informal, indeed literally colloquial, manner. But now their comportment is more sacramental, in keeping with the theological significance of the Transfiguration.

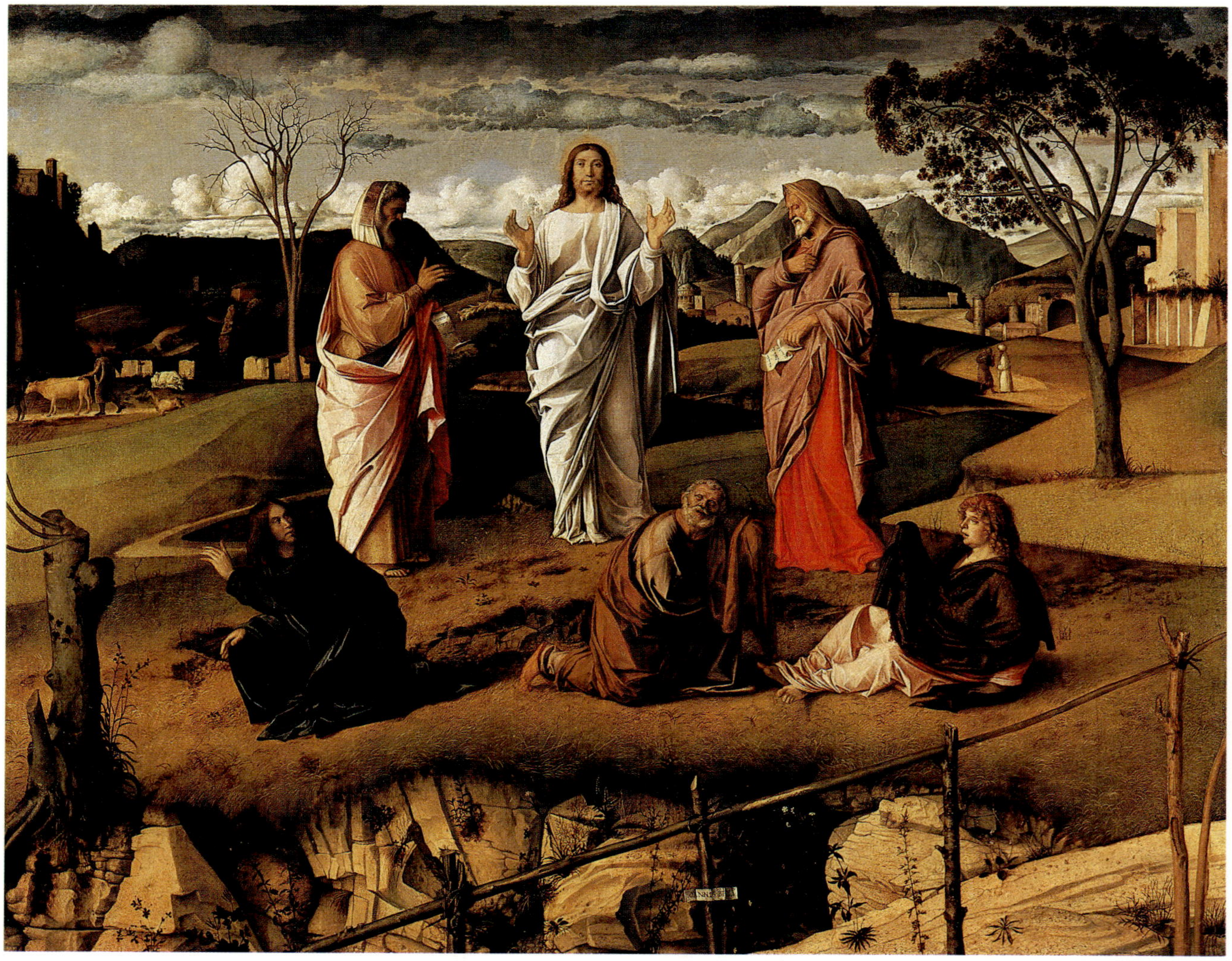

*102.* Transfiguration, *Museo di Capodimonte, Naples. Photo: Scala/Art Resource, New York.*

Bellini's painting was almost certainly commissioned for the funerary chapel of Archdeacon Alberto Fioccardo of Vicenza, which was dedicated to Christ in the cathedral of that city.[32] Fioccardo's testament of 8 July 1467 refers to the chapel construction as already underway ("incepta") and provides for its being "completed honorably and sumptuously" with an iron gate, a typical feature of private chapels in the Middle Ages and Renaissance.[33] The style of Bellini's altarpiece, which could certainly have been commissioned by 1467, suggests a date between 1475 and 1480, that is, after the Pesaro altarpiece, but it was not unusual that Fioccardo and his heirs had to wait so long for the chapel's crowning glory.[34]

Bellini apparently represented the Transfiguration for a third and final time, in a painting contemporary with the Naples panel, which survives only as two fragments, one with the bust of Christ and the other with the artist's signature, IOANNES BELLI / NUS ME PINXIT. (fig. 104).[35] Christ's incandescent white garments and exalted expression indicate what the subject must have been. Although the fragment has often been dated circa 1500, the geometrical formation of Christ's head and the drapery folds resemble his handling in much earlier works.

*103.* Transfiguration, *detail, Christ. Photo: Scala/Art Resource, New York.*

Bellini's next surviving narrative altarpiece depicted a related theme, the *Resur-*

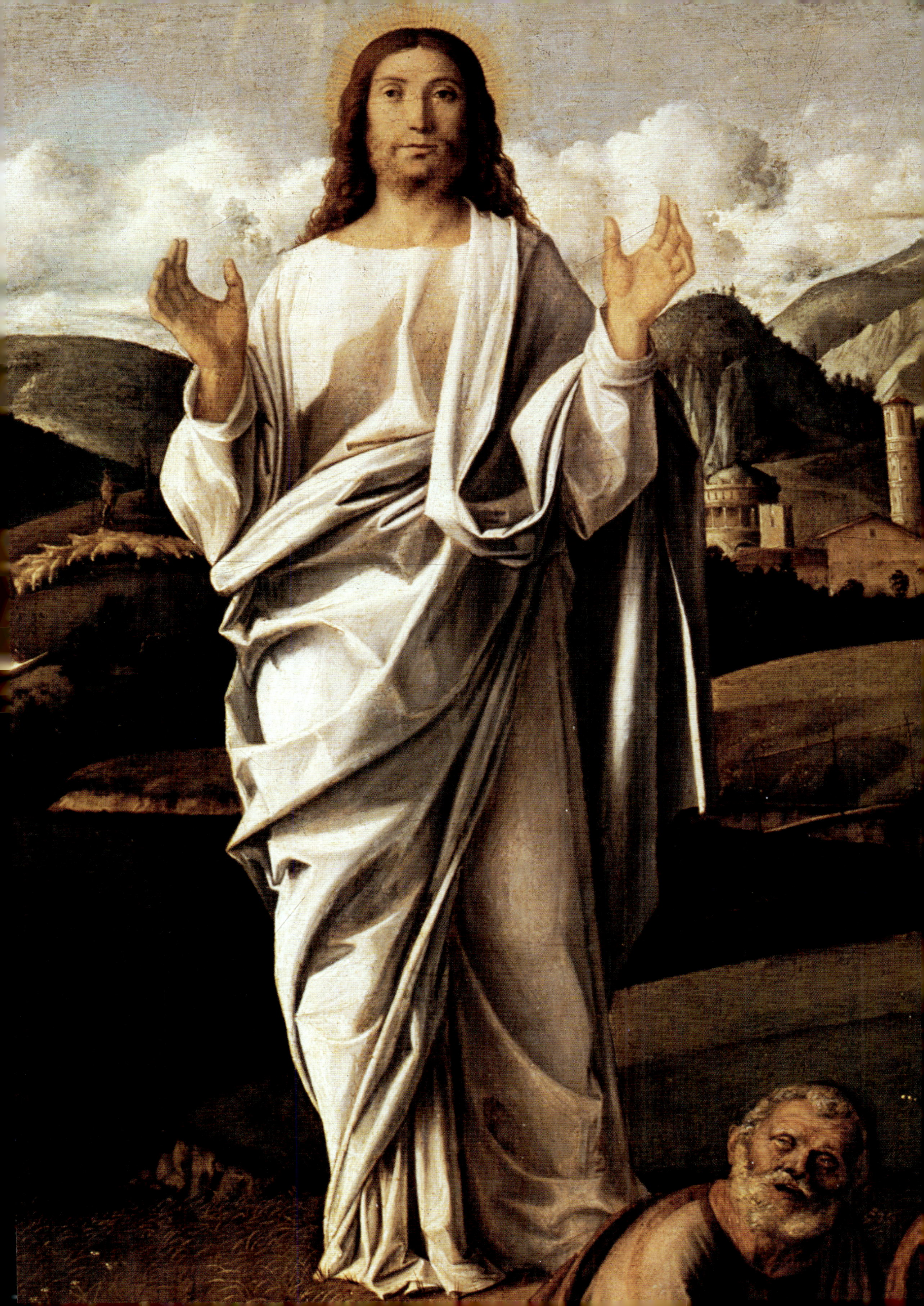

*rection of Christ*, commissioned by the Venetian patrician Marco Zorzi (Giorgio) for his family funerary chapel in San Michele in Isola (figs. 105, 106).[36] Because much of the relevant documentation survives, something of the thinking and practical mechanism of Zorzi's patronage can be reconstructed.

Founded in 1212, the Camaldolese church of San Michele in Isola, the island between Venice and Murano, had fallen into disrepair by the mid-fifteenth century. A rebuilding campaign began in 1469, and Mauro Codussi (Coducci) was employed to design the new construction. On 5 June 1475, the chapel to the right of the high altar was conceded to Marco Zorzi. The monks granted him permission to "have constructed a chapel in honor of . . . the glorious Virgin Mother Mary, in which chapel he might build a tomb for his body and for [the bodies of] his heirs and successors . . . and have erected an altar in honor of the glorious Virgin Mary."[37] Thus the chapel was always intended as the funerary chapel for Zorzi's family, a common arrangement: a chapel or altar was not just the locus of worship, it was a burial place, and future generations of the line would be interred there, with their ancestors. At San Michele not only the founder's mother but his son and eventually his descendants were all buried in the Zorzi Chapel.[38]

In the concession of 1475, Zorzi had agreed to furnish the altar with all that was necessary, "all the things and ornaments needed for celebration of Mass and all other divine offices," and he was also obligated to endow the Masses to be said there, in honor of the Virgin and for the benefit of his soul and the souls of his kinfolk. These customary provisions were guaranteed in perpetuity—at least, that was the intention, because souls are immortal—by the foundation of a *commessaria* to allocate appropriate funds after the donor's death. Nor was Marco Zorzi exceptional in endowing and constructing his funerary chapel before his death; so did many of his contemporaries, including Archdeacon Fioccardo of Vicenza and other patrons of Bellini. But Zorzi's endowment of his family funerary chapel differed in one regard: Zorzi seems to have changed his mind about the dedication of his altar, for by the time Bellini came to paint the altarpiece, the subject was no longer the Virgin Mary but the Resurrection.

Work seems to have proceeded apace, and by summer 1479, when Zorzi's mother requested burial there, she also provided funding for daily Masses to be said at the altar.[39] This implies that the chapel was complete, and the date is consistent with the style of Bellini's altarpiece.

Sansovino, writing in 1581, noted the Zorzi *Resurrection* and mentioned Bellini's use of oil, and in 1646 Ridolfi admired the armed custodians at the tomb, the mountainous landscape with its trees and animals, and the Three Marys walking in the distance.[40] The vista appealed to others: it was copied in a Bellinesque drawing evidently for use by the shop (fig. 107) and appears again and again in other paintings produced over more than two decades.[41]

Once again, Bellini has given almost half of the composition to sky, coloristically rich and atmospheric, streaked by cirrus clouds tinted red by the dawn. Christ appears there in a position of easy contrapposto, his feet rendered to suggest his standing on the cloudy air. His upward motion and the force of displaced air moving around him are suggested by his flying banner, windblown hair, and loincloth that swirls away from his body—a motif possibly derived from Rogier van der Weyden and used earlier by Bellini in his *Crucifixion* (fig. 5). Christ's posture is echoed ironically by the guard who stands below to the right. Armed and in armor, he looks toward the Resurrected and grasps his spear with both hands, his gesture the worldly and martial counterpoint to the blessing gesture of the Prince of Peace. The repetition of red and white underscores the connection.

Dramatic contrast is reiterated by the soldier in the left foreground who turns his back on the viewer to behold the miracle and by another guard who sleeps against the rocks. With one end of his loincloth pulled from his body, this oblivious soldier sprawls on the ground, providing a counterpart to Christ. The protagonist, highest and most active, is set against and above the lowest, most inert figure.

Just perceptibly larger than the other figures, central and almost frontal, Christ easily dominates this complex scene. Whereas the other figures are seen in naturalistic relations of scale to one another and to their environment, Christ is not —cannot be—delimited by spatial boundaries. This abnegation of the laws of nature, together with Christ's violation of gravity, endows the miracle with a visual conviction that is matched by the psychological and spiritual conviction of the Lord's demeanor and the behavior of the others—the slow, somber steps of his approaching mourners, the dazed wonderment of the awakened soldiers, and the unmindfulness of the other guards.

Light floods the scene from the left, or rather from the direction of Christ's right, blessing hand. The direction of light in the painting thus coincides with light that enters the Zorzi Chapel from an oculus window in the south wall (fig. 106). On earth, the soldiers and their weapons cast shadows against the rocks and the ground, while in heaven, Christ casts shadows against himself to confirm the reality of his triumphant Resurrection. As in his earlier works, Bellini depicted light and atmosphere not only for the sake of naturalism—armor that reflects light and color, for example—but also to unite his composition and to convey mood and meaning.

By the time Bellini had completed the *Transfiguration* and the *Resurrection*, he was the unrivaled master of sacred images in landscape settings. At the same moment he conquered architectural space, in his altarpiece for the Observant Franciscan church of San Giobbe in Venice (figs. 108–10).[42]

In the San Giobbe altarpiece, Bellini placed the Madonna and Child and saints in a church setting, and so logical does this seem that we take for granted what was a remarkable innovation, the first such composition in Venetian art and one of the first in Italian art. The altarpiece was painted for the second altar on the right of San Giobbe, where the original marble frame may still be seen (figs. 111–

*Overleaf:*
*104.* Christ *(fragment), Gallerie dell'Accademia, Venice. Photo: Giacomelli Fotografia, Venice.*

*105.* Resurrection of Christ, *Gemäldegalerie, Staatliche Museen Preussischer Kulturbesitz, Berlin (West). Photo: Jörg P. Anders.*

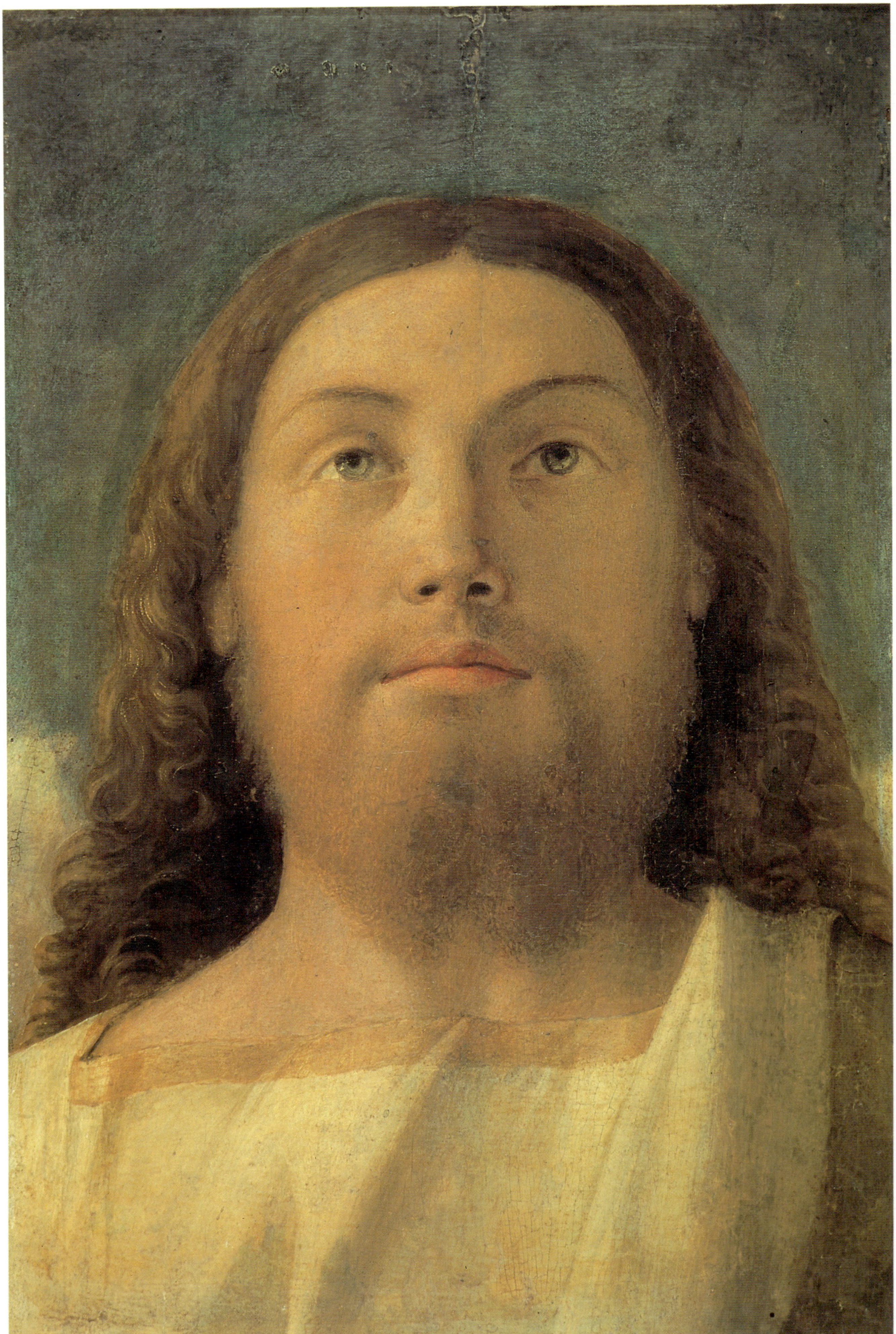

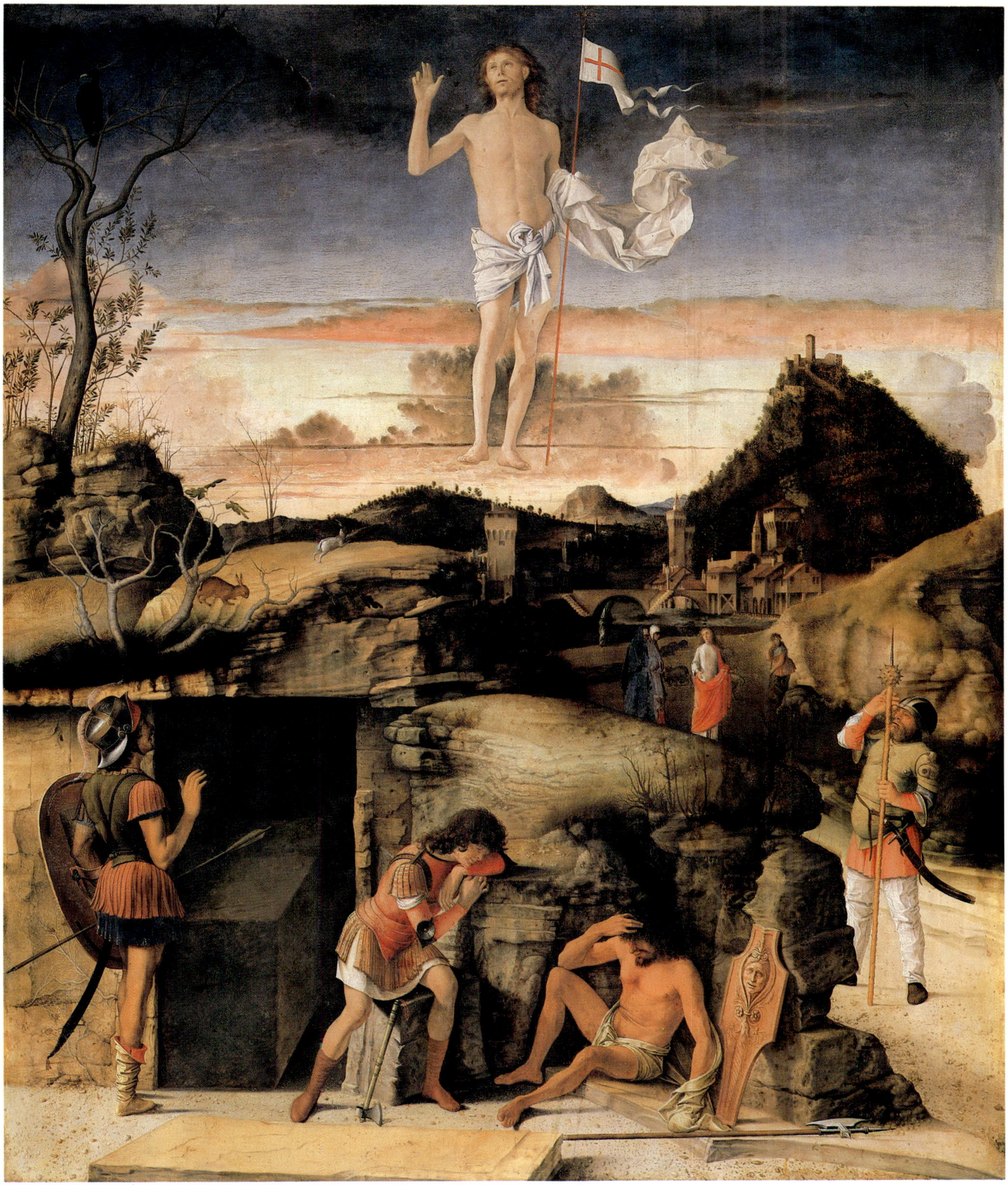

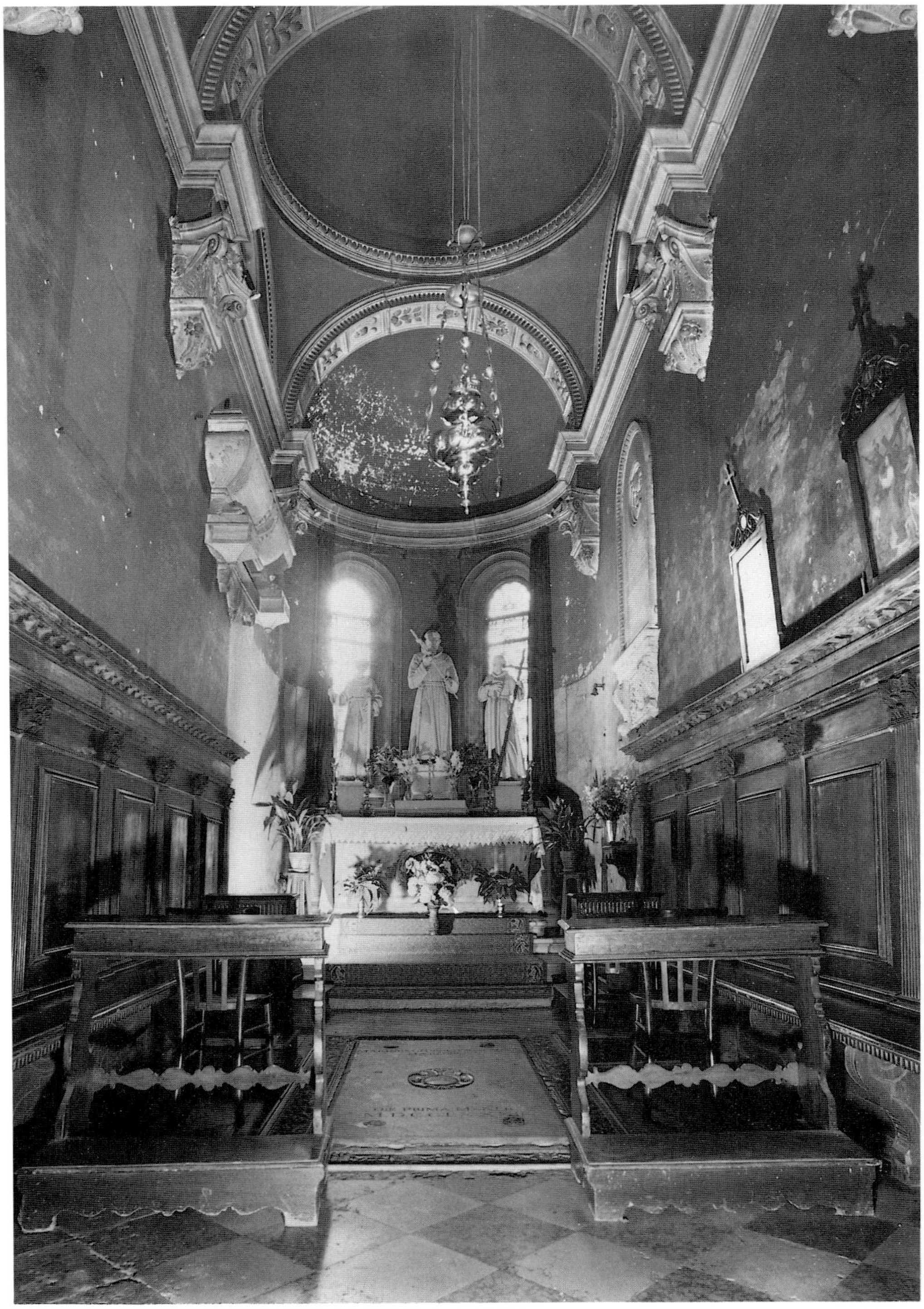

*106. Zorzi Chapel of the Resurrection, San Michele in Isola, Venice. Photo: Gianfranco Spinazzi, Venice.*

13). As in SS. Giovanni e Paolo (fig. 83), panel and frame display an illusionistic continuity of design and space, so that the beholder's world becomes the prelude to the sacred realm of the painting. The duplication of motifs in the actual and fictive architecture may indicate that Bellini was involved in plans for the altar itself; perhaps it was his own design, executed in stone.[43]

At SS. Giovanni e Paolo, the pictorial architecture opened at the sides and back, revealing the sky. For the San Giobbe altarpiece, Bellini constructed the apse of a church, with richly veined marble paneling and a gold-ground mosaic. This

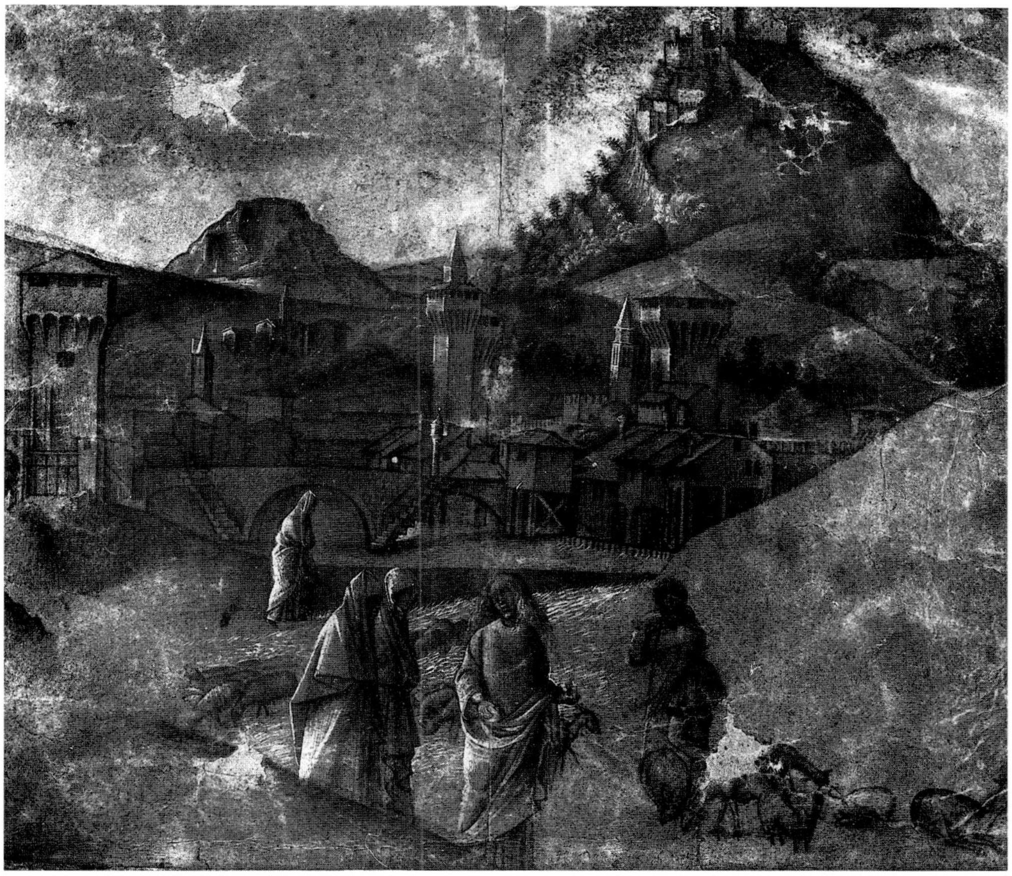

107. *Bellini studio,* View of Monselice: Landscape with Buildings, the Three Marys, and Saint John, *brush drawing, Biblioteca and Pinacoteca Ambrosiana, Milan.*

was no mere exercise in illusionism, although Bellini's command of perspective is dazzling. His architectural invention was conceived to express the meaning of this altarpiece.

Bellini raised the Madonna and Child high on a pedestal, signing his name, IOANNES BELLINVS, on a cartellino affixed to the base. The three singing boys of the SS. Giovanni e Paolo altarpiece have been replaced at San Giobbe by angels who play celestial music on prestigious instruments, the lute and the *lira da braccio*. Their elegance befits Bellini's luxurious setting and honors Job, a patron of music.[44]

To the proper right of the altarpiece, the position of honor and closest to the high altar of San Giobbe, are Francis, John the Baptist, and, nearest the Child, Job (Giobbe), venerated as a saint in Venice and a titular saint of this church.[45] Counterbalancing them are Sebastian, Dominic, and the Franciscan bishop Louis of Toulouse.[46] Each triad is grouped in triangular formation but oriented in different directions, and the lower, broader pyramid of the three musical angels in the center echoes the formula. This geometry, seemingly natural but carefully contrived, has a close parallel in the contemporary work of Leonardo da Vinci, notably the unfinished *Adoration of the Magi* (fig. 114), the keynote of the new High Renaissance style in Florence. The underlying qualities that characterize Leonardo's *Adoration* also distinguish Bellini's San Giobbe altarpiece, more

*Overleaf:*
108. *San Giobbe altarpiece, Gallerie dell'Accademia, Venice. Photo: Giacomelli Fotografia, Venice.*

109. *San Giobbe altarpiece, detail, Saint Francis. Photo: Giacomelli Fotografia, Venice.*

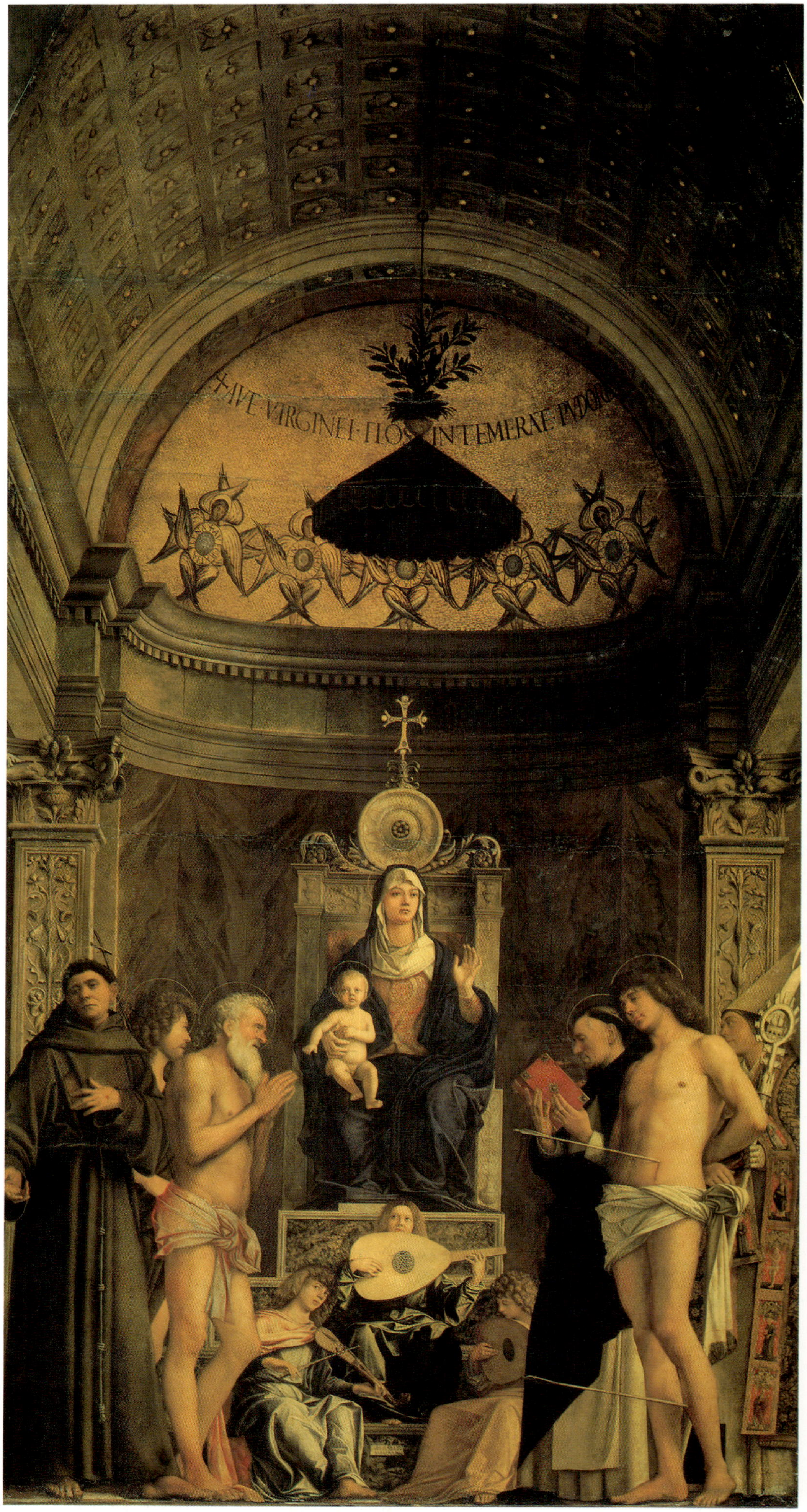
AVE·VIRGINEI·FLOS INTEMERATAE·PVDOR

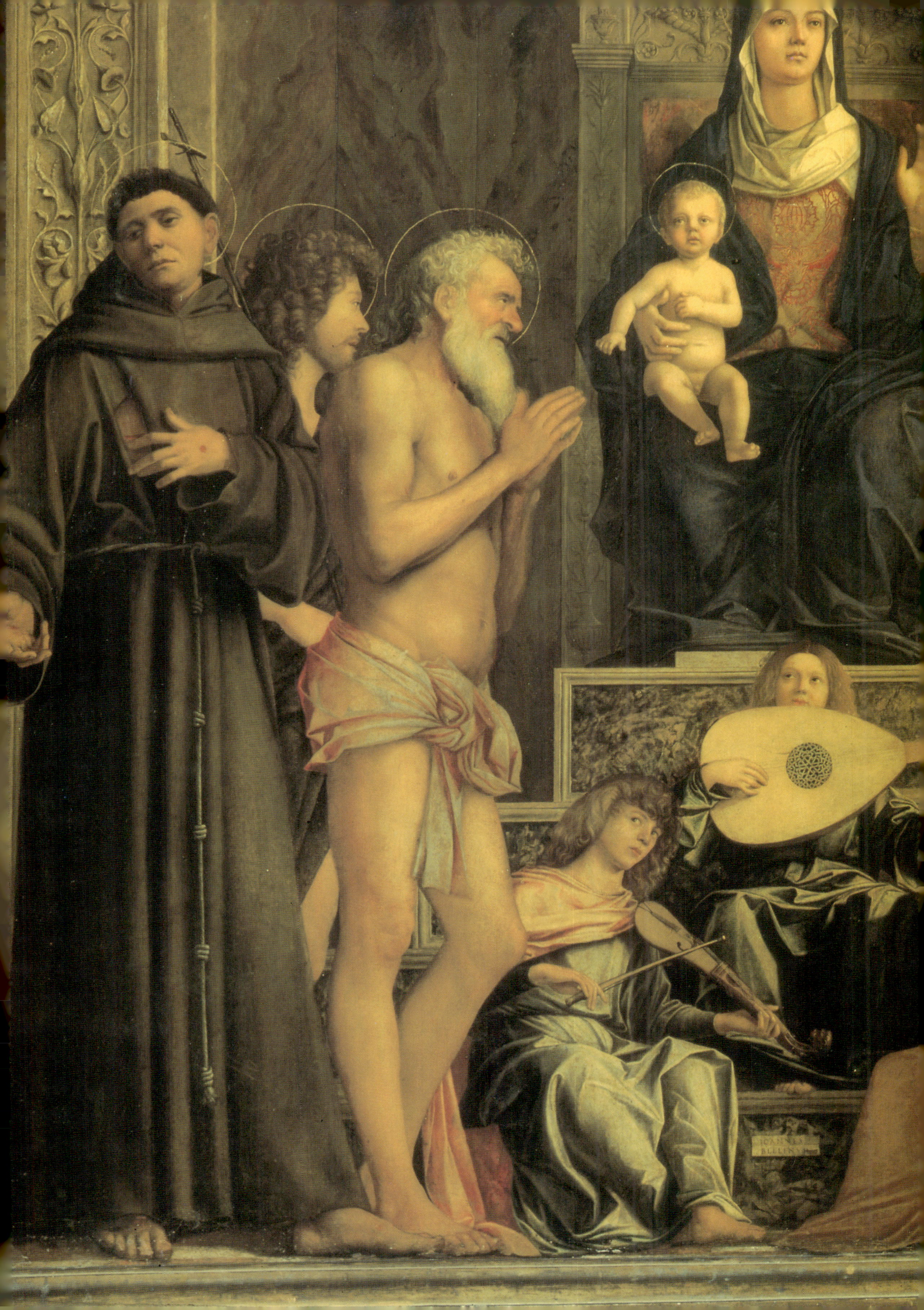

tightly composed than such earlier works as the *Resurrection* (fig. 105). And like Leonardo, Bellini sought to create individuals in whom unseen character and spirit are fully and harmoniously expressed in outward appearance.

Francis turns toward us, inviting our worshipful contemplation of the Child's future sacrifice by revealing the stigmata.[47] Francis's prayers on our behalf will be granted because he displays these wounds, inflicted by Christ himself.[48] Such emphasis on the Passion, implicit in the Infant's gesture and explicit in the behavior of Francis, is consonant with Franciscan spirituality, which demands our compassionate response. Bellini's architectural illusion provides access to the sacred realm that is merely visual, a matter of the senses; only when we emulate Francis's compassion may we join the sacra conversazione psychologically and spiritually. Bellini's visualization of faith encourages us to do so, as Ridolfi recognized: these are beings who "ravish souls."

Bellini's figures occupy an illusionistic church, recalling Piero della Francesca's Brera altarpiece (fig. 115). Piero, who may have introduced to Italian art the Netherlandish conception of a church interior for the Madonna and saints, had created an ideal realm modeled on the contemporary style of Leon Battista Alberti.[49] Like the San Giobbe altarpiece, Piero's work was commissioned for a church of the *Osservanza*, and it may be that the Observant Franciscans themselves had something to do with Bellini's use of an ecclesiastical setting. If Bellini had gone to Pesaro to execute or install his *Coronation* altarpiece—another Franciscan commission—he might well have seen Piero's work in nearby Urbino. Indeed, the resemblances between the two altarpieces go far beyond the architectural conceit. Each anticipates the Child's death—by his sleep in Piero's picture, in Bellini's by his gesture, which seems almost the negation of blessing or an evocation of the dead Christ of the Pietà. Each includes a Dominican saint: Peter Martyr in the one, Dominic himself in the other. Piero's figure of Jerome, to Mary's right, is the counterpart of Bellini's Job. Two of the same saints, the Baptist and Francis, appear in each holy congregation. And the San Giobbe Francis combines elements of Piero's characterization, in particular the action of the left hand, with aspects of Bellini's own *Saint Francis*, painted in the mid-1470s (fig. 77). Perhaps Bellini changed the facial type of this Francis, who is more ascetic and idiosyncratic in the earlier painting, in response to the more regular features of Piero's Francis. But if Bellini had Piero's saint in mind, he infused his adaptation of the model with a gentler, more Franciscan compassion: instead of standing upright and presenting his attribute, an exquisite crystal cross, which symbolizes compassion for the Passion, Bellini's Francis expresses himself directly and personally by the tilt of his head and his embracing gesture. He does not hold an object to explain himself, but himself personifies compassion and addressing us, seeks to compel compassion in us.

These altarpieces, painted within several years of each other, differ in other ways and for all their similarities belong to different worlds—and different art historical

*110. San Giobbe altarpiece, detail, Saint Sebastian. Photo: Giacomelli Fotografia, Venice.*

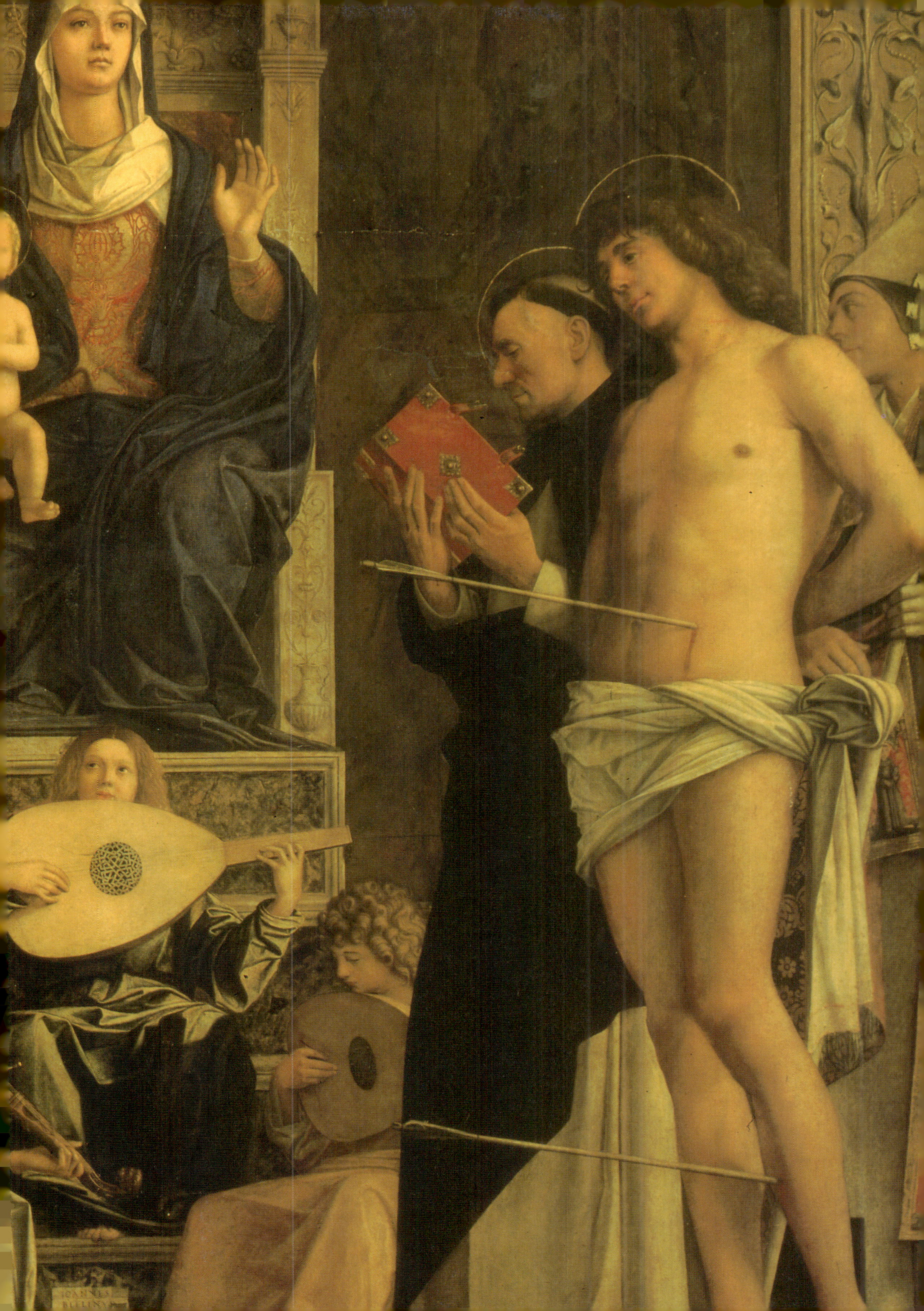

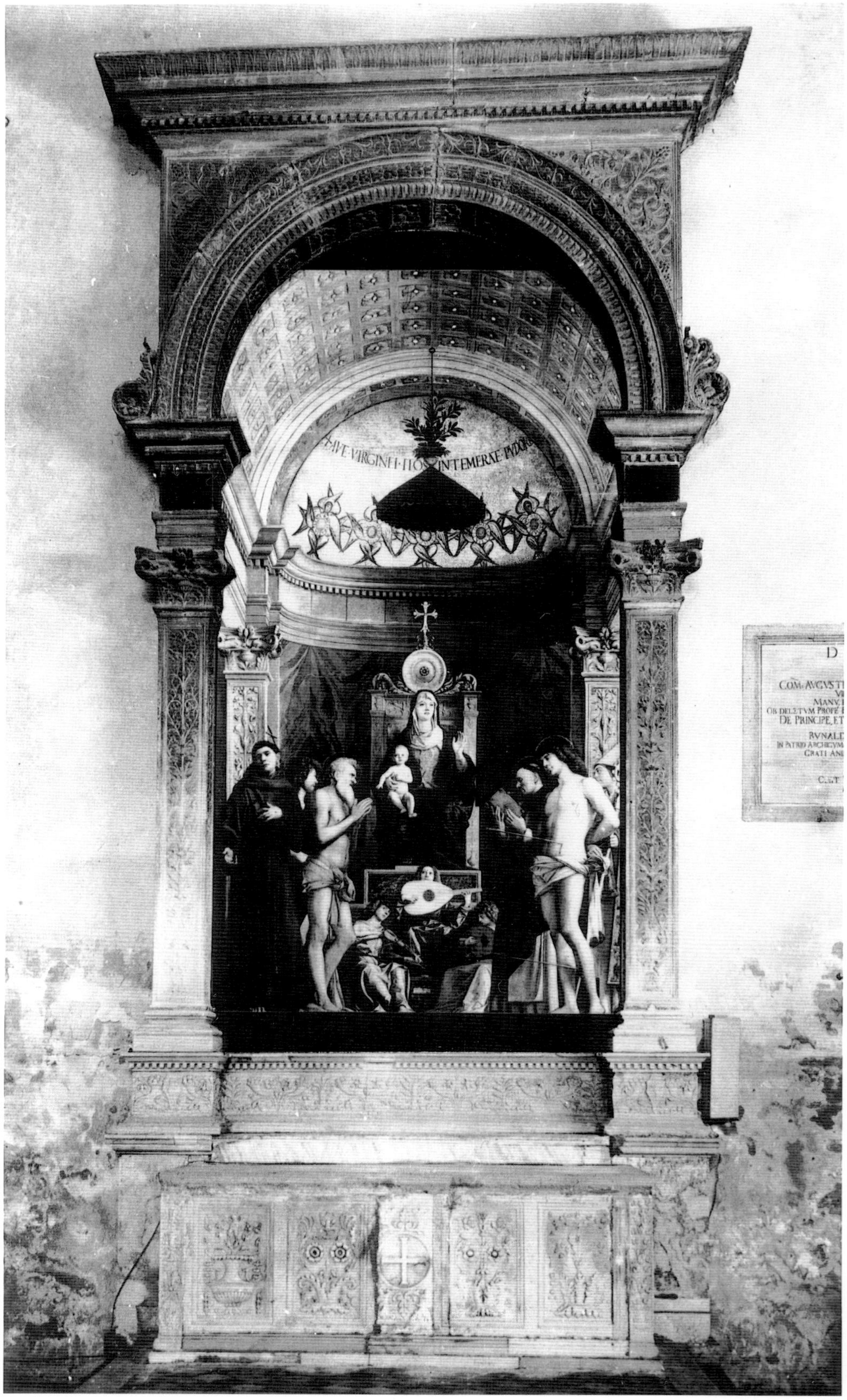

*111. Reconstruction of San Giobbe altarpiece in its frame. Photo: Gianfranco Spinazzi, Venice, and Osvaldo Böhm, Venice. Montage: Author.*

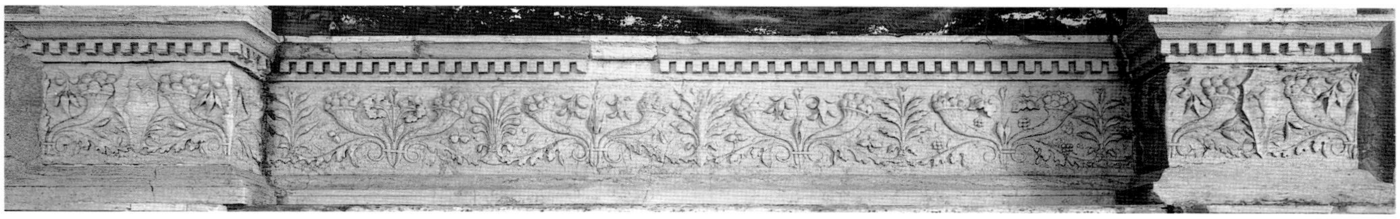

*112. Frame of San Giobbe altarpiece, detail, coat of arms. Photo: Osvaldo Böhm, Venice.*

eras. Bellini tightened the geometry of his composition. Placing his figures closer to the beholder in the foreground—concomitant with the intermediary role of Francis—he also placed them further back in his illusionistic church, simultaneously making the viewpoint even lower: we are to kneel before this image. Mary herself, raised on her throne, occupies the place of the altar in the apse. Her left hand recalls the praying gesture of the orant: she is the priest of Bellini's illusionistic church, and her Son is her eucharistic offering.[50] That this sacrificial, eucharistic imagery should be represented in a church is obviously appropriate: but why this church?

Piero's cool white light, his crystalline vision—embodied in Francis's cross—and his clear colors have become in Bellini's altarpiece warm, golden, and complex. Unlike Piero's Albertian church of white marble, Bellini's Byzantinizing architecture is best understood in reference to the ducal chapel of San Marco, that most sacred shrine of the Venetian Republic (fig. 11). This was both an aesthetic and a symbolic choice. According to tradition, Venice had been founded on March 25, the feast of the Annunciation, and so the Virgin Mary was considered the protectress of the Serene Republic, which, by analogy, identified itself with Christ Incarnate. San Marco was thus a fitting environment for the Madonna and Child in Venice. And so Bellini took San Marco as his model for the richly veined panels of marble and the mosaic with its golden tesserae.

Bellini's mosaic is made of irregular daubs of golden color, imitating the tesserae they depict and painted closer together in the highlights. Their warm tonality and colorism suffuse the scene; like the church it evokes, Bellini's San Marco seems filled with golden light and air. Color and light create form: the golden tesserae are described by color, not by their contours, which blur and even cease to exist. In the tesserae, in areas of drapery, and in highlights, Bellini applied paint comparatively thickly, and the texture of this impasto—now all but obliterated by early attempts at conservation—is bound with the atmospheric effects of his modeling, "balancing and fusing harmonies into grateful chords."[51] This visual unity, Bellini's tapestry of color-light, is comparable to the monochromatic harmony of Leonardo's chiaroscuro and sfumatura; it is the coloristic Venetian counterpart of the Florentine vision.

Bellini's mosaic determines not only the style and mood of his altarpiece: it is iconographically significant. Each mosaic seraph carries an inscription of the angelic salutation, "Ave Gratia Plena" (Hail, Full of Grace), and this suggests that Mary's praying gesture is to be associated with Gabriel's greeting at the An-

*113. Interior of San Giobbe, Venice. Photo: Osvaldo Böhm, Venice.*

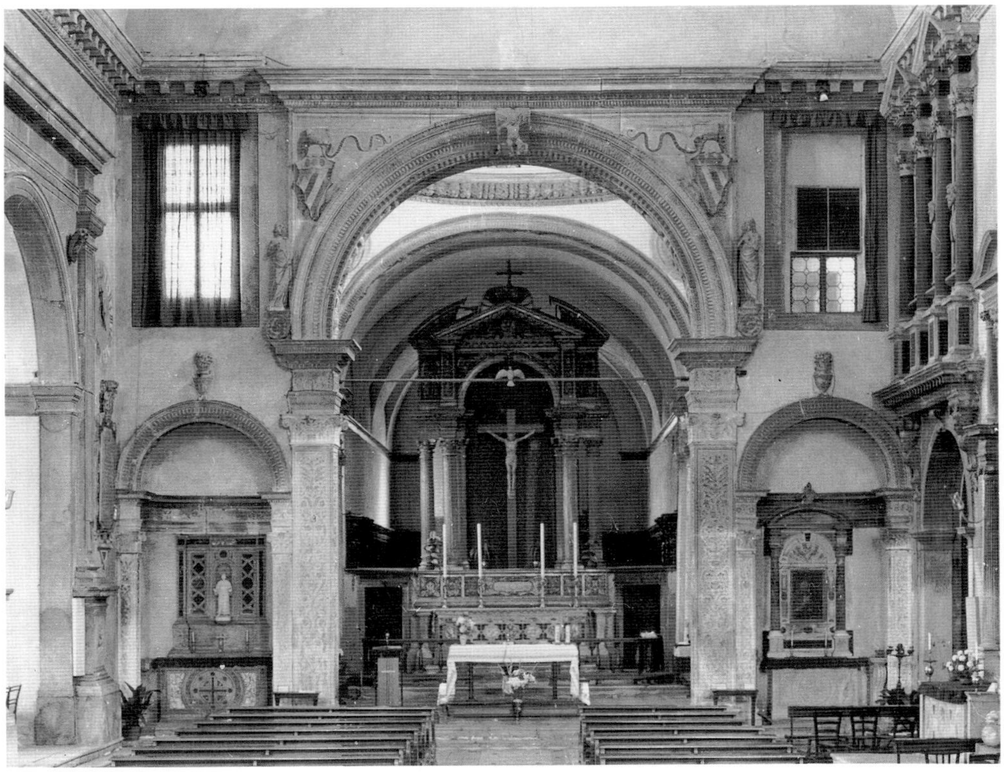

nunciation: we have been reminded of the founding of Venice on the feast of the Annunciation. The other inscription of the mosaic is also addressed to the Madonna and once again praises her purity: +AVE VIRGINEI FLOS INTEMERATE PUDORIS (Hail, undefiled flower of virgin modesty). In the context of a Franciscan church, these inscriptions clearly refer to the Immaculate Conception, Mary's birth free of the stain of Original Sin, and indeed the angelic salutation was taken as prima facie evidence of Mary's privilege. Laurel branches affixed to the baldachin above Mary's throne symbolize her purity. Bellini's combination of ideas—the Virgin's immaculacy, the humanity of Christ, and the Republic of Venice, enshrined in San Marco—is resonant, suggestive, and timely. In a bull dated 27 February 1476, Sixtus IV granted indulgences to all who attended services on the feast of the Conception, 8 December: like all Franciscans—including the confreres of San Giobbe—Sixtus ardently defended belief in the Immaculate Conception.

In the San Giobbe altarpiece, for the first time in Venetian art, Bellini represented a completely closed architectural space, the apse of a church resembling the ducal chapel of San Marco, opening illusionistically from the Lombardesque interior of San Giobbe. Clearly, he wanted more than spatial illusion: he might have achieved that just as well, if not better, without introducing a Byzantine apse into the aisle of a Lombardesque church. The answer lies in the patronage of San Giobbe. Doge Cristoforo Moro had endowed the church generously during his life, as early as 1461, and assured that his support would continue after his death by provisions of his testament of 1470, with a codicil of 1471. When the doge

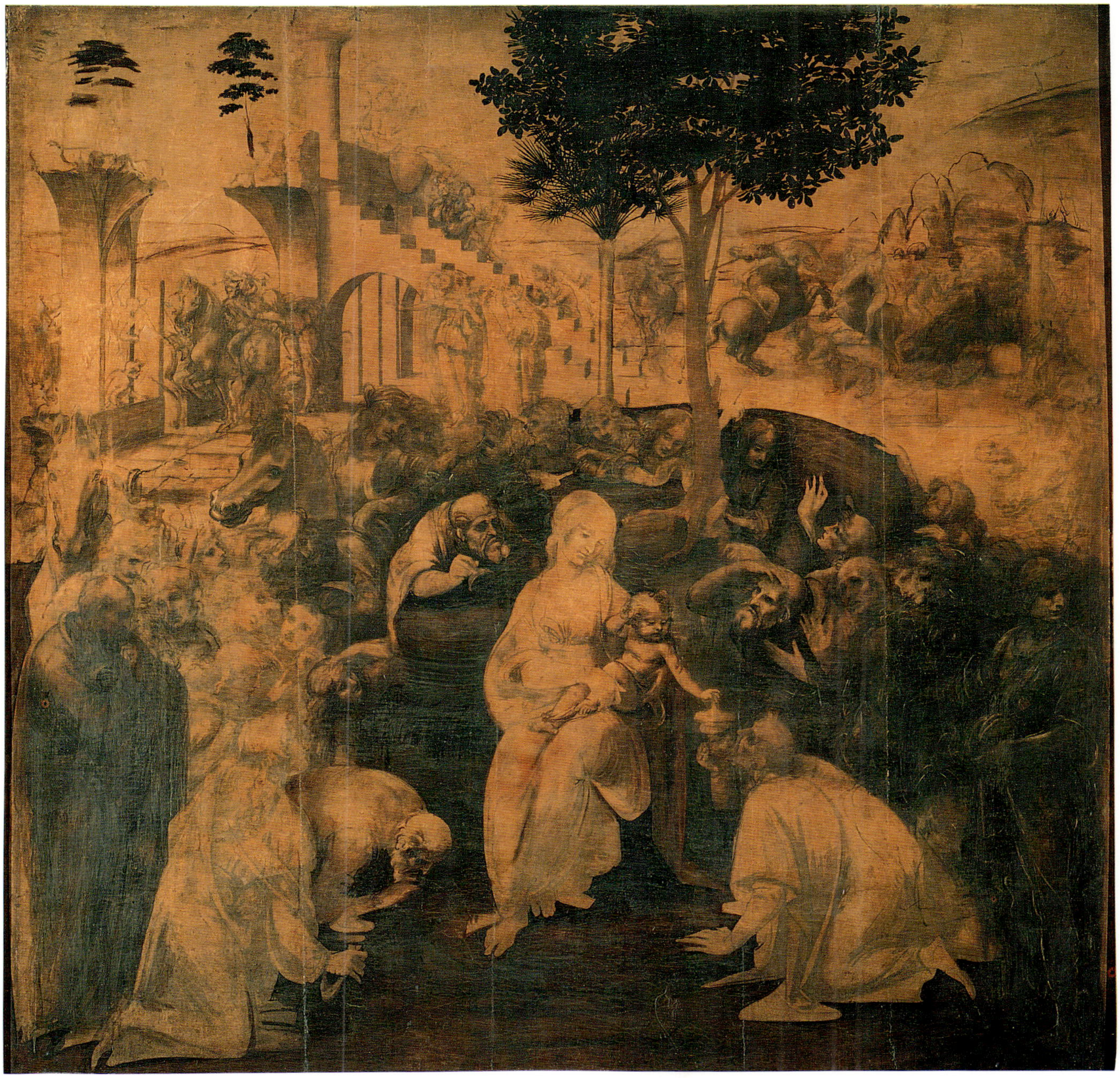

*114. Leonardo da Vinci,* Adoration of the Magi, *Galleria degli Uffizi, Florence. Photo: Scala/Art Resource, New York.*

died in 1471, he was interred before the high altar—dedicated, in compliance with his bequest, not to Job but to Bernardino of Siena.[52] Thus displaced from the high altar, Job was given the second altar on the right, as we have seen. It seems that Bellini and his patrons meant to compensate Job for the loss of the high altar to Bernardino by the ecclesiatical illusion of the altarpiece, by its great size—by far the largest altarpiece in the church, and the largest surviving work in Bellini's oeuvre—and by its visual splendor. Bernardino, declared a patron of Venice at Moro's behest, was honored by an altar in the actual San Marco; and in effect Job was similarly honored by an altar in Bellini's San Marco, recreated in the San Giobbe altarpiece.

The ducal associations of San Giobbe also explain another detail of Bellini's composition, the umbrella or baldachin suspended above the Virgin's throne.

*115. Piero della Francesca,* Madonna and Child and Saints with Federigo da Montefeltro, *Pinacoteca di Brera, Milan. Photo: Sovrintendenza per i Beni Artistici e Storici, Milan.*

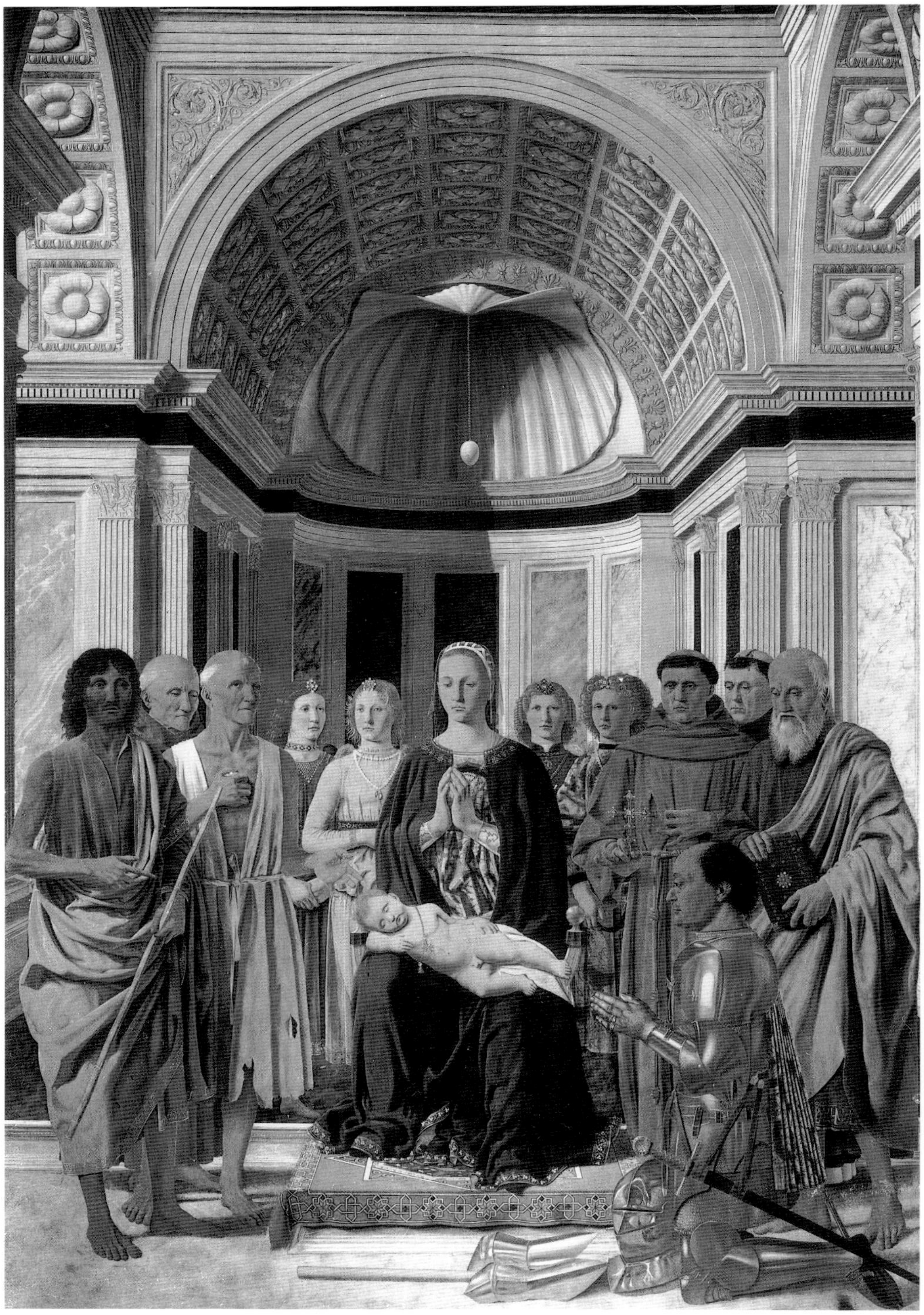

Altars were commonly adorned in this way, and here the baldachin is associated with the Madonna enthroned in the place of the altar in Bellini's imaginary church. In Venice, however, a baldachin of the sort depicted in the San Giobbe altarpiece had a particular civic significance. According to the official (and purposefully fictionalized) histories of the *Serenissima*, in 1177 Doge Ziani had been given a ceremonial umbrella very like this baldachin, at the insistence of Pope Alexander III: this event was described in the final chapter of the so-called Story of Ancona, which recounted Venice's successful intervention in the war between pontiff and emperor.[53] The umbrella, like other symbolic objects Alexander gave Ziani, was

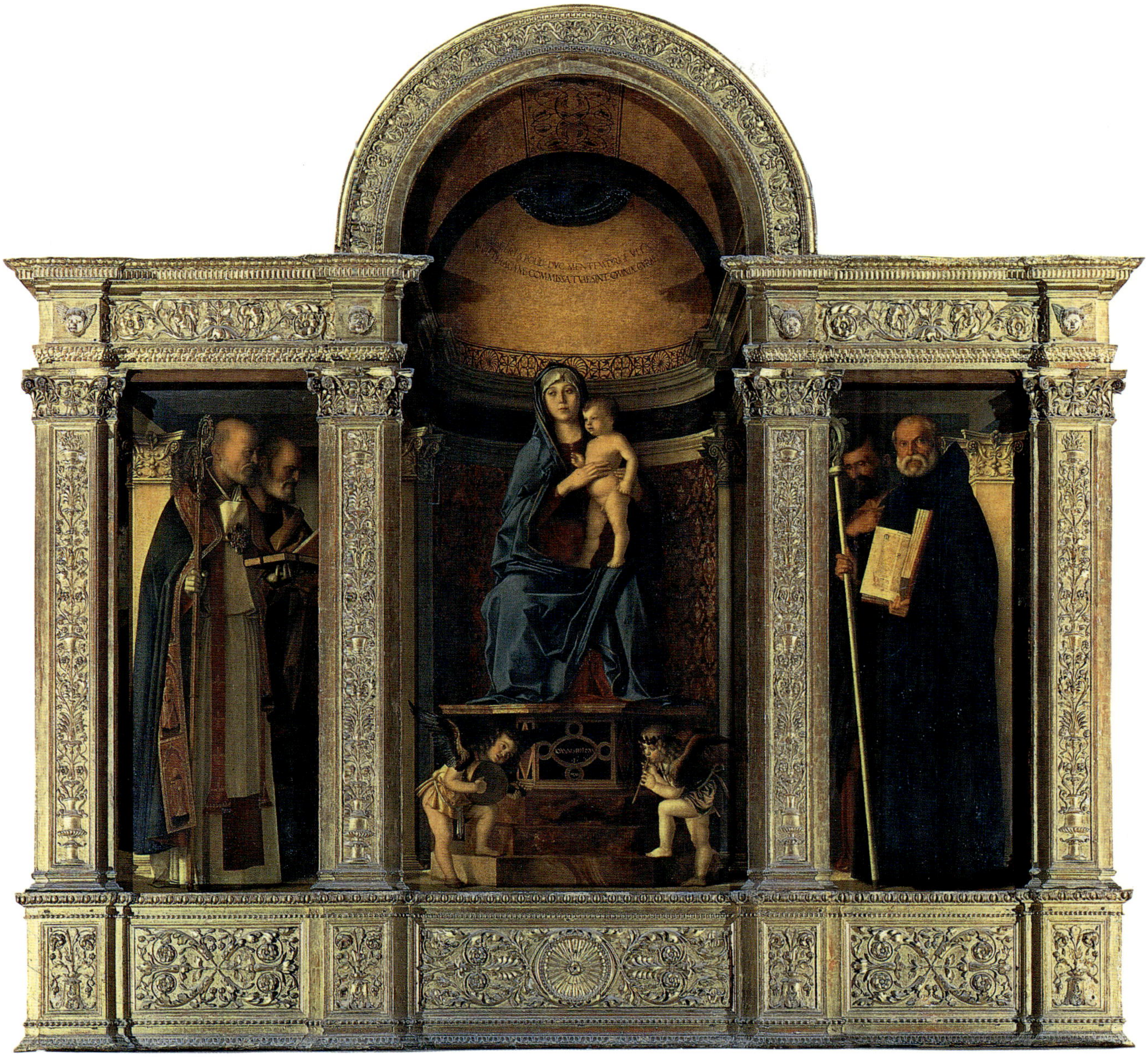

*116. Frari triptych* (Madonna and Child with Saints Peter, Nicholas, Benedict, and Mark), *Pesaro Chapel, Sacristy, Santa Maria Gloriosa dei Frari, Venice. Photo: Scala/Art Resource, New York.*

perforce inherently associated with the privileges that the pope granted to the doge, to the ducal chapel of San Marco, and to the Republic of Venice. In the San Giobbe altarpiece, the umbrella honors the Virgin and Child in San Marco, which is another way of saying that it honors the personification of Venice as the Virgin and as Christ Incarnate, conceived, like the republic, on 25 March. The identification of Venice with both Mary and Christ was a commonplace of Venetian imagery, written and visual.[54] Bellini makes these associations explicit by references to the Annunciation, when the Incarnation was accomplished. Recalling the Annunciation with Mary's gesture and with the mosaic inscription "Ave Gratia Plena," Bellini was also commemorating the traditional date of the foundation of Venice on 25 March in the year 421.

If we imagine San Giobbe as it was at the time of its consecration, then Bellini's

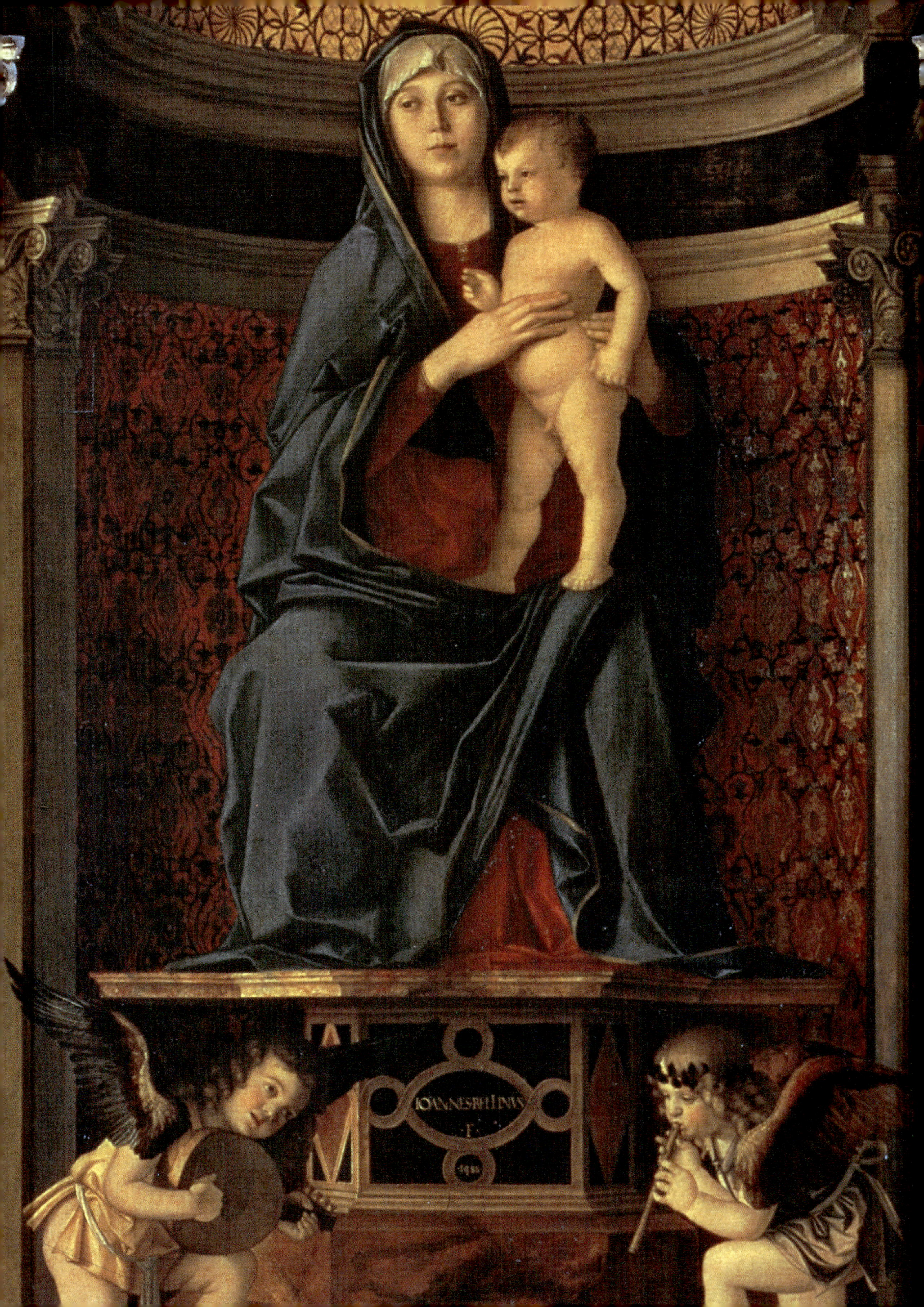
IOANNES BELLINVS
·F·

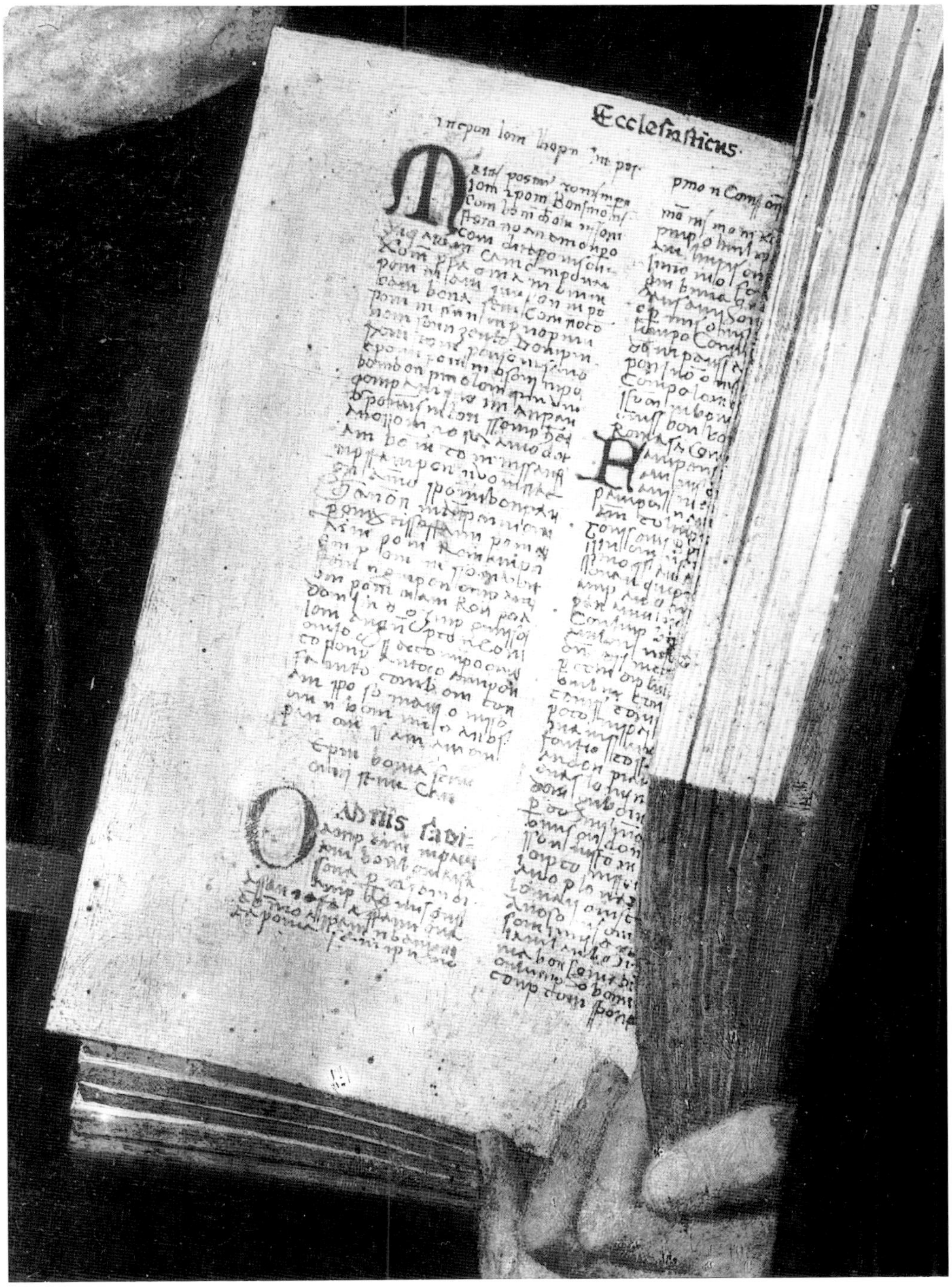


*118. Frari triptych, detail, Bible of Saint Benedict. Photo: Osvaldo Böhm, Venice.*

altarpiece stands out in splendid isolation as a rival *cappella maggiore*. And surely he and his patrons intended to provide this distinction for Job, venerated in the vicinity since the fourteenth century and deprived of the high altar by Bernardino's civic and ducal cult. Thus Bellini's evocations of San Marco are more than a general reminder of the ducal chapel: the clarity of his architectural illusionism is necessary to establish a high altar—a second high altar—for the displaced titular saint of San Giobbe.

When did Bellini paint the San Giobbe altarpiece? The painting was first mentioned in print by Marc'Antonio Sabellico, the official historian of the republic, in his *De urbis situ*, evidently published between 1487 and 1489.[55] Sabellico described

*117. Frari triptych, detail, Madonna and Child. Photo: Scala/Art Resource, New York.*

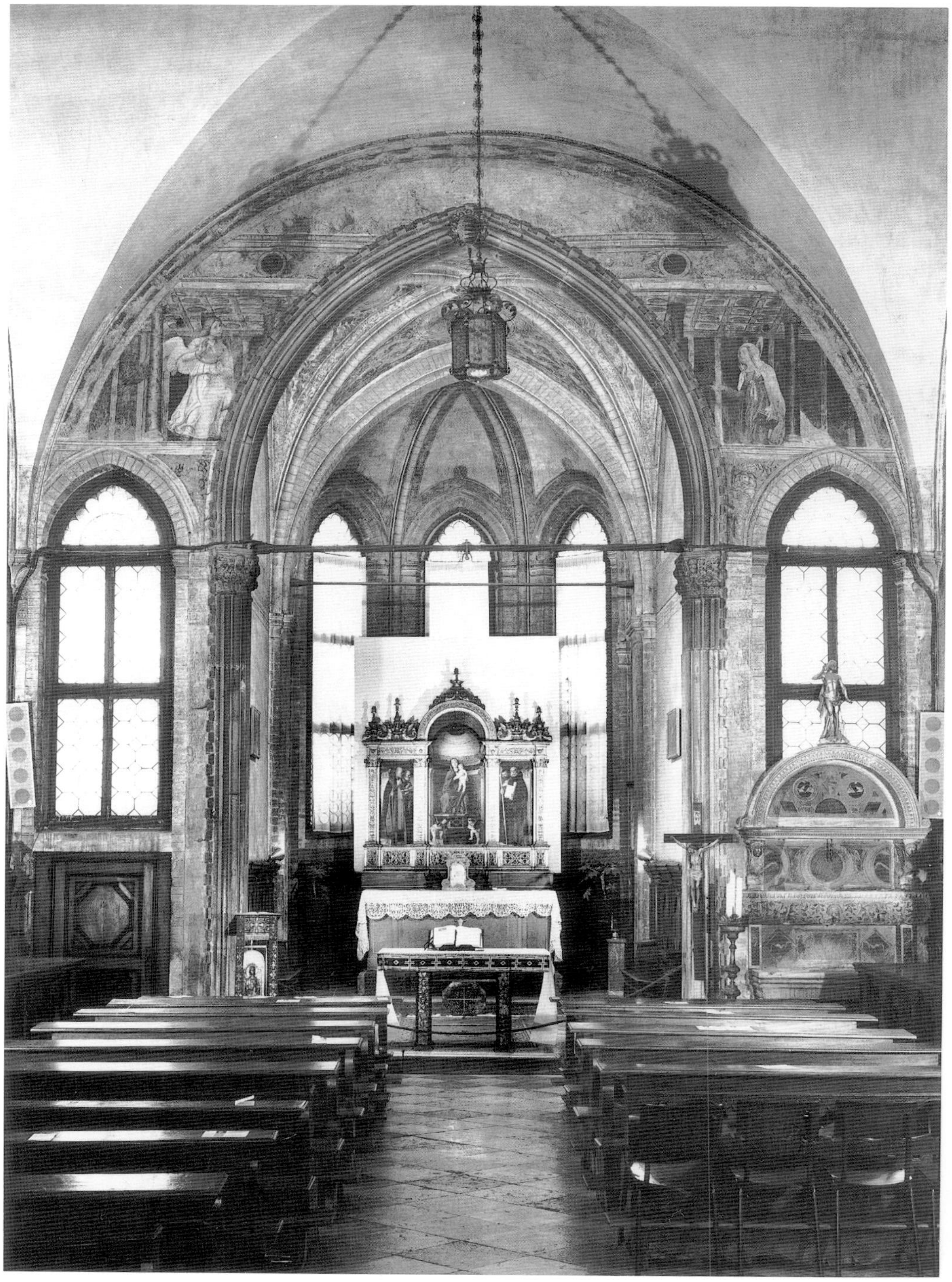

*119. Pesaro Chapel of the Immaculate Virgin, Sacristy, Santa Maria Gloriosa dei Frari, Venice. Photo: Gianfranco Spinazzi, Venice.*

it as one of Bellini's early works, an indication that must be taken seriously, given the early date of the commentary. (Bellini must have been in his forties when it was painted: *early* is a relative term.) Comparison with paintings generally placed in the 1470s confirms Sabellico's implication. The altarpiece seems to be a work of the very late 1470s, 1480 at the latest. The saints themselves may provide a further confirmation of the date. Job's dermatological woes, like Sebastian's wounds, recalled plague sores, and both martyrs were invoked against the plague: but which plague? Perhaps the commission may be associated with the terrible epidemic of 1478.[56]

Bellini played a variation on his own theme in his second and last commission for a Venetian Franciscan church, the Frari triptych signed and dated 1488: IOANNES BELINVS. / F. / 1488 (figs. 116, 117).[57] The Virgin and Child in the central panel are joined in the wings by Saints Nicholas and Peter to their right and Benedict and Mark to their left.[58] The inscription in the mosaic above the Madonna is a quotation from the office that Sixtus had approved in 1478 for the feast of the Immaculate Conception, honored also in the San Giobbe altarpiece: "Ianua Certa Poli Duc mentem Dirige Vitam / Quae Peragam Commissa Tuae Sint Omnia Curae" (Sure Gate of Heaven, lead my mind, direct my life, may all that I do be committed to thy care).[59] At the same time, Benedict presents another text central to the cult of Mary's immaculacy, Ecclesiasticus 24, legible in the Bible that he commands us to read by his forceful gaze (fig. 118).

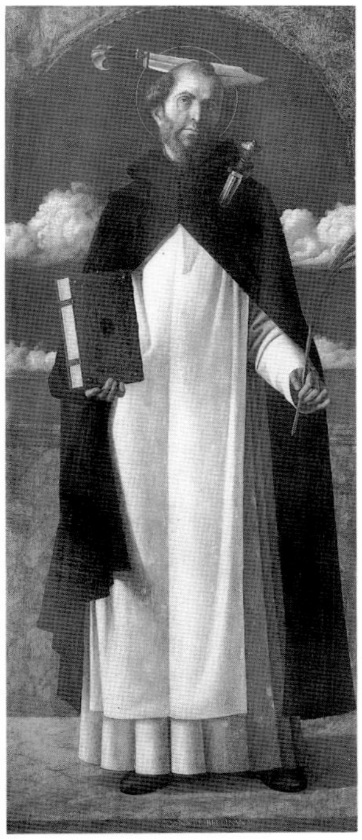

*120. Giovanni Bellini with assistance,* Saint Peter Martyr, *Pinacoteca Provinciale, Bari. Photo: Pinacoteca Provinciale, Bari.*

The triptych remains in its original carved and gilded wooden frame on the altar of the Frari sacristy chapel, endowed in 1478 by the sons of Pietro Pesaro and Franceschina Tron in memory of their mother, who died in that year (fig. 119). Pietro Pesaro and his sons are honored by the presence of their onomastic saints in the altarpiece, while Franceschina is remembered in the inscription of her grave in the pavement before the altar; this grave became the tomb of her descendants as well.

Bellini created an illusionistic architecture that is completed by the actual forms of the frame, as in the Pesaro *Coronation*, and is essentially unrelated to the architecture of the chapel itself, as at San Giobbe. Again recalling San Giobbe, Bellini's setting evokes San Marco with its golden mosaics, but the allusion to the ducal chapel is less complete, and a brocade cloth replaces the Byzantinizing panels of veined marble in the apse.

By 1488, when Bellini signed the Frari altarpiece, the triptych format had become outmoded elsewhere in Italy, though it remained popular in Venice well into the sixteenth century. Bellini produced at least two other triptychs or polyptychs approximately contemporary with this one, although they do not survive intact. The *Saint Peter Martyr* in Bari is all that remains of one of these (fig. 120); and two panels of another such altarpiece, representing *Saint Augustine*(?) and *Saint Benedict*, both painted with studio assistance, are preserved in Zagreb.[60]

In his work for the Frari, Bellini exploited the triptych format to represent the apse of a church, with Mary as priest and altar and Christ the eucharistic offering (as in San Giobbe), flanked by saintly communicants in the wings. Their spaces are accessible to and yet separate from the central sanctuary. The flanking chambers represent the pastophories of a Byzantinizing chapel or church, where the Eucharist is kept before celebration of the Mass. Like actual pastophories, they open into the central space of this fictive church and also at the other side to reveal strips of land and sky. The painting is lit as though illuminated through one of these lateral openings, behind Nicholas, and the pattern of light and shade so carefully observed by Bellini is the mortar of his illusionistic church, binding the three panels of his triptych no less forcefully than his perspectival illusion. Here, perhaps even more than in San Giobbe, particles of air fill the picture space; like transparent golden tesserae, they combine to create Bellini's coloristic universe.

In the San Giobbe altarpiece, golds and browns are emphasized (recalling the Pesaro *Coronation*) with greens and complicated "shot," or *changeant,* colors. In the triptych, Bellini combined whites, reds, and black: Mark's gown and Benedict's Bible, both startling in contrast to Benedict's black habit; the red brocade behind Mary, which changes tint in the changing light; the red of Mary's gown; and shades of red repeated in the saints to her right.

Geometry also plays a role in Bellini's unity of forms and spaces. The composition of the group is condensed in comparison with San Giobbe, especially in the placement of the flanking saints and the contour of the Virgin. The rectangular forms of the enthroned Madonna and Child in the earlier work have now become a pyramid of sacred figures and polygonal pedestal. By placing the sacred beings on a pedestal in the apse, Bellini recalls earlier northern Italian altarpieces that combine painted and carved images with a sculpture on a pedestal in a niche. His pyramidal group is enframed in depth by the semicircular apse and set between the rectangular spaces of the wings. Bellini achieved this imposition of geometry on figures and composition with such graceful naturalism that the intellectual clarity and control of his conception may not be immediately apparent. This geometrical and mathematical harmony of forms is Bellini's equivalent of the pyramidal formulations in contemporary and later works by Leonardo, Michelangelo, and Raphael. It is a hallmark of the new High Renaissance style.

Concomitant with this formal harmony is a new mood of hopefulness, evident also in Bellini's later devotional images of the Madonna. Now the Christ turns to bless Nicholas and Peter, onomastic saint of the deceased father of the Pesaro family; and Benedict, patron of the leading member of the house, draws us in through his forceful gaze and the Bible. The text, and the veneration of the Immaculate Virgin that it signifies, establish the beholder's relation to the image: very different from the scarred hand that Francis extends toward the viewer in the San Giobbe altarpiece, wherein Christ is oblivious to human presence. In the triptych, salvation is proffered by means of Scripture, whereas in the earlier altarpiece, we are urged to imitate Christ in a more personal way: only perfect compassion for his suffering, embodied by Francis, can bring redemption. Where the inscriptions of the San Giobbe altarpiece praise the Virgin Mary's purity, the Frari triptych prays for her guidance—"Lead my mind, Direct my life"—a prayer to be spoken by the living when they worship in the funerary chapel of their kinfolk. The comportment of Mary and her Son leave no doubt that the prayer will be answered.

## Bellini in the New Century: The Last Altarpieces

Bellini's first altarpiece of the sixteenth century was his last major altarpiece with a narrative theme, the *Baptism of Christ*, commissioned by the Vicentine citizen and Count Palatine GianBattista Graziano Garzadori for his family funerary chapel in Santa Corona (figs. 121, 122).[61]

Garzadori had made a pilgrimage to the Holy Land—no easy voyage in those days—and had sworn an oath to honor his patron saint, John the Baptist, on his safe return. True to his word, having returned from the banks of the River Jordan and the site of the Holy Sepulcher, he endowed his chapel in the Dominican church of Vicenza, dedicating the altar to his onomastic saint and providing for his own burial there. A two-part inscription, with the patron's arms, is written on the fourth and fifth piers of the nave, facing his altar: ANNO / .M.D., and BAP. GRATIANVS / EX HIEROSOLYMIS / SOSPES / HOC SACELLVM / DIVO IOANNI / DICAVIT (In the year of our Lord 1500, Battista Graziano, safely returned from Jerusalem, dedicated this chapel to Saint John). On the pilasters flanking the altar is the inscription DIVINO CVLTVI.

Garzadori had been conceded the right to build his chapel on 2 November 1500, the year commemorated in the dedicatory inscription. His agreement with the Dominicans was much the same as Marco Zorzi's with the Camaldulensian fathers of San Michele or that of the Pesaro with the Franciscan friars of Santa Maria Gloriosa dei Frari. In exchange for an endowment, the priests of Santa Corona were obligated to say Mass at the Garzadori altar for the benefit of the donor and his wife, Paola. Garzadori was granted permission to construct a family tomb and to decorate the chapel with reliefs, inscriptions, his coat of arms—and, implicitly, a painting.[62] Garzadori, his wife, and his sons were buried beneath the pavement in front of their altar—the tombs no longer survive, but the inscriptions were recorded—and their nephew's descendants considered this the family sepulcher more than a century after GianBattista's death.[63]

The altar itself, probably the work of a local artist, Rocco da Vicenza, is splendidly carved and embellished with gilding, with azure relief backgrounds, and with marbles, porphyry, and serpentine (fig. 123).[64] Carved garlands adorn the columns, an elegant motif used also by the Lombardo family, as in the monument of Andrea Vendramin in SS. Giovanni e Paolo in Venice, and recalling the ancient Roman custom, which survives even today, of decorating tombs with flowered wreaths. Work began in 1501, and the columns were in place in 1502.[65] These years suggest the date of Bellini's altarpiece as well, contemporary with such works as the *Madonna of the Meadow* and the portrait of *Doge Leonardo Loredan* (figs. 43, 149).

The *Baptism of Christ* is lit from the right, or east, as though from the apse of the church. A monumental landscape provides the setting, mountains and a sky tinted

*Overleaf:*
121. Baptism of Christ, *Garzadori Chapel of Saint John the Baptist, Santa Corona, Vicenza. Courtesy Palazzo Chiericati, Vicenza. Photo: Fototechnica, Vicenza.*

122. Baptism of Christ, *detail, Christ. Photo: Osvaldo Böhm, Venice.*

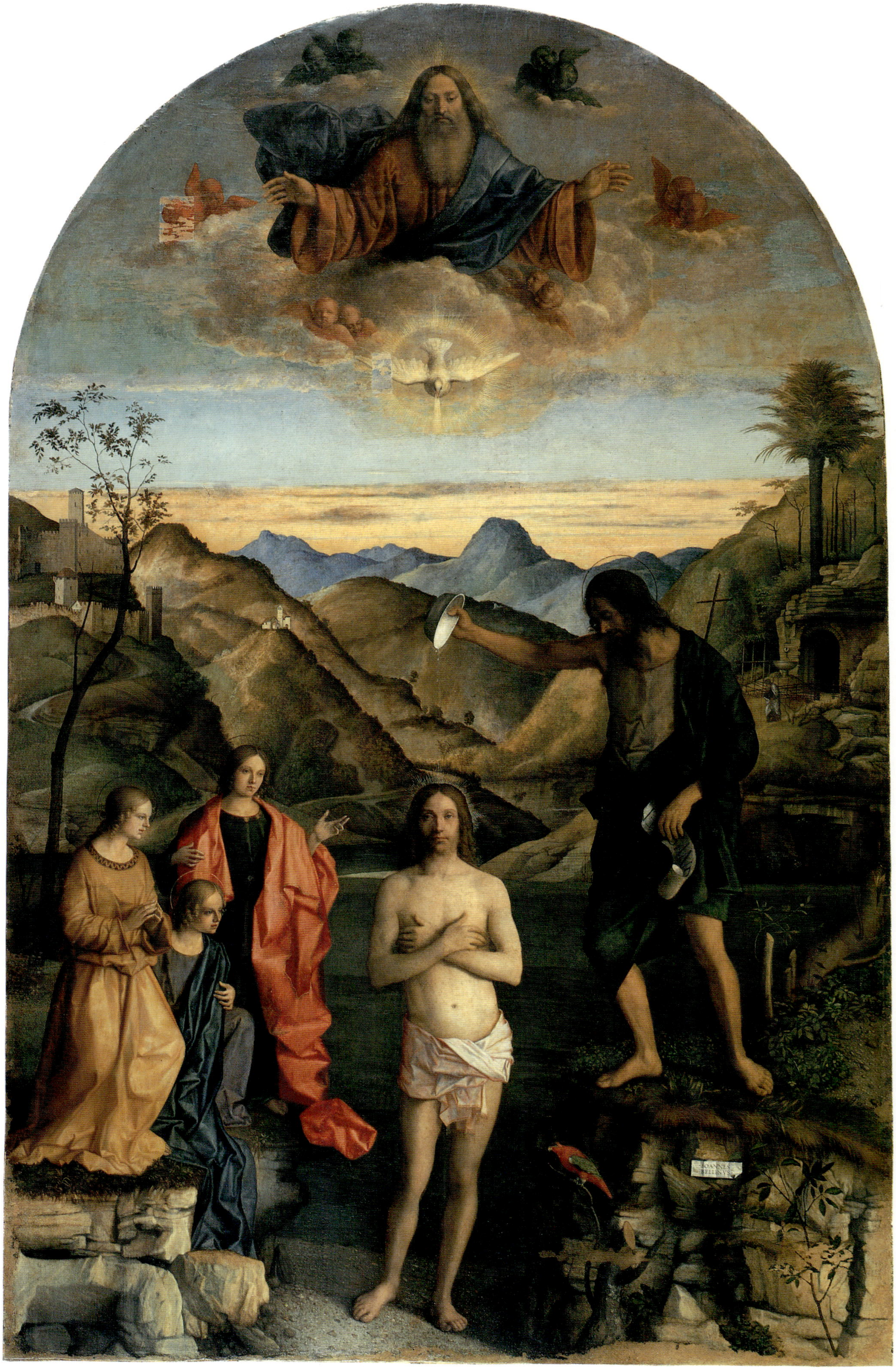
IOANNES
BELLINVS

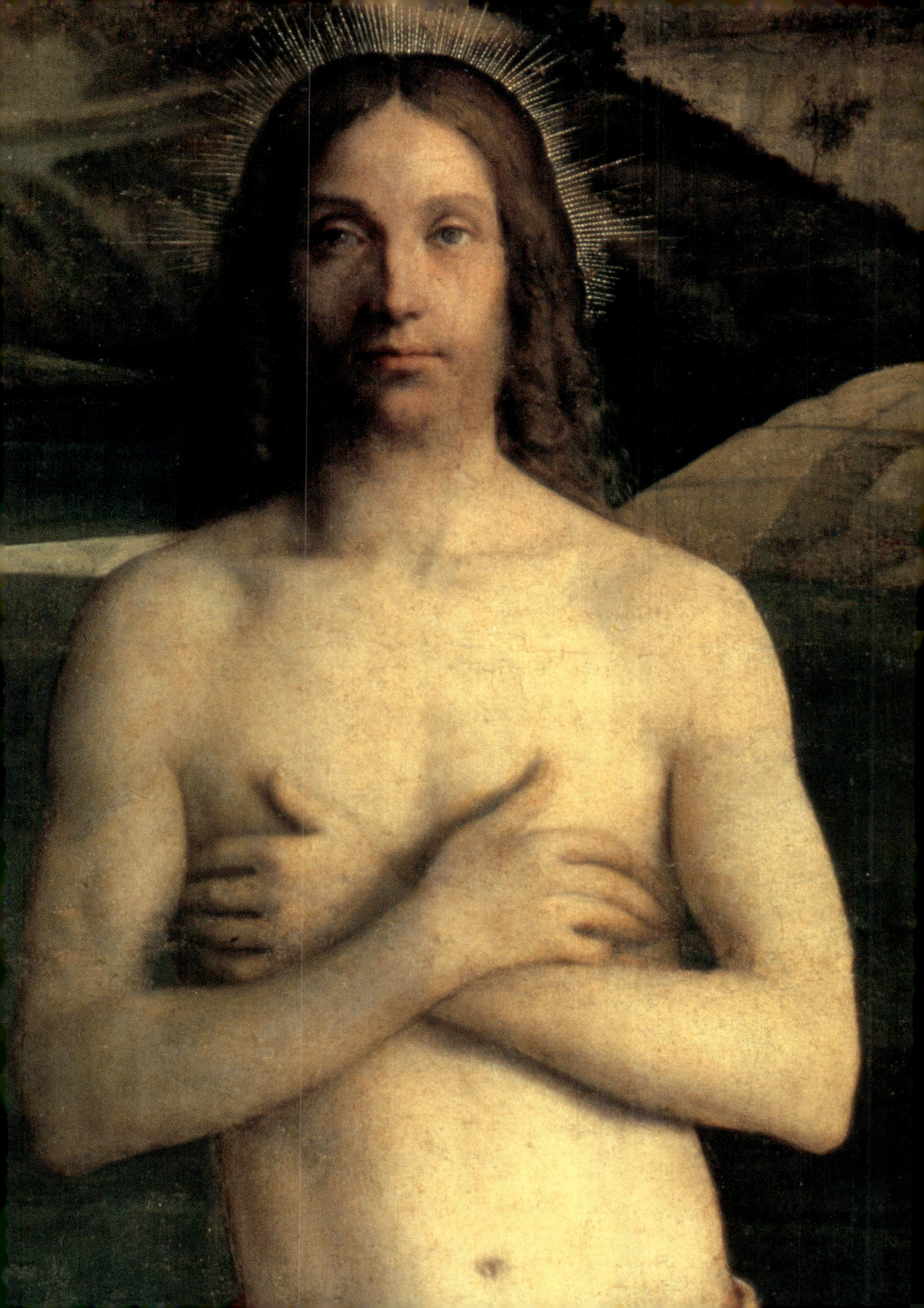

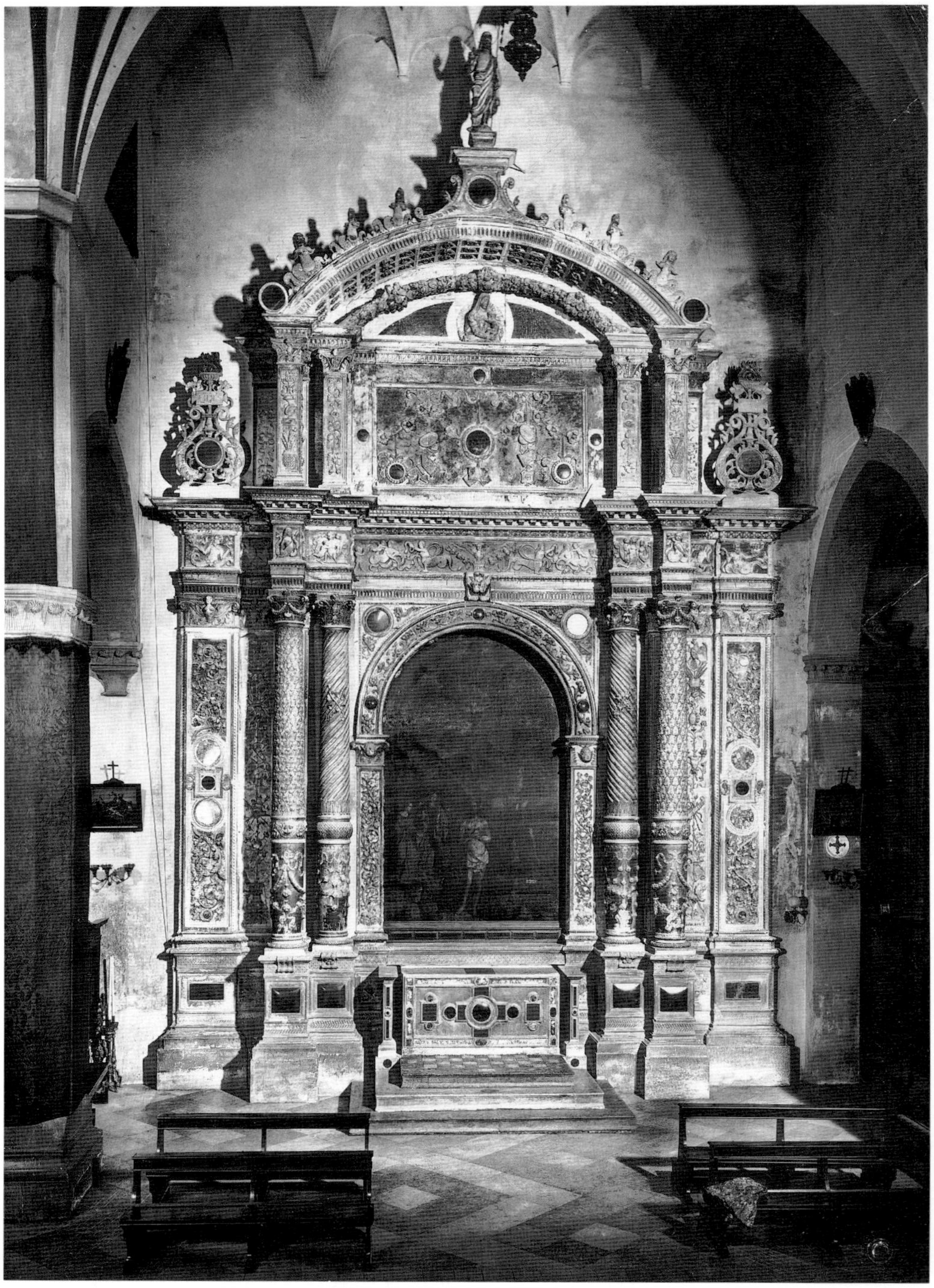

*123. Chapel of Saint John the Baptist, Santa Corona, Vicenza. Photo: Alinari, Florence.*

gold by the glow that accompanies God the Father and the Holy Spirit, who come to acknowledge Christ at the moment of his baptism: "This is my Son in whom I am well pleased." The Savior stands on the shore of the River Jordan with its pebbles opalescent in the sunlight. The center foreground belongs to Christ, the only frontal figure, calm and unmoving as he beholds the viewer. Christ's white loincloth is pink-red in the shadows, taking its color from the reds worn by others and perhaps reflecting the red of the heavenly Father. But the altar is dedicated to John the Baptist, and he is given the distinction of height, raised above Christ on the rocks of the riverbank, his halo slightly interrupting the profile of the distant mountains.

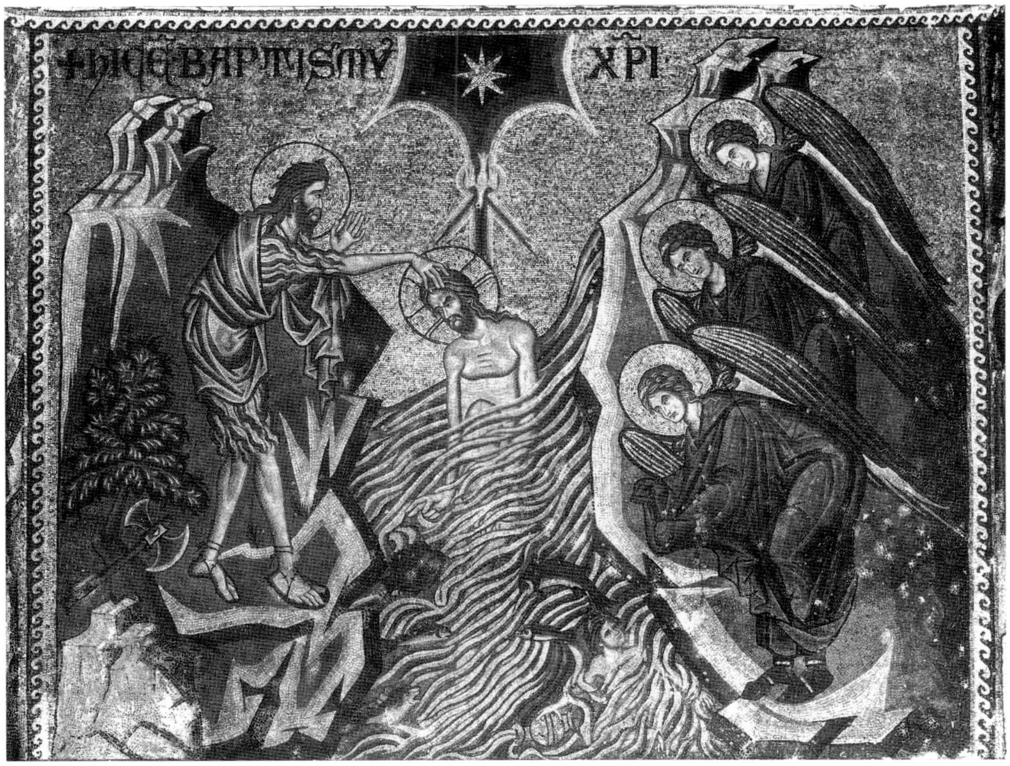

124. Baptism, *mosaic, Basilica di San Marco, Venice. Photo: Osvaldo Böhm, Venice.*

Counterbalancing John, but lower in the picture space, are three angels on the opposite bank, come to witness the baptism. The one closest to us begins to genuflect; the second, who holds Christ's blue gown over his shoulder, is already kneeling, as though completing the action begun by the first; and the third, who has the Lord's red mantle draped around his neck, stands to look and gesture at Christ, as though obeying the injunction inscribed on the Baptist's scroll, "Ecce Agnus Dei" (Behold the Lamb of God). The red mantle cascades from the angel's shoulder to the ground, echoing the lines of the mountains behind him and playing against the contour of Christ's figure. The color, the brightest and warmest in the composition, and the active silhouette become the abstract equivalent of the spiritual excitement here, which none of the actors expresses directly but which is sensed in such details as this, in the eruption of the clouds around God the Father, or in the swell of the mountains.

The angels, the elevated figure of the Baptist, and the central figure of Christ—these elements of Bellini's design would have been familiar from traditional depictions of the Baptism. The thirteenth-century mosaic *Baptism* in San Marco, for example, depicts John standing on the shore, above the central figure of Christ, and three angelic witnesses genuflecting on the opposite bank (fig. 124). Their colors—the blue, brown, green, and red of their garments and the gold of their wings—may have influenced Bellini's palette. The gold mosaic ground has become golden sky in Bellini's painting, his naturalistic metaphor for God's presence.

Bellini's younger contemporary, Cima da Conegliano, also consulted this sac-

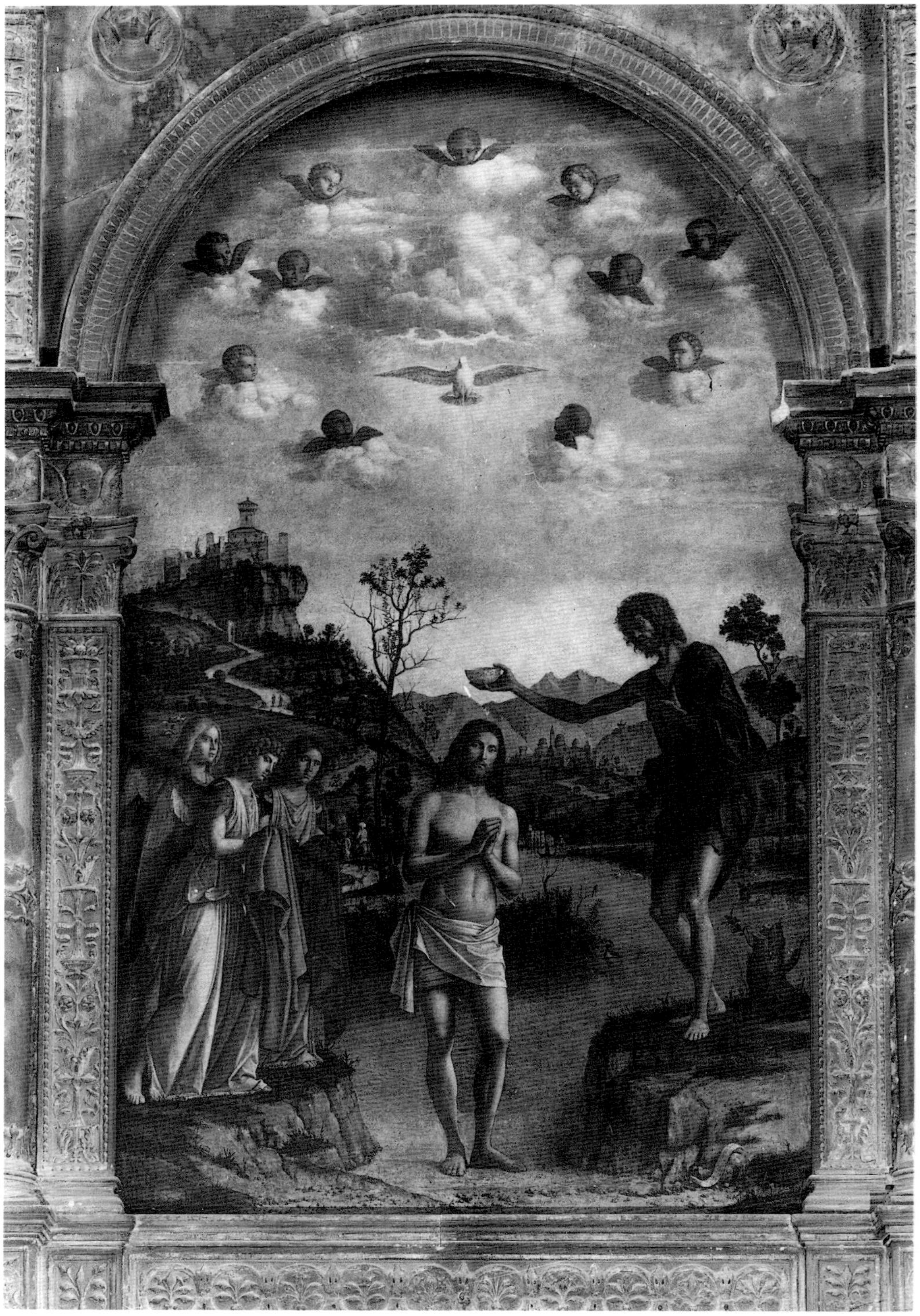

*125. Cima da Conegliano,* Baptism, *San Giovanni in Bragora, Venice. Photo: Osvaldo Böhm, Venice.*

rosanct model when he painted a Baptism for the high altar of San Giovanni in Bragora, Venice, in 1494 (fig. 125). Bellini may have had Cima's painting in mind when he conceived his own work, but his emendations are more important than his borrowings. Bellini's horizon line is higher and his sky more richly and warmly colored than Cima's. Bellini's air is denser, almost palpable, and forms in the distance have been smoothed and generalized, their details subsumed in the mist. Cima's angels stand together, leaning slightly toward Christ, as they do in

*126. San Zaccaria altarpiece, San Zaccaria, Venice. Photo: Osvaldo Böhm, Venice.*

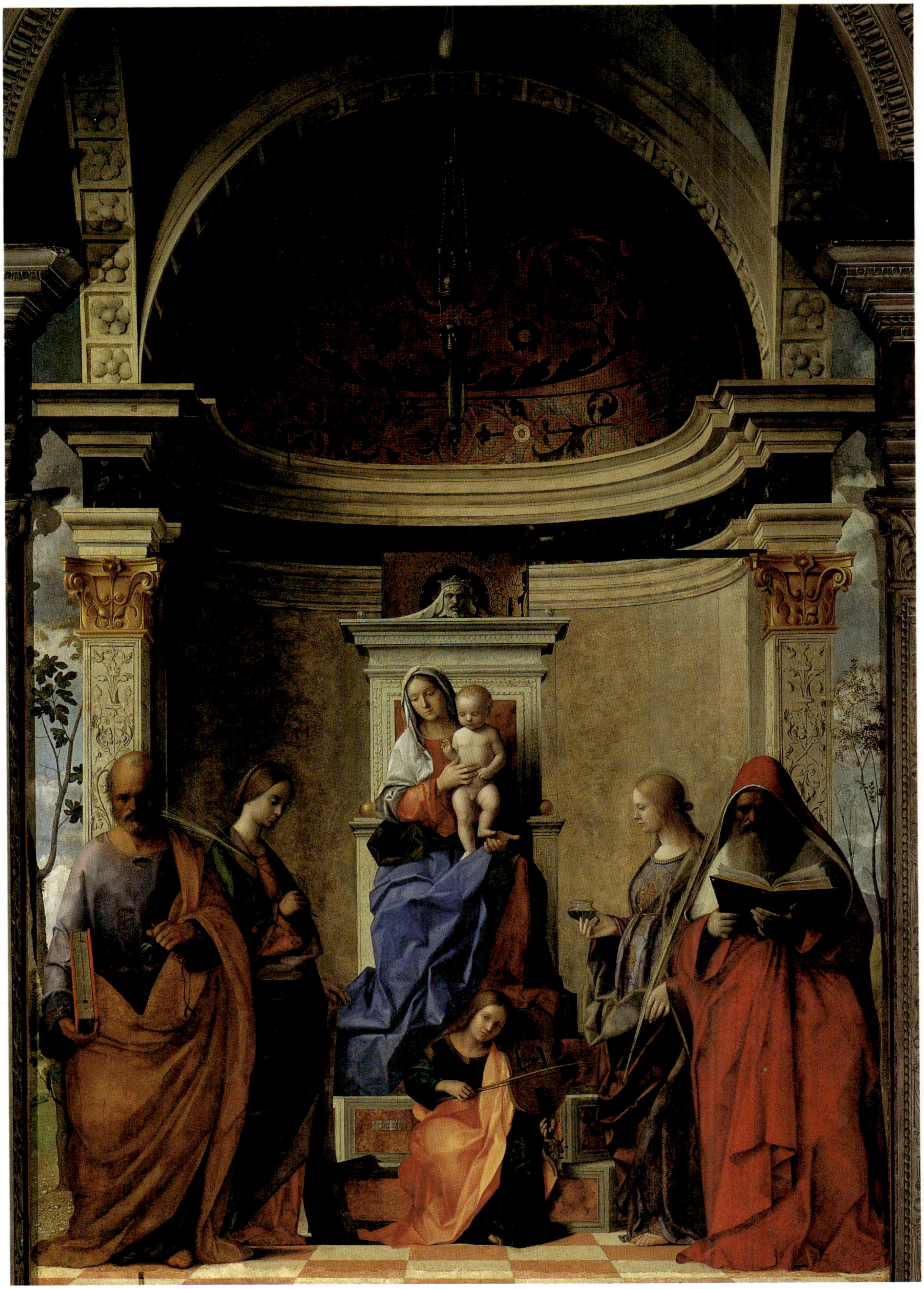

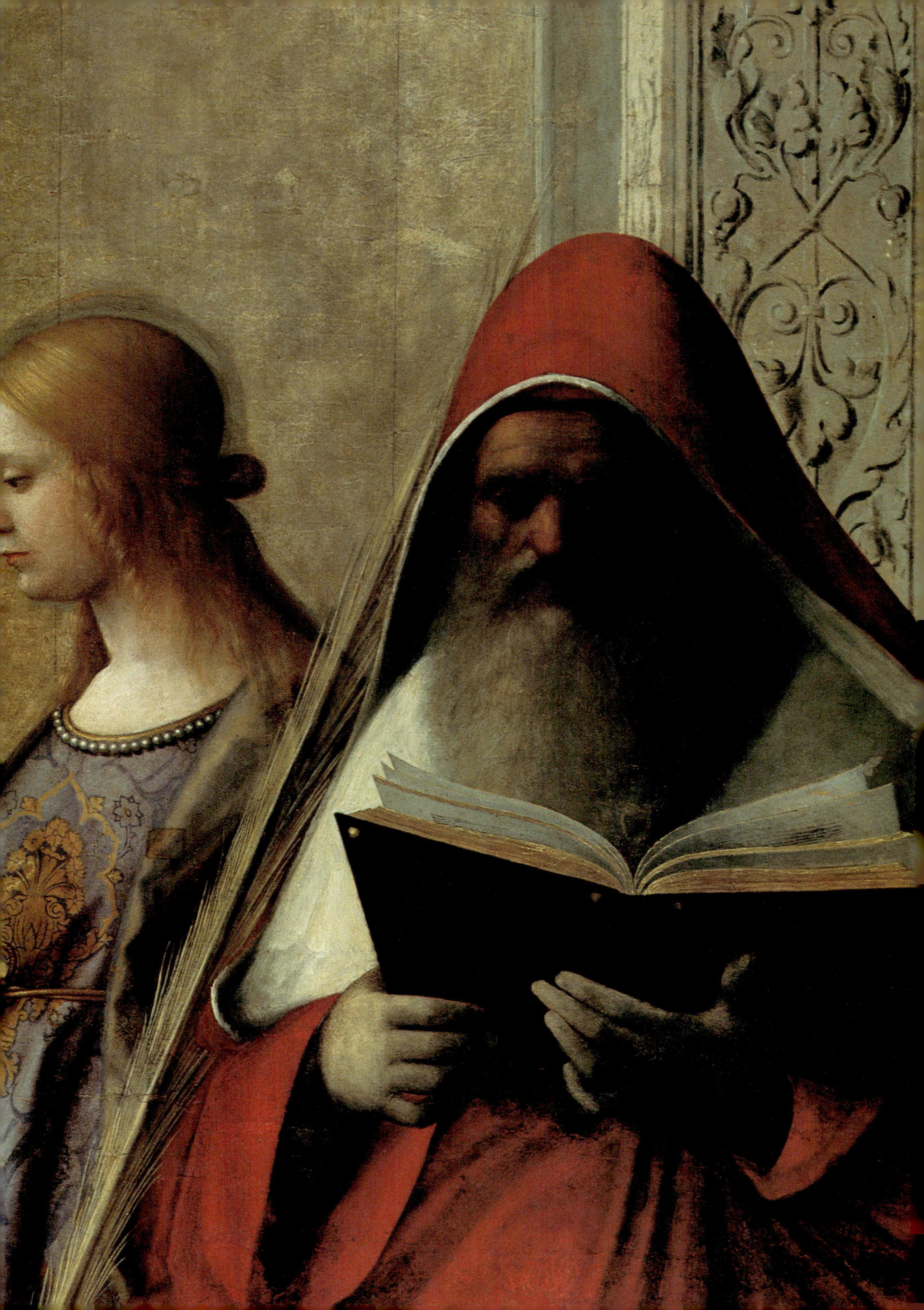

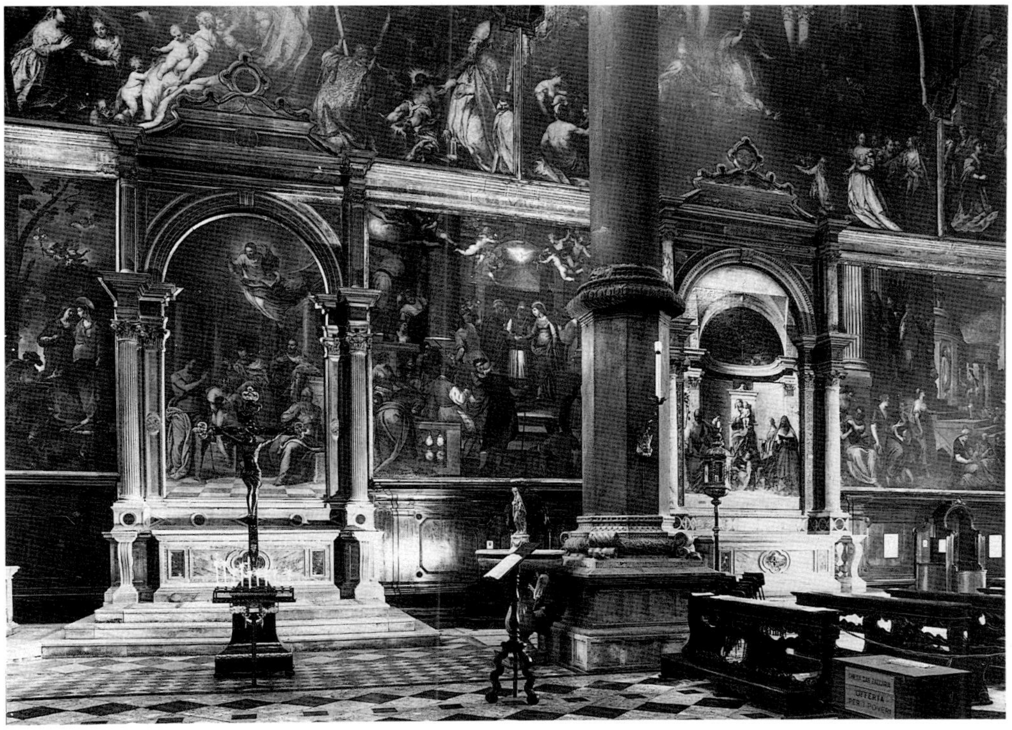

*128. San Zaccaria altarpiece in situ, San Zaccaria, Venice. Photo: Gianfranco Spinazzi, Venice.*

the mosaic prototype at San Marco. Their descendants in Bellini's *Baptism* move in positions that are musically related almost as the graceful motions of a dance, yet seeming natural and self-determined. Whereas in Cima's composition the Baptist and Christ stand in transitory postures, in Bellini's scene their positions and actions have become self-contained and self-sustaining. But more is involved.

In Cima's composition, John's head and shoulders are seen against the sky—again, as in the San Marco mosaic—and he extends his arm to raise his cup or bowl above Christ's head. Bellini has chosen a different moment in the drama and has adjusted the scene accordingly. Now the Baptist, who is contained within the earthly sphere, tilts his vessel above Christ's head. The cup is aligned with Christ, with the Holy Dove, and with God the Father: the instrument of baptism, placed on this central axis, thus sheds divine grace on the Son as the visual expression of God's acknowledgment. John the Baptist is necessary, but subsidiary; he is God's agent who fulfills the prophecy told of Jesus, but the Creator determines and guides his action. As the water of the Jordan falls on Jesus, we see what was revealed to John, the divinity that shines in Christ, first made apparent to the world at the Baptism.

The successor of the Frari triptych, and Bellini's last great altarpiece of the Madonna, is the San Zaccaria *Madonna and Saints*, signed and dated in 1505: IOANNES BELLINVS / MCCCCCV (figs. 126, 127). Unfortunately, the altarpiece has been removed from its frame and perhaps from its original site in the church.[66] Once again one must restore what has been lost in the mind's eye. The effect would have been much like that of the destroyed SS. Giovanni e Paolo altarpiece or the San Giobbe altarpiece (figs. 106–8); surely here too Bellini's illu-

*127. San Zaccaria altarpiece, detail, Saint Jerome. Photo: Osvaldo Böhm, Venice.*

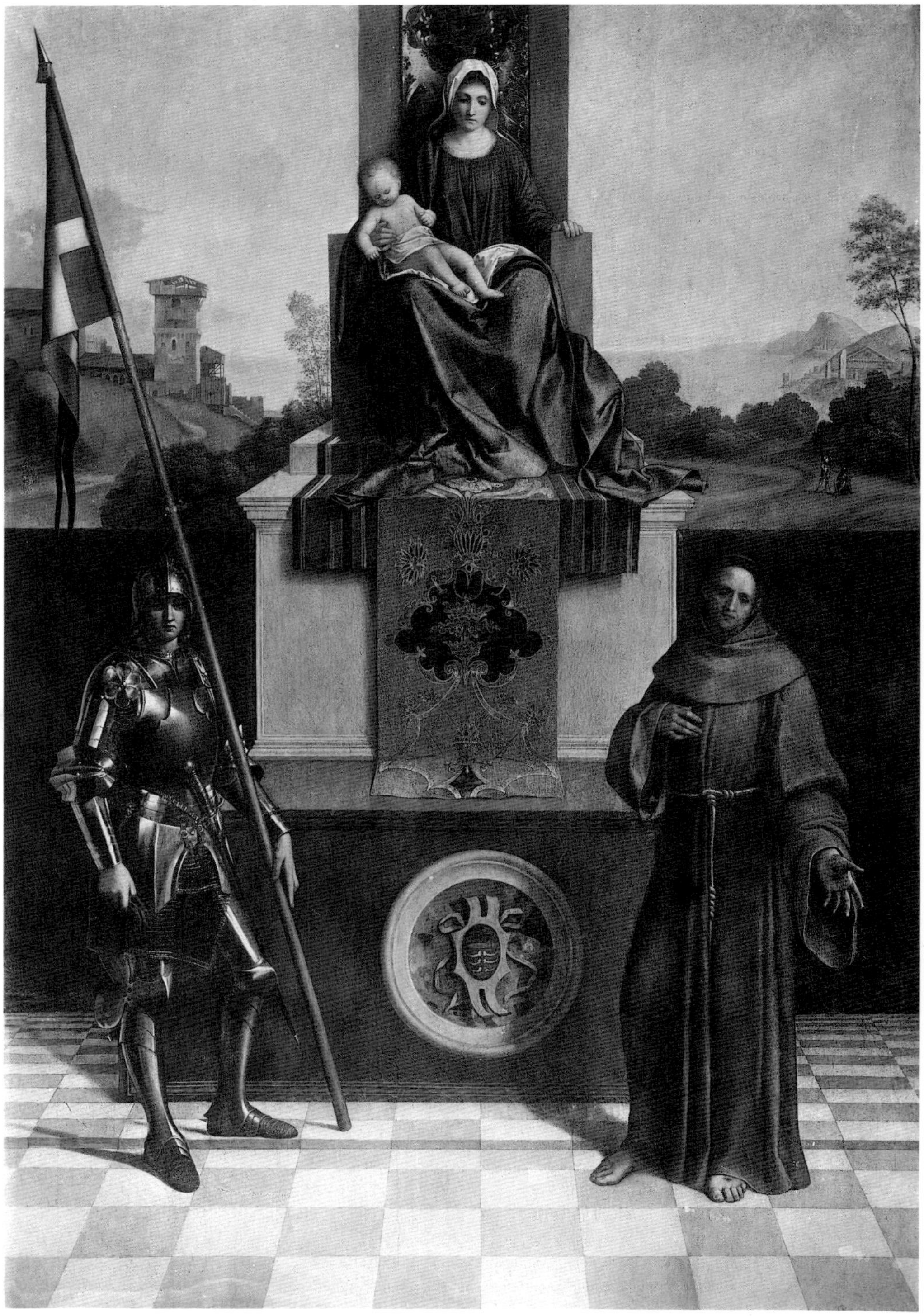

*129. Giorgione, Castelfranco altarpiece, San Liberale, Castelfranco Veneto. Photo: Alinari/Art Resource, New York.*

sionistic architecture was completed by the stone enframement of the altar itself, an effect that the present frame attempts to replicate (fig. 128).[67]

In this late work, as in the San Giobbe altarpiece and the Frari triptych, Bellini elevated the Virgin and Child in the apse of his fictive church, in the place of the altar (figs. 108–10, 116, 117). A silver and crystal lamp, like the sacred light above the consecrated altar of any church, hangs above them, an ostrich egg, symbolizing the Virgin Birth of Christ, attached to its chain.[68] The throne is decorated with

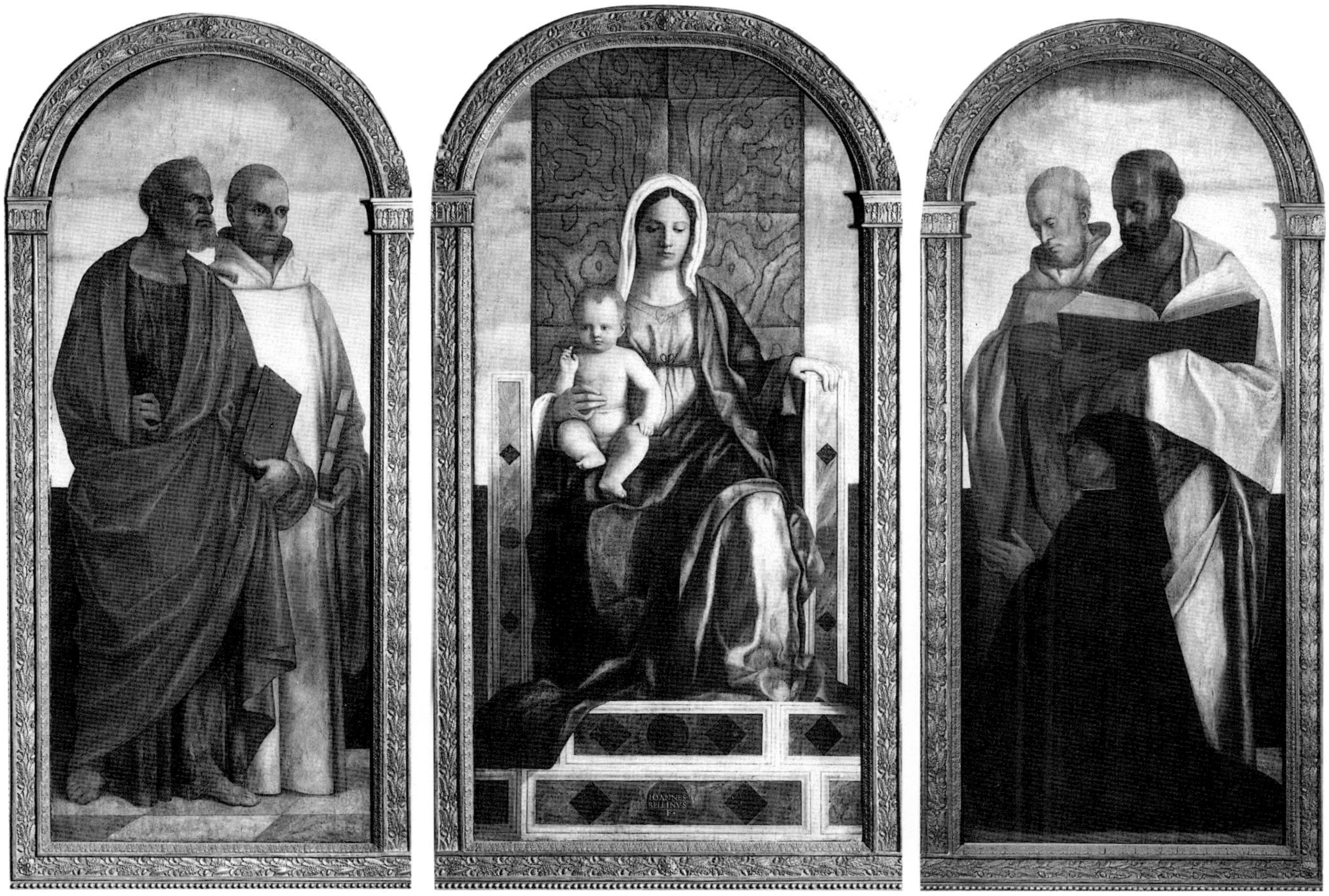

130. *Giovanni Bellini with assistance,* Madonna and Child and Saints with Donor Pietro Priuli, *triptych, Kunstsammlungen der Stadt, Düsseldorf. Photo: Fr. Pohlhammer.*

a carved head perhaps representing King David, reminding us of their lineage, and a brocade panel behind the throne is another luxurious regal insignia. The gold mosaic in the semidome is decorated with a pattern of green leaves and some startling touches of red and white, which pretends to catch the ambient light. An angel sits at the feet of Mary and Christ, serenading them and us with the *lira da braccio*. As in San Giobbe, the saints stand immediately to either side of the throne, but now the interior of Bellini's church is open at the sides, recalling the treatment of the Frari triptych or the *Madonna and Saints* formerly in SS. Giovanni e Paolo.

Views of landscape and sky are wider here than in the Frari triptych, and the architectural space considerably taller. The San Zaccaria altarpiece has a newly spacious and airy quality, flooded by light from the left, as though from its own aerial vista. This pictorial light coincides with light that enters the church from the west, an indication that the painting was made for the north or left aisle of the church, where it is now displayed. The Virgin and blessing Child turn toward this light: their beneficent response to the beholder is thus conflated with illumination, at once naturalistic and symbolic. This directional and spiritual bias toward the right is echoed by the musical angel, so that imagined sound reiterates the invitation of sight to approach the celestial throne.

The sense of light and air, of volume and monumentality endow this composition with a new nobility and harmony, an amplitude that is both visual and

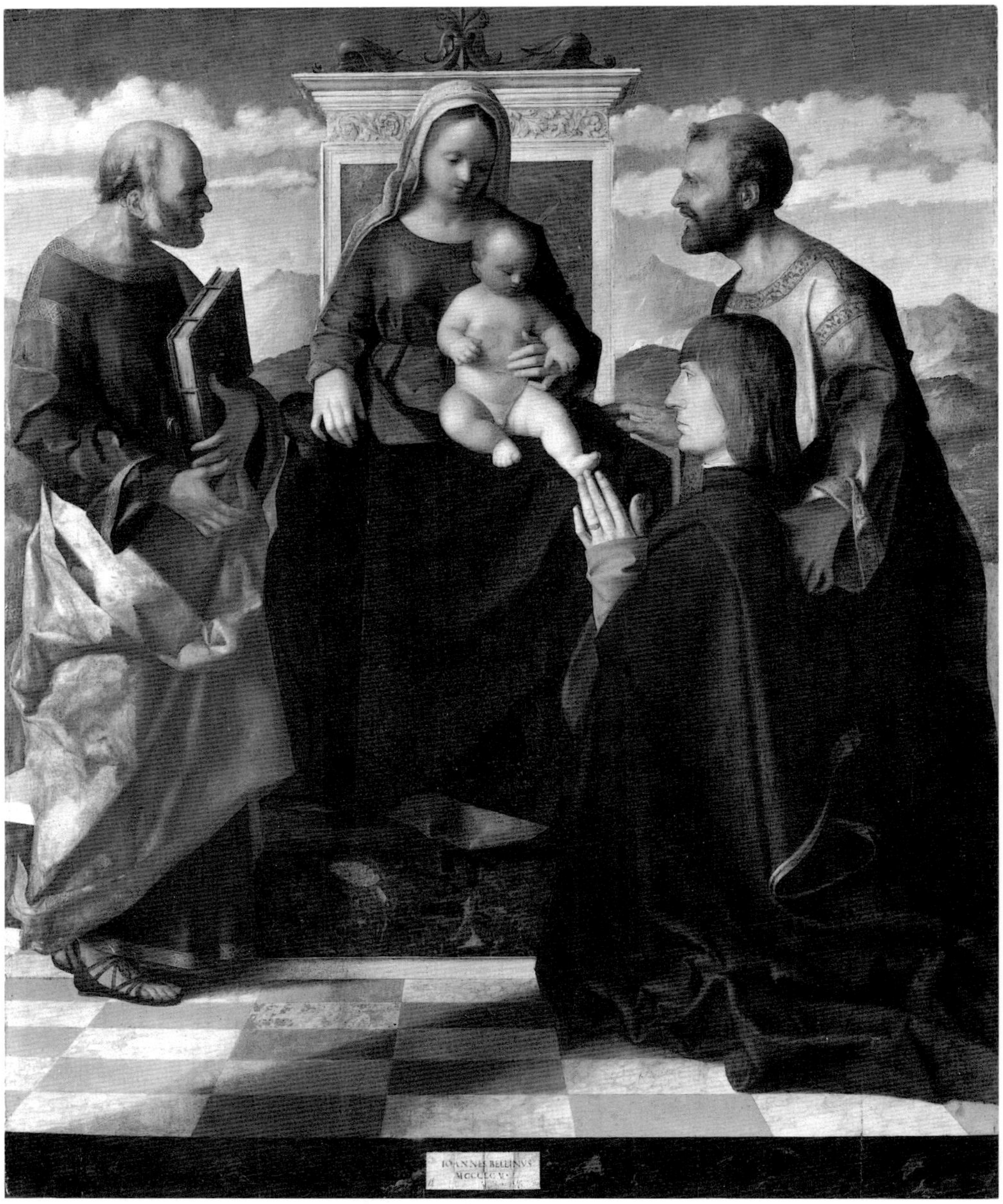

131. *Giovanni Bellini with assistance,* Madonna and Child with Saints Peter and Paul and a Donor *(Cornbury Park altarpiece), Birmingham Museum and Art Gallery. Published by permission of Birmingham Museum and Art Gallery.*

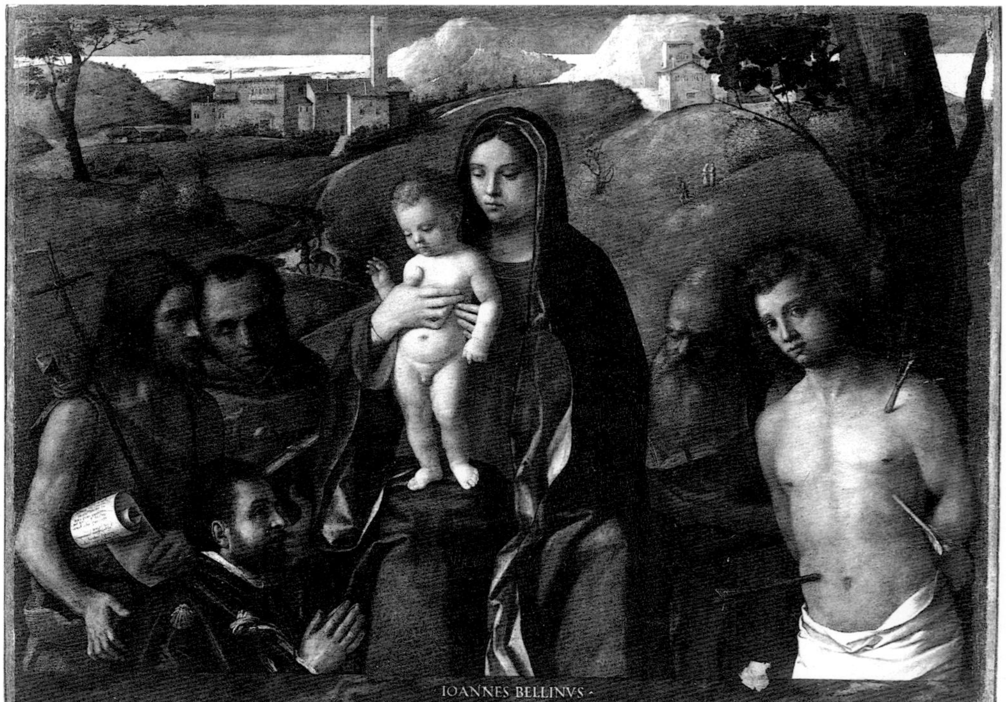


132. *Giovanni Bellini with assistance,* Madonna and Child with Saints and Donor Giacomo Dolfin *(donor repainted), Dolfin Chapel, Sacristy, San Francesco della Vigna, Venice. Photo: Soprintendenza ai Beni Artistici e Storici, Venice.*

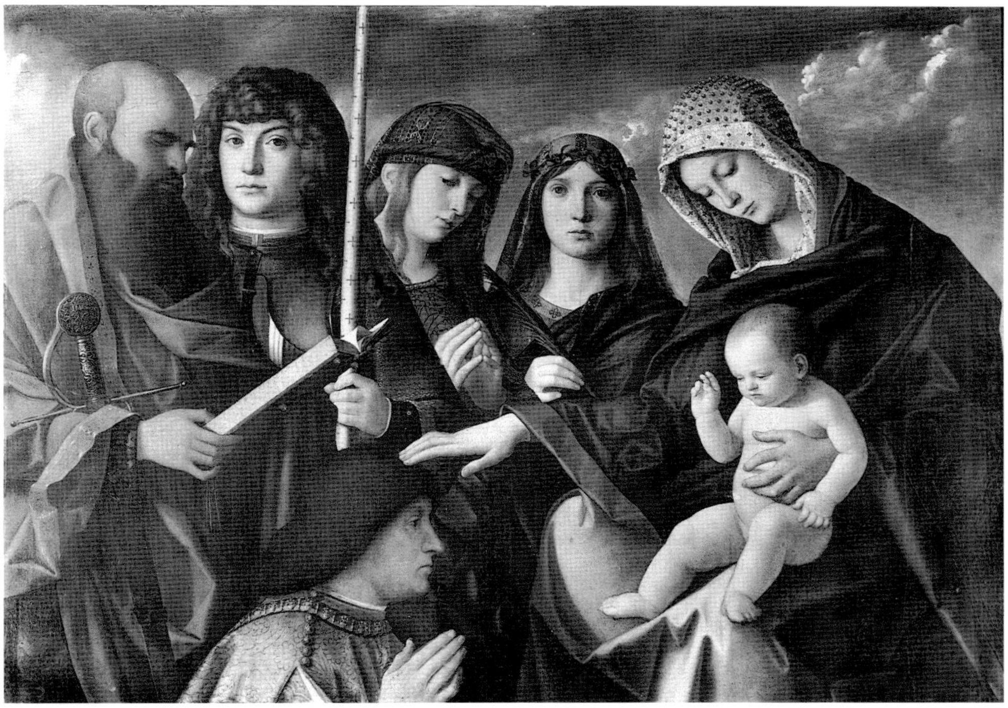

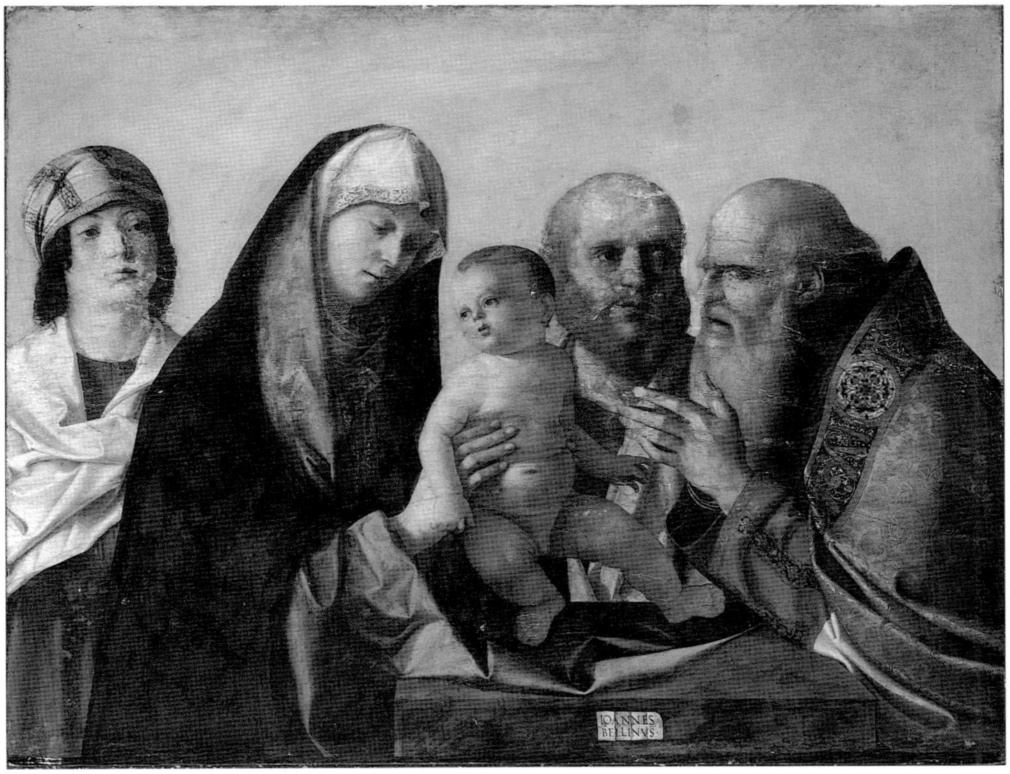


*133. Shop of Giovanni Bellini,* Madonna and Child with Saints and Donor, *The Pierpont Morgan Library, New York.*

*134. Shop of Giovanni Bellini,* Presentation of the Christ Child in the Temple, *Metropolitan Museum of Art, Anonymous Gift, 1968.*

psychological. Its polychromatic sophistication is unequaled in Venetian art at this date.[69] Perhaps Bellini was influenced by the composition of Giorgione's Castelfranco altarpiece (fig. 129), as has frequently been argued, but the younger man's debt to the old master is undeniable: the Francis in Giorgione's picture is copied after Bellini's in the San Giobbe altarpiece.

In his work for San Zaccaria, Bellini redefined his conception of feminine beauty, making the Madonna and Saints Lucy and Catherine of Alexandria more slender than their predecessors in his art, with smaller heads in proportion to their

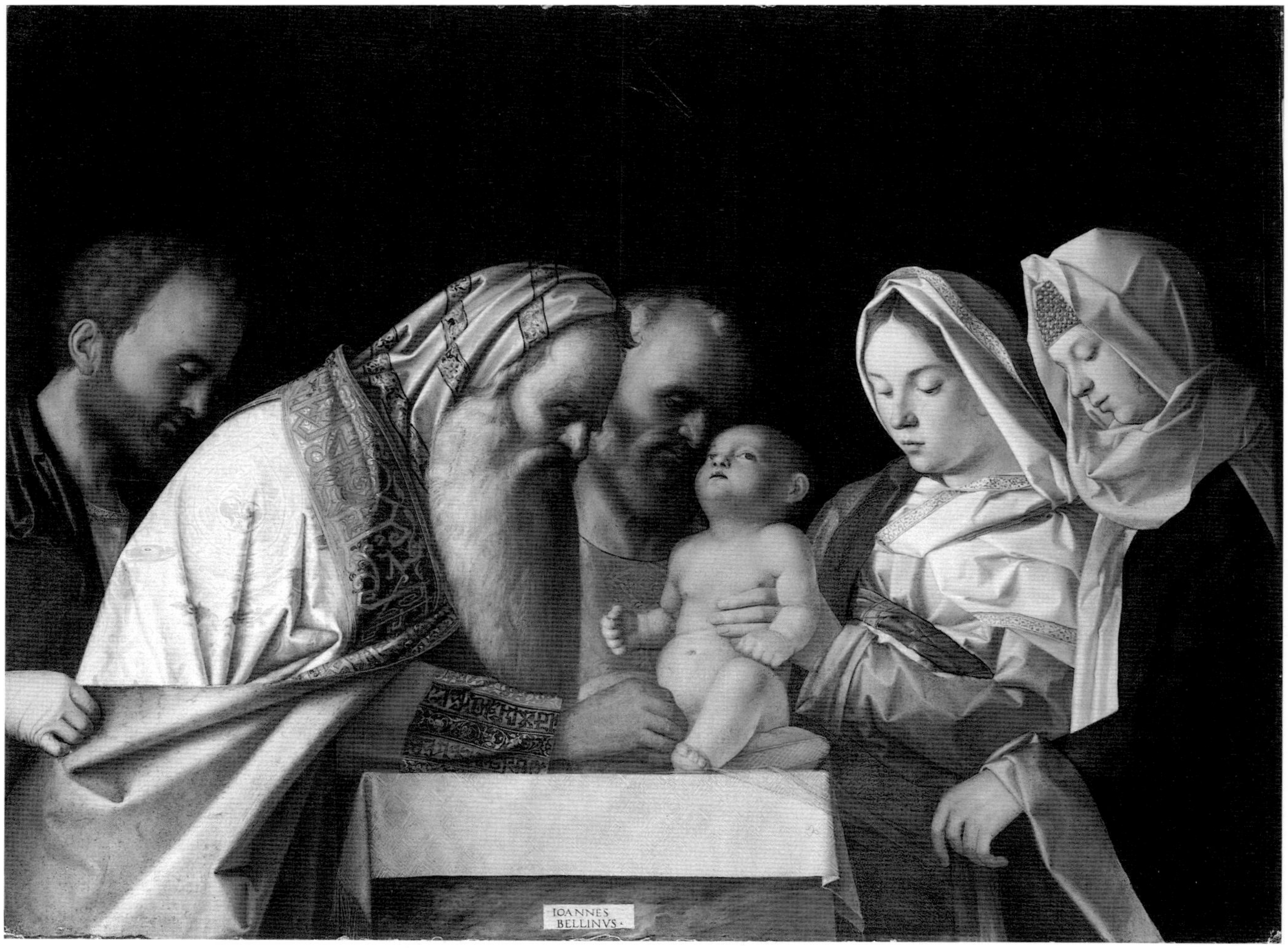


*135. Giovanni Bellini with assistance,* Circumcision of the Christ Child, *National Gallery, London.*

bodies. They have a new, that is, cinquecentesque, elegance. They also express a new mood of reverence, or rather they express this in a new way. The women are martyr saints, each holding her martyr's palm, and they offer their martyrdoms to Christ, Catherine's symbolized by her wheel, Lucy's by her crystal vessel. These saints and their male companions all have veiled eyes, and the shadows on their faces are deepest around the eyes, which is naturalistic, to be sure, but also expressive, especially in the Saint Jerome. Shadows here take on a newly important role in Bellini's art, emphasizing the volume of the head surrounded by the hood, defining form while consuming its contours in the dark, concealing the expression of the face while expressing the depth of the saint's emotion. The imprecision of the shadowed face as form becomes its strength: compelled to complete shapes in the imagination, the viewer must also specify the emotions of the saint. Thus the beholder invests in the image, becomes Bellini's collaborator, and participates in the worship of the holy congregation. Peter proffers the invitation to do so, holding the keys to the kingdom of heaven and standing in the position of honor, to the proper right of the celestial throne. He looks down at us: our psychological access to the altarpiece is through heaven's gatekeeper.

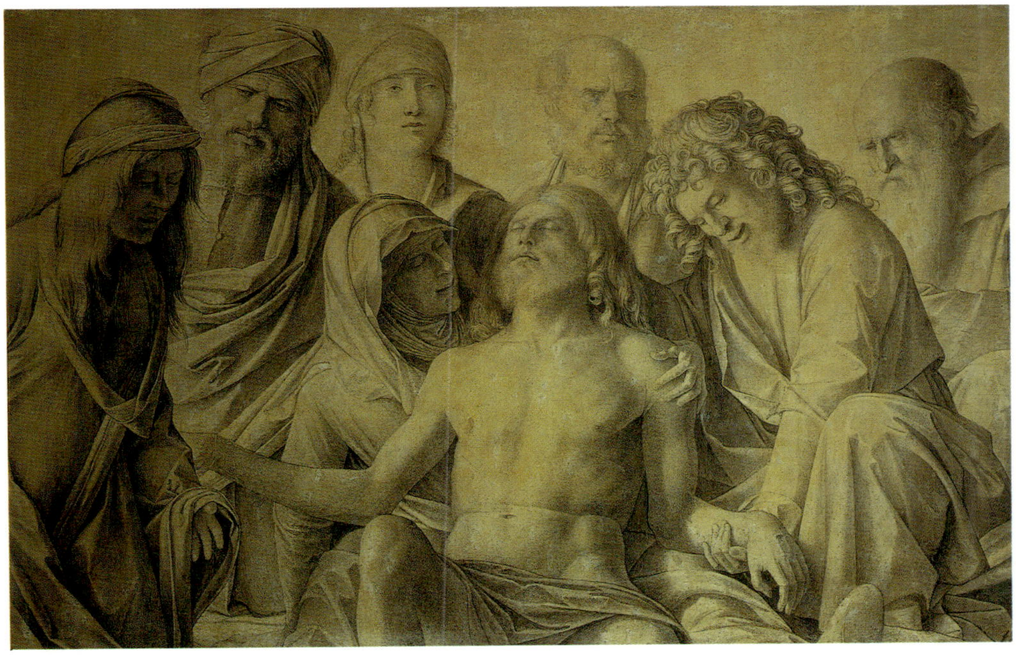

*136. Giovanni Bellini with possible assistance,* Lamentation *(Uffizi* Pietà*), Galleria degli Uffizi, Florence. Photo: Nimatallah/Art Resource, New York.*

The height of the Virgin and Child in the composition is emphasized by the low viewpoint and downward direction of their glances and tilt of their heads. What is the meaning of the way in which Christ raises his foot above the Virgin's outstretched hand? Does his action anticipate the Resurrection, when he will step out of the tomb in this way?[70] Easter was celebrated at San Zaccaria with a ducal procession that was one of the most significant and prestigious civic rituals of the republic.[71] Perhaps Bellini intended to evoke the Resurrection of the adult in the stance of the Child, so that the imagery of his altarpiece would have special relevance for this sacred and political celebration on the occasion of Christ's triumph over death.

Compared to Bellini's undisputed autograph works of the early sixteenth century, such as the Vicenza *Baptism* and the San Zaccaria *Madonna and Saints*, other sixteenth-century altarpieces associated with him must be recognized as designs by the master that were executed largely if not entirely by his shop, even though one was painted for a distinguished patrician, the procurator Pietro di Lorenzo Priuli.[72] The Priuli altarpiece, a triptych, was commissioned for the chapel of the Cross in San Michele in Isola and was probably painted a year or two after the San Zaccaria altarpiece (fig. 130). The donor kneels in prayer to the left of the Virgin and Blessing Child—not to their right, as one would expect—and Christ's benediction seems more for the benefit of the beholder than for the soul of Pietro Priuli. The unusual spiritual diffidence of this situation may reflect the donor's wishes: he was a man in whom deep piety was combined with profound modesty.[73] Perhaps these same virtues prevented his wresting from Bellini the memorial that Priuli deserved.

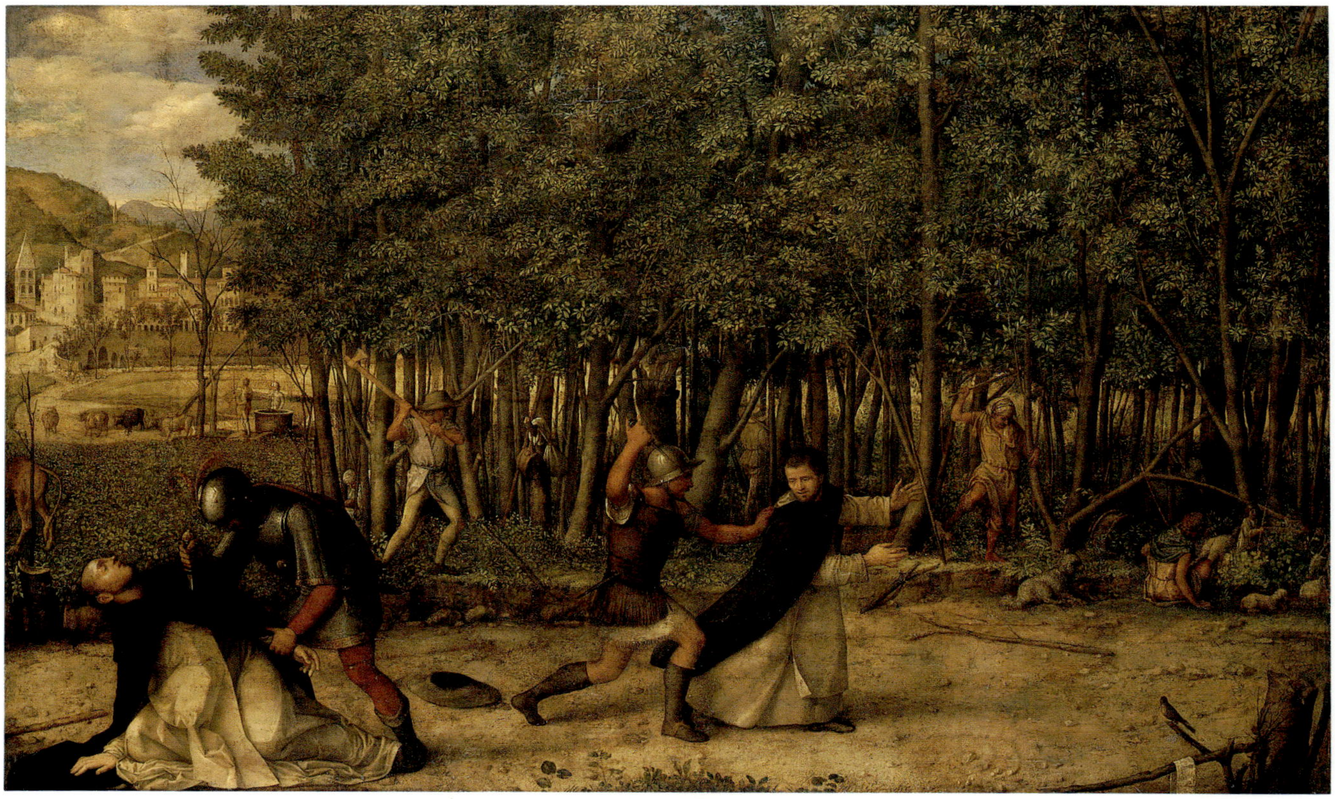

*137. Giovanni Bellini with assistance,* Death of Saint Peter Martyr, *National Gallery, London.*

Other sixteenth-century works of collaboration, in which sometimes only the design and sometimes a part of the execution may be credited to Bellini himself, include the *Madonna and Child with Saints Peter and Paul and a Donor* in Birmingham, signed and dated in 1505 (fig. 131);[74] the altarpiece commissioned by the nobleman Giacomo Dolfin for his funerary chapel in San Francesco della Vigna, which is signed and dated 1507 (fig. 132);[75] and, similar to this work in the use of partial figures, the Morgan Library *Madonna and Child with Saints and Donor*, which once belonged to Cardinal Rezzonico and later came into the possession of Antonio Canova (fig. 133).[76]

Bellini also used half- or three-quarter-length figures for narrative scenes, in particular the *Presentation of the Christ Child in the Temple* and the *Circumcision of the Christ Child*; at least some of these compositions must have been painted as altarpieces, judging from their scale (figs. 134, 135).[77] Others, perhaps first intended as private devotional images, were transformed into altarpieces by the provisions of their owners' testaments, in the same way as the *Madonna and Child* in the Madonna dell'Orto in Venice (fig. 64). This was the case with the half-length *Circumcision* that adorned the funerary chapel of the nobleman Pietro q. Giovanni Capello (or Cappello) and his wife in San Zaccaria, endowed in 1524, eight years after Bellini's death.[78] Capello's altarpiece may have been replaced in his chapel by a later, inferior copy, although its poor condition makes certainty impossible, and Bellini's composition is better represented by the version now in London (fig. 135).[79] The finest of these half-length narratives is the Uffizi *Pietà* or *Lam-*

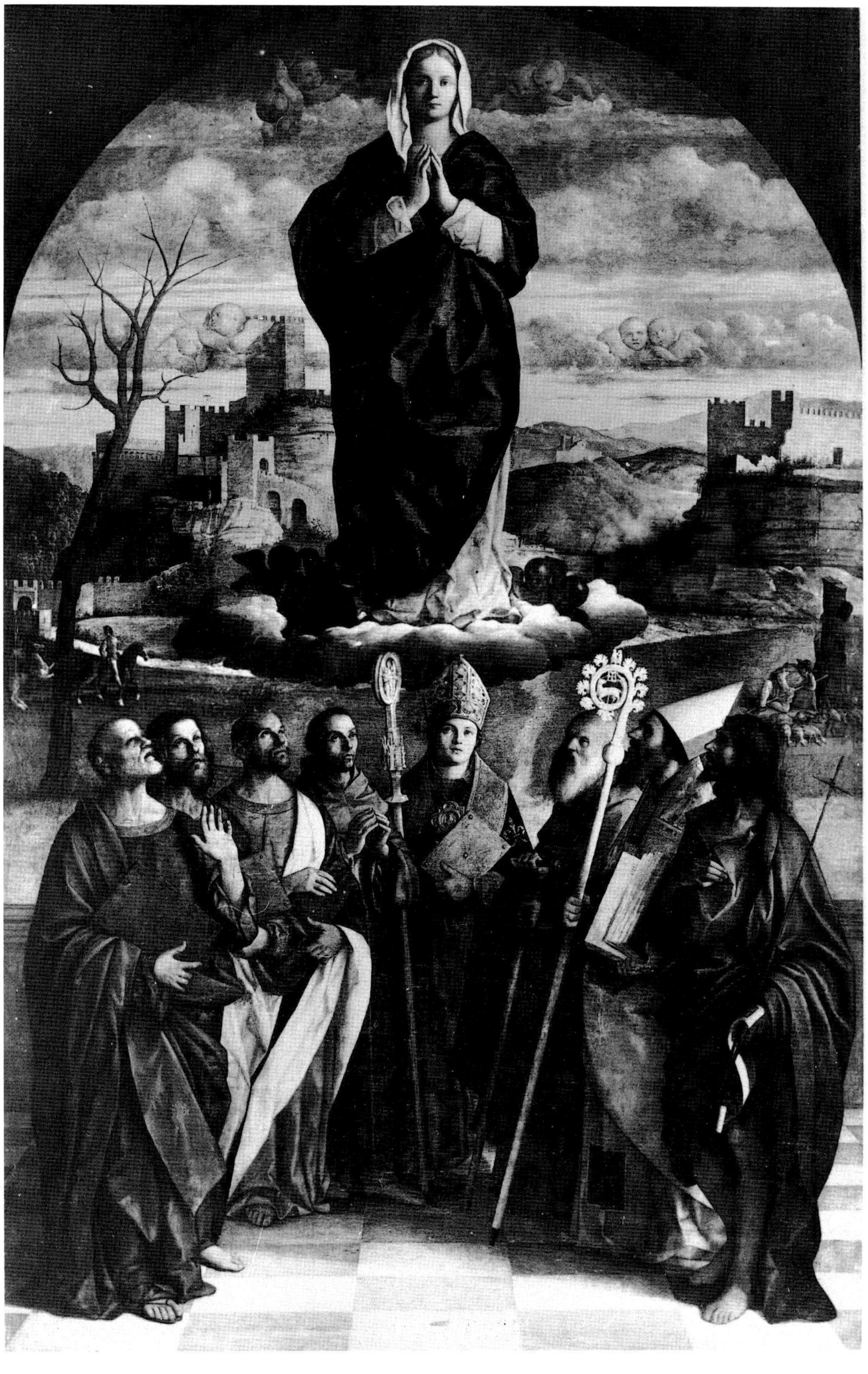

*138. Shop of Giovanni Bellini,* Immaculate Conception, *San Pietro Martire, Murano. Photo: Archivio Fotografico del Museo Correr, Venice.*

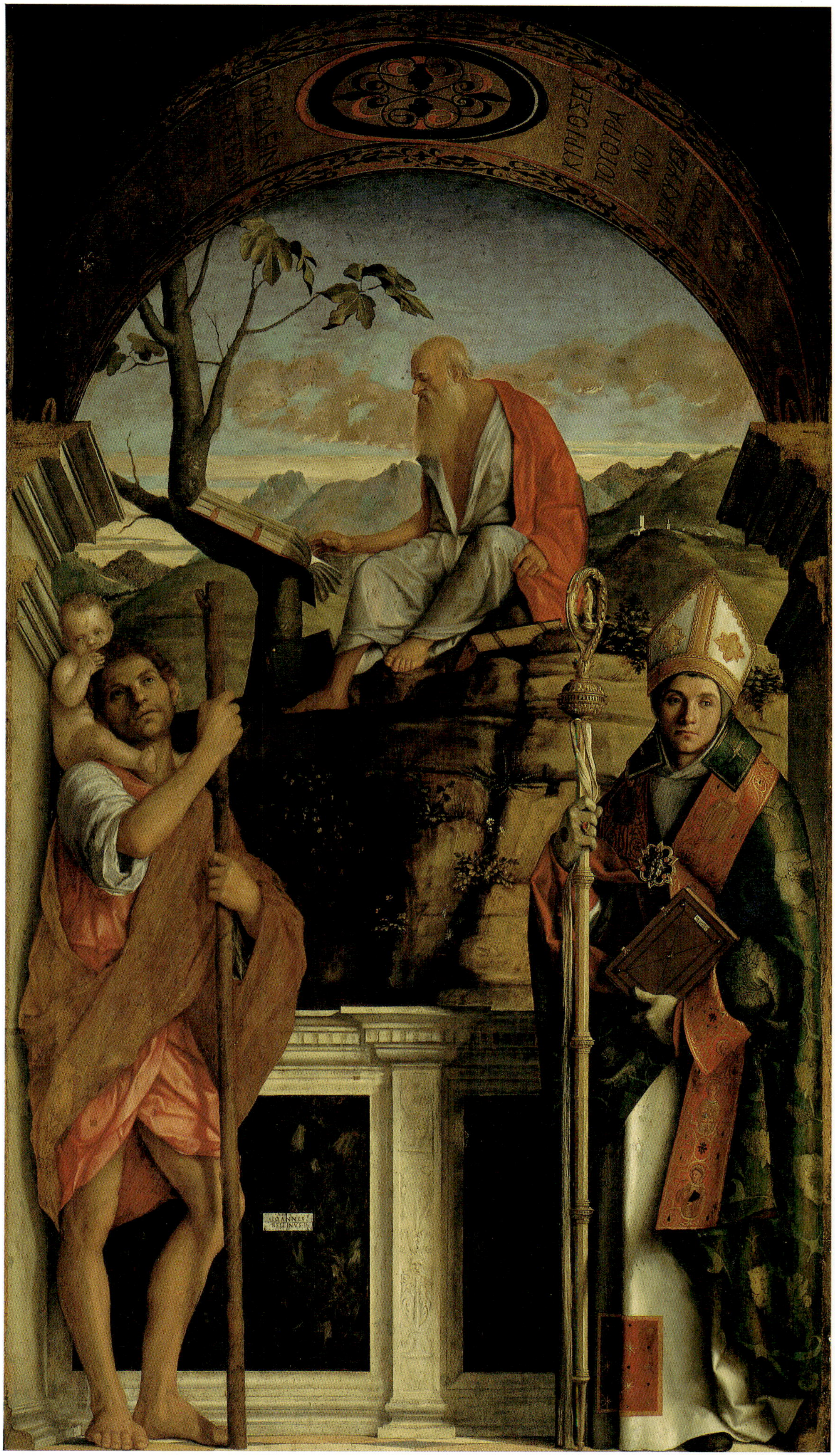
IOANNES
BELLINVS

*entation*, a grisaille dating circa 1490, perhaps painted with assistance (fig. 136). This work, however, was probably intended as a *simile* to be used as a workshop model.[80]

Comparable to the *Circumcision* and related compositions in scale, and, so to speak, in flexibility of purpose (it may have served as a devotional image, an altarpiece, or both) is the *Death of Saint Peter Martyr*, dating circa 1509 (fig. 137).[81] Here Bellini created a forest with dense rows of trees that fill the height of the canvas, closing the picture space. The martyr's death takes place in the foreground at the left, in front of a clearing in the woods. The only unrestricted view into the distance thus provides the background for the only figures set in the foreground. This scene of violence threatens to break the picture plane, and the surface tension is increased by the counterbalancing forms of a fence and tree stump at the right. A white scroll is displayed on the fence, but the signature that it carries is probably a later addition or replacement.[82]

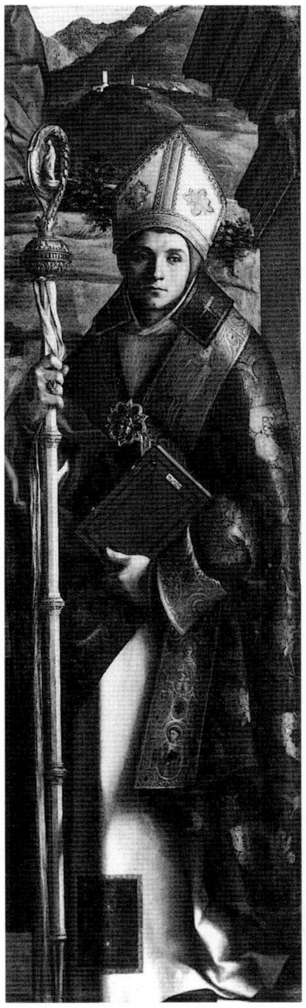

*140. San Giovanni Crisostomo altarpiece, detail, Saint Louis of Toulouse. Photo: Giacomelli Fotografia, Venice.*

With his last breath, and with his own blood, Peter writes the word *Credo*, I believe, on the ground, the opening word of the Creed in the Ordinary of the Mass and a final affirmation of his faith. Thus Peter answers his murderer, the heretic Pietro da Balsamo, called Carino, and by implication all who attack the faith: the scene is clearly relevant to the challenge of the Reformers, a Counter-Reformatory image *avant la lettre*. The martyr's face expresses his calm acceptance of his unjust suffering and death. The red of Peter's blood is echoed by red details in the garment of his assassin, the color hot and bright against the shining metal of his armor. Meanwhile, one of the saint's confreres, Bl. Brother Dominic, flees his would-be assassin in the center of the scene, slightly further back in space; but even as he runs out of harm's way, and out of the picture, Dominic looks back toward Peter.

While this terrible and bloody drama is enacted in the foreground, in the background woods other figures, oblivious to the horror, go on about their business. Some of these subsidiary characters are the pacific bucolic types who often inhabit Bellini's world, such as the shepherd seated to the far right. But others, for all their ignorance of the martyrdom, are nonetheless involved in activities that echo its violence, even though they are seemingly innocent: they hack at the branches of trees, wielding their axes with an almost hostile energy, cutting down their inanimate victims the way the heretics assault Peter and his companion.

Perhaps because of his advancing age, or because of the unceasing demands of his work in the Great Council Hall of the Ducal Palace, or even because of his (or his patrons') changing interests—or indeed for all of these reasons—Bellini produced only two more large-scale altarpieces in his last years. The high altarpiece painted for Santa Maria degli Angeli in Murano was later transferred to San Pietro Martire there (fig. 138).[83] This panel has recently been restored, and Bellini's contribution was revealed beneath layers of overpainting and discoloration. The depiction of the Virgin Mary recalls his *Madonna and Child* of 1510 (fig. 44),

*139. San Giovanni Crisostomo altarpiece, altar of Saint Jerome, San Giovanno Crisostomo, Venice. Photo: Giacomelli Fotografia, Venice.*

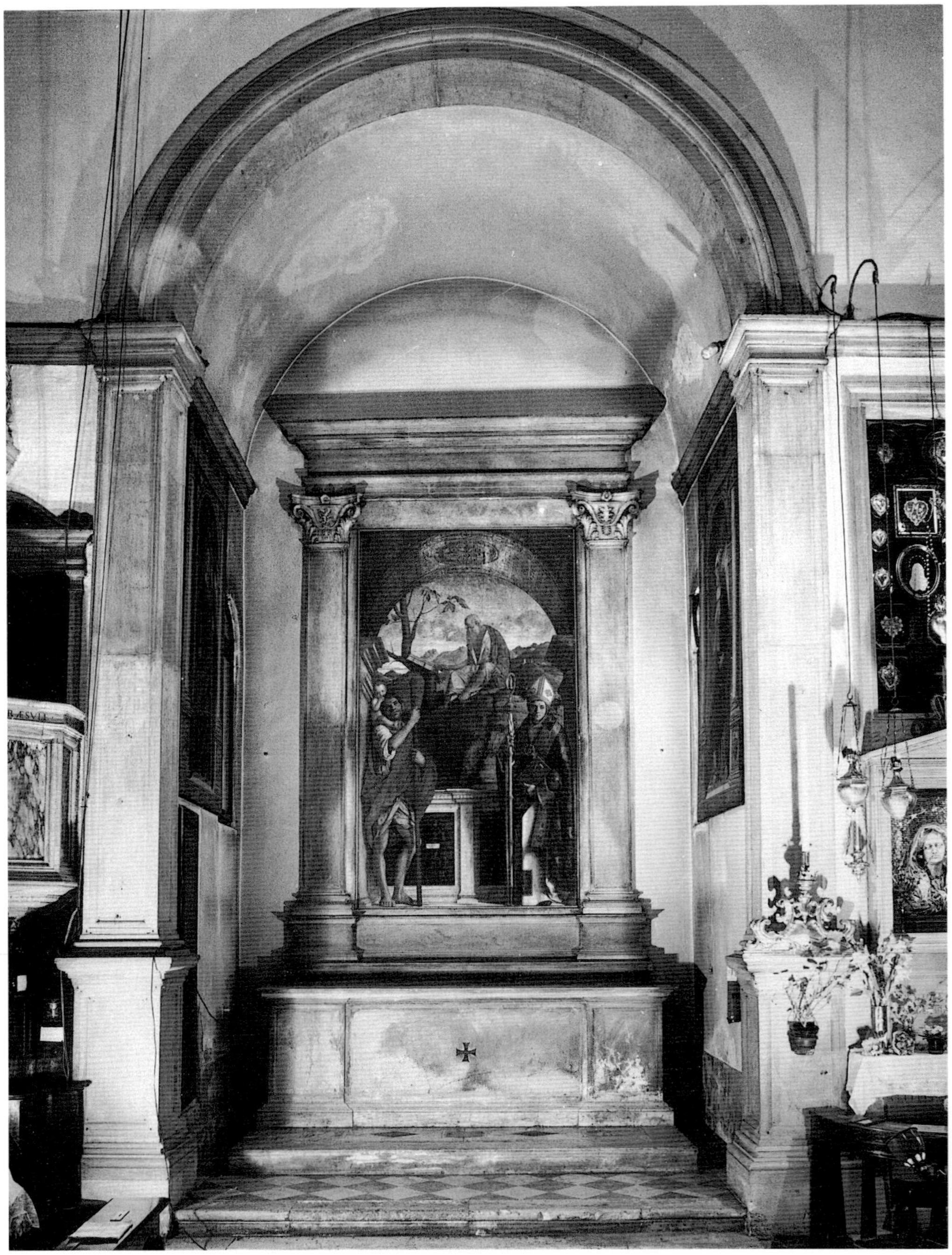

*141. Chapel of Saint Jerome, San Giovanni Crisostomo, Venice. Photo: Gianfranco Spinazzi, Venice.*

the approximate date of the altarpiece, which, however, was executed largely by assistants.

The subject of this work is not a dramatic narrative, the *Assumption*, as is often stated, but a doctrine, the *Immaculate Conception*—an important distinction that explains the stasis of the scene. The composition does resemble narratives of the Assumption, and this is purposeful: the assumption of Mary's body into heaven, that is, her exemption from the corruption of flesh, was considered prima facie evidence of her conception free of sin. The eight saints who accompany Mary do not observe her triumphant entrance into heaven, however, but bear witness to belief in her immaculacy, which was still being debated in the sixteenth century

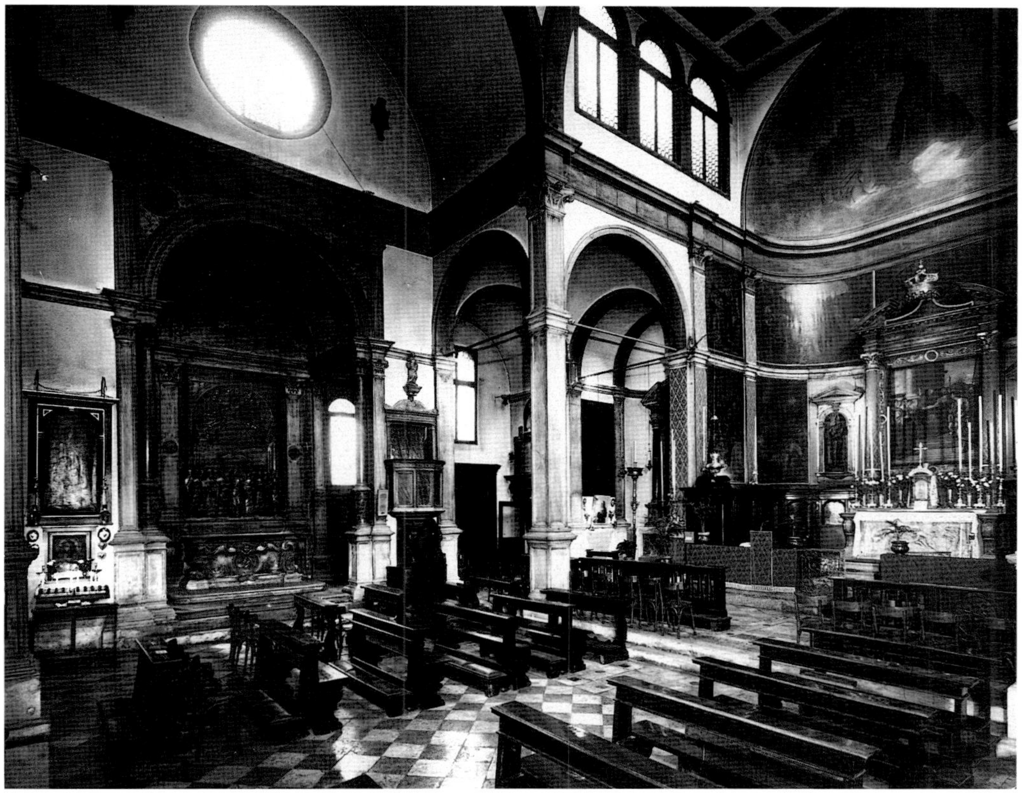

142. *San Giovanni Crisostomo, Venice; Tullio Lombardo,* Coronation of the Virgin, *Bernabò Chapel, at left. Photo: Osvaldo Böhm, Venice.*

and indeed was not declared dogma until 1854.[84] Bellini's assembly of saints includes familiar champions of the Virgin's Immaculate Conception, notably Francis and Louis of Toulouse, who is central in the composition, together with Peter, John the Evangelist, Mark, Anthony Abbot, Augustine, and John the Baptist. (Of this congregation, only the three apostles, Peter, Mark, and the Evangelist, were present at the Assumption.) Attesting to their faith in the Immaculate Conception, Bellini's witnesses gather in the semicircular formation long associated in art with groups of pupils or supporters of a belief.[85]

Bellini's last altarpiece was painted for the church of San Giovanni Crisostomo, signed and dated in 1513, just three years before his death: the inscription MDXIII / IOANNES BELLINVS. P. is written on a cartellino affixed to a low wall or balustrade in the foreground (figs. 139–41).[86] The donor was Giorgio Diletti, a wealthy merchant who lived in the parish.[87] But neither Diletti's wealth nor the subject of his altarpiece enabled him—or more accurately, his widow—to extract a commission from Bellini at a time when far more powerful patrons, including Venetian nobles and the Marchesa Isabella d'Este, were unable to do so. Rather it was because Diletti, a confrere of the Scuola Grande di San Marco, had ceded the altar to the confraternity in his will. Giovanni Bellini, like his brother Gentile, and like their father before them, was also a member of the scuola, and if his official and artistic involvement was less than that of Gentile—whose specialization in narrative painting was put to the service of their confraternity—he was nonetheless clearly committed to the organization.[88] The San Giovanni Crisostomo commission enabled Giovanni to serve his scuola, albeit at a distance, but in the genre of which he was the supreme master.

The San Giovanni Crisostomo altarpiece remains on the altar for which it was painted and is related to its site by rather remarkable means. In earlier altarpieces, Bellini had exploited the resemblance between imaginary and real architectural forms to define the relation of fictive and actual space. The conception is like that of the parapet in Bellini's small devotional images, such as the *Madonna degli alberetti* (fig. 34), the architectonic illusion that provides the point (or plane) of contact between worshiper and sacred beings.

At San Giovanni Crisostomo, Bellini elaborated on this tradition to achieve a powerful new effect. As in earlier works, Bellini's illusionistic architecture is completed by the reality of the altar enframement, at least at the sides, where stone pilasters combine with painted ones.[89] But now the vault at the top of the picture space is unrelated to the rectangular enframement, and the fictive structure no longer refers only to the space immediately before the altar. Instead, Bellini's architecture, both real and fictive, echoes that of Tullio Lombardo's relief of the *Coronation of the Virgin* on the altar across the nave, which the sculptor had completed by 1502 (fig. 142).[90] In a sense, Bellini had anticipated this effect, with its intimations of the *paragone,* at San Giobbe, where the illusionistic chapel of his altarpiece is perforce juxtaposed with the actual chapel opposite. But at San Giovanni Crisostomo, the correspondence is more complete, and the space of the church itself becomes involved with the illusion. Bellini accomplished nothing less than a redefinition of the relation of viewer to image.[91]

Three saints, Jerome, Christopher, and Louis of Toulouse, are represented, in accordance with the wishes of the donor.[92] Altarpieces with narrative subjects, such as the *Transfiguration* or the *Coronation of the Virgin*, or with the Virgin and Child accompanied by saints were far more common than groupings of three or more saints. But Bellini's composition was not without precedent, the most immediate example being the high altarpiece of this same church, completed by Sebastiano del Piombo in 1511 (fig. 143).[93]

In Sebastiano's painting, the titular saint of San Giovanni Crisostomo sits in profile, writing in his book. His seat is raised on a stepped platform and set back in the picture space. In the paved area of the foreground, John the Baptist, in three-quarter profile, approaches from the left, and behind him stand two more men, one of them probably Saint Onophrius. Three women saints at the right counterbalance this group: Mary Magdalen, Agnes, and Catherine, the onomastic saint of the donor, who faces the beholder for that very reason. The picture space behind them and in back of the titular saint is closed; to the right it opens asymmetrically to a landscape vista. Jacopo Bellini had experimented with this kind of asymmetrical composition combining open and closed spaces, and the conception had been further developed in Giovanni's paintings, including the very early *Saint Jerome in the Wilderness* (fig. 1). Sebastiano was indebted to Giovanni Bellini also for the sense of surrounding atmospheric light.

Bellini in turn took the younger master's work into account in designing his

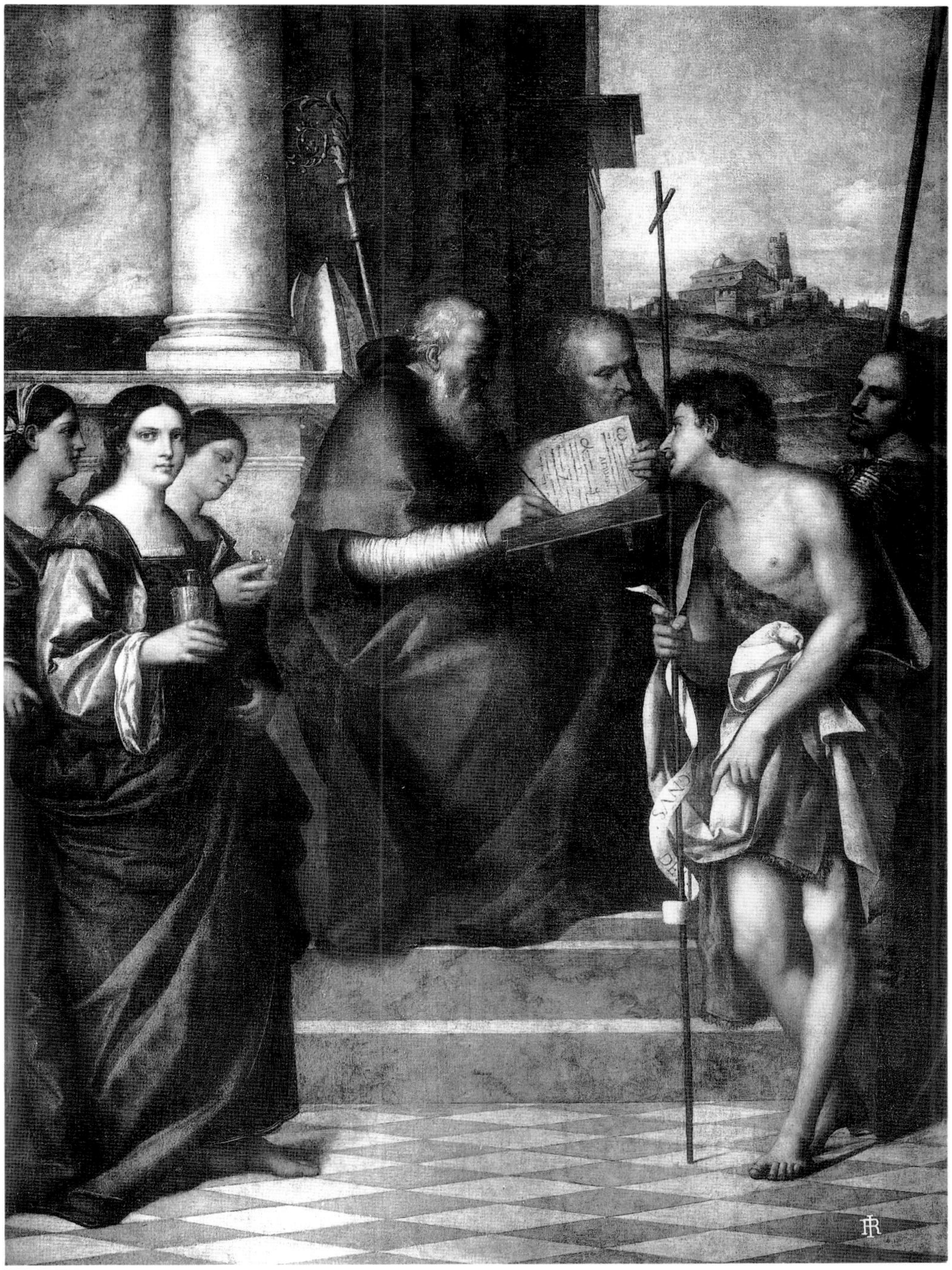

143. *Sebastiano del Piombo, San Giovanni Crisostomo altarpiece, San Giovanni Crisostomo, Venice. Photo: Osvaldo Böhm, Venice.*

altarpiece for San Giovanni Crisostomo. His picture space, like Sebastiano's, combines open and closed areas but is divided differently: two parallel planes, one above and behind the other, are separated by the balustrade. The idea of such a scheme seems to have been in the air in early sixteenth-century Venice and the Veneto. The arrangement recalls that of Giorgione's Castelfranco *Madonna*, completed some eight or more years earlier and perhaps known to Bellini. Similarly, Cima da Conegliano, in an altarpiece approximately contemporary with Giorgione's, had juxtaposed an architectural foreground with a landscape background. Titian had painted a variation on the theme in his Saint Mark altarpiece, commissioned for the church of Santo Spirito in Isola, probably circa 1510–11, and thus contemporary with Bellini's work (fig. 144).[94] But Bellini's interpretation of this idea has none of the youthful brashness, the pulsating, nervous energy of the Titian. Titian's earthly physicality and drama are in opposition—perhaps intentional opposition—to the spiritual quietude and intimate psychology of Bellini. He has masked the logical disparities of foreground and background so that they are not at first apparent; only after we have been drawn into the altarpiece do we realize that Bellini has removed us from our world to a sacred realm.

As in Sebastiano's composition, here too the titular saint, Jerome, is set further back in the picture space, higher than the other figures, and in profile.[95] In Sebastiano's altarpiece, however, the saints are related by various psychological means, and their congregation seems almost informal, especially the trio of female saints. In Bellini's image, the three protagonists are separated, preoccupied with their own thoughts. In the San Zaccaria altarpiece, Bellini had already suggested the essential isolation of the human condition: individuals are alone even among their fellows, and alone they must approach God. In the San Giovanni Crisostomo altarpiece, the isolation is more complete: each is alone before a God who is no longer visible to the senses. This separation—too gentle to seem an alienation—is stretched almost to the breaking point: it is almost a rupture.

What unites the saints, in spite of their isolation, is a shared contemplative mood. Moreover—and in Bellini's art, most important—light binds the landscape and architectural spaces, hence the holy beings who inhabit them. Coming from the right (west) and slightly in front of the altarpiece, this light, which corresponds to the late afternoon light of the church (the effect is impossible to capture in photographs) is also a means of relating the sacred realm to our world. The transparent shadow cast by Christopher's staff on his leg seems to be caused by this actual light. As in such smaller images as the *Madonna degli alberetti* of 1487 (fig. 34) or the *Madonna and Child* of 1510 (fig. 44), Bellini has used light more than perspectival illusion to make the experience of the sacred accessible to the beholder. We are invited to enter the sacred realm not by the usual illusionistic perspectival means, comprehensible to the intellect and immediate in their effect, but by the atmospheric light that unites our world and that of the saints, which surrounds us as it does them, which acts on our emotions, affecting us psychologically and spiritually.

The meaning of this mysterious scene is explained by the inscription of the mosaic vault, here written in Greek rather than Latin, the language of Bellini's other inscriptions.[96] These words, from the second verse of the fourteenth psalm, are an admonition: "The Lord looks down from heaven upon the children of men, to see if there are any that act wisely, that seek after God."[97] But whereas the text admonishes us, the image more gently shows us the way to act wisely, to seek God. Very old and learned, Jerome approaches God through his sacred text; he sits beneath a symbolic fig tree, where the Lord may look down upon him: "When you were under the fig tree, I saw you" (John 1:23). Very young, the compassionate

*144. Titian, Saint Mark altarpiece, Santa Maria della Salute, Venice. Photo: Osvaldo Böhm, Venice.*

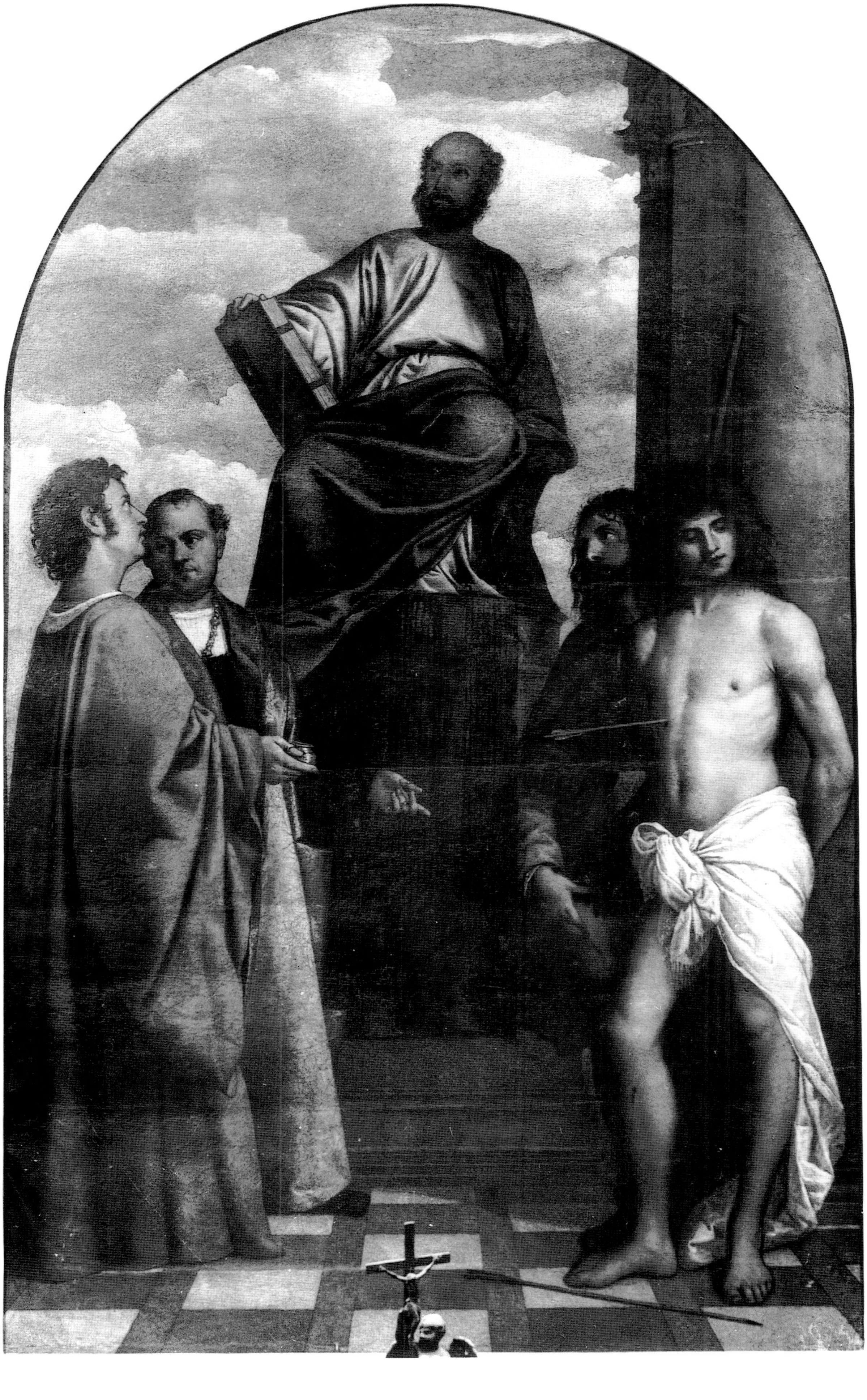

Franciscan Saint Louis holds the Lord in his heart, and Christopher, midway between the others in age, physically takes up Christ's burden. Alluding to the imagery of the ages of man, these three saints exemplify three ways of seeking God. Because each person must seek the Lord in his own way, each saint is separate: in spite of a common purpose, each is alone before God.

The clear atmosphere of the early works has become dense, almost crepuscular, as though the mosaic at the top of the image not only defined its setting but determined its pictorial language. The mosaic is not merely a Byzantinizing motif; it provides the chromatic and luministic keynote of the painting. Bellini's brushstrokes are comparable to the golden and colored tesserae of a mosaic, and like those lustrous pieces of glass or stone, they suggest forms by patches of color and light rather than precise definition with uninterrupted contours. Bellini's art emulates and evokes the sense of sight—but this sensuous experience is the means whereby the master addresses the spirit of the beholder. Perhaps unconsciously at first, but eventually and inevitably we understand the inherent transience of physical sight, the instability of changing light and atmosphere, the fragility of earthly experience. Through the senses, Bellini leads us to abandon the senses, to realize a higher truth.

# Part Two: Secular Painting

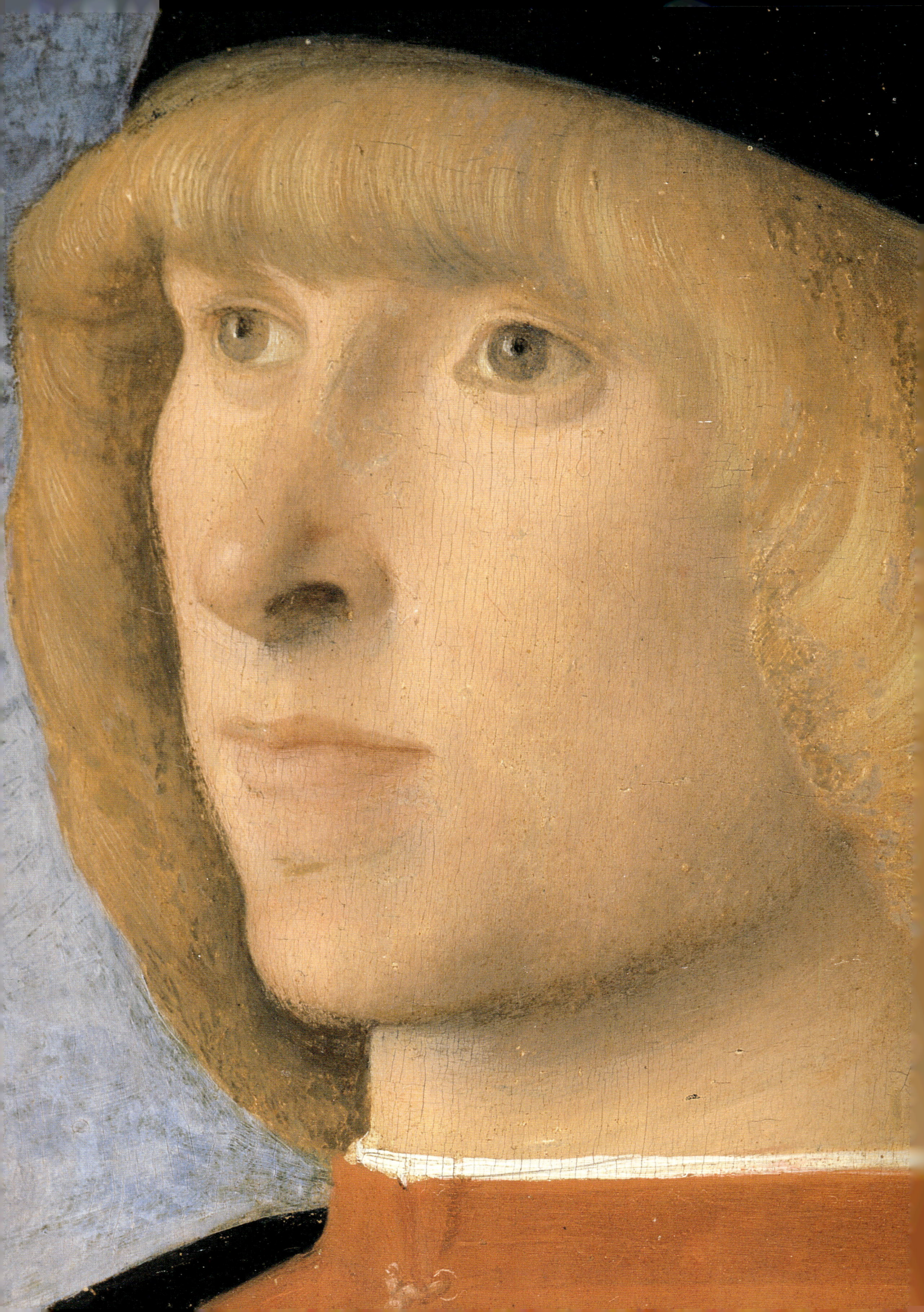

# 3 Portraits and Patricians

*Image of the soul and of the body*
—Andrea Navagero

In his funeral oration for Doge Leonardo Loredan (doge 1501–21), Andrea Navagero praised the son of the deceased nobleman in the words used as an epigraph to this chapter: "immagine dell'anima e del corpo." Had he seen Bellini's painting of the doge himself, the orator might have described it with those same words, for in this portrait both the physical likeness of the man and his inner being are shown to us with such conviction that Loredan seems present, vital, and knowable despite the nearly half a millennium that separates us from him (fig. 149). To understand this masterpiece, we must consider not only its precedents in Bellini's earlier portraiture but also the psychology and sociology of his Venetian compatriots, which Bellini knew how to represent and which are the true subject of such portraits by him. Indeed, the first authors to consider Bellini as a portraitist implied this connection between his paintings and Venetian society, and what they have to say reveals a great deal about his art and his milieu.

Marcantonio Michiel, writing a few years after Bellini's death, mentioned only five portraits (and a possible sixth) by him in the collections of Venetian noblemen. None of these can be identified—once again we are given provenances without pictures—and in any case, Michiel's list was far from complete. Its brevity notwithstanding, however, the compilation is informative: Michiel named not only the owners but the subjects of Bellini's portraits and revealed something of the artist's circle of acquaintance and patronage. Of the four owners mentioned, three were patricians, and one, Leonico Tomeo, was a philosopher and professor at Padua; Bellini was not only the artist of the nobility but had associations among the community of humanists and scholars in Padua as well as in Venice. Tomeo had a portrait of himself by Bellini, painted when the philosopher was much younger; "now," Michiel lamented in 1530, "it is all flaking, yellowed, and obscured."[1] (Tomeo also had a portrait of his father by Bellini's father; family portraits by the Bellini seem to have been a Tomeo tradition.) Michiel's choice of words—"flaking, yellowed, obscured"—suggests that the philosopher's portrait was painted primarily in oil, tempera being less subject to these woes. Given Tomeo's profession, his painting may have resembled the Bellinesque portraits in Bergamo and Milan, both dating circa 1475–80, in which the sitters' antique garments are meant to suggest erudition. The anonymous young man of the Milan portrait wears both a wreath and togalike drapery tied over one shoulder

*145. Shop of Giovanni Bellini,* Portrait of a Humanist, *Castello Sforzesco, Milan.*

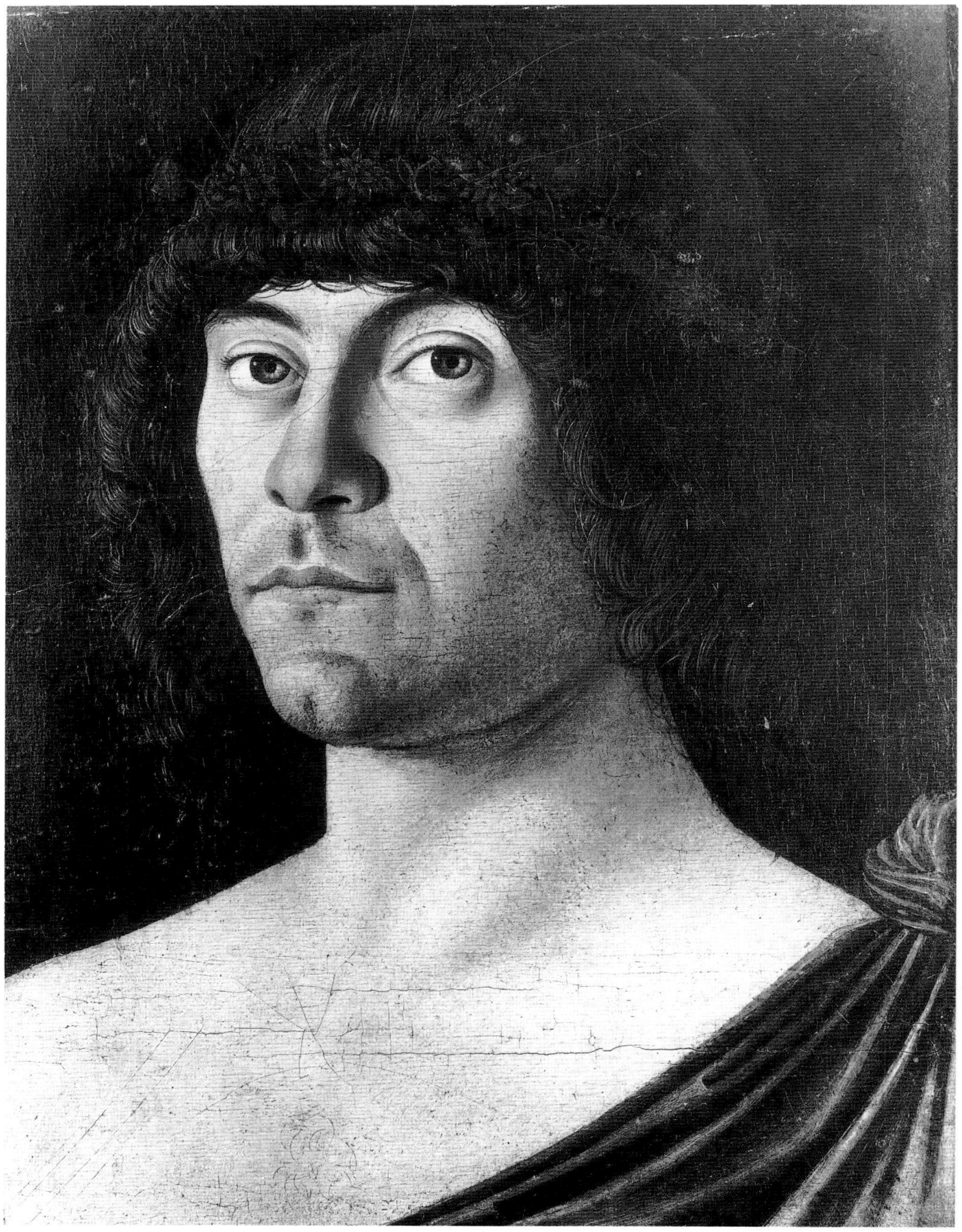

(fig. 145). In the Bergamo picture, the subject wears a green drapery that reveals enough of his neck and chest to imply classical nudity, hence classical learning (fig. 146).[2]

The other Bellini portraits that Michiel saw belonged to his patrician compatriots. Jeronimo Marcello displayed the portrait of his distinguished forebear Giacomo, Generalissimo da mar, captain general of the Venetian fleet, who died of wounds received at the Battle of Gallipoli.[3] This work probably resembled the Bellinesque portrait of another Venetian general, Giovanni Emo, Provveditore Generale in the war with Ferrara, which has often been ascribed to Bellini but is not by him (fig. 147).[4] However, the assertiveness of this military man, the attempt to illustrate appropriate pugnacity in his "leonine" features, in the thick

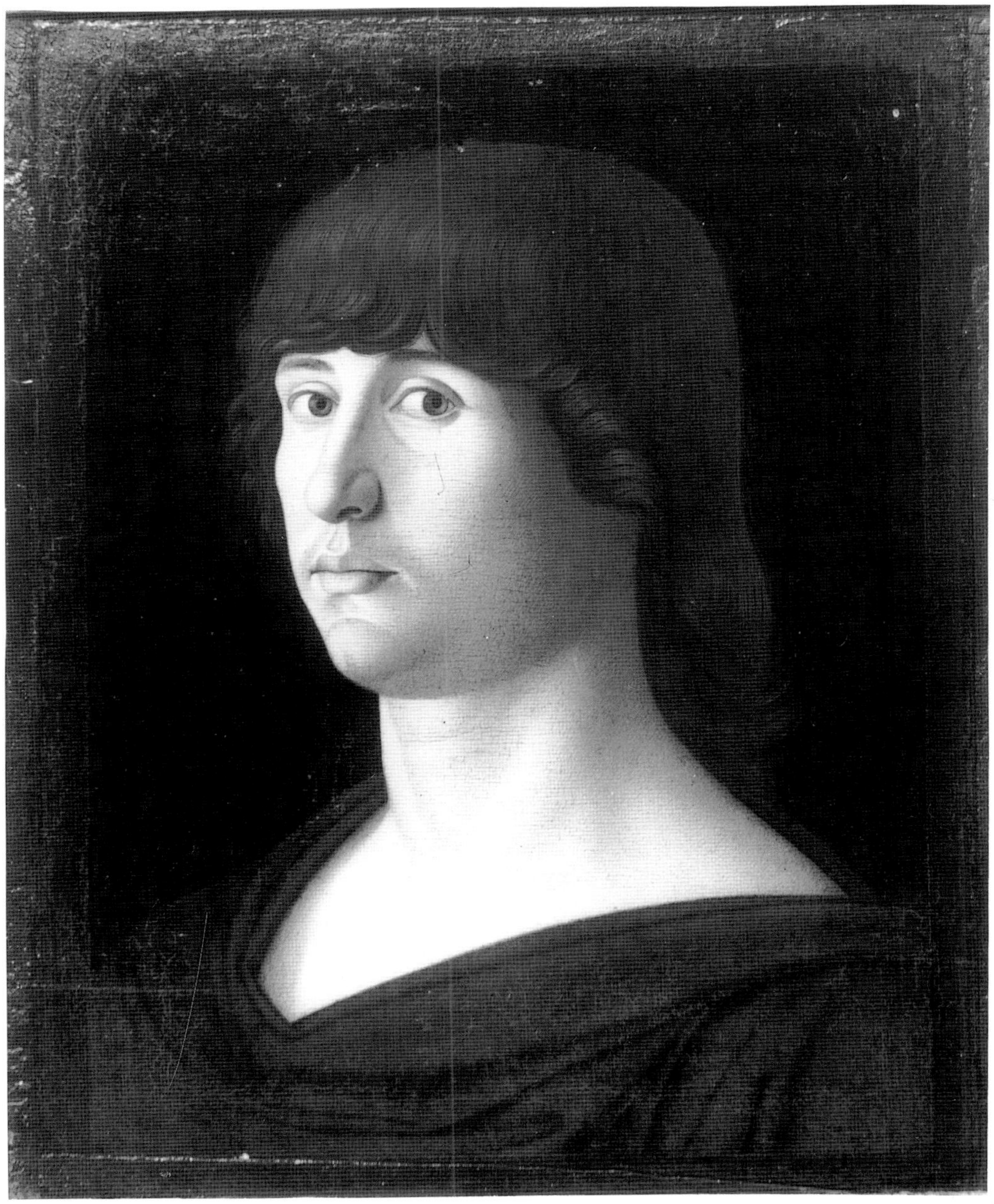

146. *Giovanni Bellini with assistance(?),* Portrait of a Humanist, *Accademia Carrara, Bergamo.*

cylinder of his neck, and even in the convolutions of his cap, a mark of office, as well as the use of the three-quarter face—all this suggests the way in which Bellini would have portrayed a man of arms, such as Generalissimo Marcello, in the portrait that Michiel saw.[5] The two pictures may also have been close in date, because Emo died in 1483, just a year before Marcello, and Emo's portrait, presumably like the lost Bellini, is in the style of the late 1470s or early 1480s. If the Bellinesque author of the *Emo* has reflected the master's interpretation of Marcello as a warrior, which appears likely, then Bellini may be credited with having anticipated the idealized characterization of such condottieri as the *Bartolommeo Colleoni* by Andrea del Verrocchio, although Bellini's portrait was certainly a recognizable likeness, whereas Verrocchio's statue is a bellicose fiction.[6]

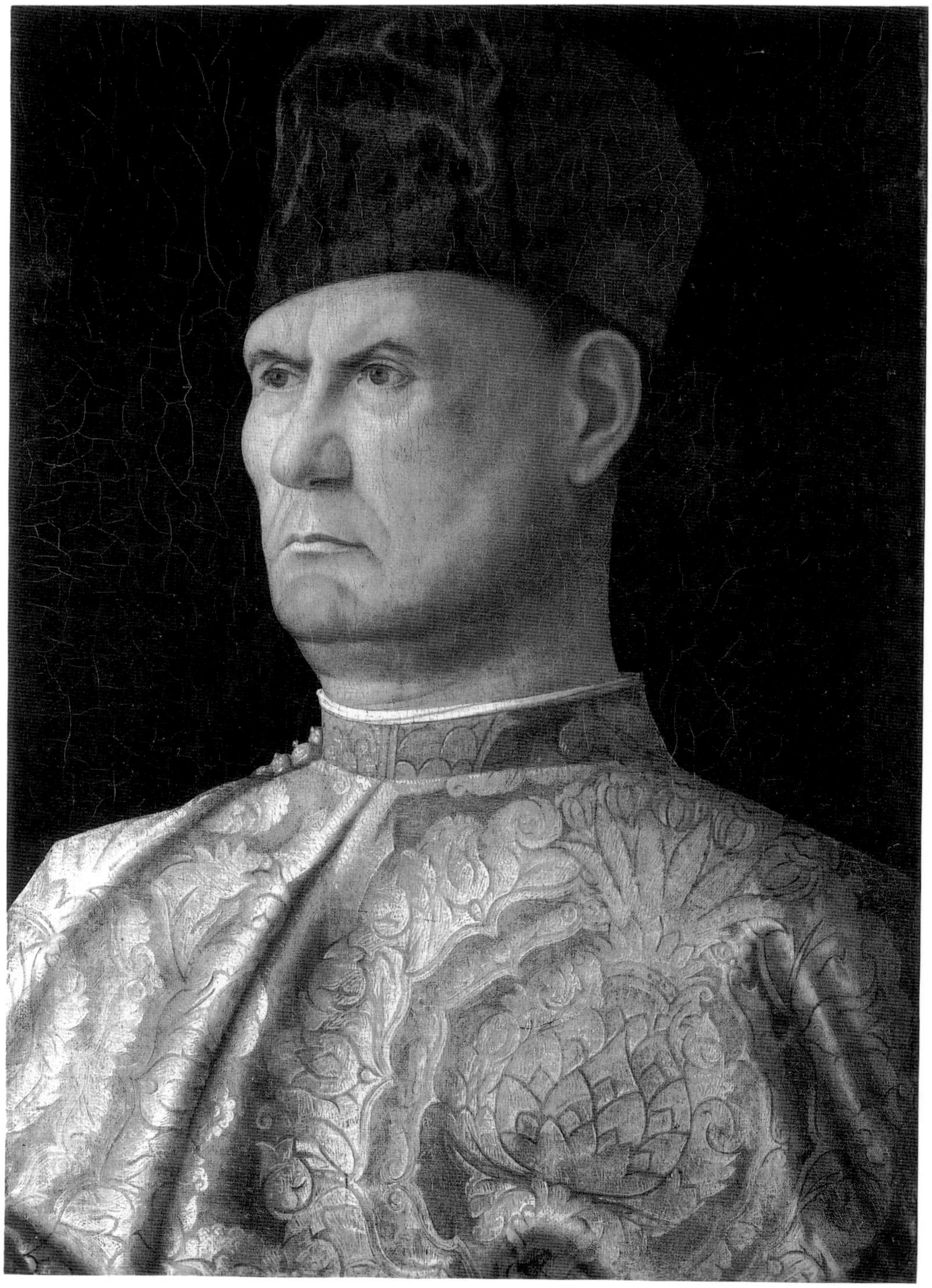

*147. Shop of Giovanni Bellini,* Portrait of Giovanni Emo, *National Gallery of Art, Washington, Samuel H. Kress Collection.*

Gabriel Vendramin—who, by 1530, when Michiel visited him, had come into possession of Jacopo Bellini's drawing book—also owned three portraits by Giovanni Bellini, including two unnamed noblemen depicted in profile.[7] Michiel was specific about this point, evidently because the profile was exceptional in Bellini's oeuvre. None of the independent portraits associated with him today is a profile: all are three-quarter or frontal.[8]

Michiel was also specific about another distinguishing feature of Bellini's por-

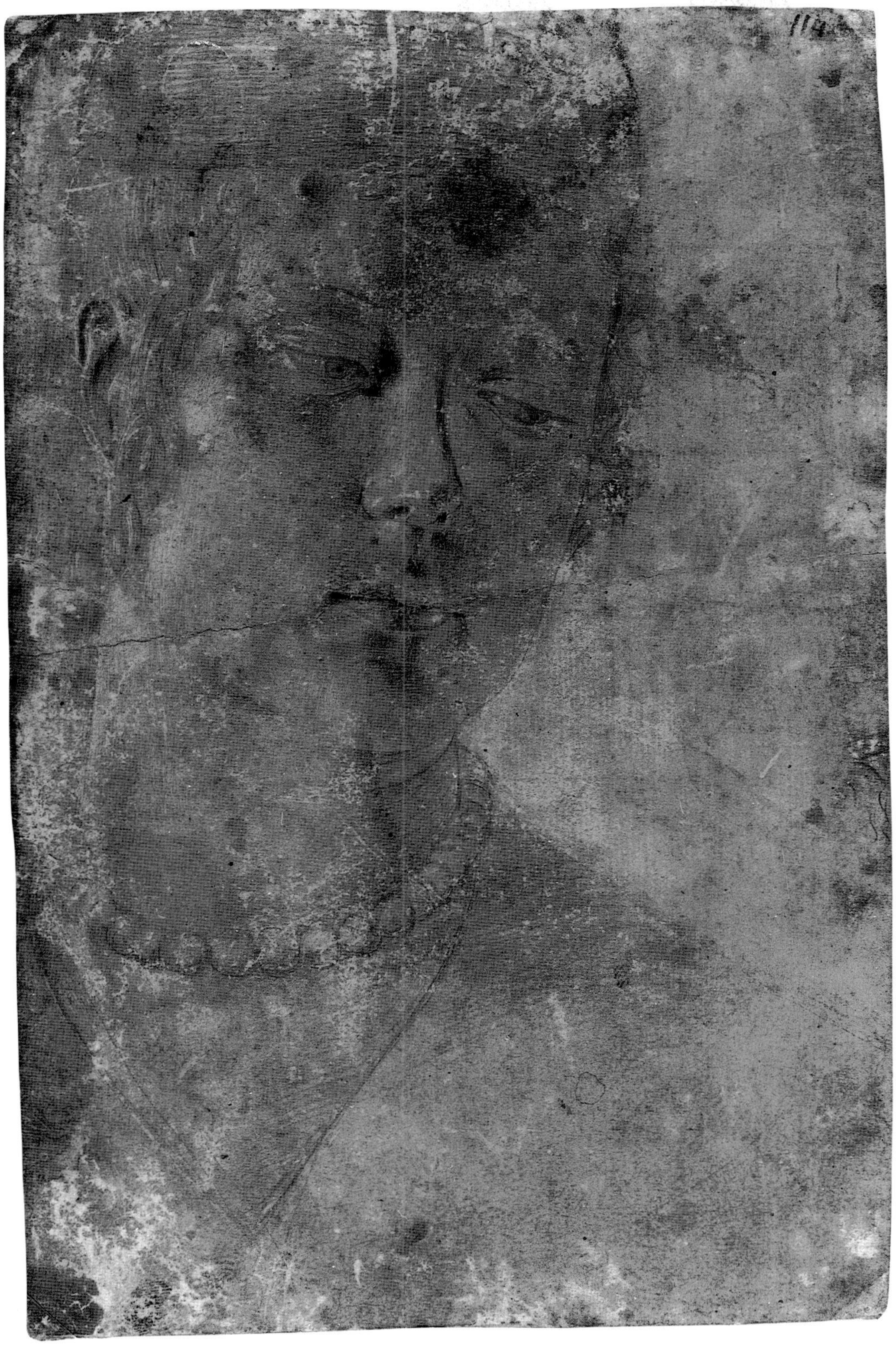


148. *Attributed to Giovanni Bellini,* Portrait of a Woman, *drawing, Gallerie dell'Accademia, Venice. Photo: Soprintendenza ai Beni Artistici e Storici, Venice.*

traits—their size. All were small images, like the "little portrait" owned by Jeronimo Marcello and the "three little portraits" in the Vendramin collection.[9] But Taddeo Contarini, who owned a *Portacroce* by Bellini, also had a *quadretto,* a small picture of a woman by the master, "portrayed from life [*al naturale*] to the shoulders," Michiel adds.[10] "Small," then, can mean "as if from nature," by implication, "life-size." This is the "possible sixth" portrait: Michiel's description leaves some doubt about whether he, and indeed Contarini or Bellini himself, regarded this "little painting" as a portrait or, as the author seems to suggest, as a picture of a woman, that is, a picture of which the subject is a woman, in the sense that another painting might have as its subject a Madonna, an allegory, or even a gazelle.[11] (The lines drawn between certain types of image, especially portraits and pictures of women, are indistinct in Venice, and we shall return to a consideration of this problem.) No painted portrait or picture of a woman by Bellini survives, although the fine silverpoint drawing in the Accademia of Venice gives some indication of the lost images (fig. 148).[12] At any rate, judging from Michiel and other contemporary evidence, the subjects of Bellini's portraits were overwhelmingly male and patrician, with an occasional humanist scholar among them. They were almost always represented in frontal or three-quarter view, life-size or smaller images. At least once Bellini also made a portrait as a manuscript illumination. Raffaele Zovenzoni's volume of Latin songs, the *Istrias*, which he sent to the bishop of Trent in 1474, was adorned with Bellini's portrait of the author. The codex itself has been preserved, but unhappily without this image.[13]

To this list of portraits by Bellini—or at least portraits considered to be by him according to those who owned them, during his lifetime or at most fourteen years after his death—we may add at least one picture that was perhaps concealed from Michiel. The portrait that "got away" belonged to Pietro Bembo, and the subject was his mistress: Bembo had composed two sonnets inspired by the image and by his desire to imitate Petrarch's sonnet on the portrait of his beloved Laura by Simone Martini. But by 1529–30, when Michiel visited Bembo's house in Padua, the humanist poet was a respectably married man. (Later still he became a cardinal of the church.) Michiel saw a portrait by Jacopo Bellini and a profile of Gentile da Fabriano—but no mistress by Giovanni.[14] Her image, like Petrarch's *Laura*, now survives only in the words of her lover (evoking Petrarch's sonnet): "O image, celestial and pure, / Which shines in my eyes more than the sun," and "Are these those beautiful eyes."[15] Surely the painting that inspired these verses was lovelier than the few, very unimpressive portraits (or images) of women optimistically, not to say impossibly, associated with Bellini's name today. Ridolfi, at least, considered it worthy of inclusion as a "marvel of art": his *Maraviglie dell'arte*, published more than a century after Michiel made his notes, included the picture and the poems, as well as a portrait of Bembo himself, also attributed to Bellini (cf. fig. 161).[16]

At first we may find it difficult to understand the enthusiasm of Bellini's contemporaries, including such luminaries as Bembo and Isabella d'Este, for such portraits as these and many others associated with him, and indeed often signed with his name.[17] Part of the problem is that few autograph portraits by Bellini survive, and many portraits associated with him are poorly preserved. In addition, Bellini and his patrons had an ideal in mind that takes some adjustment on our part. To be sure, their penchant for family portraits comes as no surprise; it seems the Venetian Renaissance equivalent of the family photograph album. But the Tuscan Vasari, writing some thirty years later and from a different vantage point than Michiel, was struck by it, and his impressions are revealing. To Vasari, perhaps himself desirous of such patronage, the Venetians seemed to have a mania for portraiture. And he indicated that this fashion had much to do with Bellini himself. According to Vasari, Bellini made "a great name for himself" as a portraitist. Indeed, "Because he [Bellini] painted portraits from the life, it became the custom in that city [Venice] that anyone who was anyone had his portrait painted by him or by other masters, as is evident in all the houses of Venice, which are chock-full of these portraits, in which one sees in painting up to the fourth generation of the family's descendents."[18] The four generations of portraits (even if a slight exaggeration) are clearly related to the obsessive concern of the Venetian patriciate for the purity of their family lines, a concern reflected also by Michiel, who named the subjects of the portraits when he could and indicated their kinship to the owners. Himself a patrician, Michiel took for granted the worth of such genealogical information and only touched on a point that was more significant to Vasari, the artist.

Writing about Contarini's picture of a woman, Michiel had mentioned that it was "painted from the life." In the first edition of his Lives (1550), Vasari likewise specified that Bellini "painted portraits from the life," and he repeated this assertion in the second edition (1568). "Giovanni's first works were some life portraits [*ritratti di naturale*]," Vasari wrote, "which pleased a great deal, and particularly that of Doge Loredan; although others say it to have been Giovanni Mocenigo."[19] Vasari seems to have been mistaken in his details. The portrait of Loredan (fig. 149) was not one of Bellini's early works—it is among his latest—and the earliest portrait known by Bellini is dated 1474, when the artist was in his late thirties or early forties: hardly, therefore, one of "Giovanni's first works" (fig. 150). If Bellini painted independent portraits significantly earlier than this one, none seems to have survived. In any case, the substantive gist of Vasari's text—that Bellini's portraits were painted from the life—is certainly correct. And the truth of that statement is implicit in the contemporary inscription once written on the back of the panel in Venetian dialect: "Joerg Fugger adì XX zugno MCCCCLXXIIII" (Jörg Fugger on 20 June 1474).[20]

Assuming that the attribution to Bellini is correct, as seems likely, the inscription identified the *Fugger* as his earliest surviving dated work. The portrait of the young German merchant may disappoint at first; its conservatism, even awkwardness—notably in the relationship of the figure to the picture field and of the head to the torso—differs markedly from contemporary works by Bellini of sacred subjects. The surface of the portrait is abraded, and there are some areas of loss and repaint in the eyes, brows, and cheeks. The mouth and contour are well preserved, however, and the X ray of the panel reveals the strength of Bellini's drawing and the beauty of his conception: the volume of Fugger's head, painted against a blue ground, is almost sculptural in form and delicate in its coloring and modeling, which Bellini achieved with oil and glazes (fig. 151).[21] Moreover, when

*Overleaf:*
*149.* Portrait of Doge Leonardo Loredan, *National Gallery, London.*

*150.* Portrait of Jörg Fugger, *Norton Simon Museum, Pasadena. Courtesy Norton Simon Art Foundation.*

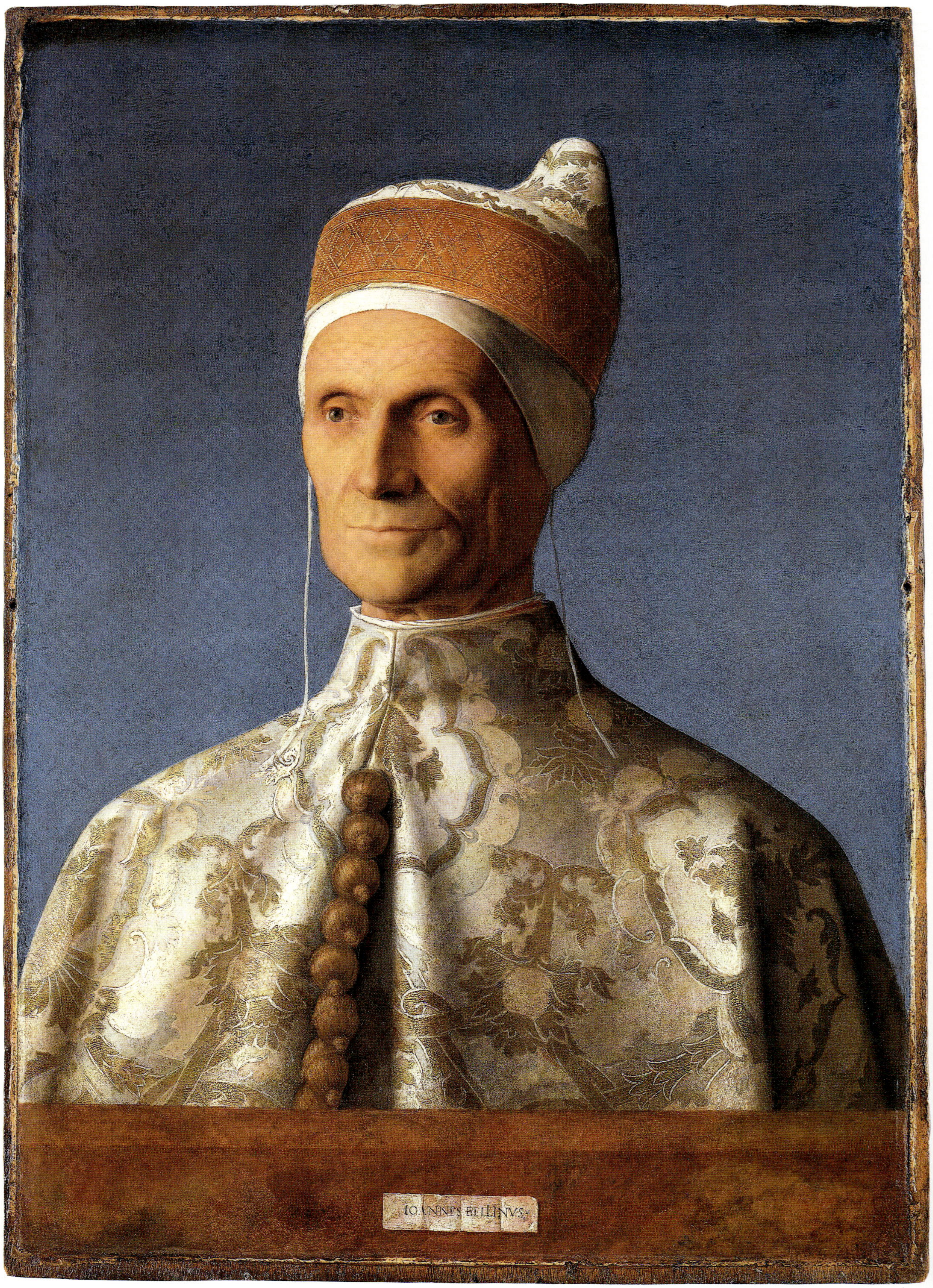
IOANNES BELLINVS

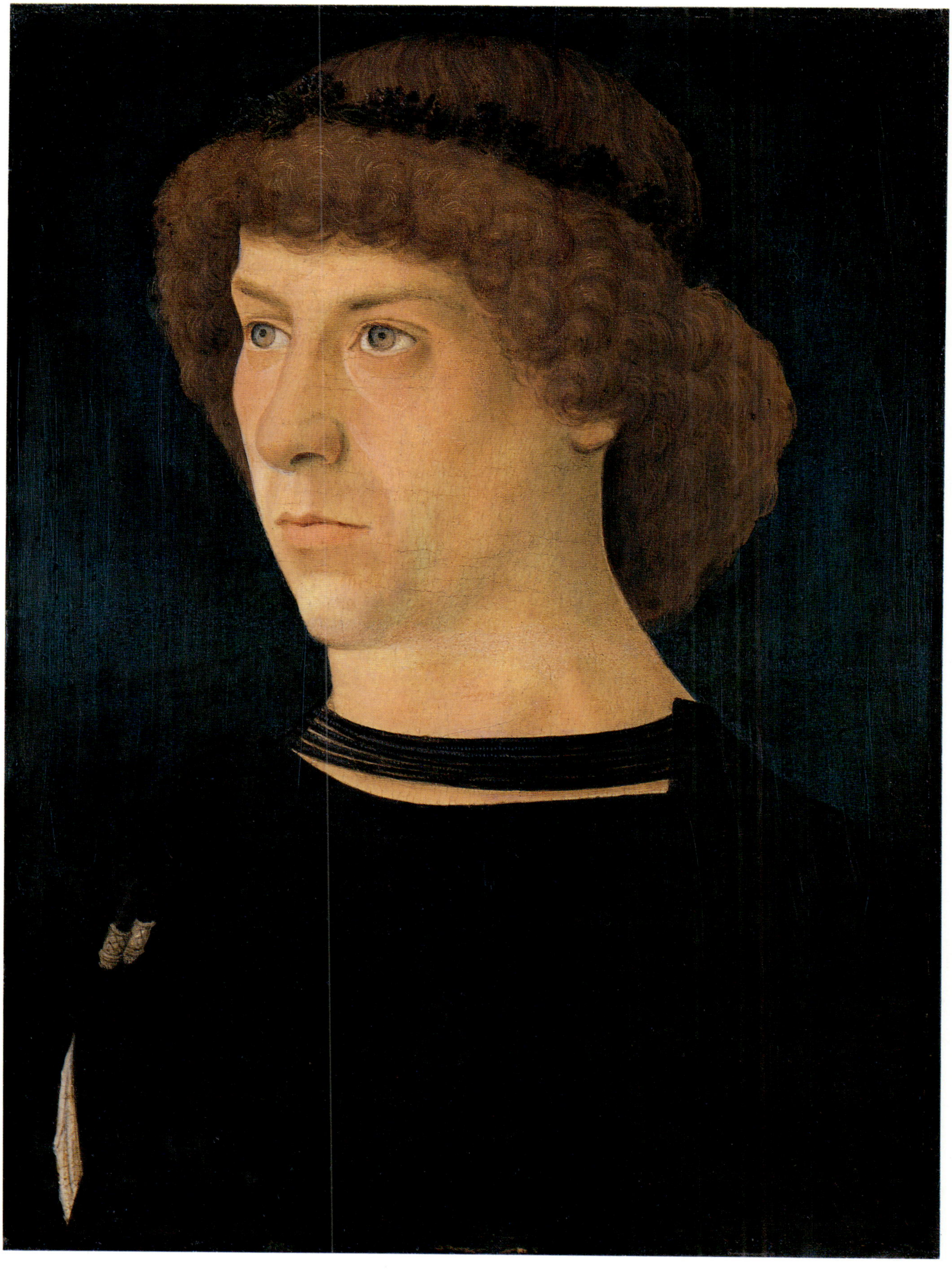

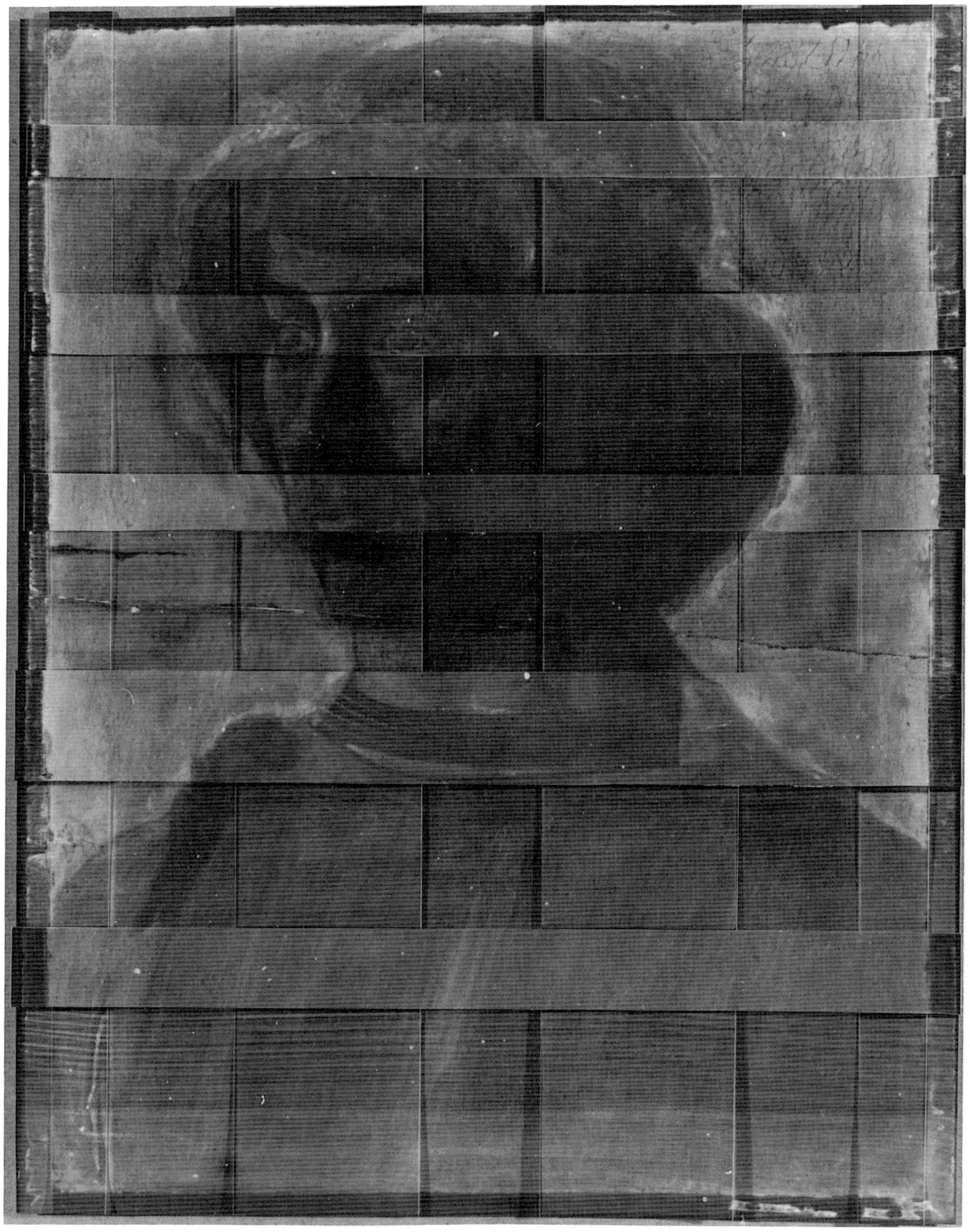

*151. X ray of* Portrait of Jörg Fugger, *Norton Simon Museum, Pasadena. Courtesy Norton Simon Art Foundation.*

it was completed in summer 1474, the *Jörg Fugger* was one of the first frontal or three-quarter portraits in Italian art.[22]

Since the early fifteenth century, when independent portraiture was enthusiastically revived in Italy, the standard format had been the profile. The classical pedigree for this type was endorsed by the *ekphrasis* (description) of a lost portrait by Apelles, court painter to Alexander the Great and perhaps the most esteemed painter of antiquity: Quintilian (followed centuries later by Alberti) had described how Apelles used the profile to portray the one-eyed king Antigonus—the format nicely solved the problem of his disfigurement—and at least one fifteenth-century master, Piero della Francesca, exploited the profile in a similar way to represent the one-eyed ruler Federigo da Montefeltro (cf. fig. 115).[23] This was part of a diptych, the other wing being the portrait of Federigo's consort, Battista, painted perhaps two years before Bellini's *Jörg Fugger*. (Battista died in 1472.) In such a diptych, the male subject would normally have been represented to the beholder's right (*dexter*), and the woman to the left (*sinister*), because she was presumed morally inferior, according to the quaint belief espoused in the Middle Ages and Renaissance. But the positions were reversed here to conceal Federigo's deformity. The profile was not used only for the blind or deformed. Considered the most characteristic view of a face, the profile seemed the type preferred by classical antiquity: numerous coins and medals, which provided the prototype for painted Italian portraits of the quattrocento, represented the face in profile. Jacopo Bellini used this type in his drawings and in his donor portrait of Lionello d'Este in the Louvre *Madonna of Humility*. Even anonymous doodlers, such as the scribe who recorded the actions of the Senato Terra for the year 1483 (*modo veneto*), chose the profile when he made a sketch bordering on caricature of Doge Marco Barbarigo (fig. 152). This type (if not this example) had the advantage of stasis, appropriate to the raison d'être of portraiture, namely, the preservation of the individual's identity, as Alberti had explained.[24] Anything transitory—movement, including facial expression and emotion—would contradict this artistic attempt at immortality. But if the purpose of portraiture is redefined to include the depiction of character and mood, then the profile is no longer suitable. The sitter must behold the beholder.

Northerners, not Italians, were the first to realize this. Jan van Eyck represented his subjects in full-face, and sometimes full-figure, long before Italian masters were willing to follow suit.[25] Perhaps Fugger, being German, was familiar with northern traditions and himself requested being portrayed in three-quarter view. But it is worth recalling that only two independent profile portraits may be associated with Bellini: the two mentioned by Michiel in the Vendramin collection. Otherwise, the three-quarter or full-face in portraiture seems to have been Bellini's consistent choice, even for donor portraits. The diffident presentation of Fugger's personality is also characteristic of Bellini: his glance is directed out of the picture space; he does not look at the viewer. Fugger remains self-contained—but not aloof, because the liveliness and open expression of his face suggest at least the possibility of psychological contact.

In these features and qualities, the *Jörg Fugger* is typical of Bellini's portraiture: face in three-quarter view, the figure bust-length (like other Italian portraits until the early sixteenth century), hands concealed behind the edge of the panel, which is sometimes buttressed by a parapet, and the figure usually seen against a neutral dark ground, such as the dark blue used here (also figs. 145–47). The compositional formula was originally Jan van Eyck's—and the date of the Fugger portrait proves that Bellini knew it (and the oil medium) or perhaps had independently reinvented it before Antonello da Messina's arrival in Venice.[26] What may seem Antonellesque in Bellini's portraits, or, for that matter, Bellinesque in Antonello's,

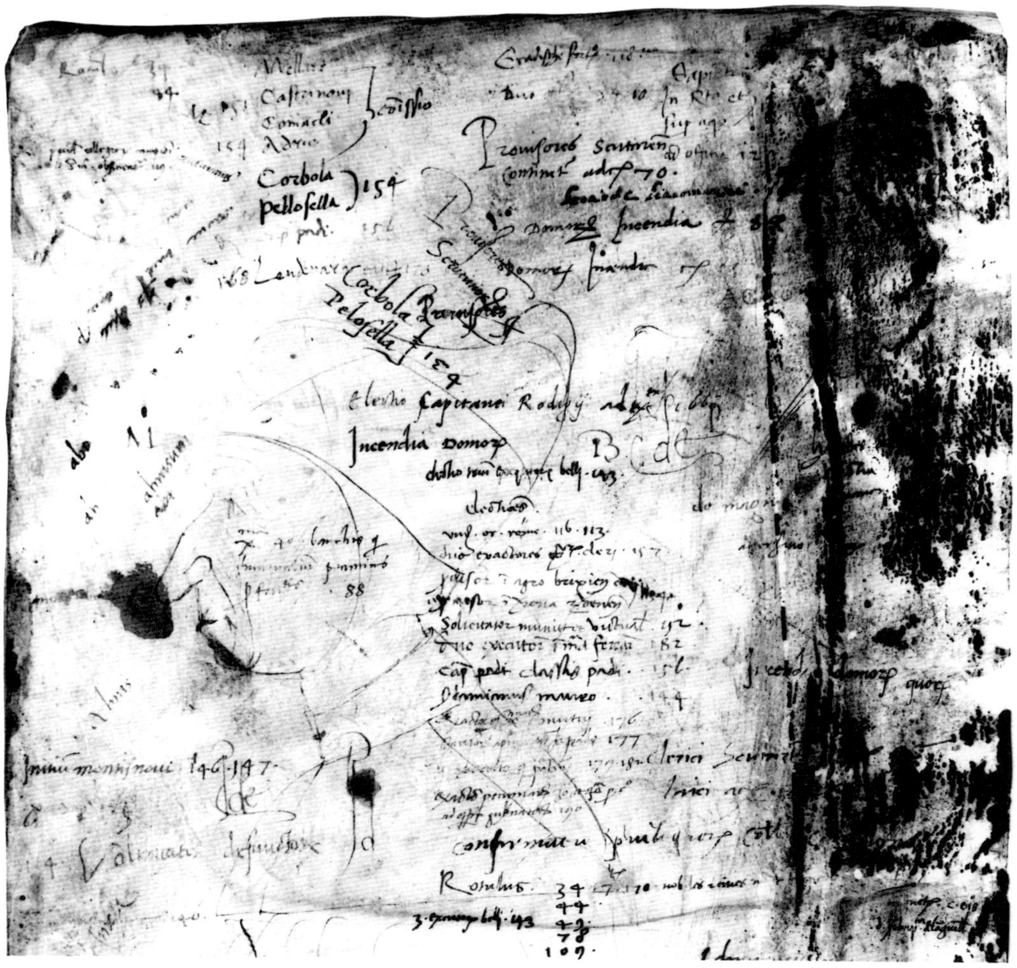

*152. Anonymous Fifteenth-Century Venetian,* Profile Portrait (Caricature) of Doge Marco Barbarigo, *Senato Terra, Registro 8 (1478–1483), folio 200 (modern folio 201v), Archivio di Stato, Venice. Photo: Archivio di Stato, Venice.*

probably derives from their common northern source. Were the surface of Bellini's painting better preserved, it would no doubt resemble Netherlandish works in modeling and handling as well.

Set against his black garment and the dark blue ground (its color repeating the blue of the eyes), Fugger's face is distinguished as the lightest and brightest area of the picture. (Bellini had already used a dark ground for the *Pietà* in Bergamo, a work of the 1450s; fig. 47.) The face is further emphasized by its volumetric existence in space; seen at an angle, it is the most forcefully three-dimensional form in the composition. Bellini combines a sense of monumentality with an interest in shapes that decorate the surface, contrasting small, complicated shapes (tassels, hair, wreath) with large, broad areas (the garment, flesh, and background). Fugger's wreath suggests his humanist learning—or at least his aspirations—like the classicizing draperies worn by the men in the Bellinesque portraits in Milan (with a wreath) and in Bergamo.

Close in date to the *Jörg Fugger* is the portrait of a boy in the Barber Institute (fig. 153). Unfortunately, little remains of the original painted surface beyond the boy's brown hair (cf. fig. 60) and the parapet. Yet, the composition itself survives intact, and enough remains of the boy's demeanor to demonstrate the tenderness of Bellini's characterization. The figure, seen to a point just below

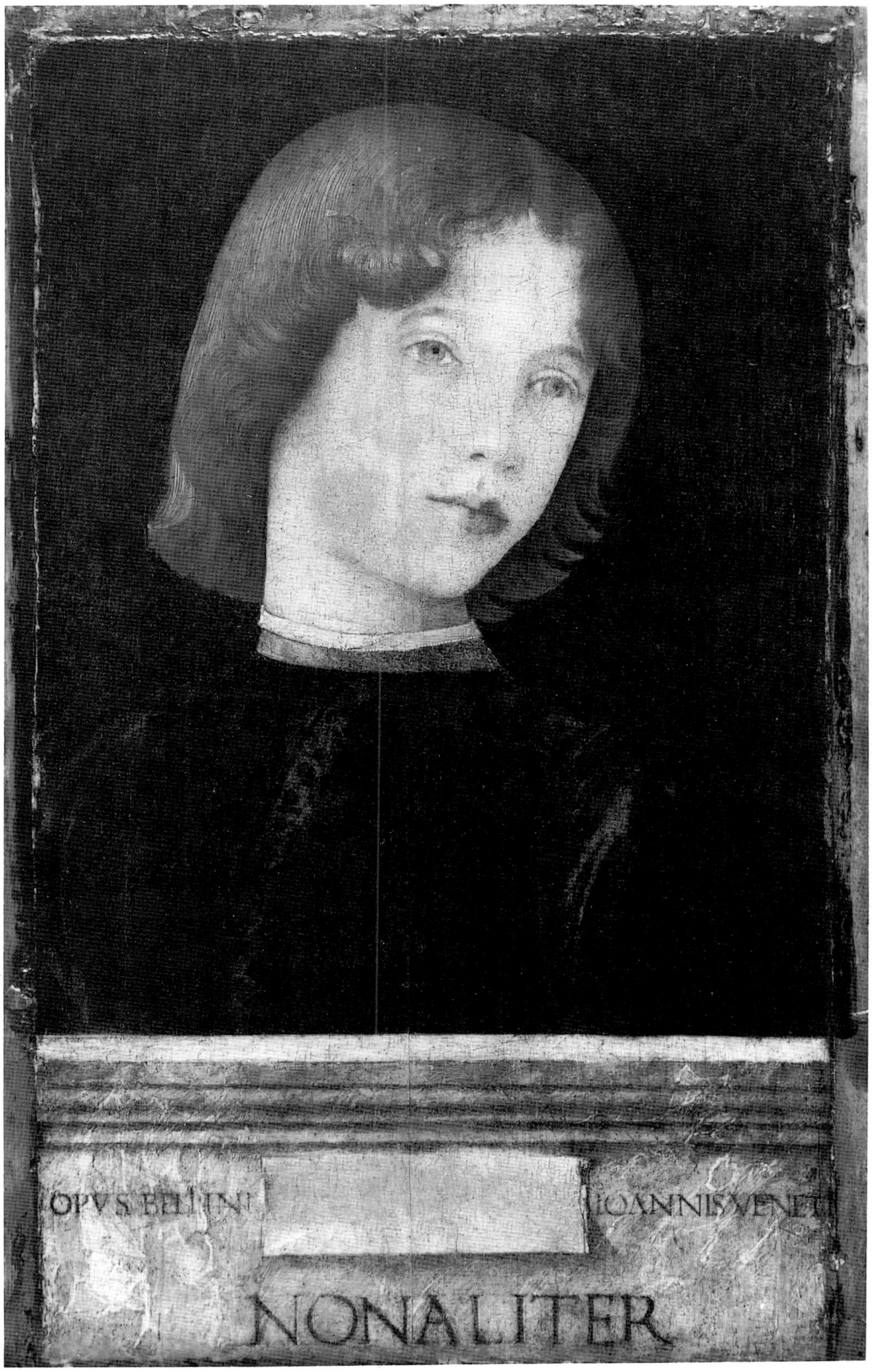


153. Portrait of a Boy, *Barber Institute of Fine Arts, Birmingham. Courtesy The Barber Institute of Fine Arts, The University of Birmingham.*

the shoulders, moves with considerable freedom, turned in contrapposto, and with the face almost frontal. The background is a deep blue-green, the pigment applied thinly over white: originally the dark ground must have seemed luminous, the figure glowing against it.[27] This spatially neutral setting is given a point of reference in the parapet. The marble of the parapet—the best preserved part of the painting—was painted largely with lead white, mixed with yellow, red ochre, and some vermillion; red-brown ochre was used for the boy's jacket, modeled with carbon black, now so abraded that it is robbed of its rich coloristic effects.

A cartellino is affixed to the parapet, but whatever inscription may have been written there does not survive. The work is signed on the face of the parapet itself, OPVS BELLINI / IOANNIS VENETI, a form of the signature explained either by the portrait's having been painted outside of Venice (perhaps in Pesaro, given the likely date in the early 1470s) and/or its representing a foreign (non-Venetian) subject.[28] The parapet also carries another inscription, NONALITER, presumably translated "Not otherwise." Perhaps the explanation of this text lies in the picture that apparently once adorned the back of the portrait, a painting of a skull, an unmistakable and somewhat gruesome reminder of death. Perhaps this boy was portrayed in an independent portrait—in itself unusual for one so young —because he was the sole legitimate male heir of his deceased father, hence the only hope for his family's future.[29]

Jörg Fugger was a German, and the young boy was almost certainly not a Venetian. But most of Bellini's portraits represent his countrymen, and their portraits are rather differently conceived. In these first two works as in other portraits by Bellini or his shop, the sitter's garments reveal social status (perforce) or political position in the Venetian regime, as the hat and brocade coat of Giovanni Emo indicate his military rank (fig. 147), or the costume of the young man in the Padua portrait identifies him as a senator or Chancellery Secretary (fig. 154). In general, however, attributes per se are excluded from Bellini's portraits: his sitters do not hold books or contemplate symbolic objects, they are not bedecked with emblematic references to their identities, they do not look at us—and these restrictions illustrate the psychology and sociology of the Venetian patricians who were Bellini's accustomed subjects.[30]

Bellini's portraits of the *Young Senator* (fig. 154) and the two patricians in Rome (figs. 155, 156), both seen against the sky and behind a parapet, are cases in point.[31] The handling and psychological refinement of these portraits are more skillfully conceived than in the *Jörg Fugger*, and at the same time the Venetians seem more withdrawn than the German. This aloofness made Bellini's conception appropriate to the portrayal of the Venetian patriciate. Completely self-sufficient—their psychological containment concomitant with the physical containment of composition and posture—these men turn from us. Absorbed in their thoughts, they are as unlike the Bellinesque humanist scholars in comportment as in dress. Their high-minded expressions (especially in the Padua portrait) recall the demeanor of

Bellini's donor figures who contemplate the Virgin and Child, and the sitters' remoteness from us is not so much concealment of the self as an act of suppression. The individual is subjugated to the class, and the class to the needs of the state. That was the ideal, the self-defined, self-created myth of Venice.

At the same time, Bellini's subjects seem complete and knowable personalities, though they hold themselves (or are held) aloof from us. Bellini achieved this by his concentration on the face: its contours, shapes, highlights, and shadows are treated not only as forms and qualities to be carefully observed and presented but as the visual record of the subject's experience and character. Nothing is allowed to compete with the face, no hands, no attributes (except clothing itself). Attributes, including emblemata, would be too explicit and hence limiting. By telling us what the subject's presumed interests may be (as Fugger's wreath suggests his humanism), or what his present situation is or was, attributes distract attention from the individual. The patrician sitters reveal nothing—while yet revealing everything about their class.

Impassivity is a primary characteristic of these portraits, an ideal of comportment extolled by patricians for patricians. One may think of Francesco Barbaro's exhortation to his son at the time of a death in the family: "We have been so born and so trained that we can bear everything with equanimity."[32] Portrait busts made for the court of Naples by Francesco Laurana (c. 1430–c. 1502) share some of these idealized qualities, and, not coincidentally, Laurana, born in Zara, was a Venetian national. His sculpted portraits, however, are more highly stylized and generalized than Bellini's paintings, which always record idiosyncracies of appearance (or at least appear to do so).[33] Oblivious to the beholder's presence, Bellini's subjects invite speculation not about their actions but about their psychology; in this way, the viewer, drawn to penetrate these characters, and yet denied customary visual instructions (attributes, gestures, explicit facial expressions), is compelled to invest his or her own emotions and character in the image in order to complete it. Many portraits were produced in Bellini's shop and many outside it, all repeating his compositional formula. But none of Bellini's contemporaries was able to represent the inner man as he did, and that (not the composition per se, or other stylistic quotations) is what distinguishes his autograph portraits. The consummate proof is Bellini's portrait of Doge Leonardo Loredan, painted at the beginning of Loredan's dogate, probably in 1501 or 1502 (fig. 149).[34]

Loredan is seen with his face almost frontal and his shoulders turned at a slight angle to the picture space, showing somewhat more of the figure than in Bellini's earlier portraits. The essentially frontal view of Loredan's portrait is noteworthy in itself. This allows Bellini to draw a physiognomical map of the doge, as it were, and in this approach his art is more closely related to Jan van Eyck's portraiture than to any contemporary Italian work. Details of appearance are endowed with significance in the definition of idealized character.[35] Moreover, although almost all portraiture associated with Bellini is three-quarter or full-face, the profile was

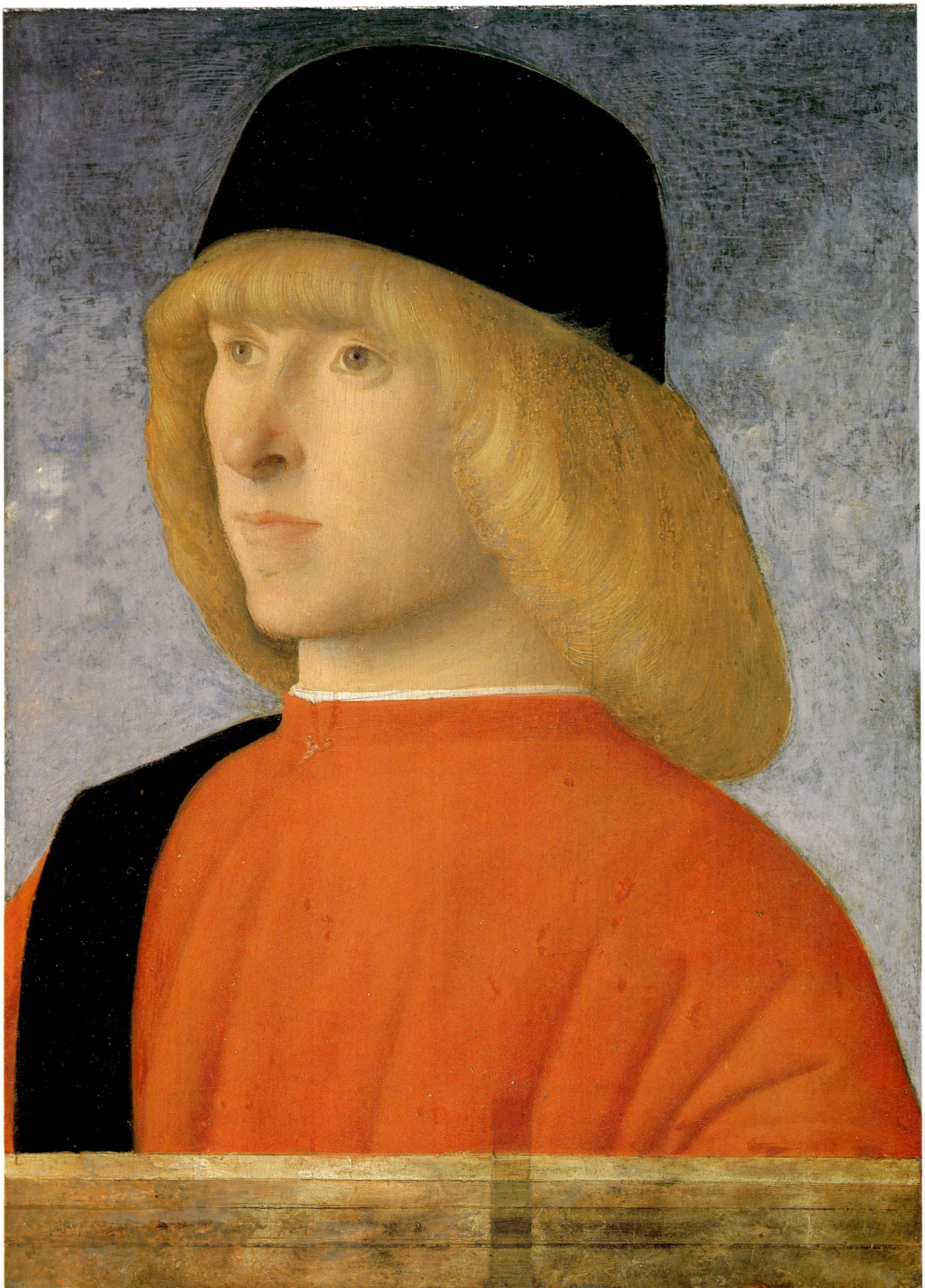

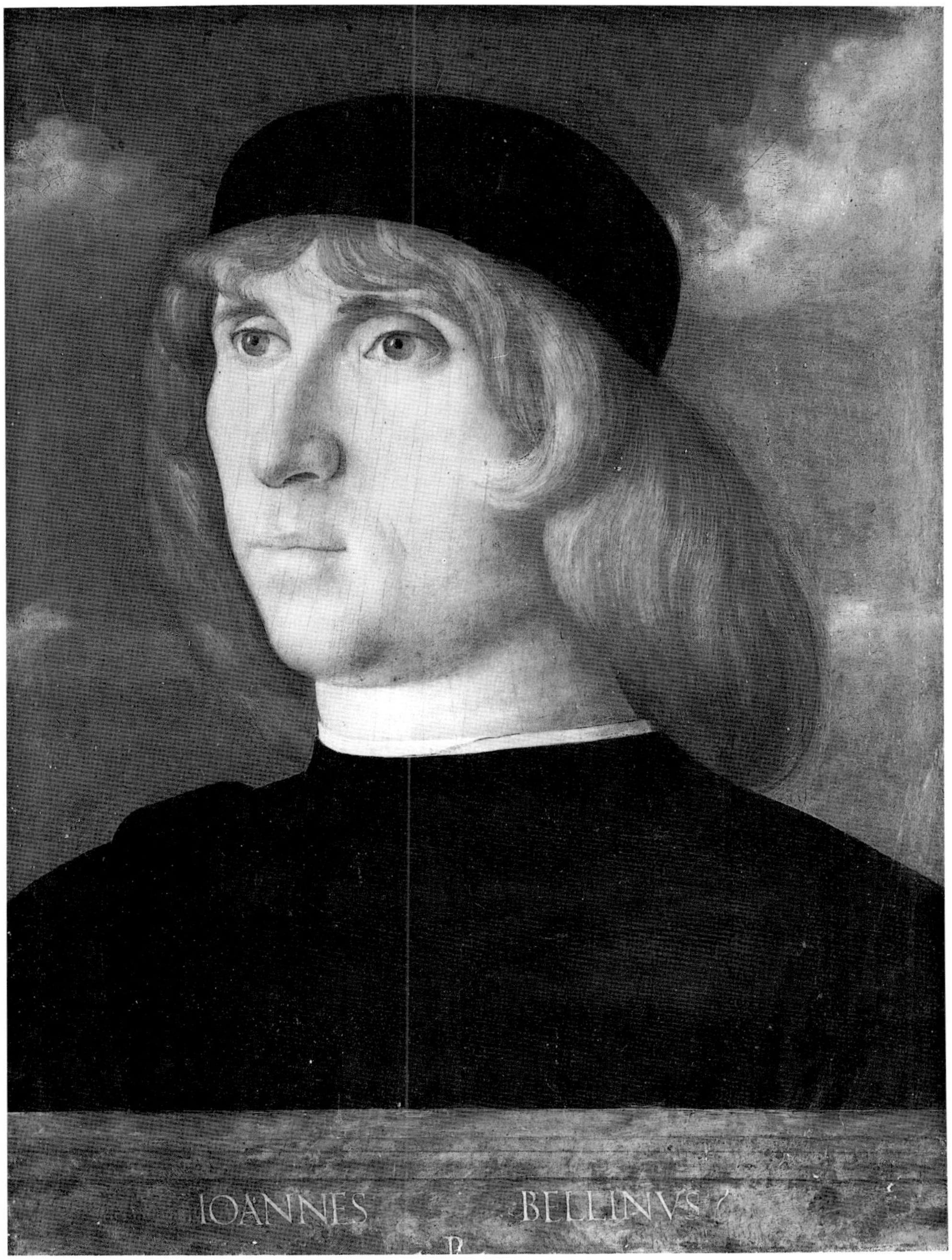


*155. Giovanni Bellini with assistance,* Portrait of a Patrician, *Pinacoteca Capitolina, Rome. Photo: Archivio Fotografico del Museo Correr, Venice.*

still preferred for depictions of doges, even for portraits of Leonardo Loredan by such other masters as Carpaccio (fig. 157).[36]

Giovanni Bellini endowed the doge with greatness, creating the perfect Venetian nobleman in this portrait. In reality, his protagonist was unlikeable and indeed something of a scoundrel. Loredan had been elected not for "maritime or terrestrial merits but only because he was born well-connected," according to Sanuto, who characterized him as "rather choleric but savvy in government"; and an inquest held to examine the doge's financial dealings after his death in 1521 eventually fined his estate 2,700 ducats.[37] But we must not let unpleasant reality intrude on our understanding of the myth of Venice any more than Bellini did in creating *Leonardo Loredan*.

*154.* Portrait of a Young Senator, *Museo Civico, Padua. Photo: Museo Civico, Padua.*

*156.* Portrait of a Patrician, *Galleria degli Uffizi, Florence. Photo: Archivio Fotografico del Museo Correr, Venice.*

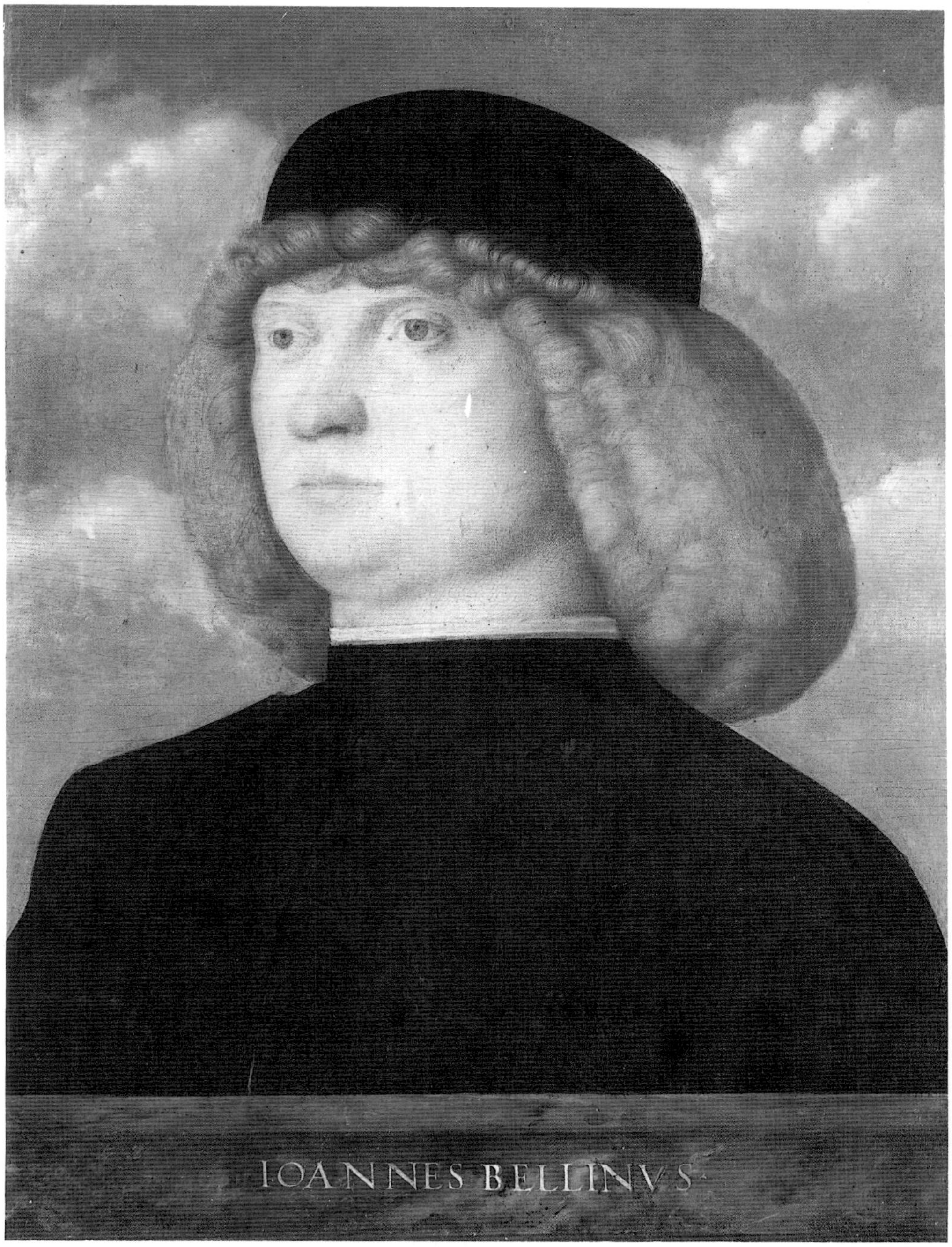


The conservatism of the regime is reflected in such ducal portraits as Carpaccio's: the insistence on the profile, especially during Loredan's dogate, must be seen as an intentional archaism at a time when other Venetian nobles were commonly portrayed full-face (but perhaps not quite frontal) or three-quarter view.[38] Bellini's *Loredan* was evidently one of the first frontal portraits of a reigning doge. Such frontality was more often associated with sacred characters, not mortals. The doge's portrait is distinguished from its fifteenth-century predecessors and from other portrayals of Loredan himself not merely by the frontality of the face but also by the self-possession and tranquility of his character, portrayed with such conviction by Bellini. We are reminded that the traditional epithet for the doge was Serene—even though Loredan assumed the dogate at a time of desperate

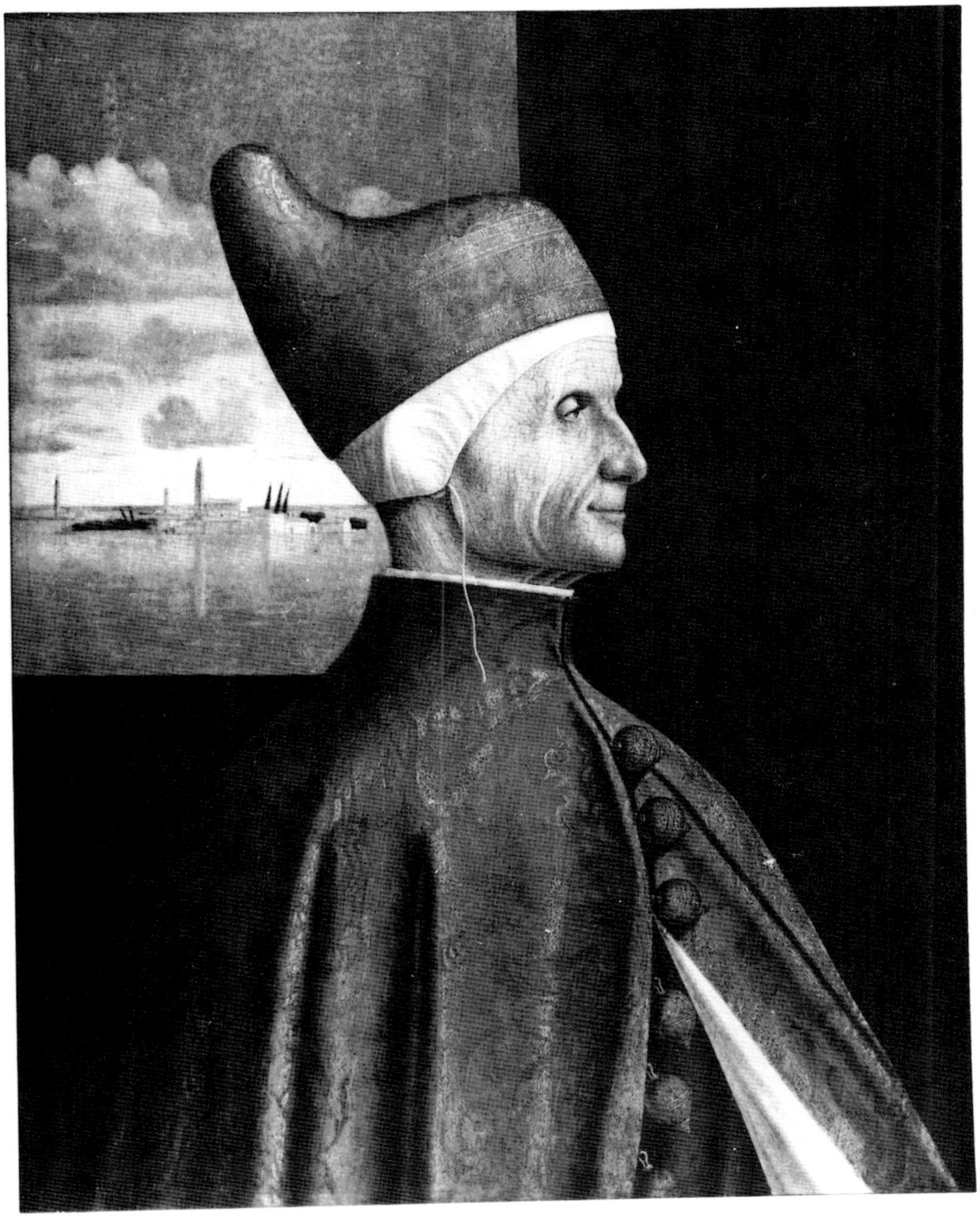

157. *Vittore Carpaccio (attributed),* Doge Leonardo Loredan, *Galleria dell'Accademia, Bergamo. Photo: Archivio Fotografico del Museo Correr, Venice.*

struggle in the war with Turkey.[39] The faces of some of Bellini's other portraits have a diffidence or even wistfulness inherently unlike this calm assurance, and the combination of Loredan's expression and his frontality endows his portrait with a quality akin to that of sacred images. Dürer's *Self-Portrait* of 1500 exploits (more complete) frontality and facial expression in much the same way, although with more overt reference to depictions of Christ and with a different, entirely personal purpose. But the quiet allusions to sacred imagery in the *Loredan* are entirely apposite vis-à-vis the subject's public life, referring to the rhetoric—verbal and visual—of the Serene Republic. Thus the parapet (signed IOANNES BELLINUS.) reminds us of the timeless ideal of the sacred paintings. This is appropriate for portraiture in general, given the Renaissance credo that a man might live on in his image, to paraphrase Alberti. But Bellini's parapet is especially suitable for his portrait of the doge, because the doge, the elected "first among equals" of the Venetian governing aristocracy, was endowed with spiritual as well as political authority. That is another reason why Bellini concealed the hands in the portrait of Leonardo Loredan and focused on the face alone: the portrait becomes more formal, more timeless thereby.

In the *Portrait of a Dominican Friar as Saint Peter Martyr* painted almost fifteen years later, circa 1515, perhaps with studio assistance, Bellini finally allowed a subject's hand to appear: X rays reveal that the right hand, which now holds a martyr's palm (part of the painting's transformation to Peter Martyr), originally grasped a scroll (fig. 158).[40] The knife, bloody head wound, and halo are also additions, and the dark ground was originally green, contrasting vividly with the black of the Dominican habit.[41] But the hand was always intended to rest on the surface of the parapet, and this makes the portrait more informal, more accessible: the hand almost, but not quite, breaks through the picture plane to our space. Whoever altered the painting understood the implications of this and, in adding the palm, broke through that pictorial barrier. This accessibility was more than physical: originally the lips were slightly parted, suggesting the Dominican's active response to the beholder.

With this painting in mind, and looking again at the *Loredan*, one understands that the concealment of the hands is essential to the hierarchic and timeless dignity of the ducal portrait: it is another aspect of his sacred identity. This sacral character is explicit in the garments that Loredan and all other doges wore: the tight-fitting cap, the pointed ducal corno, and the mantle with its round buttons, essentially immutable despite the vagaries of fashion. The earliest surviving images of Loredan's predecessors show them dressed essentially as he is—for example, Doge Dandolo in 1339 (fig. 72)—and all of his successors also dressed this way, including Lodovico Manin, the last doge, who served until Napoleon deposed him in 1797 and ended a thousand years of Venetian history.

Bellini adjusted details of Loredan's costume and figure to endow the portrait with lifelikeness and energy. The central axis of the doge's figure, for example, does not coincide with the central axis of the panel. This, with the asymmetrical pose, frees Loredan from rigid centrality in the composition and creates a subtly varied silhouette against the blue ground. The blue is lighter than in Bellini's earlier portraits, more suggestive of an atmospheric environment (though this is due in part to its superior state of preservation).[42] Differentiated by light and shade, the row of buttons is irregular, and the ties of the ducal cap move, conveying an impression of the doge's mobility. Bellini leads us to understand that the doge has the power of movement—a primary characteristic of life, the "breath and motion" Vasari so admired in Leonardo's art—and this movement is achieved without disturbing Loredan's hierarchic stasis, which endows him with a timeless dignity implying immortality. In his characterization of the doge, Bellini has thus

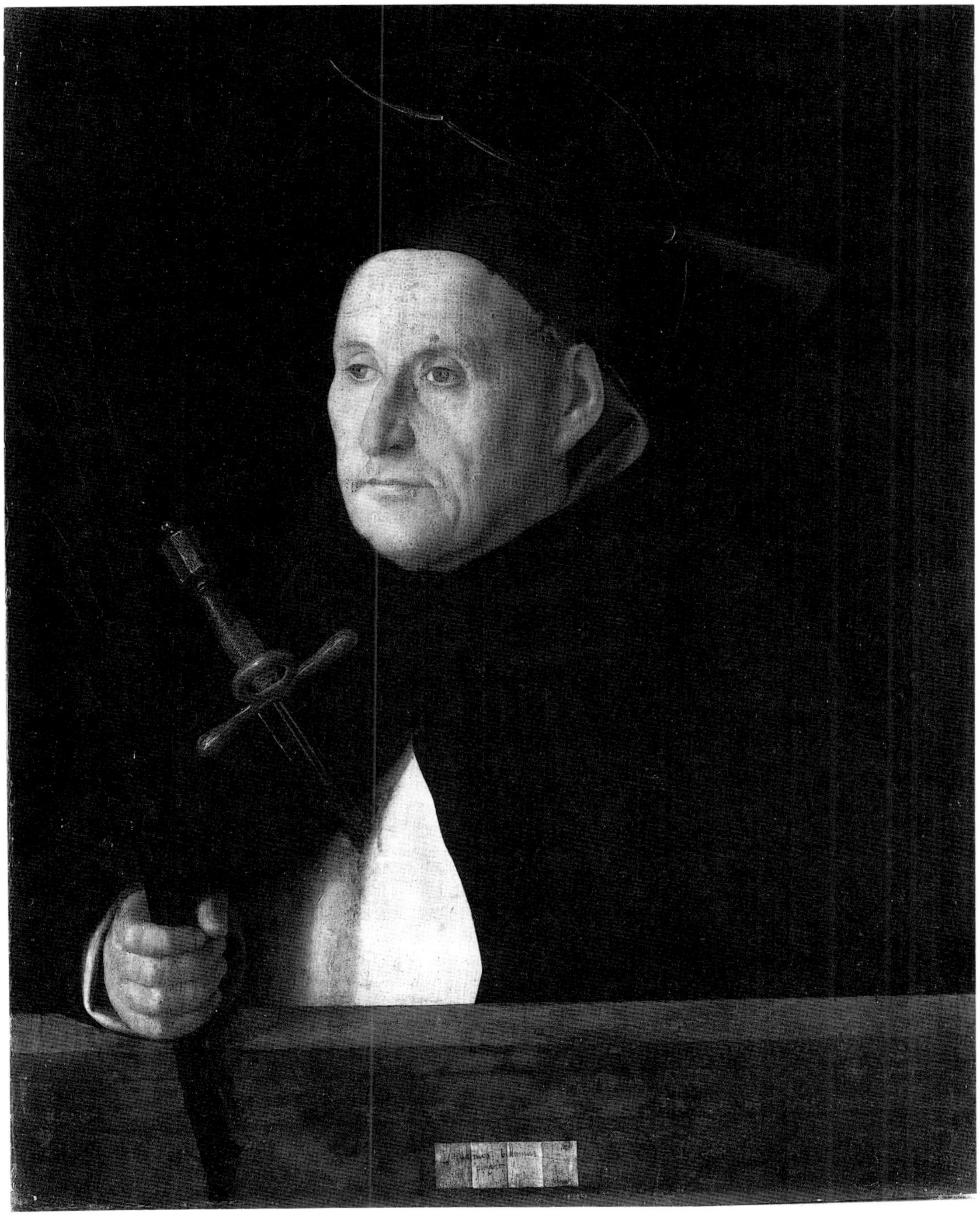

*158.* Portrait of a Dominican Friar as Saint Peter Martyr, *National Gallery, London.*

combined the self-contradictory elements of stasis and movement, transitoriness and permanence, individuality and idealism.

Bellini also combined different ways of handling paint in the portrait, and this is not merely a "technicality" but is important to our understanding of the image. Touches of color—shades of yellow, not metallic gold pigment—suggest the embroidery of the brocade and the border of the corno. Dots and dashes of various dimensions mimic the threads and their light-reflecting properties. The top layer of the brocade is a semitransparent oil glaze mixed with brown iron oxide pigment.[43] But Bellini painted the face rather differently, with glazes of different colors, with delicate gradations of light and shadow that blur contours, suggesting an enveloping atmosphere and compelling the viewer's attention: the doge seems an immanent presence, just behind the parapet that separates his spaceless realm from our world, and yet the soft definition of his face—the imprecision of the forms—suggests distance. (This is intentional: the painting is very well preserved.) It is as though Loredan's face were slightly out of focus, and one wants to concentrate one's vision to sharpen the features. To put it another way, this atmospheric treatment of the portrait involves the viewer, engaging his or her cooperation with the artist in the creation (or re-creation) of the doge's presence. The physical act of seeing, which is generally an unconscious, automatic action by the viewer before an image, now becomes purposeful, motivated by the compelling desire, or necessity, to complete the image. In doing so, the viewer attempts to endow the visage of the doge with emotional or psychological qualities to match the visual precision for which the eye strives.[44]

The doge's expression is calm and self-contained: like many of Bellini's figures, historical and sacred, Loredan does not glance directly at the viewer. But his expression is not unfriendly, and his mouth seems almost to smile. This is intended to suggest that he is alive—like the famous smile of Leonardo's *Gioconda*.[45] Anything more specific, however, comes from the viewer's attempt—invited or compelled by Bellini—to know the doge: like the forms of his face, his personality and character seem close, yet he remains out of reach. Involving us in the act of seeing, Bellini involves us in the act of defining the doge's personality.

This was not Bellini's only portrayal of Leonardo Loredan; he also designed a group portrait of the doge with four of his senators or kinsmen, signed and dated 1507 (fig. 159).[46] Loredan is visibly older than he seems in the earlier portrait by Bellini; never a healthy man, he had been aged by his high office.[47] The group portrait is evidently identical with that admired by Ridolfi in Ca' Loredan in Campo Santo Stefano: "The portrait of Doge Leonardo Loredan seated at a small table and two of his sons and others of his family to either side, very vivacious figures."[48] In other words, like Barbarigo's votive picture (figs. 68, 69), this seems to have been private property and not a gift presented to the Palazzo Ducale. Bellini had assistance in the execution. But the conception was his own remarkable innovation.

Bellini's portraits of individuals provided the perfect visualization of the social and political ideals of the patriciate. In this representation, the master gave expression to the patrician ideal incarnate in the group. The group portrait embodies the Venetian patrician corporate mentality, in which the noble gerontocracy unite around the figure of Doge Loredan—not only mature or old men but men whose shared experience was perceived as essential to their successful group government.[49] This mentality led Bellini to create a new type of portraiture, all but unprecedented in Italian (or indeed in European) art, a portrait of five men seated together. To be sure, groups of men, members of confraternities, and many more

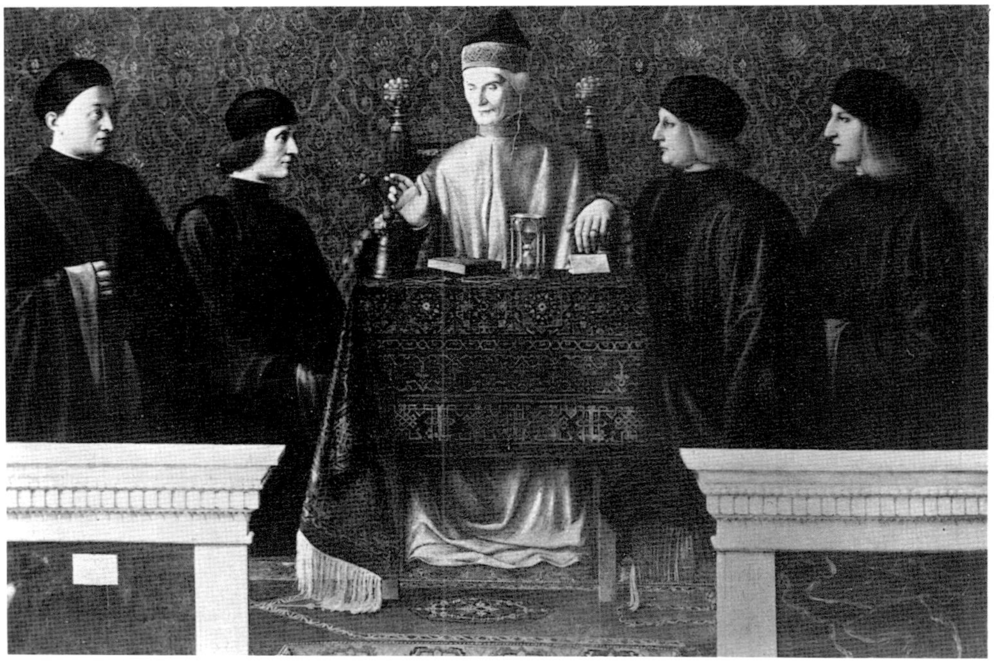

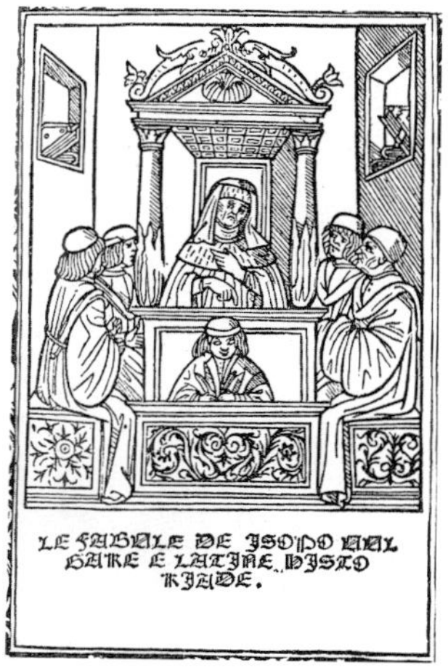


than five in number, might be represented as bystanders in narrative paintings decorating their scuole, including paintings by Bellini and his brother (figs. 184, 185); and portrait groups might be incorporated into Madonna paintings as donor figures, as in Bellini's votive picture for the Procuratia de Ultra (fig. 67) or Titian's *Madonna of the Ca' Pesaro*, the altarpiece of a family funerary chapel.[50] Two or even three men might be portrayed together, in the traditional half-length format long associated with portraiture.[51] But nothing nothing seems fully comparable to Bellini's "corporate group portrait" at this date, or indeed long thereafter—nothing, that is, except the tombs of scholars[52] and the frontispieces of books of Aesop's Fables published in 1497 and 1502 (fig. 160). Here, as in other late works, the master availed himself of the ideas of book illustrators, in this case adapting their motifs to a new purpose and investing them with new meaning.

Bellini also used another compositional source for the *Loredan and His Kinsmen*, surely even more familiar to contemporaries than the woodcuts and imbued with profound symbolic significance: the sacred imagery of the Madonna enthroned with saints and/or kneeling donors. The implication is that the doge, the head of state, is comparable to the King of Heaven. In the Maggior Consiglio, the doge was enthroned beneath Guariento's great fresco of the *Coronation of the Virgin* surrounded by the court of heaven: the rulers of Venice were identified as the earthly equivalent of their sacred exempla (fig. 66). Bellini's group portrait represents this political ideal of the Great Council in a nutshell, and here the declamatory gesture of the doge, Christ's surrogate, seemingly becomes a blessing for his people (fig. 159). Loredan's right hand is almost identical with that of the contemporary Bellinesque *Blessing Christ* (half-length and frontal) in Ottawa or of the early *Blessing Redeemer* in Paris (fig. 56).[53]

*159. Giovanni Bellini with assistance,* Doge Leonardo Loredan and His Kinsmen, *Staatliche Museen zu Berlin, East Germany. Courtesy Staatliche Museen zu Berlin, DDR, Gemäldegalerie.*

*160. Anonymous Sixteenth-Century Venetian, frontispiece,* Aesop's Fables *(Venice, 1502). From Victor Massena d'Essling,* Etudes sur l'art de la Gravure sur bois a Venise, *vol. 1 (Florence and Paris, 1907).*

The court of heaven on earth is embodied in the four patricians who accompany Loredan, all turning toward him so that they are seen essentially in profile, and the lower parts of their figures masked by the marble balustrade that carries a cartellino with Bellini's signature and the date. This balustrade opens in the center to reveal the doge seated at a small table, as Ridolfi described him. An Anatolian carpet covers the table; another carpet lies on the floor; and a rich floral pattern decorates the wall behind the figures, possibly representing the tooled leather sometimes used as a wall covering in Venice. The setting, by far the most lavish in Bellini's oeuvre, is richly patterned and colored, with red and gold tones predominating. It is a splendid environment for the doge, surrounded by his colleagues in their red-and-black robes of office.

The doge's chair is like a throne, suggesting a formal audience or council, and on the table before him are objects both practical and symbolic: a book, a piece of paper, an hourglass,[54] and a bell to summon his secretaries. The book and paper suggest the administrative duties that were the birthright and burden of the patriciate. Loredan's left hand rests on the arm of his throne and seems to point to the paper: perhaps a specific act is commemorated here. But it is not Bellini's symbolism that makes this portrait great: it is the psychological perception and conviction of his characterizations, which we can compare with his earlier portraits of Loredan or of Loredan's immediate predecessor, Agostino Barbarigo (fig. 69).

The same psychological and stylistic qualities that distinguish the ducal portraits mark another sixteenth-century patrician portrait by Bellini, the so-called Pietro Bembo in the collection of the Queen of England, which was probably painted in the years between 1505 and 1510 (fig. 161).[55] The portrait repeats the familiar Bellinesque formula—a bust-length figure seen behind a parapet with a cartellino (signed "Ioannes bellinus"), face turned to one side so that the glance avoids the viewer. But now Bellini has added a rich landscape setting, replacing the neutral backgrounds or skies of earlier works (cf. figs. 154, 155, 156).

The atmospheric handling of the landscape is matched by (or determines) an increased freedom of handling in the figure. Man and environment meld in this envelope of air, fused by light, shadow, and contour. The varied outlines of the man's shoulders, hair, and cap are echoed by—but do not coincide with—the large forms of the landscape. The interior forms of the subject's face, more softly described than the contours of his figure, similarly introduce movements and rhythms comparable to smaller forms in the landscape. But these are not pieces of a jigsaw puzzle; they do not match precisely and tediously in a tight pattern. Fluctuations and directions of movement, rather than identical shapes, are echoed and varied.

*161.* Portrait of a Man ("Pietro Bembo"), *Hampton Court, Her Majesty Queen Elizabeth II, on deposit at the National Gallery, London. Copyright reserved to Her Majesty Queen Elizabeth II.*

The other autograph work that exemplifies Bellini's late portraiture is the *Saint Dominic*, signed and dated 1515 (fig. 162). Labeled "Sanct'.Dominic" on the book and signed IOA[N]NIS BELLINI OP. on a cartellino, the canvas may be taken as Bellini's farewell to the genre—and yet it may not have been intended as a

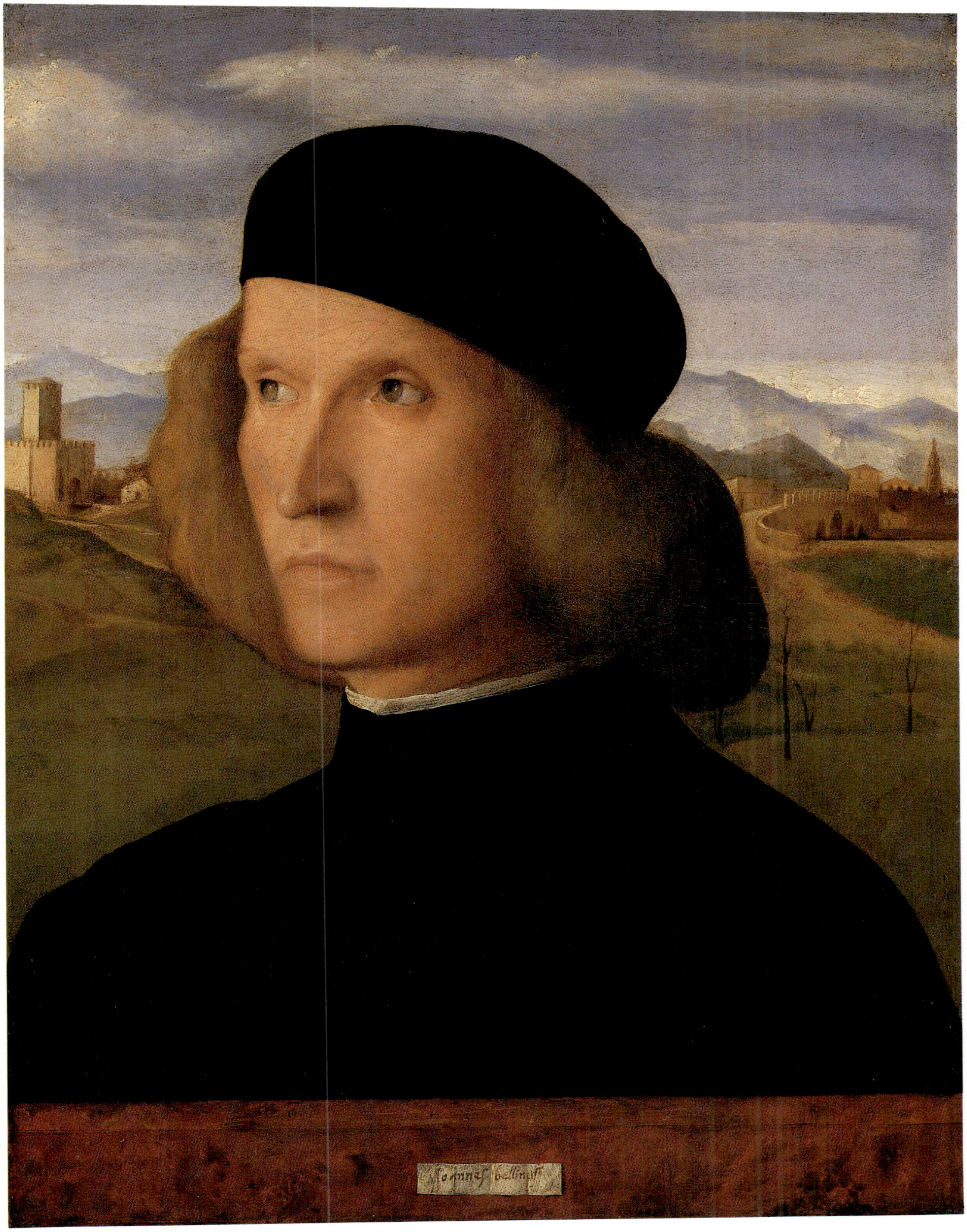

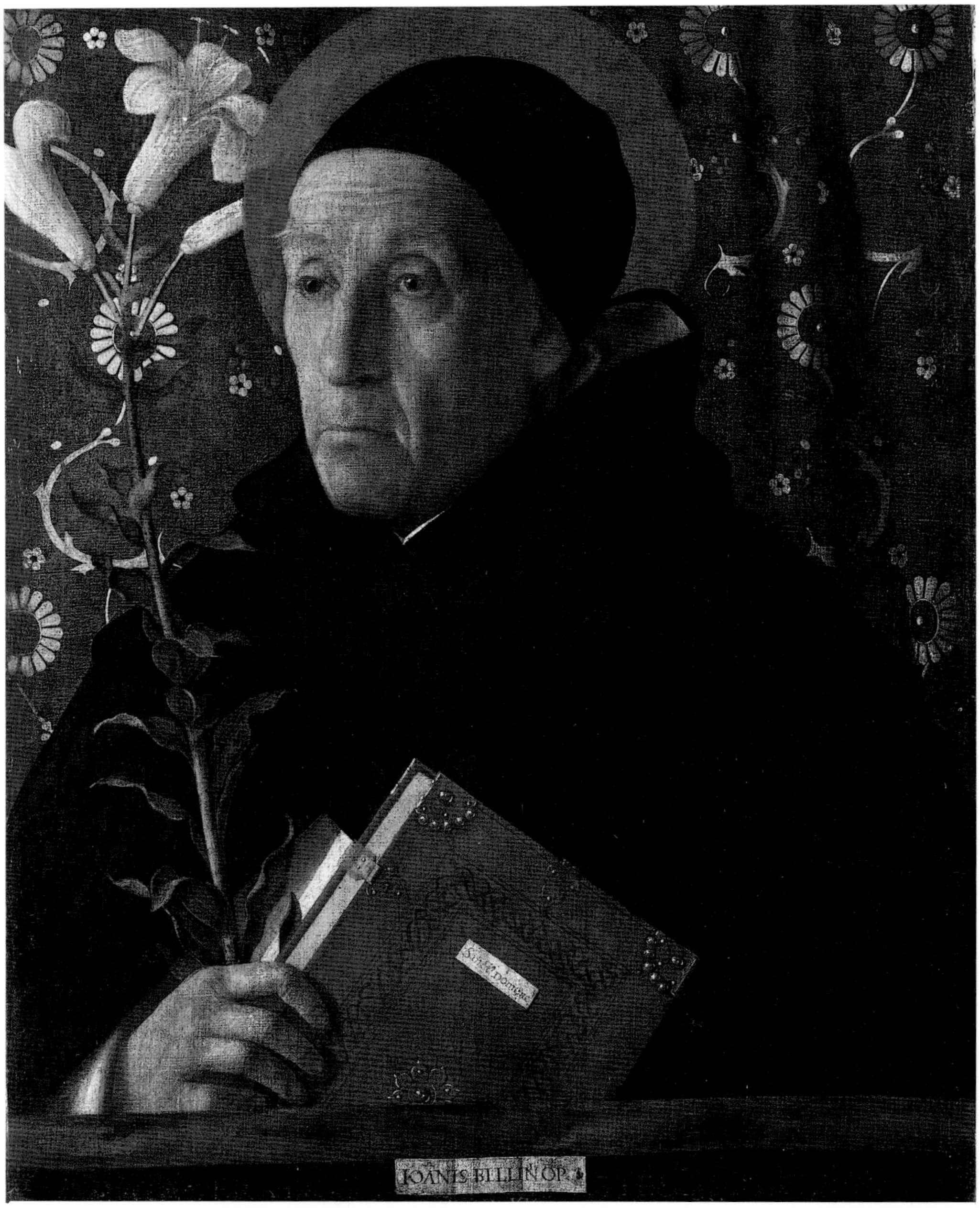

162. Portrait of Fra' Teodoro d'Urbino as Saint Dominic, *National Gallery, London.*

portrait in the traditional sense, despite identifying the sitter on the parapet: IMAGO FRATRIS / M.DXV / THEODORI URBINATIS. While this inscription may well be correct, the name of Fra Teodoro of Urbino was evidently added (with the date) by another hand after Bellini completed the painting.[56] In any case, the year on the painting is consistent with Bellini's style at the end of his life: the *Dominic* is comparable to the *Noah* in Besançon (fig. 180) and the altarpiece in San Giovanni Crisostomo (figs. 139, 140). Bellini would probably have known Fra Teodoro and his confreres at SS. Giovanni e Paolo. The master was associated with the great Dominican church from the beginning of his career until the end of his life: his first undisputed, major altarpiece was painted for that church (fig. 106); between the death of his brother, Gentile, in 1506, until his own death, he was engaged in painting the murals of the Scuola Grande di San Marco adjacent to SS.

Giovanni e Paolo (figs. 184, 185); and the Bellini were buried behind the apse of the church at the Scuola di Sant'Orsola.[57]

Although the *Dominic* is surely a likeness—the specificity of the features leave no doubt on this point—perhaps it is not a portrait per se. This is one of those strange Venetian paintings that frustrates strict identification as "portraiture" and seems to combine (or blur) two categories of imagery that were readily distinguishable elsewhere.[58] Contarini's *quadretto* of a woman was probably another of these pictures; as we recall, Michiel himself seemed uncertain whether to call it a portrait. Elsewhere, in sixteenth-century Florence or Rome, for example, an individual might be portrayed in the guise of his or her saintly or classical namesake, or conversely an individual might serve as a model for the artist's depiction of a personage in a sacred or secular painting. (Raphael's *School of Athens* and Michelangelo's *Last Judgment*, to cite two illustrious examples, are populated by such figures.) In the case of Bellini's late work, however, the two are combined differently: the characterization of the individual is as forceful and convincing as in any portrait, yet the subject of the painting seems to be Dominic—not Fra Teodoro as the saint. The lily, Dominic's traditional attribute, his halo, and his book were always intended as parts of the composition, unlike the attributes of Peter Martyr that were added to the image of an anonymous Dominican (fig. 158).[59] If this *Dominic* is the painting formerly in the collection of the Pesaro family, which seems likely, then the wording of their inventory listing is significant: "Giovanni Bellini, 'St. Dominic with the lily,' on canvas."[60] This is how Bellini had earlier represented the same saint in a painting possibly done for Alfonso d'Este in 1501 (fig. 163).[61] We recognize Dominic because of his attributes even though his face is more youthful and generalized in this earlier image than in the *Fra' Teodoro as Saint Dominic* (fig. 162). And one senses that the London painting represents the saint and not his follower because of certain compositional elements never found in Bellinesque portraits but instead the common property of his sacred images: not only the attributes that the figure holds (and always held), the halo of course, the cloth in the background—but the inclusion of his hand. (The *Dominican as Saint Peter Martyr* is the sole exception in this regard.) Bellini painted a sacred image, basing his visualization of Dominic on the visage of Brother Teodoro. Later, in response to the power of this likeness, someone other than Bellini inscribed the subject's name and transformed a devotional picture into a portrait.

The "Teodoro/Dominic" is exceptional because it records the subject's name. But aside from Bellini's ducal portraits, the donors of certain altarpieces and devotional pictures, and the *Jörg Fugger*, none of Bellini's subjects is identified, and only the quasi-portrait of the old Dominican is identified by an inscription, an addition to the picture, as we have seen. Yet, in spite of this anonymity, to understand Bellini's portraits we must know his sitters, or more precisely, their class.

The bearing of Bellini's subjects is as much an identifying attribute as what they wear. Although there are no inscriptions, emblems, or other devices to guide us,

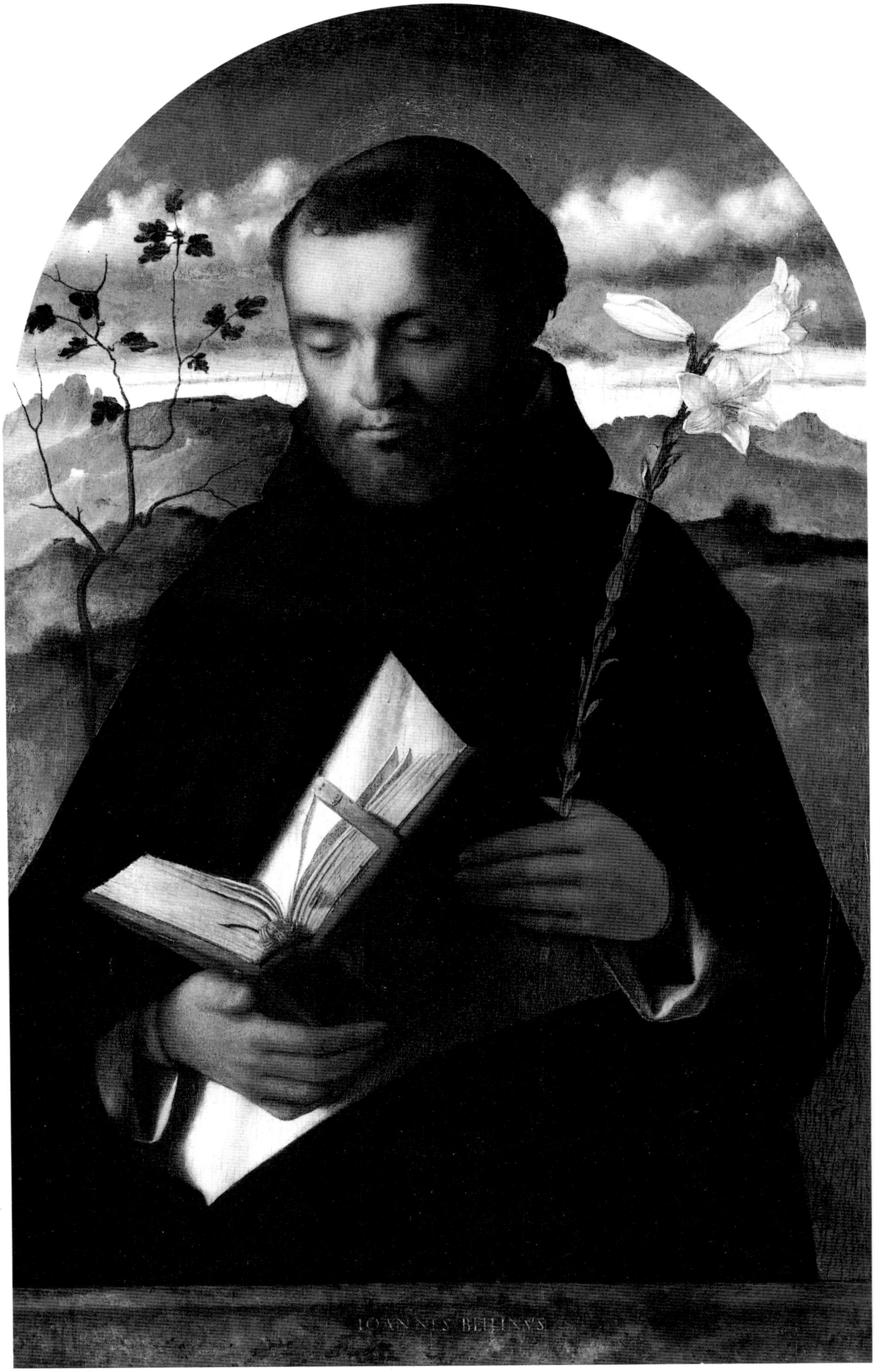
IOANNES BELLINVS

it is clear that Bellini's portraits represent the Venetian noblemen and *cittadini originari* who were the primary patrons of his altarpieces and his public commissions as well. Bellini, in short, was the artist of patrician Venice, and it is patrician ideals, patrician sociology, psychology, and spirituality, that he represented and that the ruling class clearly considered him best able to represent. In this age the self-defined patriciate of Venice became increasingly preoccupied, not to say obsessed, with its genealogical purity. Beginning at the turn of the fifteenth century, as Stanley Chojnacki has recently discussed, new legislation defined patrician status with increasing precision and exclusivity.[62] The culmination came at the beginning of the sixteenth century with the so-called *Libri d'Oro*, the Golden Books, in which were registered—in accordance with the law—all marriages between noblemen and noblewomen, and all births resulting from these unions, for legitimate descent from the legitimate marriage of patrician parents was the exacting requirement for noble status. Rules governing the *cittadinanza originaria* were almost as strict. This specificity regarding legitimacy and genealogy clearly had to do less with ideals of morality than with power (and its frequent companion, money). The basic fact of Venetian political life was the patrician monopoly of government service: noble status was the one requirement for eligibility for office—hence for the considerable financial and political benefits of office. Similarly, original citizenship was the entrée to lucrative employment in the Chancellery. But "bread and butter issues" were only part of the matter. In fifteenth-century Venice, young nobles—those twenty- to twenty-five-year-old men just entering the Maggior Consiglio—were endowed with symbolic significance as the embodiment of patrician mythology, aspirations, and ideals.[63]

These interrelated aims of the self-defined, self-perpetuating patriciate—their exclusivism as a class and their exclusive right to hold office—were given institutional expression in the ritual processes by which male patricians passed from youth to adulthood. Decorum, respect for officialdom, obeisance to procedure and to legal limitations regarding different ages, and above all a submission of individual interests to the needs of the state—these dicta constituted the patrician ideology that served both public and private needs.[64] Patrician decorum and the amalgamation of individual and group are the subject of Bellini's portraits: the sitters' restraint and concealment of their hands, the omission of ostentatious attributes such as a comparatively wealthy or well-placed Florentine might wish to see included (one can be sure that the men with wreaths or "indecorous" classicizing garments are not patricians)—these artistic decisions were consonant with the self-image of Bellini's noble patrons and the original citizens who emulated them.

Age is also significant. Most noblemen became eligible for membership in the Great Council at twenty-five, though some might join even earlier, if they were lucky in the Barbarella, the state lottery that permitted this privilege. Bellini's noble subjects were already sitting in the Great Council—theirs are the mature and thoughtful visages of responsible members of the patriciate, not the eager

*163. Giovanni Bellini with possible assistance,* Saint Dominic, *Collection of Frederick R. and Jan Mayer.*

and carefree faces of liminal youths. That age is not a worthy subject for artistic preservation: it is by definition transitional, and the sooner the transition is accomplished (by the Barbarella, legislative measures, or the passage of time), the better for all concerned. Bellini's only twenty-one-year-old subject was apparently the German Jörg Fugger, and his only child, the *Boy* in the Barber Art Institute, was evidently also not Venetian. The subjects of the late "Dominican portraits" were not noble (or had given up the patrician life), and one of these paintings was not even intended as a portrait per se. Bellini's Venetian subjects were adult patricians (or original citizens), responsible and active participants in the regime, or so their images and written propaganda assert. When the subject is arguably in his twenties, his success in winning early Council membership (or a significant position in the Chancellery) may have provided the occasion for his being portrayed.

Because the experience and situation of young Venetian patricians were identical in so many important ways, the persona of Bellini's subjects can be reconstructed, an enterprise legitimated also by the intentional suppression of individual inclinations both in the portraits and indeed in actuality. Whatever idiosyncracies, private inclinations, or desires might characterize a young nobleman would be (or were declared to be) subject to the needs of family and state—which were presumed to coincide with government service. To be sure, human beings, not even Venetian patricians, are not so easily and so consistently suppressed, but the public commemoration of inappropriate individuality could certainly be restrained or eliminated—and certainly not recorded in portraiture—just as public disapprobation could make gratifying personal needs prohibitive in social, psychological, and of course financial terms. The stuff of patrician portraiture in Venice, then, is not the slightly neurotic nervousness of Botticelli's *Young Man with a Medal of Cosimo de' Medici*, the watchful vivacity of Castagno's *Young Man*, or the convincing assertiveness of Perugino's *Francesco delle Opere*. Their informal individuality would be unwelcome and unsuitable in Venice, where every portrait of a patrician is by definition an official portrait. In Venice, possible failures of character are concealed behind an idealized mask.

Although we may know nothing, not even the name, of any individual subject of most of Bellini's portraits, we know much about all of them because each records much the same life experience. First, as we have seen, almost all (by Bellini or from his immediate circle) represent men of approximately the same age. Bellini and his shop portrayed a combination of individual likeness—we might almost say biological likeness—and idealized identity. And that is why, in Venice as nowhere else, genres seem confused: portraiture was not defined as in Florence or Perugia or Rome. Just as the features of one nobleman are recorded in a portrait that represents his class and lineage, so may the features of one person be portrayed in a depiction of that individual as the embodiment of a class—a Dominican friar, for example, or Flora, or Laura the poetess or courtesan.[65]

Perhaps Bellini's portrayal of Bembo's beloved and the "little picture" seen by Michiel in the Contarini collection were pictures of this sort. But more often, Bellini's portraits represent the protagonists of the societal process, elucidating the stages and nature of patrician adulthood, the symbolic embodiments of the patriciate's evolving definition of itself as a ruling class.[66]

In Florence, humanistic virtue was supposed to characterize the elite, whereas in Venice, the governing elite was self-defined according to lineage, and this distinction is reflected in the different conceptions of portraiture in the two centers. In Venice, without the appropriate genealogy, no individual, however gifted, could hope to achieve political status: government was a monopoly of the patriciate. This noble race was not to indulge ordinary human emotions, as Francesco Barbaro reminded his son. Nor was the Venetian patrician to indulge personal likes (and dislikes) in the way in which he lived his life. Francesco's grandson, Zaccaria's son Ermolao, tried to do so, to "live for letters" rather than for the state, and he died in disgrace.[67]

A Venetian patrician might escape the regime, as Ermolao Barbaro did, but more commonly noblemen yielded individuality to the needs of lineage and state. Publically, officially, they expressed only praise and acceptance, never criticism, of their system.[68] Precisely this apparently complacent compliance, this uncritical embrace of the regime, distinguishes Bellini's compatriots from their contemporaries in other states. The face presented by the Venetian patrician to the world, and by all accounts, even to himself, is tranquil, assured, imperturbable. Bellini's portraits ennoble that face and those convictions.

*In the purest part of heaven, dancing the mystic bacchic dance with the gods of Olympus*
—Bessarion

# 4 "Roaming at His Will"
## Allegories and Mythologies

Mythological subjects and allegories, sacred and secular, concerned Bellini and his patrons primarily during the later part of his career.[1] For this reason, and because Bellini is so closely associated in our minds with sacred subjects, his secular allegories and mythologies seem anomalous—though not in ways that have been assumed. What is remarkable about these works by Bellini is not that he painted them in spite of a presumed personal reluctance to do so but rather that he painted them at all, given the Venetian attitude toward humanistic studies.

Quattrocento Venice was not a friendly environment for the *studia humanitatis:* the fundamental issue is not whether Bellini was interested in classical subjects but why his Venetian patrons were uninterested in buying them. Surely it was not for lack of "inspiration" or information. The Republic of Venice had received (and eventually lost) the precious gift of Petrarch's humanistic library almost a century before Bellini's time, an endowment that was magnificently enriched by Cardinal Bessarion's bequest of his own collection in 1472. Responding to the profound and inherent Byzantine Hellenism of the republic, the Greek Bessarion felt that he had found a second Constantinople in Venice, and this misled him into believing the city to be an appropriate recipient of his library: "Among all the cities of Italy, I don't know of any to which I could entrust more safely my beloved books."[2] But the Venetians were not interested in the study of the classics for their own sake, at least not before the end of the fifteenth century, when Aldus Manutius took advantage of the treasure trove of books and manuscripts in the Biblioteca di San Marco to found a new industry, the publication of ancient—especially Greek—texts. The first great monuments of Venetian classicizing literature, notably Sannazzaro's *Arcadia* and the *Hypnerotomachia Poliphili*, attributed to the Roman Francesco Colonna and published by Aldus, belong to this period.[3] Even at that comparatively late date vis-à-vis the state of humanistic studies elsewhere in Italy, however, the Venetian patriciate was too busy running things to take more than dillettantish notice: their monopoly of government service effectively precluded the possibility of a patrician's serious dedication to such studies, or, for that matter, the significant employment by the regime of professional humanists.[4] When the

*164.* Pagan Allegory, *Stanley Moss Collection, New York. Photo: Stanley Moss, New York.*

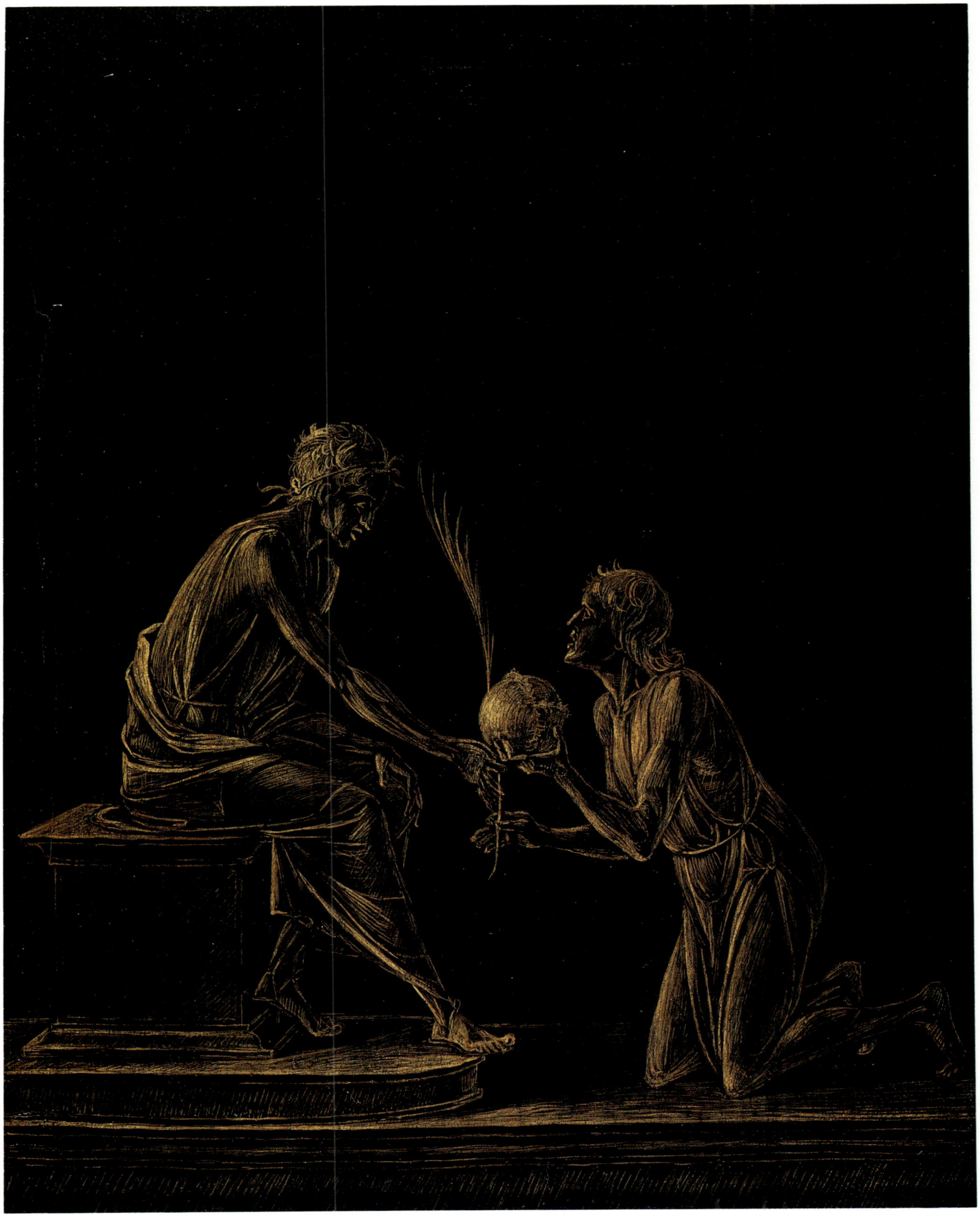

republic finally established the Scuola di San Marco in 1451, long after other states had founded similar academies, the curriculum emphasized the study of the Greek language—not primarily to permit the reading of ancient texts but for the more mundane and pragmatic purpose of preparing citizens for eventual government service. The small group of patrician humanists who had gathered around Doge Francesco Foscari (doge, 1423–57)—the first generation of humanists in Venice—were primarily concerned with promoting his new policy of mainland expansion; the kinds of classicizing literature that interested them were above all the political genres that could be exploited to serve the state, oratory, for example, or texts explaining and extolling the regime. Such men do not make good patrons of classicizing art. Indeed, Bellini's so-called *Pagan Allegory*, dating from the late 1450s or early 1460s, is among the first known Venetian representations of such material (fig. 164).[5] And this early Venetian picture of a classical subject was part of a decorative object—not an "easel" or large-scale mural painting; until the turn of the sixteenth century in Venice, such subjects were evidently banished to the intimate and secondary territory of personal furnishings.

Bellini's small panel surely formed part of a larger whole. Almost identical in size to his later *Allegories* in the Accademia, this picture probably originally served the same purpose as they seem to have done, namely, to decorate a *restello*. Bellini's early *Blood of the Redeemer* was evidently also intended to adorn an object—in this case, a tabernacle of the Host (fig. 57). Restelli were luxurious secular objects, elaborate and costly mirrors enframed with carved and gilded wood, and surrounded by small paintings, the ostensible practical purpose of all this being the convenient storage (and the true purpose, the display) of toilet articles that were themselves luxurious, such as decorated combs, and to clean them, long brushes of horsehair with elegant fittings. The first mention of a restello seems to occur in an inventory of 1457 of a Murano household: if Bellini's *Allegory* was made for such an object, then it has the distinction of having been among the first of its kind, as well as one of the first such subjects in Venetian art.[6]

Painted in gold on a black ground, Bellini's picture is like a gilded drawing or manuscript illumination; it is almost jewel-like, and the object that it once adorned must have been splendid. In technique, the panel resembles the handling of the cherubim surrounding Saint Vincent Ferrer, also painted in gold striations on black (fig. 186), or the fictive reliefs on the parapet in the *Blood of the Redeemer*, which are related in their antique subject matter as well (fig. 57). With a fine brush, Bellini applied the gold sometimes in long striations, sometimes in shorter strokes that bend back on themselves, and sometimes in cross-hatching. The strokes almost merge to suggest highlight, whereas their absence, the absence of gold, leaves the black as shadow, including cast shadows. It is a tour de force of a drawing technique that becomes coloristic painting.

The subject of the *Pagan Allegory*, which remains an enigma, was probably always intended to be arcane—like the *Hypnerotomachia*, to take a frustrating lit-

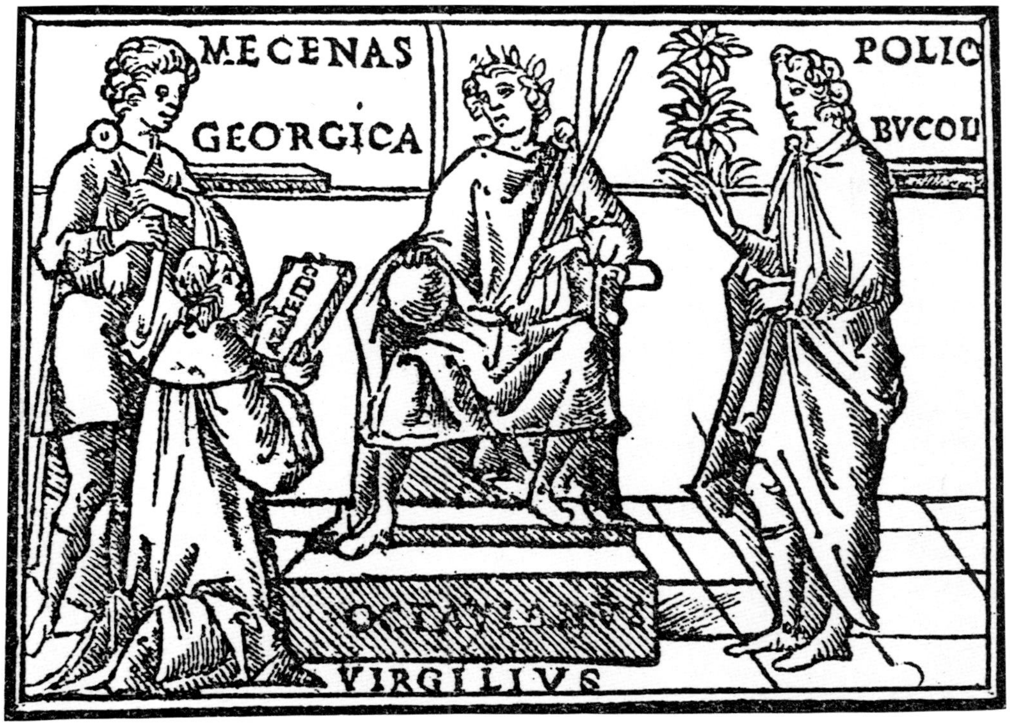


*165. Anonymous Sixteenth-Century Venetian, frontispiece, Virgil,* Opera *(Venice, 1507). From Victor Massena d'Essling,* Etudes sur l'art de la Gravure sur bois a Venise, *vol. 1 (Florence and Paris, 1907).*

erary parallel—but was perhaps more readily understood in relation to the other panels that must have accompanied it.[7] A man is seated in profile at the left of the composition. Surely he is a ruler or a god: seated on a block that resembles an ancient altar, he wears a diadem and a tunic with a mantle. The other figure, more modestly dressed, kneels to offer a palm branch and an orb. The way in which the orb is decorated with leaves (possibly myrtle) recalls the bands of precious metal and/or gems that adorn the orbs of Christian rulers, but now turned sideways rather than upright. The palm frond, too, is familiar in the context of Christian imagery—martyrs hold palm branches, and Christ's path is covered with fronds in the Entry into Jerusalem—but here the palm has been restored to its ancient usage as a sign or offering of peace. Yet the supplicant's demeanor is not one of defeat; his sensitive and animated face suggests an intellectual or cultural offering to his prince. The idiosyncratic refinement of his features and the relationship between the two men may suggest an association like that of Octavian and Virgil, a ruler who is patron and recipient of the offerings of art and culture, as in the frontispiece of Virgil's works published in Venice in 1508 (fig. 165). In Bellini's composition, the two appear to address each other, and whatever the subject of their discourse, the artist has endowed it with considerable energy.

The near-certainty that this work was once accompanied by others like it, and the classicizing reliefs of the *Blood of the Redeemer*, painted at approximately the same time, demonstrate Bellini's willingness to depict antique themes and his ability to do so with considerable sympathy and skill. Even such details as the cameolike clasp of one angel's garment in the Rimini *Pietà* or the reliefs on the throne in the *Sacred Allegory* confirm Bellini's familiarity with ancient art (figs. 60,

79). Looking at his father's drawings, Bellini would have found further encouragement, were it needed, for his interest in antiquity.[8] One should recall, too, the quotation from Propertius inscribed on the parapet of the Brera *Pietà* (fig. 49). Whether this was suggested by the patron or the artist himself, it signifies Bellini's familiarity with at least part of that classical author's poetry. In addition, Ridolfi knew two large paintings with classical subjects by Bellini, one bearing his signature. Ridolfi saw these works, evidently murals, in the fifteenth-century Grimani Palace at San Marcuola and identified the theme as *Cosmografia*, with figures of Ptolemy, Strabo, Pliny, and Pomponius Mella.[9] The Grimani paintings have been lost; who can say what other classicizing subjects may have been painted by Bellini but have gone unrecorded?

Giovanni Bellini and his brothers owned antiquities—Gentile had a *Venus*, Giovanni and Nicolò a bust of Plato that they hawked to Isabella d'Este.[10] Among Bellini's patrons were at least two humanist scholars, Raffaele Zovenzoni, who memorialized the antique *Venus* in an epigram, and Leonico Tomeo, professor at Padua. Among his friends, Bellini counted such men of learning as Pietro Bembo and Pandolpho Collenuccio of Pesaro.[11] It seems clear that the artist lacked neither knowledge nor inclination but rather opportunity to treat classical themes. What he painted—or did not paint—is explained by the needs and desires of his patrons, and not by any lack of interest or expertise.

Bellini's next surviving works of this sort—independent images representing classicizing themes—are the five *Allegories* in the Accademia, painted in the late 1480s and early 1490s (figs. 166–71, 173). When they were produced, the master was occupied with his far more demanding and prestigious work in the Ducal Palace, to say nothing of such major private commissions as the Barbarigo votive picture and the Frari triptych. Moreover, Bellini could certainly reject or avoid commissions when he wished.[12] By their very existence, the *Allegories* may be considered an illustration of Bellini's interest in such subjects.

For a hundred years and more, these panels have been associated with the restello belonging to Vincenzo Catena and mentioned by him in his last will. G. B. Cavalcaselle first suggested this provenance, but technical and stylistic evidence indicate that the fifth panel does not belong with the first four.[13] There is little reason to believe, moreover, that Bellini's *Allegories* once belonged to Catena, who may or may not have been the original owner of the restello cited in his will of 1525—but not in his testament written a dozen years earlier—and whose restello may or may not have been decorated with any of these pictures. Bellini had apparently painted a restello at the beginning of his career, of which the *Pagan Allegory* is all that remains, and perhaps others were graced with pictures by him. However attractive, the association of the Accademia panels with the restello mentioned in Catena's testament seems merely fortuitous.

In any case, what Catena wrote in 1525 is at once imprecise and revealing, whether he was referring to any of these works or to others now lost to us:

*166. Giovanni Bellini with assistance,* Fortune, *Gallerie dell'Accademia, Venice.*

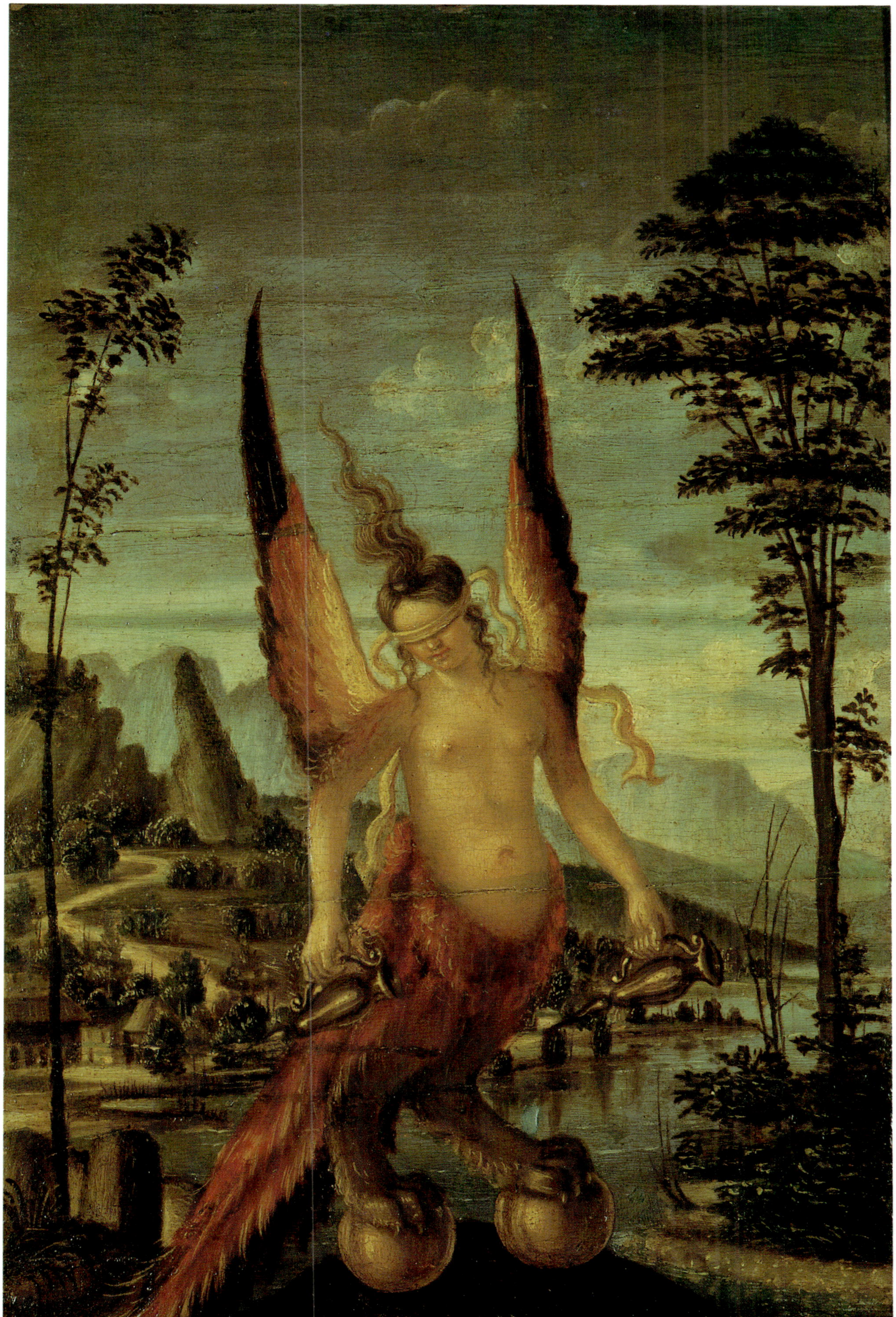

"Item, I leave to the aforementioned misser Antonio [de Marsilio], all my rings, mounted in gold, first my diamond and my emerald and two carnelians mounted in gold, and also I leave my restello of walnut with certain little figures in it painted by the hand of misser Giovanni Bellini, and also all my nudes in relief made of terracotta."[14] Placing his restello in the context of his jewels and terracotta reliefs, Catena confirms the exquisite preciousness of the thing while asserting its character as a work of art, set with autograph paintings by Bellini. His attribution may be taken more seriously than that of most testators; at least these "little figures" were painted by the master himself. Moreover, Catena's language may imply that the object had covers: Bellini's paintings are "in" (*dentro*) the restello. But aside from mentioning that these pictures include figures, Catena said nothing about content, and the description could refer just as well to the early *Pagan Allegory*, or indeed to another work by Bellini now lost or unrecognized.

If the works in the Accademia did not belong to Catena, then at least we have the consolation of knowing that Bellini painted other classicizing subjects, Catena's among them. One of those works is likely the fifth panel in the Accademia, displayed with the four others that were obviously conceived as a group, but smaller than they, in a somewhat different style, and painted on a different support (fig. 166). This work seems to be a painting by Bellini in the early 1490s, albeit with some assistance, a picture that would have belonged to yet another restello.[15]

If Bellini was a law-abiding citizen of the republic, however, then he would not have painted a restello for Catena or indeed for anyone else after 1489, for that December the Senate decreed that such objects should not be made, bought, or sold. "For some time," the indignant senators declaimed, "it has been the custom to make new expenditures that are entirely vain and superfluous, . . . that is, restelli and gilded chests [*chasse*], very sumptuous and of [monetary] value. And now, let it be decreed that all the said restelli and gilded chests be de facto prohibited and forbidden, so that from now on they cannot be used or possessed in any manner, under all the penalties and strictures contained in the legislation [*parte*] of ornaments of rooms; this applies to those who desire to possess them, as to masters who work on them." The senators then forbade expensive wedding cakes and women's fur pieces.[16] These so-called sumptuary laws, meant to curb frivolous spending, were frequently and conspicuously flouted by many Venetians. In the same year, the Senate felt compelled to reiterate its opposition to marzipan, which had already been declared a controlled substance in 1476 and 1483.[17] In any case, the date of the law pertaining to restelli is consistent with the style of at least the first four *Allegories*: perhaps the restello was legal after all, if just under the wire.

As in mural painting and in other narrative cycles, in the four *Allegories* the direction of light is consistent, tying the group together and indicating the original placement of the panels. The direction of movement in each scene confirms this. The two compositions with male protagonists were originally pendants,

*167. Rearrangement of panels from a restello by Giovanni Bellini. Photos: Soprintendenza ai Beni Artistici e Storici, Venice. Montage: Author.*

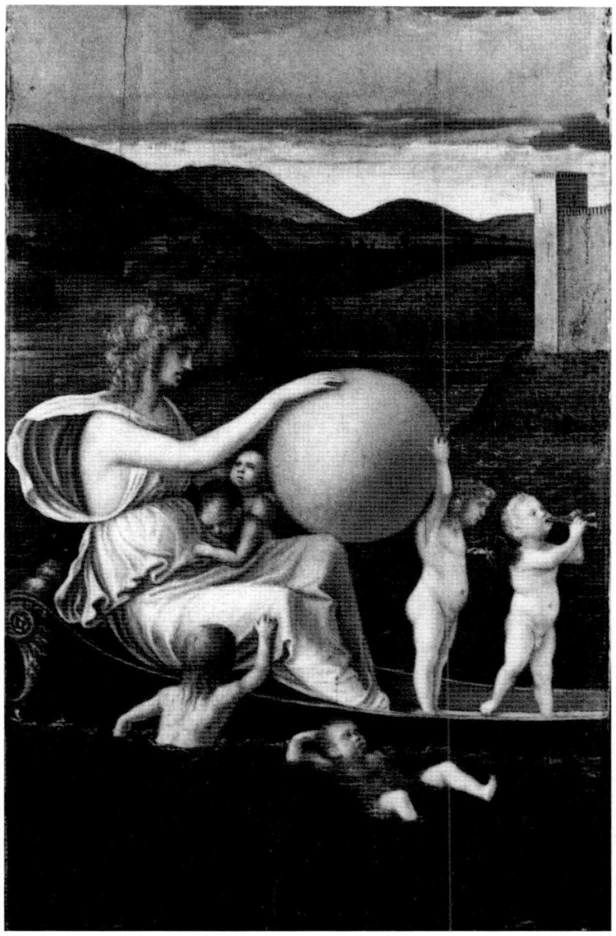

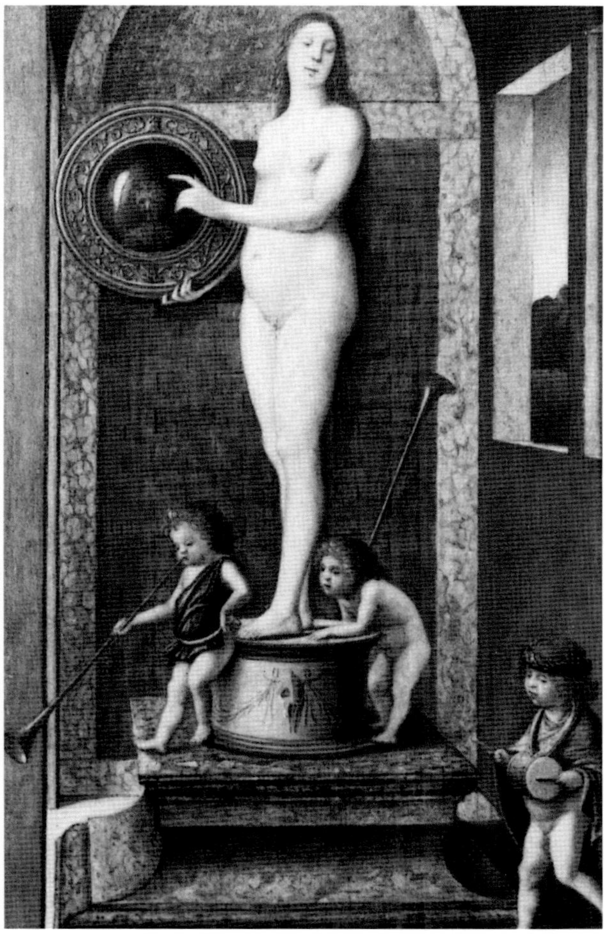

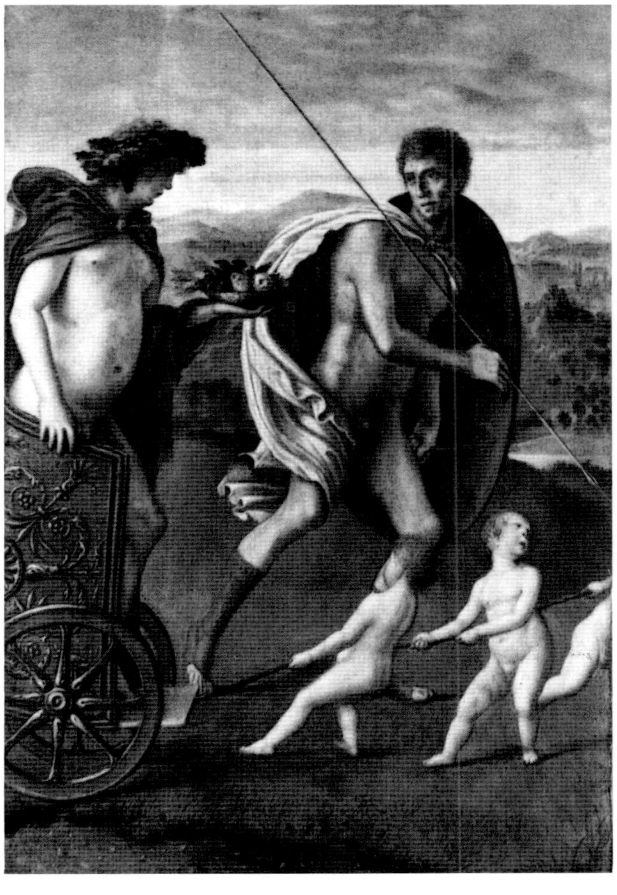

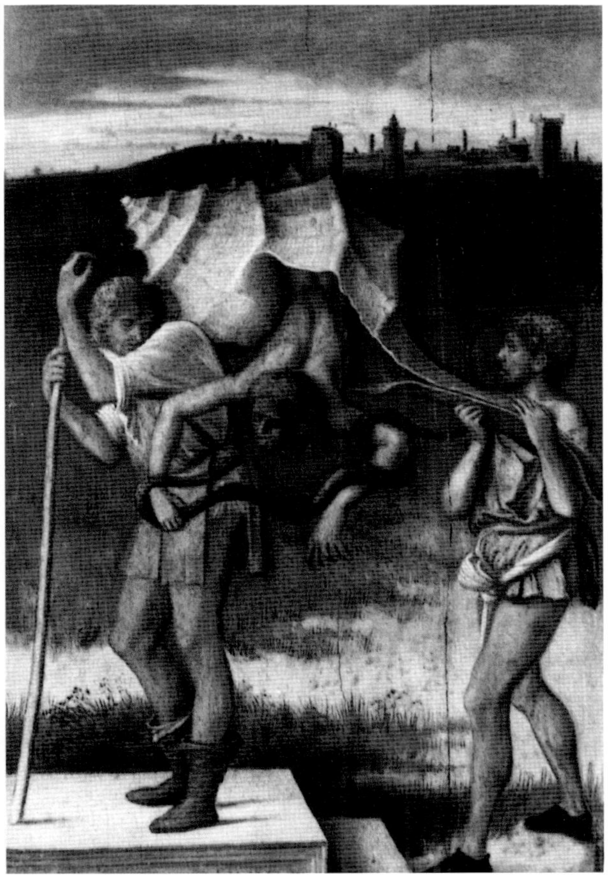

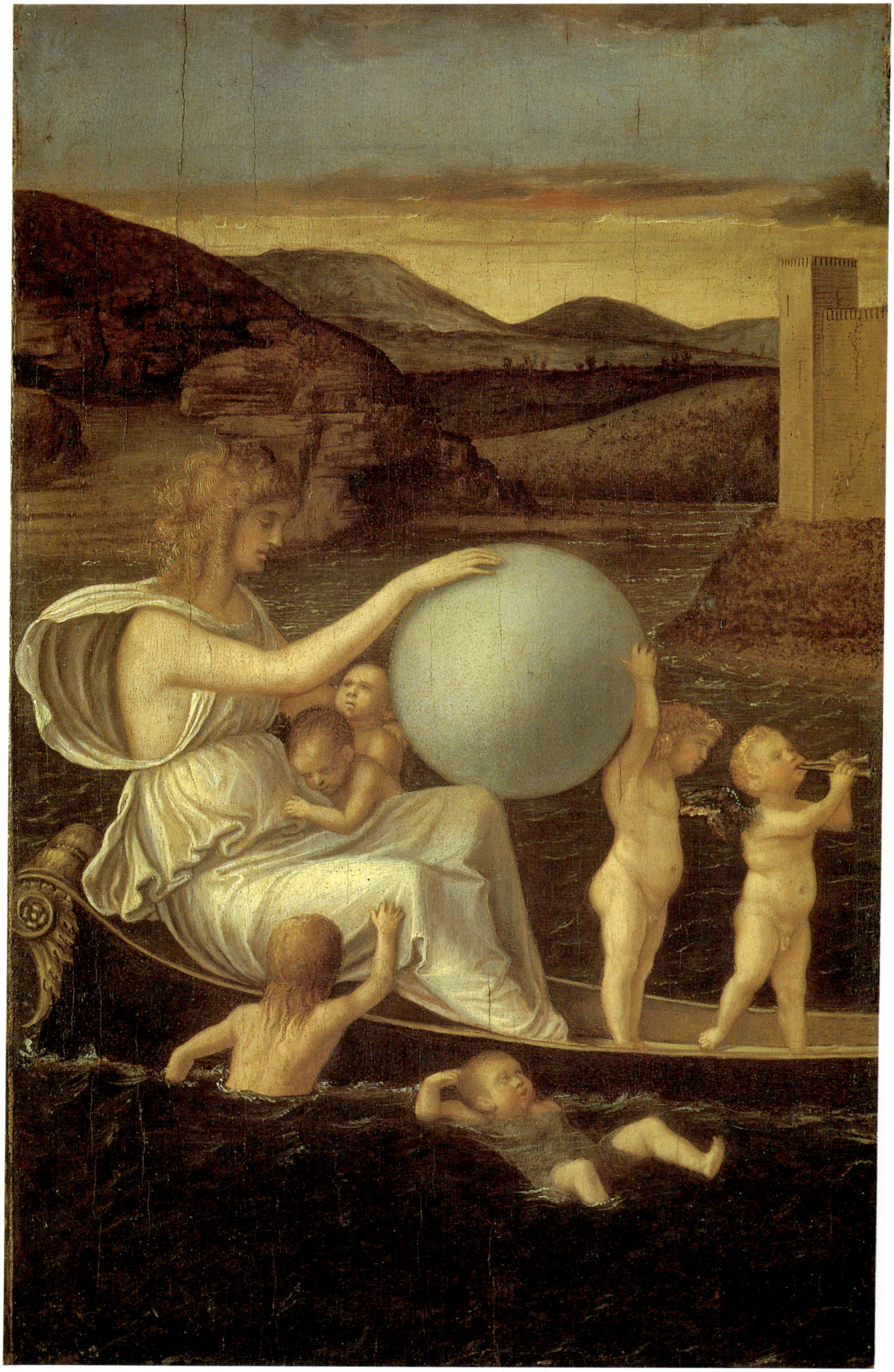

with "Bacchus" on the left and the signature at the bottom of the "Snail" panel, IOANNES BELLINVS.P. The compositions of the remaining two paintings, with female protagonists, indicate that the water scene was to the left and the woman with the mirror to the right. These horizontal pairings form logical vertical pairings as well, corresponding to the direction of the action in each scene. When the four panels are rearranged in this way, male and female are juxtaposed (fig. 167).

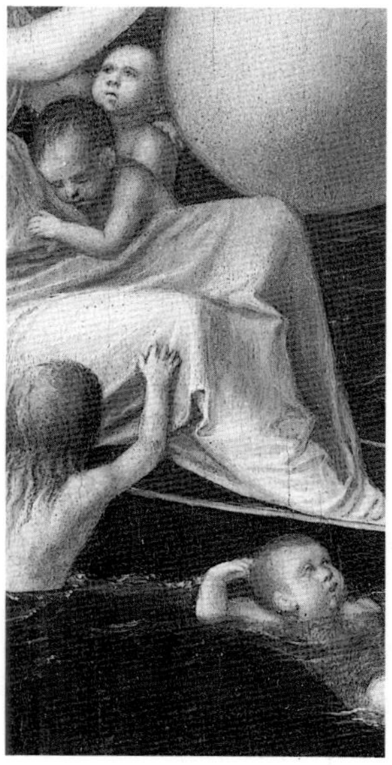

*169.* Melancholy, *detail, children. Photo: Giacomelli Fotografia, Venice.*

Bellini has also distinguished the figures according to their classicism, especially in the case of the female figures, contrasting the nude, a nonclassical northern type, with the classicizing woman in the boat. Each is paired with a male figure of comparable classicism or nonclassicism. Bellini further distinguished the figures morally, with one member of each sex embodying something virtuous and the other something invidious.[18] Hence, virtue and vice seem to have been allocated equally between the two sexes and between the two modes, classical and nonclassical. Suggestions regarding any of the panels obviously must be consistent both visually and symbolically for all four—they form a cycle—and it is worth remembering that Bellini himself was capable of "fantastic inventions," as Pietro Bembo reminded Isabella d'Este.[19] Perhaps these compositions have caused scholars so much iconographic confusion precisely because they were Bellini's personal fantasy, not a compilation of more readily recognizable symbols imposed by a patron.

The first scene represents *Melancholy* (fig. 168). The same attribute, the globe of Fortune, and the same characters, a woman and several infants, reappear in two paintings by Lucas Cranach representing *Melancholia*, the name inscribed on one of them.[20] Similarly, Dürer depicted *Melancolia I* with a globe and a putto in his engraving of 1514. Bellini's *Melancholy* sails in a boat, but how it is propelled is unexplained: the mechanics of her progress are concealed by the cropping of the picture, perhaps to signify that her voyage is uncontrolled and unguided, aimless like her musings in the characterizations by Cranach and Dürer. Bellini further confirmed her identity as Melancholy by a remarkable detail, the expressive faces (fig. 169). The incisive characterizations of these figures, all the more extraordinary given their small size, was anticipated by the early *Pagan Allegory*.

*168.* Melancholy, *restello panel, Gallerie dell'Accademia, Venice. Photo: Giacomelli Fotografia, Venice.*

*Overleaf:*
*170.* Truth: Self-Knowledge, *restello panel, Gallerie dell'Accademia, Venice. Photo: Giacomelli Fotografia, Venice.*

*171.* Perseverance, *restello panel, Gallerie dell'Accademia, Venice. Photo: Giacomelli Fotografia, Venice.*

Melancholy frowns and her little companions are woebegone, but the nude woman in the next panel smiles at us as she presents her attribute, a mirror with its reflected image, and the accompanying children celebrate her with raucous, gleeful music (fig. 170). Mirrors were associated with self-knowledge in art and literature, and this seems consistent both with the action of Bellini's figure—naked, like all truth—and with her placement on a pedestal resembling an ancient altar. The nude is Self-Knowledge, which she commends to the beholder with her gesture of indication and admonition, as though to say, "Know thyself."

The admonition, more humorous than severe, is ironically underscored by the inclusion of the panel on a mirrored object: Self-Knowledge shows the viewer to

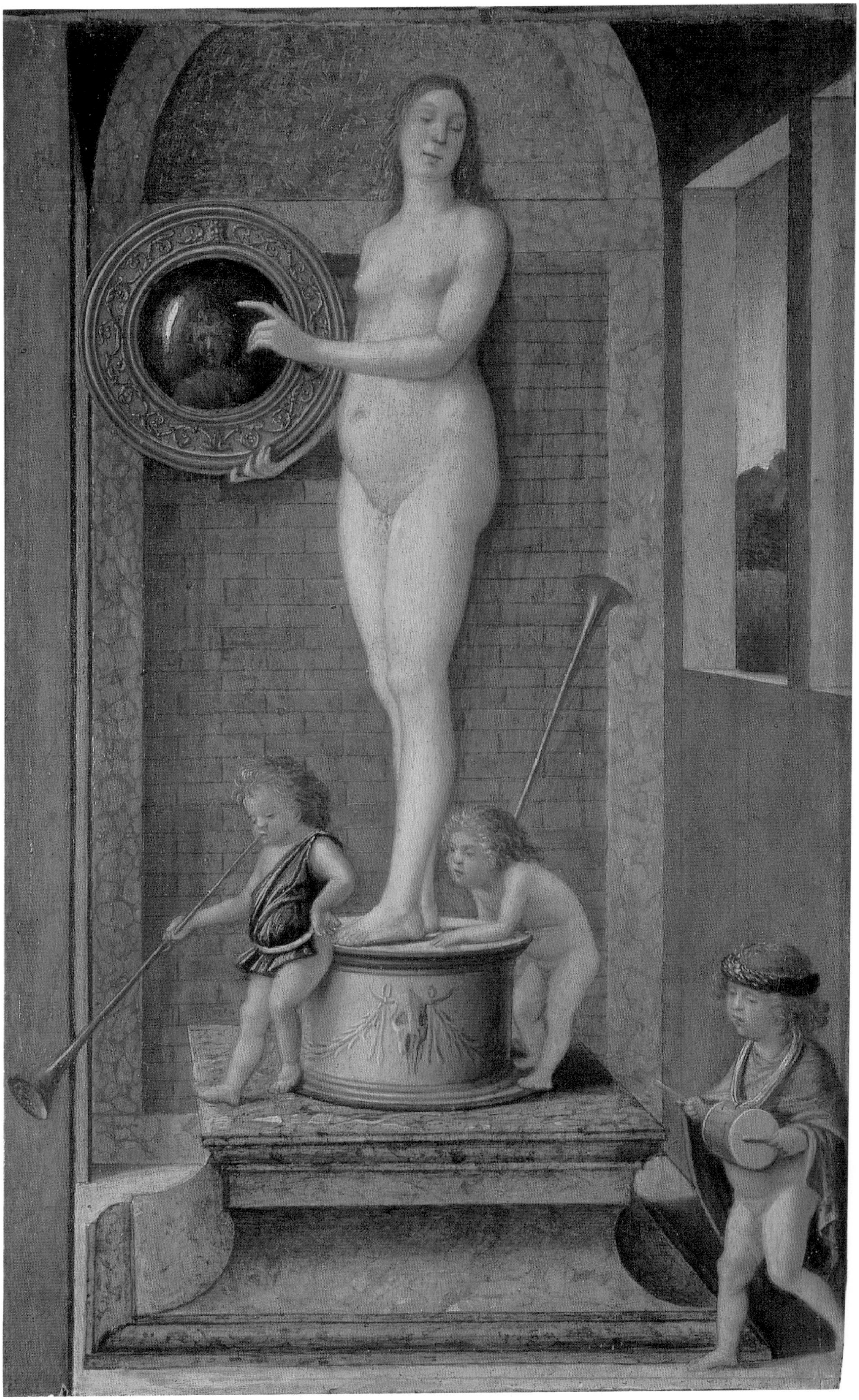

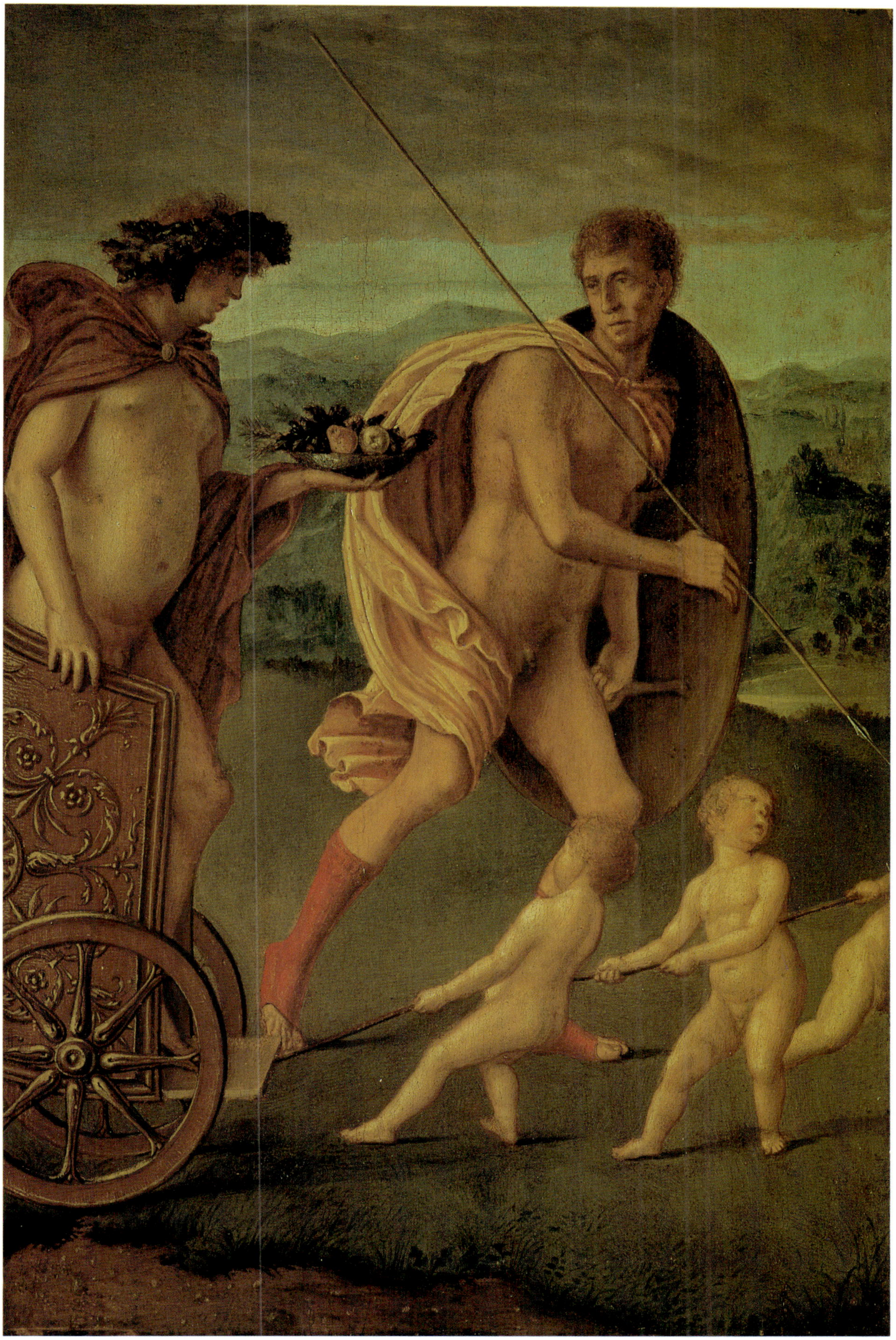

himself even as he considers his actual reflection in the mirror of the restello.[21] The mirror reflection, characterized as such by Bellini's handling of the paint, represents the bust of a figure in red, clearly alive, and almost certainly male, given the cut of the garment and the details of the face.[22] Bellini's painted reflection explicitly refers to the viewer, presented by the only figure of the cycle who addresses the beholder directly. What Self-Knowledge shows us is not herself but ourselves, or the self of the original beholder or representative viewer.

Self-Knowledge stands on her classicizing pedestal like an ancient sculptural monument, but this reference is contradicted by her distinctly unclassical physique, an antipode to the classical ideal of feminine beauty. She resembles fifteenth-century Netherlandish and German nudes in her proportions: small breasts, full hips, a swelling abdomen. One recalls the *Eve* sculpted by Antonio Rizzo in 1476 for the Arco Foscari of the Ducal Palace.[23] Was Bellini playing aesthetic games with different conceptions of beauty and style? His contrast of the nude and her surroundings suggests this. Bellini may even have had a particular northern model in mind, for his nude holds a mirror that reflects an image, and this detail suggests Bellini's knowledge of a celebrated lost painting by Jan van Eyck of a woman in her bath. Quite unlike Self-Knowledge, however, van Eyck's nude contemplates her own reflection and is oblivious to our presence.[24]

In Bellini's third composition, a Bacchuslike figure rides a chariot drawn by three hard-working children (fig. 171). The man's full face, slightly distended stomach, and flaccid flesh give him an indolent look, perhaps appropriate, though completely unlike traditional depictions of ancient gods. He has a contemporary counterpart in Italian art, however: the marble *Bacchus* carved by Michelangelo in 1496–98 in Rome—a few years after Michelangelo's stay in Venice in 1494.[25] To be sure, Michelangelo's god is inebriated and perhaps younger than Bellini's figure, but the characterization of the ancient deity as physically unfit is so unusual that it may signify a connection between the two works. The heavy wreaths are also similar. If Michelangelo did see Bellini's picture, then the Florentine's visit in 1494 provides a terminus ante quem for the Venetian's work.

The man with Bellini's Bacchus is sometimes called Mars, but he may be a nameless soldier rather than the ancient god of war. His profession is not in doubt: he is armed and wears a martial cape and leggings. His physique, quite unlike Bacchus's, is athletic and lean. Walking resolutely forward, he nonetheless looks back at his companion with a wary expression. Bacchus does not return his gaze, is self-absorbed, or rather concerned only with his attribute, a bowl of fruit. That he takes—or, rather, is taken along—the same path is evidently a matter of indifference to him, the result not of any effort on his part but due entirely to the labor of the three infants. The two men are thus contrasted in every way, in demeanor, in action (or inaction), in personality, and in physical characteristics. Is Bellini indicating that the way of virtue is difficult but not without pleasurable rewards? Edgar Wind suggested this appealing notion that revelry is an acceptable

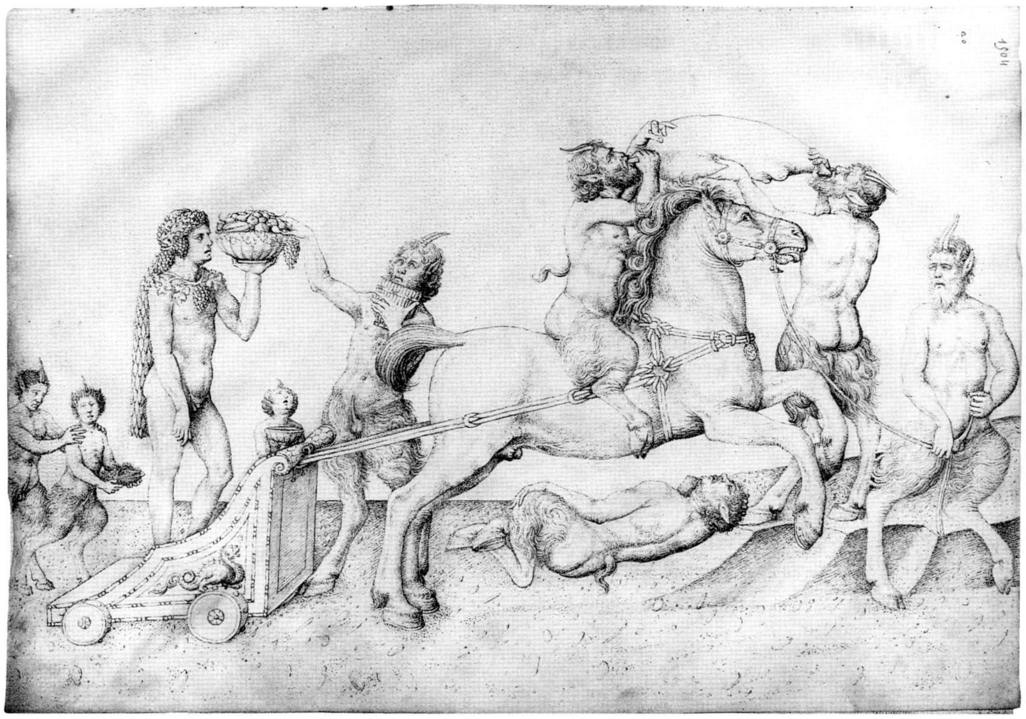

172. *Jacopo Bellini,* Procession of Bacchus, *drawing book, folio 40, Musée du Louvre, Paris. Photo: Musées Nationaux, Paris.*

reward of virtue.[26] But I think that Bellini would not have so clearly personified the two protagonists as opposites if he did not intend also an opposition of their intentions. The Venetian humanist Giovanni Caldiera provided a verbal portrait of *Accidia*, Sloth, that helps to explain Bellini's characterization of Bacchus. His "petulance of the flesh" has enervated him, leaving him indolent and useless, unable even to pursue remembered pleasures of the flesh.[27] Bellini's subject seems to be the specter of indolent pleasure that tempts the virtuous man, Perseverance or Self-Denial, and his Bacchus recalls a drawing by his father in which the god similarly offers a basket of fruit (fig. 172). The temptation is real, and in Jacopo's drawing a satyr helps himself to the fruit while others drink the god's wine. In Giovanni's painting, the soldier is also well aware of Bacchus's temptation, but he perseveres nonetheless. To summarize Caldiera, "The key to the avoidance of sin is ascetic self-denial."[28]

The last panel (fig. 173) is the one that Bellini signed, perhaps with the same kind of trenchant wit seen in the *Self-Knowledge*. In this scene, two men carry another in a rather peculiar vessel, a realistically painted shell (a lightning whelk) from which the passenger emerges like a resident snail. A snake is wrapped around his right arm, and with the left he grasps it near the head: the two seem to be not only looking at each other but hissing.

Is the meaning of this composition sinister or virtuous? Is it an allegory of Sloth or False Prophecy, Patience or Wisdom?[29] All of these possibilities have been proposed. If the other three panels have been correctly identified here, however, then this last one must surely represent a vice and not a virtue, in order to complete the cycle. The most sensible solution may be found in an image surely known to

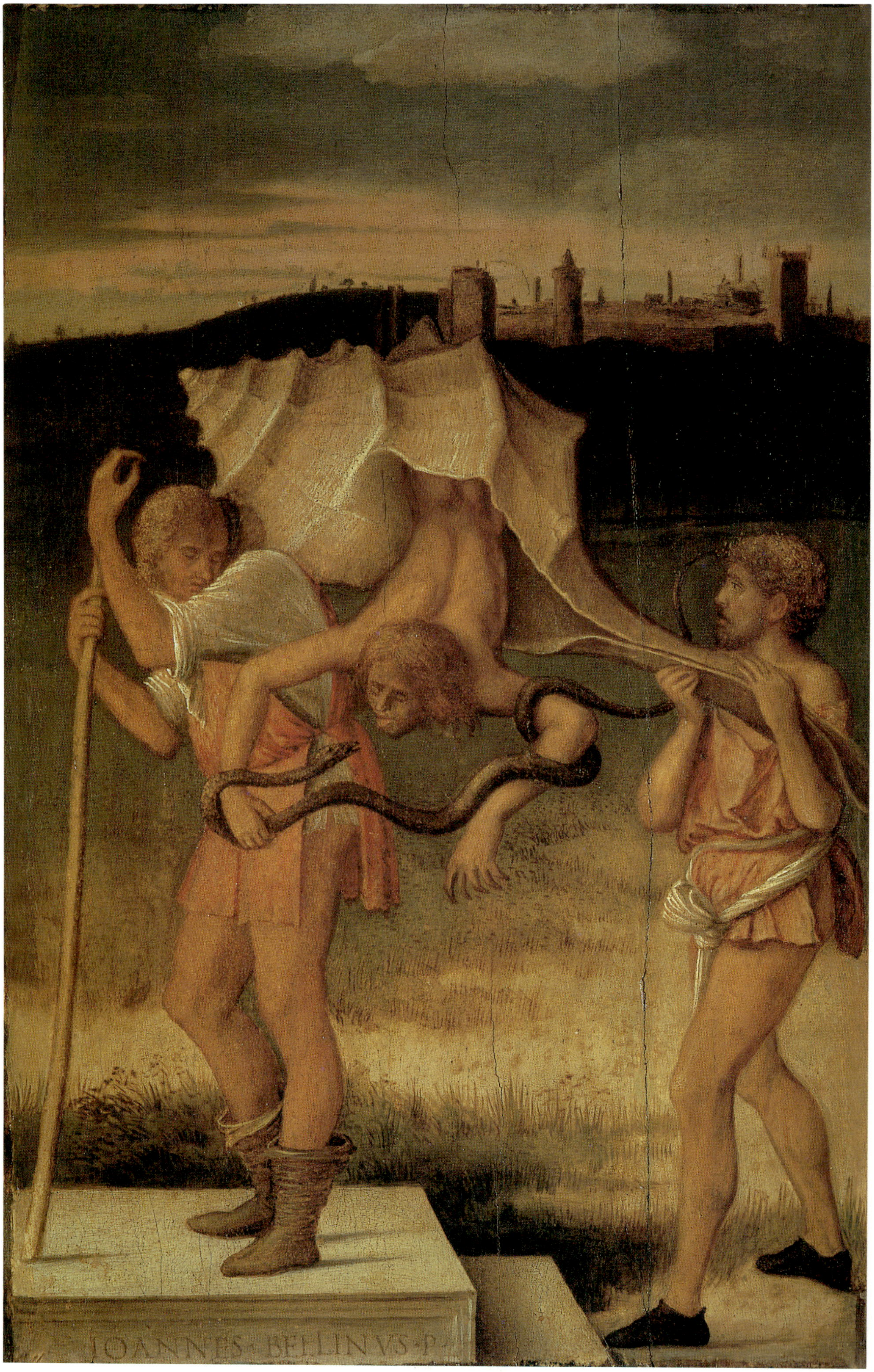
IOANNES · BELLINVS · P

Bellini: Giotto's figure of *Invidia* in the Arena Chapel. Protruding from the mouth of Giotto's *Envy* is a snake that turns back to look her in the eye. Admittedly, unlike *Invidia*, Bellini's figure and serpent are separate creatures. But the way in which they address each other implies their complicity, and the grotesque hybrid monster surely suggests obscene evil rather than virtue.

In the scene that was paired horizontally with this one, the "Soldier and Bacchus," a virtuous man perseveres despite the temptations of pleasure. Like Truth/Self-Knowledge, the other virtuous allegory, he is self-motivated and active. The vices, on the contrary, are characterized as self-indulgent and passive: Melancholy floats aimlessly, Envy is carried by two men, even slothful Bacchus is transported by others. Thus reconstructed and analyzed, Bellini's group seems complete, both visually and symbolically.

What of the fifth Accademia panel (fig. 166)? The figure personifies Fortune: blindfolded, indifferent, and disinterested, she dispenses blessings and perhaps misfortune. She is a monstrous yet beautiful female creature, a winged harpy. Each claw rests on a golden globe, and we understand that her bearing is none too steady as she pours libations from golden vases.[30] Was Bellini's *Fortune* originally the companion of these other allegorical figures? Visual indications and technical differences confirm that it was not. The direction of light and shade is consistent in the first four panels but not in the fifth, which also differs significantly in size, 27 × 19 centimeters, shorter and narrower than the others (all approximately 34 × 22 centimeters). Finally, the landscape is more detailed than in the other scenes, and the horizon significantly lower. But though we may conclude that this composition does not form part of the same group as the first four, we may nonetheless reassert its association with Bellini and his shop.

Bellini's little allegorical paintings were all made to embellish decorative objects, most probably restelli. His first commission for a large-scale composition of this sort seems to have come about as a result of Andrea Mantegna's death, when Bellini agreed to complete the classical cycle that his brother-in-law had begun for the Venetian nobleman Francesco di Giorgio Corner. Francesco Corner was a very well connected patrician indeed: his aunt was Catherine, queen of Cyprus. At his behest, the Gonzaga had allowed Mantegna to accept Corner's commission, probably in 1505; the paintings were intended to decorate Corner's *camerino* (a small study).[31] When Mantegna died on 13 September 1506, one canvas and two panels had been completed and other canvases prepared for painting. These were eventually sent to Venice, and presumably at least one of the unpainted canvases was given to Bellini, evidently in early 1507.[32] What Mantegna had begun, Bellini now finished.

Bellini had had considerable experience in mural painting, primarily in his work for the Sala del Maggior Consiglio. In 1506, in accordance with his brother's dying wish, he had accepted the commission to complete another important cycle of murals, which Gentile had begun for the Albergo, or meeting room, of the

173. Envy, *restello panel, Gallerie dell'Accademia, Venice. Photo: Giacomelli Fotografia, Venice.*

Scuola Grande di San Marco. But the *Continence of Scipio* seems to be the only surviving work of its sort—a mural painting for a private residence—produced in Bellini's shop (fig. 174).[33] Like other murals painted in Venice since the mid-fifteenth century, this was on canvas, lighter and hence more practical than panel, and more durable than fresco in the damp Venetian climate.

At the beginning of their careers, Bellini and Mantegna had both painted almost identical compositions of the *Agony in the Garden*, alluding to a common source, the drawing by Jacopo (figs. 73–75). Their professional relationship ended with the Corner commission, which again allows the comparison of two almost identical works by them. Just a few years earlier, Bellini had rejected Isabella d'Este's request for a composition of a similar subject—something allegorical, for her *studiolo*—because, he said, he was reluctant to be compared to Mantegna, who had already demonstrated his genius with such themes.[34] Yet now, for a noble Venetian patron, Bellini was willing to set aside his ostensible objections and to agree to paint a decorative mural the format of which Mantegna had already decided. Moreover, Bellini was doing this at the same time as he was refusing Isabella's renewed efforts to wrest from him an allegorical or classical subject. He could not be persuaded, according to their mutual friend Pietro Bembo—who himself owned one or two works by the master—because Bellini was accustomed to "roam at his will" in his art: "Very precise terms do not suit his style, being accustomed, as he says, always to roam at his will in paintings."[35] Michele Vianello had also advised the marchesa not to try to force any particular *istoria* on Bellini.[36] When Bellini and Isabella finally came to some sort of agreement, Bembo was to write a program that would please not only patron but artist; the marchesa herself expressed concern that the subject satisfy Bellini, and Bembo replied that he would try to accommodate both of them.[37]

Yet only a year or two later, Bellini was willing to subjugate his will to Mantegna's to fulfill the Corner commission, which involved much the kind of subject that he refused to paint for Isabella. The explanations for this evident inconsistency are not mutually exclusive: it was perhaps easier for the master to get on his professional high horse when dealing with a commission from a foreigner like Isabella d'Este than one from a powerful Venetian patrician; and his unwillingness to accept a dictated program might be overcome in the case of the Corner project, when perhaps a sense of obligation to his deceased brother-in-law and to his nephews motivated Bellini (app. 1: Family Tree). The fact that Mantegna had died may have alleviated Bellini's stated concern about their being compared. In any case, though he clearly objected to taking orders, Bellini did not object to classical or allegorical subjects per se. Indeed, statements about him by those who knew Bellini suggest that the contrary was true, that imaginative secular subjects appealed to him—so long as the imagination involved was his own.

That was not the case with the Corner commission, however, and the results seem to prove the truth of what Vianello had written to Isabella in another con-

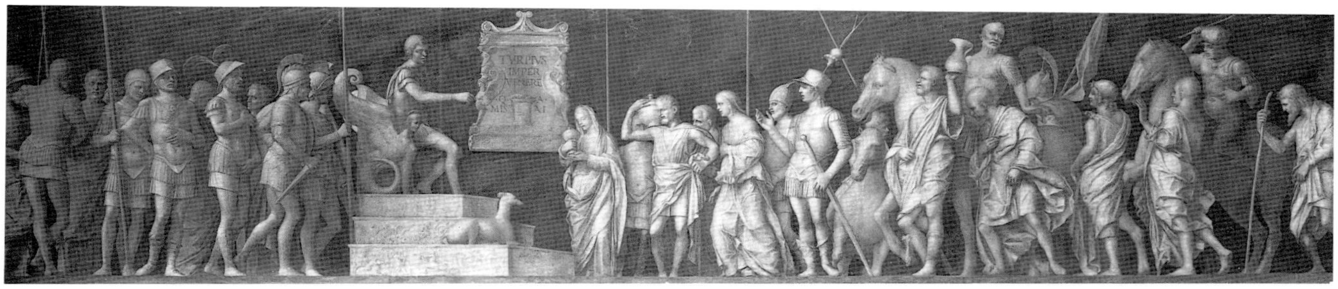

*174. Giovanni Bellini and shop,* Continence of Publius Cornelius Scipio, *National Gallery of Art, Washington, Samuel H. Kress Collection.*

text: a patron will get a better picture from Bellini if Bellini himself chooses the theme.[38] The *Continence of Scipio* narrates an episode from the life of Publius Cornelius Scipio Africanus, the most distinguished and celebrated member of the ancient Roman Gens Cornelia and an ancestor of the Cornaro, according to their own self-aggrandizing (fictional) genealogy (fig. 174).[39] The painting is inscribed TVRPIVS / IMPER / VENERE[M] / Q.[QUAM] A.[ALIENA] / MIS[ERICORDIA] A[DIUVAR], meaning, To exact love is more degrading than to be aided by the compassion of others.[40] Written on a plaque next to Scipio's throne, the words may be imagined spoken by him as he addresses his hostages taken after the conquest of Cartagena. The old woman standing nearby is identified as the wife of Mandonius, who pleads for Scipio's protection of the captive women. To the right, Prince Albricus stands with his betrothed, who has been restored to him thanks to the continence of Scipio, the virtuous ancestor of the Corner. Thus Bellini's painting and the complete cycle nicely illustrated the typical attitude of the Venetian patriciate toward classical history and humanist learning: their study and citation were motivated primarily by social and political concerns, in this case the distinguished origins of a ruling noble family whose genealogy determined its authority to govern. The theme of female chastity, which seems to run through the cycle like a leitmotif, is also germane to these patrician conceptions of antiquity and genealogy, for—as Francesco Barbaro had written, belaboring an obvious point—the purity of the noble family's lineage is founded on the purity of its wives and mothers.[41]

The Scipio friezes, Bellini's and Mantegna's alike, are distinguished by the use of grisaille and by the low viewpoint determined by the setting of the paintings, which were intended as fictive reliefs to be set high on the wall of Francesco Corner's camerino. The illusionistic viewpoint and the imitation of sculpted relief would have made these paintings inherently part of the room they originally decorated, and when the cycle was in place, as George Knox has explained, the effect must have been quite unlike other contemporary rooms decorated with paintings. The studiolo of Isabella d'Este and the *camerino d'alabastro* of her brother Alfonso were decorated with easel paintings, including the *Feast of the Gods*, which Bellini painted for the duke in 1514 (figs. 175, 176). In Venice, public rooms such as the *alberghi* of scuole and the Great Council Hall itself were effectively transformed into immense enframements, with murals that were seen as though from

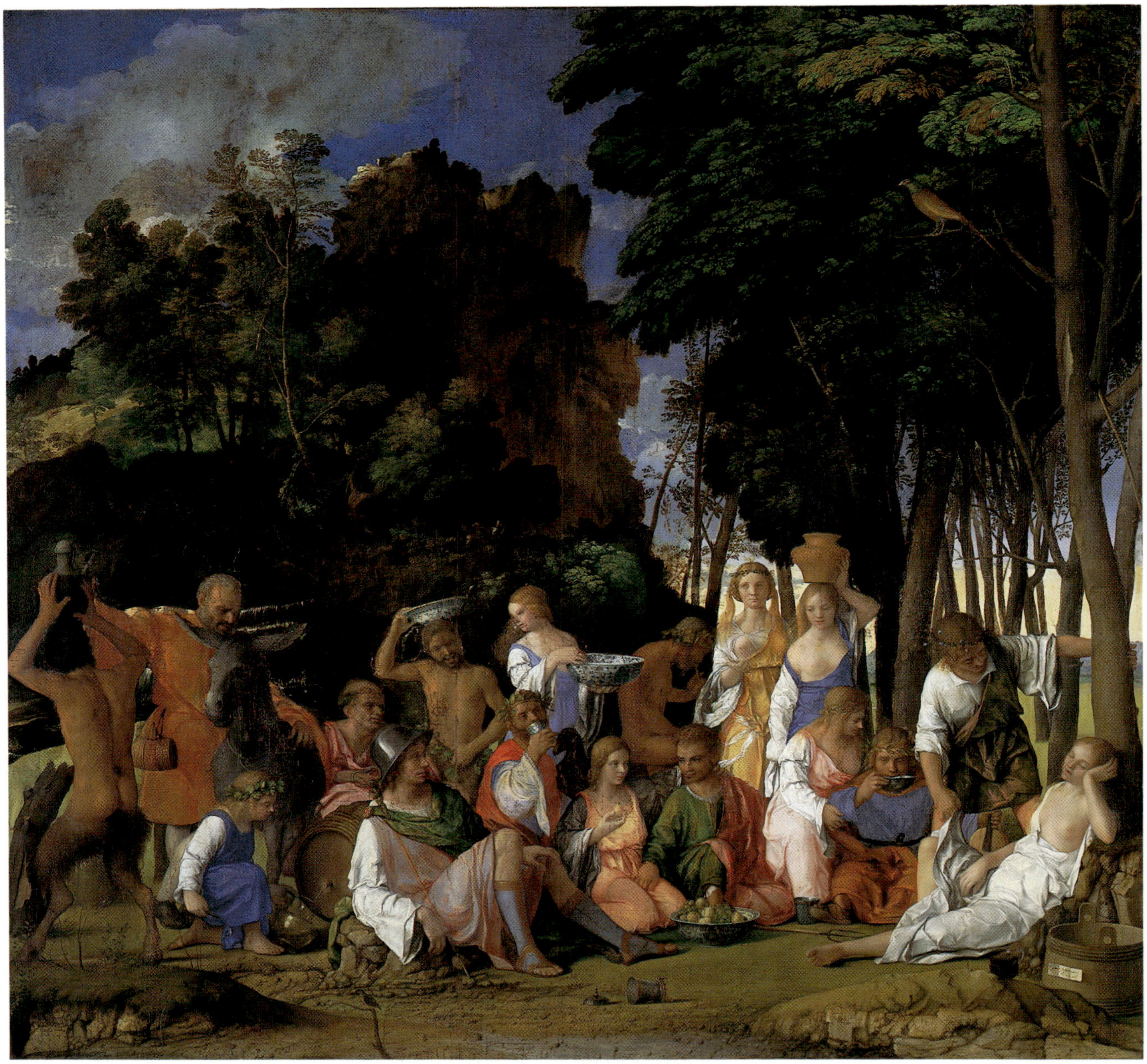

*175.* Feast of the Gods, *National Gallery of Art, Washington, Widener Collection.*

*176.* Feast of the Gods, *detail, National Gallery of Art, Washington, Widener Collection.*

eye level, framed by wooden paneling below and carved wooden ceilings above. The actual vantage point of the viewer was not taken into account, but ignored. In the camerino of Francesco Corner, however, the mural paintings were more completely and specifically integrated with their surroundings, by means of their optical illusion.[42] And this conception was Mantegna's: from the very early frescoes in the Eremitani in Padua to the *Camera degli Sposi* in Mantua, Mantegna had conceived of mural decoration in this way, in contrast to the characteristic Venetian approach, which refused to subject perfection of form to the distortions of perspective.

Bellini, naturally, was obligated to follow Mantegna in this, and he did so. But Bellini's frieze reveals an approach to sculpture and to antiquity that differs completely from Mantegna's, despite their shared predetermined characteristics. Mantegna was always an antiquarian, and his glyphic style was ideally suited to the

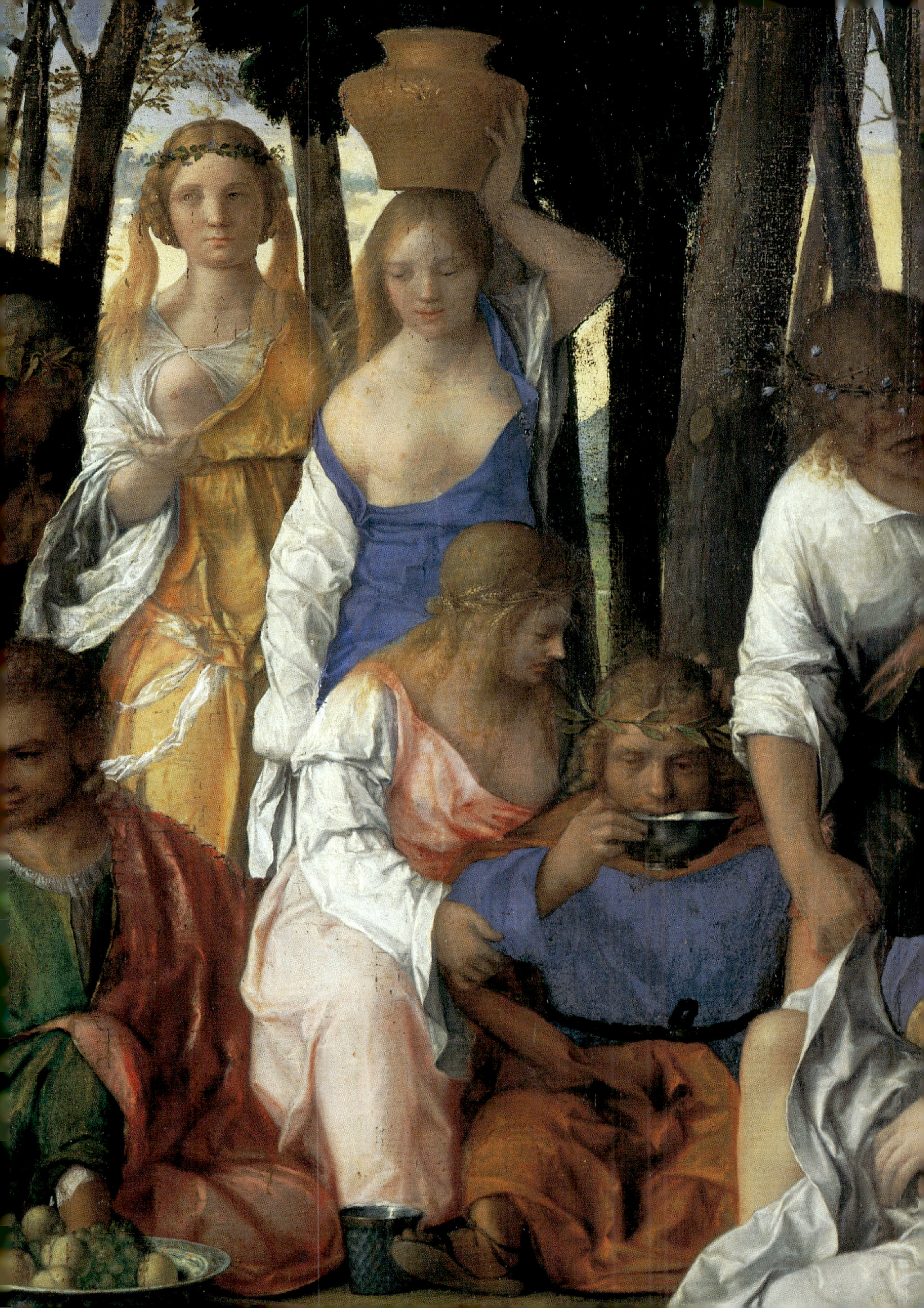

grisaille technique. With his colorism, Bellini instead replicated Pygmalion's trick: stone becomes flesh. The Venetian's classicism is lyrical and calm, resembling the contemporary sculpture of Tullio Lombardo but embued with a different, warmer sentiment (fig. 142). In this, as in other ways, the frieze prepared the way for the *Feast of the Gods*, signed and dated in 1514.

Mythological subjects on this scale—the size of the *Scipio* or the *Feast*—were not only more or less new to Bellini: they were essentially new to Venetian art in the early sixteenth century. Bellini had evidently not painted these themes on such a scale—no Venetian had—because no patron had provided the impetus. In this genre, the typical experience of his studio had been smaller easel paintings, including the *Orpheus* in Washington, and of course panels for decorative objects like restelli. The contrast with the situation in Florence or Mantua is vast. Already in the 1470s and 1480s, Florentine and Mantuan humanism had educated the taste, encouraged the enthusiasm, and sometimes written the programs for such works as Botticelli's *Birth of Venus* and *Primavera* or Mantegna's *Triumphs of Caesar*. Nothing comparable to these compositions, or to the mythological subjects painted by their contemporaries Piero di Cosimo and Antonio Pollaiuolo, exists in Venetian painting of the same date. If Giovanni Bellini never painted anything resembling the *Feast* in subject before 1514,[43] then we must remember that the same is true of his father, Jacopo (who drew such themes but apparently never had a commission to paint one), of his brother Gentile, of Carpaccio, or of Cima, whose first mythological paintings—very small paintings at that—were executed at the turn of the new century. This is true of Venetian literature as well: Bellini's great mythological work is the contemporary of the *Arcadia* and *Hypnerotomachia Poliphili*, works with little prehistory in Venice. And, significantly, the *Feast* was commissioned not by a Venetian but by Duke Alfonso d'Este of Ferrara. Indeed, this was also the case for Titian's first great mythological commissions: his early patrons for these works were Alfonso d'Este and Philip II of Spain.[44] Apparently Titian's Venetian clients, like Bellini's, were still primarily or exclusively interested in sacred themes or portraiture. The only significant exception to this Venetian rule was Giorgione, who painted a small group of mythological themes for a coterie of Venetian "young Turks"—and who thereby helped change Venetian taste. But none of these works is large: they are easel paintings, not murals. Such paintings as the Bellinesque *Infant Bacchus* and the much-debated *Orpheus* reflect this new interest of Venetian patrons and Bellini's willingness to satisfy them.[45]

The *Feast of the Gods* was the first painting completed for the camerino d'alabastro of the duke of Ferrara, and the signature alludes to this foreign patronage by specifying the artist's nationality: "Joannes bellinus venetus / M.D.XIII." (figs. 175, 176).[46] Alfonso's commission, like that of his sister Isabella, represents a new attitude regarding the status of artists and the acquisition of art. These ardent collectors and others like them were concerned with acquiring paintings by particular artists: Francesco Corner wanted Mantegna in Mantua to execute murals for his palace in Venice; Isabella wanted a mythology by Bellini for her studiolo in Ferrara, and when that was not forthcoming she accepted a *Presepio*. The artist, not the subject, mattered most.[47]

With the obvious exception of Titian's alterations to the composition, notably the landscape at the left, the *Feast of the Gods* is essentially of a piece. We may assume that Bellini himself, if not responsible for the choice of subject, was at least "pleased" to paint it, and may have had a say in its selection. Bembo's letter to Isabella d'Este, quoted here, and other contemporary comments substantiate these postulations. In any case, Bellini certainly determined the way in which his Ovidian subject was interpreted.

Having claimed this much, it is necessary to explain what the subject is, for though the customary title of the painting, *Feast of the Gods*, is appropriate to the picture's present appearance, it may not accurately describe what Bellini intended. It had generally been assumed that this kind of subject was antithetical to Bellini's creative personality and that, in consequence, he produced a restrained congregation of rustics where he should have conjured the erotic abandon of the ancient gods. Philipp Fehl, however, has argued that Bellini's subject was not the account of Priapus and his amorous misadventure with the nymph Lotis (or Vesta), as Ovid recounted twice, in the *Fasti* and *Metamorphoses*, but the commentary on yet another version of the story according to the Italian translation of the *Metamorphoses*, the *Ovidio volgarizato*, published already in 1370 and reprinted in Venice in 1497.[48] One may easily imagine that Bellini himself owned such a book (fig. 178).

In the *Metamorphoses*, Ovid himself merely encapsulated the story he told in greater detail in the *Fasti*; thus the poet explained the origin of the water lotus: "as the slow rustics still relate, Lotis, a nymph, while fleeing from Priapus' vile pursuit, had taken refuge in this shape, changed as to features but still keeping her name."[49] Not this brief excursis in the poem but the translation and commentary by Giovanni de' Bonsignori provided Bellini's *primary* text. Having first corrected what may have seemed Ovid's sin of omission in the narrative by incorporating into the *Metamorphoses* the fuller (and more comprehensible) account of Lotis's story from the *Fasti*, Bonsignori then burdened the ribald tale with a Christian moral. "Once the nymph Lotos," as he calls her,

> went outside the city with other ladies to offer sacrifice to Bacchus. One called Priapus was there, who was enamored of Lotos. He had such a large member that it would have been large even for the foal of an ass, for which reason the women had chased him out of the city. Now Priapus was waiting by the shore of that lake [where Bacchus was worshiped] to see Lotos. . . . He went before Lotos and pleaded gently that she "marry" him, but Lotos despised him. When it was night, the nymphs and other women went to sleep, and Priapus went quietly to mount [*cavalcare*] the nymph Lotos. And when he reached her, he took her garments to uncover her. And here is master Argesto

coming on one of his ass foals, and he tied the ass to a tree. Then the ass started to bray so strongly that all the women awoke, Lotos began to flee, and Priapus was following her with his immeasurable member. But meanwhile, for divine mercy, Lotos was changed into the tree called "Lotos."[50]

To this emendation of the *Metamorphosis* of Lotos (or Lotis), the fourteenth-century commentator Bonsignori appended an allegory, as he explains:

> When the feast of Bacchus came, men and women went by day and night singing his praises. They put on festive garments unlike the clothing they wore at other times, and for eight days it was permitted to each man and the women to sin carnally and without prohibition. The feast of Bacchus was celebrated principally in Thebes. . . . Outside the city was a lake along which was a temple of the god Bacchus. . . . The women came to this place to sacrifice, and each lover waited . . . to take his pleasure with his mistresses. Among them was Priapus, who had been banished from the city because he had both the nature and the member of an ass. And notwithstanding this [orgiastic feast], there were a number of women who observed chastity, and they were so praised that their fame became perpetual. Among them was Lotos, who fled to the hills before Priapus, her [would-be] lover. Argesto, who arrived on his ass foal, was a priest who came to make sacrifice; and a tree in that place is called "Lotos" in memory of that woman who in those times of sacrificial offerings would always pray at the foot of that tree.[51]

Reading Bonsignori's text, as Bellini must have done, we come to a very different understanding of the "feast," which was intended to represent not a festival of the gods but rather a celebration of the citizens of Thebes, specially dressed for the occasion and behaving with more abandon than was their custom, but still not so wantonly that we (or they) forget the perpetual fame of those who preserved their chastity. In short, the reason that Bellini's figures look like country folk and not like the gods and heroes of antiquity is precisely because this was the cast of characters his script required him to represent.

Without their attributes, these men and women of the *Feast* would never be identified as divinities; and these objects were added to the surface of the painting. Whoever inserted the attributes that have transformed the mortal Thebans into the immortal Jupiter and Hera, Neptune and Amphitrite, and Apollo and Mercury was apparently changing the original conception when he altered the composition. To be sure, Bellini made such "last-minute" alterations on the surface in other works, but it seems unknowable whether these changes were intended from the start. Most authors (including Fehl) have assumed that they were the work of another master, perhaps Titian. But to assert that Bellini may not always have intended such modifications does not preclude the possibility that these and other changes were made by him. Nothing in style, handling, or medium distinguishes

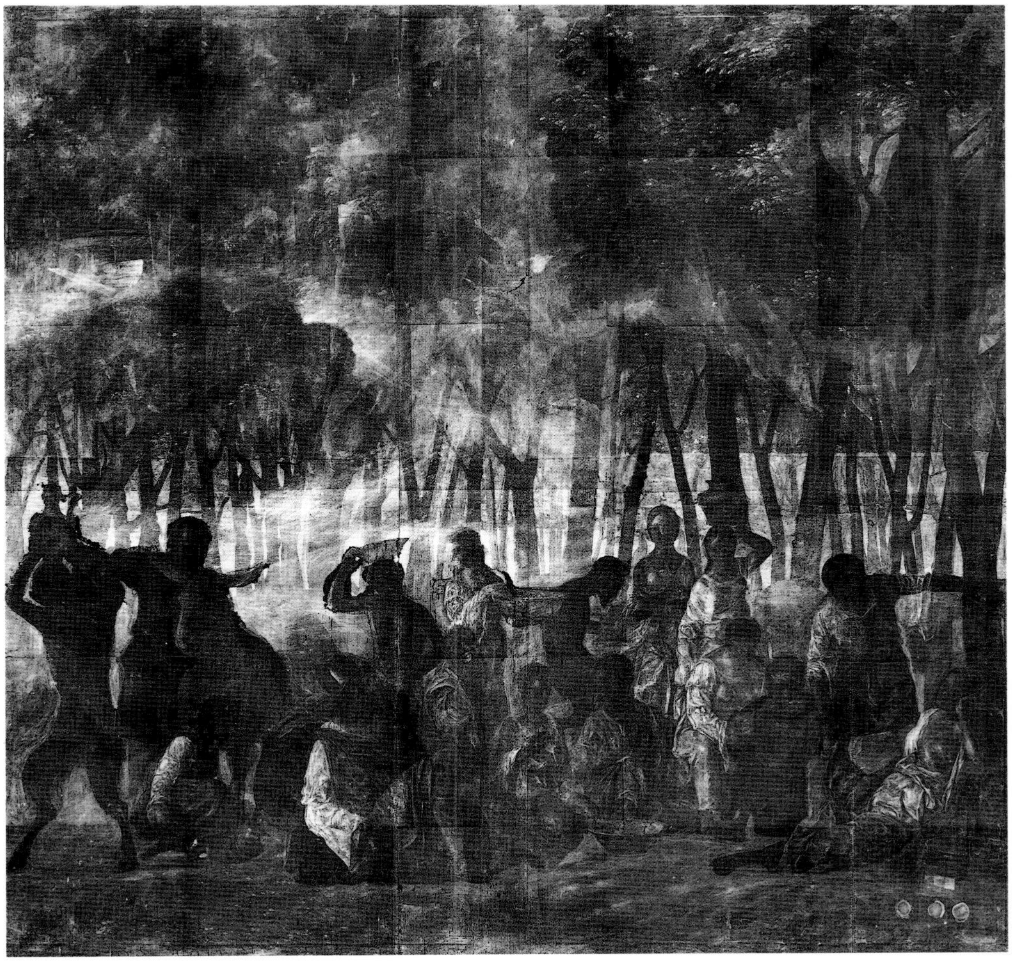

177. *X ray of* Feast of the Gods, *National Gallery of Art, Washington, Widener Collection.*

them from Bellini's treatment elsewhere in the painting, including other changes made on the picture surface. The kingfisher perched in the lower left foreground is another such emendation, and the breasts that at first were more decorously covered, as X rays reveal (fig. 177), may have been bared by Bellini himself.

A hand that was meant to rest languidly on a rock now holds Mercury's caduceus with its living snakes, and a mortal toper is deified by Neptune's attribute, a trident, here resembling a pitchfork, lying near him on the ground. A Theban woman now becomes Amphitrite, the recipient of her divine husband's caress. She holds a quince, symbol of matrimony. The quince may allude to conjugal rights, which were celebrated in Thebes, as Bonsignori explains, for eight days a year without benefit of lawful matrimony. So conspicuously held, or presented, the quince is certainly symbolic: but as with the pitchfork-trident, the reference is teasing and ironic. This irony is typical of Bellini's humor and indicates that all the alterations in the figures are by him, added as he collated Bonsignori's commentary with the ovidian text. Evidently the commentary suggested to Bellini his characterization of the gods as mortals: archaeological accuracy and heroic dignity are sacrificed in favor of mocking wit and good-humored ribaldry.

Next to the sleeping Lotis, a man guzzles his wine. The extension of his left arm, awkwardly inserted between Priapus's legs, allows this individual to hold the lira da braccio, and thus to be known as the god of music, Apollo. With advertent irony, he underscores the salaciousness of Priapus's seemingly tender approach to his beloved. Priapus's lust is visualized by the modeling and coloration of his garments to represent his tumescence. This stylistic lasciviousness is surely Bellini's work.

There is also no doubt about one notable change in Bellini's composition, and that is the landscape on the left. While concealing Bellini's original screen of trees, which was consistent with the setting at the right and resembled the background of the *Death of Saint Peter Martyr*, Titian was obliterating yet another landscape (figs. 137, 177). That is, this part of the canvas was painted three times, originally by Bellini, whose landscape was hidden first by one setting, perhaps painted by Dosso Dossi, and then again by another—Titian's massive trees and rocks, which are visible today.[52]

Titian's landscape is magnificent, but it oppresses Bellini's *Feast*. Especially now that the painting has been restored, one is aware of the sense of a space filled with light and air—but Titian has almost blocked the sun and stifled the atmosphere. Almost, but fortunately not quite, for light and air still envelop the scene; cast shadows are permeated by light, the setting sun tints the sky on the horizon visible between and behind Bellini's trees on the right, and a soft breeze moves through the grove. When one nymph or lady approaches, her sleeve and girdle sway with the wind, and her long blond hair, bound in tresses on either side of her head, casts a shadow on her neck. Light glints on the metal cup held by Apollo and on the empty beaker that lies in the center foreground, like a symbolic fulcrum around which the drowsy Thebans gather. Softer, glowing light gleams on the blue-and-white ceramics, and it shines through the glass pitcher that Bacchus fills with wine. The god, represented as a child, was perhaps the only divinity always meant by Bellini to attend this feast, the feast of Bacchus. This is Ovid's "boy . . . whose weapons are scented locks, soft garlands," slightly tipsy and drowsy, a little boy "with form beautiful as a girl's."[53] Perhaps that is one reason why the master represented the god as a child—to distinguish the boy-god from all the other figures present, human adults, men and women (and/or nymphs), who have come to worship him, the satyrs who traditionally attend bacchic occasions, and of course the protagonists of the story, Lotis and Priapus. But there was also another reason for this depiction of Bacchus: the god took the form of a child on the day of the winter solstice, the day when the feast was celebrated.[54]

Bellini almost certainly knew not only Ovid's texts and Bonsignori's commentary on Lotis and Priapus but also the woodcut illustration of the story in the Venetian edition of the *Ovidio volgarizato* of 1501 (fig. 178).[55] But the overt sexuality of the illustration has been replaced by a gentler eroticism—not only the intimate gesture of Neptune but the tender solicitude of Hera, and even the quiet, tentative way in which Priapus initiates his attempt on Lotis's chastity. And the crude energy of the woodcut has become rhythmic and silent in the painting.

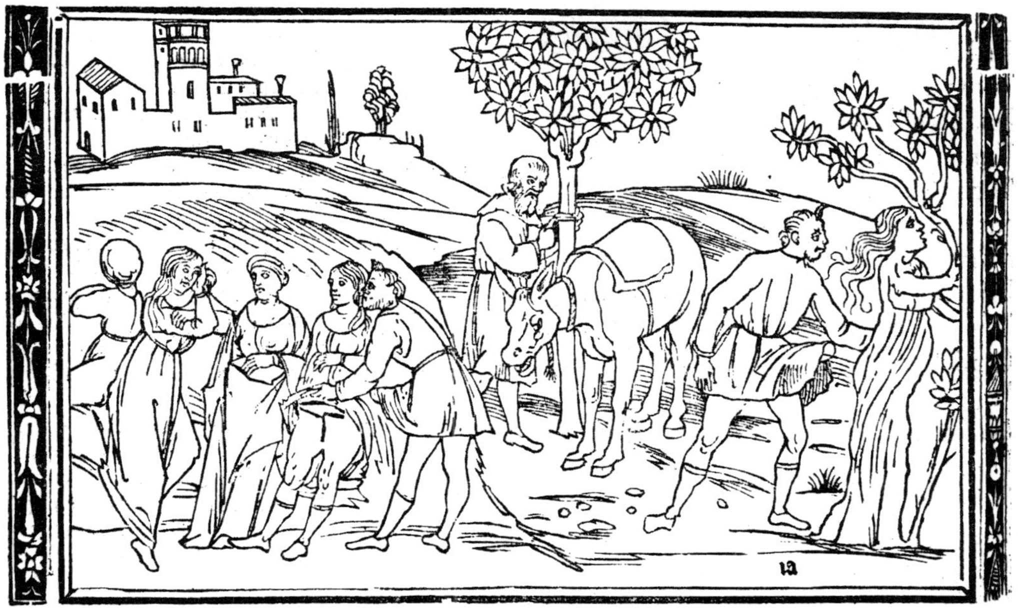

*178. Anonymous Sixteenth-Century Venetian, woodcut, Ovid,* Metamorphoses, *folio 98v (Venice, 1509). Princeton University Library. Photo: Princeton University Library.*

Indeed, silence is crucial here: it is evening, as Ovid tells us and as Bellini's low sun makes apparent; the feasters have become quiet; and one of them, Lotis, has fallen into oblivious, vulnerable sleep. If we hear anything, it is the sound of the waterfall in the distance and the single note of the satyr's pipe. But in an instant, all will change with the braying of an ass.

Bellini's Thebans-become-gods are arranged in a semicircle in the foreground, enclosing as though in a sacred precinct a beaker, now empty of wine, and a bowl piled with fruit. Behind this group, standing and seated figures extend and open the composition, each figure related to the next by variations of poses and gestures: actions are not repeated but rather echoed, so that the figural relationships become a succession of notes to form passages of a musical theme. Color harmonies reiterate this symphonic theme—shades of white, ultramarine blue, red, pink, orange, green, and brown, all illuminated from within, taking their light from the white gesso ground. Outlines do not exist here, but rather impasto and luminous layerings of color define form.

Bellini's composition became the origin of Titian's ardent *Bacchanal of the Andrians*, which is in many ways an emendation of the earlier work, and also its deathknell, in a sense, announcing the end of one era and the beginning of the next. But it was Bellini's art that engendered Titian's, and at the end of his own life, perhaps Titian recalled the introverted mood of his old master's mythology when he painted his own last *poesia,* the elegiac *Nymph and Shepherd* in Vienna.[56] Titian's bacchanals for Alfonso d'Este, painted to accompany Bellini's *Feast*, were the works of a young man. In his old age, however, Titian, like Bellini before him, knew the terrible truth that death is always near: not merely inevitable, but omnipresent. The ostensible subject of their late mythologies—Bellini's *Feast*, Titian's *Nymph and Shepherd*—is the celebration of life and love, but their awareness of mortality explains the depth of feeling, the pensiveness, the dark undercurrents of these great works, so similar in psychology in spite of their stylistic differences.

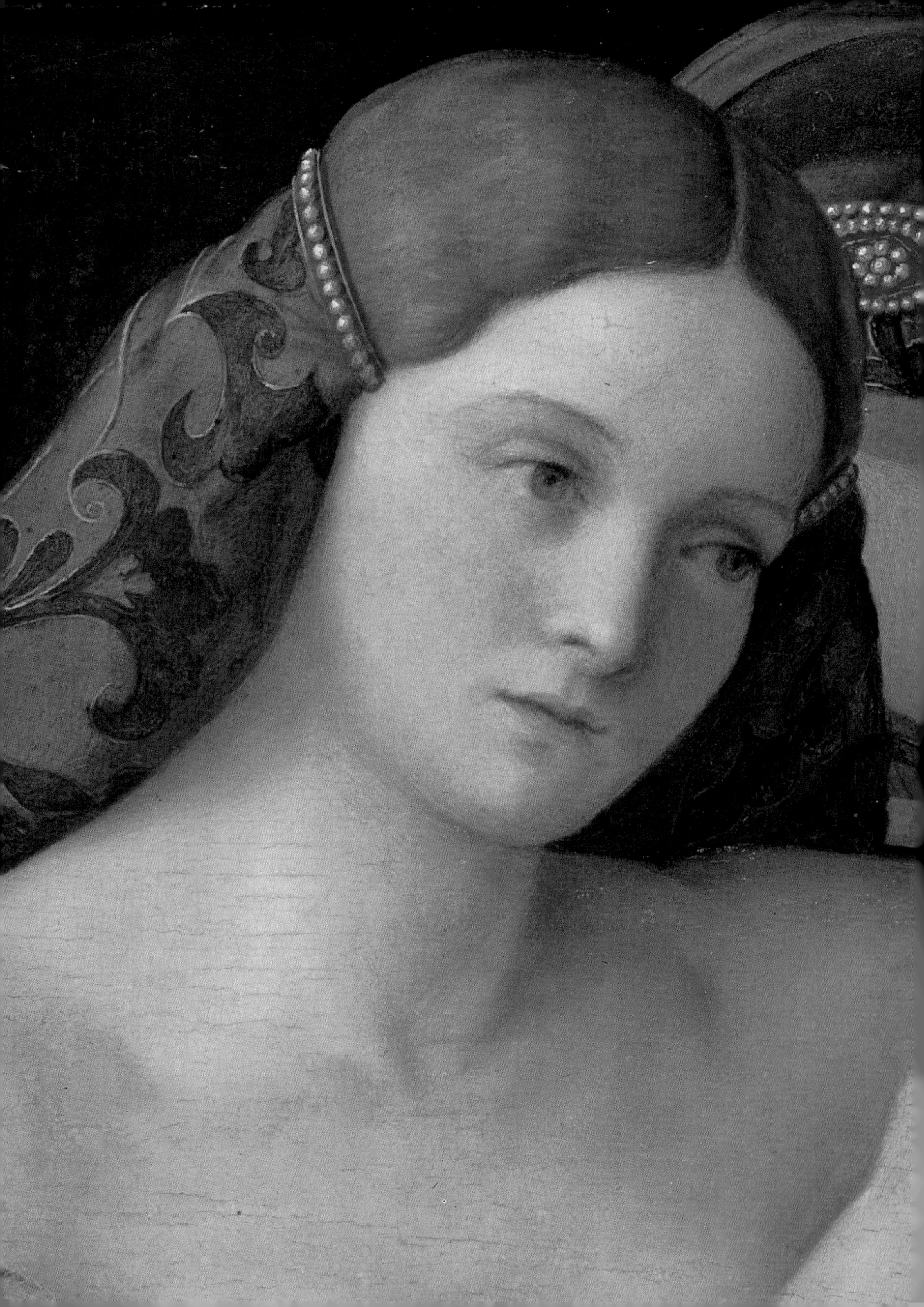

# Epilogue: "Celestial Honors"
## Old Bellini and Young Titian

*His fame will be renewed from century to century until the last breaths of the world.*
—Carlo Ridolfi

In spite of his extreme old age, Bellini had far from exhausted his creative energy: he continued to grow, and he continued to paint until the end of his life. Unfortunately, one of Bellini's most important last works, a *Madonna* for the sister of the French king, has been lost.[1] We shall probably never know what this picture looked like, which was Bellini's farewell to the theme with which he had always been so closely associated. But other works done toward the end of his life suggest his grappling with a sense of his own mortality; they share a kind of personal old-age style achieved by comparatively few masters (Titian among them), and in subject they seem somehow autobiographical, no matter for whom they may have been painted.[2]

Bellini's *Christ Crowned with Thorns*, completed in the first years of the new century, is one of these works (fig. 61).[3] Representing a subject that Bellini had evidently abandoned thirty years earlier, the *Christ* is retrospective in that sense, introspective in spirituality and mood, and innovative in its painterly handling (an effect exaggerated by abrasion), which anticipates the style of his last works. What the *Christ* heralds culminated in Bellini's *Derision of Noah* (fig. 180).

The *Peter Martyr*, painted circa 1509 (fig. 100), represents a scene of bloodshed, and the *Martyrdom of Saint Mark* (fig. 185), which the master did not live to complete, also depicts a violent murder, but Bellini's *Derision of Noah*, a composition almost devoid of physical action, narrates a far more powerful drama than either of these collaborative works, and with considerable psychological insight. The painting may be dated circa 1513–14, contemporary with the *Feast of the Gods*, with which it shares certain stylistic features—the patterns of drapery, for example, and the painterly handling—though the *Feast* is much better preserved.[4]

Often identified as the "Drunkenness of Noah," the picture represents the aftermath of his intoxication, when Noah, unconscious and naked, having allowed his mantle to fall from him in his helplessness, was mocked by one son, Ham, and covered by the other two, Shem and Japheth (Gen. 9:18–27).[5] Whereas they exemplified filial duty, Ham failed Noah and was punished by a terrible curse: "A slave of slaves shall he be to his brothers" (Gen. 9:25). According to Christian exegeses, the ugly episode was deeply significant in general, because Noah, as a "new Adam," the "first man" in the new beginning after the flood, was a prototype of Christ, and in particular, because the derision of Noah anticipated the mocking of Christ. In the *Biblia Pauperum*, illustrations of the *Mocking of Christ* and of the *Derision of Noah* were juxtaposed with the explanatory inscription "Noah signifies Christ, whom the Jews mocked, stripping him naked and crowning him with thorns, just as the unfaithful sons of Noah mocked his folly."[6] As Noah's nudity anticipates the nakedness of Christ on the cross, the wine that intoxicated the Old Testament hero prefigures the wine of the Eucharist, and the vines that he planted allude to Christ, who said, "I am the vine" (John 15:5; Eccles. 24:17–20).[7] Thus Bellini's composition intentionally recalls traditional depictions of the Lamentation: Noah's sleep and derision, set against a background of vines, anticipate the mocking and death of the Lord.

Bellini seems to have taken major components of his composition from a modest woodcut illustration of the *Derision* in the *Biblica italica* published in Venice in 1493: here he found the setting of the scene in the vineyard, basic elements of Noah's posture, the wine cup discarded on the ground, and the three sons turning in different directions, two averting their glance while Ham looks at his father's shame (fig. 179).[8] But Bellini transformed this bland composition (fig. 180). The setting is compressed, the background closed by the dense grape vines, while the figures crowd together. Noah lies on his side, posture reversed and even more frontal than his prototype in the woodcut and facing the beholder, but of course oblivious to any audience, sleeping the unwholesome sleep of drunkenness.

Nothing is restful about Noah's slumber, and nothing dignified. Lying on the bare ground with his head on a rock, Noah puts one hand to his face to cushion himself from this hard pillow.[9] His other arm is bent over his head in the gesture that also betokened sleep in classical antiquity, in the *Barberini Faun*, for example, and Noah's legs fall akimbo in much the same way as those of his drunken mythological predecessor. Noah's eyes and mouth are deeply shadowed, and this darkness seems to express his spiritual condition. He appears delicate next to his robust sons, and certainly pathetic in his nakedness—very unlike Bellini's characterizations of the old Job as a heroic nude (figs. 79, 108). Near Noah's head are grapes, instrument of his shame and symbol of our ultimate salvation. Wine threatens to spill from a cup in the center foreground: its precarious balance suggests the unsteadiness of insobriety and the uneasiness of Noah's sleep.

Highlights on the grapes are painted with heavy daubs of white, and thick strokes of white highlight the rim of the cup and its inner edge, reflecting the moisture of the wine within it. Noah's hair, beard, and flesh, by contrast, are very thinly painted, and though the poor condition of the canvas exaggerates the effect, it seems that Bellini intended this delicacy of handling here, purposefully blurring edges so that one substance merges imperceptibly into the next. The painting surface becomes a fabric of interwoven strokes of color and light, exploiting the weave of the fine canvas, which is visible throughout the composition. Bellini an-

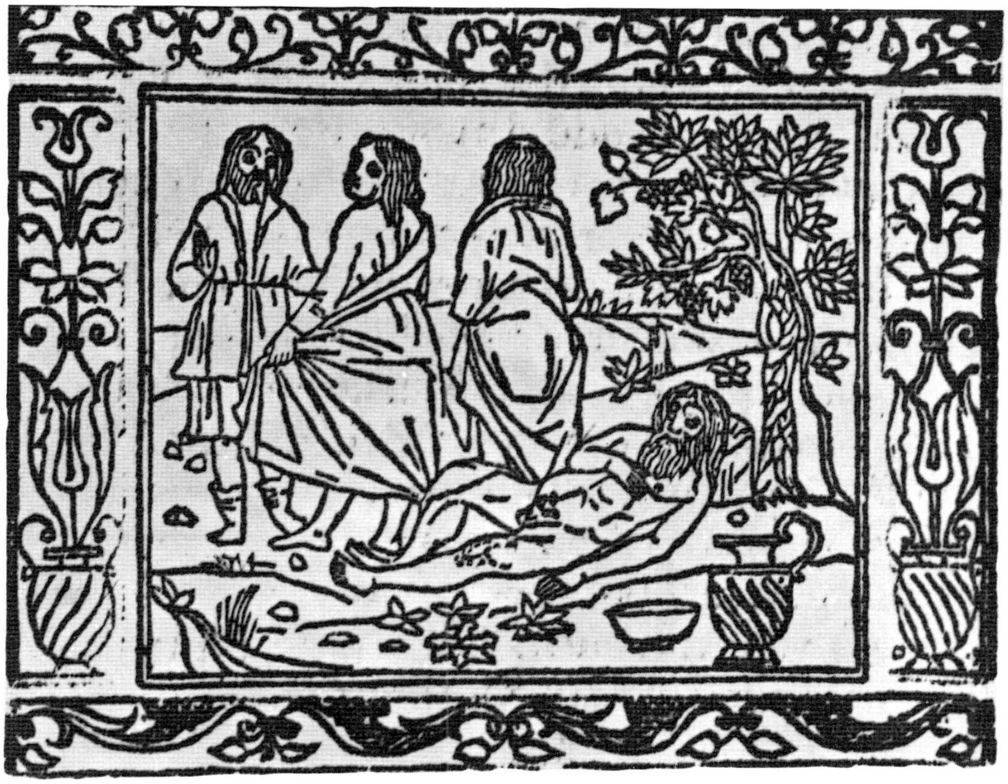

*179. Anonymous Fifteenth-Century Venetian, woodcut,* Biblia italica, *folio 3v (Venice, 1493), Biblioteca Nazionale Marciana, Venice.*

ticipated this colorism in other works, as in the background of the Uffizi *Allegory*, the *Christ* in Stockholm, and the *Feast of the Gods*, but expressed it most fully here.

The cropping of the vines above and of the figures to left and right condense the composition, forcing the scene forward, toward the beholder. This very crowding expresses drama, and the only release from the claustrophobic density comes in the center foreground, where Noah's wine cup sits conspicuously. But the cup's centrality is visual, not mathematical: the axis lies slightly to the right, and the resulting pull between these two foci intensifies the drama.

Japheth bends forward and inward to arrange the mantle over his father. His dutiful action is anticipated and assisted at the left by his brother Shem, who leans toward him while lifting Noah's mantle. This creates a shadowed void above Noah, comparable in shape and pictorial function to the cup and to the space around it. These accoutrements of his shame—the empty mantle, bare ground, and almost empty cup—thus associated in the eye, seem to collude against Noah, as it were, and, surrounding his figure, emphasize his vulnerability and humiliation. But the most explicit expression of his shame is in the face of his son Ham.

Ham's face is more fully lighted than those of his brothers, and the scorn thus exposed distorts his features, making them almost grotesque: his regular features have become horrible because of the character they reveal. He laughs at his father, and his laughter is both frightening and sinister. Leaning back from Noah, he places his hands on one brother's arm and on the other's shoulder, as though simultaneously inviting their collaboration in his mockery and hindering

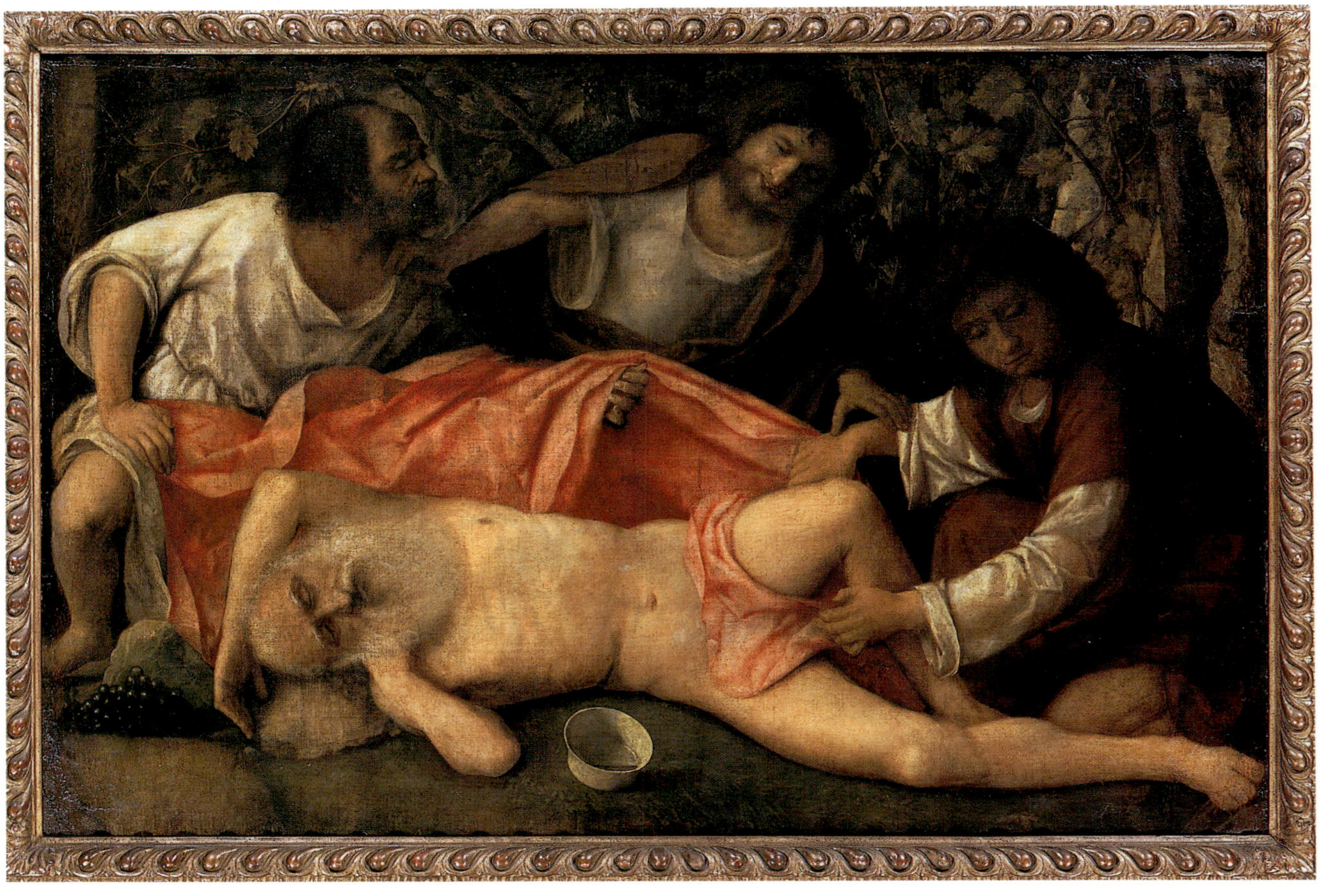

*180.* Derision of Noah, *Musée des Beaux-Arts, Besançon. Courtesy Besançon, Musée des Beaux-Arts et d'Archéologie. Photo: Ch. Choffet, Besançon.*

the accomplishment of their filial duty. Noah's helplessness is the more terrifying because of his vulnerability to Ham's wickedness.

This deeply disturbing work is not the only clause in Bellini's visual testament, however. The multivalence of his artistic personality was perhaps never so remarkable as at the end of his life, for while Bellini was painting the *Noah* he was also working on another composition in the new secular genre of Venetian cinquecento art, the *Woman with a Mirror* (fig. 181). This painting represents the master's final statement on what had been a leitmotif of his oeuvre, the professional self-awareness of the painter and the significance of his art. Bellini was perhaps eighty when he signed and dated it in 1515: "Joannes bellinus faciebat M.D.X.V." (fig. 182).[10]

Sight itself is a theme of this painting. Bellini's concern with the sense of sight was conscious, perhaps self-conscious, in the way of early sixteenth-century Italian artists preoccupied with the *paragone,* the competitive comparison of the representational arts, painting and sculpture. Bellini's conception of form here, the proportions of the figure, and even the facial type are more closely related to contemporary reliefs by Tullio Lombardo than to any ancient model or contemporary

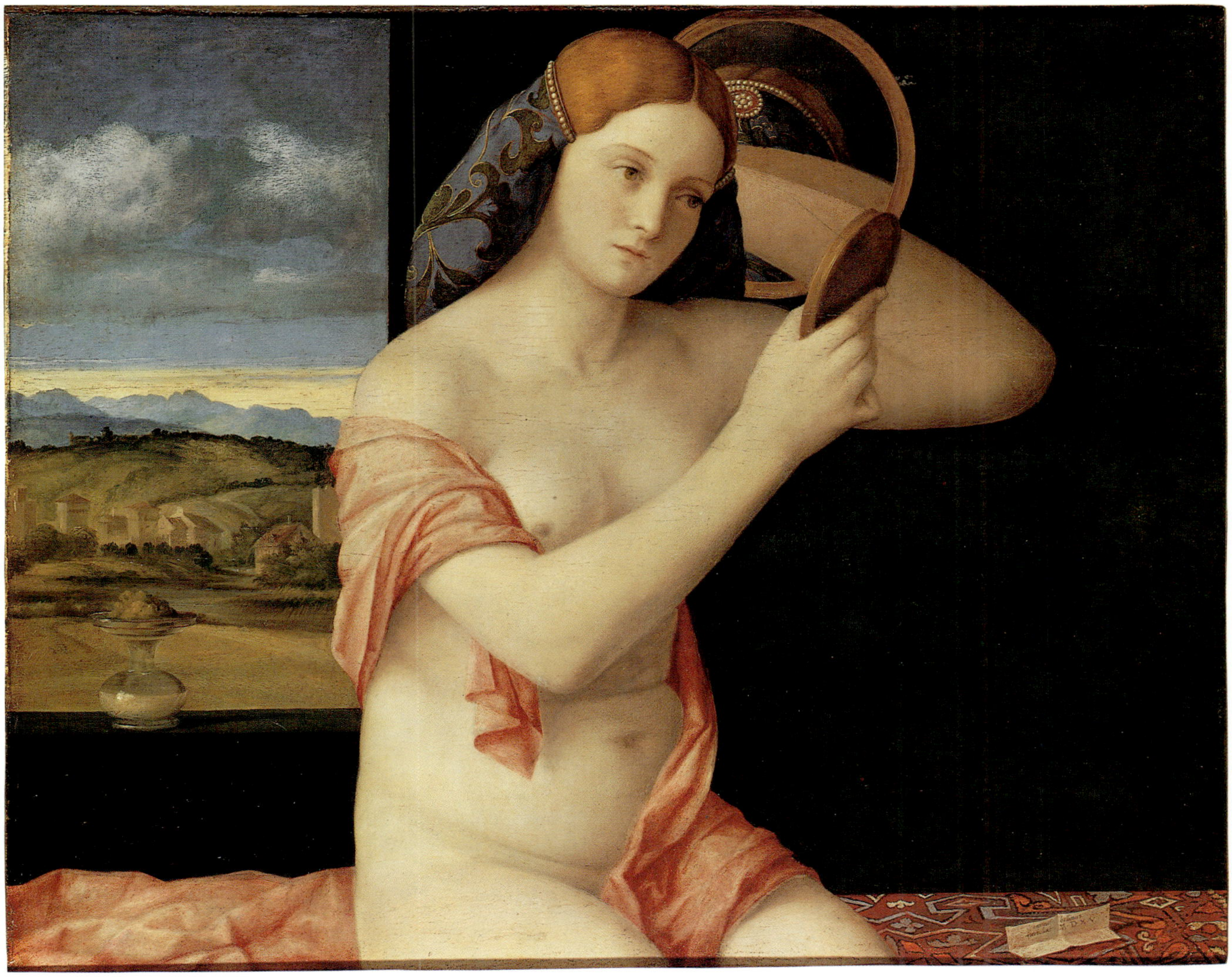

painting.[11] Simply put, the paragone debate was about this question: Which art form, painting or sculpture, can best achieve the purpose of art, which is to imitate nature? Sculptors argued that theirs was the superior art because actual volume in space is a primary characteristic of reality, and sculpture exists in three dimensions. Painters, however, asserted that this presumed benefit of sculpture required the beholder to move physically around the work in order to see its aspects, whereas a picture could present different points of view simultaneously. This was the gist of the argument that concerned Giorgione and some unnamed sculptors, according to the Venetian Paolo Pino, who wrote that "our painter . . . to the perpetual confusion of sculptors, painted in a picture of Saint George, armed, standing, leaning on the shaft of a lance, with the feet at the very edges of a limpid and clear spring, in which the entire figure was reflected, seen foreshortened up to the top of the head; . . . the back and one side of the entire figure was reflected in a mirror resting against a tree trunk. Giorgione simulated another mirror on the other side, in which one saw all the other side of Saint George, the artist wishing to sustain his point that a painter can make the whole figure visible in one glance, something that a sculpture cannot do."[12]

*181.* Woman with a Mirror, *Kunsthistorisches Museum, Vienna. Photo: Kunsthistorisches Museum, Vienna.*

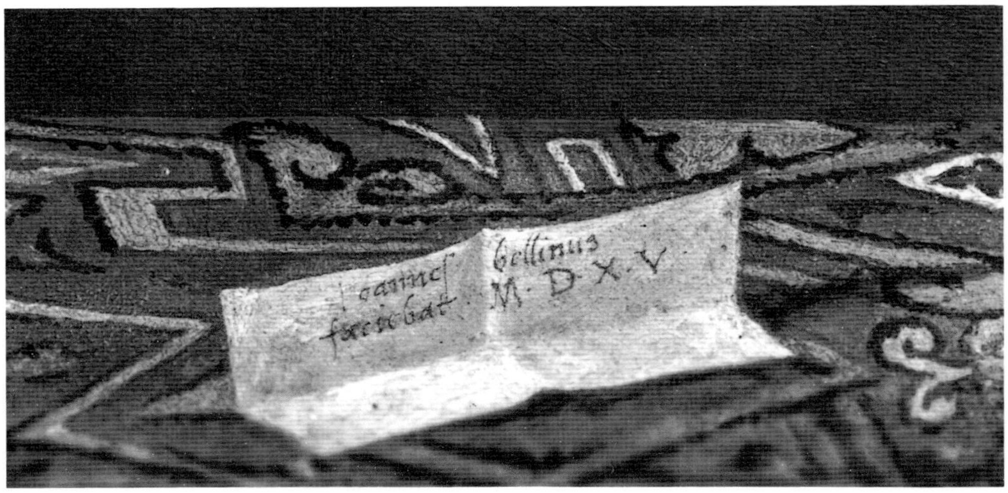

*182.* Woman with a Mirror, *detail, signature. Photo: Kunsthistorisches Museum, Vienna.*

The painting by Giorgione has been lost, but the late panel by Bellini demonstrates the old master's interest in precisely these issues. Bellini's picture is less programmatic and contrived than Giorgione's must have been; it is imbued with the tranquil self-assurance that Bellini had earned over seven decades of mastery. And Giorgione had proved his point with an image of a man in armor—not coincidentally, his patron, Saint George. Bellini, instead, depicted a nude female, the theme of the paragone *par excellence*. Apelles had painted several female nudes for Alexander the Great, including Venus, as explained by Pliny, whose writings were much in vogue among Venetian humanists beginning in the late fifteenth century. Artists and scholars took to heart Pliny's discussion of the difficulty of representing female beauty: here was the subject that epitomized the fundamental problems of art—the relation between beauty of character (which is invisible) and physical loveliness, and the creation of perfect beauty in art, something that may not be possible in nature. Painting a beautiful woman, the artist may demonstrate "the beauty of painting."[13]

The *Woman with a Mirror* is signed and dated 1515—five years after Giorgione's death and one year before the death of Bellini himself. Even in the sixteenth century, however, Bellini did not date all his works; this inscription—like that of the *Feast of the Gods*—has something of the quality of a testimonial, and the apparently casual placement of the cartellino on the table implies both intimacy and the artist's actuality: his signature, as in others of his sixteenth-century works, has become an integral part of the composition—not merely a label applied to the surface—as though he, too, had been in this room and had left his name as a record of his presence. This was not his first painting to deal with mirrors, mirror reflections, and the possibilities inherent in these things: the restello *Self-Knowledge* preceded it, perhaps by as much as a quarter of a century. But then Bellini was concerned primarily with the allegorical implications of the mirror and with the inclusion in its reflection of someone outside the painting. In his late work, mirrors are exploited in a different way, and the picture is self-referential, completing itself within itself.

A young woman sits in the foreground of a room with a window and landscape view to the left. She is in the immediate foreground of the picture space, pushed forward by the table or bench on which she sits, her legs cropped by the lower edge of the canvas. Unlike the parapets of most of Bellini's sacred paintings and portraits, this table propels the woman out of the picture space into our world: she exists both within and in front of the picture plane.

The woman is nude except for a red fabric that winds from her right arm and around her back to fall over her left thigh. Both her flesh and this red have been robbed of their chromatic richness by overcleaning with a harsh solvent; the modeling was originally more volumetric and the color deeper (cf. figs. 127, 140). Together the red fabric and the woman's raised right arm constitute a variant of the traditional Venus Pudica pose, and in a general, nonarchaeological way perhaps we are intended to recall classical types of Venus, who was often represented with a mirror as her attribute, especially in Hellenistic art. Holding a small mirror in her right hand so as to see the back of her head in a larger mirror on the wall, the woman arranges her hair or adjusts her brocade hair covering, embroidered with pearls.[14] The pearls also evoke Venus, and if this is she, then the goddess has been represented in a contemporary guise, in a sixteenth-century Venetian interior, with a fashionable Venetian *reticella* on her hair, and a typical Veneto landscape seen through the window. If this is not Venus, then Bellini has represented a contemporary woman—or ideal woman—as "a Venus," or, more generally, as a goddess or personification of beauty. The ambivalent characterization of Bellini's figure in this sense—the uncertainty regarding her identity—recalls his *Fra Teodoro of Urbino as Saint Dominic* and even more is akin to contemporary works by Titian and other masters that similarly seem to confound attempts to categorize them. And the woman's pensive mood recalls the elegiac poetry of the *Feast of the Gods*. At the same time, Bellini has set the stage for Titian's later depictions of Venus in contemporary settings, such as the *Venus of Urbino*, painted circa 1536, and for Titian's images of Venus with musicians as competitive allegories of the senses in which sight is victorious.[15]

This returns us to the theme of the paragone, which was Bellini's subtext here (and Titian's as well), encapsulated in the mirror.[16] That is to say, Bellini's picture is about seeing: while we look at the woman and at her mirror reflection, she looks at herself and into the mirror on the wall—into which she gazes indirectly, through the intermediation of her hand mirror. In other words, we see the back of her head, which, without the wall mirror, would be hidden from view, and the lady sees a similar view of herself in her hand mirror, reflecting the reflection. Here again, Bellini was representing a motif also employed by Titian, a motif close to their Venetian hearts in part because it allowed them to differentiate with varied handling of paint and with modulation of hue the glassy quality of the reflected image as opposed to its source (fig. 183). Titian's canvas in the Louvre —which represents a woman, possibly a courtesan, and certainly not Venus—

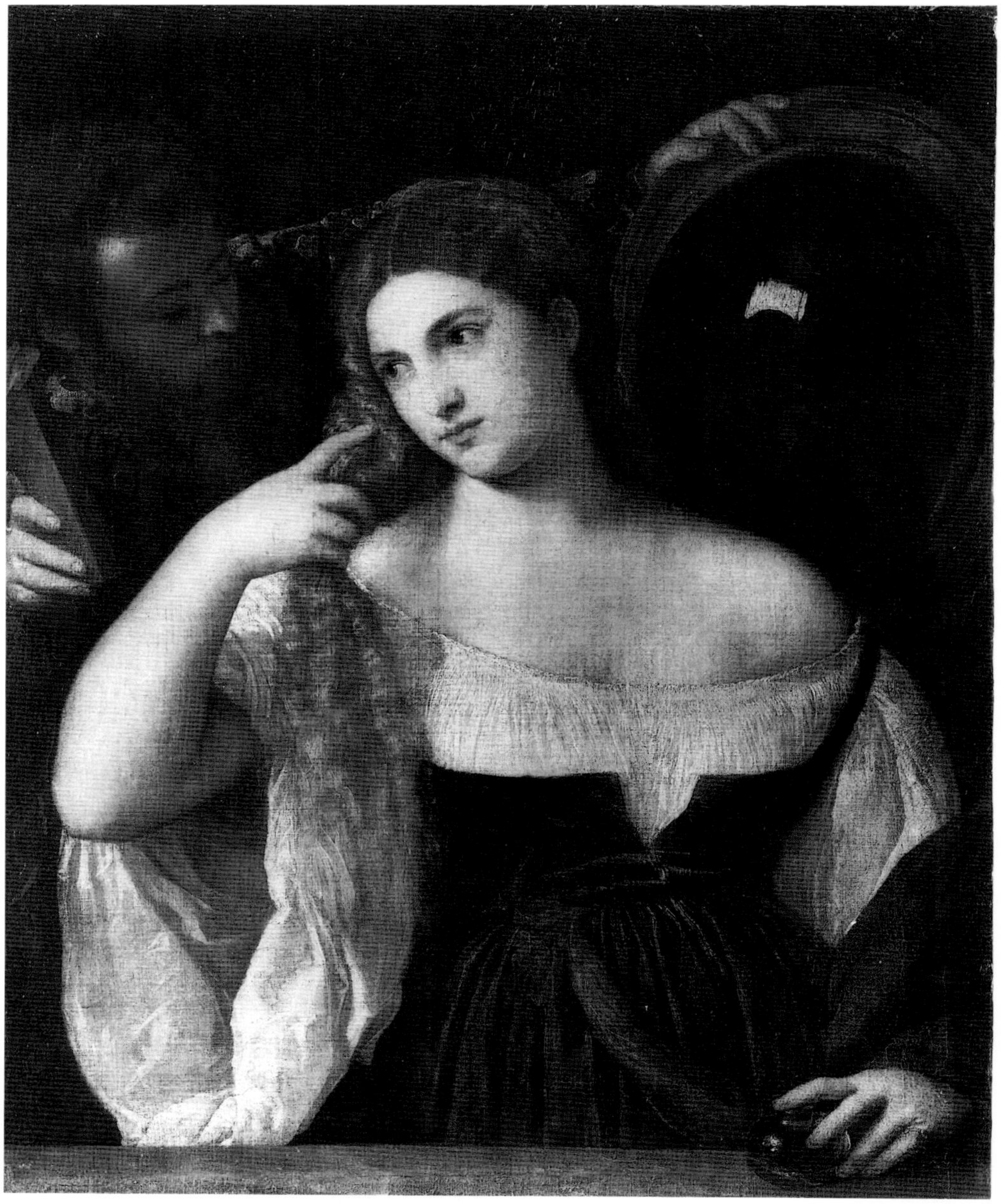

*183. Titian,* Woman with a Mirror, *Musée du Louvre, Paris. Photo: Musées Nationaux, Paris.*

is contemporary with Bellini's painting: but Bellini signed and dated his canvas, and Titian did not, so one cannot know for a fact which was painted before the other.[17] The younger artist was pointing the way toward the painterly "loaded brush" style of such Baroque masters as Peter Paul Rubens, and the old Bellini was practicing and anticipating the more closely defined, classical manner of such seventeenth-century painters as Nicolas Poussin. The dichotomy of styles between old Bellini and young Titian is not a distinction between an older, implicitly outmoded manner of painting and a bold, new one, destined to replace it, but rather a contrast between two equal possibilities, each of which had a very rich future in art. That Rubens made copies of Titian's works, while Poussin (or his follower) also copied Bellini's *Feast of the Gods* illustrates the point.

Bellini's *Woman with a Mirror* is the simultaneous and differentiated depiction of different kinds of experiences of seeing, which involve also distinct levels of reality—source and reflection and reflected reflection. Bellini played a variation on this theme with a device familiar from fifteenth-century Flemish painting, from which the mirror imagery may also have originated, and that is the clear glass vase, partially filled with water, set on the windowsill, casting a shadow and allowing us to see through glass and liquid. Bellini confirms both the transparency and the substantiality of the vase and liquid. The vase contains flowers, too indistinct to name. These flowers, together with the trees and plants of the landscape, are juxtaposed with the floral and plant motifs of the brocade reticella and the richly patterned oriental carpet on the table or ledge: another contrast of different realities, nature's and the artist's. Thus Bellini reminds us that the purpose of the Renaissance artist is to reflect nature, to mirror and to recreate reality. In so doing, Bellini imitates the Creator whose creation is mirrored in art. This is Bellini's true last will and testament.

*Family of Giovanni Bellini*

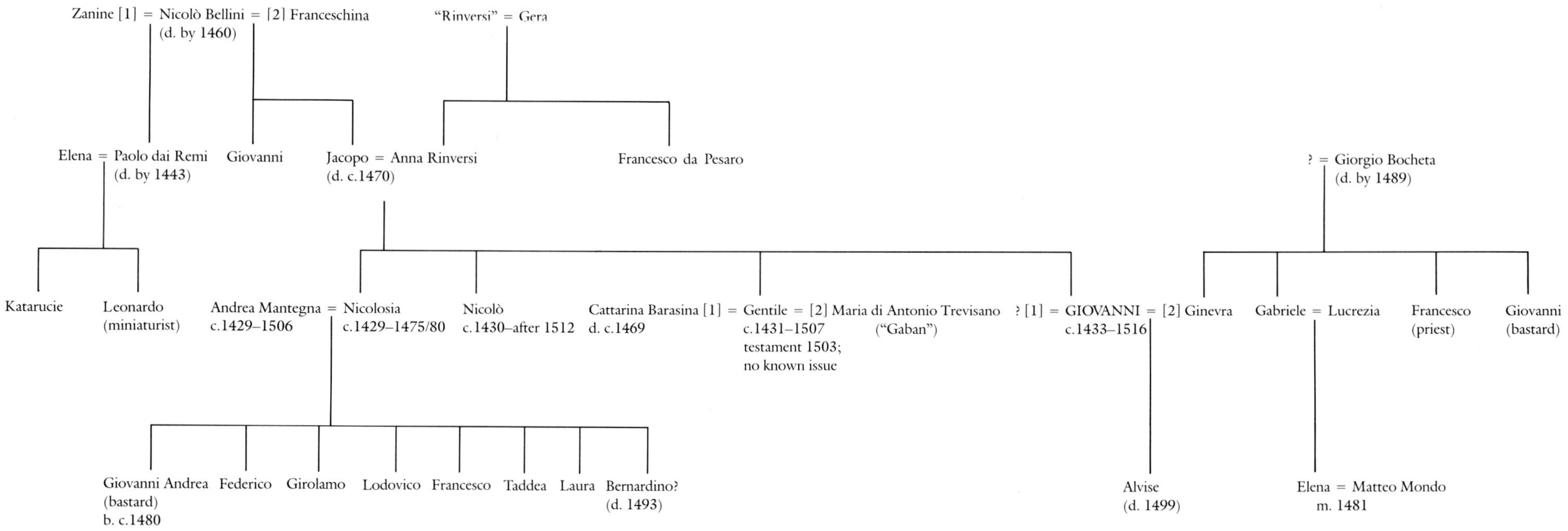

# Appendix 1
## Family Tree and Chronology

I acknowledge especially the chronologies published by Stefano Bottari, *Tutta la pittura di Giovanni Bellini* (Milan, 1963), 1:20–21, 2:16–18, and Renato Ghiotto and Terisio Pignatti, *L'Opera completa di Giovanni Bellini* (Milan, 1969), pp. 83–84. I have also used Lightbown, *Mantegna*, and Rodolfo Signorini, "Mantegna's Unknown Sons: A Rediscovered Epitaph," *Journal of the Warburg and Courtauld Institutes* 49 (1986): 233–35. I have added material derived from archival research and have compiled information from various sources to present as complete a picture as possible of Bellini's career.

1429
Jacopo Bellini's wife, Anna Rinversi, being pregnant, makes a will on 6 February (app. 2, no. 1).

1434 ca.
Birth of Giovanni Bellini.

1453
Marriage of his sister Nicolosia and Andrea Mantegna.

1459
2 April, witnesses document for notary Giuseppe Moisis; living at San Lio, Venice (app. 2, no. 5).

1459?
Signs altarpiece of Gattamelata Chapel in Sant'Antonio, Padua, with Jacopo and Gentile Bellini (app. 2, no. 6; Jacopo had earlier collaborated with one of his sons, unnamed but presumably Gentile, in the painting of a high altarpiece on canvas representing three saints; see Paoletti, *Raccolta*, p. 9).

1460–64
Dates of Carità triptychs, possibly painted in part by Giovanni Bellini (fig. 187).

1464
Signs one of two (lost) paintings for the Scuola di San Gerolamo (Ridolfi, *Maraviglie*, 1:64).

1468–71
Paints altarpiece of Saint John the Evangelist, formerly in Santa Maria della Carità, with a predella by Lauro Padovano (app. 4 at nn. 9–10).

1470
24 April, agrees to paint *The Flood with Noah's Ark* for the Scuola Grande di San Marco, which was probably never executed or, if completed, destroyed in the fire of 1484 (app. 2, no. 7).

1470
Jacopo still alive on 26 August (Paoletti, *Raccolta*, p. 11).

1471
Jacopo's widow, Anna Rinversi, makes a will dated 25 November (app. 2, no. 9).

1472
Date formerly inscribed on the *Pietà* (pl. 25) in the Ducal Palace (A. M. Zanetti, *Della pittura veneziana*, p. 49).

1472
Date inscribed on lost *Crucifixion with the Three Maries and Doctors of the Church* in the Refectory of Santa Maria della Carità (Ridolfi, *Maraviglie*, 1:64).

1473
The Signoria decides to redecorate the Sala del Maggior Consiglio with canvas murals depicting the "story of Ancona," as recorded by Marino Sanuto, *Cronaca veneziana*, Venice, Biblioteca Nazionale Marciana, MSS Ital. Cl. VII.cxxv (7460), fol. 340v.

1474
Date of lost portrait of Raffaele Zovenzoni, included in the manuscript *Istrias*.

1474
Date 20 June 1474 written on the back of the *Portrait of Jörg Fugger* (fig. 150).

1479
29 August, appointed to work in the Sala del Maggior Consiglio (app. 2, no. 11).

1479
3 September, Gentile Bellini goes to Constantinople, ostensibly to paint the portrait of Mehmet II but also to act as an informant for the Serenissima. (See Zorzi, "Notizie," p. 484; N.B. the language with which the Great Council referred to Gentile Bellini's voyage in app. 2, no. 12: "in the service of our Dominion").

1481
Giovanni Bellini witnesses marriage contract of Elena Zorzi and Matteo Mando on 9 May (app. 1: Family Tree, app. 2, no. 11).

1483
26 February 1482, m.v., Giovanni Bellini is called "painter of our Dominion" because of his excellence and is released from obligation to pay fees to the painters' confraternity (app. 2, no. 13).

1483
30 June, will of Gaspare Trissino of Vicenza providing for payments to Bellini for a *Resurrection* for the Trissino funerary chapel in the cathedral of that city (see Bottari, *Bellini*, 1:21).

1484
Listed as a member of the Scuola Grande di San Marco (Paoletti, *Raccolta*, p. 13. Paoletti adds that Bellini was also a member of the Scuola di San Cristoforo dei Mercanti, of which Gentile da Fabriano had been a brother as well. Both Giovanni and Gentile Bellini were also members of the Scuola Grande della Misericordia).

1485
30 July, guarantees the dowry of his (second?) wife, Ginevra Bocheta; living at Santa Marina, Venice (app. 2, no. 14). That Giovanni Bellini was living in the parish of San Lio in 1459, while his parents resided at San Gimignano, implies that he was already married.

1486
Is a deacon of the Scuola Grande di San Marco (app. 2, no. 15).

1487
Signs *Madonna degli alberetti* (fig. 34).

1487
Witnesses contract in house of the humanist Pandolfo Collenuccio, procurator of Varano in Venice (app. 2, no. 16).

1488
Signs Frari triptych (figs. 116, 117).

1488
Signs votive picture of Doge Agostino Barbarigo (figs. 68, 69).

1488
On 28 July, working with his brother Gentile in the Sala del Maggior Consiglio (app. 2, nos. 17–18).

1489
23 September, his wife, Ginevra, makes her will; they live at Santa Marina (app. 2, no. 19).

1490
Signs *Supper at Emmaus* for the Cornaro (figs. 188, 189).

1492
25 March, resumes work in the Sala del Maggior Consiglio (app. 2, nos. 20, 22).

1494
14 July, Giorgio Diletti makes his will, providing for his funerary chapel in San Giovanni Crisostomo (figs. 139–41).

1497
10 August, Donato Civalelli makes his testament, allocating three hundred ducats for an altarpiece by Bellini for the church of Santa Maria in Zara (app. 2, no. 24).

1497
4 October, Bellini has refused to paint a view of Paris on a painting for Marchese Francesco Gonzaga, who asks the artist to paint instead a subject of his own choosing (app. 2, no. 25).

1497
12 October, promises to paint another subject for the marchese (app. 2, no. 26).

1498
14 December, Bellini's son, Alvise, makes his will; Bellini's wife, Ginevra Boscheta, is already deceased (app. 2, no. 28).

1499
Alvise Bellini is dead.

1500
Garzadori chapel of Saint John the Baptist in Santa Corona, Vicenza, is dedicated (figs. 121–23; app. 2, no. 29).

1501
Bellini is working in the Ducal Palace and has almost completed the *Saint Dominic* (fig. 163) for Alfonso d'Este (app. 2, no. 34).

1504
July, Bellini sends a *Nativity* (*Presepio*) to Mantua for Isabella d'Este, who intends to display it in a bedroom (app. 2, nos. 39, 48).

1505
Signs the San Zaccaria altarpiece (figs. 126, 127).

1505
Date of the *Madonna and Child with Saints and Donor* in Birmingham, signed by Bellini but executed by the shop (fig. 181).

1505
Date of the *Saint Jerome* in Washington, executed with assistance.

1506
7 February, Dürer writes to Pirckheimer: Bellini is the greatest painter in Venice (app. 2, no. 52).

1506
7 February 1505, m.v., testament of Giacomo Dolfin: Bellini's altarpiece for Dolfin's funerary chapel in San Francesco della Vigna is almost complete (fig. 132; app. 2, no. 53).

1507
18 February, testament of Gentile Bellini (app. 2, no. 55).

1507
23 February, burial of Gentile Bellini (app. 2, no. 56).

1507
7 March, agrees to complete Gentile's unfinished *Saint Mark Preaching in Alexandria* for the Scuola Grande di San Marco (fig. 184; app. 2, no. 57).

1507
28 September, replaces the deceased Alvise Vivarini in the completion of a painting for the Sala del Maggior Consiglio (app. 2, no. 58).

1507
Signs the *Doge Leonardo Loredan and His Kinsmen* (fig. 159), executed with assistance.

1509
Date written on the back of the *Death of Saint Peter Martyr* in the Courtauld Institute.

1509
Date of the *Madonna and Child*, now in Detroit (fig. 45).

1510
Date of the *Madonna and Child*, now in Milan (fig. 44).

1513
Date of the San Giovanni Crisostomo altarpiece (figs. 139, 140).

1514
Signs the *Feast of the Gods* (figs. 175, 176).

1514
13 November, receives final payment for the *Feast* from Alfonso d'Este (app. 2, no. 62).

1515
27 February, working in the Sala del Maggior Consiglio (app. 2, no. 64).

1515
4 July, agrees to paint the *Martyrdom of Saint Mark* for the Scuola Grande di San Marco (fig. 185; app. 3).

1515
Signs *Woman with a Mirror*, now in Vienna (fig. 181).

1515
Date of the *Fra' Teodoro* (fig. 162).

1516
15 January 1515, m.v., the *Madonna* for the Lady d'Alençon is almost complete (app. 2, no. 63).

1516
30 January, the Dominicans of SS. Giovanni e Paolo agree to lend a silver crown to Bellini again for approximately two days (app. 2, no. 66).

1516
29 November, death of Giovanni Bellini (app. 2, no. 67).

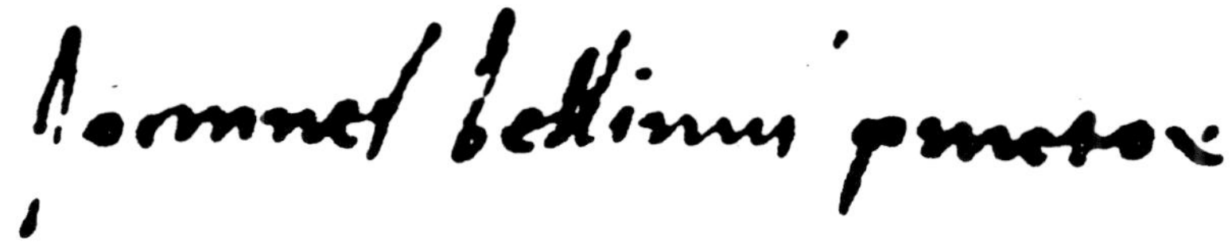

# Appendix 2
## Documents and Sources

1. 1429, 6 February (1428, m.v.). Testament of Anna Rinversi, wife of Jacopo Bellini. Pregnant with her first child and living with her husband, Jacopo, in the parish of San Gimignano, Anna names her mother and her uncle as her commissaries and the child who is to be born as a primary beneficiary of her estate: "Ego Anna uxor Iacobi Belin pictoris de confinio S. Zeminiani. . . . gravida, . . . volo hoc meum esse ultimum testamentum in quo commissarios meos constituo, ordino, ac esse volo donam Zeram dilectam genitricem meam, et ser Franciscum de Pesaro, avunculum meum. . . . Residuo omnium bonorum meorum presentorum et futuorum aducorum inordinatorum . . . dimitto filio meo vel filie vel quam portiam et hac presenti mea gravidatione vel perturitione." (ASV, Testamenti, Enrico Salomoni, Busta 946, no. 313; see also Paoletti, *Raccolta*, pp. 5–6. On p. 5, Paoletti publishes the will of Jacopo's father, Nicolò, 11 April 1424 [ASV, Notarile, Lorenzo Buscarino, Busta 545, Protocollo].)

2. 1440, 18 September (1439, m.v.). Jacopo's brother Giovanni, also a painter, is working with him. (ASV, Cancellaria Inferiore, Atti di Vittore Pomino, Busta 149, Protocollo 1439, c. 55t; Fiocco, "Giovanni e la famiglia," p. 6.)

3. 1443, 23 August. Jacopo takes as his assistant his sister's son Leonardo q. Paolo. (ASV, Cancellaria Inferiore, Atti di Francesco Elmis, Busta 74, fasc. xxviii, c. 20; see also Paoletti, *Raccolta*, pp. 7–8.)

4. 1453, 25 February. The Scuola Grande di San Giovanni Evangelista (of which Jacopo had been a member since 1437), grants a subvention to him because of the imminent marriage of his daughter Nicolosia to Andrea Mantegna: "Ducati vinti per nome de ser Iachomo Belin depintor per sovinzion del maridar de Nicholoxa sua fia." (See Paoletti, *Raccolta*, pp. 6, 9, citing ASV, Scuola Grande di San Giovanni Evangelista, Registro 72.)

5. 1459, 2 April. Giovanni Bellini signs as a witness of the testament of Margarita, wife of the medical doctor Artinio; Bellini is living at San Lio: "Testis ser Johanes filis magistrii Jacobii Belin [contrata] S. Leonis." (ASV, Notarile, Guiseppe Moisis, Busta 727, no. 32, fols. 1v, 2v.) This is the first archival mention of Giovanni Bellini. His living apart from his parents, residents of the parish of San Gimignano, suggests that he was already married. N.B. the 10 June 1482 will of Marieta, the pregnant wife of "Giovanni the painter of the contrata of San Gemignano": "Ego Marieta uxor magistri Joannis pictoris de confinio Sancti Geminiani . . . gravida . . . dimitto magistro Joanni marito et commissario meo" (ASV, Testamenti Lorenzo Stella, Busta 876, no. 528). It is uncertain whether this Giovanni is Giovanni Bellini, and Marieta therefore his first wife, but the document is worth noting because this notary worked for the artist's family on other occasions (nos. 19, 28) and because the Bellini family were sometime residents of San Gimignano, although Giovanni Bellini was documented as a parishoner of San Lio in 1459 (no. 5) and of Santa Marina in 1481 and in 1485 (no. 12). See also no. 14, below.

6. 1459 or 1460? Jacopo, Gentile, and Giovanni Bellini sign the altarpiece of the Gattamelata Chapel of Saint Francis in Sant'Antonio, Padua: "Iacobi Bellini Veneti Patris, ac Gentilis, e Ioannis Natorum opus. MCCCCIX [*sic*]."

7. 1470, 24 April. Bellini's agreement with the Scuola Grande di San Marco to paint a canvas of *The Flood with the Ark of Noah*: "Fo deliberato de dar el teller in cavo de la Schuola . . . a ser Zuan Bellin nel qual die far el deluvio et l'arca de Noe cum le sue pertinentie. . . . [Signed] Io Zuan Bellini sono contento di quanto e sopra scripto sopra." (See Molmenti, "Pittori Bellini," p. 228, and Paoletti, *Raccolta*, pp. 11–12.)

8. 1471, 11 May. Letter from Elisabetta Morosini to her brothers Pietro and Marco di Paolo: "I warmly pray you, messer Marco, that it please you for the friendship I understand you have with Gentile or Giovanni Bellini the painters to learn from them somehow whether they wish to teach the reason of drawing (or design) to our priest Domenico." (Published by F.S., "Aneddoto," *Nuovo archivio veneto* 2 [1891]: 382. The letter is said to be in ASV, Atti Carlo Bruni di Loreo, but I have been unable to find it. "F.S." is not identified in the journal.)

9. 1471, 25 November. Testament of Anna Rinversi. Widowed and bedridden, Anna names Francesco di Alvise di Giovanni her only commissary, and leaves all her works of art to her son Gentile, including gessos, marbles, reliefs, paintings, drawing books, and everything else pertinent to pictures and to painting. Gentile and his brother Nicolò share equally in the rest of the estate, and Nicolò also receives the fabric from a brown dress. "Ego Anna relicta magistri Iacobi Bellino pictoris veneti sana mente et intellectu . . . , licet corpore infirma et jacens in lecto. . . . Volo et statuo esse meum solum comissarium ser Franciscum de Aloysio de Iohanne Venetum. . . . dimitto Gentili filio meo omnia laboreria de zessio, de marmore et de releviis, quadros dessignatos, et omnes libros de dessigniis, et alia omnia pertinentia pictorie et ad dipingendum que fuerunt quondam prefati magistri Iacobi Bellino viri mei. Et residuum omnium et singularum bonorum meorum . . . dimitto prefato Gentili et Nicolao filiis meis et dicti quondam magistri Iacobi equaliter. Et ultra dictum residuum dimitto dicto Nicolao unam meam vestem pani brunii a meo dorso." (ASV, Cancellaria Inferiore, Francesco Elmis, Busta 361, Protocollo, fol. 65v, no. 173.)

10. 1473, 18 April. Letter from Antonio di Choradi in Pera to his brother-in-law, the stonemason ser Nicolò Gruatto. He requests Gruatto to order a painting of Christ from Lazzaro Bastiani. He gives the desired measurements and adds that, in case Bastiani is dead or unwilling to do the work, Gruatto should order the picture from Bellini instead: "Apresso andatte da Lazaro Bastian che stano sopra el champo di San Polo che chusi li schrivo a lui e fateme far uno quadreto . . . con la figura di misser Iesù Cristo che siano belo chome li schrivo a lui, o se per chaxo che idio el guarda el fusse morto, over lo nol volesse far, andate da Ziane Belino e mostrateli el mio e ditege il volio a quel modo chome stano quelo con quela soaza d'oro polita e bela." The commission went to Bastiani, who was indeed still alive (he died in 1512) and who completed the picture in 1474. (For the letter in the commissaria of Bartolomeo Gruato, ASV, Scuola Grande della Misericordia, Busta 23, see Paoletti, *Raccolta*, p. 12, and also Henry Thode, "Neue archivalische Forschungen über venezianische Kunst," *Repertorium für Kunstwissenschaft* 18 [1895]: 193.)

11. 1479, 29 August. A deliberation of the Maggior Consiglio, 350 in favor, 11 against, and 4 abstentions, regarding Gentile Bellini's departure for Constantinople and Giovanni Bellini's appointment to continue the work in the Sala del Maggior Consiglio, including his right to the next available *sansaria* (broker's patent) of the Fondaco dei Tedeschi for his lifetime, reimbursement of expenses for materials, and an annual stipend of 80 ducats, assuming that his work is worthy: "Quum fidelis civis noster Gentilis Belinus pictor, qui instaurabat figuras et picturas huius Sale Maioris Consilii, de mandato nostri Dominii profiscitur Constantinopolim ad serviendum nostro Dominio . . . . Vadit pars, quod auctoritate huius Consilii, fidelis civis noster Johannes Belinus pictor egregius deputetur ad dictum opus instaurandum, renovandumque. Et teneatur id instaurare atque renovare quando ut ubi fuerit opus, ac sibi mandabitur per provisores nostros Salis: qui sibi providere debeant expensis nostris de coloribus et aliis rebus eidem operi necessariis. Verum quia omnis mercenarius dignus est mercede sua, captum sit, quod in premium laborum suorum, prima sansaria Fontici que vacabit auctoritate istius Consilii sibi conferatur in vita sua." (ASV, Maggior Consiglio, Deliberazioni, vol. Regina, 1455–79, fol. 192r [new fol. 200r]. This information was later recorded also by the Colleggio [ASV, Collegio, Notatorio-Registro 12, Anno 1474–1481, fol. 127v (new fol. 128v), 1 July 1480]. The act of 1479 was previously published by Lorenzi, *Monumenti*, pp. 88–89; I have corrected his minor errors in this transcription, and in all those that follow. On p. 91, Lorenzi published the record of the Collegio dated 1 July 1480.)

12. 1481, 9 May. Giovanni Bellini "the painter" signs as a witness of the marriage of his kinswoman Elena di Gabriele di Giorgio (see app. 1: Family Tree and nos. 19, 28, and 68) to Matteo Mando; Bellini is living in Santa Marina, where Gabriele di Giorgio (Zorzi) and the new husband also reside (Bellini and the Giorgio family eventually shared a tomb; see no. 68.): "In contrata Sante Marine in domo ser Gabrielis Georgii . . . ser Matheus Mando quondam Joannis de contrata Sante Marine . . . tempore contractus matrimonii dicta dona Elena filie ser Gabrielis Giorgii. . . . Testis Dominus Johannes Bellinus pinctor, ser Victor de Rubeis tintor, Sancte Marine." (ASV, Cancellaria Inferiore, Notai, Busta 124, Giovanni Antonio Mando, fol. 22r.)

13. 1483, 26 February (1482, m.v.). The Collegio calls Giovanni Bellini "painter of our Dominion" and releases him from the obligation to pay fees to the painters' confraternity. He is urged to free himself from other obligations in order to complete the work in the Great Council Hall: "Joannes Bellinus per egregium ingenium suum in arte picture pictor nostri Dominii est appellatus, et Ideo assumptus ad renovandam Salam Maioris Consilii et a nostro Dominio publice permiatus utque ad eam solam rem vacare possit liber ab omni alia cura. Per intrascriptos Dominos Consiliarios exemptus factus fuit ab omnibus officiis et beneficiis scollae seu fratalae pictorum." (ASV, Collegio, Notatorio-Registro

13, Anno 1481–1489, fol. 22r [new 25r]; Lorenzi, *Monumenti*, p. 92.)

14. 1485, 30 July. Giovanni Bellini guarantees the dowry of his wife, Ginevra Bocheta; they are living at Santa Marina: "Plenam et irrevocabilem securitatem facio ego Ioannes Bellino q.d. [quondam] Jacobi pictor de confinio Sancte Marine cum meis heredibus et successoribus tibi Zenevre uxori mee dilecte et succesoribus tuis de tota illa repromissa magna vel parva que tempore tue desponsationis dotis nomine pro te mihi dari promissa fuit. Que quidem dos seu repromissa fuit in totum ducatos quingentorum auri. Et quia de illis inter denarios numerata, et res mobiles de comuni concordio extimatas mihi bene solutum fuit et integre satisfactum existit adeo quod nihil inde remansit unde te aut heredes vel successores tuos amplius requirere seu moletare valeam per ullum ingenium sive modum. Ideo te cum heredibus et successoribus tuis quietam perpetuo reddo pariter et securam." (ASV, Notarile, Lorenzo Stella, Busta 875, no. 162; Paoletti, *Raccolta*, p. 13; see also no. 5, regarding Marieta, who may have been Bellini's first wife.)

15. 1486. Giovanni Bellini is a deacon of the Scuola Grande di San Marco. (ASV, Scuola Grande di San Marco, Busta 202, unpag.)

16. 1487, 17 May. Giovanni Bellini witnesses a document signed in the house of the Pesarese humanist Pandolfo Collenuccio: "magistro Johanne Bellino pictor quondam domini Jacobi, de confinis S. Marine." (See M. Morici, "Documenti," *Rassegna bibliografica dell'arte italiana* 7 [1904]: 90. I have been unable to find this document. Perhaps Bellini had already met Collenuccio in Pesaro, assuming that the artist went to that city to paint the *Coronation of the Virgin* [pl. 38]. For the humanist and diplomat, see Eduardo Melfi, in *Dizionario biografico degli italiani* [Rome, 1982], vol. 27, s.v. "Collenuccio, Pandolfo.")

17. 1488, 28 July. Alvise Vivarini notes that Giovanni and Gentile Bellini are working in the Sala del Maggior Consiglio; he too wishes to work there. (ASV, Provveditori al Sal, Busta 59, fols. 181r–v [new fols. 151r–v].)

18. 1488, July. Another record of the same request by Alvise Vivarini. (ASV, Collegio, Notatorio-Registro 13, Anno 1481–1489, fol. 168v [new fol. 171v].)

19. 1489, 23 September. Testament of Bellini's wife, Ginevra Bocheta, naming three commissaries, her brother, her cousin, and her husband. Gentile Bellini witnesses the document. Giovanni Bellini is to be her primary beneficiary, and after his death, their son, Alvise, is to inherit the estate. She also leaves a bequest of 25 ducats to her nephew Sebastiano when he reaches age 20. If he should die before that time, the 25 ducats are to go instead to the son of another Giovanni, the natural son of her deceased father: "Ego Zenevra uxor egregy viri ser Ioannis Bellini pictoris de confinio Sancte Marine. . . . Constituo meos fidei commissarios d. presbiterum Franciscum Bocheta fratrem meum, egregium virum ser Gabrielem q[uondam] Georgii consobrinum meum, et suprascriptum ser Ioannem Bellinum maritum meum. . . . Residuum vero omnium bonorum meorum, etc., dimitto suprascripto ser Ioanni Bellino marito meo dilecto in vita sua tantum, sed post eius mortem volo dotum meum residuum devinire in Alovisum filium meum . . . et quod dentur ducati 25 omnino Sebastiano nepoti meo quando pervenerit ad etatem annorum 20. Verum si dictus Sebastianus obiret ante dictam etatem . . . , tunc volo quod dicti ducati 25 dentur filius ser Ioannis filii naturalis q[uondam] patris mei." (ASV, Testamenti, Lorenzo Stella, Busta 877, no. 829, and Busta 877, Registro, fol. 60v, no. 214.)

20. 1492, 25 March. Giovanni Bellini resumed his work in the Sala del Maggior Consiglio for a fee of five ducats a month, or sixty ducats per annum. (See no. 22.)

21. 1494. Giovanni Bellini is a deacon of the Scuola Grande di San Marco. (ASV, Scuola Grande di San Marco, Busta 202, unpag.; see app. 3 at n. 3.)

22. 1495, 23 December. Reference to Bellini's having resumed work in the Sala del Maggior Consiglio on 25 March 1492 (no. 20). His is the first name in the list of artists working there, the others being Alvise Vivarini (see nos. 17, 18), Cristoforo da Parma, Marco Marziale, Vincenzo da Treviso, Francesco Bissolo, and two boys assisting them. Alvise Vivarini was paid the same stipend as Bellini, five ducats a month, while the others all received lesser amounts. (ASV, Consiglio de' Dieci, Misto Registro 26 [1493–1495], fols. 199r–200r, and Provveditori al Sal, Busta 2, fols. 74v–76v).

23. 1496, 26 November. Beginning of correspondence pertaining to Bellini's painting a picture for Isabella d'Este; letter from Alberto da Bologna to the marchesa: "Yesterday evening Your Most Illustrious Lord [Gian Francesco Gonzaga] told me that Giovanni Bellini, who is a most excellent painter, will do a painting for the studiolo." (First published by Alessandro Luzio in 1888; but now see Brown with Lorenzoni, *Isabella*, p. 157. The letter is preserved in the Archivio di Stato, Mantua [hereafter abbreviated ASM], Busta 1439, c. 317. Because Brown's recent volume makes the Italian texts readily and accurately available, I give only brief English translations or summaries of passages of significance regarding Bellini. See also J. M. Fletcher, "Isabella and Giovanni.")

24. 1497, 10 August. Testament of the knight Donato Civalelli, providing three hundred ducats for an altarpiece by Giovanni Bellini. This is to furnish a chapel to be dedicated to the Virgin in the Benedictine church of Santa Maria in Zara, where he and his deceased brother (buried in Padua) are eventually to be reinterred: "Ego Donatus Cievalelus eques nobilis iadrensis de confinio Sancti Johannis Novi. . . . Item volo et ordino quod residuarii mei teneantur et sint obligati in termino anni unius cum eorum comoditate portavi facere corpus meus iadrem simul cum cadavere quondam domini Hyeronimi fratris mei quod est Padue . . . et sepeliatur dictum cadaver meum et cadaver supra scriptum quondam fratris mei apud ecclesiam Sancte Marie ordinis Sancti Benedicti. In qua ecclesia volo quod de bonis meis fiat capella in honorem Virginis Mariae . . . in qua expendatur ducati tercenti [*sic*] auri simul cum eius palla altaris, quam fieri volo per dominum Joannes Bellino." (ASV, Testamenti, Pietro Florian, Busta 408, no. 95.)

25. 1497, 4 October. Letter from Marchese Francesco Gonzaga to Giovanni Bellini: "In the past few days we have had sent to you a painting on which we wish that you paint the city of Paris and because you responded [to the messenger] that not ever having seen it [you don't want to paint it], we are content and thus we defer to your judgment regarding what should be painted." (Luzio, "Disegni," p. 277.)

26. 1497, 12 October. Letter from Giovanni Bellini to Marchese Gonzaga: "Most Illustrious Lord . . . from Your Excellency's letter I have understood that you have changed your opinion that I paint the city of Paris on the picture that I have. And this because I have never seen it [Paris]. Then Your Excellency, for his humanity and benignity, defers himself to my judgment that I paint in said picture that which seems [appropriate] to me. I, Your Excellency, am for doing as much as Your Illustrious Lordship has commissioned me to do, and thus I shall push myself with my little skill to do that which will be pleasing to Your Excellency, again with my soul more secure for having served you, having understood some of Your Lordship's imagination, but I shall not cease, as I have said, from giving my every care to content Your Most Illustrious Lordship, to whom, as a good servant, I continuously recommend myself. . . . Giovanni Bellini." ("Ill.me et Ex.mo Domine observandissime. Per littere di Vostra Signoria ho intexo quella esser mutata di opinione ch'io faci la cità de Paris sopra el quadro io ho. Et questo per non l'haver io veduta. Poi V. Ex.ma S. per sua humanità et benignità si remette al juditio mio che faci sopra dicto quadro quello ad me pare. Io, Sr. Ex.mo, sum per far quanto da la Illustrissima Signoria Vostra mi è stà comesso, et cussì afforceromi cum el mio picolo ingegno de far cosa che sii grata a V. Ex. Ancor che cum animo più securo l'haria servita, havendo intexo qualche sua fantaxia, ma non risterò, come ho dicto, di ponere ogni mia cura per contentar Vostra Illustrissima Signoria, a la qual come ben servitore di continuo mi racomando. Venetiis die XII.mo octobris 1497. E.V.S. Johannes Bellinus"). (Luzio, "Disegni," 277. This letter has apparently been lost. See Fletcher, "Isabella and Giovanni," p. 710.)

27. 1498, 26 April. Letter from Isabella d'Este to Cecilia Bergamini-Visconti, asking to borrow her portrait by Leonardo da Vinci to compare with "certain beautiful portraits by the hand of Giovanni Bellini" ("certi belli retracti de man di Zoanne Bellino"). (Adolfo Venturi and Alessandro Luzio, "Nuovi documenti su Leonardo da Vinci," *Archivio storico dell'arte* 1 [1888]: 45.)

28. 1498, 14 December. Testament of Giovanni Bellini's son, Alvise, naming as his only commissary Lucrezia, the wife of his kinsman Gabriele de Giorgio, who had been his mother's commissary (see no. 19). Making his father his primary beneficiary, Alvise specifies that Lucrezia is to inherit the estate after Giovanni's death, which implies (as did Ginevra's testament) that Giovanni Bellini had no other children living in 1498. Alvise also refers to his mother as deceased: "Ego Alovisius Bellinus natus d. Ioannis Bellini de confinio Sancte Marine, . . . corpore languens. . . . Constituo meam solam fidei commissariam dominam Lucretiam consortem ser Gabrielis de Georgio amitam meam. . . . Residuum vero omnium bonorum meorum . . . dimitto suprascripto domino Ioanni patri meo dilectissimo. Sed quoniam per quondam Zenevram olim matrem meam dimisit mihi per suum testamentum dotem suam post mortem . . . dicti genitoris mei. Ideo dimitto totam ipsam dotem suprascripte domine Lucretie amite et commissarie mee post mortem dicti mei patris." (ASV, Testamenti, Lorenzo Stella, Busta 877, no. 755.)

29. 1500. Garzadori Chapel of Saint John the Baptist in Santa Corona, Vicenza, is dedicated (figs. 121, 123).

30. 1501, 2 March. Letter from Michele Vianello to Isabella d'Este: "I have been with Giovanni Bellini. . . . described the need and desire of [the marchesa regarding her commission], and the story in the manner Your Most Illustrious Ladyship desires, [and] the said Giovanni Bellini responded that he was constrained by the Venetian state to continue the work begun in the Palazzo Ducale . . . ; yet he will do the work for Your Excellency and will steal the time. . . . Again, I advise Your Ladyship that the said Giovanni Bellini has many

other works to do, so that it will not be possible to have his work all that soon. I think . . . it will be within a year and a half. . . . Regarding the price, he asked me for 150 ducats." Vianello, who acted as the marchesa's agent, thought he could get the fee reduced to 100 ducats. (ASM, Busta 1439, c. 317, transcribed in Brown with Lorenzoni, *Isabella*, p. 157.)

31. 1501, 1 April. Letter from Vianello to Isabella d'Este: Bellini requires information regarding the measurements of the painting and asks for a "downpayment" of twenty-five ducats. (ASM, Busta 1439, c. 318, transcribed in Brown with Lorenzoni, *Isabella*, p. 158.)

32. 1501, 25 June. Letter from Vianello to Isabella d'Este: "Today . . . I have received a letter from you and with it . . . the 25 ducats to give to Giovanni Bellini who is at the [Bellini's?] villa: he will remain there, according to what they told me at his house, about five days. . . . he [Bellini] has told me he is very desirous of serving Your Ladyship. But as for that narrative ("istoria") which Your Ladyship has given him, one cannot say how very unwillingly he would do it because he knows the judgment of Your Ladyship and then [because] it would be compared ("va al parangone") with those works ("quele opere") by Andrea [Mantegna], . . . and he says that in this narrative . . . there is nothing good . . . and he does it as very unwillingly as one can say, so that I doubt that he will serve Your Excellency as Your Excellency desires. So that, if it appears to Your Excellency to give him the liberty to do what he pleases, I am most certain that Your Ladyship will be much better served." (ASM, Busta 1439, c. 319, transcribed in Brown with Lorenzoni, *Isabella*, p. 159.)

33. 1501, 28 June. Isabella d'Este to Vianello: "If Giovanni Bellini would do that narrative ("historia") with such reluctance, as you have described, we shall be content to submit to his judgment, provided that he paint some ancient narrative or fable either of his own invention or pretending to be one that represents something ancient, and of beautiful meaning. . . . The measurements of the picture have not changed since you were here and saw the place where it is to be hung." (ASM, Busta 2993, Libro 12, c. 62v, transcribed in Brown with Lorenzoni, *Isabella*, p. 160. On 20 December 1501, Isabella wrote again to Vianello complaining that she did not know whether Bellini had begun work, and if he could not complete the painting as promised she wanted her twenty-five ducats back [ASM, Busta 2993, Libro 13, c. 16v, in Brown with Lorenzoni, *Isabella*, p. 160].)

34. 1501, 3 August. Letter from Lorenzo da Pavia to Isabella d'Este: Giovanni Bellini is completing a small and very beautiful painting of *Saint Dominic* for her brother, Alfonso d'Este (fig. 163). (Luzio, "Disegni," p. 278. The letter is ASM, Busta 1439, cc. 310–11. See Fletcher, "Isabella and Giovanni," p. 707.)

35. 1502, 4 January. Vianello to Isabella: "Giovanni Bellini has been very occupied and he has [also] been sick for many days." He promised to complete the marchesa's painting by the end of September. (ASM, Busta 1439, ca. 316 [Vianello's letter] and Busta 2993, Copialettere, Libro 13, c. 22v [Isabella's reply], and also Libro 14, c. 11v, her letter of 10 August 1502, expressing concern that Bellini may not have begun her picture. If he has not, she wants her twenty-five ducats to be reimbursed. All are transcribed in Brown and Lorenzoni, *Isabella*, p. 161.)

36. 1502, 10 September. Letter from Lorenzo da Pavia to Isabella d'Este: Bellini assures her that he will paint "a fantasy in his own way" ("una fantasia a suo modo"). (ASM, Busta 2993, c. 32, summarized in Fletcher, "Isabella," p. 708.)

37. 1502, 15 September. Isabella d'Este to Vianello: "You can recall that many months ago we gave the commission to Giovanni Bellini to make for us a painting for the ornament of our study, and how he has yet to finish the picture. . . . We don't care any more to have that painting, and if, in its place, he [Bellini] wishes to make for us a *Nativity* ("presepio"), we shall remain very content. . . . We desire this *Nativity* to include a Saint John the Baptist and the animals near the Madonna and Our Lord God [and] Saint Joseph." (ASM, Busta 2993, Libro 14, cc. 16r–v, transcribed in Brown with Lorenzoni, *Isabella*, p. 162.)

38. 1502, 15 October. Vianello to Isabella: "I received a letter from Your Excellency a few days ago about the painting by Giovanni Bellini, who has not been in town these days . . . ; but now he has come and I have talked with him, and he tells me that he is content to paint the *Nativity* and to do excellent things; and if Your Ladyship wants it on the same canvas that was prepared for Your Ladyship's camerino he will begin at once; and for the price he wants the same figure that he wanted to do the narrative, that is, 100 ducats." (ASM, Busta 1440, c. 124, transcribed in Brown with Lorenzoni, *Isabella*, p. 163. Fletcher, "Isabella and Giovanni," p. 708, plausibly suggests that Bellini may have been out of town in connection with the *Baptism* in Vicenza [fig. 121]).

39. 1502, 20 October. Letter from Isabella d'Este to Vianello: "We are content that master Giovanni Bellini will do the *Nativity* for us in place of the narrative. . . . But our desire is that it not be of the size that we wanted for the narrative . . . because our intention is to put it in a bedroom. As for the price, it does not seem convenient that he be

given as much as we had offered to give him for the narrative in which there would have been more figures than there will be in the *Nativity*: you can offer him 40 or 50 ducats. . . . If for some reason he shows himself inclined to abandon the *Nativity* and to do some other of his new inventions of the Madonna, we shall be content that he do so: [but] the truth is that we shall be more content with the *Nativity*." (ASM, Busta 2993, Libro 14, cc. 25v–26r, transcribed in Brown with Lorenzoni, *Isabella*, p. 163.)

40. 1502, 3 November. Letter from Vianello to Isabella d'Este: "I have been to find [Bellini] and to tell him of Your Excellency's intentions regarding the *Nativity*, and that Your Excellency wants there to be in said painting a St. John the Baptist; he [Bellini] replied to me that he was content to serve Your Excellency, but that it appeared to him that it was inappropriate ("fuori de propoxito") to have this saint present in the *Nativity* and that, pleasing Your Most Illustrious Ladyship, he would do instead a *Madonna and Child*, with the Baptist and some distant vistas ("luntani") and other fantasies which would much more suit this picture and fit in much better. . . . as for the price, we have come to an agreement on 50 ducats." (ASM, Busta 1440, c. 125, transcribed in Brown and Lorenzoni, *Isabella*, p. 164.)

41. 1502, 12 November. Letter from Isabella d'Este to Vianello: "Since it is decided that Bellini is to paint in place of the *Nativity* a picture of the Madonna and Child with St. John the Baptist, it would please us and we desire that he also include a St. Jerome with the other inventions that will occur to him." (ASM, Busta 2993, Libro 14, c. 37v, transcribed in Brown with Lorenzoni, *Isabella*, p. 164.)

42. 1502, 22 November. Letter from Isabella d'Este to Vianello: the marchesa had changed her mind and decided that she wanted Bellini to paint a *Nativity* without St. John the Baptist. "Whether the manner of painting should be on canvas or on wood, we refer to him," but she is sending the required measurements. (ASM, Busta 2993, Libro 14, c. 51, transcribed in Brown with Lorenzoni, *Isabella*, pp. 164–65. See also Fletcher, "Isabella and Giovanni," p. 709, for letters from Lorenzo da Pavia to the marchesa on 17 June and 6 October 1503.)

43. 1503, 8 October. Letter from Francesco Malatesta to Isabella d'Este: "Master Lorenzo [da Pavia] has given me to understand that it will not be possible for me to see the picture that Giovanni Bellini is painting because he never shows anyone anything of his that is not finished." (ASM, Busta 1440, c. 299, transcribed in Brown with Lorenzoni, *Isabella*, p. 165.)

44. 1504, 3 January. Letter from Lorenzo da Pavia to Isabella d'Este: Bellini needs another one and a half months because it is winter and his pigments will not dry properly. (Charles Yriarte, "Isabelle d'Este et les artistes de son temps," *Gazette des Beaux-Arts* 15 [1896]: 220.)

45. 1504, 10 April. Letter from Isabella d'Este to Alvise Marcello: The marchesa has been waiting three years for a painting by Giovanni Bellini and has already paid him twenty-five ducats. He has never offered any excuse for all the delay ("non ha pur facta una minima scusa"), and now she wants her money returned, "not so much for the recovery of the cash, as not to endure the injury received from Bellini." (ASM, Busta 2994, Libro 17, cc. 14v–15, transcribed in Brown with Lorenzoni, *Isabella*, pp. 165–66.)

46. 1504, 2 July. Letter from Giovanni Bellini to Isabella d'Este: "Most Illustrious Lady, if my deference in executing the desire of Your Ladyship, and not any less my own, regarding the work promised to Your Ladyship has been tedious to the aforesaid Most Illustrious Lady, of whom, kneeling, I ask pardon, supplicating the excellent Lady, for her customary kindness, if she would attribute it to my innumerable occupations and not to disregard for the concerns of Your Excellency, which concerns continuously, as her most perfect servant, I have carved in my heart; praying Our Lord God that in the passage of time if I have not satisfied Your Ladyship, as she had in mind, at least in this work she remain content, which, however, if it be not thus to the satisfaction of the immense wisdom and experience of Your Ladyship, I would attribute this to the tenuity of my weak knowledge. To the Lady I recommend and offer myself in humility. From Venice, July 2, 1504, Your Most Humble Servant of this Dominion, Giovanni Bellini the painter" ("Illustrissima Signora, se'l deferir mio in exequir el desiderio di Vostra Signoria, e non men mio, cercha l'opera a quella promessa, è stato tedioxo ala prefata Illustrissima Signoria Vostra, da quella, flexis genibus, ne chiedo perdono, supplicando la prelibata, per solita sua benignità, se degni attribuirlo a le innumerabel occupation mie e non ad oblivion de cosse di Vostra Signoria, le quale continuamente, como perfectissimo servidor de quella, me sono scolpite nel cuore; pregando el Signor Nostro Idio che se in longeza di tempo non ho cusì satisfacto ala prefata Signoria Vostra, como era de mente de quella, saltim in essa opera rimanga contenta, la quale però se non cusì satisfacesse ala inmensa sapientia e praticha de l'antedicta Signoria Vostra, lo attribuischa ala tenuità del debel saper mio. A la qual humiliter mi ricomando et offerischo. Ex Venetiis die II Julii 1504. Eiusdem Dominationis Vestre humilimus servitor Johannes Bellinus pictor"). (ASM, Raccolta

d'Autografi, Cassetta 7, c. 686, transcribed in Brown with Lorenzoni, *Isabella*, pp. 166–67. This is the only letter by Bellini that seems to have survived. See no. 26.)

47. 1504, 6 July. Letter from Lorenzo da Pavia to Isabella d'Este: "This morning I have been with Giovanni Bellini . . . he has completed the painting, . . . and it truly is a beautiful thing, done better than I had believed, and I know it will please Your Excellency, and in this painting he [Bellini] has much invested himself for the greatest honor for respect of messer Andrea Mantegna, even if it be true that in invention ("invencione") it cannot approach the most excellent messer Andrea." Another patron will buy the painting if the marchesa does not forgive Bellini, but Lorenzo da Pavia urges her to acquire it for her collection, because it is one of the master's finest works, and he is very old. If she is content, "he [Bellini] wishes to have made a beautiful frame" for the painting. (ASM, Busta 1890, c. 336, published by Braghirolli, "Carteggio," pp. 382–83. See also two other letters from Lorenzo da Pavia to the marchesa: ASM, Busta 1890, c. 337, 16 July 1507, and c. 341, 13 August 1504. Lorenzo was disturbed at the poor quality of the wood panel but considered the painting very beautiful, although he thought the figures too small for their setting. These letters were transcribed by Luzio, "Isabella d'Este e Giulio II," *Rivista d'arte* anno 12, vol. 2 [1909]: 861–62.)

48. 1504, 9 July. Letter from Isabella d'Este to Giovanni Bellini: "If the painting of the picture that you have made in our name corresponds to your fame, as we hope, we shall remain pleased with you, and we pardon the injury that we have received by your tardiness. . . . consign it to Lorenzo da Pavia, who will give you the [balance of] twenty-five ducats. . . . We pray you to pack it in such a way that it can be carried easily and without danger." (ASM, Busta 2994, Libro 17, c. 29v, transcribed in Brown with Lorenzoni, *Isabella*, p. 167.)

49. 1505, 1 January. Letter from Pietro Bembo to Isabella d'Este: "Bellini . . . is very well disposed to serve Your Excellency as soon as the measurements or canvas is sent. It will be necessary that the invention that Your Excellency writes to me . . . be accommodated to the fantasy of him who has to paint it: . . . very precise terms do not suit his style, accustomed as he says always to roam at his will in paintings" ("Il Bellini . . . è ottimamente disposto a servire V. E. ogni volta che le siano mandate le misure o telaro. La invenzione che mi scrive V. S. che io truovi al disegno, bisognerà che l'accomodi alla fantasia di lui chel ha a fare: il quale ha piacere che molto signati termini non si diano al suo stile, uso come dice di sempre vagare a sua voglia nelle pitture." (Gaye, *Carteggio inedito*, 2:71–73.)

50. 1505, 27 August. Letter from Pietro Bembo to Isabella d'Este: "I have not forgotten my promise to do everything possible to get Giovanni Bellini to accept the commission for a painting for Your Excellency's camerino. . . . we [Bembo and another friend of Bellini] have given such battle that it seems the castle will cede. A warm letter from Your Excellency [to Bellini] . . . I am certain would not be written in vain." (Carlo D'Arco, *Delle arti e degli artefici di Mantova, Notizie raccolte ed illustrate con disegni e con documenti*, vol. 2 [Mantua, 1857], p. 60.)

51. 1505, 19 October. Letter from Isabella d'Este to Giovanni Bellini: "Messer Giovanni, However much our desire may have been to have a picture painted with a narrative ("historia") from your hand to place in our studio near those of your brother-in-law Mantegna, . . . we accept the *Nativity* in place of the narrative, . . . [the *Nativity*] pleases us very much, holding it as dear as any painting that we have. . . . [we pray] that you will agree to paint [another] painting, and we leave to you the responsibility of conceiving the poetic theme ("inventiva poetica")." (ASM, Busta 2294, c. 130, published by D'Arco, *Delle arti*, p. 60.)

52. 1506, 7 February. Letter from Albrecht Dürer in Venice to Wilibald Pirckheimer in Nuremberg: "I have many good friends among the Italians who want me not to eat and drink with their painters, for many of them are my enemies and copy my work in the churches and wherever they can find it; afterwards they criticise it and claim that it is not done in the antique style and say it is not good, but Giambellin has praised me highly to many gentlemen. He would willingly have something of mine, and came himself to me and asked me to do something for him, and said he would pay well for it, and everyone tells me what an upright man he is, so that I am really friendly with him. He is very old and yet he is the best painter of all." (Translated by Roger Fry, *Records of Journeys to Venice and the Low Countries*, The Humanist's Library, ed. Lewis Einstein, vol. 6 [Boston, 1913], p. 6.)

53. 1506, 7 February (1505, m.v.). Testament of Jacomo Dolfin (fig. 132). (See chap. 2, at n. 75.)

54. 1506, 13 September. Death of Andrea Mantegna.

55. 1507, 18 February (1506, m.v.). Testament of Gentile Bellini. (ASV, Testamenti, Bernardo Cavanis, Busta 271, no. 307; see also app. 3, n. 1.)

56. 1507, 23 February. Gentile Bellini is buried, as recorded by Marino Sanuto: "I note today that Gentile Bellini, excellent painter, was buried at SS. Giovanni e Paolo; he had been sent to the father of the present Turkish sultan [Mehmet], by whom he was knighted. I've made a note of

this here because he is famous. He was . . . years old, and is survived by his brother Giovanni Bellini, who is the most excellent painter in Italy. Likewise, Andrea Mantegna has died in recent months in Mantua" (*Diarii*, 6:552.)

57. 1507, 7 March. Giovanni Bellini agrees to complete his brother's painting for the Scuola Grande di San Marco and accepts the same contractual conditions as Gentile, with the understanding that he will have to deal with only one member of the confraternity, Marco Pelegrin, in matters regarding money and everything else. The members agree that Pelegrin is to see that the work is completed to his satisfaction: "Essendo manchà de questa vita messer Zentil Bellin nostro fradello et essendo romaxo el teller la principiado per la scuola non compido. . . . El dito messer Zuane [Bellini] e contento de conpirlo con quella medema condicion e pati havea fato el dito condam suo fradelo misser Zentil . . . dechiarando che el dito messer Zuane vuol che misser Marco Pelegrin sia quello habia a governar questa cossa e non voler haver a far con altri che con lui si de haverli danari come ogn'altra cossa. Onde misser Piero de Alberto e compagni mete la parte chel dito misser Marco Pelegrin habia ogni libertà de poder far el tuto zercha al conpir de dito teller come li parerà e piacerà." (ASV, Scuola Grande di San Marco, Not. 17, 1498–1530, c. 33; Molmenti, "Pittori Bellini," p. 233.)

58. 1507, 28 September. Giovanni Bellini is urged to complete "with his customary diligence" the three main paintings in the Sala del Maggior Consiglio, including one begun by Alvise Vivarini, *Otto Recommending Peace to His Father Frederick Barbarossa*, and two of Bellini's own compositions, one of which he had not yet begun. He is asked not to be so preoccupied with other obligations as he had been previously so that their project may be finished at last. Three other painters, including Carpaccio, are hired to assist him: "Essendo di non mediocre ornamento dela sala nostra da Gran Conseglio de ultimar tandem li tre quadri principiati de pictura, videlicet quello del quondam Alvixe Vivarin et li altri doi restano, uno dei qualli non è ancor principiato, siche poi compir si possino el resto de dicta sala che non resti pui impedita come fina hora è stato et che una volta dicta sala finita et expedita sia: come si convien alo ornamento di quella. . . . Havendossi etiam per questo effecto el fidelissimo citadin nostro Zuan Bellin per la obligation lui ha di usar ogni solita diligentia cum la solartia sua de imponer fine a simel opera deli prefati tre quadri dummodo habia in agiuto [aiuto] suo li infrascripti nominati pictori: . . . maistro Vector dicto Scarpaza [Carpaccio] . . . , maistro Vector quondam Mathio . . . et Hieronimo depentor." (ASV, Provveditori al Sal, Busta 6, vol. 4 [1413–1514], fols. 183v–184r; see also Lorenzi, *Monumenti*, p. 142.)

59. 1508, 10 December. Bellini heads an artists' arbitration commission to determine Giorgione's payment for the façade of the Fondaco dei Tedeschi, in consequence of Giorgione's complaint of 8 November (ASV, Notatorio dei Provveditori al Sal, Busta 62, no. 3, c. 123v). Also on the commission are Lazzaro Bastiani, Vittor Carpaccio, and Vittor di Matteo (who assisted Bellini in the Sala del Maggior Consiglio): "Ser Lazaro Bastian, ser Vettor Scarpaza, et ser Vethor di Mathio, per nominati da ser Zuan Belin, depintori constituidi ala presentia dì magnifici s[ignori] m[essier] Caroso da Cha da Pesaro, messier Zuan Zentani, messier Marin Griti, et messier Aluvise Sanudo, dignissimi provedadori al Sal, come deputadi ellecti dipentori a veder quello pol valer la pictura facta sopra la faza davanti del fontego di Todeschi, et fatta per maistro Zorzi da Castelfranco, et zurati dachordo dixeno a juditio et parer suo meritar el dicto maistro per dicta pictura ducati cento et cinquanta intuto." (ASV, Notatorio dei Provveditori al Sal, Busta 63, c. 95r; cf. Ruggero Maschio, "Per Giorgione: Una verifica dei documenti d'archivio," *Antichità viva* 17, nos. 4–5 [1978]: 5–11, who published the sources with some minor errors and with incorrect archival references.)

60. 1511. Giovanni and Nicolò Bellini sell their father's antique bust of Plato to Isabella d'Este. (Brown, "Testa de Platone antica," and Brown with A. M. Lorenzoni, "The Grotta of Isabella d'Este, II," *Gazette des Beaux-Arts* 97 [1978]: 77.)

61. 1513, 31 May. Letter addressed by Titian to the Council of Ten requesting the privilege of working in the Great Council Hall with the same "conditions, obligations, and exemptions as misser Giovanni Bellini," and two boys to assist him, "cum i modi, condition, obligation, et exemption ha misser Zuan Bellini, et do zoveni che voio tuor apresso de mi." (ASV, Consiglio de' Dieci, Misto, Registro 35, fol. 103v–104r [new fols. 236v–237r]).

62. 1514, 14 November. Alfonso d'Este sends a final payment of eighty-five gold ducats to Giovanni Bellini for the *Feast of the Gods* (figs. 175, 176). (Campori, "Tiziano," p. 581. Professor John Shearman has reexamined the document, which is ASE, Camera Ducale, Libri camerali diversi 249, fol. 140. I thank him for most generously sharing this information with me before the publication of his article on Raphael and Alfonso d'Este.)

63. 1515, 27 February (1514, m.v.). An assistant working with Giovanni Bellini in the Sala del Maggior Consiglio is to be paid eight ducats. (ASV, Provveditori al Sal, Busta 60, fol. 176v.)

64. 1515, 4–5 July. Convention between Bellini and the Scuola Grande di San Marco: "de far uno teller de tella sopra el qual se die far depenzer una historia de misser S. Marco, come essendo in Alexandria el ditto fo strassinato per terra da quelli mori infideli. El qual teller die esser sopra la porta de Albergo grando tra uno muro et l'altro per mezo l'altro teller depento che se trova sopra la bancha dove stano el vardian et compagni. El qual teller die esser fatto per el dito messer Zuan Belin cum i patti, tempi, pretio, et condition infrascritti, et primo: Dieno el ditto vardian et compagni dar al ditto messer Zuanne le telle andarano a far el ditto teller a spexe dela scuola. Sia etiam obligato el ditto meser Zuane depenzer suso el ditto teller la historia soprascritta, cum suo casamenti, figure, animali, et tutto quello achadera a tutte sue spese. . . . si de colori, come de ogni altra cosa in tutta perfection, come se convien a quel luogo, et come rechiede la excellentia dela virtù del ditto messer Zuanne, meiorando el teller che se trova al incontro el qual fece messer Zentil suo fradello. Promettemo [il guardian e compagni] dar al ditto messer Zuanne per sua merce de depenzer el sopra scritto teller quel medemo pretio have messer Zentil soprascritto, cum queli medemi modi et patti have ditto messer Zentil. Se obliga el ditto messer Zuanne dar compido el ditto teller a tutta perfection in tanto tempo quanto dete, el soprascritto messer Zentil el sopraniminato teller cum queli modi precisi. Siano obligati i soprascritti vardian et compagni dar al ditto messer Zuanne de presenti per capara del soprascritto lavor fatto sara el teller ducati 10 de contadi. Siano anchora obligati i soprascritti . . . dar al ditto messer Zuanne de tempo in tempo danari segondo esso messer Zuanne lavorara. El qual lavor deba de tempo in tempo el ditto vardian et . . . messer Andrea provededor . . . andar a vedar et secondo el proceder del lavor tanto dar al ditto messer Zuanne. . . . come per parte presa in capitolo zeneral appar . . . 1515 adì 4 luio. [Signed] Io Vettor Ziliol, vardian grando . . . , Io Andrea Ruzier, provedador . . . , Io Zuan Belin son contento de quanto è soprascritto." Giovanni acknowledged payment of the ten ducats one day later: "1515 adì 5 luio—Recevi mi Zuan Belin da meser Vetor Ziliol . . . ducati diese . . . per parte del lavor soprascrito." (ASV, Scuola Grande di San Marco, Registro 17, fol. 60; see also app. 3, with a partial translation of this document at n. 9.)

65. 1516, 15 January (1515, m.v.). Letter from Gaspare a Vidua to Giovanni Badoer regarding Giovanni Bellini's *Madonna* for the sister of the king of France. (See chap. 1, at nn. 102–3, 129.)

66. 1516, 30 January. *Liber Consiliorum* of the Dominican convent of SS. Giovanni e Paolo: the chapter votes to lend a silver crown to Bellini. (ASV, SS. Giovanni e Paolo, Busta 11, vol. C, fol. 77v.)

67. 1516, 29 November. Marino Sanuto records the artist's death: "One heard this morning Giovanni Bellini, the excellent painter, is dead. He was . . . years old; his fame is known throughout the world, and old though he was, he painted excellently. He was interred at SS. Giovanni e Paolo in his tomb, where his brother Gentile Bellini, likewise an excellent painter, is also buried" ("Se intese questa matina esser morto Zuan Belin optimo pytor, havia anni . . . la cui fama è nota per il mondo, et cussi vechio come l'era, dipenzeva per excellentia. Fu sepulto a San Zane Polo in la soa arca, dove *etiam* è sepulto Zentil Belin suo fradelo *etiam* optimo pytor"). (*Diarii*, 23: 256.)

68. Description of Bellini's family tomb, located in the cemetary of the Scuola di Sant'Orsola behind the apse of SS. Giovanni e Paolo, which he and his kinsman Gabriele Giorgio had purchased from the Abbati family: "Sepultura Domini Gabrielii Georgii, et Domini Joannii Bellini pictori excellentissimi alias esse solebat D. Pauli, et Antonii Abbati est in cimiterio Sancte Ursule ad instar capse muro cappelle S. Ursule affixa iuxta sepulturam D. Fantini Lauredano in parte meridionali estque insignita tali Epitaphio, in fronte sepulture, et sub Epitaphio habet insigne cum sex pillii [Sepultura de Polo et Antonio Abbati / Fradelli et di so heredi]." (*Iscrizioni sepolcrali, ed altre, nelle chiese di Venezia*, Venice, Biblioteca Correr, MS Gradenigo 201, vol. 1, fol. 120r. Professor William Barcham kindly brought this manuscript to my attention. See also Rodolfo Gallo, which includes the tomb inscription ["Scuola di S. Orsola," p. 20]. Bellini probably purchased the tomb at the time of Gentile's death, and Gentile was buried there, as Sanuto noted [see no. 67].)

69. 1521, 17 May. Will of Elena Trevisan, bequeathing her painting of *Christ* by Giovanni Bellini. (See chap. 1 at n. 98.)

70. 1524. Giovanni Capello is interred at San Zaccaria, and his altar is decorated with a *Circumcision* by Bellini (cf. fig. 135). (See chap. 2 at nn. 77–78.)

71. 1528, 16 May. Codicil of the will of Jeronimo Hollivier, bequeathing his *Madonna* by Bellini to the Madonna dell'Orto. (See chap. 1 at nn. 85–87.)

[1531, 22 January (1530, m.v.). Will of Marieta, widow of Vittore Belliniano, who had completed Bellini's *Martyrdom of Saint Mark* (fig. 185) in 1526. (ASV, Testamenti, Gerolamo Canal, Busta 191, no. 472.)]

[1548, 18 March. Testament of Maria, widow of Giovanni Bellini of San Stae: this Maria was the widow of another man by the same name as the painter. (ASV, Testamenti Giacomo De Raspi, Busta 835, no. 287.)]

# Appendix 3
## The Scuola Grande di San Marco

The obvious degree of studio participation in many late works signed by Bellini or from his shop demonstrates that his noble countrymen often had no more facility than foreign princes in extracting works from the old master. But one "patron" could claim Bellini's attention with a unique and undeniable authority, and that was his elder brother Gentile.

On 18 February 1507, dictating his will on his deathbed, Gentile enjoined Giovanni to complete the great work of decorating the Scuola Grande di San Marco for which he, Gentile, had contracted but would obviously be unable to achieve. Gentile had almost completed the first painting for the cycle, the *Preaching of Saint Mark in Alexandria* (fig. 184); only when Giovanni had finished it would he inherit their father's book of drawings. If Giovanni did not complete the painting, however, the drawing book was to remain part of Gentile's estate, to be administered by four commissaries: his widow, his "dearest brother," and two friends, confreres of the Scuola Grande di San Marco.[1]

Gentile had been associated with the scuola for decades, as had Jacopo Bellini before him, and his professional responsibility toward his confreres clearly meant a great deal to him.[2] Giovanni Bellini himself had also signed an agreement with the confraternity, in 1470, but it seems that he never fulfilled this obligation, though he served the scuola in other ways. Twenty-two years later, in 1492, with his brother, Giovanni had agreed to paint the entire Saint Mark cycle for the scuola, in memory of their father's earlier work there, which had been destroyed by fire in 1485, and with the understanding that no other painter would be employed on the project.[3] But Giovanni had done little or nothing for the cycle: perhaps, therefore, Gentile had good reason to be concerned. With the promise of Jacopo's drawings as reward, however, Giovanni did fulfill his brother's last wish and the obligation to their confraternity.

Gentile Bellini was buried on 23 February. Within two weeks, on 7 March, Giovanni Bellini signed an agreement with the scuola: "Because our confrere, messer Gentile Bellini, has died, and because the canvas mural he had begun for the scuola is unfinished . . . the said messer Giovanni [Bellini] is content to complete it with the same conditions and agreements to which his late brother messer Gentile had agreed." The only noted addition to the previous agreement was that Giovanni specified that he would deal only with one member of the scuola, a friend of the Bellini brothers, Marco Pelegrin.[4] Bellini's agreement with the scuola assured him of the same rights (as well as obligations) as his brother had had, including, it seems, some discretion regarding the subject of his mural and its interpretation.

Gentile had presumably been working on the *Preaching of Saint Mark in Alexandria* since 1504, the date of his agreement, and certainly the composition and much of the execution are his. By 9 March 1505, the work was well underway, and Gentile presented a design for the next narrative, representing the saint's *Martyrdom*.[5] Even though the *Preaching* was near completion when Gentile died, however, the canvas reveals Giovanni's hand.[6] A luminous atmosphere pervades the scene, an Alexandria that evokes both the Piazza di San Marco and the saint's Scuola Grande, thus anticipating Mark's ultimate triumph. The setting was surely Gentile's idea, but this luminosity is quite unlike his more arid treatment of the similar composition for the Scuola Grande di San Giovanni Evangelista. The portraits of scuola members who witness Mark's sermon, moreover, clearly include many added by Giovanni after Gentile's death.[7] (The figure of Mark himself, however, is

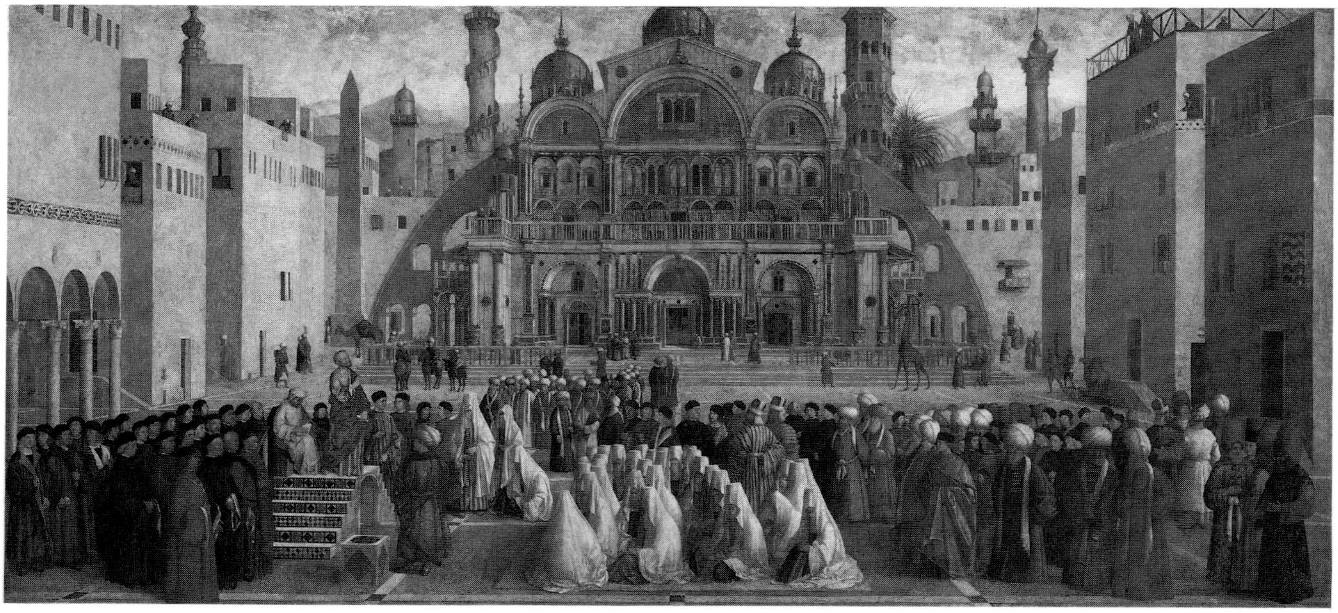

*184. Gentile and Giovanni Bellini,* Preaching of Saint Mark in Alexandria, *Pinacoteca di Brera, Milan. Photo: Scala/Art Resource, New York .*

largely a later repainting.) Painted with a livelier touch that endows the figures themselves with vivacity, these portraits are more convincingly conceived as volumes surrounded by light and air and are more believable portrayals of individuals of character and energy.

Having finished this composition, which Gentile had begun, Giovanni started the next narrative in the cycle, the *Martyrdom of Saint Mark*, which Giovanni himself did not live to complete (fig. 185). The only mural still in situ, on the entrance wall of the former albergo of the scuola (now the library of the Ospedale Civile), the work was signed and dated by Giovanni's follower Vittore Belliniano in 1526, ten years after the master's death (MDXXVI / VICTOR BELLINIANUS).[8] The *Saint Mark Preaching in Alexandria* was originally on the opposite wall, as Bellini's agreement with the scuola makes clear:

> [The painter is] to make a mural of canvas on which he will paint a story of Saint Mark: how the saint was dragged on the earth by those infidel Moors in Alexandria. Said mural is to be above the door of the large albergo between one [side] wall and the other, opposite the other mural painting which is found above the bench where the guardian and scuola officials sit [that is, the *Preaching*]. Said painting is to be made by the said messer Giovanni Bellini, with the agreements . . . described herein, and first of all, the said guardian and officers must provide the said messer Giovanni the canvases that are going to be used for the said mural canvas, at the expense of the scuola. The said messer Giovanni is likewise obligated to paint on the said mural canvas the narrative described above, with its buildings, figures, animals, and all that is necessary, all at his expense . . . colors, as all other things, of the highest quality, as is appropriate to this place, and as is required by the excellence of the virtue of the said messer Giovanni, surpassing the mural that is found opposite, which was made by his brother messer Gentile. . . . We [the guardian and officers] promise to give to the said messer Giovanni for his materials for painting the aforementioned mural that same price that the above-mentioned messer Gentile had, with the same modes and agreements that the said messer Gentile had.

The guardian and officers contracted to pay Bellini from "time to time" according to his progress on the work, and they stated their intention to "go to see from time to time" how he was proceding. Bellini received a modest initial payment of 10 ducats and signed the agreement: "I Giovanni Bellini am content with what is written above."[9]

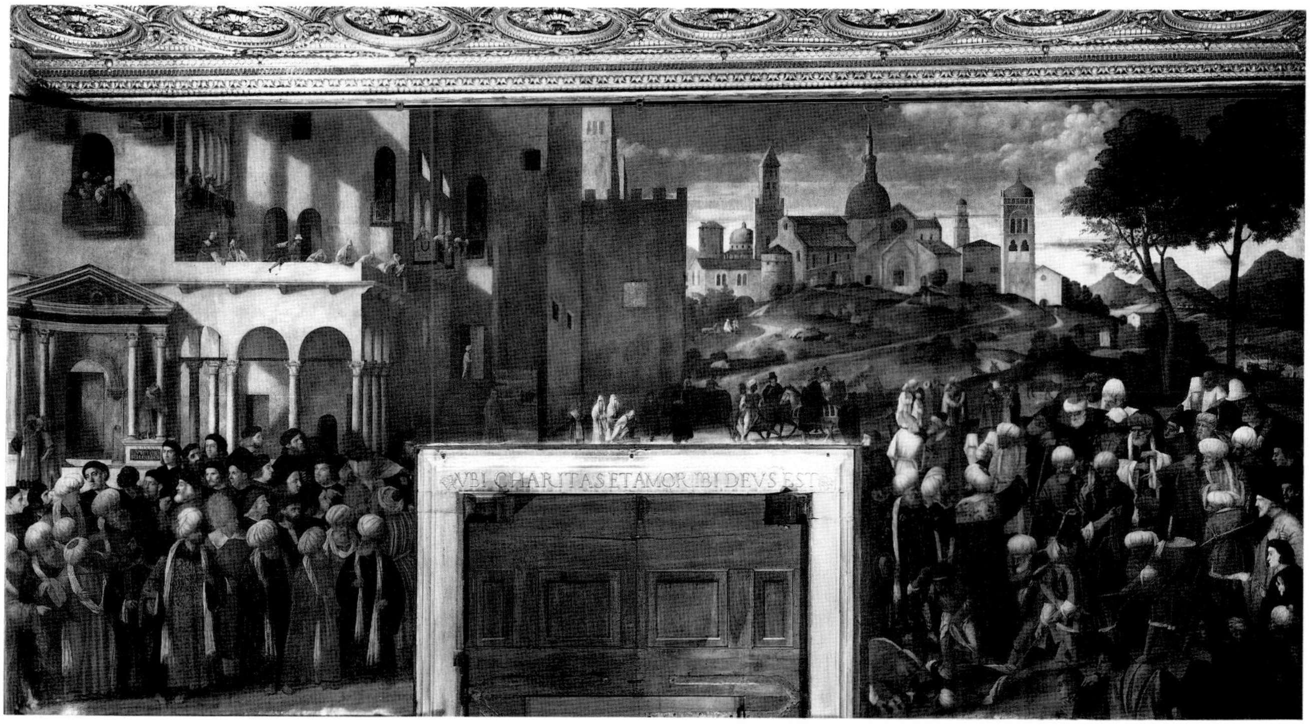


*185. Giovanni Bellini and Vittore Belliniano,* Martyrdom of Saint Mark, *Ospedale Civile, Venice (ex-Scuola Grande di San Marco, Albergo). Photo: Soprintendenza ai Beni Artistici e Storici, Venice.*

Even though the *Martyrdom* was not completed until 1526, Bellini conceived the composition, possibly with reference to the design that his brother had presented for the scuola's approval in 1505. It seems, however, that if he was consulting Gentile's project, Giovanni made considerable adjustments: none of the older man's scuola paintings resembles this one in its freedom of movement and in the importance of the landscape. I am convinced, moreover, that Giovanni painted much of the *Martyrdom* himself.[10] One may recognize Giovanni Bellini in the sunlight that bathes the buildings on the left and in the atmosphere that envelops the scene throughout the composition. In the rhythmic unification of the crowd, far more energetic and imaginative than the static tableaux of his brother (or of other scuola painters), one sees Giovanni's mind at work, reinventing the old formula and charging it with new drama. Similarly, in some (certainly not all) of the portraits included in the crowd at the left, and among some of the hostile crowd at the right, one finds the visual and psychological vigor and specificity characteristic of Giovanni Bellini, qualities far beyond the capabilities of Vittore Belliniano. The handling of drapery is sometimes very close to that of the *Feast of the Gods* (figs. 175, 176) and the *Derision of Noah* (fig. 180). This important painting deserves recognition as one of Bellini's most significant late works, for all that he did not live to complete it.[11]

# Appendix 4
## Attributions and Other Dilemmas

### Disputed Attributions

Although the Correr *Transfiguration* (fig. 9), originally measuring approximately 1.5 meters in height, is large compared to Bellini's other early works, it is not monumental: the small forms throughout the painting belie the composition's actual dimensions. Bellini's first monumental work in both scale and character seems to have been the polyptych for the Scuola di San Vincenzo Ferrer in the Dominican church of SS. Giovanni e Paolo (fig. 186)—but the attribution and date are problematic.[1] Here the three main panels, which represent the titular saint of the altar flanked by Saints Christopher and Sebastian, measure 1.67 meters high, and each figure fills the height of his picture field. It is the very size and scale of the images—combined with their poor condition—that accounts in large part for the harshness of the style compared with other early works by Bellini.

The central panel depicts the great Spanish preacher Vincent Ferrer, who had died in 1419 and was canonized in 1455 by Callistus III (the same pope who recognized the feast of the Transfiguration). Vincent had been venerated as a saint by his confreres and followers well before 1455, however, both in hopeful anticipation of his canonization and as a means in itself of promoting that end.[2]

According to the *mariegola,* or rule book, of the Venetian Scuola di San Vincenzo, the confraternity was established already in 1450, five years before the saint's canonization, and the scuola had already dedicated an altar to Saint Vincent Ferrer in SS. Giovanni e Paolo.[3] Moreover, records beginning in 1453 document the purchase of wood to build (or rebuild?) the saint's altar, which was already complete by 1454.[4] These indications of a date in the mid-1450s are consistent with the canonization of the saint in 1455: rather than waiting a decade after the canonization to honor the new saint, as has been argued, more likely the Dominicans of SS. Giovanni e Paolo and the members of the confraternity of Vincent Ferrer anticipated the pope's official action.[5]

Did this altar have an altarpiece, and if so, is it the polyptych seen there today? Who painted it? And when? In other words, if it is by Bellini, is the polyptych contemporary with the Correr *Transfiguration* (fig. 9), or does it postdate the London *Agony in the Garden* (fig. 73)? The choice of colors in the *Transfiguration* may be compared to the palette of the Saint Vincent altarpiece, and when one takes into account the notable difference of scale between these works, the resemblances seem closer still, in the use of gold striations, for example. The polyptych is of uneven quality, and it may be that the altarpiece is so confusing to art historians (including the writer) because it is a pastiche. But the main panels seem to be essentially by Bellini in the mid-1450s and are remarkably inventive, if not so fine in their execution as one might expect or wish.

*186. Giovanni Bellini and assistants, polyptych of Saint Vincent Ferrer, SS. Giovanni e Paolo, Venice. Photo: Osvaldo Böhm, Venice.*

This altarpiece is among the earliest images of Vincent, and it is entirely possible that one of the older confreres of SS. Giovanni e Paolo knew the saint and that his appearance was part of "living memory."[6] In any case, Bellini's portrayal of him has portraitlike specificity, though it is not a portrait per se but was intended rather to be taken for a likeness in much the same way as Paolo Uccello's *Sir John Hawkwood*, painted almost twenty

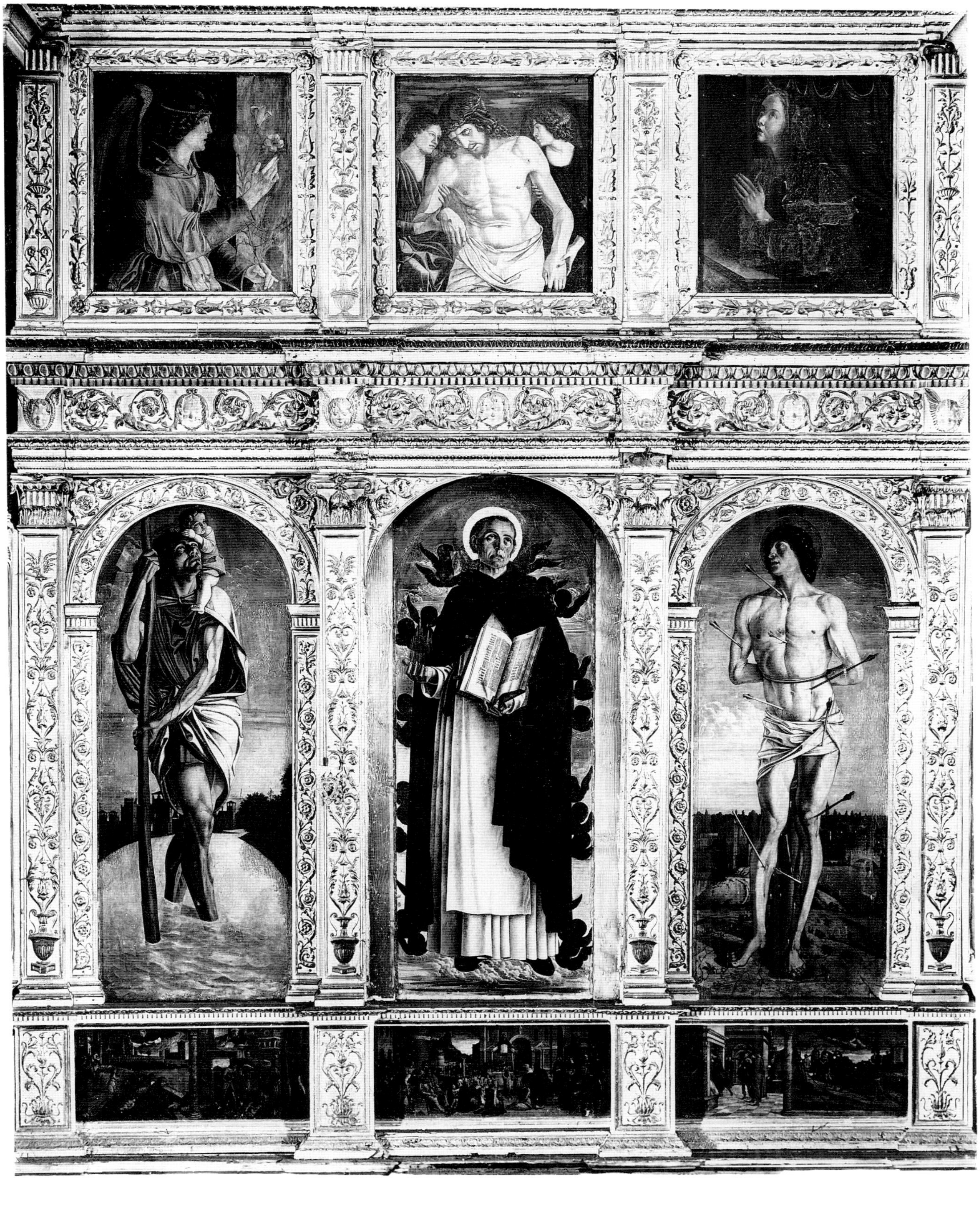

years earlier, or Andrea del Verrocchio's *Colleoni*, completed at the end of the century. This portraitlike treatment of Vincent may in turn have influenced the conception of the flanking saints, whose physiognomies are also idiosyncratic, unlike their more idealized counterparts in other works by Bellini. The Sebastian, to Vincent's right, is particularly unlike later characterizations of him in Bellini's art, and very close to Mantegna both physically (the sharp modeling) and emotionally (figs.7, 75, 79, 110).

The Saint Christopher represents a noteworthy innovation in Renaissance art, one of the first depictions of the *figura serpentinata*, as Craig Hugh Smyth has remarked.[7] The way in which the Infant clings to Christopher, moreover, anticipates Bellini's treatment of the same figures in his San Giovanni Crisostomo altarpiece, signed in 1513, approximately sixty years later than the polyptych (fig. 139). If the SS. Giovanni e Paolo saints are not entirely by Bellini's hand, surely someone close to him was involved—perhaps even Jacopo or Gentile.

The three predella panels, which illustrate miracles of Saint Vincent Ferrer, are patently not by Bellini but by another artist. Such a division of labor was not uncommon: about ten years earlier, for example, Uccello received the commission for the predella (the *Miracle of the Host*) for the *Communion of the Apostles* altarpiece painted several years later by Joos van Ghent.[8] And according to Marcantonio Michiel, writing in the 1520s, Bellini himself shared a commission in this way on at least one other occasion: his lost altarpiece of John the Evangelist, painted for Santa Maria della Carità between 1468 and 1471, had a predella with scenes from the saint's life by the miniaturist Lauro Padovano.[9] The Carità altarpiece itself has been destroyed, but the predella may survive. This predella without a pala, representing episodes from the life of the Evangelist, is clearly by the same artist who painted the predella of Vincent Ferrer. If Michiel was correct and if the predella of the Evangelist is indeed part of Bellini's otherwise destroyed altarpiece for the Carità, then we can identify the artist of both predellas as Lauro Padovano. Given that the altarpiece of the Evangelist was painted between 1468 and 1471, then either the predella of Vincent Ferrer, very similar in style, is a work of approximately the same date, or the style of Lauro Padovano, a pedestrian illustrator, did not change much in the course of a decade or more. To be sure, the Saint John predella panels may have formed part of another work, unrelated to Bellini's lost altarpiece of the Evangelist. It is possible, moreover, that the Vincent predella was added to the altarpiece after the main panels had been painted, and the disparity of styles in the pala may thus be related to a disparity of date: the present frame of the altarpiece is not the original one, but demonstrably later, dating circa 1523;[10] at least one more panel (representing *God the Father*) was once part of the polyptych but has been lost; and it seems clear that the present combination of elements is a conglomeration of works by different masters, perhaps painted at different times. But Giovanni Bellini conceived the main panels of the saints and the upper panels in which Gabriel and the Annunciate Virgin flank the dead Christ supported by angels—all familiar Bellinesque types. Although Bellini had assistance or collaboration in the execution of this commission, the ideas are his.

The confusion surrounding this work will probably never be resolved; vast though the Venetian archives may be, they have not preserved all the answers, and certainly not all the answers to questions that probably did not trouble the members of the confraternity of Saint Vincent as they bedevil us today. Nonetheless, in spite of the uncertainty about its history, the altarpiece in SS. Giovanni e Paolo illustrates something of Bellini's extraordinary process of growth.

Bellini's altarpiece of John the Evangelist, formerly in the church of the Carità, is the only work for the Carità associated with the master's name in Renaissance sources. It is a serious loss: this documented work was the missing link in the reconstructed chain of accomplishments between Bellini's *Transfiguration* in the Correr (fig. 9), his first altarpiece, to Pesaro, his first triumph on the large scale (figs. 86–90). In place of the lost Carità altarpiece, we have four conundrums, four triptychs from the same church, which are undeniably works of collaboration and clearly not good enough to have been painted

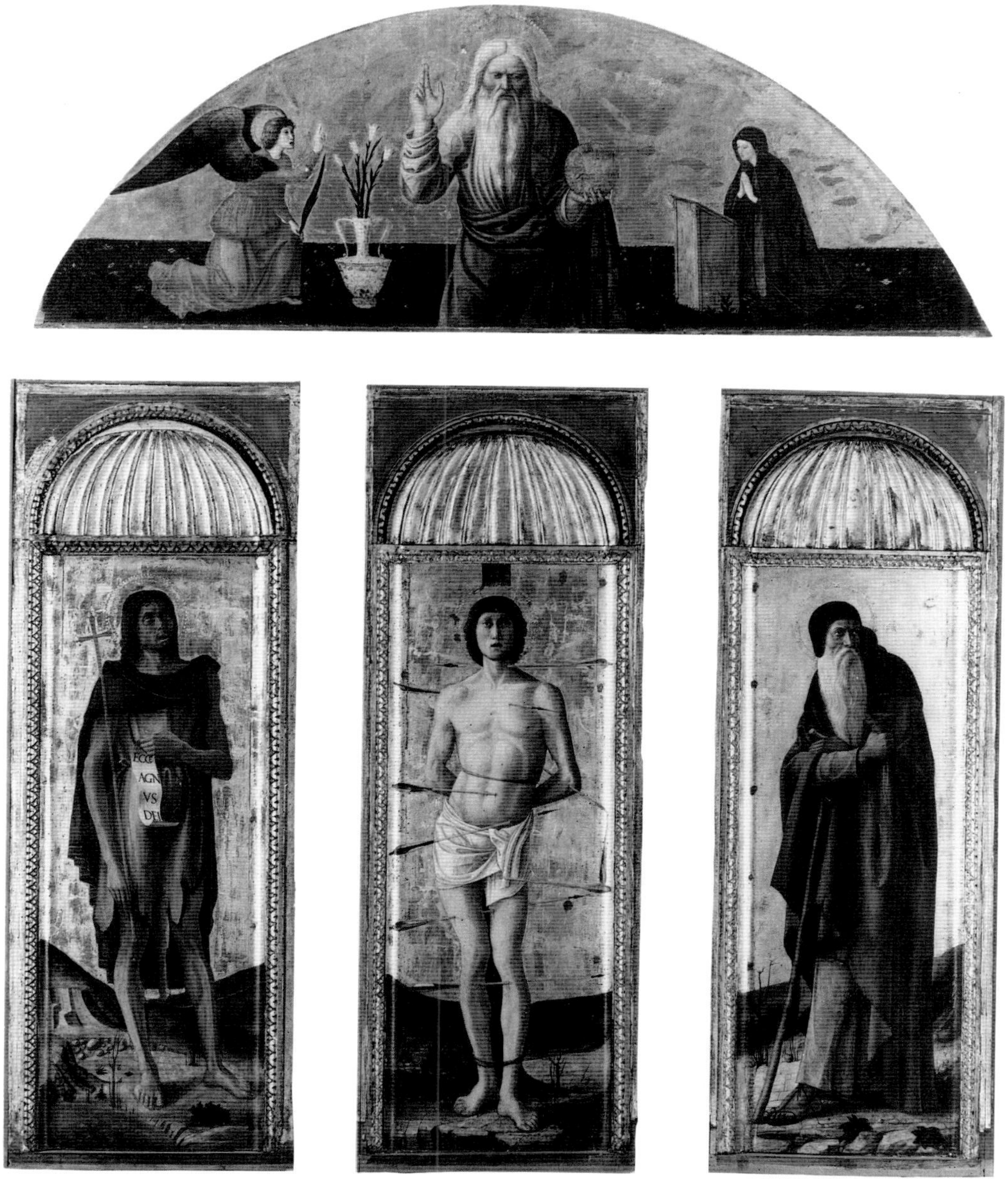

*187. Giovanni Bellini?,* Saint Anthony Abbot, *right wing, Carità triptych of Saint Sebastian; Gallerie dell'Accademia, Venice. Photo: Osvaldo Böhm, Venice.*

entirely by Giovanni Bellini or even under his direct supervision. But he may have been one of a group of collaborators, which surely included other artists in the Bellini family sphere of influence: presumably Jacopo himself was involved, perhaps also Gentile, and undeniably others, nameless and second-rate associates of these men.[11] The most powerful figures of these four Carità triptychs are the *Saint Anthony Abbot* panel from the Saint Sebastian altarpiece (fig. 187) and the Donatellesque *Saint John the Baptist* from the Saint Lawrence triptych: if Giovanni Bellini is to be seen anywhere in these works it is in these panels, the best of a damaged lot. The *Baptist* has incised outlines, which seems anomalous in Bellini's work, but he may well have adjusted his manner and handling here (and perhaps in other parts of the altarpieces) to accommodate the styles of his collaborators.

## The *Supper at Emmaus*

The *Supper at Emmaus* in the crossing of San Salvador is almost certainly not the original of Bellini's much-repeated composition, as Sansovino thought; more likely, it is a version of the lost original known from an engraving by Pietro Monaco, inscribed "Ioannes Bellinus Pinxit MCCCCLXXXX" (figs. 188, 189).[12]

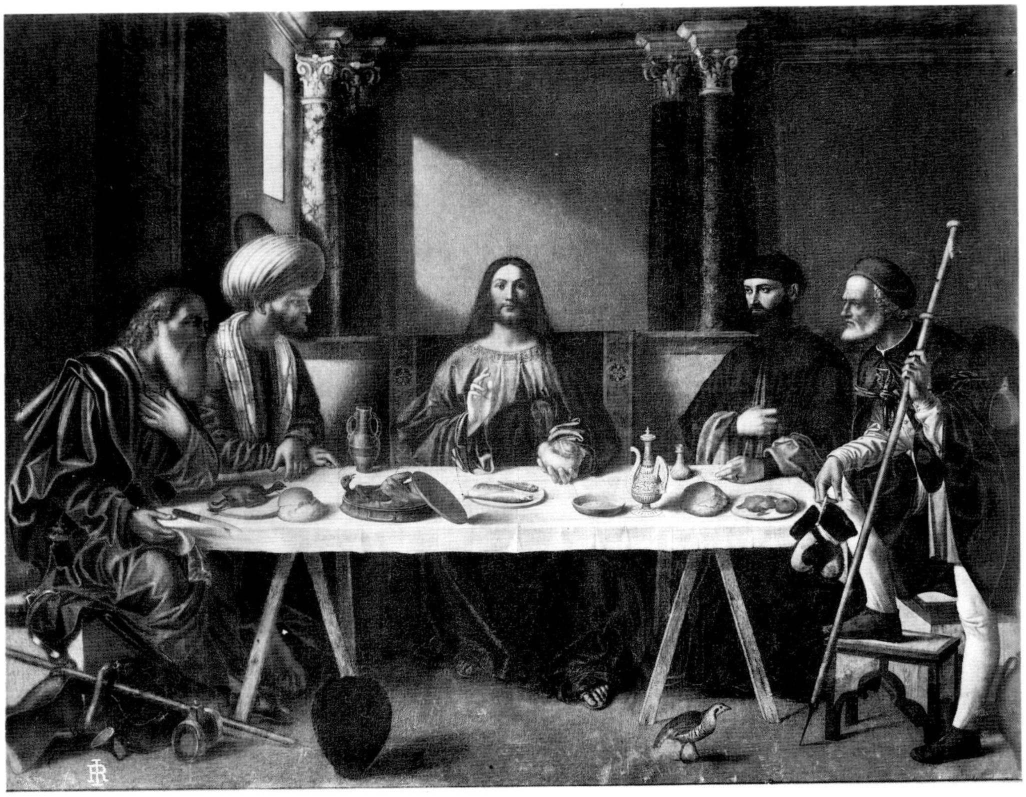

*188. Giovanni Bellini with assistance,* Supper at Emmaus, *San Salvatore, Venice. Photo: Osvaldo Böhm, Venice.*

Whether the canvas in San Salvador is partly by Bellini seems impossible to determine, given the poor condition of the work. Although this painting and the presumed "original" recorded in the engraving have some differences, the essentials of the composition are the same, and they merit attention, for this work was certainly one of Bellini's most innovative compositions.

Christ is seated in the center of the scene, frontal (the only frontal figure) and still. In type, he resembles the fragment from an altarpiece in the Accademia and the grand characterization of Christ in the Naples *Transfiguration*, albeit with a head smaller in proportion to the body (figs. 102–4). In the *Supper at Emmaus*, sunlight that floods into the scene from a window at the left creates a trapezoid of illumination on the wall behind Christ. A strong cast shadow in the engraving suggests that the painting it reproduced was similarly lighted. The pattern and effects of this light are carefully observed, but this seemingly natural light is a supernatural manifestation. Coming from Christ's proper right, from the side of Christ's blessing hand, the light is the means whereby Christ's companions recognize him. (This detail is changed in the engraving because of the reversal of direction which that technique entails.) The window from which the divine light enters the room where they gather is the only visible source of illumination in the painting, and yet it is clearly not the cause of the cast shadows that appear throughout. These are determined by another, natural light source, which also enters the room from the proper right, but from somewhere in front of the picture plane. The shadows that it causes fall diagonally and cannot be associated with the light from the window, which belongs to Christ alone.

Bellini himself had anticipated this dramatic treatment of light in his *Annunciation* canvases, made in the 1490s as organ covers or doors for the Madonna dell'Orto and executed primarily (or entirely) by an assistant (fig. 190).[13] Here light accompanies the Archangel Gabriel as he enters the Virgin's chamber. This light is more diffuse and hence naturalistic than Christ's illumination at Emmaus but nonetheless functions in much the same way, visually and symbolically, as a supernatural accoutrement of the angel's manifestation.

The room where Christ sits with his four companions at Emmaus, one of the more

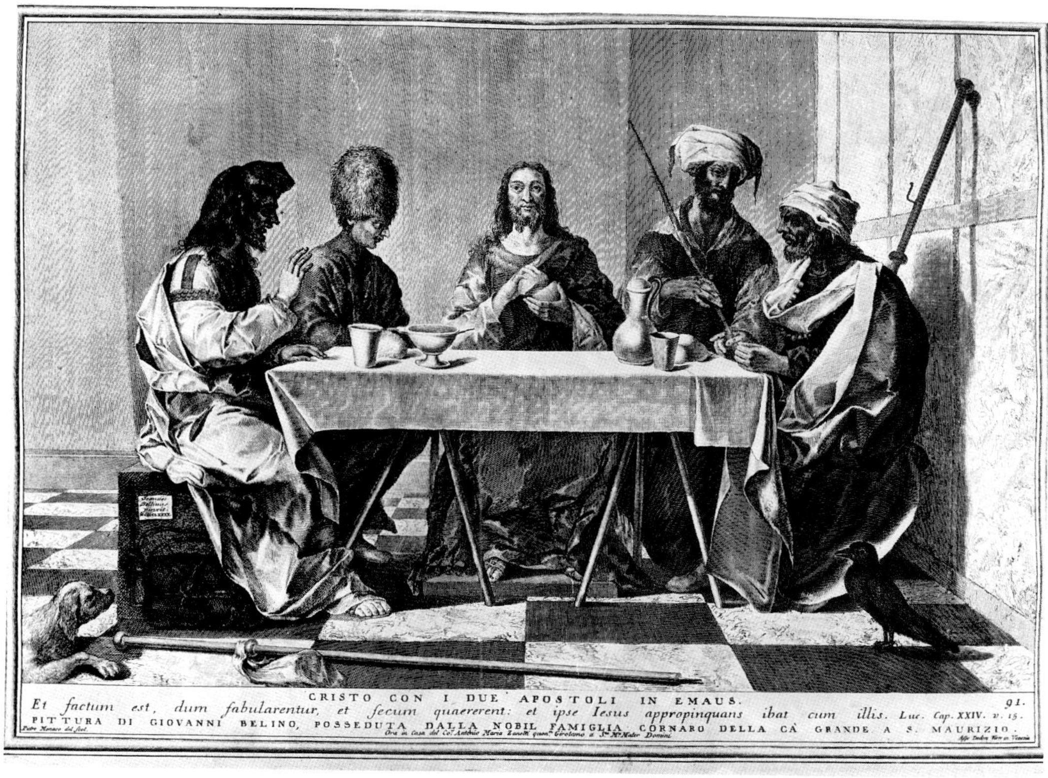


*189. Pietro Monaco after Giovanni Bellini,* Supper at Emmaus, *engraving, British Museum, London. Photo: Archivio Fotografico del Museo Correr, Milan.*

remarkable settings for a painting in the 1490s, was also anticipated by the elaborate architectural interior that Bellini had designed for the Annunciate Virgin. We are shown the left window wall of the inn at Emmaus, where the window is flanked left and right by paired columns with Corinthian capitals. Another pair punctuate the wall behind Christ, so that columns enframe him to either side: these make the setting symmetrical, echoing the Lord's frontal and central figure, even though the room itself—or what we see of it—is asymmetrical. A patterned carpet, rather like the cloths of honor that Bellini used in his Madonna paintings, hangs on a ledge behind Christ.

The carpet or cloth betokens Christ's kingship and sets him apart from his surroundings: he is both the focal point of the composition and the focus of everyone's attention, but at the same time he is isolated from the setting visually as he seems isolated psychologically, unaware of his companions. And yet the action that he performs is for their salvation. The two men at the left are evidently Cleopas and Simon, two of the disciples, who had met Christ on the road to Emmaus. Luke, the only evangelist to include the event in his Gospel, described their experience: "That very day two of them were going to . . . Emmaus . . . , and talking with each other about all these things that had happened. While they were talking and discussing together, Jesus himself drew near and went with them. But their eyes were kept from recognizing him" (Luke 24:13–35). Learning that it was his own death that they had been discussing and lamenting, Christ explained to them that this suffering had been necessary for him to "enter into his glory." At Emmaus, the three stopped to take dinner together, and "when he was at table with them," Luke continued, Jesus "took the bread and blessed, and broke it, and gave it to them. And their eyes were opened and they recognized him; and he vanished out of their sight" (Luke 24:30–31).

Bellini has depicted Christ blessing the bread, which he will share with the disciples, these first earthly recipients of the Eucharist after his death and Resurrection. At this moment, "their eyes were opened." Two other men witness the event, an old man dressed as a pilgrim with a walking staff and a younger man with a short dark beard, who is dressed in late fifteenth-century Venetian garb. This can only be a portrait, presumably of the donor. And here, by including the donor among the actors of the great biblical drama, Bellini

*190. Studio of Giovanni Bellini,* Archangel Gabriel *and* Annunciate Virgin, *Gallerie dell'Accademia, Venice. Photo: Soprintendenza ai Beni Artistici e Storici, Venice.*

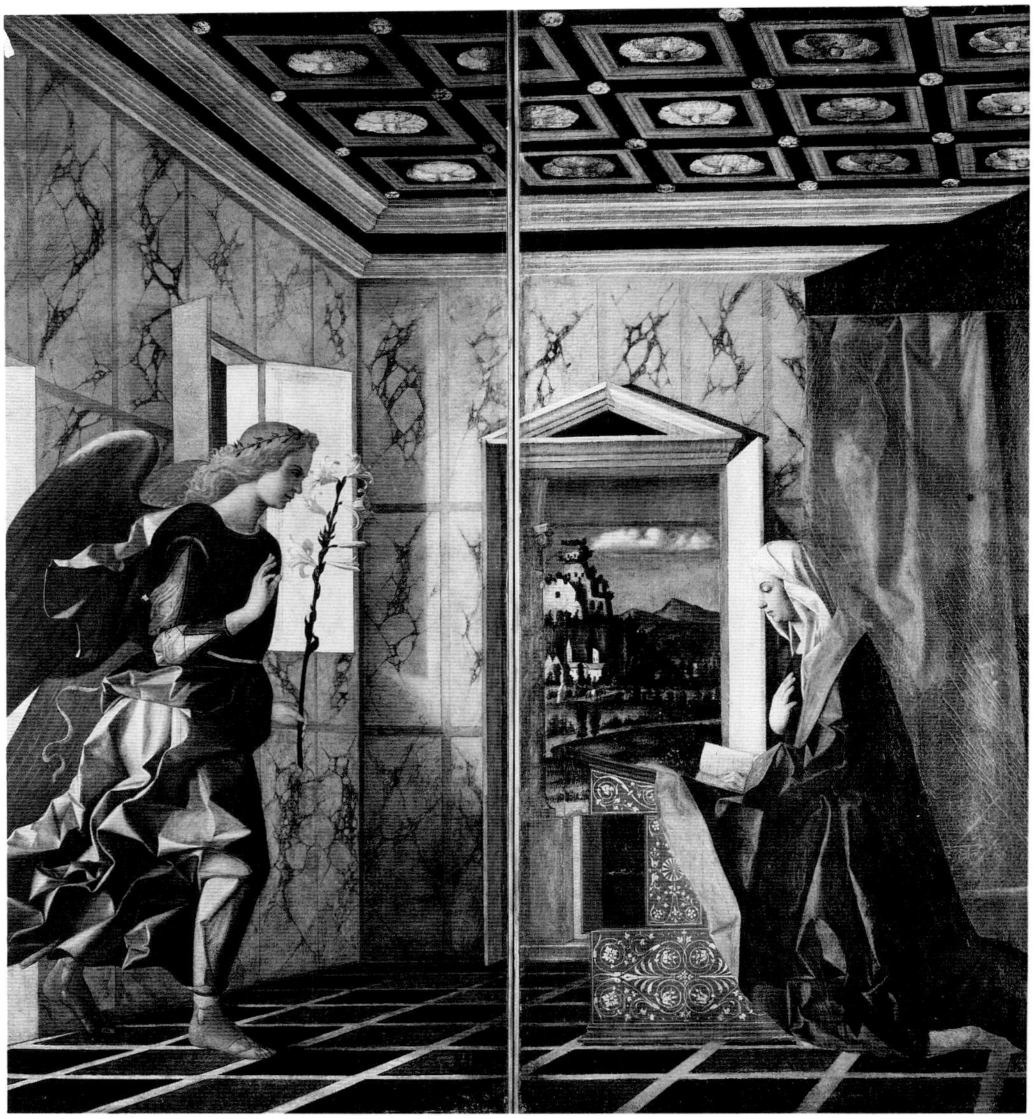

achieved another of his quiet revolutions. Although donors had already entered sacred narratives early in the fourteenth century, the context had been devotional and funerary. A notable example, and one undoubtedly known to Bellini, is the *Last Judgment* on the west wall of the Arena Chapel in Padua, which includes the figure of the patron, Enrico Scrovegni, kneeling before the Madonna to present a model of his funerary chapel.[14] Donors and their associates often join the train of the Magi in scenes of the Adoration, sometimes even impersonating the Three Wise Men. Innumerable examples of such donor portraits also populate the narrative paintings commissioned by the confraternities of Venice, though these often represent events in which contemporaries or figures from the recent past actually participated. Be that as it may, none of them is exactly comparable to Bellini's composition, which was a private commission originally displayed in a home: here only four witnesses flank the figure of Christ, and the donor is present at his side, as one of the first communicants at this eucharistic meal offered by the Lord himself. Perhaps that is why Bellini also included a quail, that familiar symbol of humility, on the pavement beneath the donor's feet—such daring may have required a symbolic "corrective." One precedent for this kind of donor portrait may be found in a work designed by Bellini, but painted with assistance. This is not a large-scale narrative painting, however, but a small half-length *Madonna and Child with Saints Paul and George*, the latter evidently a portrait of the donor (fig. 36). But in the *Supper at Emmaus*, the donor does not merely witness Christ's actions: he is the beneficiary. And that is quite remarkable.

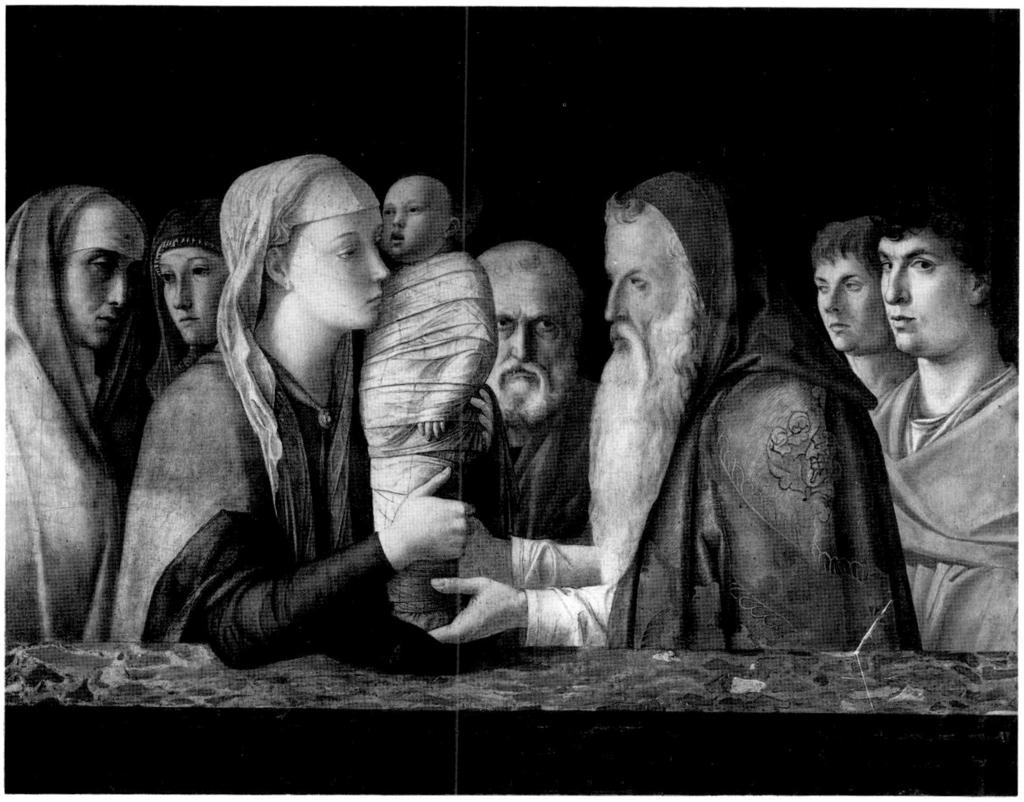

191. *Studio of Giovanni Bellini,* Presentation of the Christ Child in the Temple, *Museo Querini Stampalia, Venice. Photo: Archivio Fotografico del Museo Correr, Venice.*

## Giovanni Bellini and Andrea Mantegna

The artistic relationship between Bellini and Mantegna is problematic and vexing. The two artists were closest in the 1450s and early 1460s—that is, when Mantegna was still living in Padua and when Bellini may also have been employed there, working with his father and brother on the Gattamelata altarpiece. The same models inspired both Bellini and Mantegna, above all the art of classical antiquity and the sculpture of Donatello (fig. 8), and also, quite naturally, the work of Jacopo Bellini and of Squarcione, Mantegna's master. Such early works by Giovanni Bellini as the *Transfiguration* (fig. 9)—with an apocryphal monogram of Mantegna—and the *Dead Christ* (fig. 53), both in the Correr, come very close to Mantegna's art. But in two works of the late 1450s or early 1460s, the *Agony in the Garden* (fig. 73) and the *Pietà* in the Brera (fig. 49) Bellini seems to have declared his independence both from Mantegna and from the school of Padua.[15] The *Agony in the Garden*, so closely related to Mantegna's paintings of the same subject (the San Zeno predella and fig. 75), seems especially to represent a purposeful break with Bellini's first style. Thereafter, despite sometimes extraordinary variations in manner, he gave himself completely to the painting of ambient light—light as metaphor and light as substance. How, then, are we to explain Bellini's later Mantegnesque episodes?

Such paintings as Bellini's *Blessing Redeemer* (fig. 56), his *Saint Francis* (fig. 77), or the restello panel representing *Truth* (fig. 170) reveal his almost experimental interest in other styles, in these cases, the art of the Netherlands. Beginning in the 1460s, Bellini's use of oil and glazes demonstrates a concern much deeper than a taste for foreign motifs or figure types. Bellini's self-awareness as an artist, encapsulated in the form of his signature on the cartellino, also motivated his later approaches to Mantegna. However, whereas in his earlier works Bellini approximated both Mantegna's types and his sculptural style, in his later years the Venetian transformed his brother-in-law's art. That is, Bellini took Mantegna's compositions or formulas but not his style; he expressed these borrowed ideas in his own language. It is perhaps more to be expected that an artist's copy of another master's compositions is predicated on a stylistic sympathy between them; one may think

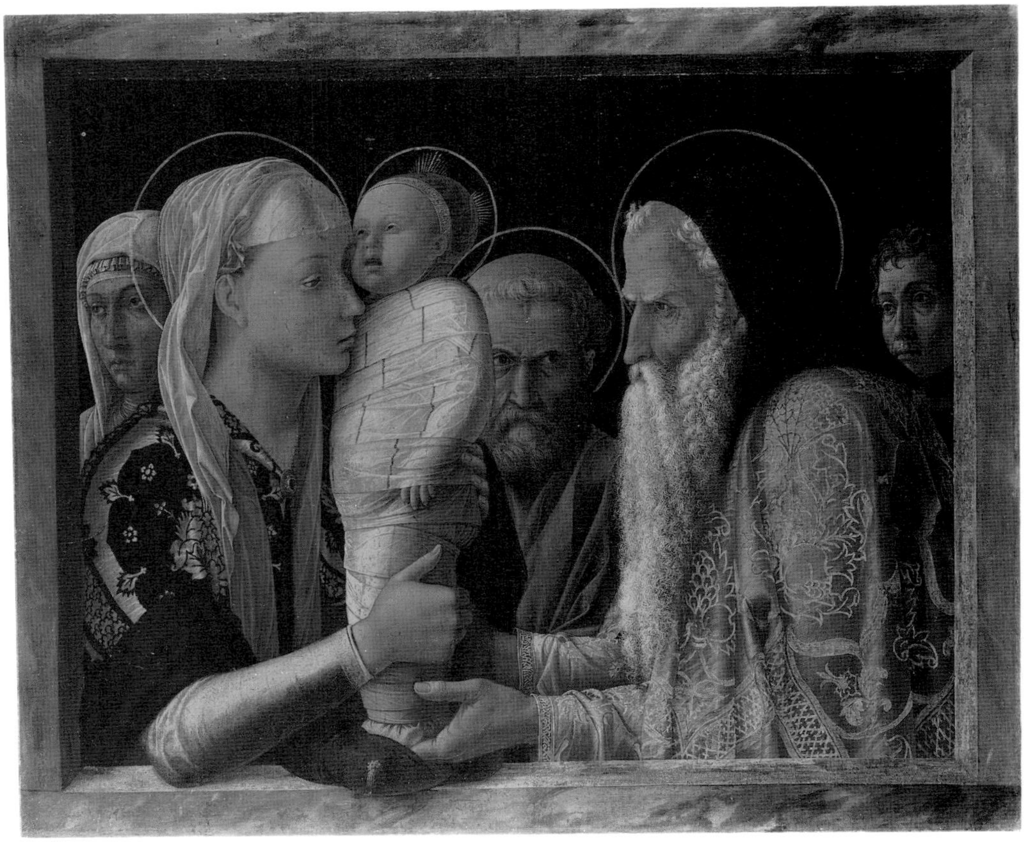

*192. Andrea Mantegna,* Presentation of the Christ Child in the Temple, *Gemäldegalerie, Staatliche Museen Preussischer Kulturbesitz, Berlin (West). Photo: Jörg P. Anders.*

of Rubens's copying Titian, for example, or Michelangelo's borrowings from Quercia. But for Bellini, on several occasions, copying Mantegna seems to have been a means whereby the younger master challenged his kinsman, purposefully putting forward his own stylistic solution to identical compositional and narrative problems. The first such work is the *Agony in the Garden* (fig. 73), and the last is the *Continence of Scipio* (fig. 174).

In one regard, the most significant of these Bellinesque versions of Mantegna seems to be the unfinished *Presentation of the Christ Child in the Temple*, which is probably a work of the mid-1460s (figs. 191, 192). However, the relationship of the two paintings is unclear. Moreover, the Venetian work, while undeniably Bellinesque, is in fact unworthy of him, an inferior, albeit photogenic, painting. The drawing of Christ's right cheek and of Mary's right eye is distorted, and the shadowing of Mary's head is impossibly crude for Bellini. Incised lines in these and other figures, unexpected and perhaps nonexistent in Bellini's autograph work, may be related to the fact that the *Presentation* is a copy—perhaps even a copy of a lost copy by Bellini after Mantegna. Nonetheless, even if I am correct in removing the panel from his oeuvre (a decision that I expect will be unpopular and debated), the fact remains that it illustrates yet another Bellinesque translation of a composition by Mantegna, perhaps more important for the idea involved—the use of the half-length format for a narrative scene—than in itself.[16] And this idea, which Bellini and his studio exploited in numerous compositions of such subjects as the *Circumcision* (fig. 135), may have been introduced to Italian art by his father. Jacopo Bellini's half-length *Lamentation* in the Louvre drawing book is an example dating from the 1450s (cf. fig. 136).[17] But what is the date of Mantegna's *Presentation*?

It has been argued that Mantegna painted this picture circa 1455 as a votive offering after his wife, Nicolosia Bellini, survived the difficult birth of one of their children (fig. 192).[18] The two witnesses of the *Presentation* are supposed to be Mantegna and Nicolosia, but these identifications seem unlikely. There is no evidence regarding the appearance of Nicolosia, and undisputed portraits of Mantegna himself (in the Camera degli Sposi and in the artist's funerary chapel in Sant'Andrea, Mantua) both show a face with markedly thinner

*193.* Descent of Christ into Limbo, *City of Bristol Museum Art Gallery.*

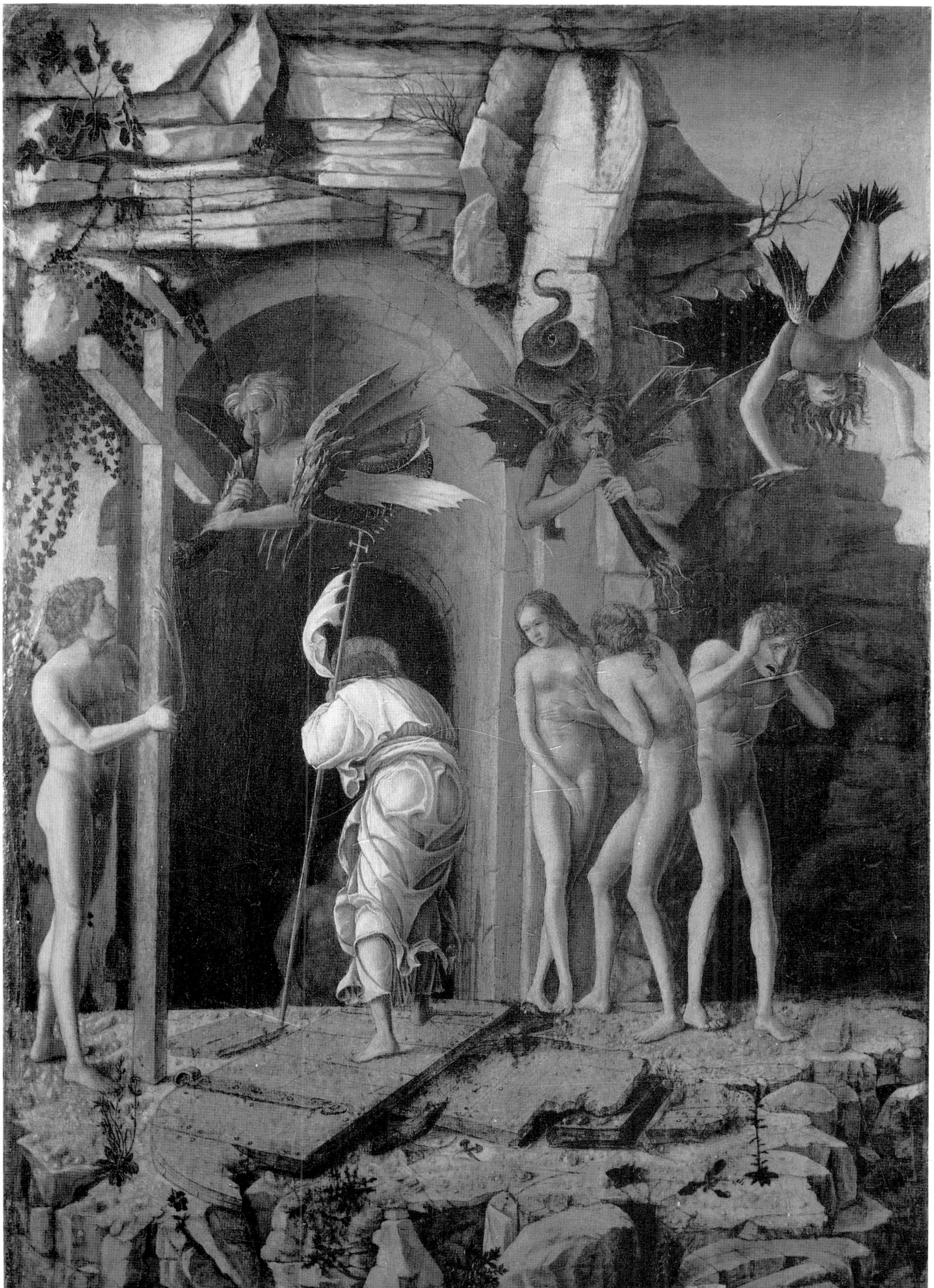

lips and a differently shaped nose. If the painting is detached from these dubious iconographic moorings, its date becomes open to debate. The *Presentation* may in fact be a work of the 1460s, but in any case, it is undeniably a masterpiece by Mantegna, whereas the Bellinesque version is a very inferior work. For this reason, and also because of a long-standing art historical habit of seeing Mantegna as the innovator and Bellini as the follower, it has almost always been assumed that the Paduan's composition inspired the Venetian work. However, though certain elements are distinctly Mantegnesque, notably the forms of the Virgin's wimple and the type of the Christ Child, others seem more typical of Bellini, including the use of the dark ground (cf. fig. 47) and the figures of Joseph and the rabbi. These figures recur in such Bellinesque works as the monochrome *Lamentation* (fig. 136), the late *Presentation* in Vienna, and the drawing ascribed to Bellini in the Uffizi.[19] Moreover, the Bellinesque panel in Venice is considerably larger than Mantegna's canvas (105 × 80 cm. as opposed to 68.9 × 86.3 cm.) and includes two additional figures at left and right. Camesasca long ago argued that Mantegna's work was based on Bellini: this possibility should not be discounted, though I suspect that the original work has been lost.[20]

The most intriguing of Bellini's copies after Mantegna is the *Descent of Christ into Limbo*—indisputably a copy and indisputably an autograph work, which may be dated in the 1470s (figs. 193, 194).[21] Bellini's *Descent* is painted on vellum: in this regard it is the closest approximation we have of the master's work in miniature painting, documented by Zovenzoni's reference to his lost portrait in a manuscript dated 1474. This is the approximate date of the *Descent* as well; it comes between the Pesaro *Coronation* and the *Resurrection* painted for San Michele in Isola (figs. 86, 105). Mantegnesque engravings provided Bellini's source for the composition: and this in itself is significant, because such a model lacks those components most distinctive in Bellini's art: color and light. Perhaps it was for this reason that he determined to copy the work. Unfortunately, Bellini's painting has been mounted on wood and varnished, and this past mistreatment has obscured his palette and dulled the luminosity of the scene, which may be imagined by reference to his approximately contemporary predella panels in the *Coronation* altarpiece. The handling seems freer in the *Descent*, however, and the brush strokes at the edges of things are thinly applied so that contours are slightly blurred: Bellini's painterly translation of Mantegna's sculptural line.

The composition of the *Descent into Limbo* is related to two drawings, in the Lehman Collection in the Metropolitan Museum and in the Ecole des Beaux-Arts in Paris (fig. 195). The latter, which is in the same sense or direction as the engraving, and almost the same size, is generally considered to have been Bellini's immediate model because it shares certain features with his painting that are not found in the Mantegnesque print. For these reasons, Byam Shaw has argued for an attribution to Bellini and considers the drawing the artist's intermediate step between Mantegna's composition and the painting.[22] The drawing seems Bellinesque to me, with elements of Mantegna's style to be explained by the fact that it is a record of a work by that master. But the question is difficult, perhaps impossible to resolve. No drawing has been attributed to Giovanni Bellini without some dispute. And the argument often concerns the alternate possibility of an attribution to Mantegna.

This is as ironic as it is frustrating, considering that Giovanni Bellini's painting style is so different from Mantegna's even when they most closely approximate each other and that Bellini's career involved the production of numerous replicas and variants, which would seem to require the use of drawings as studio records. The one sheet that is most closely related to a painting by Bellini, however, the landscape drawing of the background scene of his *Resurrection* altarpiece, was produced after the fact—that is, as a record of the motif rather than as a preparatory study (figs. 105, 107). Moreover, the motif was repeated more outside Bellini's studio than within it. Paintings rather than drawings per se seem to have served Bellini's shop as records of compositions—the Uffizi *Lamentation* is evidently a case in point—and Giovanni Bellini himself often drew directly on the panel, perhaps without making any preliminary sketches on paper. Underdrawing is visible in

194. *After Andrea Mantegna,* Descent of Christ into Limbo, *engraving, Metropolitan Museum of Art, Gift of Philip Hofer, 1932.*

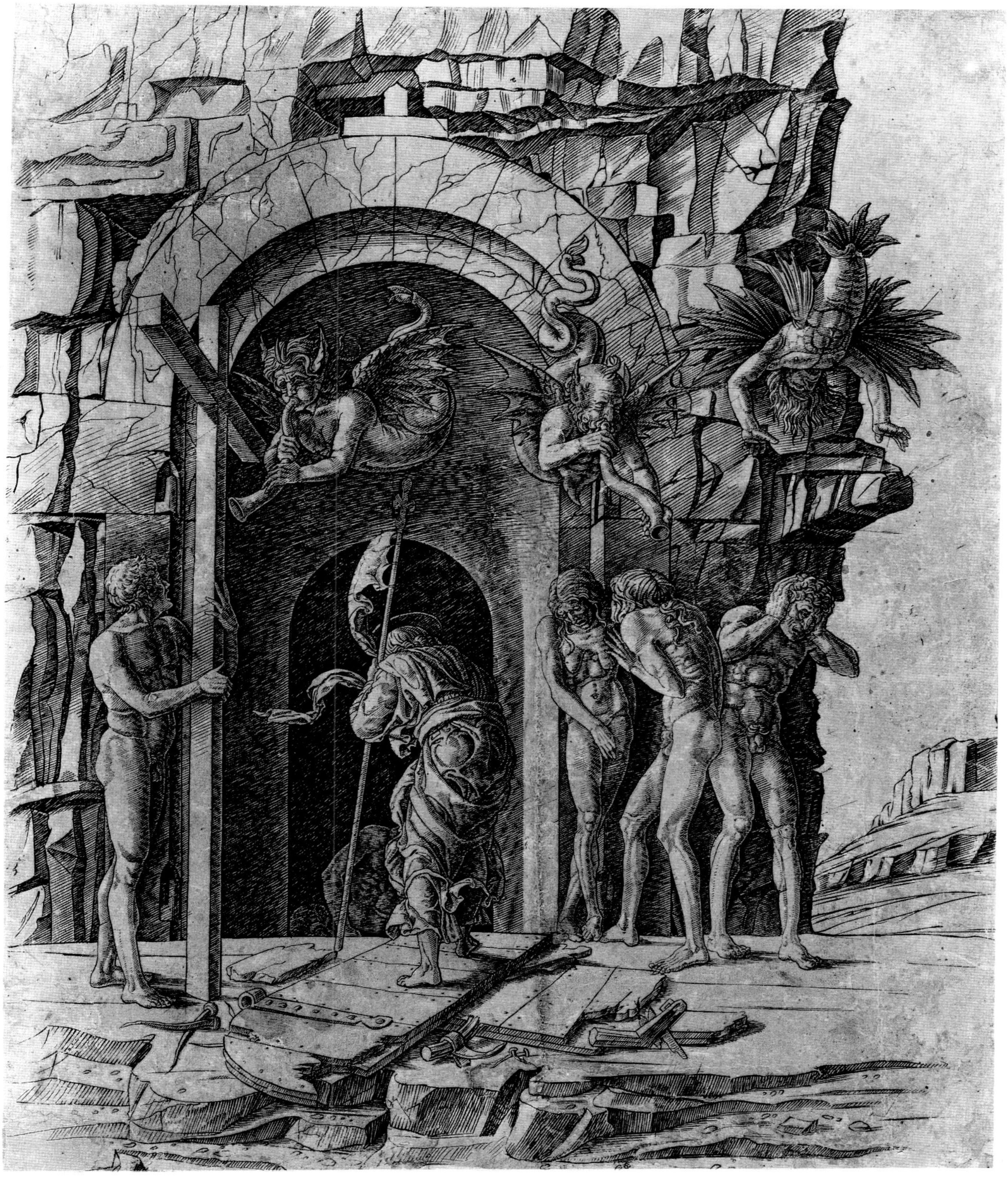

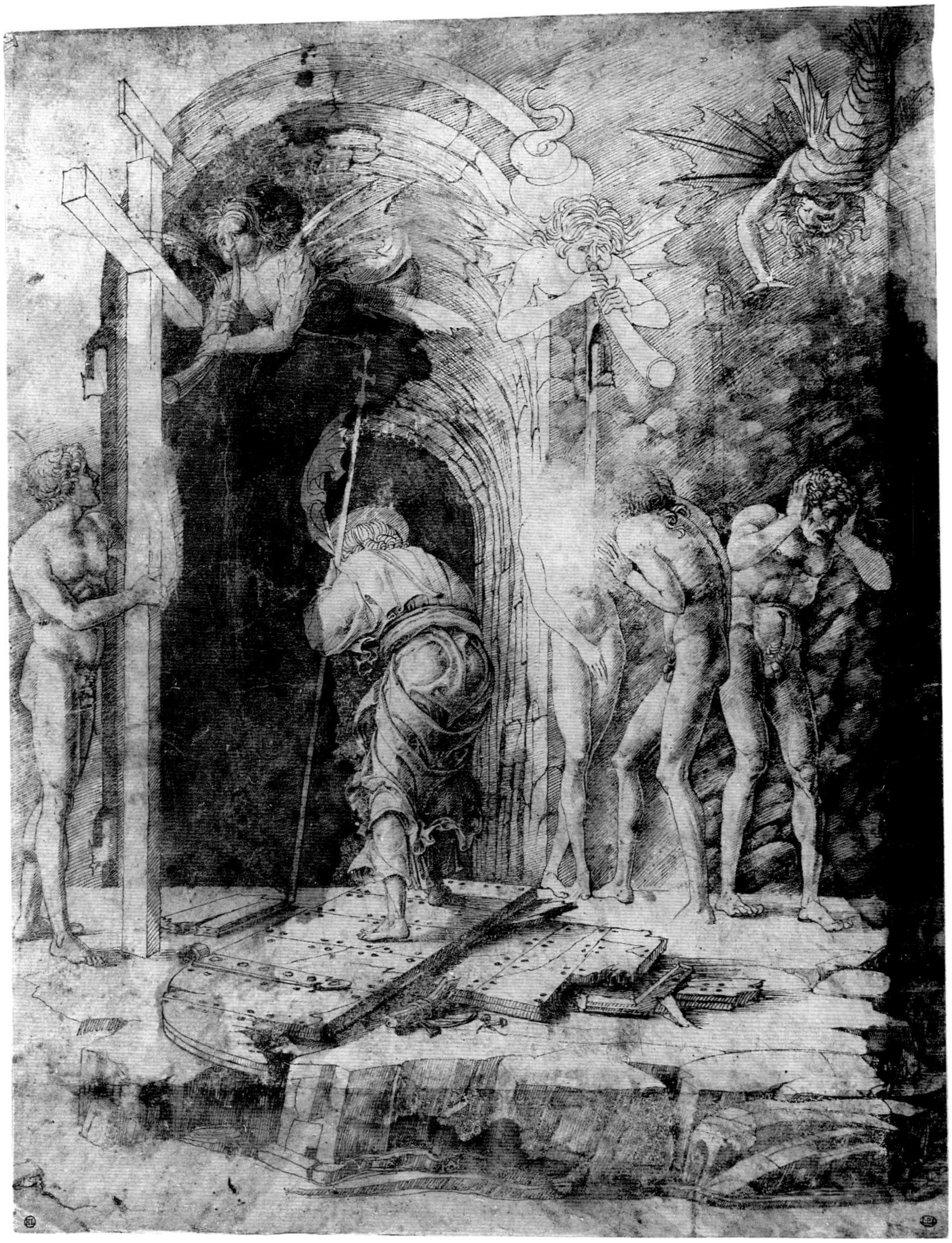

*195. Attributed to Giovanni Bellini,* Descent of Christ into Limbo, *drawing, Ecole Nationale Supérieure des Beaux-Arts, Paris.*

works produced throughout his career, where the paint has worn thin. That drawings by Bellini (or reasonably attributed to him) are generally unrelated to his paintings is explained in part by this practice and perhaps by reference to his father's use of drawing: apparently, few of Jacopo Bellini's sketches were preparatory studies for his paintings but rather represent experiments and possibilities. Giovanni Bellini also seems to have used drawing in this way, as a kind of visual thinking, in such sheets as the two *Lamentations* (figs. 55, 58). If the drawings of the *Descent into Limbo* are in fact by Bellini, they would thus represent a departure from his rule, explained by the fact that he was copying the work of another master.

# Appendix 5
## Checklists

### Part 1. Works by Giovanni Bellini

The checklist is arranged according to city. When a collection contains more than one painting, the listing is arranged alphabetically by title, sacred works preceding secular subjects. All works are on panel unless otherwise stated. (When the kind of wood is known, that information is included.) Measurements are given in centimeters, height before width. These figures are taken primarily from museum catalogs and from information provided by owners. Medium is specified only when the information is based on analysis of the pigments, because visual evidence is often insufficient to make a judgment in this matter.

Bergamo, Accademia Carrara
*Dead Christ with the Virgin Mary and Saint John the Evangelist*, tempera, 42 × 32 (fig. 47)
*Madonna and Child* (Lochis *Madonna*), oil, 47 × 34 (fig. 30)
*Madonna of the Pear* (Morelli *Madonna*), oil, 84.3 × 65.5 (fig. 35)
Berlin, Gemäldegalerie (Staatliche Museen)
*Dead Christ with Two Angels*, poplar panel, 83 × 67.5 (fig. 59)
*Resurrection of Christ*, poplar panel transferred to canvas, 148 × 128 (fig. 105)
*Portrait of a Young Man*, poplar panel, 32 × 26
Besançon, Musée des Beaux-Arts
*Derision of Noah*, canvas, 103 × 157 (fig. 180)
Birmingham, Barber Institute of Fine Arts
*Saint Jerome in the Wilderness*, 48 × 35.8 (fig. 1)
*Portrait of a Boy*, oil?, 38 × 23 (fig. 153) *See also* Part 2, Florence, Private Collection
Boston, Isabella Stewart Gardner Museum
*Madonna and Sleeping Child*, 61 × 43 (fig. 23)
Bristol, City Art Gallery
*Descent of Christ into Limbo*, parchment, 52 × 37.4 (fig. 193)
Florence, Galleria degli Uffizi
*Pietà* (*Lamentation*), tempera, 74 × 118 (fig. 136)
*Sacred Allegory* (*Meditation on the Passion*), oil, 73 × 119 (figs. 79, 80)
Hampton Court, Her Majesty Queen Elizabeth II
*Portrait of a Man*, 43 × 34, on loan to the National Gallery, London (fig. 161)
London, National Gallery
*Agony in the Garden*, 81 × 127 (fig. 73)
*Blood of the Redeemer*, 47 × 34 (fig. 57)
*Madonna of the Meadow*, transferred to canvas from panel, 67 × 86 (fig. 43)
*Portrait of Fra' Teodoro d'Urbino as Saint Dominic*, canvas, 63 × 49.5 (fig. 162)
*Doge Leonardo Loredan*, oil on poplar panel, 61.5 × 45 (fig. 149)
*Portrait of a Dominican with the Attributes of Saint Peter Martyr*, poplar panel, 59 × 48 (fig. 158)
Milan, Bagatti Valsecchi Collection
*Saint Giustina*, 129 × 55 (fig. 84)
Milan, Museo Poldi-Pezzoli
*Dead Christ*, 48 × 38 (fig. 54)
Milan, Pinacoteca di Brera
*Dead Christ with the Madonna and Saint John the Evangelist*, 107 × 86 (fig. 49)
*Madonna and Child* (*Madonna greca*), tempera, 62 × 82 (fig. 27)
*Madonna and Child*, dated 1510, primarily oil, 118 × 85 (fig. 44)
Murano, San Pietro Martire
Votive picture of Doge Agostino Barbarigo (*Madonna and Child with Saints Mark and Augustine, and Doge Barbarigo*), dated 1488, oil on canvas, 200 × 320 (figs. 68, 69)
Naples, Gallerie Nazionali di Capodimonte
*Transfiguration*, oil, 115 × 151.5 (fig. 102)
New York, Frick Collection
*Saint Francis in Ecstasy*, tempera and oil, 120 × 137 (fig. 77)
New York, Metropolitan Museum of Art
*Madonna and Sleeping Child* (Davis *Madonna*), tempera, 72.4 × 46.3 (fig. 14)
New York, Mr. Stanley Moss
*Pagan Allegory*, 31 × 25 (fig. 164)
Padua, Museo Civico
*Portrait of a Young Senator*, 35 × 26.4 (fig. 154)
Paris, Musée du Louvre
*Blessing Redeemer*, 58 × 44 (fig. 56)
Pasadena, Norton Simon Museum
*Portrait of Jörg Fugger*, dated 1474 (formerly on the back), oil?, poplar panel, 26 × 20 (fig. 150)
Pavia, Civico Museo Malaspina, on

## Part 2. Works by Giovanni Bellini with Assistance and Uncertain Attributions

Ferrara, Pinacoteca Nazionale
Jacopo Bellini, *Adoration of the Magi* (predella panel), probable collaboration, 28.5 × 57
*See also* Padua, Museo Civico, *and* Venice, Museo Civico Correr
Florence, Galleria Corsini
*Crucifixion*, 57 × 45
Florence, Galleria degli Uffizi
*Portrait of a Man*, oil on panel, 31 × 26
Florence, private collection
*Memento mori*, 30.5 × 21.5
*See also* Birmingham
Fort Worth, Kimbell Museum
*Madonna and Child*, tempera and oil, 82.5 × 58 (fig. 31)
Glasgow, Art Gallery
*Madonna and Child*, 62 × 47.6
Harewood House, Earl of Harewood
*Madonna and Child with Donor*, 80 × 70 (fig. 38)
Kansas City, W. Rockhill Nelson Gallery and M. Atkins Museum of Fine Arts (Kress Collection)
*Madonna and Child*, 74 × 56.5
London, National Gallery
*Madonna of the Pomegranate*, poplar panel, 91 × 65
*Circumcision of the Christ Child*, 75 × 102 (fig. 135)
*Dead Christ with Two Angels*, 94.5 × 71.5
*Death of Saint Peter Martyr*, 100 × 165 (fig. 137)
Milan, Castello Sforzesco (Civiche Raccolte d'Arte)
*Madonna and Child* (Trivulzio *Madonna*), 78 × 54 (fig. 22)
*Portrait of a Humanist*, 35 × 28 (fig. 145)
Milan, Pinacoteca di Brera
*Preaching of Saint Mark in Alexandria*, canvas, 347 × 770, begun by Gentile Bellini (fig. 184)
Murano, San Pietro Martire
*Immaculate Conception*, 350 × 190 (fig. 138)
New York, Brooklyn Museum
*Portrait of a Young Man*, 25 × 19
New York, Metropolitan Museum of Art
*Madonna and Child*, oil, 88.9 × 71.1
*Madonna and Blessing Child* (Lehman *Madonna*), 54 × 39 (fig. 21)
New York, Pierpont Morgan Library
*Madonna and Child with Saints and Donor*, 75 × 109.2 (fig. 133)
Padua, Museo Civico
Jacopo Bellini, *Descent of Christ into Limbo* (predella panel), probable collaboration, 28.5 × 58
*See also* Ferrara, Pinacoteca Nazionale, *and* Venice, Museo Civico Correr
Paris, Musée du Louvre
*Madonna and Child with Saints Peter and Sebastian*, 84 × 61 (fig. 37)
*Portrait of a Young Man*, 32 × 26
Philadelphia, John G. Johnson Collection
*Madonna and Child*, 61 × 41 (fig. 20)
Rome, Galleria Capitolina
*Portrait of a Patrician*, 34 × 25 (fig. 155)
Rovigo, Accademia dei Concordi
*Christ Carrying the Cross*, oil, 48.5 × 27
Saint Bonaventure (New York), Saint Bonaventure University, Friedsam Library
*Madonna and Child with Donor*, 92 × 70 (fig. 39)
Venice, Museo Civico Correr
Jacopo Bellini, *Crucifixion* (predella panel), probable collaboration, 28.5 × 57 (fig. 3)
*See also* Ferrara, Pinacoteca Nazionale, *and* Padua, Museo Civico
Venice, Gallerie dell'Accademia
Carità triptychs, possible collaboration with Jacopo Bellini and others:
Triptych of Saint Lawrence
*Saint Lawrence*, 103 × 45
*Saint John the Baptist*, 103 × 45
*Saint Anthony of Padua*, 127 × 48
*Madonna* and *Angels*, fragments of lunette
Triptych of Saint Sebastian
*Saint Sebastian*, 103 × 45
*Saint John the Baptist*, 127 × 48
*Saint Anthony Abbot*, 103 × 45 (fig. 187)
*Annunciation*, lunette, 59 × 170
Triptych of the Nativity
*Nativity*, 103 × 45
*Saint Francis*, 127 × 48
*Saint Victor*, 127 × 48
*Trinity*, lunette, 60 × 166
Triptych of the Madonna
*Madonna and Child*, 127 × 48
*Saint Jerome*, 127 × 48
*Saint Louis of Toulouse*, 127 × 48
*Dead Christ and Two Angels*, lunette, 60 × 166
*Lamentation*, canvas, possible collaboration with Rocco Marconi, 444 × 312 (fig. 52)
*Madonna and Child with Saints John the Baptist and a Female Saint* (Giovanelli *Sacra Conversazione*), 54 × 76 (fig. 42)
*Madonna and Child with Saints Paul and George*, 66 × 88 (fig. 36)
Madonna dell'Orto Organ Doors, with Pier Maria Pennacchi(?)
*Annunciation* (*Archangel Gabriel* and *Annunciate Virgin*) and *Saint Peter*, three canvases, 224 × 106 each (fig. 190)
*Fortune*, fir panel, 27 × 19 (fig. 166)
Venice, San Francesco della Vigna
*Madonna and Child with Saints John the Baptist, Francis, Jerome, and Sebastian, and Donor Giacomo Dolfin* (Dolfin *Madonna*), dated 1507, 90 × 145 (fig. 132)

Venice, San Salvatore
*Supper at Emmaus*, canvas, possible collaboration of Giovanni Bellini, 260 × 375 (figs. 188, 189)
Venice, SS. Giovanni e Paolo
Polyptych of Saint Vincent Ferrer (fig. 186), collaboration with Lauro Padovano (and others?): main panels, 167 × 67; upper panels, 67 × 72 each; predella panels attributed to Lauro Padovano, 36 × 60 each
Venice, ex-Scuola Grande di San Marco (Ospedale Civile)
*Martyrdom of Saint Mark*, dated 1526, canvas, begun by Giovanni Bellini and completed by Vittore Belliniano, 362 × 771 (fig. 185)
Washington, National Gallery of Art
*Madonna and Child*, 72 × 53.2
*Madonna and Child*, 75 × 58.5
*Saint Jerome*, dated 1505(?), 49 × 39
*Infant Bacchus*, transferred to muslin on wood from panel, 48 × 36.8
*Orpheus*, transferred to canvas from panel, 39.5 × 81
*Portrait of a Young Man in Red*, 32 × 26.5
*Portrait of a Young Man*, 31 × 25
*Portrait of a Man*, 30 × 20
*Continence of Publius Cornelius Scipio*, tempera on canvas, 74.8 × 356.2 (fig. 174)
Zagreb, Strossmayer National Gallery
*Saint Augustine* and *Saint Benedict*, panels from an altarpiece, 108 × 40 each
Collection of Frederick R. and Jan Mayer
*Saint Dominic*, panel, 43 × 28 (fig. 163)

## Part 3. Checklist of Recorded Lost Works

DATED WORKS

1459 or 1460?
Altarpiece of the Gattamelata Chapel of Saint Francis in Sant'Antonio, Padua, signed and dated by Jacopo, Gentile, and Giovanni Bellini (see app. 2, no. 6).

1464
Two paintings for the Compagnia di San Gerolamo, one representing Jerome and his confreres at the walls of their convent, the other showing the saint reading in his study, with other brothers. This painting was signed and dated, according to Carlo Ridolfi (*Maraviglie*, 1:64.)

1468–71
Altarpiece of Saint John the Evangelist with a predella by Lauro Padovano, in Santa Maria della Carità. (Mentioned by Michiel, *Anonimo Morelliano*, p. 114. The predella may be identified with the panel illustrating the legend of Drusiana, now in the Wittelsbach collection. For arguments regarding its attribution and the lost altarpiece by Bellini, see Robertson, *Bellini*, pp. 47–48.)

1472
A Crucifix with the Three Marys and Doctors of the Church in the Rectory of Santa Maria della Carità. (Sansovino repeated the information in *Venetia*, ed. Stringa, p. 185a.)

1474
Miniature portrait of *Raffaele Zovenzoni*, formerly illuminating the *Istrias*, MS in Milan, Biblioteca Trivulziana.

1474 c.
Altarpiece of Saint Catherine (*Madonna and Child and Saints*), Venice, SS. Giovanni e Paolo (fig. 82).

1483 c.
*Resurrection*, commissioned by Gaspare Trissino for his funerary chapel in the Cathedral of Vicenza.

1497 c.
*Madonna* altarpiece, commissioned by Donato Civalelli for Santa Maria, Zara (app. 2, no. 24).

1504
*Presepio* (*Nativity*) for a bedroom of Isabella d'Este (app. 2, no. 47).

1515
*Madonna*, commissioned by the republic for the sister of the king of France (app. 2, no. 65).

UNDATED LOST WORKS

This compendium is compiled from sources indicated in brief after each listing.

*Sacred subjects:*
*Christ Carrying the Cross*, in the house of Taddeo Contarini (Michiel)

Head of *Christ in Majesty*, in the house of Giovanni Antonio Venier (Michiel)

Head of *Christ in Majesty*, signed, in the Albergo of the Scuola Grande di Santa Maria della Carità (Michiel, with an attribution to "Andrea" Bellini)

*Christ*, bequeathed by Elena Trevisan to her son (app. 2, no. 69)

*Christ in the House of the Pharisee (Saint Mary Magdalen Washing the Feet of Christ)*, San Salvatore, chapel of the Sacrament (Sansovino, *Venetia*)

*Madonna Enthroned Reading the Office*, in the collection of Procurator Simon Zen (Sansovino, *Dialogo*)

*Madonna* altarpiece of the Scuola de' Cinturari, San Felice (Ridolfi; Sansovino, *Venetia*)

*Madonna* altarpiece of the Grimani family, Santa Maria Maggiore (Sansovino, *Venetia*)

*Madonna*, in the Sacristy of Santo Spirito (Sansovino, *Venetia*)

*Miracle of the Relic of the Cross*, second canvas of the cycle in the Albergo of the Scuola Grande di San Giovanni Evangelista (Sansovino, *Venetia*)

*Nativity* and *Passion of Christ*, collaborative works, in the Scuola Grande di San Giovanni Evangelista (Sansovino, *Venetia*) N.B. the three canvases of the Infancy cycle, ascribed to Jacopo, Gentile, and Giovanni Bellini in the collection of Stanley Moss, New York, and two belonging to the same series, now in the Galleria Sabauda, Turin. These have been identified with the San Giovanni Evangelista cycle; see Howard Collins, "Major Narrative Paintings by Jacopo Bellini," *Art Bulletin* 64 (1982): 466–72. Giovanni Bellini's contribution to these seems to me doubtful, and minimal at most.

*Saint Catherine*, in San Giminiano (Ridolfi)

*Saint Jerome in the Desert with Saints Francis and Clare*, triptych, formerly on the first altar on the left in Santa Maria dei Miracoli, which was completed in 1489 (Boschini, *Ricche minere*; Ridolfi; Sansovino, *Venetia*)

*Stigmatization of Saint Francis* (Boschini, *Carta*)

*Secular subjects:*

Portraits:
- *Pietro Bembo* (Ridolfi)
- *Bembo's Mistress* (Bembo; Ridolfi)
- *Leonico Tomeo* (Michiel)
- *Generalissimo Jacopo Marcello* (Michiel)
- *Filippo Vendramin* (Michiel)
- Two Profile Portraits of Gentlemen (Michiel)
- Bust-length picture of a woman, in the house of Taddeo Contarini (Michiel)

Classical theme:
- Two large paintings of *Cosmografia*, with figures of Ptolemy, Strabo, Pliny, and Pomponio Mella, in the Grimani Palace (Ridolfi)

Ducal Palace:
- Large paintings in the Sala del Collegio with portraits of doges and other figures (Ridolfi)
- Paintings (subjects unspecified) in the Pregadi (Sansovino, *Dialogo*)
- Paintings in the Sala del Maggior Consiglio:
- *Doge Sebastiano Ziani and Pope Alexander III at Santa Maria della Carità*
- *Naval Battle of Doge Ziani and the Emperor's Son Otto*

*Peace Treaty of Pope Alexander and Emperor Frederick Barbarossa*, begun by Alvise Vivarini and completed after 1507 by Bellini. Bellini began working in the Great Council Hall in 1479. On the lost paintings, see Sansovino, *Venetia*, ed. Stringa, pp. 235a–37a. See also Sansovino, *Lettera*, pp. 23–29, esp. pp. 26ff. Norbert Huse has compared the various sixteenth-century sources to reconstruct the decoration of the hall (*Bellini*, pp. 56–71). In addition, see Wolfgang Wolters, *Bilderschmuck*, pp. 161–81.

# Notes

Cross-references to the text are indicated by references to note citations, for example, "see above, chap. 2 at n. 12." Frequently cited sources are abbreviated in the notes and given full citation in the Select Bibliography.

## Introduction: Young Bellini

*Note to epigraph*: Boschini, *Carta del navegar pitoresco*, p. 665.

1. An article published over seventy years ago by Roberto Longhi continues to influence the art historical view of Bellini, especially in Italy ("Piero dei Franceschi," pp. 198–221, 241–56). See also Boskovits, "Giovanni Bellini," pp. 386–93; Del Bravo, "Giovanni Bellini in relazione al Valla," pp. 691–704; and S. J. Freedberg, *Painting in Italy, 1500 to 1600*, Pelican History of Art (Harmondsworth, 1970), pp. 78–84, 109–10. Giles Robertson, *Giovanni Bellini*, also presented Bellini's career in terms of his relationship to Mantegna and to other masters. Cf. the review by David Rosand in *Art Quarterly* 33 (1970): 72–74. But Robertson himself noted that there was no evidence to assume that Bellini was a "slow-starter" compared to Mantegna ("Earlier Works," pp. 45–59). For a discussion of Bellini's influence on his contemporaries, see the important essay by Smyth, "Venice," pp. 209–49.

2. Giuseppe Biadego, *Variazioni e divagazioni a proposito di due sonetti di Giorgio Sommariva in onore di Gentile e Giovanni Bellini* (Verona, 1907), p. 14, quoting a sonnet written when Jacopo Bellini was still alive, and therefore by 1470. The sonnet distinguishes between the "great Giovanni" and "good Gentile" and puns on their family name: "Dui bei fratelli." Another contemporary poet, Andrea Squarzòla (d. 1510), likewise preferred "the sublime and excellent hand of Giovanni" to Gentile's art; for the sonnet "Da tutti son la gigantea chiamata," see Rossi, "Canzoniere inedito," pp. 47–48.

3. In the *Istrias*, dated 1474 and dedicated to the bishop of Trent, Zovenzoni described Bellini as "nobilissimus pictor Joannes Bellinus." See Ziliotto, *Raffaele Zovenzoni*, pp. 54–55, 164, and chap. 1 at n. 7, and chap. 3 at n. 13, below. Felice Feliciano, a friend of Mantegna's, described Bellini as "famosissimo in orbe pictori Joanni bellino" in a letter written between 1474 and 1475, dedicated to an unknown friend, possibly Paolo Bevilacqua. See Pratilli, "Felice Feliciano," p. 63.

4. Liburnio, *Opere gentile ed amorse*, p. 8r, sonnet 30, "O quanto a te Natura e ciel arride/Ioanni mio." Liburnio praised Bellini again in *Le selvette* (Venice, 1513), dedicated to Isabella d'Este; N.B. *selvetta* 6, "il pintore messer Giovan Bellino . . . tra gli altri maestri degno d'immortalità" (n.p.). The humanist Zovenzoni also compared Bellini to Apelles by evoking Alexander: "Ioanni Bello Bellino Pictori Clarissimo./Qui facis ora tuis spirantia, Belle, tabellis/dignus Alexandro principe pictor eras." See Ziliotto, *Zovenzoni*, p. 78, carme no. 28.

5. "Er ist sehr alt und ist noch der pest im gemoll." See Hans Rupprich, ed., *Dürer: Schriftlicher Nachlass* (Berlin, 1956), 1:43–44.

6. Alluding to the story told of Apelles and Protogenes in Pliny's *Natural History*, Camerarius described Bellini's amazed admiration of Dürer's beautiful lines, due to his consummate skill and not to special brushes. See Smith, "Dürer and Bellini, Apelles and Protogenes," pp. 326–29.

7. At least we know what he looked like: for three certain portraits of Bellini and one possible likeness, see Jörgen Rapp, "Das Tizian-Porträt in Kopenhagen: ein Bildnis des Giovanni Bellini," *Zeitschrift für Kunstgeschichte* 50 (1987): 359–74, esp. pp. 365–67, for Belliniano's drawing, Gambello's medal, and the anonymous drawing of Bellini on his deathbed.

8. Documents pertaining to Gentile have been conveniently published in Meyer zur Capellen, *Gentile Bellini*. For a chronology of Giovanni's life and transcriptions of documents relating to him, see apps. 1, 2. According to one contemporary poem, the old Bellini enjoyed a homosexual relationship with a boy. Morelli evidently knew but suppressed the poem, preserved in a manuscript in the Biblioteca Nazionale Marciana, Venice; it was rediscovered by Jennifer Fletcher, "Some Venetian 15th Century Painters and Their Responses to the Antique," *Venezia e l'archeologia*, ed. Gustavo Traversari (Venice, 1989), in press.

9. For the historical situation, see, among others, Cessi, *Storia della Repubblica*; Gilbert, "Venice in Crisis," pp. 274–92; Kretschmayr, *Geschichte von Venedig*; Lane, *Venice*, esp. pp. 225–352; and Libby, "Venetian History," pp. 7–45.

10. App. 2, no. 67. Dennis Romano has found that apprenticeship might begin between the ages of six and eight, rather than the more

customary thirteen or fourteen, especially if the boy were studying within the family. See Romano's forthcoming volume, *Apprenticeship in Early Renaissance Venice*.

11. This is assuming an almost assembly-line production of infant Bellini from 1429, when the first child was born (probably Nicolosia), followed by Giovanni's older brothers Nicolò and Gentile. Anna's first testament, dated 6 February 1428, was written during her first pregnancy, a customary precaution at that time, given the dangers inherent in childbirth (app. 2, no. 1). The child whose birth she was expecting must have been either Nicolò or, more likely, Nicolosia, named, as was customary, for their paternal grandfather. If the first child had been the boy Nicolò, why repeat the name for the girl Nicolosia? That would have been a redundant departure from tradition, whereas if Nicolosia were the firstborn, Jacopo might well use the name again for his first son. For naming customs, see Christiane Klapisch-Zuber, "The Name 'Remade': The Transmission of Given Names in Florence in the Fourteenth and Fifteenth Centuries" [1980], pp. 283–309, in Klapisch-Zuber, *Women, Family, and Ritual*. See also Gibbons, "New Evidence," pp. 54–58, and Meyer zur Capellen, *Gentile Bellini*, p. 10. Gentile was identified as older than Giovanni by their admiring contemporary Pescennio (Francesco Negro) in the *Peri archon*, confirmed in turn by the record of the inscription with which Jacopo and his painter sons signed the altarpiece of the Gattamelata Chapel in Sant'Antonio, Padua, naming Giovanni last, after Gentile. See Giovanni Mercati, "Appendice alla memoria su Pescennio Francesco Negro," in Mercati, *Ultimi contributi*, p. 38* [*sic*], and Valerio Polidoro in app. 2, no. 6, for the altarpiece.

12. Anna Rinversi's will of 1471 omitted mention of two of Jacopo's children: not only Giovanni but also Nicolosia (app. 2, no. 9). So far as I can determine, Nicolosia died between 1475 and 1480. Anna Rinversi also omitted mention of any of her grandchildren. To be sure, Anna may have excluded Nicolosia because the girl's dowry was considered her share of the family estate; this accorded with Venetian law. Yet Anna might have bequeathed her daughter some small amount of money or a gift as a "sign of love," a common practice. On the treatment of daughters in their parents' wills, see Stanley Chojnacki, "Dowries and Kinsmen," and Chojnacki, "Patrician Women." For a case in point, see the will of Giovanni Bellini's grandfather, Nicolò, 11 April 1424 (ASV, Notarile, Lorenzo Buscrino, Busta 545, Protocollo, published by Paoletti, *Raccolta*, p. 5). Eugenio Billanovich argues unconvincingly that Vasari meant to suggest Bellini's illegitimacy ("Note," pp. 369–70). In any case, Vasari would be an unreliable source for such information. For an analysis of Bellini's Madonna imagery based on the assumption of his illegitimacy, see Kristeva, "Motherhood," pp. 237–70.

13. As executor of her will, Anna designated a friend instead of one or more of her children, which would have been customary. This departure from the rule may indicate that her exclusion of Giovanni was not intended to stigmatize him, but that all her arrangements were idiosyncratic. N.B. also that, like his mother before him, Gentile Bellini omitted one of his brothers from his will, for Nicolò was still living when Gentile died and yet was not mentioned (app. 2, no. 55). Nicolò survived Gentile by at least six years; see Brown, "'Una testa di Platone,'" pp. 372–77.

14. Venetian law had required the registration of *cittadini originari* since 1305, and beginning in 1486, "original citizens," like patricians, were required to prove legitimacy by registering births with the Avogaria di Comun. See Andrea da Mosto, *L'Archivio di Stato di Venezia* (Rome, 1937), 1:73–74, with a list of citizen families, including the Bellini. For the social class, see Stephen R. Ell, "Citizenship and Immigration in Venice: 1305–1500" (Ph.D. diss., University of Chicago, 1976); Brown, *Venetian Narrative Painting*, pp. 13–15, 23–28, 51; and Neff, "Chancellery Secretaries," esp. pp. 370–71, for Alvise di Giovanni Bellini's chancellery service in 1486, which is documented in ASV, Consiglio dei Dieci, Misti, fil. 9, c. 203r; Reg. 27, fol. 33v; and Reg. 28, fol. 124.

15. Restoration has confirmed that the signature is "of a piece with the picture surface." See Hamish Miles, *Handbook of the Barber Institute of Fine Arts*, 2d ed. (Birmingham, 1983), p. 3. The *Saint Jerome* was restored by Herbert Lank in 1973. Giovanni Bellini's signature contrasts significantly with his father's assured epigraphy in drawings in the Louvre sketchbook, e.g., fols. 44–45, dating in the 1450s (Degenhart and Schmitt, *Jacopo Bellini*, pls. 52–53).

16. Letter 22, trans. in P. Schaff and H. Wace, ed., *Nicene and Post-Nicene Fathers* (New York, 1893), 6: 24–35. See also Meiss, "Scholarship and Penitence," pp. 134–40.

17. See fols. 18v and 22v in the Louvre album (Degenhart and Schmitt, *Jacopo Bellini*, pls. 17, 24). See also the painting attributed to Jacopo Bellini in Verona, Museo del Castelvecchio.

18. Richard Offner noted the stylistic significance of scale in *Italian Primitives at Yale University* (New Haven, 1924), p. 26. See also Lipman, "Florentine Profile Portrait," pp. 94–95.

19. I thank Lilian Armstrong for her helpful bibliographic suggestions regarding the miniaturist. See esp. Giordana Mariani Canova, "Per Leonardo Bellini," *Arte veneta* 22

(1968): 9–14; Mariani Canova, *La miniatura veneta del Rinascimento* (Venice, 1969), pp. 22–24, 103–4, 142–45; Lino Moretti, "Leonardo Bellini," pp. 58–66; and Robertson, *Bellini*, p. 16. Robertson ascribes the miniatures in the Arsenal MS "Life of St. George" to Bellini. More recently, Christiane Joost-Gaugier has attributed two illuminations in a manuscript of Strabo's *De Situ Orbis Geographia* (Albi, Bibliothèque Rochegude, MS 4) to Bellini ("Pair of Miniatures, " pp. 48–71). The only undisputed miniature by him, however, is the *Descent of Christ into Limbo*, for which see app. 4 and fig. 193.

20. For the *Adoration* in the Pinacoteca Nazionale, Ferrara, see Volpe, "Donazione," pp. 73–78; for the *Descent*, see Lucio Grossato, *Il Museo Civico di Padova: Dipinti e sculture dal XIV al XIX secolo* (Venice, 1957), p. 30, no. 66; and for the *Crucifixion*, Mariacher, *Museo Correr*, pp. 54–55. Rodolfo Pallucchini also attributes the small altar with seven saints in the Museo Piersanti, Matelica, to Giovanni Bellini circa 1450, based on his father's design (*Bellini*, p. 127). See also Colin Eisler, "Anthony Abbot and Bernardino of Siena," p. 36.

21. Eisler, "Anthony Abbot and Bernardino of Siena," pp. 32–40, two articles by Boskovits, "Per Jacopo Bellini pittore," and "Giovanni Bellini," with a color plate of the panel, which is in a private collection in New York, and most recently Christiansen, "Venetian Painting." I thank Professor Eisler for discussing this problematic altarpiece with me.

22. For the chapel dedication, see Antonio Sartori, *Documenti per la storia dell'arte a Padova*, ed. Clemente Fillarini, Fonti e studi per la storia del Santo a Padova, Fonti, vol. 3 (Vicenza, 1976), p. 81, citing a document of 24 July 1472. The chapel may have originally been dedicated to Francis alone, and in any case Bernardino's cult in the chapel seems to have been forgotten at a later date; see Polidoro, *Le Religiose memorie*, pp. 24v, 33r–v, 35r–v, and table 2. For the inscription and Polidoro's confusion of the date of the altarpiece, see app. 2, no. 6. Presumably the date recorded by Polidoro, "MCCCCIX," should read "MCCCCLX" (1460) or "MCCCCLIX" (1459; just after completion of the chapel itself). I do not follow Sartori's logic in arguing that the altarpiece was painted after 1471 (*Documenti*, p. 80). Gattamelata made his will in 1441 and died in 1444. The chapel construction seems to have been complete in 1458, but the altarpiece could have been commissioned and begun at any time after 1441. The final payment for the chapel decoration is dated 6 November 1477 (Sartori, *Documenti*, p. 32, also pp. 32–33, 180).

23. I am grateful to Dott.ssa Maria Urbani of the Curia Patriarcale for her assistance regarding the San Marco mosaics. The south transept of San Marco is the ducal precinct, which may indicate that Bernardino's cult was promoted by the doges even before Cristoforo Moro (doge, 1462–71) acted to make him a patron saint of the republic; see chap. 2 at n. 52. Four saints are depicted in the mosaic: Anthony Abbot, Bernardino, Vincent Ferrer, and Paul the Hermit. Anthony and Vincent were executed by Maestro Silvestro, who signed and dated the first figure in 1458. The other two saints are contemporary works by Maestro Antonio di Jacopo. This seems a more promising straw to grasp than the Gattamelata Chapel as a provenance for the Bellini altarpiece, and in any case the combination of saints reminds us that the pairing of Anthony Abbot and Bernardino in the left wing does not guarantee the presence of Anthony of Padua and Francis in the other (lost or missing) panel.

24. App. 2, no. 5.

25. Marilyn Aronberg Lavin notes that Uccello's *Corpus Domini* predella was completed in 1468, almost five years before the main panel was begun by Joos van Ghent. The final payment is dated 1474 ("Altar of Corpus Domini," p. 10 for the dates); see also app. 4.

26. The Bellini surely collaborated on many commissions other than the Gattamelata altarpiece, of which the only undisputed (if garbled) survival is its signature and date. Nothing about the style or subject of these four panels is so distinctive as to preclude their having formed part of another work by the Bellini. Giandomenico Romanelli, *Museo Correr* (Milan, 1984), p. 69, says the *Crucifixion*, hence the altarpiece of which it formed a part, may have come from the convent of San Zaccaria in Venice.

27. N.B. also fols. 18r, 37, and 74 in the Louvre book (Degenhart and Schmitt, *Jacopo Bellini*, pls. 16, 42, 69, 93). On Bellini's use of landscape, see also Eugenio Battisti, "Le origini religiose del paesaggio veneto," *Archivio di filosofia* 1 (1980): 227–46, and André Chastel, "Venezia e la pittura del Nord," pp. 104–8 in *Venezia e la Germania* (Milan, 1986).

28. See Meiss, "'Highlands' in the Lowlands: Jan van Eyck, the Master of Flémalle, and the Franco-Italian Tradition" (1961), in Meiss, *Painter's Choice*, pp. 36–59. Meiss suggests that the Eyckian *Crucifixion* evidently came to Padua in the mid-1450s. Mantegna's conception of space is more Eyckian than Bellini's: it seems that Bellini's work is a few years earlier and that his composition more distantly related to the northern prototypes.

29. The picture is sometimes identified with a *Transfiguration* by Bellini formerly in San Salvatore (Salvador); see the commentary on the life of Mantegna in Vasari, *Vite*, ed. Milanesi (hereafter cited as

Vasari-Milanesi), 3:429–30. But cf. the doubts expressed by Mariacher, *Museo Correr*, p. 47. The panel was restored by Mauro Pellicioli in 1950. N.B. also the fragment of a head of Christ in the Accademia (fig. 104), which must have come from yet another depiction of the *Transfiguration* by Bellini. Another possibility is that the painting now in the Correr was commissioned for the hospital or oratory of San Giobbe; see n. 31, below.

30. See G. H. Guyot, in *New Catholic Encyclopedia*, s.v. "Transfiguration."

31. Robertson, *Bellini*, p. 30. One thinks of the hospital and later church of San Giobbe, although Job in the wings does not preclude association with San Salvador.

32. For the meaning of the miracle and its association in the Gospels with the theme of his sufferings, see Carlston, "Transfiguration and Resurrection," pp. 233–40, and Kenny, "Transfiguration and Agony," pp. 444–52. Elijah's predicted ascension and return anticipate Christ's; see G. J. Dyer, in *New Catholic Encyclopedia*, s.v. "Elia (Second Coming of)"; and B. McGrath, *New Catholic Encyclopedia*, s.v. "Elia (Elijah)."

33. For the relationship of the Transfiguration and the Agony in the Garden, see Guyot, "Transfiguration," pp. 243–44; and esp. Kenny, "Transfiguration and Agony," p. 444. Kenny notes that although both miracles occurred at night (Luke 9:37), the apostles were vividly conscious of color—the glowing white robes of Christ in one case, red drops of blood in the other.

34. On clouds and the supernatural, see Meiss, *Bellini's St. Francis*, p. 31; and also Carlston, "Transfiguration and Resurrection," p. 238.

35. For a comparison of Mantegna's painting with the very similar work by Bellini, see above, chap. 1 at nn. 131–33.

36. See also Theodor Hetzer, *Tizian*, esp. pp. 35–41.

## Chapter 1. Images for Private Devotion

1. *Dialogo*, unpaginated, but on what would be p. 27: "Et oltra i quadri [di Bellini] per la Città si trovano diverse opere in San Iob, in San zaccaria, nel Pregai [Pregadi], certi Quadri, Et si veggono alcune nostre donne molte belle e devote."

2. See Julia Kristeva, "Motherhood," pp. 237–70. N.B. also Freud's theories about Leonardo's illegitimate birth, first published in 1910 (*Leonardo da Vinci and a Memory of His Childhood*, trans. Alan Tyson, ed. James Strachey [New York, 1964]). An alternative psychological art history of the Madonnas would relate them to the artist's probable first marriage and the possible loss of a child or children (see app. 2, no. 5). It is almost inconceivable that Bellini was not married before 1485, when he guaranteed the dowry of the woman who was presumably his second wife (app. 2, no. 14). Yet the artist's only documented child was Alvise, the son of this marriage, who predeceased Bellini (app. 2, no. 28). I first discussed the imagery and meaning of these paintings in "Icon and Vision." Bellini's Madonnas may be compared to Luca della Robbia's reliefs (John Pope-Hennessy, *Luca della Robbia* [Ithaca, 1980], p. 66).

3. Inescapable awareness of infant mortality may have distanced mortal mothers (and fathers) from their children, at least until the newborn had survived the first perilous stages of development. N.B. the Florentine custom of sending newborns to wetnurses; see Christiane Klapisch-Zuber, "Blood Parents and Milk Parents: Wet Nursing in Florence, 1300–1530," pp. 132–64, in Klapisch-Zuber, *Women, Family, and Ritual*. Stanley Chojnacki informs me that in Venice infant care was probably more often entrusted to wetnurses employed in the parents' home. Medieval and Renaissance childrearing seems cold-blooded by modern standards, and in both Florence and Venice, children belonged to the paternal line. Thus, a child whose father had died would be separated from his mother if she did not remain in her deceased husband's household. See Klapisch-Zuber, "Childhood in Tuscany at the Beginning of the Fifteenth Century" and "The 'Cruel Mother': Maternity, Widowhood, and Dowry in Florence in the Fourteenth and Fifteenth Centuries," pp. 94–116, 117–31, in her *Women, Family, and Ritual*; Chojnacki, "The Power of Love: Wives and Husbands in Late Medieval Venice," pp. 126–48, in *Women and Power in the Middle Ages*, ed. Mary Erler and Maryanne Kowalski (Athens, Ga., 1988), esp. 132, 136, n. 49; James Bruce Ross, "The Middle-Class Child in Urban Italy, Fourteenth to Early Sixteenth Century," pp. 183–228, in *The History of Childhood*, ed. Lloyd de Mause (New York, 1974); and the classic study by Philippe Ariès, *Centuries of Childhood: A Social History of Family Life* [1960], tr. Robert Baldick (New York, 1962). Venetian treatises on children often show even less concern with nurturing than do Florentine publications; see King, "Caldiera and the Barbaros," p. 46.

4. Goffen, "Icon and Vision," p. 507 and nn. 112–16.

5. William Durandus [Guglielmus Durantis, c. 1230–96], *The Symbolism of Churches and Church Ornaments*, trans. J. M. Neale and B. Webb (London, 1893), p. 43. This volume is the first book of Durandus's *Rationale Divinorum Officiorum*.

6. Andrea Dandolo [Andreae Danduli, Ducis Venetiarum], *Chronica per extensum descripta*, ed. Ester Pastorello, in *Rerum italicarum scriptores: Raccolta degli storici italiani dal cinquecento al millecinquecento*, ed. L. A. Muratori, vol. 12, pt. 1 (Bologna, 1938), p. 109; Alberto Rizzi and Lorenzo Lazzarini, "La Madonna Nicopeia," *Quaderni della*

*Soprintendenza ai Beni Artistici e Storici di Venezia* 8 (1979): 11–21; and Rizzi, "Un'icona costantinopolitana del XII secolo a Venezia: La Madonna Nicopeia," *Thesaurismata* 17 (1980): 289–307.

7. For Bellini's lost portrait of Zovenzoni, see chap. 3 at n. 13. Similarly, when the Venetian nobleman Jacopo Antonio Marcello could not meet with the knights of the Crescent, he sent instead a manuscript life of their patron saint, including a portrait of himself. Marcello's portrait has been attributed to Bellini by Giles Robertson and to Mantegna by Millard Meiss (Meiss, *Mantegna*; Robertson, *Bellini*, pp. 17–21).

8. Leon Battista Alberti, *On Painting and On Sculpture: The Latin Texts of* De Pictura *and* De Statua, ed. and trans. Cecil Grayson (London, 1972), p. 61.

9. The primary exception is the kneeling donor; see, e.g., fig. 68.

10. From Bessarion's letter of 1468 to Doge Cristoforo Moro, stating his intention to give his manuscript collection to the republic. See Geanakoplos, *Interaction*, p. 177.

11. See Goffen, *Piety and Patronage*, p. 133.

12. Zeri with Gardner, *Italian Paintings*, pp. 5–6.

13. In a studio work formerly in the Contini Bonacossi Collection in Florence, the Virgin prays over her sleeping Child, who is covered with a drapery like a winding cloth.

14. See Bynum, "Body of Christ"; Steinberg, *Sexuality of Christ*; and, on the related themes of sex and sexuality in art, Goffen, "Renaissance Dreams."

15. See Goffen, *Spirituality in Conflict*, p. 67.

16. See Goffen, "Icon and Vision," p. 503 and nn. 87–89, and *Piety and Patronage*, pp. 121–22, 230, n. 39. Cyrilla Barr cites a confraternity inventory that lists such a pillow, to be used in the funeral services of defunct members ("A Renaissance Artist in the Service of a Singing Confraternity," n. 22, in *Life and Death in Fifteenth-Century Florence*, ed. Marcel Tetel, Ronald G. Witt, and Goffen [Durham, N.C., 1989]). N.B. also the custom of carrying relics on cushions in procession.

17. Belonging to the Museo Civico Malaspina of Pavia, inventory no. 22, the panel is now displayed in the Castello of that city. See Adriano Peroni et al., *Pavia, Pinacoteca Malaspina* (Milan, 1981), p. 162. The panel seems to have been cut on all sides and originally had a rounded top, like the Davis *Madonna* (fig. 14); see U. Bicchi, *Pinacoteca Civica di Pavia* (Milan, 1958), p. 45. According to Carlo Gamba, the cloth of honor is not original but a later addition (*Giovanni Bellini* [Milan, 1937], p. 42).

18. Similar motifs and ideas had originated perhaps twenty years earlier in the art of Jan van Eyck, in such paintings as the portraits of Arnolfini and his wife or of the man inscribed "Timotheos" (in Greek) and "Lael Souvenir" (Long Memory). See Martin Davies, *Early Netherlandish School*, National Gallery Catalogues, 2d ed. rev. (London, 1955), pp. 38–40, 41. For the conception of the artist's signing his painting as witness, see Panofsky, *Early Netherlandish Painting*, p. 203. For Bellini's signature as the equivalent of Luke's genuflection (fig. 12), as an assertion of the artist's role as creator of the image and as witness to its reality, see Goffen, "Icon and Vision," pp. 510–11. Note also the signature of the Brera *Pietà* (fig. 49).

19. See chap. 3 at n. 32, and the forthcoming article by Martha Feldman, "The Academy of Domenico Venier: Poetry and Music in Venice around 1550," which Professor Feldman kindly made available to me before publication.

20. The Davis *Madonna* was adapted by Bartolomeo Vivarini in a composition of 1481 in the de Young Museum, San Francisco (Rodolfo Pallucchini, *Giovanni Bellini* (Milan, 1959), p. 126, fig. 195). Another very early Madonna composition by Bellini, c. 1460, is known only in two studio variants or replicas, in Amsterdam, the Rijksmuseum, and Berlin, Staatliche Museen, no. 1177. The motif of Mary's hands then reappeared in two later autograph works, the *Madonna greca* and the *Madonna and Blessing Child* (figs. 27, 29), and in two studio variants of the type, in the National Gallery of Art, Washington (Kress Collection), and in the Museo di Castelvecchio, Verona. Regarding the Trivulzio *Madonna* in the Sforzesco, N.B. Evelyn Sandberg-Vavalà's tentative attribution to Bellini's follower Bastiani ("Lazzaro Bastiani's Madonnas," *Burlington Magazine* 59 [1931]: 132). The Johnson *Madonna* has been heavily repainted, notably in the faces, in Mary's right hand, and in Christ's leg, making certain attribution difficult if not impossible. The Lehman *Madonna* was heavily restored by Duveen. The Lehman panel has also been overpainted; see John Pope-Hennessy with Laurence B. Kanter, *The Robert Lehman Collection*, vol. 1: *Italian Painting* (New York and Princeton, N.J., 1987), pp. 337–39. On replicas, variants, and collaboration in Bellini's shop, see Tietze-Conrat, "Unpublished *Madonna*"; Tietze, "Meister und Werkstätte"; and the following articles by Felton Gibbons: "Giovanni Bellini and Rocco Marconi," *Art Bulletin* 44 (1962): 127–31; "The Bellinesque Painter Marco Bello," *Arte veneta* 16 (1962): 42–48; and "Practices in Bellini's Workshop." Gibbons's analysis of the Bellini shop seems to be correct: the master assigned a composition to an associate and worked with him on the first version, or matrix, which was repeated thereafter by the assistant with little or no further participation by Bellini. But N.B. that the

Detroit *Madonna* of 1509 (fig. 45), painted with assistance, precedes the autograph Brera *Madonna* by a year (fig. 44).

21. The Trivulzio *Madonna* carries a fragmentary signature that seems to be a later addition. The contemporaneous inscription of Bellini's name on many panels that none but the most optimistic or misguided critic would attribute to him and the variation in the form of the signature were discussed by Gronau, "Signaturen."

22. Rollin van N. Hadley, director of the Gardner Museum, and Kristin Mortimer, the curator, generously made the museum files on the *Madonna* available to me, including records of Gabrielle Kopelman's restoration in 1975. See Philip Hendy, *European and American Paintings in the Isabella Stewart Gardner Museum* (Boston, 1974), pp. 8–20. Repaintings include the first two letters of the signature, IOANNES BELLIN/VS P., and most of Mary's face, neck, and brooch (the restorations being based on the Frizzoni *Madonna*; fig. 26). The figure of Christ is better preserved, with the exception of the repainted left thigh.

23. Moschini Marconi, *Gallerie dell'Accademia*, pp. 65–66. Formerly in the Magistrato della Milizia del Mare in the Palazzo Ducale, the *Madonna* was restored by Mauro Pellicioli in 1938–39; the reinforced outlines are probably his. The sky is clearly ruined. Antonio Vivarini and Giovanni d'Alemagna also painted such altarpieces in which the central panel of Madonna and sleeping Child is flanked by the figures of standing saints.

24. The sky background is completely repainted in the Frizzoni *Madonna*, and the painting has suffered from a clumsy transfer from panel to canvas, but the figures themselves are nonetheless a little better preserved than in the Gardner painting. The reinforced outlines in the Frizzoni *Madonna* may be due to the restorer Pellicioli.

25. To a considerable degree, Bellini defined these facial shadows in the underdrawing, executed in charcoal with touches of color. See Paola Zanolini, "Il restauro della Madonna greca," pp. 10–13, and Antonietta Gallone Galassi, "L'analisi del colore," pp. 14–15, both in Rosalba Tardito et al., *Giovanni Bellini a Milano* (Milan, 1987). Gallone Galassi notes that Bellini mixed costly lapis lazuli with less expensive azurite for the blues. All the colors are combined with lead white. Mary's gown is red lake, with a transparent layer of lake. The medium is egg tempera mixed in some areas with a resinous substance, probably bitumen. Zanolini explains that the panel was prepared with gesso and glue with traces of oil. Mary's mantle and Christ's garment are thickly painted, but the color is applied in very thin layers in the flesh and in the strips of azure sky to either side of the cloth. This azure was later (perhaps in the sixteenth century) covered with gold, of which traces are still visible around the Greek inscriptions. The letters, however, are original.

26. Bellini may have been assisted in executing this panel, but the condition is very poor, and it is possible that a restorer provided the "collaboration." Christ's face is completely repainted, and perhaps as much as two-thirds of the original surface is lost. When the *Madonna* was displayed in the magistracy of the Monte Nuovissimo in the Palazzo dei Camerlenghi in 1559, it was transformed into a triptych by Vitrulio Buonconsiglio. See Moschini Marconi, *Gallerie dell'Accademia*, pp. 66–67.

27. Bellini may also have had in mind the ancient prototype of the Pergamene *Fallen Gaul*, an example of which was later in the collection of the Venetian nobleman Dominico Grimani. He bequeathed the statue in the Museo Archeologico, Venice, no. 57, in 1523.

28. Restored in 1938–39 by Mauro Pellicioli. Impasto—or its ghost—is apparent here and indeed almost throughout Bellini's oeuvre in the whites and highlights. Studio variants of the Contarini composition include: Galleria Sabauda, Turin; Staatliche Museen, Berlin; and Rijksmuseum, Amsterdam.

29. See Smyth, "Venice."

30. The landscape is well preserved. None of the surviving autograph works painted between the Davis and the Contarini panels has a landscape background, but numerous shop works and collaborations by Bellini and assistants do have such settings, and lost compositions by him probably did so as well.

31. Giovanni Bellini's *Madonna* (fig. 33), now in the Accademia, was formerly in the Scuola della Carità. Restored by Pellicioli in 1938, it is in comparatively good condition. Cf. Mantegna's *Madonna and Child with Cherubim* in the Pinacoteca di Brera, Milan (Kristeller, *Andrea Mantegna*, pp. 306–8).

32. Bellini reprised the Child's posture for the Metropolitan *Madonna and Child*, no. 08.183.1, painted c. 1490 with studio assistance, and in several variants of this composition.

33. See also the portrait of *Jörg Fugger* (fig. 150).

34. Federico Zeri and Francesco Rossi suggest that Bellini may have been assisted in executing the background, especially the little figures at left, but otherwise consider the painting "in grandissima parte autografo." Restored and cleaned seven times since c. 1880 (inter alia by Mauro Pellicioli in 1932 and by Marcella Sorteni in 1979), the panel is in good condition. Painted as an image of private devotion, it was placed in the Carmelite nunnery of Sant'Anna, Albino, in the first half of the sixteenth century, evidently as part of abbess Lucrezia Agliardi-Vertova's dowry. The panel eventually came into the possession

of Giovanni Morelli. See Zeri and Rossi, *Raccolta*, pp. 128–29.

35. It is possible that this painting is a pastiche; N.B. the slick surface.

36. N.B. the Bellini studio *Madonna and Child with Saint John the Baptist*, Rome, Galleria Doria Pamphili.

37. Fry, *Bellini*, p. 34. Some of this glow is dirty varnish.

38. Bellini used violet more than any of his contemporaries, obtaining the color either by mixing ultramarine and red lake or by using violet lakes. See Lazzarini, "Colore," p. 142.

39. N.B. the similar treatment in Raphael's contemporary *Madonna of the Meadow* in the Kunsthistorisches Museum, Vienna. Marco Boschini often compared Bellini and Raphael, for example, in *La Carta del navegar pitoresco*, p. 46. N.B. also Alfonso d'Este's interest in obtaining works by both artists, which he evidently intended to display together; see chap. 4 at n. 44.

40. Bellini added several of these details late in the execution of the painting; they are not present in the underpainting, a fact revealed when the picture was transferred to canvas. See Ruhemann with Plesters, *Cleaning of Paintings*, pp. 156–61. The same is true of some landscape details of the portrait of a man in the collection of Queen Elizabeth II; see chap. 3 at n. 55 and fig. 161.

41. Cesare Ripa suggests that the stork with a serpent in its beak and sitting on a rock may signify Religion (*La più che novissima iconologia* [Padua, 1630], pt. 3, p. 12). For other interpretations of this group, see Wind, "Eloquence of Symbols," and Cast, "Stork and Serpent."

42. For the historiographic tradition, see Libby, "Venetian History," pp. 7–45.

43. The painting was restored in 1986, and this cleaning revealed the identity of the animal, previously thought to be a monkey because of disfiguring varnish (or alteration by an earlier restorer?).

44. N.B. also the sketchy underdrawing of the *Madonna greca* (fig. 27), and cf. the highly finished drawings beneath the surface of other paintings, such as those in the Metropolitan Museum (no. 08.183.1) and in the Harewood Collection (fig. 38). Although these underdrawings seem to be by Bellini himself, the final execution involved assistance. I postulate that Bellini provided such finished drawings in *some* cases precisely in order to guide his assistants.

45. The painting was transferred to canvas in the nineteenth century, however, and it is possible that some underdrawing may have been destroyed in the process; but N.B. Bellini's late surface additions in other works (above, n. 40). The greens are composed of copper resinate and lead white, with some lead tin yellow in the lining of the Virgin's mantle; the blues are azurite and lapis lazuli for her mantle; her red gown is red lake. The medium is primarily oil, although tempera was used in the light blues. See Zanolini, "La Madonna con Bambino benedicente," and Gallone Galassi, "L'analisi del colore," in Tardito, et al., *Bellini a Milano*, pp. 20–29.

46. Bellini incorporated similar images into altarpieces, such as the SS. Giovanni e Paolo polyptych (fig. 186 and app. 4), and the Pesaro *Coronation* (figs. 86–90). For another early example of this imagery, N.B. the destroyed painting by Squarcione, formerly in Berlin, the Kaiser-Friedrich-Museum; see Boskovits, "Giovanni Bellini," p. 387.

47. On this imagery, see Goffen, "Masaccio's Trinity," pp. 489–504, esp. pp. 497, 499.

48. The word *pietas* appears twenty-three times in the Bible; see Dobrzeniecki, "Mediaeval Sources," p. 5. Bellini's Rimini *Pietà* (fig. 60) was described as "imago domini nostri Iesu Christi Salvatoris mortui et sublati de cruce in formam pietatis"; see above, chap. 1 at nn. 95–96.

49. I shall use the terms *pietà* and *Dead Christ* interchangeably. On Mary as co-redeemer, see Dobrzeniecki, "Mediaeval Sources," p. 15; Cabrol, *De Corredemptione*; and Goffen, *Piety and Patronage*, pp. 61, 76 with further bibliography.

50. For anachronistic compositions that include saints who were not contemporaries of the Virgin and Child, see figs. 36, 37, 40–42.

51. Panofsky, "Imago Pietatis," and "Reintegration." Cf. Dobrzeniecki, "Mediaeval Sources." He is wrong to discount Panofsky's interpretation of the *Imago Pietatis* as a non-narrative *Andachtsbild* and right to insist on its narrative element. These paintings certainly have a narrative aspect, and this was understood by their first viewers, as Dobrzeniecki indicates. But they are clearly not narratives in the same way as those compositions that represent full-length figures in more complete spatial and chronological settings (e.g., fig. 52). These half-length images of the Passion are hybrids, combining the narrative and devotional, non-narrative modes of representation. See also above at n. 59.

52. Although the original frame has been lost, the paint edges confirm that the composition is complete.

53. The background was recognizably green when J. A. Crowe and G. B. Cavalcaselle studied the painting (*History of Painting*, 1:143 and n. 3).

54. A much-debated drawing in the Accademia is ascribed to Bellini and associated with the Brera *Pietà* by Hans Tietze and Erica Tietze-Conrat, *Drawings of Venetian Painters*, 1:89, no. 323. Giles Robertson sees a relationship between the drawing and Bellini's Correr *Dead Christ* (figs. 53, 55) but is nonetheless inclined to ascribe the sheet to Mantegna (*Bellini*, p. 24).

55. For Jacopo Bellini's comparable interest in heroic nudity, N.B. the drawing of a classical nude, evidently based on a sculpture or high relief, fol. 76 in the Louvre book (ill. in Degenhart and Schmitt, *Jacopo Bellini*, pl. 95). But unlike his son, the elder Bellini evidently did not translate these ancient types into a Christian context.

56. *Propertius*, trans. H. E. Butler (Loeb Classical Library, 1912; repr. 1976), *Sexti Properti Elegiarum, Liber Primus*, 21.1.3: "Quid nostro gemitu turgentia lumina torques." Charles Brink recognized Bellini's reference; see Robertson, *Bellini*, p. 55, n. 1. Propertius's work was available and circulated in manuscript copies long before the publication of a printed edition in Venice in 1472, which Hans Belting wrongly considers the post quem for the painting (*Giovanni Bellini Pietà*, p. 30). For example, Petrarch owned a manuscript of the ancient poet's Elegies that was transcribed for Salutati by 1380. See Ronald G. Witt, *Hercules at the Crossroads: The Life, Works, and Thought of Coluccio Salutati* (Durham, N.C., 1983), pp. 184–90. Perhaps the death of a Christian soldier at the fall of Constantinople in 1453 explains the sad inscription on the *Pietà*, for the poem by Propertius from which Bellini was quoting is addressed to a fallen warrior.

57. The cartellino that still displays the signature is wide enough to have included a date as well, and the high placement of the name implies a continuation of the inscription. See Zanetti, *Della pittura veneziana*, p. 49. N.B. the *Dead Christ with Mary and John the Evangelist in the Tomb* cited by Carlo Ridolfi in the Magistrato dell'Avogaria in the Ducal Palace (*Maraviglie*, p. 64). Boschini's more explicit description proves that this is the same painting, which would have been moved from its presumed original location in the chapel of Saint Nicholas, destroyed in the early sixteenth century; see Zanetti, *Descrizione*, p. 135; Detlev von Hadeln, "Beiträge zur Geschichte des Dogenpalastes," *Jahrbuch der königlich preussischen Kunstsammlungen*, Beiheft, 32 (1911): 1–33, esp. pp. 4–5; and n. 58 below for the chapel.

58. The presence of Saints Mark and Nicholas and the use of canvas indicate that the work was painted as a mural for the ducal Cappella di San Nicolò, which is substantiated by Ridolfi's evident allusion to Bellini's painting in the palace in 1646 (cited above in n. 57). (The low viewpoint indicates that the canvas was placed high on the wall.) No other provenance seems likely. The fourteenth-century chapel or church dedicated to Saint Nicholas, located at the south end of the Ducal Palace courtyard, was destroyed c. 1525. This is to be distinguished from the doge's private chapel, located at the opposite end of the courtyard, and apparently not identified as the chapel of Saint Nicholas until the early sixteenth century. See Pincus, *Arco Foscari*, pp. 22–23, n. 27, and Bassi, "Appunti," pp. 35–37. See also above, chap. 1 at nn. 105–8.

59. These additions were removed by Mauro Pellicioli in the 1948 restoration of the painting. N.B. also the mid-sixteenth-century adaptation of Bellini's *Madonna and Blessing Child* (fig. 29) for the Monte Nuovissimo.

60. Despite the authentic signature, many scholars have been inclined to credit this work to Gentile Bellini because its presumed "dryness" of style, especially in the figures of the flanking saints, seems more typical of him than of Giovanni (fig. 110). Much of this dryness is due to the poor preservation of the painting, however, and if the saints are less forceful in character and design, this may have to do more with the nature of the commission than with a putative division of labor between the brothers. The handling is typical of Giovanni, with impasto in some parts (e.g., the crown of thorns), and pigment thinly applied in other areas. Yellow pigment, not gilding, was used to paint gold objects and details. Finally, if Gentile had collaborated with his younger brother here, as is frequently suggested, one would expect that his signature would have come first: but this cannot be the case, because of the placement of Giovanni Bellini's name on the cartellino. Cf. app. 2, no. 6. The *Pietà* will be restored by Ottorino Nonfarmale, who kindly allowed me to examine it in his studio.

61. See also Meyer zur Capellen, *Gentile Bellini*, pp. 12–13. For the destroyed Ducal Palace murals by the Bellini and others, all lost in the fire of 1577, see Huse, *Studien zu Bellini*, pp. 56–71, and above, app. 5, pt. 3. For the provenance of the *Pietà*, see n. 58 above.

62. Emile Mâle, *L'art religieux de la fin du moyen âge en France: Etude sur l'iconographie du moyen âge et sur ses sources d'inspiration*, 3d ed. (Paris, 1925), pp. 98ff., 269, on the half-length images of the Christ as "abbreviations" of the Mass of Saint Gregory.

63. There are no stigmata in the hands of the Poldi *Christ*, but the painting is clearly finished. Perhaps the wounds were removed in an overzealous cleaning.

64. On van der Weyden's expression of emotion, see Panofsky, *Early Netherlandish Painting*, 1:249. For the Petrarchan comingling of joy and sorrow, the one making the other more keenly felt, see Martha Feldman's forthcoming essay, "The Academy of Domenico Venier: Poetry and Music in Venice around 1550."

65. Davies, *Earlier Italian Schools*, pp. 60–61. For valuable technical information about the painting, see Braham, Wyld, and Plesters, "Blood of the Redeemer." For the type of Christ and the use of such images as tabernacle doors, see

Colin Eisler, "Golden Christ," and Horster, "Mantuae Sanguis," esp. pp. 151–56. According to Horster, Bellini's picture is the first Venetian depiction of this Tuscan type.

66. Whether the blood of Christ should be venerated was a matter of considerable discussion in the mid-fifteenth century, the question being whether the blood shed by Jesus in the Passion, which must have been human blood, was hypostatically united with Christ after the Resurrection, and hence worthy of veneration. See Horster, "Mantuae Sanguis," pp. 161–64; for the Venetian veneration of a relic of the blood preserved in the Frari, see Goffen, *Piety and Patronage*, p. 21.

67. Horster, "Mantuae Sanguis," p. 158, identifies the angel with the chalice as the "Angelus Missae," citing Saint Ambrose in the canon prayer "De sacramentis," 4.6.27.

68. Saxl, "Pagan Sacrifice," pp. 344, 351–52. On the left are an altar, and, among other figures, a man in ancient dress holding a small sacrificial vessel in his left hand and lifting his right to perform the act of libation with a patera. The inscription on the altar reads: DIS MANIB / AVR[EL]IVS. / ( . . . )TI, the rest being hidden by Christ's hand. The wording indicates that this is a sacrifice to the dead, as Saxl explained. On the right, according to Saxl, are Porsena and Mucius Scaevola, but this interpretation was rejected by Davies, who saw in Christ's gesture an obliteration of the pagan ritual, not an adumbration of his sacrifice (*Earlier Italian Schools*, p. 60). More recently, Bellini's fictive relief has been explained as an archaeologically correct depiction of a pagan offering of incense in a *thymiaterion,* a basin of burning coals. See Thomas M. Troy, "Classical Reliefs and Statues in Later Quattrocento Religious Paintings" (Ph.D. diss., University of California at Berkeley, 1980), p. 250.

69. For the drawing, no. 436 in the Louvre, see Tietze and Tietze-Conrat, *Drawings*, 1:88–89, no. 319. The Tietzes consider the drawing to be "probably . . . from Bellini's late period." Robertson instead seems inclined to place the sheet c. 1472, but with an attribution to Andrea Mantegna (*Bellini*, p. 25).

70. See Saxl, "Pagan Sacrifice," pp. 343–44, for the quattrocento emphasis on the wounds as signs of love, the lance wound being called the "amatorium lavacrum," the "Laver of Love."

71. This may be the painting mentioned by Vasari in San Francesco della Vigna, who says the king of France (Louis XII) practically forced the Venetians to give it to him (Vasari-Milanesi, 3:163, and Gamba, *Giovanni Bellini*, p. 161). See also above, Epilogue at n. 3, and cf. n. 101, below.

72. On these technical and interpretive issues, see chap. 3 above at nn. 42–44.

73. The aged master who painted this tragic image had suffered the most terrible losses: he had seen both his wife and his only son predecease him. No matter who may have commissioned this picture, perhaps we may see in its intense emotion a reflection of Bellini's psychology.

74. Ringbom, *Icon to Narrative*.

75. For the panel in the Museum of Art, Toledo, Ohio, see Richter, "*Christ Carrying the Cross*." The recent restoration makes clear that the painting is not by Bellini. See also Hendy, "*Christ Carrying the Cross*." The Gardner panel has the delightful if dubious distinction of having been attributed to Giorgione in Ghiotto and Pignatti, *L'Opera completa*, p. 108, no. 200, and to Bellini in Virgilio Lilli and Pietro Zampetti, *L'Opera completa di Giorgione*, Classici dell'arte 16 (Milan, 1968), p. 97, no. 47. The Rovigo version, painted in oil on panel, was restored by Laura Mora in 1983–84; see Mauro Lucco, pp. 30–31, in Pier Luigi Fantelli and Lucco, *Catalogo della Pinacoteca dell' Accademia dei Concordi di Rovigo*, Fondazione Giorgio Cini, Cataloghi di raccolte d'arte, n.s., 17 (Vicenza, 1985). For a variant ascribed to Bello in Budapest, Musée des Beaux-Arts, see Anchise Tempestini, "Marco Bello tra Giovanni Bellini e Vincenzo Catena," p. 320, in *Scritti di storia dell'arte in onore di Federico Zeri*, vol. 1, ed. Mauro Natale (Milan, 1984).

76. See Anderson, "Christ Carrying the Cross," on the painting attributed either to Giorgione or to Titian, c. 1508–9.

77. In 1550 and again in 1568, in the second edition of his Lives, Vasari credited Giorgione with the painting. But, perhaps unaware of his self-contradiction, Vasari also attributed the picture to Titian in this edition. Presumably he was basing this assertion on testimony from Titian himself—but Titian was not known to be a disinterested witness of his own accomplishments.

78. For Franciscanism and its influence in an earlier period of Italian art, see Goffen, *Spirituality in Conflict*, and *Piety and Patronage*, chaps. 1, 2. On Incarnation theology in the fifteenth century, see O'Malley, *Praise and Blame*; and for its visualization in art in the display of Christ's nude body, Steinberg, *Sexuality of Christ*.

79. Perhaps his text is represented in the open Bible that lies on the parapet in the Kimbell version, as suggested by R. F. Brown et al., *Catalogue of the Collection*, Kimbell Art Museum (Fort Worth, 1972), pp. 27–29. Or perhaps Bellini did not intend to be so literal. In the Berlin variant of this composition, painted with assistance, the Infant sucks his fingers in a naturalistic, childlike way.

80. That restoration was completed in 1869; the organ was originally located near the door of the Cappella di San Mauro and the old sacristy, in the right nave. The altar was constructed of wood and considered too ruined to merit preserva-

tion. Bellini's *Madonna* was restored early in the nineteenth century and given a new frame at that time. See Zanetti, *Chiesa della Madonna*, pp. 45–46, 86. For the restoration in 1968 by Antonio Lazzarin, see Valcanover, *Restauri*, p. 44.

81. Joannes Georgius Palferus [Palferius], *Memorabilia venetiarum monumenta antiquis recentioribusque lapidibus insculpta*, Venice, Biblioteca Nazionale Marciana, MS Lat. Cl. X, cod. cxlix (3657), fol. 191v, and Cicogna, *Inscrizioni*, 2:260, n. 22, and p. 261. See also Biblioteca Correr, MS Gradenigo 201, fol. 181r. In the absence of Navagero's testament, which I have not been able to find, one cannot be certain that he endowed the altar at his tomb site, but his patronage seems likely, given his social position and the use of the word *monumentum* in the inscription, suggesting a reference to more than the tomb slab itself.

82. Navagero, son of Michiel Navagero, was Luogotenente of Udine. He was married twice, in 1442 and again in 1452, and was survived by three sons: Bernardo, Francesco, and Michiel. See Cicogna, *Inscrizioni*, p. 260, and ASV, Barbaro, 5:467–68.

83. Renaissance terminology does not distinguish between an altar and a chapel; the words are used interchangeably.

84. If Bellini's customary procedure were to offer "ready-made" Madonna paintings to his patrons, this would explain the absence of documentation: bills of sale or receipts instead of contracts would have been drawn for these transactions, and such documents are unlikely to have been preserved.

85. Herbert Lank restored the Harewood *Madonna* in 1968. The paint surface is very worn, revealing underdrawing (hatching and cross-hatching), especially in the donor's face and in the Virgin's neck. The *Madonna* was tentatively identified with the Hollivier picture by Gronau, *Giovanni Bellini*, p. 209, no. 112, with a list of copies. The donor wears a red gown and black stola, identifying him either as a Venetian senator, hence noble, or a ranking secretary in the Chancellery, that is, a *cittadino originario*. The Hollivier, or Olivieri, were original citizens, as were the Bellini; see Andrea da Mosto, *L'Archivio di Stato di Venezia* (Rome, 1937), 1:76, and above, Intro., at n. 14. But the age of this donor seems to preclude his having achieved significant rank in the Chancellery, if a citizen, or any position higher than senator, if noble. The same is true of Bellini's *Young Senator* (fig. 154) and the *Young Patrician* (fig. 155). On the significance of age, see Robert Finlay, "The Venetian Republic as a Gerontocracy: Age and Politics in the Renaissance," *Journal of Medieval and Renaissance Studies* 8 (1978): 157–78. For the garments, see the *Memorie dell'illustre famiglia de' Freschi, Cittadini originarii veneti* (Biblioteca Nazionale Marciana, MS Ital. VII.165 [8867]); P. Brown, *Venetian Narrative Painting*, p. 26, n. 81; and esp. Neff, "Chancellery Secretaries," p. 8, n. 1. The illustrations in the MS *Memorie* seem to suggest that the width and placement of the stola may be distinguishing features.

86. N.B. also the *Madonna and Child with Donor*, formerly in the collections of the marquess of Londonderry and of Lady Mairi Bury, no. 73 in the Christie's (London) sale of 8 July 1977. Related to these pictures are compositions in which the Mother and Child are accompanied by one saint, who may represent the onomastic or patron saint of the donor, such as the Bellinesque panel in the Galleria Doria Pamphili, Rome.

87. Jeronimo (Girolamo) Hollivier q. Barthesaris, 29 June 1524, in ASV, Girolamo Canali, Busta 190, no. 339. See also Paoletti, *Raccolta*, p. 15. It is not known where the painting was displayed in the Madonna dell'Orto or indeed whether the provisions of Hollivier's will were executed. The clause regarding his burial appears in his testament. For the bequest of the painting, see the codicil, 16 May 1528, fols. 84r–v: "Vollgio ett hordeno che el quadro della Nostra Dona fatto per man de Zuan Bellin che a el rettratto della bona memoria del q[uondam] messer Marcho fo mio fradello vollgio ett hordeno quello sia soazado de inttaio dorado e fatto ttantto bello e sonttuoxo quantto posibel posi esser, e quello sia posto in lla giexia de Madona Sancta Maria dell'Ortto in lluogo de palla a quallche uno delli allttari della ditta giexia de Madona Sancta Maria dell'Ortto hoveramentte della sagresttia sechondo chome parera ai padri della ditta giexia."

88. N.B. also the eventual transformation of two other devotional images to altarpieces, the *Madonna of the Pear* (fig. 35) and the *Circumcision* (fig. 135).

89. For the Cranach, see Anthony F. Janson, *Great Paintings from the John and Mable Ringling Museum of Art* (New York, 1986), pp. 16–17. For Carpaccio, see Jan Lauts, *Carpaccio: Paintings and Drawings* (London, 1962), pp. 232–33.

90. On Carpaccio's cycle for the Scuola di Sant'Orsola, which was located next to SS. Giovanni e Paolo in Venice, see P. Brown, *Venetian Narrative Painting*, pp. 56–59, 279–82; Lauts, *Carpaccio*, pp. 18–26, 227–30; and Moschini Marconi, *Accademia*, pp. 97–105. The cycle was restored by Ottorino Nonfarmale in 1982–85. The inventory made by the commissaries of the estate of Damian Michiel of Santa Maria Formosa, dated 25 January 1530, m.v. (*modo veneto*), includes "four paintings of the Madonna" among the household furnishings, together with such items as "eight silver forks" (ASV, SS. Giovanni e

Paolo, Busta M, fasc. xxxviii, no. 4, fol. 8r).

91. See Julius S. Held, "A Tomb by Cornelius Engebrechtsz.," *Oud-Holland* 67 (1952): 233–37.

92. See Paul F. Watson, "A *Desco da Parto* by Bartolomeo di Fruosino," *Art Bulletin* 61 (1974): 4–9, and Goffen, "Renaissance Dreams," pp. 701–2.

93. Dominici, *Regola*, pp. 34–35. The *Regola* was written c. 1405.

94. Dante's famous verse expresses the same belief, addressing the Virgin as daughter of her son, "Figlia del tuo Figlio." For Guariento's fresco, which was severely damaged by fire in 1577, covered by Tintoretto's *Paradiso*, and finally, in 1906, detached and removed to the Sala dell'Armamento, see Sinding-Larsen, *Christ in the Council Hall*, p. 45, and Wolters, *Bilderschmuck*, pp. 292–93. For dolls representing the Christ Child, see Christiane Klapisch-Zuber, "Holy Dolls: Play and Piety in Florence in the Quattrocento," in her *Women, Family, and Ritual*, pp. 310–29.

95. Vasari, who was in Rimini in 1547–48, identified a *Pietà* in San Francesco as a work painted by Bellini for Sigismondo Malatesta, who died in 1468 (Vasari-Milanesi, 3:170). But Vasari described a composition with only two putti, whereas Bellini's has four. Was Vasari referring to this painting? Or, intending this painting, did he mistake its patronage? Perhaps Sigismondo's *Pietà* was presented by his heirs and successors to their friend and counselor Migliorati. His will is preserved in Rimini, Archivio Notarile, Atti Mangiaroli, 1499; see Campana, "Notizie," p. 419.

96. The passage reads: "Cui capelle ipse test[at]or reliquit testatoris tabulam depictam manu Iohannis Bellini, in qua est depicta imago domini nostri Iesu Christi Salvatoris mortui et sublati de cruce in formam pietatis" (Rimini, Archivio Notarile, Atti di Andrea Mangiaroli, 1499, fol. 64r, published in Campana, "Notizie," pp. 417–19). The painting was also listed in an inventory of Migliorati's possessions, compiled after his death in February 1499: "An ancona or panel in which is painted the image of Our Lord Jesus Christ in the form of a Pietà, descended from the Cross." There is no evidence, however, that Migliorati ever got his chapel; and the painting by Bellini was instead kept in the sacristy of San Francesco, where Vasari later saw it.

97. But cf. the *Ecce Homo* noted by Boschini in the Procuratia de Citra. See Zanetti, *Descrizione*, p. 158.

98. This clause is from the codicil to the will of Elena Trevisan, 17 December 1521, amending the testament of March 1520: "Io Helena Trivisan consorte del M.co misser Vito Antonio fo de misser Marco dela contra[da] de S. Sten . . . per il presente mio codicillo lasso in segno de amor uno Cristo fato per man de Zuan Belin et la Croxe dorada cum il crucefixo darzento et il tabernaculo . . . el pregi dio per lanima mia" (ASV, Notarile, Bartolameo Raspi, Busta 446, no. 168). See also Gustav Ludwig, "Nachrichter," pp. 90–91. Domenico's having taken monastic vows necessitated his mother's codicil, excluding him from a major share of his mother's estate, which he otherwise would have inherited with his brothers, in accordance with the original provisions of her testament. For Elena's father, Grand Chancellor Giovanni Dedo (or Diedo), see Neff, "Chancellery Secretaries," pp. 269, 418–19.

99. See Brown, with Lorenzoni, *Isabella*, pp. 149–67, and N.B. the letters of Isabella and Lorenzo transcribed on pp. 162ff. Her painting is sometimes associated with the *Nativity* in Washington; see Hans Tietze and Erica Tietze-Conrat, "*Allendale Nativity*."

100. "Item mi attrovo una bella Nostra Donna de man de Zan Bellin, et uno altro quadro di Oloferne, voglio chel sia dato a m[esser] Jer.mo [Gerolamo q. Paolo] Contarini, da esser goduti per loro fratelli" (ASV, Notarile, Testamenti Cesare Ziliol, Busta 1261, no. 884, 1 and 21 February 1578). I speculate that this painting may be the *Madonna* bequeathed to the Accademia of Venice by Girolamo Contarini in 1838 (fig. 32).

101. As recorded by Marino Sanuto, *Diarii*, 10:col. 150, April 1510. See also Giangorgio Zorzi, "Notizie," p. 484. Louis reigned from 1462 to 1515. Cf. n. 71, above.

102. "Habiamo deliberato . . . donar a la Illustrissima Madama de Lanson [Alençon] uno quadro de pictura de la imagine de la gloriosa Vergene, questo piuii excellente et perfecto che esser el possi: et poiche in questa nostra cita [città] ne habiamo pur ritrovati alcuni pulcherimi, ma vechii et alcuni hanno varie oppositione, iusta li appetiti de quelli li hanno visti, consistendo questa cosa ne la volunta et desyderio de chi l'ha à goder, et desyderando nuy imprimis satisfare à la Excellentia sua, habiamo deliberato pel dicto effecto farne far uno novo in tuta belleza et perfectione. Et perho volemo et commettemovi che . . . debiate far intender questo desyderio et invention nostra a la prefata Illustrissima Madama cercando intender el suo voler et piacer circa la grandeza et qualita de detto quadro. Lo esser de la gloriosa S. Verzene cum el fiolo, qual figure la voria li fusseno dai canti, et de qual grandeza, et in summa ogni altra particularita necessaria" (ASV, Capi del Consiglio de' Dieci, Lettere, Filza 16, [anno] 1515, no. 383). See also Ludwig, "Nachrichter," p. 90.

103. "Magnifico et Cl.mo Domino Joanni Baduerio doctori [et eq]uiti, oratori veneto [ad Christianissi]mam M[ajesta]tem Francorum [pro]ficiscenti. . . . Solicito etiam la perfection del quadro de la Ill.ma sorela del Cristianissimo che in vero

sara bela cosa. El maistro è Zuan Bellin et pochissimo li mancha à compirlo perfectamente. . . . Duc. Venetiis Die xv Januarii [1515, m.v., i.e., modern 1516]. Servitor et Compadre G[aspare] a Vidua" (ASV, Procuratori di San Marco de Citra, Misti, Busta 57 [the Commissaria of Francesco Badoer, fasc. x–xxii], fasc. xxii, b). See also Ludwig, "Nachrichter," p. 90.

104. For the provenance, see chap. 1, n. 58.

105. For the groans described in the inscription of the Brera painting, see above, chap. 1 at n. 56. N.B. also a lost work recorded by Sansovino in the Ridotto dei Procuratori de Sopra (in the Procuratia Vecchia) in which Bellini represented the Madonna with Saints Mark and Theodore, patrons of the republic; *Venetia città nobilissima et singolare*, ed. Giovanni Stringa (Venice, 1604), p. 216b.

106. The decoration of the chapel in 1319 is documented by ASV, Maggior Consiglio, Deliberazioni, Fronesis (1318–1325), fol. 28v, published by Lorenzi: "Quia Ecclesia beati Nicolai de Palacio est tota nuda picturis, capta fuit pars, quod . . . debeant expendi et poni in laborerio picturarum dicte Ecclesie pingendo in ea hystoriam Pape [Alexander] quando fuit veneciis cum domino Imperatore [Frederick Barbarossa] et alia que videbuntur" (*Monumenti*, p. 12, no. 36).

107. On the Venetian cult of Saint Nicholas and his chapel in the Palazzo Ducale, see Muir, *Civic Ritual*, pp. 88–89, 97–101, 132–33. N.B. the oxymoronic juxtaposition of conflicting emotions in Petrarch, among others; see above at n. 64.

108. See above at n. 59 for the sixteenth-century alterations to this work; and above at n. 118 for these kinds of donations by doges and other state officials.

109. See app. 2, no. 11.

110. See app. 3. Giovanni had painted two works for the Scuola di San Gerolamo, one of them signed and dated 1464, according to Ridolfi, *Maraviglie*, 1:64. For the pictorial decoration, see Humfrey, "St. Jerome Cycle."

111. The painting was formerly in the magistracy of the Milizia del Mar in the palace, but even if the *Madonna* was not commissioned for the Palazzo Ducale, its scale proves that it was made either as an altarpiece (presumably a triptych or polyptych) or as a votive picture. For the provenance, see Moschini Marconi, *Accademia*, p. 66. Regarding Bellini's stylistic flexibility, I wonder whether he influenced his friend Bembo's conception of different styles in the *Prose della volgar lingua* of 1525. For the author's emphasis on "the Ciceronian maxims of decorum, variation, and separation of stylistic levels," see Feldman, "Academy of Domenico Venier."

112. The violet is much worn but original. See Moschini Marconi, *Accademia*, pp. 65–66, no. 66; and, for Bellini's preference for this color, see above, n. 38.

113. On the related imagery of the Joyful Pietà, in which Mary smiles over the body of her dead Son, see Tadeusz Dobrzeniecki, "Mediaeval Sources," pp. 23–24 and n. 88.

114. For the provenance, see Bottari, *Tutta la pittura*, 1:37. N.B. the small *Madonna and Child* cited by Boschini in the Tribunale in the "Suprema stanza" of the Heads of the Council of Ten in the palace; perhaps this is the same painting? See Zanetti, *Descrizione*, p. 114.

115. See Brian Pullan, *Rich and Poor*, p. 138, with bibliography in n. 19.

116. Ridolfi, *Maraviglie*, 1:27–28. On p. 28, n. 6, von Hadeln identified the three procurators. Marco Boschini also cited the painting (*Ricche minere*, p. 73, and Zanetti, *Descrizione*, p. 161). The signature and date, which were inscribed on a cartellino on the lower step of Mary's throne, were lost when the canvas was cut. See Elisabeth C. G. Packard, "Bellini Painting." The painting was executed in two stages; see Eric M. Zafran, *Fifty Old Master Paintings from the Walters Art Gallery* (Baltimore, 1988), p. 46.

117. Barbarigo was doge 1487–1501. His painting was restored by Ottorino Nonfarmale. See Valcanover et al., *Pala Barbarigo*, esp. the technical report by Lorenzo Lazzarini ("Le analisi di laboratorio," pp. 23–28).

118. According to Sinding-Larsen, the custom of hanging doges' votive pictures in the palace council rooms evidently began with Leonardo Loredan, doge 1501–21 (*Christ in the Council Hall*, pp. 30–42). But N.B. a payment to Gentile Bellini on 22 January 1487 (1486, m.v.) for the canvas for a painting of Doge Marco Barbarigo, Agostino Barbarigo's brother and immediate predecessor in the dogate; ASV, Provveditori al Sal, Busta 61, fol. 149v (new fol. 120v), published by Lorenzi, *Monumenti*, p. 101.

119. On the ducal insignia and those additions, including ermine, on the occasion of a public "coming or going in triumph," *andata in trionfo,* see Sinding-Larsen, *Christ in the Council Hall*, pp. 156–58.

120. According to the diarist Girolamo Priuli; see Brunetti, "Due dogi," p. 283. In recording the doge's death, Sanudo copied an anonymous Latin biography of Barbarigo, describing his hot temper, avarice, arrogance, and general obnoxiousness ("Vita serenissimi principis, domini Augustini Barbadici, noviter defuncti," cols. 114–15, in *Diarii*, vol. 4 [Venice, 1880], ed. Nicolò Barozzi). For more dispassionate accounts, see Franco Gaeta, *Dizionario biografico degli italiani*, 6:47–49; da Mosto, *Dogi*, pp. 260–66; and Filippo Nani-Mocenigo, "Testamento del Doge Agostino Barbarigo," *Nuovo archivio veneto*, n.s., anno 9, vol. 17, pt. 1 (1909): 234–61. The doge grew his beard as a sign of mourning after the death of his only son.

121. Davies, *Earlier Italian Schools*, pp. 544–47, no. 750; Meyer zur Capellen, *Gentile Bellini*, pp. 154–55;

and Puppi, "Pala votiva." To be sure, it was a donor's prerogative to select his saintly patrons, but the way in which a scene is interpreted reflects the artist's judgment.

122. Perhaps Saint Christopher was included as an intermediary against the plague, presumably the serious outbreak that occurred in 1478, the first year of Mocenigo's dogate.

123. ASV, Notarile, de Floriani, Busta 416, c. 6: 17 July 1501 with a codicil of 15 August.

124. "Item, nui hordinemo che la pala nostra granda ch'è in la crozolla del palazo la sia mandada al monastero de Santa Maria di Anzolli predetto, et per esser ben conforme quela figura di Nostra Dona coi anzolli ad esser messa sopra al suo altar grande de la sua gesia, ma che i nostri chomissari la debia farla adornarla sì de sotto chome da i ladi et de sopra per modo che la sia ben adornatta per contento nostro et de quele venerabilli done. Et quanto plus presto sarà messa tal palla in opera, tanto plus speremo in la beata Verzene Maria, habia esser nostra avvochata apresso el nostro summo chreator Idio. Et che nostri zeneri, nì nostre fie, nì nostri nevodi non posino demeterla nì in la chasa granda nostra nì in altro luogo salvo sopra l'altar grando de quelo devotissimo et religioso monastero; la qual semo zerti che in ogni tempo la habi a pregare Idio per l'anima nostra e de tuti i altri nostri che sono pasatti de questa vita" (ASV, Notarile, de Fiorini, Busta 416, c. 6). The doge's provisions for appropriate framing of the picture anticipated Hollivier's similar concerns; see n. 87 above. N.B. also Barbarigo's use of the word *pala,* "altarpiece," to describe his painting, even though it served no such function until long after it was executed.

125. See Goffen, *Piety and Patronage*, pp. 130–31 and notes. The painting is signed and dated 1339, the year of the doge's demise. The lunette format of Bastiani's painting (fig. 71) indicates that it too was made for a tomb, which, however, does not survive.

126. See chap. 3 at nn. 41–42. A later, Venetian example of such imagery is Titian's Pesaro *Madonna*, the altarpiece of a funerary chapel, in which Bishop Jacopo Pesaro is presented to the Virgin and Child by Saint Peter, in reference to the donor's papal service. For Titian's *Madonna*, see Goffen, *Piety and Patronage*, chap. 4.

127. King, "Caldiera," p. 27, alluding to Caldiera's *De iconomia*. See also her article "Personal, Domestic, and Republican Values," and her recent volume, *Venetian Humanism*, sec. 2 and pp. 344–45 for a profile of Caldiera. For the possible association of Bellini's landscape settings with Venetian rule of the mainland, see above, at n. 30.

128. "Die 30 [January, 1516] Capitulum fuit per cunsilium q. mutuaretur corona de argento pulcra ex novo domine Johanj Belino ex.mo pictori et hoc per duos dies vel circha" (ASV, SS. Giovanni e Paolo, Busta 11, vol. C, Liber Consiliorum, fol. 77v). The dating in the volume is "normal"—that is, not Venetian style (m.v.). On the crown itself, see also ibid., Registro XI, Liber consiliorum, fol. 53v, 11 May 1511; the brothers decide to have a silver crown made for the altar dedicated to Mary in the church. This seems to be the piece that Bellini borrowed five years later. Dr. Bonnie Blackburn generously called these passages to my attention, which had been previously noted by Puppi in *La grande vetrata della Basilica di San Giovanni e Paolo* (Venice, 1985), p. 19.

129. See above at nn. 100–103.

130. For Bellini's accurate depiction of an Anatolian carpet, see fig. 159 and Johanna Zick-Nissen, "Eine Gruppe von Gebetstep-pichen und ihre Datierung," *Berliner Museen*, N.F., 11 (1961): 6–14.

131. Jacopo's drawing in the British Museum sketchbook, fols. 43v–44r, dating c. 1455–60, is contemporary with Mantegna's picture. I credit Jacopo rather than his son-in-law with the conception because the asymmetrical composition is typical of the older artist and is seen even in his earlier drawings in the Louvre book, begun in the 1430s. For the dates of the drawings, see Degenhart and Schmitt, *Jacopo Bellini*, p. 13. For Mantegna's picture, see Davies, *Earlier Italian Schools*, pp. 59, 335–36; Kristeller, *Mantegna*, pp. 468–69, docs. 6, 7; and Lightbown, *Mantegna*, p. 404, suggesting a date c. 1455—that is, before the San Zeno predella *Agony* (Musée des Beaux-Arts, Tours), which is also close to Bellini's composition. The San Zeno altarpiece was painted between 1456 and 1459; see Lightbown, *Mantegna*, pp. 406–7, and Puppi, *Trittico*. Giovanni Bellini's *Agony in the Garden* was restored by Helmut Ruhemann in 1967.

132. The possibility of Marcello's patronage was discussed by Crowe and Cavalcaselle, *Painting in North Italy*, 2:85; Kristeller, *Mantegna*, pp. 468–69, docs. 6, 7; and Lightbown, *Mantegna*, p. 404. For Marcello's manuscript life of Saint Maurice, with illuminations attributed to Mantegna, see above, chap. 3, n. 8.

133. The mourning putti of the early *Crucifixion* are the predecessors of this apparition (fig. 5).

134. See Meiss, *St. Francis*. On the history of the saint's characterization in art, see Goffen, *Spirituality in Conflict*, chap. 2. Bellini painted with a mixture of tempera and oil on an unusually thin layer of gesso, applying oil glazes over the tempera; see William Suhr's conservation report of 1942, pp. 2–3, in the curatorial records of the Frick Collection. (Suhr restored the painting in 1942 and cleaned it lightly in 1964.) Bellini's combination of media is typical of works executed in the period of transition from tempera to oil. The

use of tempera is concealed from the eye, however, and has no apparent effect on Bellini's style and handling of the picture surface, which have all the characteristics of oil. See Stout, "Mixed Technique," pp. 69, 71, and Johnson and Packard, "Methods." In 1986, Maryan Ainsworth of the Metropolitan Museum of Art examined the *Francis* with infrared reflectography that reveals Bellini's freehand sketching, possibly in charcoal, for such details as the saint's head, hands, and feet, and more finished (perhaps traced) drawings for the architecture. Ainsworth also noted the use of a gray tone applied with hatching strokes as underpainting for the trees at upper left and for the donkey, and she considered that the rabbit may have been painted "as an afterthought." Her report is filed in the Frick's curatorial records for the painting.

135. As William Suhr recorded in 1942, p. 1, the sides and bottom of the composition are complete: the edges of the paint film leave a ¼-inch margin of the panel unpainted. At the top, however, the paint film continues to the edge of the panel, indicating a loss. Suhr's notes are found in the curatorial records of the Frick Collection. This loss may measure approximately 8⅛ inches, according to Everett Fahy and Keith Christiansen of the Metropolitan Museum of Art and to Ria O'Foghludha of Columbia University, who were able to examine the painting out of its frame and generously shared their observations with me. The painting consists of two panels connected by butterfly joints, the lower panel measuring 28½ inches in height, and the upper, only 20⅝ inches. The two panels were cut from the same piece of wood, and if they were originally of the same dimensions, as one might expect, then the difference between them represents the area that has been lost. See also above at nn. 139–40.

136. For Leo's blessing, see Fleming, *Bonaventure to Bellini*. For other interpretations, see Meiss, *St. Francis*; and Turner, *Vision of Landscape*, pp. 57–65.

137. On the Franciscan "cult of personality," see Goffen, *Spirituality in Conflict*, esp. chap. 2, and Rosalind B. Brooke, "The Lives of St. Francis of Assisi," in *Latin Biography*, ed. T. A. Dorey, Studies in Latin Literature and Its Influence (London, 1967), pp. 177–98. Bellini's saint became the prototype for the Francis in Titian's Pesaro *Madonna*, completed in 1526; see Goffen, *Piety and Patronage*, chap. 4. N.B. also Giorgione's adaptation of Bellini's *Francis* in the Castelfranco *Madonna*.

138. Thomas of Celano, *First Life of St. Francis*, 2.18, trans. Placid Hermann, in Marion A. Habig, ed., *St. Francis of Assisi, Writings and Early Biographies: English Omnibus of Sources for the Life of St. Francis* (Chicago, 1973), p. 332. For the Latin text, see Celano, *Vita Prima S. Francisci Assisiensis et eiusdem Legenda ad Usum Chori* (Quaracchi, 1926), p. 132.

139. Goffen, *Spirituality in Conflict*, pp. 14–22, 26, 41–42, 80–81. The controversy regarding the saint's stigmatization continued throughout the fifteenth and sixteenth centuries; see Goffen, "Sixtus IV," p. 221. Bellini's picture clearly never included the wound in the side, though thinly painted wounds in the feet might have been incorrectly removed in an early attempt at restoration. This seems unlikely, however, in view of Suhr's comment that "on the whole the paint film is in excellent condition," even though the panel had been "repeatedly restored in the past"; see his report of 1942, pp. 2, 4, in the curatorial records of the Frick Collection.

140. See Meiss, *St. Francis*, p. 27. Meiss considered the composition to be essentially complete and noted that no additional form or figure is revealed by X rays. Cf. Fletcher, "Provenance." Fletcher is too optimistic regarding the ownership of the painting, which belonged to "Zuan Michiel" and was then evidently purchased by Taddeo Contarini, in whose house it was seen in 1525 by Marcantonio Michiel. The Michiel family was very large, including several documented Zuans, any of whom might have owned the *Francis*—and none of whom can be definitively associated with it. There are too many of them, and no mention of the painting (in their wills, for example), aside from Marcantonio's pithy reference. Nor is there any evidence to suggest that the picture was ever intended or used as an altarpiece. A painting of the *Stigmatization* ascribed to Bellini by Boschini cannot be the work now in the Frick Collection, unless the author was inaccurate in his account of the composition. Boschini explicitly describes the way in which rays from Christ's wounds penetrate the saint's flesh, as in Bellini's Pesaro *Coronation* predella of the *Stigmatization* (fig. 89). See Boschini, *Carta del navegar pitoresco*, p. 344.

141. Meiss, *St. Francis*, p. 23. For Francis's emphasis on the Passion, see Goffen, *Spirituality in Conflict*, esp. chap. 2. The dramatically illuminated laurel may also signify the Burning Bush; see Fleming, *Bonaventure to Bellini*, pp. 48–56.

142. Meiss, *St. Francis*, p. 23.

143. Ibid., p. 22, fig. 41, citing Howard McP. Davis.

144. As noted by Meiss, *St. Francis*, p. 14. See also Meiss, "Jan van Eyck and the Italian Renaissance" (1956), in his *Painter's Choice*, pp. 19–35; Wiess, "Jan van Eyck"; and Campbell, "Netherlandish Pictures."

145. For fifteenth-century stage sets, see Peter Meredith and John E. Tailby, *The Staging of Religious Drama in Europe in the Later Middle Ages: Texts and Documents in English Translation* (Kalamazoo, Mich., 1983), pp. 85–86, and Timothy Verdon, "Donatello and the Theater: Stage Space and Projected Space in the San Lorenzo Pulpits," *Artibus et Historiae* 14 (1986): 49. For Bellini's

painting, see Antonio Paolucci in *Gli Uffizi, catalogo generale* (Florence, 1979), p. 161.

146. This painting has variously been interpreted to represent the pilgrimage of the soul (Ludwig, "Bellinis Madonna am Zee"); a sacra conversazione (Rasmo, "Sacra Conversazione"); an allegory of Mercy and Justice (Verdier, "Allegorie"); and a "Paradise Garden" (Braunfels, "Paradiesgärtlein"). The most extensive consideration of the picture's imagery is Coltellacci and Lattanzi, "Studi belliniani." Norbert Huse follows Rasmo and Verdier in associating this painting with the work done for Isabella d'Este between 1502 and 1504 (*Studien*, pp. 82–86). Giles Robertson agreed with this suggestion in his review of Huse's volume (*Burlington Magazine* 108 [1976]: 33–34). But the date seems far too late to me. I agree with Braunfels, who argued for a date c. 1488 ("Paradiesgärtlein," p. 12).

147. It was the condition of the figure in black and white that first led observers astray: she seems to have no feet and to hover miraculously above the ground. In fact, this apparent anomaly is due to the transparency of the pigment. She is not supernatural, she does not float in air, her feet are visible if faded, and they support her on the pavement in the normal way of mortal feet. Cf. Susan J. Delaney, "Iconography," who argues that the figure is levitating and therefore represents Hope and who identifies this woman's companion as Faith and the tree as Charity, the three virtues seen here as Job's daughters ("Iconography," pp. 332, 334). But the colors that they wear are unsuitable for Faith, traditionally associated with green, and Hope, who wears white but surely not black.

148. Christ identified himself as "the green tree" (Luke 23:31); see Land, "Poetry of Bellini's *Allegory*," p. 63.

149. See *The Golden Legend of Jacobus de Voragine*, trans. and ed. Granger Ryan and Helmut Ripperger (New York, 1969), p. 89, and *Acta Sanctorum*, 1 January, p. 603, no. 4, and p. 604, no. 8. Ludwig noted that Bellini's group of the saint and centaur resembles a woodcut published in an edition of the *Golden Legend* printed in Venice in 1518, probably reproducing an older image or an older type ("Bellinis Madonna am See," pp. 163–86). In the background of Bellini's *Allegory*, the donkey may be related to another story told of Saint Anthony (*Golden Legend*, p. 102).

150. Sinding-Larsen, *Christ in the Council Hall*, pp. 48–49.

151. Sansovino, *Venetia*, pp. 124r–v, cited by Sinding-Larsen, *Christ in the Council Hall*, pp. 48–49.

## Chapter 2: Images for Public Devotion

*Note to epigraph*: Ridolfi on the saints of the San Giobbe altarpiece (figs. 108–10): "D'arie così gentili e di movimenti così suavi, che rapiscono gli animi, qual maniere di figure destano somma divotione nelle mente de' fedeli" (*Maraviglie*, 1:66).

1. For the lost altarpiece of the Gattamelata Chapel of the Santo in Padua, see the Introduction at nn. 20–22, and app. 2, no. 6. Other early altarpieces ascribed to Bellini are problematic for various reasons; see app. 4 for the SS. Giovanni e Paolo polyptych (fig. 186), the Carità triptychs (fig. 187), and the lost Carità altarpiece of Saint John. Bellini's first signed and dated altarpiece is the Frari triptych of 1488 (figs. 116, 117).

2. Bellini's *Sacra Conversazione* was commissioned by the confraternity of Catherine of Siena for the first altar on the right in SS. Giovanni e Paolo, the great Dominican church of Venice. The scuola's patronage may have been assisted by the noble Bragadin family; in 1506, Marco q. Giovanni Bragadin bequeathed funds for masses, candles, and oil for the lamp of the altar of Saint Catherine, where he was to be interred (ASV, SS. Giovanni e Paolo, Busta P, fasc. x, no. 207, fol. 493v). Bellini's altarpiece was in poor condition by 1550, when the confraternity of Saint Catherine, which had merged with that of Saint Vincent, allocated funds for its restoration (ibid., no. 7, c. 12r, and no. 188). By 1726 the church had granted the confraternity permission to replace Bellini's work with a new altarpiece (ibid., no. 157). For the lost altarpiece, see Rona Goffen, "Bellini's Altarpieces, Inside and Out," *Source* 5 (1985): 23–28. For the polyptych of the Scuola di San Vincenzo Ferrer in the same church, see app. 4 and fig. 186. On the early history of the sacra conversazione, see Goffen, "*Conversatio*."

3. The *Saint Giustina* was commissioned by the Borromeo for a monument in San Francesco Grande in Milan, which was under construction in 1471. See Bernard Berenson, *The Study and Criticism of Italian Art*, 3d ser. (London, 1916), pp. 38–61. For the style of the lost altarpiece, N.B. also the Pesaro *Coronation* (figs. 86–90).

4. Testament of Saint Francis (1226), trans. Benen Fahy, in Marion A. Habig, ed., *St. Francis of Assisi, Writings and Early Biographies: English Omnibus of the Sources for the Life of St. Francis* (Chicago, 1972), p. 67. For the Latin text, see *Die Opuscula des hl. Franziskus von Assisi*, ed. Kajetan Esser, Spicilegium Bonaventurianum, 13 (Grottaferrata, 1976), pp. 438–39.

5. Zanotto, *Pinacoteca Veneta*, 1:index, p. 9. Zanotto also admired the delicate gradations of light and shade but criticized traces of "the old hardness, and especially in the hands." He was referring to the "harder" drawing of earlier works, such as the Pesaro *Coronation*, as opposed to the colorism of the Naples *Transfiguration*. As Michael Hirst reminds me, we would know much

more about Bellini's palette if the watercolor copy, published in black and white by Roger Fry, could be found; the copy is the frontispiece of Fry's *Bellini.*

6. Ridolfi, *Maraviglie*, 1:65–66. However, Ridolfi mentioned "the great panel of St. Catherine of Siena," Bellini's lost altarpiece, before recounting the story of his attempt to learn Antonello's secret of oil painting. The implication is that Bellini's work was painted before Antonello's arrival in Venice. Cf. Vasari-Milanesi, 2:570–71. Regarding Bellini's "disguise": as an "original citizen," he would have dressed like a gentleman; see chap. 1, n. 85.

7. Crowe and Cavalcaselle, *History of Painting*, 1:154. Discussing the Pesaro *Coronation* on p. 167, the authors praise Bellini's adept handling of oil. For Bellini's pigments and media, see Lorenzo Lazzarini, "Le analisi di laboratorio," in *La pala Barbarigo di Giovanni Bellini*, Quaderni della Soprintendenza ai Beni Artistici e Storici di Venezia, 3 (Venice, 1983), pp. 23–28; Lazzarini, "Colore nei pittori veneziani," pp. 138–39, 142–43; Packard, "Bellini Painting"; Paola Zanolini and Antonietta Gallone Galassi in Tardito et al., *Giovanni Bellini a Milano* (Milan, n.d. [1987]), pp. 10–18, 20–29; and the technical discussion of the *Saint Francis*, nn. 134–35 for chap. 1, above.

8. Sansovino, *Venetia*, ed. Martinioni, 1:155–56.

9. Mather, "Messina's Altar-Piece"; Wilde, "Pala di San Cassiano." For a more convincing interpretation, see Robertson, "Architectural Setting," and esp. Robins, "Paintings of Antonello."

10. Berenson considered that the San Cassiano figures "witness to the influence the Venetian exerted upon the Sicilian" ("A Madonna at Vienna and Antonello's S. Cassiano Altar-Piece" [1916], in *Study and Criticism*, p. 106, n. 1).

11. But N.B. the poor condition of many works; the palette of the Frizzoni *Madonna*, for instance, seems light in part because of abrasion (fig. 26). Similarly, the pale blue of the Davis *Madonna* is in fact the underpainting applied by Bellini, the color itself having been removed (fig. 14).

12. I consider that the lost work and the Pesaro altarpiece were produced at about the same time but that the *Coronation* was completed after the *Sacra Conversazione*. For the date, see Meiss, *St. Francis*, pp. 41–42; Pallucchini, *Bellini*, p. 57; Smyth, "Emergence of High Renaissance," pp. 227–28, and above, at nn. 14–15. It is not known whether Bellini went to Pesaro to paint the altarpiece, but if he did so, he would probably have found kinfolk there (app. 1: Family Tree).

13. The painting is signed IOANNES BELLINVS., below Christ's right foot, on the polygonal base of the throne. The *Coronation* was the high altarpiece of San Francesco but had been moved to the first (westernmost) chapel on the left by 1610. See Carolyn Wilson, "Giovanni Bellini's Pesaro Altarpiece: Studies in Its Context and Meaning" (Ph.D. diss., Institute of Fine Arts, 1976), p. 112, app. 4. The *Coronation* was restored lightly in 1915 and more completely at the Istituto Centrale del Restauro di Roma in 1948. See Brandi: "Cleaning of Pictures," p. 184; "Factual Observations"; and "Postilla." Both the *Coronation* and the *Pietà* were restored in 1988 by the Istituto Centrale, Enea, and the Vatican Museum laboratories, under the direction of Marisa Tabasso. The two panels were exhibited together in Pesaro in 1988–89; Ileana Chiappini di Sorio's "Ancora sulla pala di Giovanni Bellini a Pesaro: precisazioni e ipotesi," in *La pala restaurata*, is in press (Venice, 1989).

14. Jacobus de Voragine, *The Golden Legend*, trans. and ed. Granger Ryan and Helmut Ripperger (New York, 1969), p. 452. Here Mary's soul is enthroned; her body arrived later (p. 454).

15. Federico Zeri reconstructed the altarpiece in "Cinque schede."

16. For Bellini's knowledge of music, see Winternitz: "*Lira da Braccio*," and *Musical Instruments*, pp. 39, 44, 97, and 188, n. 3.

17. Ileana Chiappini di Sorio informs me that the *Pietà* is complete, that is, uncut, and that evidence on the backs of the two panels confirms that they were once attached. Because of their different frames, however, she argues that the two were not connected by Bellini but perhaps combined at some later date. (The frame of the *Pietà* is inferior in quality and carved with somewhat different foliate motifs, as Chiappini di Sorio has discussed in *Bellini*, pp. 22–24.) I disagree with her conclusions. Other explanations may account for the differences between the frames, including the possibility that damage necessitated replacing the *Pietà* frame or that its high placement (confirmed by the painting's low vantage point) permitted compromise or variation. One must also ask why the *Pietà* would have been added to the *Coronation* if this were not Bellini's intention. Giovanni Andrea Lazzarini, in Becci, *Catalogo*, p. 20, referred to Bellini's painting "with all its ornaments above and around [the main image], which one can count among the most noteworthy pictures in our city" ("con tutti i suoi ornamenti sopra ed intorno, e si può questa contare tra le più insigni pitture della nostra Città"). Gustavo Frizzoni identified the Vatican *Pietà* as a missing element of the *Coronation* altarpiece ("Per la reintegrazione della pala del Bellini," *Emporium* [1913]: 227–28; and Frizzoni, "For the Reintegration of a Great Altarpiece," *Burlington Magazine* 22 [1913]: 260–69). Note the "small Deposition of Christ from the Cross" ascribed to Bellini in a list of paintings in the sac-

risty of San Francesco compiled by Domenico Bonamini in 1797 and published by G. Vaccaj, "Quadri delle chiese di Pesaro asportate dai francesi," *Rassegna marchigiana* 2 (1923–24): 245–48. Vaccaj concluded that this was the crowning panel of the *Coronation* but was not convinced that it was the same work now found in the Vatican. More recently, see Wilson, "Altarpiece," app. 3, with a summary of the confusing provenance of the *Pietà*. She also cites a description of the altarpiece by Giuseppe Oddi in 1736–37, written in connection with the canonization proceedings of Bl. Michelina, who is depicted in a pilaster of the frame. Oddi does not mention a *Pietà* above the *Coronation*, but neither does he mention the predella; he was writing not for art historians but for an ecclesiastical court concerned with only one detail of the altarpiece. Chiappini di Sorio, *Bellini,* considers the Vatican panel too small to have been set atop the *Coronation*. But, as I argue above, the *Pietà* was possibly accompanied by other panels, and it is associated with the *Coronation* visually and iconographically. If the Vatican panel was not originally part of the *Coronation* altarpiece, then another painting, similar in subject and composition, must have been.

18. For the spiritual and historical significance of the stigmatization of Francis, see Goffen, *Spirituality in Conflict*, pp. 14–22, 26, 41–42.

19. The face of the dead Jesus differs somewhat from that of the King of Heaven, but so do the faces of Saints Francis and Paul in the Coronation differ from themselves in the predella.

20. For Francis and the use of the vernacular, see Goffen, "*Conversatio*," and *Spirituality in Conflict*, p. 25.

21. Voragine frequently quoted Jerome in the description of Mary's glorification (*Golden Legend*, pp. 456–58).

22. "Thronum paratum conscende: coronam gemmis ornatam suscipe. . . . Et virgo. . . . Non reclamabo: non renitar: sed reverendo quodam mentis assensu voluntati tuae annuens: eademque quando te genui: protuli verba: nunc repeto dicens. Ecce ancilla domini: fiat mihi secundum verbum tuum [Luke 1:38]" (Giustiniani, *Opera*, fols. xlix r–v). Not all descriptions of the Assunta are the same; cf. Mary's readiness as described in Voragine's *Golden Legend* on the Assumption, "My heart is ready, O Lord!" and so on (p. 451).

23. Voragine quotes Gerardus: " 'The most ineffable Trinity Itself applauds her with unceasing dance' " (*Golden Legend*, p. 458).

24. The illusionistic repetition of the frame in the fictive architecture resembles the lost Saint Catherine altarpiece (fig. 82). But the *Coronation* frame is carved and gilded wood: the continuity of altarpiece and frame, like that of Mantegna's altarpiece for San Zeno in Verona, creates an illusion that is self-referential—painting and frame are related to each other but related to the viewer's world only by association.

25. The monument was identified by Ludwig and Bode, "Altarbilder," p. 137, n. 1. See also Fahy, "New Evidence." Wilson's and my own interpretation of the building's reference to the Heavenly Jerusalem is probably correct even if the fortress is based on the castello of Gradara, conquered by Alessandro Sforza in 1467. See Wilson, "Bellini's Pesaro Altarpiece," pp. 139–45. Bellini used the same fortress again in the background of the Barbarigo votive picture (fig. 68), as Roger Fry noted (*Bellini*, p. 37).

26. N.B. also symbolic windows that represent Christ as Savior, God the Father, the Trinity, and/or the concept of salvation; see Carla Gottlieb, "The Mystical Window in Paintings of the Salvator Mundi," *Gazette des Beaux-Arts* 56 (1960): 313–32.

27. See app. 5, pt. 3.

28. Voragine, *Golden Legend*, p. 337.

29. For the Franciscan pope, see Goffen, "Sixtus IV," pp. 218–62, and p. 255 and n. 135 for the assault on his coronation day.

30. It has been thought that the *Coronation* was commissioned by Costanzo Sforza, lord of Pesaro, or even by his father, Alessandro. But there are no grounds for this association and one good reason to disassociate it: none of the ruling family's onomastic saints appears in the composition. For the mechanism of patronage by the mendicant orders, see Goffen, *Piety and Patronage*, pp. 83–84.

31. The heads of Peter and James are repainted in the Naples *Transfiguration*. Branches of the tree on the right are an addition, perhaps of the sixteenth century; originally the tree was bare. The man in the background who approaches the Oriental is also an addition. See R. Causa, *Catalogo della IV Mostra dei restauri* (Naples, 1960), pp. 55–57. According to Roger Fry, the buildings in the background between Christ and Elijah are monuments of Ravenna, the mausoleum of Theodoric and the campanile of Sant'Apollinare in Classe (*Bellini*, p. 27). But these may be general types, not specific buildings. The plants were identified by Minio, "Iconografia," pp. 166–67.

32. Edoardo Arslan's association of the altarpiece and the Cathedral of Vicenza is convincing and generally accepted; see his *Catalogo*, pp. 27–28, 35, and "Studi belliniani," pp. 47–48; Barbarano de Mironi, *Historia ecclesiastica della città, territorio e diocesi di Vicenza, Libri I–VI* (Vicenza, 1649–1762), 5:29; and Gronau, *Bellini*, p. 204, n. 66.

33. Fioccardo's words: "Honorifice et sumptuose compleatur cum ferriata quae claudi possit, eam salizando cum quadretis seu lapidibus vivus albis et rubeis" (Arslan, *Catalogo*, p. 28). The Capella Fioccardo

was the second chapel on the left aisle: the entire left aisle of the cathedral was under construction in the 1460s and '70s, and this perhaps led the various patrons to press for completion of their chapels (ibid., pp. 26–28). According to Arslan, the exterior arch is original, the vaults are reconstructed, and the exterior socle is restored, using original elements. N.B. also the sixth chapel, rebuilt under the patronage of Gaspare Trissino in 1483 with a *Resurrection of Christ* for its altar by Bellini. For family chapels with gates, see Goffen, *Piety and Patronage*, p. 38.

34. In Venice, Benedetto Pesaro and his brothers waited a decade between beginning construction of their chapel in Santa Maria Gloriosa dei Frari and the installation of their altarpiece by Giovanni Bellini, signed and dated in 1488 (figs. 116–19).

35. Moschini Marconi, *Accademia*, pp. 74–75; Huse, *Bellini*, p. 53.

36. The painting was "restored" in 1731 (ASV, S. Michele in Isola, Busta 27, Entrata-Uscita 1730–1740, fol. 145v). See also Meneghin, *S. Michele*, 1:323, n. 85. The Zorzi Chapel measures approximately 9 × 21 ft. (3 × 7 m.). It is lighted by two round-arched windows placed approximately 5 feet from the pavement; the altarpiece would have been set between these windows. The intrados of the arch above the semidome is decorated with putto heads and what seems to be grain, alluding to the theme of rebirth.

37. ASV, Convento S. Michele in Isola, Busta 2, Registro 1, c. 184r–v. Parts of this document were transcribed and published by Ludwig and Bode, "Altarbilder," 131–32, with an old busta number and with some minor errors, which I have corrected in the following transcription: "[5 June in S. Michele] . . . presentibus viro nobili domino Petro Loredano spectabilis domino Laurentii, Marco Antonio q. [i.e., *quondam*, "the former"] Francisci de Florentia pictore et M.o [magistro] Moreto magistri Martini de Bergomo [Coducci]. . . . Ibique cum sit quod spectabilis vir dominus Marcus Georgio q. magnifici domini Bertutii . . . in ipso monasterio construi facere unam capellam ad honorem et nomen gloriosae virginis matris Mariae, in qua etiam construi posset unam arcam pro cadevere suo et suorum heredum et successorum. . . . de novo totaliter renovari et fabricari cum capellis de novo fiendis. Et supplex ac humiliter requisiverit Rdu. d. abbatem et suos fres. [fratres] quatenus velit et sibi placeat impartivi et concedere unam ex illis capellis denuo fiendis, et in ipsa construi facere posset unum altare ad nomen gloriosae virginis Mariae et ipsum fulciri omnibus necessariis ac etiam unam arcam pro cadavere suo et suorum heredum et successorum offerens se exburtare nedum expensas fabricae ipsius capellae, videlicet ducatos centu[m] auri de presenti et omnes alias expensas necessarias pro fulcimentis et ornamentis ipsius altaris et ipsam capellam dotare aliquali convenienti dote et introytu prout eius conscientiae videbitur et placuerit, ut quotidie in ea in perpetuum celebretur una missa pro remissione suorum delictorum et remedio animae sue et suorum progenitorum ac heredum et successorum suorum. . . . omnes monaci professi in eodem monasterio habentes vocem in capitolo, et representantes maiorem partem sui capituli unanimes et concordes nemine eorum dissentiente aut discrepante pro se et successores suos jure perpetue et irrevocabilis concessionis dederunt concesserunt et traditerunt spectabili domino Marco Giorgio presenti et acceptanti et stipulanti et recipienti pro se suisque heredibus et successoribus illam Capellam de novo construendam apud altare magnum ad manum dextram cum libertate potestate et auctoritate construi faciendi in ea unum altare ad momen et honorem gloriose virginis matris Mariae et ipsum fabricare et omnibus rebus et ornamentis sibi necessariis pro celebranda missa et alia divina officia, et unam archam tantum pro se et heredibus et successoribus suis." As the concession makes clear, the original intention was to dedicate the altar to the Virgin.

38. On 31 August 1479, Zorzi's mother, Cristina, made her will, requesting burial in the sepulcher that he had had constructed. The monks were to say daily Masses for her soul in the family chapel. The notary's copy of her holograph testament is ASV, Notarile Natale Colona, Busta 360, no. 101, fol. 71v: "Ego Cristina relicta quondam messer Bertucy Georgio [Zorzi] . . . ho statuito de mia propria mano sopra el prexente foio nottar el testamento et ultima mia volonta. . . . Volgio che'l mio chorpo sia messo a San Michiel de Muran nel'archa ha fato far Marco mio fiol, al qual monastier laso ducati dodese ogni an[n]o da poi el mio manchar de la prexente vita con chondizion che i diti frati siano tegnuti farmi dir hogni dì una messa in dita chapela per l'anima mia." The relevant clause from Cristina Zorzi's testament is also recorded in ASV, Convento S. Michele in Isola, Busta 2, Reg. 1, c. 284v. The transcriptions of the will and of this clause in Ludwig and Bode, "Altarbilder," p. 133, have several errors, the most important being the insertion of the words "della ressuretione" in the S. Michele register: the chapel is not in fact identified there as the Chapel of the Resurrection. In 1515, some forty years after the concession of the chapel, Marco Zorzi made his own holograph will, likewise requesting burial in the family sepulcher: "volgio che el corpo mio sia sepulto a San Michiel de Murano in l'archa che io fici far nela chapela a mi concesa fino de l'ano 1475 adì 5 zugno per quel missier l'abate con il suo chapitolo" (ASV, Notarile, Pietro Florian, Busta 408, no. 214, dated 12 March 1515). A note on

the verso indicates that Marco Zorzi died just over two weeks later, on 27 March. Zorzi's son Bertuccio was also buried in the chapel, "dressed in the habit of the Camaldulensian brothers of San Michele" (ASV, Notarile, Giacomo Grasolario, Busta 1183, no. 93, 12 November 1523). The widow of one of his descendants was later interred in the chapel; her tomb on the north wall identifies: "Contarena Zorzi, widow of the former Marc'Antonio, died January, 1569." An inscribed plaque with the family arms commemorates "Marino Zorzi, for himself and his heirs, March 1, 1782"—three centuries after the original endowment by Bellini's patron, Marco Zorzi.

39. According to Vittorio Meneghin, the family tomb was originally inscribed "Marcus Georgio Bertucci Filius Sibi et Posteris V. Fieri Fecit. 1477," but this was later changed by a Marino Zorzi in 1782 (*S. Michele*, 1:302, n. 14). See also n. 38, above.

40. Sansovino, *Venetia*, p. 85, and Ridolfi, *Maraviglie*, 1:66–67. According to Ludwig and Bode, the landscape is Monselice, in the south of the Euganean hills; here, as on other occasions, Bellini was accurate—or at least evocative—in his recording of a place ("Altarbilder," p. 137).

41. See Tietze and Tietze-Conrat, *Drawings*, 1:92–93, no. 347. Bellini's recycling of motifs—his artistic economy—characterized not only his autograph works but the immense production of his shop and indeed of artists working throughout the Veneto in his sphere of influence. This "parsimonious" practice was continued by Venetians throughout the following century, Titian providing a notable case in point. See Tietze, "Early Version."

42. Some of the material here is found in my "Bellini, S. Giobbe," with additional archival and historical information. It seems that Bellini's patron was the Scuola di San Giobbe, assisted by the unknown patron whose generosity (if not his identity) is recalled by the shields with the rearing horses (figs. 111, 112). The scuola's patronage is suggested by the conspicuous placement of Job in Bellini's altarpiece and by the record of an "altarpiece with its saints" in an inventory of 1753 (ASV, Scuole Piccole e Suffragi, Busta 375, "Libro di Avensari della Scolla di San Gibbe [*sic*] L'anno 1753"). Elizabeth Hamer Jones consolidated the colors in 1971.

43. N.B. that in 1476, Gentile Bellini designed a pulpit for the Scuola Grande di San Marco, to which both he and Giovanni belonged. The pulpit was executed by the sculptor Antonio Rizzo, obviously capable of having produced his own design but in this instance following a project by a painter. See Sohm, *Scuola Grande*, p. 242. The frame of Giovanni Bellini's Frari triptych (fig. 116), also related illusionistically to the painted architecture, is inscribed on the back with the name of the carver; see Goffen, *Piety and Patronage*, p. 190, n. 38. See also Creighton Gilbert, "Peintres," on the division of labor.

44. See Kathi Meyer, "St. Job as a Patron of Music," *Art Bulletin* 36 (1954): 21–31. These instruments were highly regarded, hence worthy of celestial musicians.

45. The exemplar of faith and patience, Job was a traditional patron of hospitals, as indeed at San Giobbe, built near a hospital dedicated to him already in the fourteenth century. For Job and the imagery of Christ's redeeming sacrifice, see Frederick Hartt, "Carpaccio's Meditation on the Passion," *Art Bulletin* 22 (1940): 25–35; and Zeri with Gardner, *Italian Paintings*, pp. 15–16.

46. For the life and imagery of this saint, see Goffen, *Spirituality in Conflict*, app. 2.

47. The stigma in his right foot is also visible. In a seventeenth-century Corpus Christi procession in Venice, Dominic was paired with Francis, the two great mendicant saints appearing as companions of the doge: perhaps this repeated an older conception, relevant also to their presence in this altarpiece with its ducal and political resonance. For the procession, see Muir, *Civic Ritual*, p. 230. For the civic imagery of Bellini's altarpiece, see above at nn. 50–51.

48. See above, chap. 1 at n. 138, for the prayer of Thomas of Celano describing this intermediation. N.B. that Celano quotes the Book of Job both at the beginning of this prayer and at the end of the following section of the biography of Francis.

49. M. A. Lavin, "Montefeltro Altarpiece"; Shearman, "Logic and Realism"; and Meiss, *Painter's Choice*, pp. 105–50.

50. Christ's gestures evoke his sacrifice as in depictions of the Pietà. For the roles of Mary and Christ, see also Carra Ferguson O'Meara, "'In the Hearth of the Virginal Womb': The Iconography of the Holocaust in Late Medieval Art," *Art Bulletin* 63 (1981): 75–88; Otto Semmelroth, *Mary, Archetype of the Church*, trans. Maria von Eroes and John Devlin (New York, 1963), pp. 130–31; and Sinanoglou, "Christ Child."

51. Crowe and Cavalcaselle, *History of Painting*, 1:163.

52. The saint had predicted Moro's election to the dogate; see Goffen, *Piety and Patronage*, app. 1. For the doge's bequest, see ASV, San Giobbe, Busta 8, "Stampa al Laudo del Venerando Monastero di S. Giobbe contro la Veneranda Schola di San Bernardino in San Giobbe." Bernardino had died in 1446 and was canonized in 1450. The church was identified with reference to both Job and Bernardino as early as 1461 in a bull issued by Pope Pius II on 30 June, alluding to Doge Moro's support: "Ecclesiae olim Job nuncupatae sub invocatione

dicti Sancti Bernardini" (ASVat, Registro Vaticano 514, Pii Secundi Bulla Secretae Lib. I, fol. 60v). Professor Martin Lowry most generously brought this document to my attention. See also ASV, San Giobbe, Busta 1, fol. 44r, the testament of Cataruza Polani, 23 April 1464, establishing a fund at "Sancto Job et Bernardino," and fol. 37r, a copy of the testament of Petrus de Peracisco (?), 11 May 1489, requesting burial "in Sto. Job dicto St. Bernardino." The church was dedicated in 1493.

53. The story is also known as the Peace of Venice or Donation of Alexander. See Goffen, *Piety and Patronage*, p. 148, with bibliography; Muir, *Civic Ritual*, pp. 119–34; and above, chap. 1 at nn. 106–8 and app. 5, pt. 3. For the drawing by Carpaccio in the Crocker Art Gallery, Sacramento, which shows the pope presenting Doge Ziani with an umbrella like the baldachin in Bellini's altarpiece, see Lauts, *Carpaccio*, p. 277, no. 49.

54. See Goffen, *Piety and Patronage*, chap. 5; Sinding-Larsen, *Christ in the Council Hall*, and "Immagine"; and Wolters, *Bilderschmuck*, esp. pp. 289–305.

55. "[In San Giobbe] one must see a noteworthy panel by Giovanni Bellini, which he painted at the beginning of his art" (Sabellico, *Sito di Venezia*, p. 21). The Latin edition, *De situ urbis libri tres*, was republished in 1502, and an Italian translation was printed in Venice in 1544 by Lucio Fauno. Sanudo admired the altarpiece when the church was dedicated in 1493; Marin Sanudo (Marino Sanuto), *Cronica*, Venice, Biblioteca Correr, MS Cicogna 1920, fol. 25.

56. For the bubonic plague of 1478, see Nicolò Trevisan et al., *Cronica di Venetia*, Biblioteca Nazionale Marciana, MS It. VII.519 (8438), fol. 289r. Crowe and Cavalcaselle, *History of Painting*, 1:163, implied a date c. 1478. For stylistic arguments regarding a date c. 1478–80, see also Huse, *Bellini*, pp. 48–55, and esp. Smyth, "Emergence of High Renaissance," pp. 220–24.

57. On the back of the central panel, written in ink in cursive characters, is the name of the framemaker, Jacopo da Faenza: "fece 1488. adì 15 dece[m]brio maistro iachomo de faeca." See Pietro Paoletti, "Notizie di Venezia," *L'Arte* 5 (1902): 125. This was discovered when the triptych was removed during the restoration of the chapel. Paoletti records no other inscription, and I do not know where more recent authors may have found the different version (with a date in February) commonly repeated but evidently incorrect.

58. The related drawing of Saints Benedict and Mark in the British Museum is too retouched (evidently by Rubens) to attribute with certainty, and whether it was done as a study for the triptych or as a copy is unclear. See Popham and Pouncey, *Italian Drawings*, p. 13.

59. Translated by Robertson, *Bellini*, p. 89. The significance of the text was recognized by Ettlinger, "Iconography," p. 64 and nn. 9, 54, 67. For the iconography and patronage of Bellini's triptych, see Goffen, *Piety and Patronage*, chap. 2, esp. pp. 40–61. Bellini's two inscriptions—in the apse and in Benedict's Bible—make clear that the subject of the altarpiece is the Immaculate Conception.

60. On the back of the *Saint Peter Martyr* are various rough sketches. See Gino Fogolari, "Disegni." Although it was presumably part of an altarpiece, this painting is unrelated to the two panels in the Strossmayerova Galerija, Zagreb, with which it is sometimes associated. See Gronau, *Bellini*, p. 206, and Robertson, *Bellini*, p. 89. Note also the *Madonna and Sleeping Child Enthroned*, here fig. 24, which is the fragment of a triptych or polyptych. For Bellini's sixteenth-century triptychs, see above, chap. 2 at nn. 72–74. On the form itself, see Lankheit, *Triptychon*.

61. See Bortolan, *S. Corona*, pp. 263–69, and Arslan, *Catalogo*, p. 66.

62. Archivio di Stato, Vicenza (hereafter ASVi), Convento di Santa Corona, Busta 110, "Istromenti in pergamena dal 1500 al 1508, N. 1712 a 1768," which includes on fol. 1 the following record by the prior of the convent of Santa Corona, dated 10 April 1522, the year of Garzadori's death: "Pro ornamento Templi nostri Magnificus Domine Baptista Gratianus Dignissimus Comes Palatinus per seipsum in vita pro sua quadam eximia munificentia et animi magnitudine perfecit, ut plane cognoscant priores singuli qui pro tempore erunt, et patres conventus et totius Congregationis nostrae quantum ipsi Domine Baptista debeamus et quantum pro eo et integerrima q. eius coniuge ac filiis deum orare teneamur, qui seipsum nobis totum." On fols. 1–5, the prior recorded a copy of the agreement of 26 November 1500: "D. Baptista Gratianus D. Valerii filius, Vicentinus, Comes Palatinus, et cupiens dum vivit et post mortem dignum relinquere monumentum prius ex orato Divino Numine, ut coeli favor et gratia coeptis omnibus invocanda semper adsit, feruore sacro et animo pio accensus sacellum unum Divo Ioanni Baptistae in Templo Dominicae Coronae propria impensa erigi, absolui, et dicari statuit. . . . [the brothers of the chapter are listed] concedi, tradi, et assignari, atque conferri locum ipsum vacantem prope aram Divae Mariae Virginis versus chorum, ut possit et valeat ipsum fabricare et exornare ad honorem summi Dei ac Divi Ioannis Baptistae, nec non Templi ornamentum omnes unanimes et concordes consulte agentes locum ipsum ut supra requisitum laeto animo et hilari corde tradiderunt concesserunt et assignaverunt praedicto D. Baptistae praesenti et

acceptanti." The goods and monies to be paid are specified, including grain for the convent; the chapel is conceded in perpetuity and Garzadori's obligation is perpetual, in exchange for which the priests will say Mass at his altar for his soul, and for souls of his wife, Paola, and their sons, Leonardo and Antonio, "in life and in death." The decoration of the chapel is considered on fols. 4–5: "Quod in dicto loco capellae undique finiente aliquid aliud fabricari non possit intelligendo maxime de depositis, insignibus, sepulchris, scabellis, et aliis huiusmodi impedientibus, in incommodum et deformitatem ipsius sacelli." (Bortolan published this passage in *S. Corona*, p. 264. Our transcriptions have minor variations, and perhaps Bortolan was recording another copy of the document; he did not specify his source.) Bortolan also noted that two antique statues were placed to either side of the altar (p. 268). The sculptures were eventually removed to the Museo Civico; at least one of them is now in storage there, as Dr. Wendy Steadman Sheard kindly informs me. This is inscribed, as Bortolan noted, "Iphigenia post vestales prima virgo Deo dicata." I have no information regarding the companion figure mentioned by Bortolan.

63. The tombs were inscribed: BAPTISTA GRATIANUS V.P. HUMANAE VITAE CONDITIO SEPULTURAE TANTUM HAERES EST V. P. BAP. GRATIANUS VAL. F. AB IMP. FEDERICO III. DONATUS PRAECLARIS HONORIBUS SIBI ET PAULAE UXORI CHARISS. ET LEONARDO ET ANTONIAE DULCISS. LIBERIS PRIMO AETATIS FLORE SUBREPTIS V.S.L.M. MDXXIII. See Bortolan, *S. Corona*, p. 269. The testament of GianBattista Garzadori, dictated in 1522, is preserved in ASVi, Archivio Notarile, Testamenti, 1521–1522, Libro 63. He requested burial in his tomb in Santa Corona, with his wife and sons, and asked that he be interred in the habit of a pilgrim, with the red cross on his breast: "Lasso, ordeno, et cussì per ultima mia volonta testo chel corpo mio sepulto sia in lo santo tempio de Santa Corona in la mia capella intitulata de Sancto Giovanbatista acio le cenere et ossa de Leonardo [et] Antonio mei carissimi fioli et de Paula consorte . . . et per devotione mia dal corpo mio rivestito sia de habitus de peregrino in la rosa croce hierosolimetana in petto . . . iuxta il consueto de peregrina chel Sancto Sepulchro et Sancta Terra hanno visitati." Because his sons had predeceased him, ownership of the chapel was to pass to his nephew Gerolamo. The will of Garzadori's wife, who also predeceased him, is: ASVi, Testamenti in bombacina, 22 December 1502, published by Giovanni Mantese in the *Giornale di Vicenza* in 1984.

64. Arslan, *Catalogo*, pp. 56–57. See also Bortolan and Rumor, *Guida di Vicenza*, pp. 142–43.

65. The *Cronica praeteriti temporis* records the beginning of construction: "Item del sporascritto anno [1501] Battista q. messer Valerio di Gratiani cittadino di Vicenza principiò a far le sua capella e fece far quel bel saliso di preda rossa e bianca con prefili di preda nera con un quadro di marmoreo in mezzo al detto saliso con letter intagliate. . . . Item del detto anno [1502] del mese di Dicembre il detto Battista fece mettere alla detta capella tutte quelle colone intagliate di preda con la cornice et friso di sopra dal altare" (Bortolan, *S. Corona*, p. 265).

66. Bellini's painting was presumably commissioned for the altar of the Madonna, but I have been unable to determine by whom. The only sixteenth-century reference to the altar of the Madonna in San Zaccaria is in connection with Andrea Giustinian's endowment for Masses in his holograph will of 1502, but he does not seem to have been the patron of the altar. See ASV, San Zaccaria, N. 4, "XXII Catastico, Mansionarie III," fol. 124 and the fifth unpaginated sheet after fol. 137.5, and ASV, Notarile, Testamenti Cristoforo Rizzo, Busta 1227, no. 20. An altar of the Madonna in the earlier (pre-1457) church of San Zaccaria was patronized by Lucia Morosini; in her will of 1448, she provided six soldi for a lamp (ASV, San Zaccaria, Busta 2, "XII Indice generale dell'Archivio 1800," 1:318). Her estate was still making payments to the altar of the Madonna in the new (present) church in the sixteenth century and indeed as late as 1755 (ibid., p. 319). Bellini's painting was stolen by Napoleon's troops, and, adding injury to insult, the French transferred it from panel to canvas. The picture suffered further damage when it was returned to Venice in 1815 and thereafter restored by order of the Austrian government. See Cicogna, *Inscrizioni*, 4:691. In the restoration completed by Antonio Lazzarin in 1976, the strip that had been added at the top of the altarpiece to adapt it to its new frame was removed. See Valcanover, *Restauri a Venezia*, p. 65.

67. The design of the frame may therefore preserve something of the original. In any case, the same frame design was repeated for all the altars of the nave in a redecoration of the church, which I assume was part of the alterations carried out in 1595. See Paoletti, *Architettura*, p. 63, and Franzoi and Di Stefano, *Chiese di Venezia*, p. 404.

68. On the imagery of ostrich eggs, see Meiss, "*Ovum Struthionis:* Symbol and Allusion in Piero della Francesca's Montefeltro Altarpiece" [1954], in his *Painter's Choice*, pp. 105–29.

69. For example, the mantles, especially Peter's, are painted with a mixture of orpiment (orange-colored arsenic trisulfide) and realgar (orange-red arsenic sulfide with a

resinous luster). Bellini was among the first masters to introduce this combination, used for highlights and halflights, and often combined with bitumen for shadows. See Lazzarini, "Colore," p. 142. At the same time, as Lazzarini notes, Bellini adhered to the traditional quattrocento technique of using few strata of color, painted over preparatory sketches, with the lights laid in first, then the halftones, and finally the darks.

70. See, e.g., Piero della Francesca's *Resurrection* in Sansepolcro, in which Christ places one foot on the edge of his sarcophagus, literally stepping out of the tomb (a traditional motif).

71. See Dellwing, "San Zaccaria," esp. pp. 229–34; Tramontin, *San Zaccaria*, p. 13; and Muir, *Civic Ritual*, pp. 219–23.

72. Other distinguished patrons were also powerless when it came to dealing with Bellini; N.B. the procurators who had to settle for a studio work (fig. 35) and Isabella d'Este, whose negotiations with the master were a mammoth struggle ending in compromise. Priuli's choice of a triptych reflects an apparent Venetian preference for that format, long out of favor elsewhere in Italy. N.B. also the destroyed triptych of John the Baptist, formerly in Berlin; see Gronau, *Bellini*, p. 148. For other triptychs and polyptychs by Bellini, see above, Introduction at nn. 29–34; chap. 2 at nn. 57–60; and app. 4 and 5, pt. 3. This conservative Venetian taste continued into the next generation: in 1522 Titian signed the Averoldi polyptych in Brescia, Santi Nazzaro e Celso, with the Resurrection of Christ in the central panel.

73. Priuli's tomb is in the church of San Michele in Isola under the *barco* to the south; it is a plain slab without arms, as he insisted it be, inscribed DOM/PETRUS PRIOLUS BENEDICTI/E HABITAT S. SOPHIA SIBI/SUISQ. POST. P./MDXI. His holograph will is ASV, Notarile, Testamenti Antonio Savina, Busta 1235, no. 142, 8 July 1491. See also Meneghin, *S. Michele*, 1:322, and Ludwig and Bode, "Altarbilder," pp. 142–46. Priuli was praised in Pietro Dolfin's letters: *Petri Delphini Veneti, Prioris Sacre Eremi Generalis totius Ordinis Camaldulensis, Epistolarum volumene* (Venice, 1524), vol. 3, p. 55 (Venice, Biblioteca Nazionale Marciana 7331 [=18D7]).

74. Birmingham Art Gallery, formerly in the collection of Oliver Vernon, Cornbury Park; see Campori, *Raccolta*, p. 182, and Cannon-Brookes, *Cornbury Park Bellini*.

75. Dolfin's figure was repainted later in the sixteenth century by a follower of the Bassano, but the composition itself represents Bellini's original intention. The will of Giacomo Dolfin, 7 February 1505, m.v., mentions his plans for burial in San Francesco della Vigna—after a precautionary two days during which his body is to remain "above ground"—and the "altarpiece that master Giovanni Bellini is making for me at present": "Io Iacomo Dolfin fo del messer Piero del confin de Santa Ternita [Trinita] . . . volgio che quando l'anema mia sara seperada dal corpo voio esser tegnudo sopra tera hore 48 [i.e.] zorni do et volgio esser posto a San Francesco dela Vigna vestido de suo abito. El mio corpo sia posto in la sepoltura mea in iexia de messer San Francesco dela Vigna se quella haveva fata far avanti la mia morte et se veramente quella non havesse fato far volgio che per i mie comesarii subito lasia fato far. . . . Volgio et ordeno que in la iexia predita de messer San Francesco sia fato uno altar cum la sepoltura davanti come quello dagli Grimani et sopra dito altar sia posta la mia pala over ancona laqual prexente me fa messer Zuane Beli[n] cum li suo adormamenti et cum la cortina davanti come se rechiede." (ASV, Notarile, Testamenti Cristoforo Rizzo, Busta 1228, no. 205; and, for the estate, Procuratori di San Marco de Citra, Busta 255.)

76. N.B. also the related composition in the Louvre, which belonged to the Pesaro, kinfolk of Bellini's patrons in the Frari (fig. 116); and the *Sacra Conversazione* in the Metropolitan Museum of Art, no. 49.7.1.

77. For the transformation of devotional images into altarpieces, see chap. 1 at n. 88. On half-length narratives, see Ringbom, *Icon to Narrative*. For the Bellini shop *Circumcision*, see Campori, *Raccolta*, p. 181, and Davies, *Earlier Italian Schools*, pp. 68–70. For the Bellini shop *Presentation*, see Zeri with Gardner, *Italian Paintings*, pp. 8–9. Zeri and Gardner note that there are "at least twenty-nine versions" of this composition, all works dating circa 1490 or later. See also Heinemann, *Bellini*, 1:41–44. For the earliest *Presentation* associated with Bellini, the unfinished, photogenic, and (to my eye) inferior work in the Fondazione Querini-Stampalia, Venice (fig. 191), see above, app. 4 at nn. 16–18.

78. Capello's tomb was inscribed: "Pietro Capello Joannis Procuratoris dignissimi fi[g]lio Senatori optimo M.D.XXIII."; see Cicogna, *Inscrizioni*, 2:120. Capello's wife, Maria di Bartolomeo Vendramin (a kinswoman of the great collector Andrea Vendramin), had predeceased him in 1522 and was already interred in the chapel. In her testament dated 29 July 1521 (ASV, Notarile, Testamenti Piero Bon, Busta 133, no. 461), Maria had asked to be buried "where my beloved husband wishes my body to go," fastidiously adding that she did not want to share her tomb with anyone but him and her niece Chiara ("Item ordeno . . . chel mio corpo sia sepulto dove voia andar el mio dilecto marido . . . et non voio sia posti altri corpi salvo il corpo de Chiara olim mia neza"). Finally, she provided a bequest of ten ducats to San Zaccaria, where another niece,

Paola, was a nun: "Ducati diexe lasso a l'abedessa de S. Zacharia dove è mia neza Suor Paula." Capello's holograph will is dated 8 April 1523 (ASV, Notarile Testamenti, Giacomo Grasolario, Busta 1184, no. 456), with a *cedula* dated 31 May, 1524 (ibid., Busta 1185, fols. 71v–73r). He bequeathed "300 ducats . . . to the Observant nuns of San Zaccaria, where I have had a chapel by authority of their chapter and have made my tomb where I have placed my beloved consort and thus I want to be buried [there] when it pleases God" ("Item lasso ducati 300 . . . ale done de San Zacharia hoservante nelqual luogo ho habudo una capella per auctorita del suo capitolo e ho facto la mia sepoltura dove ho facto poner la mia carissima consorte et cusì voio esser mi quando piazera a dio"). For Maria's soul, and for himself, Capello endowed masses to be said at the altar above their tomb. His commissaries and primary beneficiaries were the two nephews who inscribed the frame of the *Circumcision*: IUSTAS EFFUNDITE PRECES SACRI VIRI PRO DEFUNCTI PETRI CAPELLI ANIMA IN CUIUS MEMORIAM HOC ALTARE ANNUIS MUNERIBUS DECORATUM ET PIE ERECTUM SPECTATUR. PHILIPPUS ET JOANN. NEPOTES PIETATIS OPUS F.F. The painted epigraph was recorded by Cicogna, *Inscrizioni*, 2:119, no. 9.

79. The panel in London is much discolored; transparencies made after cleaning in 1949 reveal glowing whites, pinks, and reds. Ruhemann's analysis of the color of Catherine's robe reveals something of the way in which Bellini and his shop achieved their effects. There are several layers of color, beginning with a thin layer of gesso, tinted with pink, followed by a dark blue underpaint containing azurite and ultramarine in lead white, a light blue, with the same pigments but more white, and finally an olive-brown glaze containing copper. For the transparencies and the technical report, see the National Gallery conservation record, vols. 1, 2:3.

80. The *Lamentation* is painted in tempera; Antonio Paolucci, in *Gli Uffizi, catalogo generale* (Florence, 1979), p. 161. Cf. other examples of Bellini's work in grisaille, early (the fictive reliefs in the *Blood of the Redeemer*) and late (the *Continence of Scipio*): they do not look like this panel (figs. 57, 174). On the other hand, Bellini did not necessarily draw his compositions so carefully on the panel before completing the painting with color—where the paint has worn thin in some cases, one can see underdrawing and pentimenti far sketchier than this (figs. 27, 34, 38). In the *Madonna of the Meadow*, however, more detailed underdrawing may be concealed beneath the surface (fig. 37). See Wind, cited in Robertson, *Bellini*, p. 119. Citing Tietze's discussion of a *simile* by Mansueti, David Rosand argued that Bellini's panel was a work of the same sort; see Rosand's rev. of Robertson, *Bellini*, in *Art Quarterly* 33 (1970): 74. N.B. also Elizabeth C. G. Packard's comments on Venetian painting technique circa 1510: figures are drawn in monochrome, flesh is then tinted thinly, draperies and background are added in later stages; "Bellini Painting," p. 69.

81. The composition is known in two versions, of which that in the National Gallery, London, here fig. 127, was painted by Bellini, probably with some assistance. The clarity and brightness of color are much obscured by dirt. N.B. that the original ground is a pale yellow, according to a report by H. Ruhemann and N. S. Brommelle in 1950 in the National Gallery conservation record for the painting, vol. 2. The studio variant of the *Saint Peter Martyr*, in the Courtauld Institute, London, is said to have been inscribed on the back with the year 1509. See Stefano Bottari, *Tutta la pittura*, 2:34, no. 131. I am grateful to Professor Michael Hirst and to the staff of the Courtauld Institute for facilitating my examination of the painting while it was being restored in 1985.

82. Davies, *Earlier Italian Schools*, pp. 65–67.

83. The painting was cited by Ridolfi, *Maraviglie*, 1:70. I thank Francesco Valcanover, former Ispettore Generale, and Giovanna Nepi Scirè, Soprintendente ai Beni Culturali in Venice, for allowing me to examine the painting in restoration.

84. See Goffen, *Piety and Patronage*, chap. 3, sec. 1, and *passim*.

85. Meiss, "Masaccio and the Early Renaissance: The Circular Plan" (1963), in his *Painter's Choice*, pp. 63–81.

86. This great work is endangered by the congregation's votive candles, offered to the adjacent twentieth-century image of the Madonna. In their disregard for Bellini's altarpiece, the clergy and congregation of San Giovanni Chrisostomo are following in the unenlightened footsteps of their predecessors. In 1733 the priest of San Giovanni Chrisostomo attached a statue of Saint Anne to the altarpiece by nailing the figure to Bellini's panel. The statue was removed when the brothers of the confraternity of San Marco protested. Thus the scuola was still defending its proprietary rights 220 years after the endowment of the altar. No one seems able to defend the painting today, the Soprintendenza's protests notwithstanding. For the priest's vandalism, see Paoletti, "Scuola Grande," p. 111. Radiographs and infrareds of the painting were published by Ruggeri, "Bellini: Gerolamo, Cristoforo e Ludovico." The color is most notably damaged in the mantle of Saint Christopher. The painting was restored in 1975. During that restoration, it was discovered that the clouds are repainted; Ruggeri considers them completely false, perhaps

painted over some trace of clouds by Bellini. Bellini's pigments here have been analyzed by Lazzarini, "Colore," pp. 138–39. The altarpiece was restored by Antonio Lazzarin in 1976; see Valcanover, *Restauri a Venezia*, p. 46.

87. Diletti made his testament on 13 July 1494, the parish priest of San Giovanni Crisostomo acting as notary: "Georgius Delettis q[uondam] Joannis de confinio sancti Joannis Crisostomi. . . . Item, si et quando anima mea egressa fuerit ex corpore meo tunc volo sepelliri ad ecclesiam . . . S. Joannis Chrisostomi . . . in aliquo loco in predicta ecclesia donec quousque fiat una cappella . . . et commissariis meis pro fabricando dictam capellam . . . et palla in ea fiendis, volo expendantur ducati ducentum . . . et si dicta iocalia non sufficient . . . pro fienda dicta capella et palla, volo expendantur usque ad ducatos trecentos . . . , que quidem capella volo intituletur sub titulo Sancti Hieronimi, Sancti Ludovici, et Sancti Chrisophori, et in ea capella fiat arca mea et ibidem corpus meum sepeliatur" (ASV, Notarile, Testamenti Lodovico Talenti, Busta 955, no. 288). Diletti also provided funds for Mass to be said daily in perpetuity and for candles and lamp oil. See Odenthal, *San Giovanni Cristomo*, pp. 158–59. A copy of the will, dated 13 July 1516, is found in the parish archive of San Canciano, MS 115, fols. 29r–30r, as noted by Tramontin, *San Giovanni Grisostomo*, p. 24. Other copies of the will are preserved in the records of the Scuola Grande di San Marco in ASV, Busta M, xxii prima, no. 135, fols. 7r–8r, and xxii seconda, no. 406, fols. 2r–3v. The latter copyist's error in transcribing the name of Saint Christopher as "Chrisostomi" has caused much needless confusion about the identity of the saints. Construction of Diletti's chapel was undertaken as part of a rebuilding campaign—the older church had been destroyed by fire in 1475. Diletti, who died in 1503, was eventually buried in his chapel, but no traces of the tomb are visible. For the rebuilding campaign, directed by the energetic priest (and notary) Ludovico Talenti, who served 1480–1516—possibly honored in Bellini's altarpiece by the inclusion of Saint Louis—see, in addition to Odenthal, *San Giovanni Crisostomo*; Angelo Pinetti, "Nuovi documenti sull'architetto bergamasco Mauro Codussi," *Bergomum*, n.s., 27 (1926): 49–57; Filippo Scolari, *Nuove opere di abbellimento e ristauro nella chiesa vicariale di S. Giovanni Crisostomo in Venezia* (Venice, 1860); and Tramontin, *San Giovanni Grisostomo*, pp. 9–10. Diletti's altarpiece was not actually commissioned until after his widow's death in 1511: she had remarried but respected Diletti's wishes regarding his funerary chapel, including his granting *iuspatronato* of the altar in perpetuity to the Scuola Grande di San Marco. See ASV, Notarile, Testamenti Pietro Bono, Busta 133, no. 565; partial copies in ASV, SS. Giovanni e Paolo, Busta M xxii prima, no. 135, fols. 8v–9r, and Busta M xxii seconda, no. 406–425, fols. 4v–5r; and the parish archive of San Cancian, as noted by Odenthal, *San Giovanni Crisostomo*, p. 169.

88. See Sohm, *Scuola Grande*, pp. 242–48, and documents on pp. 259–61, 279, 280–81; and above, app. 3.

89. Elements of the frame at the level of the fictive entablature are missing, and the inner frame of the altarpiece has been removed.

90. Wilk, *Sculpture of Lombardo*, pp. 85–144.

91. Titian profited from this example in his *Assunta* for the high altar of Santa Maria Gloriosa dei Frari, begun in 1516, the year of Bellini's death. See Goffen, *Piety and Patronage*, chap. 4, sec. 5. On the *paragone,* see I. A. Richter, *Paragone: A Comparison of the Arts by Leonardo da Vinci* (London, 1949), and Leatrice Mendelsohn, *Paragoni: Benedeto Varchi's "Due Lezzioni" and Cinquecento Art Theory* (Ann Arbor, 1982).

92. Diletti was a merchant, and Christopher is the patron saint of merchants, whereas Jerome is the titular saint of the altar. For the cult of Jerome here, see Coronelli, *Guida*, p. 229. The label on Louis's Bible, inscribed "De Civitate Dei," is surely a later addition to the painting, and the implication that this is Augustine, author of the *City of God*, is incorrect. Both the ineptitude of the inscription and its placement on the back of the book—as indicated by its clasps—cast its authenticity into doubt.

93. See Rodolfo Gallo, "Per la datazione della pala di San Giovanni Grisostomo di 'Sebastian Viniziano,'" *Arte veneta* 7 (1953): 152, and Michael Hirst, *Sebastiano del Piombo* (Oxford, 1981), pp. 23–26.

94. Jaynie Anderson, "Some New Documents Relating to Giorgione's 'Castelfranco Altarpiece' and His Patron Tuzio Costanzo," *Arte veneta* 27 (1973): 290–98; Peter Humfrey, *Cima da Conegliano* (Cambridge, 1983), pp. 121–22; and Harold E. Wethey, *The Paintings of Titian, Complete Edition*, vol. 1: *The Religious Paintings* (London, 1969), p. 143. The pose of Bellini's Christopher in the San Giovanni altarpiece resembles that of Titian's Sebastian in his altarpiece.

95. As Hirst noted in *Sebastiano*, p. 25 and n. 115, Bellini himself had already represented a protagonist in profile in his Uffizi *Allegory* (fig. 79). N.B. also the *Presentation* (fig. 191).

96. Bellini may have been asked to use Greek because Greek was the language of Saint John Chrysostom, as Sebastiano reminded us in the text of the saint's book (fig. 143). The plan of the church is that of the centralized Greek cross, like other contemporary Venetian buildings, part of a Greek revival at the turn of the century in arts and letters.

For Bellini's role in this revival, see André Chastel, "Titien et le neo-byzantinisme vénitien," p. 101, in *Tiziano e il manierismo europeo*, ed. Rodolfo Pallucchini.

97. Bellini's inscription reads from the right to the left side of the vault: ΚΥΡΙΟΣΕΚ ΤΟΥΟΥΡΑ ΝΟΥ ΔΙΕΚΥΨΕΝ ΥΠΕΡΤΟΥΣ ΤΩΝ ΑΝΘΡΩΠΩΝ/ΤΟΥΙΔΕΙΝ ΕΙΕΣ-ΤΙΣΙΝΙ ΩΝ ΗΕΚΖΗΤΩΝ ΤΟΝ ΘΕΟΝ. The Psalms had been published in Greek by various Venetian editors as early as the 1480s and by Aldus Manutius between 1496 and 1498, with subsequent Aldine editions in the early sixteenth century; see Lattanzi, "Pala," p. 36 and n. 22.

## Chapter 3: Portraits and Patricians

*Note to epigraph:* Navagero, "Orazione," 1:193.

1. "Lo ritratto di esso M. Leonico [Tomeo], giovine, hora tutto caschato, inzallito et ofuscato, fu de mano di Zuan Bellino. Lo ritratto di suo padre a guazzo in profil fu di man di Jacomo Bellino." Michiel's manuscript is in the Biblioteca Marciana, MS Ital., Cl. xi, cod. lxvii. I have used the edition published by Frimmel, *Anonimo Morelliano* [hereafter cited as Michiel-Frimmel], p. 18, for Tomeo. The younger Tomeo was a professor at Padua from 1497 and died in 1531. On Niccolò Leonico Tomeo, see King, *Venetian Humanism*, pp. 432–34. On Michiel, see Fletcher, "Marcantonio Michiel."

2. The sculptor Riccio represented much the same type in the antique medium of bronze. The painting was attributed to Bellini by Longhi, with a date circa 1470–75 (*Viatico per cinque secoli di pittura veneziana* [1946], p. 56, reprinted in his *Ricerche*, vol. 10). It is inscribed on the back: JACOBUS DE . . . , but whether in reference to the sitter or to the artist (as Bernard Berenson thought) is not known. Note the inscription formerly on the back of our fig. 150, which identified the subject of the portrait.

3. "El ritratto picolo de M. Jacomo [*sic*] Marcello suo avo, Capitano general del'armata, fu de man de Zuan Bellino" (Michiel-Frimmel, p. 90). For the general's tomb, see Goffen, *Piety and Patronage*, p. 66, n. 114. The general was the paternal grandfather of Jeronimo (or Girolamo); see Barbaro, MS Correr, vol. 4, fols. 305v–6v, Tree G.

4. The subject of the portrait has been identified thanks to the detective work of Schulz, "Portrait." The painting of the general's brocade lacks the assurance with which Bellini created fabrics (cf. figs. 116, 122, 139, 140), the pattern of the folds is banal, and the face rigid. See also Meyer zur Capellen, *Gentile Bellini*, pp. 161–62.

5. Meller, "Physiognomical Theory." Warriors were meant to resemble lions in appearance as in ferocity, which explains the characterization of *Colleoni* by Verrocchio as opposed to the *Gattamelata* by Donatello, representing a more intellectual ideal of leadership.

6. For the monument, formally unveiled on 21 March 1496, see Günter Passavant, *Verrocchio: Sculptures, Paintings and Drawings*, trans. Katherine Watson (London, 1969), pp. 62–67, 185–86, pls. 62–68.

7. "Li 3 retratti picoli a guazzo, uno de M. Filippo Vendramin in un ochio e mezo, et li altri dui de do gentilhomeni gioveni in profilo furono de man de Zuan Bellino. . . . El libro grande in carta bombasina de dissegni de stil de piombo fu de man de Jacomo Bellino" (Michiel-Frimmel, pp. 106, 108). This is the book now in the British Museum. In Venetian parlance, a *gentilhomeno* is a nobleman. For an inventory of G. Vendramin's collection in 1567, see Ravà, "Camerino."

8. There is one possible quasi-exception, the portrait of Jacopo Antonio Marcello, which decorates the manuscript "Life of Saint Maurice," attributed by Robertson to Bellini in the early 1450s. But an illumination is not a panel painting, and in panel painting Bellini's consistent choice was the more modern, more complete view of the face. For the Marcello miniature, see Millard Meiss, who argued for an attribution to Mantegna (*Mantegna*, esp. p. 25, and "A Lost Portrait of Jean de Berry by the Limbourgs," *Burlington Magazine* 115 [1963]: 52, n. 14), and Lightbown, *Mantegna*, pp. 494–95. Cf. Robertson, "Earlier Works," pp. 45–59, esp. p. 47, and *Bellini*, pp. 17–21.

9. The portrait ascribed to Bellini in Tulsa would certainly have been described this way: it measures a mere 12.7 × 10.2 cm. (Suida, "Bellini's Portrait").

10. "El quadretto della donna retratta al naturale insino alle spalle fo de mano de Zuan Bellino" (Michiel-Frimmel, p. 88). The type of female portrait he may have owned is represented in sketches published by Borenius, *Picture Gallery*, pls. 3b, 16b, 17b. The painting published by Richter, "Portrait of a Lady," is surely not by the master, and neither is the panel sometimes ascribed to him in the Rijksmuseum, Amsterdam.

11. Had it lived, Girolamo Cornaro's gazelle would have stood for its portrait by Titian in 1520; Giovanni Bellini had already portrayed the animal in a painting owned by Cornaro. See Fern Rusk Shapley, "Giovanni Bellini and Cornaro's Gazelle," *Gazette des Beaux-Arts* 28 (1945): 27–30; Tietze-Conrat, "Again"; and Friedmann, "Cornaro's Gazelle."

12. Tietze and Tietze-Conrat, *Drawings*, 1:89–90, no. 324. The drawing is silverpoint on greenish gray prepared paper.

13. The codex is in the Biblioteca Trivulziana, Milan. Zovenzoni's dedicatory letter reads: "Non sinerunt ad te, id est ad meum Caesarem, accedere sed habebis expressam in

libelli pagina faciem hanc, quam nobilissimus pictor Ioannes bellinus imitatus est" (his situation does not permit his joining the lord bishop, but in the pages of this book he sends his visage imitated by the most excellent painter Giovanni Bellini). See Ziliotto, *Zovenzoni*, pp. 54–55, 164; and above, chap. 1 at n. 7. For Zovenzoni's epigrams on Jacopo and Gentile Bellini, see R. Sabbadini, *Raffaele Zovenzoni e la sua monodia Crysolorae* (Catania, 1899), pp. 12, 16–17. On transient scholars in Venice, including Zovenzoni, see King, *Venetian Humanism*, pp. 232–36, 267–69.

14. Michiel-Frimmel, p. 20. If this is correct, as one would much like it to be, it seems to confirm Jacopo's friendly and professional association with Gentile da Fabriano. (Gentile Bellini was presumably named for him.) But that is no reason to assume that Jacopo was the rowdy youth identified as Jacopo di Piero—Jacopo Bellini's patronymic was Nicolò—who was tried for assault in Florence in 1423, as is usually argued; the felon may just as well have been another Jake.

15. "O imagine mia celeste e pura, / che splendi più che 'l sole agli ochi miei . . . / credo che 'l mio [Giovanni] Bellin con la figura / t'abbia dato il costume anco di lei"; "Son questi quei begli occhi, in cui mirando senza difesa far perdei me stesso? . . . O volto, che mi stai ne l'alma impresso, / perch'io viva di me mai sempre in bando" (Sonnets 19 and 20 in Bembo, *Prose e rime*, pp. 521–23).

16. Ridolfi, *Maraviglie*, 1:73. Ridolfi quotes from the sonnets cited in the previous note. According to Vasari, Bembo's sonnet on the portrait of his mistress was Bellini's payment for the painting (*Vite*, ed. Bellosi and Rossi, p. 437). See also the second edition (1568), Vasari-Milanesi, 3:169. Sabine Eiche cites a painting listed in a seventeenth-century inventory as a portrait by Titian of "a woman who was favored of Cardinell Bembo" ("On the Dispersal of Cardinal Bembo's Collections," *Mitteilungen des Kunsthistorischen Institutes in Florenz* 27 [1983]: 356). I wonder whether this may have been Bellini's picture. Bellini's portrait of a man from Hampton Court (fig. 161) is often identified as Bembo, but this is wishful thinking; see above at n. 55.

17. Isabella d'Este wanted to borrow Cecilia Bergamina-Visconti's portrait by Leonardo to compare it with "certain beautiful portraits by the hand of Giovanni Bellini": "Essendone hogi accaduto vedere certi belli retracti de man de Zoanne Bellino siamo venute in ragionamento de le opere de Leonardo cum desiderio de vederle al parangone di queste havemo" (Adolfo Venturi and Alessandro Luzio, "Nuovi documenti su Leonardo da Vinci," *Archivio storico dell'arte* 1 [1888]: 45–46). Liburnio wrote that Alexander would have chosen "not Apelles but Bellini," had they been contemporaries (*Opere*, Sonnet 30, p. 8r).

18. Vasari, *Vite* (1550), ed. Bellosi and Rossi, pp. 433, 437. Vasari cites Bellini's portrait of *Doge Loredan* on p. 433 (our fig. 149). See also Tietze, "*Giacomo Marcello*," p. 148.

19. Vasari-Milanesi, 3:154–55. Although it is certainly possible that Bellini also portrayed Giovanni Mocenigo, there is no evidence of this, aside from Vasari. Mocenigo's dogate was 1478–85, and Loredan's 1501–21. The profile portrait of Doge Mocenigo in the Correr Museum has often been attributed to Gentile Bellini (Mariacher, *Museo Correr*, pp. 44–45). For Mocenigo's votive picture, see above, chap. 1 at n. 121.

20. This is also the date of the lost portrait of Zovenzoni; n. 13, above. The inscription was recorded by Mayer, "Portrait of Joerg Fugger," but was later destroyed when the poplar panel was thinned. Now in the Norton Simon Museum, Pasadena, the portrait was formerly owned by the counts Fugger at Oberkirchberg (Ulm). A son of Jacob Fugger (1397–1469), Jörg was born in 1453, and so was twenty-one when his portrait was painted in Venice, where members of his family had been residing and doing business since the first half of the fifteenth century. See Franz Herre, *Die Fugger in ihrer Zeit* (Augsburg, 1985), p. 28; Henry Simonsfeld, *Der Fondaco dei Tedeschi in Venedig und die deutsch-venezianischen Handelsbeziehungen* (Stuttgart, 1887), 1:61; and for the portrait of Jörg Fugger, see Goffen in Egbert Haverkamp-Begemann, *Small Paintings of the Masters* (New York, 1981), 1:31.

21. The blue is either lapis or azurite. Technical information on the painting is derived from the notes of Herbert Lank, who examined it in 1969, and Marco Grassi, who restored it in 1975–76.

22. I refer to independent painted portraits, not portraits incorporated into other compositions. Perhaps one of the first such independent portraits is Castagno's *Young Man* in the National Gallery of Art, Washington, circa 1450. See John Pope-Hennessy, *The Portrait in the Renaissance* (London and New York, 1966), p. 28; but cf. Creighton Gilbert's review in *Burlington Magazine* 110 (1968): 278–85, esp. 281–82. In part because the Castagno, if a portrait, would represent a remarkable innovation, Gilbert argues that it is in fact the depiction of a saint cut from an altarpiece. According to Irving Lavin, the first dated Renaissance portrait bust in sculpture is the *Piero de'Medici* by Mino da Fiesole in 1453 ("Sources and Meaning," p. 208).

23. Quintilian, *De institutione oratoria*, 2.13.12, discussed by Schapiro, *Words and Pictures*, p. 45 and n. 85. Leon Battista Alberti repeated the reference to the portrait of Antigonus by Apelles (without citing Quintilian) in his treatise *On Painting*

(*On Painting and On Sculpture*, ed. Grayson, pp. 78–79). On Florentine profile portraits, see Hatfield, "Five Portraits."

24. "Through painting, the faces of the dead go on living for a very long time" (*On Painting*, 2:25, in *On Painting and On Sculpture*, ed. Grayson, p. 61). See also above, chap. 1 at n. 8.

25. Full-length portraits remained extremely rare in Italy until the second decade of the sixteenth century; see Goffen, "Carpaccio's Portrait."

26. See Hadeln, "Two Portraits," pp. 4–7 and n. 10. For Bellini and Antonello, see above, chap. 2 at nn. 5–10.

27. Much lead white was used throughout, and the medium seems to be oil. I owe this and the following technical information about the painting to a report prepared for the Barber Institute in 1979, which Professor Hamish Miles generously shared with me.

28. Gamba, *Bellini*, p. 71. The Bellini themselves offered convincing proof of this hypothesis when Jacopo, Gentile, and Giovanni signed the Gattamelata altarpiece in Padua (not so far from home) as "Veneti." See app. 2, no. 6.

29. For bust portraits of children in sculpture, also comparatively rare in spite of the antique pedigree for such images, see Pope-Hennessy, *Italian Renaissance Sculpture* (*An Introduction to Italian Sculpture*, part 2), 2d ed. (London and New York, 1971), p. 49.

30. N.B. the evidence of Michiel, cited above in nn. 1, 3, 5–6, and 8–9. Some of Bellini's subjects were probably members of the distinguished but non-noble citizens' class, *cittadini originari* like the Bellini themselves and the humanist Giovanni Caldiera, who could be as ardent in their defense of the regime as any nobleman. These citizens had "a monopoly of office in the Ducal Chancery," as explained by Pullan, *Rich and Poor*, p. 22, and 99–113, 500. For Caldiera, see King, "Caldiera and the Barbaros."

31. I use the customary picture titles for the sake of convenience, but the garments indicate that Bellini's subjects may be either noblemen or "original citizens," who adopted the ideals and demeanor of the patriciate together with their wardrobe; see above, chap. 1, n. 85, and fig. 38. Age is also significant: the men in figs. 38, 154, and 155 are probably too young to be dressed this way as "original citizens" of rank in the Chancellery, but old enough to be noblemen wearing senators' robes. The portrait in Padua was restored by Antonio Lazzarin in 1964–65. See Alessandro Prosdocimi, "Restauri ad altri dipinti del Museo Civico di Padova," *Bollettino del Museo Civico di Padova* 52 (1963): 63–65, and Lucio Grossato, "Catalogo," ibid.: 67–69.

32. Margaret L. King translated and discussed this letter of 1438 in "Caldiera and the Barbaros," p. 35, n. 60. For Bembo's related views on Ciceronian decorum, echoed by Venier, among others, see Martha Feldman, "The Academy of Domenico Venier: Poetry and Music in Venice around 1550," in press; and above, chap. 1 at n. 19.

33. For the sculptor, see Pope-Hennessy, *Italian Renaissance Sculpture*, pp. 50, 67–68; and W. R. Valentiner, "Laurana's Portrait Busts of Women," *Renaissance Quarterly* 5 (1942): 273–99. On portrait busts, see ibid., pp. 45–52, and the classic study by I. Lavin, "Sources and Meaning."

34. Davies, *Earlier Italian Schools*, pp. 55–56, no. 189. Davies writes that the figure is in excellent condition and notes pentimenti in the outlines of the cap and the chin on the left. The painting was lightly cleaned by H. Ruhemann in 1963, as described in the conservation record in the National Gallery, vol. 3.

35. On the sixteenth-century definition of the individual, see Greenblatt, "Psychoanalysis and Renaissance Culture."

36. Ferdinando Bologna, "Un ritratto del doge Leonardo Loredan," *Arte antica e moderna* 5 (1959): 74–78; Lauts, *Carpaccio*, pp. 241–42. Ducal portraits on the mainland were more often frontal or nearly frontal than those made for Venice proper.

37. *I Diarii di Marino Sanuto*, vol. 4 (Venice, 1880), ed. Nicolò Barozzi, cols. 143–44. After his death, the inquisitors and the *correttori della promissione ducale* examined Loredan's records for two years before reaching their conclusion in May 1523. See da Mosto, *Dogi di Venezia*, pp. 266–75, esp. 272ff.

38. I refer to independent portraits; frontal or three-quarter views might be used in narratives or in other contexts, such as the ducal portraits in the Sala del Gran Consiglio. Meyer zur Capellen, "Dogenbildnis," notes that ducal portraits from Francesco Foscari to Loredan were profiles until Gentile Bellini's *Agostino Barbarigo* in the Harcourt Collection, Nuneham Park (his fig. 26, discussed on p. 80). Of the ducal portraits displayed in the Sala del Gran Consiglio of the Ducal Palace, some were in profile and some frontal; see Meyer zur Capellen's fig. 30, with bibliography in n. 2, and his *Gentile Bellini*, pp. 132–33, 176–90.

39. See Navagero, "Orazione," p. 182. The generalissimo in this war was another patron of Bellini's, Benedetto Pesaro (figs. 116, 117). On the war with Turkey, see Goffen, *Piety and Patronage*, chap. 2, sec. 3.

40. The signature in minuscule, "ioannes bellinnus / pinxit.," is authentic, although retouched. Bellini had also spelled his family name in this way on the earlier *Madonna* in the Madonna dell'Orto (fig. 64). See Davies, "Dipinto Belliniano."

41. See the report by Philip Hendy in 1948, in the National Gallery conservation record for this panel, 2:11.

42. Bellini achieved this aerial quality by applying the color in two layers; on the gesso ground is a mixture of ultramarine in a matrix of lead white, and over this a second layer with more ultramarine. See the notes signed by Joyce Plesters in 1964 in the conservation record of the National Gallery, London, 3:5. Plesters added that the medium seems to be oil.

43. Ibid., p. 6.

44. There may be a physiological basis for this. See Harmon, "Recognition of Faces," p. 76.

45. E. H. Gombrich, "The Mask and the Face: The Perception of Physiognomic Likeness in Life and Art" (1970), in Gombrich, *Image and Eye*, pp. 105–36.

46. Signed and dated IOANNES BELLINVS / MCCCCCVII on a cartellino affixed to the balustrade. The painting went from the Spiridon Collection, Paris, to the Nemes Collection, Munich. It was presumed destroyed in World War II, but survives in the Berliner Museen, East Berlin. The painting had been transferred from canvas to panel and measures 135 × 208 cm. See Erica Tietze-Conrat, "Giovanni Bellinis "Gruppenbild"; Crowe and Cavalcaselle, *History of Painting*, 1:179, n. 3; and Meyer zur Capellen, *Gentile Bellini*, p. 188. Bellini's imagery seems to have had little impact on Venetian (or Italian) portraiture: it was in the North that group portraits became increasingly popular.

47. His eulogist, Andrea Navagero, noted that Loredan had been weak even as a young man but that his spirit was strong (of course) and that he never spared himself in serving the state ("Orazione," p. 194). Cf. Marino Sanuto on the doge's personality (*Diarii*, 4:cols. 143, 688; 5:col. 795).

48. "In casa Loredana di Santo Stefano conservasi il ritratto del Doge Leonardo Loredano posto a sedere ad un tavolino e due suoi figliuoli ed altri della famiglia intorno che sono figure molto vivaci" (Ridolfi, *Maraviglie*, 1:72, n. 7). In his eulogy, Navagero noted that the doge had many sons, all virtuous, a rare thing, and true, though difficult to believe, and also daughters whom he married to the best men in Venice ("Orazione," p. 191).

49. See Finlay, "Venetian Republic," and Chojnacki, "Political Adulthood."

50. For the Titian, see Goffen, *Piety and Patronage*, chap. 4.

51. N.B. also the double portraits noted by Crowe and Cavalcaselle, *History of Painting*, 1:134–35, n. 2, 135, n. 1 (panels in the Louvre, no. 1156, ascribed to Cariani, and in Berlin, no. 12). A Bellinesque double portrait, the so-called *Master and Pupil*, oil on panel, 44 × 63 cm., was on sale at Sotheby's, New York, 6 June 1985 (ill. *Il Giornale dell'arte* 25 [July–Aug. 1985]: 38). A portrait ascribed to Gentile Bellini in Haarlem (F. Koenigs) shows Doge Andrea Vendramin (doge, 1476–78) and two other men; it was included in the Italian exhibition at the Royal Academy in 1930. See also Wilk, "Tullio Lombardo."

52. For examples of such tombs, see Wolters, *Scultura veneziana*, 1: 214–15, 207, 242; 2:figs. 399, 560–61.

53. Cf. the similar, rhetorical gesture of the scholar Niccolò da Monselice as depicted in his funerary monument in Padua, Sant'Antonio (Wolters, *Scultura veneziana*, 2:fig. 561). On the Ottawa panel, see Myron Laskin, Jr., *European and American Painting: Sculpture and Decorative Arts in the National Gallery of Canada*, vol. 1 (Chicago, 1986). For the genesis of the blessing gesture, see Gombrich, "Ritualized Gesture and Expression in Art" (1966), in his *Image and Eye*, pp. 63–77, esp. 63ff. Nothing is immutable, however. Recently the actor Mark Harmon was photographed for the cover of *Gentleman's Quarterly* (April 1987), his right hand "blessing."

54. For the hourglass as Assiduousness, Diligence, Eloquence, and/or Solicitude, see Cesare Ripa, *Della piu' che novissima iconologia* (Padua, 1630), pts. 1, 2:95, 189, 214; pt. 3:78. On 2:297 Ripa associates the hourglass with the judge and justice.

55. Hampton Court, on loan to the National Gallery, London. The original edges of the panel are visible on all sides. The flesh is abraded and much restored in the shadows. While the paint was still wet, Bellini apparently used the handle of his brush to define the distant bridge, and palm prints suggest that he used his hand to consolidate the paint surface in the landscape. See John Shearman, *The Early Italian Pictures in the Collection of Her Majesty the Queen* (Cambridge, 1983), pp. 41–43.

56. Davies notes that there was a "Fra Teodoro" among the Dominicans of SS. Giovanni e Paolo in 1514 (*Earlier Italian Schools*, p. 63); see also Paoletti, "Scuola Grande," p. 152.

57. Only ten months before he died in 1516, Bellini had been granted permission by the Dominicans to borrow a silver crown, which he surely wanted to use as a model, perhaps in painting his last work, a Madonna for the sister of the king of France; see chap. 1 at nn. 102–3, 128. N.B. also that Bellini's *Baptism* was painted for the Dominican church of Santa Corona in Vicenza (figs. 121, 122).

58. Hirst, *Sebastiano del Piombo*, p. 93.

59. Davies demonstrates that the attributes are original but that the frater's name was added somewhat later: the painting was conceived as a St. Dominic (*Earlier Italian Schools*, p. 62).

60. The picture seems to be identical with no. B17 in the inventory of Pietro and Giovanni Pesaro, dated 1797; see Giuseppe Fiocco, *Palazzo Pesaro* (Venice, 1925), pp. 28–29, 36, and Davies, *Earlier Italian Schools*, pp. 63–64, n. 6.

61. Formerly in London, A. L. Nicholson Collection, London, then Hickox Collection, New York, and now in the Frederick R. and Jan Mayer collection. I thank Everett Fahy for his assistance in locating the painting. Georg Gronau identified the panel with the painting of *Saint Dominic* by Bellini for Alfonso d'Este, which the artist described as "just completed" in a letter to Isabella d'Este, dated 3 August 1501 (*Giovanni Bellini*, Klassiker der Kunst, vol. 36 [Stuttgart, 1930], p. 213, no. 143). For the letter, see Alessandro Luzio, "Disegni topografici e pitture dei Bellini," *Archivio storico dell'arte* 1 (1888): 278.

62. For the patriciate, see Chojnacki, "Political Adulthood," pp. 798, 799, nn. 34, 35. For the importance attached to sons—each a future member of the Council by virtue of legitimate noble birth—see Chojnacki, "Kinship Ties," and Finlay, "Politics and Family." For the cittadinanza originaria, see the Introduction, n. 14, and chap. 4, nn. 30–31, above.

63. Chojnacki, "Political Adulthood," esp. pp. 800–806, 809.

64. Ibid., p. 810. For a citizen humanist's expression of these ideals, see King, "Personal, Domestic, and Republican Values."

65. See Held, "Flora," and Anderson, "Giorgionesque Portrait."

66. Chojnacki, "Political Adulthood," p. 809, and "Venetian Patriciate." Cf. Ruggiero, "Modernization."

67. For a penetrating discussion of patrician values, see King, "Caldiera and the Barbaros," and pp. 37–43 for Ermolao Barbaro.

68. King notes that Venetian works on the family appear to lack the attitude of nurturing concern for the individual that is present in some non-Venetian works (ibid., pp. 46–50). Venetian authors (again unlike other Italians) do not view their social world critically or offer suggestions for improvement but offer praise and acquiescence to the existing order. For the patrician "feet of clay," see Queller, *Venetian Patriciate*.

## Chapter 4: Allegories and Mythologies

*Note to epigraph:* Bessarion, on the occasion of the death of Giorgio Gemisto Pletone, quoted in Calvesi, *Hypnerotomachia*, p. 117 (as cited below, n. 3).

1. The quotation "roaming at his will," the title of this chapter, comes from a letter by Pietro Bembo to Isabella d'Este, explaining why Bellini was refusing to paint the allegory she had wanted in a second unsuccessful attempt to deal with the artist. For the letter and Bellini's dealings with Isabella, see above at n. 35 and app. 2, no. 49, as well as nos. 23, 30–51.

2. Bessarion is quoted in Gilbert, "Humanism in Venice," p. 13.

3. The author has long been identified with a Dominican priest of the same name in the convent of SS. Giovanni e Paolo, Venice, but it seems unlikely that the cleric was the Roman nobleman who wrote the *Hypnerotomachia*. See Maurizio Calvesi, "*Hypnerotomachia Poliphili*: Nuovi riscontri e nuove evidenze documentarie per Francesco Colonna signore di Preneste," *Storia dell'arte* 60 (1987): 85–136, and Silvia Squarzina Danesi, "Francesco Colonna, principe, letterato, e la sua cerchia," ibid.: 137–54.

4. This is in marked contrast to the situation in Florence. One notable exception to the typical amateur's uninterest of the Venetian patriciate in humanist studies, the nobleman Ermolao Barbaro, ended his life in exile; another, Pietro Bembo—Bellini's friend and patron—had to prove himself abroad before his countrymen entrusted him with the kind of position to which his noble birth entitled him and for which his father had intended him. On Bembo's career, see Gilbert, "Humanism in Venice," p. 23. For the plight of Ermolao Barbaro, see King, "Caldiera and the Barbaros," and *Venetian Humanism*.

5. I thank Professor C. John Henderson of Yale University for sharing his observations on the *Pagan Allegory* with me and Stanley Moss for allowing me to examine the painting. Although the attribution of this panel has sometimes been questioned, it seems to be an early autograph work of high quality. Moreover, even if one wishes to reject it and to wait for the late 1480s or early 1490s and Bellini's *Allegories* in the Accademia in Venice (figs. 166–71), the situation remains much the same: even circa 1490, Bellini's allegories were among the earliest paintings of classicizing subjects produced in Venice.

6. See the study by Gustav Ludwig, based in part on Fritz Rintelen's research: "Restello," esp. p. 199 for the inventory of 1457. Of course, there is no way of knowing when the restello listed in 1457 was made, but in the absence of any earlier documentation, we may assume that this kind of object was a comparatively recent concoction at that date.

7. A Giorgionesque painting in the National Gallery, London, seems to represent a related theme. See Newton, "Homage to a Poet."

8. Several sheets in the Louvre book depict ancient subjects, including statuary and inscriptions copied from actual antiquities known to the artist; in addition, he invented his own subjects *all'antica;* see fols. 8, 35, 36, 39, 44, 45, 76, ill. in Degenhart and Schmitt, *Jacopo Bellini*, pls. 4, 40, 41, 45, 52, 53, 95. In the album in the British Museum, N.B., for example, the nude in fol. 76 (Goloubew, *Dessins de Jacopo Bellini*, 2:no. 126).

9. Ridolfi, *Maraviglie*, 1:72. Ridolfi's language, "dipinse nella Sala due gran quadri," suggests that the pictures were murals. The Grimani Palace is on the Fondamenta delle Cappuccine. N.B. also that Bellini's handwriting is that of an educated man, befitting a cittadino originario, and that his son, Alvise, must have known Latin, a require-

ment for employment in the Chancellery. See the Introduction, n. 14, and Epilogue, n. 10.

10. For the *Venus*, see the following note. For the Plato, see the epigram by Pietro Valeriano in Biadego, *Variazioni*, p. 20, and Brown, "Testa de Platone antica."

11. See app. 2, no. 16, for Bellini and Collenuccio. For Zovenzoni's Latin epigram, no. 135, see Ziliotto, *Zovenzoni*, p. 109, and for Bellini's miniature portrait of Zovenzoni, see above, chap. 3 at n. 13. Zovenzoni taught in Venice. For the Paduan Tomeo's portrait by Bellini, see chap. 3 at n. 1 and at nn. 15–16 for Bembo's portrait of his mistress.

12. See above at nn. 34–37, on Bellini's avoidance techniques with Isabella d'Este. For the five panels, see Moschini Marconi, *Accademia*, pp. 71–73, and Nepi Scirè in Nepi Scirè and Valcanover, *Accademia*, p. 91. The panels were restored in 1979.

13. Cavalcaselle, in the 1871 edition of Crowe and Cavalcaselle, *History of Painting*, pp. 167, 170–71. Original paint edges, the nearly identical measurements of four of the five panels, the use of fir (*abies*) affixed to hardwood, and their compositional features indicate that these four are essentially intact and that they formed a group (figs. 168, 170, 171, 173). This combination of woods is typical of paintings intended for furniture. The composition of the fifth panel (fig. 169) likewise seems complete: this painting, 27 × 19 cm., would always have been different from the others in size and proportions. Moreover, the panel is fir alone, without hardwood—hence less expensive. These differences preclude the panel's association with the others; see above at nn. 15, 30. I thank Soprintendente Giovanna Nepi Scirè and Sante Luigi Savio, conservator of the Accademia, for their assistance in these technical matters.

14. ASV, Testamenti, Zaccaria di Priuli, Busta 777, no. 455, Catena's holograph will of 25 November 1525, with additions dated 15 April 1530 and 10 September 1531. The reference to Bellini's restello is in the first part of the document of 1525, fol. 2r: "Item laso al sovra schrito misser Antonio [de Marsilio fo de misser Alvise sta in champo Rusolo] tuti i mie aneli lichati in oro prima el mio diamante et la mia prasina e do chorniole lichate in oro et anchora laso el mio restelo di nogera chon zerte fegurete dentro depinte di mano de misser Juan Belino e anchora tuti i mie nudi di relievo fati di terachota." However, all references to Antonio q. Alvise and all of this clause are canceled, and in the margin, written next to each cancellation, is the word *privo*. In his first will, dated 1513—while Bellini was still alive—Catena made no mention of the restello, which may signify that it came into his possession only later. See also Giles Robertson, *Vincenzo Catena* (Edinburgh, 1954), pp. 6–8.

15. See above at nn. 13, 30. Cf. Robertson, *Bellini*, pp. 105–6, and Wind, *Feast of the Gods*, pp. 48–49, n. 14. Roberto Longhi, by contrast, gives the fifth panel (fig. 166) to Andrea Previtali and considers it unrelated in any way to the first four (*Ricerche*, p. 13).

16. "MCCCCLXXXVIII MS decembrio. Pretera perchè da poco tempo in qua se è posto in consuetudine far nove spexe al tuto vane e superflue, le qual excriedeno el privato, nè mai se ne pol trazer alguna utilità, zoè i Rastelli et chasse dorate, molto sumptuose et de valuta. Et nunc, sia azonto, che tuti i dicti Rastelli et chasse, quovismodo dorate, siane de facto prohibite et bandite, sichè da qui in avanti nullo modo se possino più uxar nè tegnir, soto tute le pene et strecture contegnude [in] la parte di ornamenti de le camere, si a quelli, che decetero havesseno ardir de tegnirle, come ai maistri che le lavorasseno. Et oltra tute le altre pene e strecture predicte, se algun maistro sarà trovado da qui in avanti lavorar alguna de le stesse casse prohibite in questo capitolo specificate, quelli che le troverano siano chi se boglia, le possino de factotuor, et siano liberamente soe" (ASV, Senato Terra, Registro 10, 1486–1489, fol. 185v [184v in the old pagination]). The text was published and discussed by Bistort, *Magistrato*, pp. 368–73.

17. ASV, Senato Terra, Registro 10, fol. 185r (formerly 184r).

18. As Wind suggested (*Feast of the Gods*, pp. 48–49, n. 14). For other views, cf. G. F. Hartlaub, "Spiegel-Bilder"; Hartlaub, *Zauber des Spiegels*, pp. 47, 49–51; and Cieri Via, "Allegorie." See also Ruggeri, "Bellini: Vanitas," with an X ray of our fig. 170; and Nepi Scirè in Nepi Scirè and Valcanover, *Accademia*, p. 91.

19. The letter is discussed and quoted above at n. 35. N.B. also Bellini's contractual arrangement with the Scuola Grande di San Marco, granting to him, as to his brother before him, narrative freedom of choice; see app. 3, n. 3.

20. See Cieri Via, "Allegorie," pp. 136–41. Cf. Hartlaub, "Spiegel–Bilder," p. 240 and n. 1.

21. This in itself precludes a frequently posited identification of the figure as Prudence: Prudence, with two heads to see simultaneously the future and the past, contemplates herself in a mirror. Cf. Goffen, "Early Italian School, XIV–XV Centuries," in Egbert Haverkamp-Begemann, ed., *Small Paintings of the Masters* (New York, 1981), 1:32.

22. Does this face allude to the patron or original owner of the object? Although whether restelli were normally made for women is not certain, it seems likely that they were, and the context of the prohibition of restelli in the act of 1489, referring also to furs and wedding cakes, implies this. But the one documented owner of a

restello by Bellini, that is, Catena, was a man, and so was the friend originally designated by Catena to inherit the precious object, prized for its painting, not its function.

23. Zovenzoni dedicated ode 163 to the *Eve*: "If your beauty was that which lives in this marble, who would be amazed if man knelt before you, Eve?" (Si tua forma fuit quae marmore vivit in isto, / quoi mirum si vir paruit, Eva, tibi?); see Ziliotto, *Zovenzoni*, p. 116. The northern qualities of the *Eve* and Zovenzoni's appreciation of her beauty prove that this type of nude was an attractive aesthetic option in Venice, though Bellini's patron may also have been a northern European whose taste is reflected in the restello nude. For Rizzo's sculptures, see also Pincus, *Arco Foscari*, pp. 228–33.

24. Cited by Vasari-Milanesi, 1:184. See also Panofsky, *Early Netherlandish Painting*, 1:3, 174. This painting was owned by Cardinal Ottaviano and described by Bartolomeo Fazio c. 1455 in *De viris illustribus* (Florence, 1745), p. 46. N.B. also Schwarz, "Mirror of the Artist," and Held, "Artis Pictoriae Amator."

25. The drunkenness of Michelangelo's *Bacchus* was intended as a moral commentary on excess, according to Condivi. Michelangelo studied Bellini's art closely, as Smyth has shown ("Emergence of High Renaissance").

26. Wind, *Feast of the Gods*, p. 48.

27. The passage from Caldiera's *De virtutibus*, fol. 52v, is translated and analyzed by King, "Personal, Domestic, and Republican Values," p. 546.

28. Ibid., p. 545.

29. Cieri Via, "Allegorie morali," p. 142; Hartlaub, "Spiegel-Bilder," p. 240; Wind, *Feast of the Gods*, p. 49, n. 14. Ludwig identified the group as the "Unmasking of Shame" and compared it to Giotto's *Envy* ("Restello," pp. 229, 239).

30. The globes and amphorae appear in other, undisputed depictions of Fortune; see Cieri Via, "Allegorie," pp. 129–33, for examples.

31. See Brown, "Mantegna," and Knox, "Camerino."

32. The two other paintings associated with the commission are the panels representing the *Vestal Virgin Tuccia* and *Sophonisba Drinking the Cup of Poison*, both now in the National Gallery, London (Davies, *Earlier Italian Schools*, pp. 340–41). But, as Knox warns, these two are not a pair ("Camerino," p. 82).

33. For Bellini's lost mural paintings in one of the Grimani palaces, see above at n. 9. According to the object file in the National Gallery, Washington, the *Scipio* canvas is painted in emulsified tempera and is better preserved on the left side than the right, which is abraded.

34. Isabella's "commission" was first given to Bellini verbally by her husband, Marchese Gianfrancesco, in 1496; see Luzio, "Disegni," p. 277, and Robertson, *Bellini*, pp. 133–52. (Perhaps Bellini often received commissions in this way, that is, orally, which would explain why no contracts have been found for his paintings for individual patrons.) Correspondence pertaining to the picture did not begin until 1501, and then negotiations were still preliminary. The allegorical painting first discussed in 1496 and in 1501 was never painted; in 1504 Bellini sent Isabella a "Presepio"—a *Nativity* or *Adoration*. This work has been lost but may be reflected in the Allendale *Nativity* in the National Gallery of Art, Washington. See Brown with Lorenzoni, *Isabella*, pp. 149–67. Isabella expressed herself delighted with Bellini's *Presepio*, which she displayed in a bedroom (cf. our fig. 65). See Braghirolli, "Carteggio," pp. 370–83, and above, app. 2, no. 51.

35. "Bellini . . . is very well disposed to serve Your Excellency as soon as the measurements or canvas is sent. It will be necessary that the invention that Your Excellency writes to me . . . be accommodated to the fantasy of him who has to paint it: . . . very precise terms do not suit his style, being accustomed, as he says, always to roam at his will in paintings." The Italian text is given in app. 2, no. 49; see also no. 50. Bembo goes on to urge Isabella's assistance with Mantegna's painting for Francesco Cornaro. See Giovanni Gaye, *Carteggio inedito*, 2:71, no. 22.

36. For Vianello's letter of 25 June 1501, see app. 2, no. 32. In addition to voicing displeasure with Isabella d'Este's text for the proposed painting, Bellini complained that he did not want his work compared with Mantegna's excellent allegories.

37. Isabella to Bembo on 2 December 1505: "Di fare una inventione a modo suo: che satisfatia al Bellino . . . et di vario et ellegante significato." See Cian, "Bembo e Isabella," p. 106. In his reply, Bembo advised that it would be best to allow Bellini "to roam at his will," as cited above in n. 35. On 11 May 1506, the marchesa again wrote Bembo, urging him to keep Bellini well disposed toward the enterprise and to compose the *poesia* to his satisfaction, "di tener ben disposto il Bellino, et di componere la poesia ad sua satisfactione" (Cian, "Bembo e Isabella," p. 108).

38. In the letter of 25 June 1501, as cited above in n. 36.

39. For this fanciful approach to genealogy, characteristic of many Venetian patricians, see Davis, *Venetian Family*.

40. Transcribed by Erwin Panofsky, cited by Fern Rusk Shapley, *Catalogue of the Italian Paintings* (Washington, D.C., 1979), 1:52–54. For the iconography of the painting and the identification of the figures depicted, see Knox, "Camerino."

41. Barbaro's *De uxoria* is discussed by King, "Caldiera and the Barbaros," and *Venetian Humanism*, pp. 92–98.

42. Knox, "Camerino," p. 83.

43. N.B., however, Bellini's lost and undated *Cosmografia* noted by Ridolfi; see above at n. 9.

44. Bellini's *Feast* was the first work completed for the studiolo, which was the intended destination of the painting from the start, as John Shearman has demonstrated. It seems that the duke also commissioned a painting from Raphael, which was to represent the *Indian Triumph of Bacchus*, already in 1514 or perhaps earlier, which was meant for the same room. Alfonso ordered a second painting from Raphael for the camerino, the *Hunt of Meleager*, begun in 1517 but never delivered. Any attempt to reconstruct the camerino must take Raphael's contributions into account, as Shearman notes. Professor Shearman most generously made available to me the manuscript of his essay "Alfonso d'Este's Camerino" before publication.

45. On these paintings, see Shapley, *Italian Paintings*, pp. 47–50, 54, and "Giovanni Bellini and Cornaro's Gazelle," *Gazette des Beaux-Arts* 28 (1945): 27–30; Tietze-Conrat, "Again"; Tietze and Tietze-Conrat, "Orfeo"; and Friedmann, "Cornaro's Gazelle."

46. Note the signature of the portrait of a boy in Birmingham, chap. 3 at nn. 27–29, and fig. 153. The first home of Bellini's *Feast*, the *Camerino d'alabastro* of Alfonso d'Este, was in his castello in Ferrara, though the precise location of the room is unknown. Wind's suggestion (*Feast of the Gods*) that Alfonso got in 1514 the mythological painting first begun by Bellini for Isabella in 1506 is unwarranted. See Carlo Dionisotti, review of Edgar Wind, *Feast of the Gods*, *Art Bulletin* 32 (1950): 237–39. Bellini received a final payment of 85 ducats in 1514 (Campori, "Tiziano," p. 581). The document is ASE, Camera Ducale, Libri camerali diversi 249, fol. 140; I owe this information to John Shearman.

47. Perhaps Alfonso got the idea of commissioning a work by Bellini from his sister. In any case, patronage of the Venetian master was in a sense part of their common heritage, for their predecessor, Lionello, had long ago employed Bellini's father, Jacopo.

48. Walker had recognized Bellini's debt to the woodcut illustration in the Venetian editions (1501) of the *Metamorphoses* but not his reliance on the translator's commentary, which, as Fehl argues, provided Bellini's primary text. See Walker, *Bellini and Titian*, p. 13, and Philipp Fehl, "Worship of Bacchus," pp. 45–51.

49. Ovid, *Metamorphoses*, 9.346–48: "Ut referunt tardi nunc denique agrestes, / Lotis in hanc nymphe, fugiens obscena Priapi, / contulerat versos, servato nomine, vultus" (trans. Frank Justus Miller, Loeb Classical Library, 1976), 4:26–27.

50. This is Fehl's translation, from "Worship of Bacchus," pp. 48–49. The Italian of Bonsignori, *Ovidio volgarizato*, fol. 78v, is given in Fehl's app. 2, p. 88.

51. Bonsignori, *Ovidio volgarizato*, fol. 79v. My translation differs slightly from Fehl's ("Feast of Bacchus," pp. 49–50).

52. The sky at the horizon on the right is probably also by Titian, and perhaps he reworked part of the landscape in the upper right. The question of who painted the second (concealed) landscape at the left probably cannot be answered. The staff of Mercury's caduceus is visible in X ray, indicating the presence of white lead; the other attributes are not visible; and all were added on the surface. Bellini exploited the white gesso ground to lighten and illuminate his forms, allowing the gesso to show through thin layers of color. This luminous effect has been lost as a result of a relining process that darkened the gesso. Aside from this and some minor losses, the painting is in excellent condition. I thank David Bull for these observations. Mr. Bull, who began restoration of the canvas in 1985, and Joyce Plesters, who analyzed the pigments, plan to publish their discoveries in *Studies in the History of Art*. See also Bull, "Bellini's-Titian's Feast." He makes the following technical observations: Silenus's orange robe of orpiment and realgar is very abraded; the greens in the trees are discolored copper resinate; and Bellini's paint is applied directly onto the priming, whereas Titian's is combined with more medium—both masters used walnut oil—and applied in thicker layers.

53. See Fehl, "Feast of Bacchus," p. 51, and Ovid, *Metamorphoses*, 3.553–56, 607, 655. References are to the Loeb edition, trans. Frank Justus Miller (Loeb Classical Library, 1977), 1:162–63, 166–67, and 170–71. The Bellinesque *Infant Bacchus* in Washington is akin to this figure in the *Feast*.

54. As Erica Tietze-Conrat suggested; see Walker, *Bellini and Titian*, p. 5, n. 10. In a paper, "Bellini's 'Feast of the Gods' and the Hypnerotomachia Poliphili," presented at the meetings of the Renaissance Society of America, New York, 1988, Anthony Colantuono found confirmation of this in the kingfisher represented at the lower left, a bird identified with the mythical Halcyon, humanist metaphor for the solstice. Professor Colantuono most generously allowed me to read his essay before publication. It seems to me that his discoveries do not contradict Fehl's interpretation. N.B. that X rays reveal that the kingfisher, like the attributes of the gods, was added on the surface, perhaps to establish or confirm what otherwise would not be clear in Bellini's initial conception of the theme. Moreover, Bellini's original combination of mortals, mythic beings, and divinity (the infant Bacchus) is comparable to the heterogenous populations necessarily inhabiting the scenes begun by Raphael and those represented by Titian in his

paintings for the camerino.

55. Walker, *Bellini and Titian*, p. 13; followed by Fehl, "Feast of Bacchus," p. 45 and fig. 9. The patron or author of the program of the painting may have informed Bellini of the various textual sources, but the woodcut illustration he surely knew firsthand. Our fig. 178 is from the 1509 ed., a reprint of 1501.

56. On Titian's autobiographical *Pietà*, with its echoes of Bellini's altarpieces, see Goffen, *Piety and Patronage*, pp. 151–54.

## Epilogue: Old Bellini and Young Titian

*Note to epigraph:* Ridolfi, *Maraviglie*, 1:75: "La cui [di Bellini] fama rinovellerassi di secolo in secolo fino à gl'ultimi respiri del Mondo." For Bellini's "celestial honors," see the fifteenth-century sonnet published by Biadego, *Variazioni*, p. 14, quoted above, Introduction at n. 2.

1. See chap. 1 at nn. 102–3, 128.

2. On the conception of "Altersstil," see Held, "Commentary." This volume of the *Art Journal*, entitled *Old-Age Style*, was edited by David Rosand. N.B. also Hans Tietze: *Tizian: Leben und Werk* (Vienna, 1936), pp. 231–52; "Jugendwerk und Alterswerk"; and "Earliest and Latest Works."

3. See chap. 1 at n. 71.

4. On the *Noah*, see Wagner, "Trunkenheit Noahs." The painting is in mediocre condition. A seam in the canvas runs vertically down the center, the edges are damaged, and there are small repaintings throughout. The slight *di sotto in su* suggests that the painting was made to be seen from below.

5. Although Noah himself identified Ham as his youngest son (Gen. 9:24), the order in which the three sons were named in the Bible suggested the order of their ages to Bellini and indeed to other artists and to commentators. Ham, therefore, is second.

6. "Noe Christum significat, quem iudei deridentes / ipsum corona spinea coronaverunt, et denudaverunt / et sicut infedeles filii eum tamquam stultum subsannaverunt" (Paul Kristeller, *Biblia Pauperum*, Graphische Gesellschaft, 2, Veröffentlichung [Berlin, 1906], pl. 21). For this typology, see Stefano Coltellacci, "Studi belliniani," p. 84, and also David C. Steinmetz, *Luther in Context* (Bloomington, 1986), pp. 99–111.

7. Augustine compared the nakedness of Noah and of Christ in *De civitate dei*, 16:1–2.

8. See Coltellacci, "Studi belliniani," p. 82.

9. The nymph of the *Feast of the Gods* sleeps in the same way (fig. 72).

10. The hand that wrote this inscription also signed the *Feast of the Gods* (figs. 175–76). See Walker, *Bellini and Titian*, pp. 95–96, citing Alwyn Cole, examiner of questioned documents, Department of the U.S. Treasury. Cole notes that the writer was "of some skill" and that neither signature has been retouched in any significant way. The *Portrait of a Man* from Hampton Court (fig. 161) has a signature very close to these, probably by the same hand. The signature of the *Dominican/Peter Martyr* in London (fig. 158), on the contrary, was probably written by someone else. The "skill" of Bellini's writing is suggestive regarding his education, perhaps to be expected of an original citizen. The painted signatures may also be compared with those written by Bellini in various documents listed in app. 2, nos. 5, 7, 12, 14, 16, 46, 64.

11. For the sculptor, see Wilk, "Tullio Lombardo," and for Bellini's awareness of his work, see above, chap. 2 at n. 90.

12. Pino, *Dialogo della pittura* [1548], p. 131. See also Vasari-Milanesi, 1:101, 4:98; Creighton E. Gilbert, "Milan and Savoldo," *Art Bulletin* 27 (1945): 124–38; and Paul Hecht, "The *Paragone* Debate: Ten Illustrations and a Comment," *Simiolus* 14 (1984): 125–27. I speculate that the *Saint George* in the Cini Collection, Venice, echoes the stance of the lost figure; Harold E. Wethey, *The Paintings of Titian*, vol. 1: *The Religious Paintings* (London, 1969), pl. 150.

13. Cropper, "Beauty of Woman," p. 176, and pp. 181–82 for the distinction between inner and outer beauty in Castiglione and Bembo, inter alia. For the importance of Pliny's Natural History (esp. 35:10, 36) to this discourse, see Ferriguto, "Venere." Wendy Stedman Sheard brought this essay to my attention.

14. The raised arm has been heavily restored, and its disproportionate width is surely due to this. The paint surface is visibly thicker in this part, and the contour has been incised. To be sure, Bellini used incised outlines for geometric shapes here (the window) and elsewhere, such as for parapets or thrones (fig. 126), but I know of no instance in which he employed incised lines for figures. I suspect that this too is due to later "restoration." X rays suggest that the white lead is denser in this arm than elsewhere in the painting. Reflectograms made by Dolf van Asperen de Boer for the Warburg Institute may shed further light on the question, but these were not made available to me.

15. For Bellini and the *Venus of Urbino*, see also Robertson, *Bellini*, p. 152. For arguments about the identity of Titian's figures, see Goffen, "Renaissance Dreams," pp. 691–701, and David Rosand, "Ermeneutica amorosa: Observations on the Interpretation of Titian's Venuses" (1976), in *Tiziano e Venezia: Convegno internazionale di Studi* (Vicenza, 1980), pp. 375–81.

16. See Schwarz, "The Mirror of the Artist," and Zucker, "Reflections on Reflections." Bellini's allusions to the paragone may also be implicit in the sculptural (Lombardesque) quality of the figure.

17. Stephan Poglayen-Neuwall, "Titian's Pictures of the Toilet of

Venus and Their Copies," *Art Bulletin* 16 (1934): 358–84; Poglayen-Neuwall, "The *Venus* of the Ca d'Oro and the Origin of the Chief Types of the *Venus at the Mirror* from the Workshop of Titian," *Art Bulletin* 29 (1947): 195–96; and Harold E. Wethey, *The Paintings of Titian*, vol. 3: *The Mythological and Historical Paintings* (London, 1975), pp. 68–70, 162–65. Wethey dates the Louvre Titian c. 1515.

## Appendix 3: The Scuola Grande di San Marco

1. 18 February 1507 (1506, m.v.) (ASV, Testamenti, Bernardo Cavanis, Busta 271, c. 307). The will has been published many times, most recently by Meyer zur Capellen, *Gentile Bellini* p. 120.

2. Jacopo Bellini worked for the scuola as early as 1444; see W. B. Wurthmann, "The *Scuole Grandi* and Venetian Art, 1260–c. 1500" (Ph.D. diss., University of Chicago, 1975), p. 174. For Jacopo Bellini's contract with the scuola in 1466 and for Gentile's continuing association with the confraternity, beginning in 1467, see Pompeo Molmenti, "I pittori Bellini: Documenti e ricerche," *Archivio Veneto*, anno 18, vol. 36 (1888): 225–28, and Molmenti, *Studi e ricerche di storia e d'arte* (Turin and Rome, 1892), pp. 126–29. On Gentile Bellini and the confraternity, see Meyer zur Capellen, "Bellini in der Scuola," pp. 104–8, and Sohm, *Scuola Grande*, esp. pp. 242–46, 259–61, 272, 278–79.

3. ASV, Scuola Grande di San Marco, Registro 16bis (1479–1503), c. 38, 24 April 1470, for the *Flood with the Ark of Noah*, which Giovanni Bellini probably did not paint. See Molmenti, "Pittori Bellini," p. 228, and Molmenti, *Studi e ricerche*, p. 130; and Sohm, *Scuola Grande*, pp. 242–43, 260, for this painting, for Giovanni Bellini's terms as deacon of the confraternity in 1486 and in 1494 (citing ASV, Scuola Grande di San Marco, Busta 202, n.p.), and for his participation in meetings. Meyer zur Capellen documents Giovanni Bellini's activity in the scuola in 1484 and 1486, and perhaps in 1476 and 1494 ("Bellini in der Scuola," 105–6, nn. 9, 11). For the scuola's acceptance of the Bellini brothers' offer—actually put forward by Gentile—to decorate the albergo, see the record of 15 July 1492, published by Paoletti, *Raccolta*, p. 14, and Paoletti, "Scuola Grande," p. 137. The choice of narratives was evidently to be made with the advice of the painter-brothers (see Sohm, *Scuola Grande*, pp. 245–46).

4. "Essendo manchà de questa vita misser Zentil Bellin nostro fradello et essendo romaxo el teller la principiado per la scuola non compido. . . . El dito messer Zuane [Bellini] he contento de conpirlo con quella medema condicion e pati havea fato el dito condam suo fradelo misser Zentil . . . dechiarando che el dito misser Zuane vuol che misser Marco Pelegrin sia quella habia a governar questa cossa e non voler haver a far con altri che con lui si de haverli danari come ognaltra cossa. Onde misser Piero de Alberto e compagni mete la parte chel dito misser Marco Pelegrin habia ogni libertà de poder far el tuto zercha al conpir de dito teller come li parerà e piacerà" (ASV, Scuola Grande di San Marco, Registro 17 [1498–1530], fol. 33; published by Molmenti, "Pittori Bellini," p. 233). For the cycle of seven paintings that once decorated the albergo of the scuola, see Humfrey, "Bellinesque Life of St. Mark Cycle," pp. 225–42. For Pelegrin's friendship with Gentile Bellini, see Sohm, *Scuola Grande*, p. 244; Pelegrin witnessed Gentile Bellini's will.

5. ASV, Scuola Grande di San Marco, Registro 17, fol. 28. See Paoletti, *Raccolta*, 1:18–19, and Sohm, *Scuola Grande*, p. 279.

6. The painting was recently restored by Pinin Brambilla Barcilon. I am grateful for her having kindly allowed me to examine it in her studio in Milan, and to Rosalba Tardito, Soprintendente ai Beni Artistici e Storici of Milan, for arranging my visit.

7. Gentile Bellini himself is among them, wearing the gold chain, insignia of his knighthood. He was first tentatively identified by Giuseppe Fiocco, "Visto da vicino," p. 7.

8. Belliniano sketched his master on his deathbed; the drawing, inscribed "Johan belljno Veneto pictor quando era morto in cathalecto," is in a private collection in England and was published by Jennifer Fletcher in the *Sunday Times Magazine*, 14 December 1975, p. 23, and by Christian Hornig, "Una nuova proposta per i 'Tre Filosofi,'" p. 49, fig. 47, in *Giorgione: Atti del Convegno Internazionale di Studio per il 5 Centenario della Nascita* (Venice, 1979). Belliniano's better-known drawing of Giovanni Bellini alive is in the Musée Condé, Chantilly.

9. The record of the agreement made 4 July 1515, was copied on 11 August. Molmenti found the document, ASV, Scuola Grande di San Marco, Registro 17, fol. 60, and it was published by Paoletti, *Raccolta*, p. 14, and Sohm, *Scuola Grande*, p. 281. See app. 2, no. 64.

10. Humfrey, "Bellinesque Life of St. Mark Cycle," p. 230, n. 8, likewise argues for Giovanni's probable authorship of the composition, despite the existence of a design by Gentile, which is documented in the scuola records of 9 March 1505 (ASV, Scuola Grande di San Marco, Registro 17, fol. 28). For this, see Paoletti, *Raccolta*, pp. 18–19, and Sohm, *Scuola Grande*, p. 279. I thank the staff of the hospital library (the present use of the albergo of the scuola) for their helpfulness when I studied the painting. For the testament of Belliniano's widow, see app. 2, following no. 71.

11. The painting is to be restored by Ottorino Nonfarmale, who

kindly allowed me to examine it in his studio. At the right edge of the canvas, the second tree and part of the mountain were painted in by Mauro Pellicioli during an earlier restoration. The man in white who beats Saint Mark looks like Bellini's work to me, as do some of the figures in the crowd at right and in the background. I further speculate that Bellini may have painted the architecture, but not the sky.

## Appendix 4: Attributions and Other Dilemmas

1. I have discussed the Vincent Ferrer panels at greater length in "Bellini and St. Vincent," pp. 277–96. Francesco Sansovino attributed the altarpiece to Bellini, but authors of later guide books to Venice variously ascribed the work to almost anyone but him (*Venetia città nobilissima et singolare* [Venice, 1581], p. 23v). Roberto Longhi reasserted the sixteenth-century attribution to Bellini, though this is still debated ("Piero dei Franceschi e lo sviluppo della pittura veneziana," *L'Arte* 17 [1914]: 241–44). Compare Luitpold Düssler, *Giovanni Bellini* (Vienna, 1949), p. 59, and Giles Robertson, *Giovanni Bellini* (Oxford, 1968), pp. 43–46. Most recently, Miklòs Boskovits has dealt with the problems of Bellini's early work ("Giovanni Bellini: Quelques suggestions sur ses débuts," *Revue du Louvre et des musées de France* 36 [1986]: 386–93). It seems to me that his arguments are often based on extremely doubtful attributions, e.g., the Carità triptychs (fig. 187) or the Pesaro *Crucifixion* (surely not by Bellini), and do not give sufficient weight to such undisputed early works as the *Saint Jerome*, the *Crucifixion*, and the *Transfiguration* (figs. 1, 5, 9).

2. Ferrer was represented as a saint by a fellow Dominican, Fra Angelico, in a fresco of 1441–42 (John Pope-Hennessy, *Fra Angelico*, 2d ed. [Ithaca, 1974], p. 205). On the use of images to promote canonization, see Goffen, *Spirituality in Conflict*, chap. 2, and, for a Venetian example, Goffen, *Piety and Patronage*, pp. 78–79. N.B. also the mosaic figure of Vincent Ferrer, signed and dated by Maestro Silvestro in 1458 in the south (ducal) transept arch of San Marco, Venice. The location suggests official approbation of the cult. See also the Introduction, n. 23.

3. ASV, SS. Giovanni e Paolo, Busta P, fasc. x, no. 117; no. 145, fol. 4; and no. 188 (copies of a lost original).

4. "Cronaca del convento de' SS. Giovanni e Paolo di Venezia," Vicenza, Biblioteca Bertoliana, G6.8.29 (1305), fol. 75.

5. Cf. Gino Fogolari, "Disegni," pp. 360–90; followed by Robertson, *Bellini*, pp. 43–53. Fogolari's arguments regarding the date of the altar itself are mistaken, as I have shown; see "Bellini and St. Vincent."

6. For the problem of likeness in the depiction of saints, especially saints whose appearance might reasonably have been recorded or described to artists by eyewitnesses, see Goffen, *Spirituality in Conflict*, chap. 2.

7. "Venice and the High Renaissance in Florence," pp. 219–20.

8. M. Lavin, "Altar of Corpus Domini in Urbino," pp. 1–24.

9. *Anonimo Morelliano*, ed. Frimmel, p. 114. For the date of the altarpiece, see Paoletti, *L'architettura*, 1:183.

10. For the work on the frame and altar in 1523–24, see the *Cronaca*, Vicenza, Biblioteca Bertolana MS 583, fols. 75 (old fol. 29r), 94 (old fol. 35v). Bonnie Blackburn kindly brought to my attention two further references to the sixteenth-century "reconstruction": ASV, SS. Giovanni e Paolo, Busta P, fasc. x, no. 207, fols. 491v, 492r-v. The decorative motifs of the frame are very close to those of the frame of Titian's *Assunta*, 1516–18. See also Arslan, "Polittico di San Zanipolo," pp. 140–41.

11. On the triptychs, all of which must have been executed between 1460 and 1471, see Arslan, "I trittici della Carità," *Bollettino d'arte*, 4th ser., 36 (1951): 305–23; Arslan, "Studi belliniani," ibid. 47 (1962): 40–58; and Robertson, *Bellini*, pp. 39–43. Colin Eisler informs me that he considers the triptychs to have been executed in the studio of Jacopo Bellini with the assistance of several masters, probably including Giovanni Bellini; see Eisler's *The Genius of Jacopo Bellini* (New York, 1989), in press.

12. This version of the painting was in the collection of Giorgio Cornaro, according to the inscription of the engraving, and according to Vasari, in the second edition (1568) of his Lives (Vasari-Milanesi, 3:164). In 1760, again according to the Monaco engraving, the painting was in the collection of Anton Maria Zanetti in Venice; then it passed to the Razumowsky collection in Vienna, where it was unfortunately destroyed by fire. See Gronau, *Giovanni Bellini*, pp. 217–18, with a listing of replicas and variants. Marilyn Aronberg Lavin reminds me that the subject is comparatively rare.

13. Pier Maria Pennacchi, according to Marco Boschini, *Le minere della pittura* (Venice, 1664), p. 414. The backs of the canvases—that is, the interior of the organ doors—were decorated with figures of saints in niches, *Peter* on the back of the Gabriel canvas, and *Paul*, now lost, formerly on the back of the Annunciate Virgin canvas. See Moschini Marconi, *Gallerie dell'Accademia di Venezia*, pp. 86–87.

14. I purposely exclude tiny figures, such as those in Masaccio's *Adoration* predella or that in Bellini's predella of the *Crucifixion of Saint Peter* (fig. 101): the effect is quite different when one is dealing with actors on a miniature scale. Masaccio also included contemporary figures

in the *Tribute Money* and in other frescoes of the Brancacci Chapel, a family funerary chapel in Santa Maria del Carmine, Florence.

15. Hans Belting has recently discussed the *Pietà* as a purposeful break with Mantegna (*Giovanni Bellini: Pietà*). I think he is wrong, however, to date Bellini's painting with reference to the first publication of Propertius, whose work was well known and available well before that printing; see above, chap. 1, n. 56.

16. For the type, see Ringbom, *Icon to Narrative*. For Mantegna's painting in Berlin, see Lightbown, *Mantegna*, pp. 404–5.

17. Degenhart and Schmitt, *Jacopo Bellini*, pl. 3.

18. Wolfgang Prinz, "Die Darstellung Christi im Tempel und die Bildnisse des Andrea Mantegna," *Jahrbuch der Berliner Museen* 12 (1962): 50–54. For the artist's family, see Rodolfo Signorini, "Mantegna's Unknown Sons: A Rediscovered Epitaph," *Journal of the Warburg and Courtauld Institutes* 49 (1986): 233–35.

19. For the drawing, see Hans Tietze and Erica Tietze-Conrat, *The Drawings of the Venetian Painters in the 15th and 16th Centuries* (New York, 1944; repr. 1970), p. 85, no. 299.

20. E. Camesasca, *Mantegna* (Milan, 1964), pp. 17, 115–16, 127–28.

21. See J. Byam Shaw, "A Giovanni Bellini at Bristol," *Burlington Magazine* 94 (1952): 157–59, and "A Further Note on the Bristol Bellini," ibid., 237; Konrad Oberhuber and Jacquelyn L. Sheehan in Jay A. Levenson, Oberhuber, and Sheehan, *Early Italian Engravings from the National Gallery of Art* (Washington, D.C., 1973), pp. 208–11; and Lightbown, *Mantegna*, pp. 491–92.

22. See Byam Shaw, "Giovanni Bellini" and "Further Note"; and cf. Robertson, *Bellini*, pp. 25–26, 75, who attributes the drawing to Mantegna. The attribution of the sheet in the Lehman Collection, which is in the opposite direction, is also disputed.

# Select Bibliography


Alberti, Leon Battista. *On Painting and On Sculpture: The Latin Texts of* De Pictura *and* De Statua. Trans. and ed. Cecil Grayson. London, 1972.

Anderson, Jaynie. "'Christ Carrying the Cross' in San Rocco: Its Commission and Miraculous History." *Arte veneta* 31 (1977): 186–88.

———. "The Giorgionesque Portrait: From Likeness to Allegory." In *Giorgione: Atti del Convegno Internazionale di Studio per il 5 centenario della nascita*, pp. 153–58. Venice, 1979.

Arslan, Edoardo. *Catalogo delle cose d'arte e di antichità d'Italia, Vicenza*. Vol. 1: *Le chiese*. Rome, 1956.

———. "Il polittico di San Zanipolo." *Bollettino d'arte*, 4th ser., 37 (1952): 127–46.

———. "Studi belliniani." *Bollettino d'arte*, 4th ser., 47 (1962): 40–58.

Bassi, Elena. "Appunti per la storia del Palazzo Ducale di Venezia, 1." *Critica d'arte* 51 (1962): 25–38, 41–53.

Becci, Antonio. *Catalogo delle pitture che si conservano nelle chiese di Pesaro*. Pesaro, 1783.

Belting, Hans. *Giovanni Bellini Pietà: Ikone und Bilderzählung in der venezianischen Malerei*. Frankfurt, 1985.

Bembo, Pietro. *Prose della volgar lingua*. Venice, 1525.

———. *Prose e rime*. Ed. Carlo Dionisotti. Turin, 1960.

Biadego, Giuseppe. *Variazioni e divagazioni a proposito di due sonetti di Giorgio Sommariva in onore di Gentile e Giovanni Bellini*. Verona, 1907.

Billanovich, Eugenio. "Note per la storia della pittura nel Veneto." *Italia medievale e umanistica* 16 (1973): 359–89.

Bistort, Giulio. *Il Magistrato alle pompe nella Republica di Venezia: Studio storico*. Venice, 1912; repr. Bologna, 1969.

Bonsignori, Giovanni de'. *Ovidio volgarizato*. Venice, 1501.

Borenius, Tancred. *The Picture Gallery of Andrea Vendramin*. London, 1923.

Bortolan, Domenico. *S. Corona, Chiesa e convento dei Domenicani in Vicenza: Memorie storiche*. Vicenza, 1889.

Bortolan, D., and S. Rumor. *Guida di Vicenza*. Vicenza, 1919.

Boschini, Marco. *La carta del navegar pitoresco* [1660]. Ed. Anna Pallucchini. Civiltà veneziana fonti e testi, 7; Fonti e documenti per la storia dell'arte veneta, 1st ser., 4. Venice and Rome, 1966.

———. *Le minere della pittura*. Venice, 1664.

———. *Le ricche minere della pittura veneziana*. 2d ed. rev. Venice, 1674.

Boskovits, Miklós. "Giovanni Bellini: Quelques suggestions sur ses débuts." *Revue du Louvre et des musées de France* 36 (1986): 386–93.

———. "Per Jacopo Bellini pittore (Postilla ad un colloquio)." *Paragone* 36 (1985): 113–23.

Bottari, Stefano. *Tutta la pittura di Giovanni Bellini*. 2 vols. Milan, 1963.

Braghirolli, Willelmo. "Carteggio di Isabella d'Este Gonzaga intorno ad un quadro di Giambellino." *Archivio veneto* 7 (1877): 370–83.

Braham, Allan, Martin Wyld, and Joyce Plesters. "Bellini's 'The Blood of the Redeemer.'" *National Gallery Technical Bulletin* 2 (1978): 11–24.

Brandi, Cesare. "The Cleaning of Pictures in Relation to Patina, Varnish, and Glazes." *Burlington Magazine* 91 (1949): 183–88.

———. "Postilla al restauro della pala del Bellini di Pesaro e del Gozzoli del 1456 della Pinacoteca di Perugia." *Bollettino dell'Istituto Centrale del Restauro* 2 (1950): 57–62.

———. "Some Factual Observations about Varnishes and Glazes." *Bollettino dell'Istituto Centrale del Restauro* 3–4 (1950): 9–29.

Braunfels, Wolfgang. "Giovanni Bellinis Paradiesgärtlein." *Das Münster* 9 (1956): 1–13.

Brown, Clifford M[alcolm]. "Andrea Mantegna and the Cornaro of Venice." *Burlington Magazine* 116 (1974): 101–3.

———. "Giovanni Bellini and Art Collecting." Letter. *Burlington Magażine* 114 (1972): 404–5.

———. "'Una testa de Platone antica con la punta dil Naso di Cera': Unpublished Negotiations between Isabella d'Este and Niccolò and Giovanni Bellini." *Art Bulletin* 51 (1969): 372–77.

Brown, Clifford M., with Anna Maria Lorenzoni. *Isabella d'Este and Lorenzo da Pavia, Documents for the History of Art and Culture in Renaissance Mantua*. Travaux d'Humanisme et Renaissance, 189. Geneva, 1982.

Brown, Patricia Fortini. *Venetian Narrative Painting in the Age of*

*Carpaccio*. New Haven and London, 1988.
Brunetti, Mario. "Due dogi sotto inchiesta: Agostino Barbarigo e Leonardo Loredan." *Archivio Veneto-Tridentino* 7 (1925): 278–329.
Bull, David. "The Restoration of Bellini's—Titian's Feast of the Gods." In *Bacchanals by Titian and Rubens*, ed. Görel Cavalli-Björkman, pp. 9–16. Nationalmusei Skriftserie, 10. Stockholm, 1987.
Byam Shaw, J. "A Giovanni Bellini at Bristol." *Burlington Magazine* 94 (1952): 152–59.
———. "A Further Note on the Bristol Bellini." *Burlington Magazine* 94 (1952): 257.
Bynum, Caroline Walker. "The Body of Christ in the Later Middle Ages: A Reply to Leo Steinberg." *Renaissance Quarterly* 39 (1986): 399–439.
Cabrol, J. B. *De Corredemptione Beatae Virginis Mariae*. Vatican City, 1950.
Campana, Augusto. "Notizie sulla 'Pietà' riminese di Giovanni Bellini." In *Scritti in onore di Mario Salmi*, 2:405–27. Rome, 1962.
Campbell, Lorne. "Notes on Netherlandish Pictures in the Veneto in the Fifteenth and Sixteenth Centuries." *Burlington Magazine* 123 (1981): 467–73.
Campori, Giuseppe. *Raccolta di cataloghi ed inventarii inediti di quadri, statue, disegni, bronzi, dorerie, smalti, medaglie, avori, ecc. dal secolo xv al secolo xix*. Modena, 1870; repr. Bologna, 1975.
———. "Tiziano e gli Estensi." *Nuova antologia di scienze, lettere ed arti*, 1st ser., 27 (1874): 581–620.
Cannon-Brookes, Peter. *The Cornbury Park Bellini: A Contribution towards the Study of the Late Paintings of Giovanni Bellini*. Birmingham, 1977.
Carlston, Charles Edwin. "Transfiguration and Resurrection." *Journal of Biblical Literature* 80 (1961): 233–40.
Cartari, Vincenzo. *Le imagini con la spositione de i dei degli antichi*. Venice, 1556.
———. *Le imagini de i Dei degli antichi*. Venice, 1571.
Cast, David. "The Stork and the Serpent: A New Interpretation of the Madonna of the Meadow by Bellini." *Art Quarterly* 32 (1969): 247–58.
Cessi, Roberto. *Storia della Repubblica di Venezia*, 2d ed. rev. 2 vols. Milan, 1968.
Chiappini di Sorio, Ileana. *Giovanni Bellini: Incoronazione della Vergine ("Pala di Pesaro")*. Venice, 1986.
Chojnacki, Stanley. "Dowries and Kinsmen in Early Renaissance Venice." *Journal of Interdisciplinary History* 5 (1975): 571–600.
———. "In Search of the Venetian Patriciate: Families and Factions in the Fourteenth Century." In *Renaissance Venice*, ed. J. R. Hale, pp. 47–90. London, 1973.
———. "Kinship Ties and Young Patricians in Fifteenth-Century Venice." *Renaissance Quarterly* 38 (1985): 240–70.
———. "Patrician Women in Early Renaissance Venice." *Studies in the Renaissance* 21 (1974): 176–203.
———. "Political Adulthood in Fifteenth-Century Venice." *American Historical Review* 91 (1986): 791–810.
Christiansen, Keith. "Venetian Painting of the Early Quattrocento." *Apollo* 125 (1987): 166–77.
Cian, Vittore. "Pietro Bembo e Isabella d'Este Gonzaga." *Giornale storico delle letteratura italiana* 9 (1887): 81–136.
Cicogna, Emanuele Antonio. *Delle inscrizioni veneziane raccolte ed illustrate*. 4 vols. Venice, 1827–34.
Cieri Via, Claudia. "Allegorie morali dalla bottega belliniana." In *Giorgione e la cultura veneta tra '400 e '500: Mito, allegoria, analisi iconologica* (Atti del Convegno, Rome, 1978), pp. 126–45. Rome, 1981.
Coltellacci, Stefano. "Studi belliniani: La *Derisione di Noè* di Besançon." In *Giorgione e la cultura veneta tra '400 e '500: Mito, allegoria, analisi iconologica* (Atti del Convegno, Rome, 1978), pp. 80–87. Rome, 1981.
Coltellacci, Stefano, and Marco Lattanzi. "Studi belliniani: Proposte iconologiche per la *Sacra allegoria* degli Uffizi." In *Giorgione e la cultura veneta tra '400 e '500: Mito, allegoria, analisi iconologica* (Atti del Convegno, Rome, 1978), pp. 59–79. Rome, 1981.
Coronelli, V. M. *Guida de' forestieri o sia Epitome diaria perpetua sagra-profana per la città di Venezia*. Venice, 1744.
Cropper, Elizabeth. "The Beauty of Woman: Problems in the Rhetoric of Renaissance Portraiture. In *Rewriting the Renaissance: The Discourses of Sexual Difference in Early Modern Europe*, ed. Margaret W. Ferguson, Maureen Quilligan, and Nancy J. Vickers, pp. 175–90. Women in Culture and Society, ed. Catharine R. Stimpson. Chicago and London, 1986.
Crowe, J. A., and G. B. Cavalcaselle. *A History of Painting in North Italy: Venice, Padua, Vicenza, Verona, Ferrara, Milan, Friuli, Brescia from the Fourteenth to the Sixteenth Century*. Ed. Tancred Borenius. Vol. 1. London, 1912.
Davies, Martin. *The Earlier Italian Schools*. National Gallery Catalogues. 2d ed. rev. London, 1961.
———. "Un dipinto Belliniano radiografato a Londra." *Arte veneta* 4 (1950): 169.
Davis, James C. *A Venetian Family and Its Fortune, 1500–1900: The Donà and the Conservation of Their Wealth*. Memoirs of the American Philosophical Society, 106. Philadelphia, 1975.
Degenhart, Bernhard, and Annegrit Schmitt. "Ein Musterblatt des Jacopo Bellini mit Zeichnungen

nach der Antike." In *Festschrift Luitpold Dussler: 28 Studien zur Archäologie und Kunstgeschichte*, pp. 139–68. Munich and Berlin, 1972.

———. *Jacopo Bellini: The Louvre Album of Drawings*. New York, 1984.

Del Bravo, Carlo. "Giovanni Bellini in relazione al Valla." *Annali di Scuola Normale Superiore di Pisa*, 3d ser., 13 (1983): 691–704. (Repr. in Del Bravo, *Le Risposte dell'arte*, pp. 97–107. Florence, 1985.)

Delaney, Susan J. "The Iconography of Giovanni Bellini's *Sacred Allegory*." *Art Bulletin* 59 (1977): 331–35.

Dellwing, Herbert. "Die Kirche San Zaccaria in Venedig: Eine ikonologische Studie." *Zeitschrift für Kunstgeschichte* 37 (1974): 224–34.

Dobrzeniecki, Tadeusz. "Mediaeval Sources of the Pietà." *Bulletin du Musée National de Varsovie* 7 (1967): 5–24.

Dominici, Bl. Giovanni. *Regola del governo di cura familiare, parte quarta: On the Education of Children*. Trans. and ed. Arthur Basil Coté. Washington, D.C., 1927.

Dussler, Luitpold. *Giovanni Bellini*. Vienna, 1949.

Eisler, Colin. "'Saints Anthony Abbot and Bernardino of Siena' Designed by Jacopo and Painted by Gentile Bellini." *Arte veneta* 39 (1985): 32–40.

———. "The Golden Christ of Cortona and the Man of Sorrows in Italy." *Art Bulletin* 51 (1969): 107–18, 233–46.

Ettlinger, Helen S. "The Iconography of the Columns in Titian's Pesaro Altarpiece." *Art Bulletin* 61 (1979): 59–67.

Fahy, Everett P., Jr. "New Evidence for Dating Giovanni Bellini's 'Coronation of the Virgin.'" *Art Bulletin* 46 (1964): 216–18.

Fehl, Philipp. "The Worship of Bacchus and Venus in Bellini's and Titian's Bacchanals for Alfonso d'Este." *Studies in the History of Art* 6 (1974): 37–95.

Ferriguto, Arnaldo. "Come nacque la Venere di Dresda." In Ferriguto, *Attraverso i "misteri" di Giorgione*, pp. 223–36. Castelfranco Veneto, 1933.

Finlay, Robert. "Politics and the Family in Renaissance Venice: The Election of Doge Andrea Gritti." *Studi veneziani*, n.s., 2 (1978): 97–117.

———. "The Venetian Republic as a Gerontocracy: Age and Politics in the Renaissance." *Journal of Medieval and Renaissance Studies* 8 (1978): 157–78.

Fiocco, Giuseppe. "Giovanni e la famiglia dei Bellini alla luce di nuovi documenti." *Vernice* 4 (1949): 6.

———. "I Disegni di Giambellino." *Arte veneta* 3 (1949): 40–54.

———. "Visto da vicino: 'La predica di San Marco' di Gentile e Giovanni Bellini." *Emporium* 88 (1938): 6–16.

Fleming, John V. *From Bonaventure to Bellini: An Essay in Franciscan Exegesis*. Princeton Essays on the Arts, 14. Princeton, N.J., 1982.

Fletcher, Jennifer. "Isabella d'Este and Giovanni Bellini's 'Presepio.'" *Burlington Magazine* 113 (1971): 703–12.

———. "Marcantonio Michiel: His Friends and Collection." *Burlington Magazine* 123 (1981): 453–67, 602–8.

———. "The Provenance of Bellini's Frick 'St. Francis.'" *Burlington Magazine* 114 (1974): 206–14.

Fogolari, Gino. "Disegni per gioco e incunabili del Giambellino." *Dedalo* 12 (1932): 360–90.

———. "I Restauri del Giambellino delle Gallerie dell'Accademia di Venezia." *Le Arti* 2 (1940): 251–55.

Franzoi, Umberto, and Dina Di Stefano. *Le chiese di Venezia*. Venice, 1976.

Friedmann, Herbert. "Cornaro's Gazelle and Bellini's *Orpheus*." *Gazette des Beaux-Arts* 32 (1947): 15–22.

Frimmel, Theodor. *See* Michiel, Marcantonio.

Frizzoni, Gustavo. "A Plea for the Reintegration of a Great Altarpiece." *Burlington Magazine* 22 (1913): 260–69.

———. "Per la reintegrazione della pala del Bellini." *Emporium* (1913): 227–28.

Fry, Roger. *Giovanni Bellini*. London, 1899.

Gallo, Rodolfo. "La Scuola di S. Orsola, i teleri del Carpaccio e la tomba di Gentile e Giovanni Bellini." *Bollettino dei musei civici veneziani* 8 (1963): 1–24.

Gamba, Carlo. *Giovanni Bellini*. Milan, 1937.

Gaye, Giovanni. *Carteggio inedito d'artisti dei secoli XIV, XV, XVI*. 3 vols. Florence, 1840; repr. Turin, 1968.

Geanakoplos, Deno John. *Interaction of the "Sibling" Byzantine and Western Cultures in the Middle Ages and Italian Renaissance (330–1600)*. New Haven and London, 1976.

Ghiotto, Renato, and Terisio Pignatti. *L'Opera completa di Giovanni Bellini detto Giambellino*. Classici dell'arte, 28. Milan, 1969.

Gibbons, Felton. "New Evidence for the Birth Dates of Gentile and Giovanni Bellini." *Art Bulletin* 45 (1963): 54–58.

———. "Practices in Giovanni Bellini's Workshop." *Pantheon* 23 (1965): 146–54.

Gilbert, Creighton. "Peintres et menuisiers au début de la Renaissance en Italie." *Revue de l'art* 37 (1977): 9–28.

Gilbert, Felix. "Humanism in Venice." In *Florence and Venice: Comparisons and Relations*. Vol. 1: *Quattrocento*, pp. 13–26. Florence, 1971.

———. "Venice in the Crisis of the League of Cambrai." In

*Renaissance Venice*, ed. J. R. Hale, pp. 274–92. London, 1973.

Giustiniani, St. Lorenzo. *Opera Divi Laurentii Iustiniani Venetiarii Prothopatriarcha*. Bressanone, 1506.

Goffen, Rona. "Bellini, S. Giobbe and Altar Egos." *Artibus et Historiae* 14 (1986): 57–70.

———. "Giovanni Bellini and the Altarpiece of St. Vincent Ferrer." In *Renaissance Studies in Honor of Craig Hugh Smyth*, ed. Andrew Morrogh et al., 2:277–96. Florence, 1985.

———. "Carpaccio's Portrait of a Young Knight: Identity and Meaning." *Arte veneta* 37 (1983): 37–48.

———. "Friar Sixtus IV and the Sistine Chapel." *Renaissance Quarterly* 39 (1986): 218–62.

———. "Icon and Vision: Giovanni Bellini's Half-Length Madonnas." *Art Bulletin* 57 (1975): 487–518.

———. "Masaccio's Trinity and the Letter to Hebrews." *Memorie Dominicane*, n.s., 11 (1980): 489–504.

———. "*Nostra Conversatio in Caelis Est*: Observations on the *Sacra Conversazione* in the Trecento." *Art Bulletin* 61 (1979): 198–222.

———. *Piety and Patronage in Renaissance Venice: Bellini, Titian, and the Franciscans*. New Haven and London, 1986.

———. "Renaissance Dreams." *Renaissance Quarterly* 40 (1987): 682–706.

———. *Spirituality in Conflict: Saint Francis and Giotto's Bardi Chapel*. University Park and London, 1988.

Goloubew [Golubew], Victor. *Les dessins de Jacopo Bellini au Louvre et au British Museum*. 2 vols. Brussels, 1908–12.

Gombrich, E. H. *The Image and the Eye: Further Studies in the Psychology of Pictorial Representation*. Ithaca, N.Y., 1982.

Greenblatt, Stephen. "Psychoanalysis and Renaissance Culture." In *Literary Theory/ Renaissance Texts*, ed. Patricia Parker and David Quint, pp. 210–24. Baltimore and London, 1986.

Gronau, Georg. *Giovanni Bellini: Des Meisters Gemälde*. Klassiker der Kunst, 36. Stuttgart, 1930.

———. "Die Signaturen des Giovanni Bellini." *Pantheon* 3 (1929): 221.

Guyot, G. H. In *New Catholic Encyclopedia*. s.v. "Transfiguration." New York, 1967.

Hadeln, Detlev von. "Two Portraits by Giovanni Bellini." *Burlington Magazine* 51 (1927): 4–7. *See also* Ridolfi, Carlo.

Harmon, Leon D. "The Recognition of Faces." *Scientific American* (1973): 71–82.

Hartlaub, G. F. "Die Spiegel-Bilder des Giovanni Bellini." *Pantheon* 30 (1942): 235–41.

———. *Zauber des Spiegels: Geschichte und Bedeutung des Spiegels in der Kunst*. Munich, 1951.

Hatfield, Rab. "Five Early Renaissance Portraits." *Art Bulletin* 47 (1965): 315–34.

Heinemann, Fritz. *Bellini e i belliniani*. Trans. Lucio Grossato and Franco Barbieri. 2 vols. Venice, 1962.

Held, Julius S. "'Artis Pictoriae Amator': An Antwerp Art Patron and His Collection." *Gazette des Beaux-Arts* 41 (1957): 74–83.

———. "Commentary." *Art Journal* 46 (1987): 127–33.

———. "Flora, Goddess and Courtesan." In *De Artibus Opuscula XL: Essays in Honor of Erwin Panofsky*, ed. Millard Meiss, 1:201–18. New York, 1961.

———. "A Tomb by Cornelius Engebrechtsz." *Oud-Holland* 67 (1952): 233–37.

Hendy, Philip. "The *Christ Carrying the Cross* at Fenway Court." *Burlington Magazine* 56 (1930): 197–203.

Hetzer, Theodor. *Aufsätze und Vorträge*. 2 vols. Leipzig, 1957.

———. *Tizian: Geschichte seiner Farbe*. Frankfurt, 1935; repr. 1969.

Horster, Marita. "'Mantuae Sanguis Preciosus.'" *Wallraf-Richartz-Jahrbuch* 25 (1963): 151–80.

Humfrey, Peter. "The Bellinesque Life of St. Mark Cycle for the Scuola Grande di San Marco in Venice in Its Original Arrangement." *Zeitschrift für Kunstgeschichte* 48 (1985): 225–42.

———. "The Life of St. Jerome Cycle from the Scuola di San Girolamo in Cannaregio." *Arte veneta* 39 (1985): 41–46.

Huse, Norbert. *Studien zu Giovanni Bellini*. Berlin and New York, 1972.

Johnson, Meryl, and Elizabeth Packard. "Methods Used for the Identification of Binding Media in Italian Paintings of the Fifteenth and Sixteenth Centuries." *Studies in Conservation* 16 (1971): 145–64.

Joost-Gaugier, Christiane. "A Pair of Miniatures by a Panel Painter: The Earliest Works of Giovanni Bellini?" *Paragone* 30 (1979): 48–71.

Kenny, Anthony. "The Transfiguration and the Agony in the Garden." *Catholic Biblical Quarterly* 19 (1957): 444–52.

Keydel, Julia Helen. "A Group of Altarpieces by Giovanni Bellini Considered in Relation to the Context for Which They Were Made." Ph.D. diss., Harvard University, 1969.

King, Margaret Leah. "Caldiera and the Barbaros on Marriage and the Family: Humanist Reflections of Venetian Realities." *Journal of Medieval and Renaissance Studies* 6 (1976): 19–50.

———. "Personal, Domestic, and Republican Values in the Moral Philosophy of Giovanni Caldiera." *Renaissance Quarterly* 28 (1975): 535–74.

———. *Venetian Humanism in an Age of Patrician Dominance.* Princeton, N.J., 1986.

Klapisch-Zuber, Christiane. *Women, Family, and Ritual in Renaissance Italy.* Trans. Lydia Cochrane. Chicago and London, 1985.

Knox, George. "The Camerino of Francesco Corner." *Arte veneta* 32 (1978): 79–84.

Kretschmayr, Heinrich. *Geschichte von Venedig.* Vols. 1 and 2. Gotha, 1905–20.

Kristeller, Paul. *Andrea Mantegna.* Ed. S. Arthur Strong. London, 1901.

Kristeva, Julia. "Motherhood According to Giovanni Bellini" [1975]. In Kristeva, *Desire in Language: A Semiotic Approach to Literature and Art*, ed. Leon S. Roudiez, trans. Thomas Gora, Alice Jardine, and Roudiez, pp. 237–70. New York, 1980.

Land, Norman E. "On the Poetry of Giovanni Bellini's *Sacred Allegory.*" *Artibus et Historiae* 5 (1984): 61–66.

Lane, Frederic C. *Venice: A Maritime Republic.* Baltimore and London, 1973.

Lankheit, Klaus. *Das Triptychon als Pathosformel.* Heidelberg, 1959.

Lattanzi, Marco. "La pala di San Giovanni Crisostomo di Giovanni Bellini: Il soggetto, la committenza, il significato." *Artibus et Historiae* 2 (1981): 29–38.

Lavin, Irving. "On the Sources and Meaning of the Renaissance Portrait Bust." *Art Quarterly* 33 (1970): 207–26.

Lavin, Marilyn Aronberg. "The Altar of Corpus Domini in Urbino: Paolo Uccello, Joos van Ghent, Piero della Francesca." *Art Bulletin* 49 (1967): 1–24.

———. "Piero della Francesca's Montefeltro Altarpiece: A Pledge of Fidelity." *Art Bulletin* 51 (1969): 367–71.

Lazzarini, Giovanni Andrea. *See* Becci, Antonio.

Lazzarini, Lorenzo. "Il colore nei pittori veneziani tra il 1480 e il 1580." *Bollettino d'arte* 5 (1983): 135–44.

Libby, Lester J., Jr. "Venetian History and Political Thought after 1509." *Studies in the Renaissance* 20 (1973): 7–45.

Liburnio, Nicolò. *Opere gentile ed amorse.* Venice, 1502.

Lightbown, Ronald. *Mantegna.* Berkeley and Los Angeles, 1986.

Lipman, Jean. "The Florentine Profile Portrait in the Quattrocento." *Art Bulletin* 18 (1936): 54–102.

Longhi, Roberto. "Piero dei Franceschi e lo sviluppo della pittura veneziana." *L'Arte* 17 (1914): 198–221, 241–56.

———. *Ricerche sulla pittura veneta, 1946–1969*, vol. 10 of *Opere complete di Roberto Longhi.* Florence, 1978.

Lorenzi, Giambattista. *Monumenti per servire alla storia del Palazzo Ducale di Venezia: Parte I, dal 1253 al 1600.* Venice, 1868.

Ludwig, Gustav. "Giovanni Bellinis sogenannte Madonna am See in den Uffizien: Eine religiöse Allegorie." *Jahrbuch der königlich preussischen Kunstsammlungen* 23 (1902): 163–86.

———. "Nachrichter über venezianische Maler." *Italienische Forschungen* 4 (1911): 85–147.

———. "Restello, Spiegel und Toilettenutensilien in Venedig zur Zeit der Renaissance." *Italienische Forschungen* 1 (1906): 185–361.

Ludwig, Gustav, and Wilhelm Bode. "Die Altarbilder der Kirche S. Michele di Murano und das Auferstehungsbild des Giovanni Bellini in der Berliner Galerie." *Jahrbuch der königlich preussischen Kunstsammlungen* 24 (1903): 131–46. *See also* Paoletti, Pietro di Osvaldo.

Luzio, Alessandro. "Disegni topografici e pitture dei Bellini." *Archivio storico dell'arte* 1 (1888): 276–78.

McHam, Sarah Blake. *See* Wilk, Sarah Blake.

Mariacher, Giovanni. *Il Museo Correr di Venezia: Dipinti dal XIV al XVI secolo.* Venice, 1957.

Mather, Frank Jewett, Jr. "Antonello da Messina's Altar-Piece of 1476." *Art Studies, Medieval, Renaissance and Modern* 2 (1924): 125–33.

Mayer, August L. "A Portrait of Joerg Fugger Ascribed to Giovanni Bellini." *Burlington Magazine* 48 (1926): 219.

Meiss, Millard. *Andrea Mantegna as Illuminator: An Episode in Renaissance Art, Humanism, and Diplomacy.* New York, 1957.

———. *Giovanni Bellini's St. Francis in the Frick Collection.* Princeton, N.J., 1964.

———. *The Painter's Choice: Problems in the Interpretation of Renaissance Art.* New York, 1976.

———. "Scholarship and Penitence in the Early Renaissance: The Image of St. Jerome." *Pantheon* 32 (1974): 134–40.

Meller, Peter. "Physiognomical Theory in Renaissance Heroic Portraits." In *The Renaissance and Mannerism: Studies in Western Art, Acts of the Twentieth International Congress of the History of Art*, 2: 53–69. Princeton, N.J., 1963.

Mendelsohn, Leatrice. *Paragoni: Benedetto Varchi's "Due Lezzioni" and Cinquecento Art Theory.* Ann Arbor, 1982.

Meneghin, Vittorino. *S. Michele in Isola di Venezia.* Vol. 1. Venice, 1962.

Mercati, Giovanni. *Ultimi contributi alla storia degli umanisti.* Fasc. 2. Studi e testi, 91. Vatican City, 1939.

Meyer zur Capellen, Jürg. "Bellini in der Scuola Grande di San Marco." *Zeitschrift für Kunstgeschichte* 43 (1980): 104–8.

———. *Gentile Bellini.* Stuttgart, 1985.

———. "Zum venezianischen Dogenbildnis in der zweiten Hälfte des Quattrocento."

*Konsthistorisk Tidskrift* 50 (1981): 70–86.

Michiel, Marcantonio. *Der Anonimo Morelliano (Marcantonio Michiel's Notizia d'opere del disegno)*. Vol. 1: *Text und Übersetzung*. Ed. Theodor Frimmel. Quellenschriften für Kunstgeschichte und Kunsttechnik des Mittelalters und der Neuzeit, N.F. 1. Vienna, 1888.

Minio, Michelangelo. "Iconografia della flora spontanea in Giovanni Bellini: Suo interesse di fonte cronologica e come tipo di intuizione biologica." *Atti dell'Istituto Veneto di Scienze, Lettere ed Arti, Classe di scienze morali e lettere* 108 (1949–50): 155–77.

Molmenti, Pompeo G. "I pittori Bellini: Documenti e ricerche." *Archivio veneto* 36 (1888): 219–34.

———. *Studi e ricerche di storia d'arte*. Turin and Rome, 1892.

Moretti, Lino. "Di Leonardo Bellini, pittore e miniatore." *Paragone* 9 (1958): 58–66.

Moschini Marconi, Sandra. *Gallerie dell'Accademia di Venezia: Opere d'arte dei secoli XIV e XV*. Rome, 1955.

Mosto, Andrea da. *I dogi di Venezia nella vita pubblica e privata*. Repr. Milan, 1966.

Muir, Edward. *Civic Ritual in Renaissance Venice*. Princeton, N.J., 1981.

Navagero, Andrea. "Orazione . . . recitata nell'esequie del Doge Leonardo Loredan." In *Orazioni, elogie e vite scritte da letterati veneti patrizi in lode di dogi, ed altri illustri soggetti*, 1: 168–97. Venice, 1798.

Neff, Mary Frances. "Chancellery Secretaries in Venetian Politics and Society, 1480–1533." Ph.D. diss., UCLA, 1985.

Nepi Scirè, Giovanna, and Francesco Valcanover. *Gallerie dell'Accademia di Venezia*. Milan, 1985.

Newton, Stella Mary. "Homage to a Poet." *Bulletin of the Metropolitan Museum of Art* (1971): 33–37.

Odenthal, Anna Maria. *Die Kirche San Giovanni Crisostomo in Venedig: Ein Beitrag zur venezianischen Sakralarchitektur des späten 15. Jahrhunderts*. Bonn, 1985.

O'Malley, John W. *Praise and Blame in Renaissance Rome: Rhetoric, Doctrine, and Reform in the Sacred Orators of the Papal Court, c. 1450–1521*. Durham, N.C., 1979.

Packard, Elizabeth C. G. "A Bellini Painting from the Procuratia di Ultra, Venice: An Exploration of Its History and Technique." *Journal of the Walters Art Gallery* 33–34 (1970–71): 64–84.

Pallucchini, Rodolfo. *Giovanni Bellini*. Milan, 1959.

———. *Giovanni Bellini, Catalogo illustrato della mostra*. 3d ed. Venice, 1949.

Panofsky, Erwin. *Early Netherlandish Painting: Its Origins and Character*. 2 vols. Cambridge, Mass., 1953.

———. "Imago Pietatis: Ein Beitrag aus Typengeschichte des 'Schmerzensmannes' und der 'Maria Mediatrix.'" In *Festschrift für M. J. Friedländer*, pp. 261–308. Leipzig, 1927.

———. "Reintegration of a Book of Hours Executed in the Workshop of the Maître des Grandes Heures de Rohan." In *Mediaeval Studies in Memory of A. Kingsley Porter*, 2: 479–99. Cambridge, Mass., 1939.

Paoletti, Pietro di Osvaldo. "La Scuola Grande di San Marco." *Rivista della città di Venezia* 8 (1929): 1–196.

———. *L'architettura e la scultura del Rinascimento in Venezia: Ricerche storico artistiche, Parte prima*. Venice, 1893.

———. *Raccolta di documenti inediti per servire alla storia della pittura veneziana nei secoli XV e XVI: Fascicolo 1, I Bellini*. Padua, 1894.

Paoletti, Pietro di Osvaldo, and Gustav Ludwig. "Neue archivalische Beiträge zur Geschichte der venezianischen Malerei." *Repertorium für Kunstwissenschaft* 22 (1899): 427–57.

Pincus, Debra. *The Arco Foscari: The Building of a Triumphal Gateway in Fifteenth Century Venice*. Outstanding Dissertations in the Fine Arts. New York and London, 1976.

Pino, Paolo. *Dialogo di pittura* [1548]. In *Scritti d'arte del cinquecento*, ed. Paola Barocchi, vol. 3: *Pittura e scultura*, pp. 93–139. Bari, 1960. Repr. Turin, 1978.

Polidoro, Valerio. *Le Religiose memorie . . . nelle quali si tratta della chiesa del glorioso S. Antonio Confessore da Padova*. Venice, 1590.

Popham, A. E., and Philip Pouncey. *Italian Drawings in the Department of Prints and Drawings in the British Museum: The Fourteenth and Fifteenth Centuries*. London, 1950.

Pratilli, Laura. "Felice Feliciano alla luce dei suoi codici." *Atti del Reale Istituto Veneto di Scienze, Lettere ed Arti, Classe di scienze morali e letteratura* 99, pt. 2 (1939–40): 33–105.

Pullan, Brian. *Rich and Poor in Renaissance Venice: The Social Institutions of a Catholic State, to 1620*. Oxford, 1971.

Puppi, Lionello. *Il trittico di Andrea Mantegna per la Basilica di San Zeno Maggiore in Verona*. Verona, 1972.

———. "La pala votiva Mocenigo della National Gallery di Londra." *Antichità viva* 8 (1969): 3–18.

Queller, Donald E. *The Venetian Patriciate: Reality versus Myth*. Urbana and Chicago, 1986.

Rasmo, N. "La Sacra Conversazione belliniana degli Uffizi e il problema della sua comprensione." *Carro minore* 5–6 (1946): 229–40.

Ravà, Aldo. "Il 'camerino delle Antigaglie' di Gabriele Vendramin." *Nuovo archivio veneto*, n.s., 77–78 (1920): 155–81.

Ricci, Corrado. *Iacopo Bellini e i suoi libri di disegni*. 2 vols. Florence, 1908.

Richardson, Joan Olivia. "Hodegetria and Venetia Virgo: Giovanni Bellini's San Giobbe Altarpiece." M.A. thesis, University of British Columbia, Vancouver, 1979.

Richter, G. M. "A Portrait of a Lady by Giovanni Bellini." *Burlington Magazine* 69 (1936): 3–4.

———. "*Christ Carrying the Cross* by Giovanni Bellini." *Burlington Magazine* 75 (1939): 95–96.

Richter, I. A. *Paragone: A Comparison of the Arts by Leonardo da Vinci*. London, 1949.

Ridolfi, Carlo. *Le Maraviglie dell'arte ovvero le vite degli illustri pittori veneti e dello stato* [1648]. Ed. Detlev von Hadeln. 2 vols. Berlin, 1914.

Ringbom, Sixten. *Icon to Narrative: The Rise of the Dramatic Close-Up in Fifteenth-Century Devotional Painting* [1965]. 2d ed. rev. Doornspijk, 1984.

Robertson, Giles. "The Architectural Setting of Antonello da Messina's San Cassiano Altarpiece." In *Studies in Late Medieval and Renaissance Painting in Honor of Millard Meiss*, ed. Irving Lavin and John Plummer, 1:368–72. New York, 1977.

———. "The Earlier Works of Giovanni Bellini." *Journal of the Warburg and Courtauld Institutes* 23 (1960): 45–59.

———. *Giovanni Bellini*. Oxford, 1968.

———. Rev. of Norbert Huse, *Studien zu Giovanni Bellini* (Berlin, 1972). *Burlington Magazine* 108 (1976): 33–34.

Robertson, Martin. "A Possible Classical Echo in Bellini." *Burlington Magazine* 121 (1979): 650–53.

Robins, Anthony W. "The Paintings of Antonello da Messina." *Connoisseur* 188 (1975): 186–93.

Rossi, Vittorio. "Il canzoniere inedito di Andrea Michieli detto Squarzòla o Strazzòla." *Giornale storico della letteratura italiana* 26 (1895): 1–91.

Röthlisberger, Marcel. "Studi su Jacopo Bellini." *Saggi e memorie di storia dell'arte* 2 (1958–59): 41–89.

Rosand, David. Rev. of Giles Robertson, *Giovanni Bellini*. *Art Quarterly* 33 (1970): 72–74.

Ruggeri, Adriana Augusti. "Giovanni Bellini: Santi Gerolamo, Cristoforo e Ludovico." In *Giorgione a Venezia*, pp. 196–202. Milan, 1978.

———. "Giovanni Bellini: Vanitas." In *Giorgione a Venezia*, pp. 34–37. Milan, 1978.

Ruggiero, Guido. "Modernization and the Mythic State in Early Renaissance Venice: The Serrata Revisited." *Viator* 10 (1979): 245–56.

Ruhemann, Helmut, with Joyce Plesters. *The Cleaning of Paintings: Problems and Potentialities*. London, 1968.

Sabellico, Marc' Antonio. *Del sito di Venezia città* [1502]. Ed. G. Meneghetti. Venice, 1957.

Sansovino, Francesco. *Dialogo di tutte cose notabili che sono in Venetia*. Venice, 1563.

———. *Lettera intorno al Palazzo Ducale e descrizione dei quadri nella Sala del Gran Consiglio esistenti prima dell'incendio del MDLXXVII*. Ed. Domenico Combi. Venice, 1829.

———. *Venetia città nobilissima et singolare*. Venice, 1581.

———. *Venetia città nobilissima et singolare*. Ed. Giustiniano Martinioni. Venice, 1663; repr. Venice, 1968.

———. *Venetia città nobilissima et singolare*. Ed. Giovanni Stringa. Venice, 1604.

Sanuto, Marino. *I Diarii di Marino Sanuto*. Ed. Rinaldo Fulin et al. 58 vols. Venice, 1879–1902.

Saxl, F. "Pagan Sacrifice in the Italian Renaissance." *Journal of the Warburg and Courtauld Institutes* 2 (1939): 346–67.

Schapiro, Meyer. *Words and Pictures: On the Literal and Symbolic in the Illustration of a Text*. Approaches to Semiotics, 11. The Hague and Paris, 1973.

Schulz, Anne Markham. "A Portrait of Giovanni Emo in the National Gallery of Art." *Studies in the History of Art* 9 (1980): 7–11.

Schwarz, Heinrich. "The Mirror of the Artist and the Mirror of the Devout: Observations on Some Paintings, Drawings, and Prints of the Fifteenth Century." In *Studies in the History of Art Dedicated to William E. Suida on His Eightieth Birthday*, pp. 94–98. New York, 1959.

Scolari, Antonio. *Documenti per la storia dell'arte a Padova*. Ed. Clemente Fillarini. Fonti e studi per la storia del Santo a Padova, vol. 4; Fonti, vol. 3. Vicenza, 1976.

Sheard, Wendy Steadman. "The Widener *Orpheus*: Attribution, Type, Invention." In *Collaboration in Italian Renaissance Art*, ed. Sheard and John T. Paoletti, pp. 189–231. New Haven and London, 1978.

Shearman, John. "The Logic and Realism of Piero della Francesca." In *Festschrift Ulrich Middeldorf*, ed. Antje Kosegarten and Pieter Tigler, 1:180–86. Berlin, 1968.

Sinanoglou, Leah. "The Christ Child as Sacrifice: A Medieval Tradition and the Corpus Christi Plays." *Speculum* 48 (1973): 491–509.

Sinding-Larsen, Staale. *Christ in the Council Hall: Studies in the Religious Iconography of the Venetian Republic*. *Acta ad Archaeologiam et Artium Historiam Pertinentia* (Institutum Romanum Norvegiae). Vol. 5. Rome, 1974.

———. "L'Immagine della Repubblica di Venezia." In *Architettura e utopia nella Venezia del Cinquecento*, pp. 40–49. Milan, 1980.

Smith, Alistair. "Dürer and Bellini: Apelles and Protogenes." *Burlington Magazine* 114 (1972): 326–29.

Smyth, Craig Hugh. "Venice and the Emergence of the High Renaissance in Florence: Observations and Questions." In *Florence and Venice: Comparisons and Relations*, vol. 1: *Quattrocento*, pp. 209–49. Florence, 1979.

Sohm, Philip L. *The Scuola Grande di San Marco, 1437–1550: The Architecture of a Venetian Lay Confraternity*. New York and London, 1982.

Steinberg, Leo. *The Sexuality of Christ in Renaissance Art and in Modern Oblivion*. New York, 1983.

Stout, Charles L. "One Aspect of the So-Called 'Mixed Technique.'" *Technical Studies* 7 (1938): 59–72.

Suida, William E. "Giovanni Bellini's Portrait of the Condottiere Bartolomeo d'Alviano." *Art Quarterly* 13 (1950): 49–58.

Tardito, Rosalba, et al. *Giovanni Bellini a Milano*. Milan, 1987.

Tietze, Hans. "An Early Version of Titian's Danae: An Analysis of Titian's Replicas." *Arte veneta* 8 (1954): 199–209.

———. "Earliest and Latest Works of Great Artists." *Gazette des Beaux-Arts* 26 (1944): 273–84.

———. "Giovanni Bellini's *Portrait of Giacomo Marcello*." *Gazette des Beaux-Arts* 31 (1947): 145–50.

———. "Jugendwerk und Alterswerk in der bildenden Kunst." *Zeitwende* 9 (1933): 220–26.

———. "Meister und Werkstätte in der Renaissancemalerei Venedigs." *Alte und neue Kunst* 1 (1952): 89–98.

Tietze, Hans, and Erica Tietze-Conrat. *The Drawings of the Venetian Painters in the 15th and 16th Centuries*. 2 vols. New York, 1944; repr. 1970.

———. "The *Allendale Nativity* in the National Gallery." *Art Bulletin* 31 (1949): 11–20.

———. "L' 'Orfeo' attribuito al Bellini della National Gallery di Washington." *Arte veneta* 3 (1949): 90–95.

Tietze-Conrat, Erica. "Again: Giovanni Bellini and Cornaro's Gazelle." *Gazette des Beaux-Arts* 29 (1946): 187–90; 30 (1946): 185.

———. "An Unpublished *Madonna* by Giovanni Bellini and the Problem of Replicas in His Shop." *Gazette des Beaux-Arts*, 6th ser., 33 (1948): 379–82.

———. "Giovanni Bellinis Gruppenbild von 1507." *Belvedere* 8 (1929): 106–8.

Tramontin, Silvio. *San Giovanni Grisostomo*. Venezia Sacra, 7. Venice, 1968.

———. *San Zaccaria*. Venezia Sacra, 13. Venice, 1979.

Turner, A. Richard. *The Vision of Landscape in Renaissance Italy*. Princeton, N.J., 1966.

Valcanover, Francesco, et al. *Restauri a Venezia, 1967–68*. Quaderni della Soprintendenza ai Beni Artistici e Storici di Venezia, 14. Venice, 1986.

———. *La pala Barbarigo di Giovanni Bellini*. Quaderni della Soprintendenza ai Beni Artistici e Storici di Venezia, 3. Venice, 1983.

Vasari, Giorgio. *Le Vite de' più eccellenti architetti, pittori, et scultori italiani, da Cimabue insino a' tempi nostri* [1550]. Ed. Luciano Bellosi and Aldo Rossi. Turin, 1986.

———. *Le Vite de' più eccellenti pittori, scultori ed architettori* [1568]. Ed. Gaetano Milanesi. Vol. 3. Florence, 1906; repr. Florence, 1973.

Vecellio, Cesare. *Degli habiti antichi, et moderni di diverse parti del mondo*. Venice, 1590.

Verdier, Philippe. "L'Allegoria della Misericordia e della Giustizia di Giambellino agli Uffizi," *Atti dell'Istituto Veneto di Scienze, Lettere ed Arti, Classe di scienze morali e lettere* 3 (1952–53): 97–115.

Volpe, Carlo. "La donazione Vedeghini Baldi a Ferrara." *Paragone* 28 (1977): 73–78.

———. "Per gli inizi di Giovanni Bellini." *Arte veneta* 32 (1978): 56–60.

Wagner, Hugo. "'Die Trunkenheit Noahs' von Giovanni Bellini." In *Michael Stettler zum 70. Geburtstag. Von Angesicht zu Angesicht: Porträtstudien*, ed. Florens Deuchler, Mechthild Flury-Lemberg, and Karel Otavsky, pp. 182–89. Bern, 1983.

Walker, John. *Bellini and Titian at Ferrara: A Study of Styles and Taste*. London, 1956.

Wiess, Roberto. "Jan van Eyck and the Italians." *Italian Studies* 11 (1956): 1–15; 12 (1957): 7–21.

Wilde, Johannes. "Die 'Pala di San Cassiano' von Antonello da Messina: Ein Rekonstruktionsversuch." *Jahrbuch der kunsthistorischen Sammlungen in Wien* 3 (1929): 57–72.

Wilk, Sarah Blake. *The Sculpture of Tullio Lombardo: Studies in Sources and Meaning*. Outstanding Dissertations in the Fine Arts. New York and London, 1978.

———. "Tullio Lombardo's 'Double Portrait' Reliefs." *Marsyas* 16 (1972–73): 67–86.

Wilson, Carolyn. "Giovanni Bellini's Pesaro Altarpiece, Studies in Its Context and Meaning." Ph.D. diss., Institute of Fine Arts, 1976.

Wind, Edgar. *Bellini's Feast of the Gods: A Study in Venetian Humanism*. Cambridge, Mass., 1948.

———. "The Eloquence of Symbols." *Burlington Magazine* 92 (1950): 349–50.

Winternitz, Emanuel. "A *Lira da Braccio* in Giovanni Bellini's *The Feast of the Gods*." *Art Bulletin* 28 (1946): 114–15.

———. *Musical Instruments and Their Symbolism in Western Art*. London, 1967.

Wolters, Wolfgang. *Der Bilderschmuck des Dogenpalastes: Untersuchungen zur Selbstdarstellung der Republik Venedig im 16. Jahrhundert*. Wiesbaden, 1983.

———. *La scultura veneziana gotica (1300–1460)*. 2 vols. Venice, 1976.

Zanetti, Antonio Maria. *Della pittura veneziana*. . . . Venice, 1771.

———. *Descrizione di tutte le pubbliche pitture della città di Venezia e isole circonvicine: O sia rinnovazione delle Ricche Minere di Marco Boschini*. Venice, 1733.

Zanetti, Vincenzo. *La Chiesa della Madonna dell'Orto in Venezia*. Venice, 1870.

Zanotto, Francesco. *Pinacoteca Veneta: Ossia Raccolta dei migliori dipinti delle chiese di Venezia*. Vol. 1. Venice, 1858.

Zeri, Federico. "Cinque schede per Carlo Crivelli." *Arte antica e moderna* (1961): 170–71.

Zeri, Federico, with Elizabeth E. Gardner. *Italian Paintings: A Catalogue of the Collection of the Metropolitan Museum of Art, Venetian School* (Vicenza, 1973).

Zeri, Federico, and Francesco Rossi. *La Raccolta Morelli nell'Accademia Carrara*. Bergamo [1986].

Ziliotto, Baccio. *Raffaele Zovenzoni: La vita, i carmi*. Trieste, 1950.

Zorzi, Giangiorgio. "Notizie di arte e di artisti nei diarii di Marino Sanudo." *Atti dell'Istituto Veneto di Scienze, Lettere ed Arti, Classe di scienze morali e lettere* 119 (1960–61): 471–604.

Zucker, Wolfgang M. "Reflections on Reflections." *Journal of Aesthetics and Art Criticism* 20 (1962): 239–50.

# Index

*All monuments and institutions are in Venice, unless otherwise noted. All paintings are by Giovanni Bellini, unless otherwise noted, and are listed by location and by title.*